ANAYA'S JOURNEY TO THE NEW HEAVEN ON EARTH

BY: ANITA QUINN BILLINGSLEA
All Illustrations By: Anita Quinn Billingslea
Photography By: My Son Chosen Billingslea and The Vonce

Studio of Books LLC
5900 Balcones Drive Suite 100
Austin, Texas 78731
www.studioofbooks.org
Hotline: (254) 800-1183

Ordering Information:
Special discounts are available on quantity purchases by corporations, associations, and others. For details, contact the publisher at the address above.

Printed in the United States of America.

ISBN-13: Hardcover   978-1-964864-81-5
          eBook   978-1-964864-82-2

Library of Congress Control Number: 2024924535

Contents

DEDICATION PAGE

I am wishing a joyful day in heaven to the one and only love of my life Ricado. Together as one during our more than forty years of marriage we were able to learn the important life lessons of harmonizing the duality of the light and dark frequencies in our lives to achieve the realization that unconditional love is eternal and now as I travel the path of the final stretch of my ascension journey to the New Heaven on Blessed Gaia Earth, I'm looking forward to the glorious reunion and celebration that awaits me. Thank you, our Prime Creator Father, Source Light for the gift of my wonderful life.

CHAPTER ONE

OUR PRAYER

Ye cannot serve God and mammon.

(Matthew 6:24)

God said. "Let the birds fly above the earth across the vault of the sky."

(Genesis 1:20)

A Prayer

Dear Father open my eyes to Your wisdom as I consider your creation.

3

At this stage of our ascension, it is important that we begin our day by giving our spiritual body food just like we give food to our physical body. Your soul needs spiritual food as soon as you awake. Drink some water first, take a shower, take your first quantum jump of the day in the shower and then follow with your daily meditations. Your Merkabah light body is the vehicle you used to descend and access the nine tenths the speed of light vibrations to enter the earth plane, and it is the same vehicle you will be using for you to ascend back home to the new heaven on earth.

Planet earth has been in the ascension process since the portal to the fourth dimension opened on December 21, 2012, and at the same time, earth entered the photon belt. Ever since this date we have been existing in a fourth dimensional simulation, first a tunnel and then a light container for our soul to complete its third dimensional life lessons on earth. Currently, there is no more third dimension earth, you are either vibrating fourth or fifth dimensional frequencies. Let us begin our journey in prayer.

Jesus of Nazareth wrote the Lord's Prayer for his seven brothers and sisters to pray when he was only fourteen years of age, and he passed this prayer on to all of us before his ascension forty days after his crucifixion on May 18, A.D. 30 back into his home in heaven. This is the most important prayer to pray before leaving your home daily, because it covers all the protection you will need throughout your blessed day.

THE LORD'S PRAYER

Our Father who art in heaven

Hallowed be thy name

Thy kingdom come thy will be done.

On earth as it is in heaven. Give us this day our daily bread.

And forgive us our trespasses as we forgive those who trespass against us.

Lead us not into temptation but deliver us from evil

For thou art the kingdom the power and glory forever and ever.

The end

This is a brief interpretation of The Lord's Prayer, and it teaches us the following lessons.

I.

The Prime Creator, Source is our Father and He has established a covenant with all of humanity to fellowship with our brother and trust in God as our Father. When you pray direct your prayer to God as His beloved child, because when we pray to God we are talking to our dad.

II.

Heaven is God's dwelling place; His home and God wants heaven to also be our home. Spiritually speaking heaven is now on planet earth because of Jesus of Nazareth and we can enter it now.

III.

God's name is hallowed when His name is considered holy and when people understand that God lives in and among them with awe and reverence and not trivialize the name of God in any way nor make God a tool for selfish purposes. God's name is worthy and deserves the highest form of honor and veneration.

IV.

God has a divine plan to replace our present world order with His kingdom of light and love. This new kingdom is not a place or system, it is just a situation where God is in control and not man. It is the kingship of God and the state in which God is really being acknowledged to be directing and giving to everyone, because God wants to reign in our hearts and in our lives. Go to God for all your needs in life.

V.

Have the desire daily for God's will to be done, because just as the angels do God's work in heaven, we should also do God's will on earth. God himself wants all His perfect will to be done down here on this earth in all our individual lives. We should never forget to stay in the perfect will of God for all our life here on earth.

VI.

We need to depend on God for everything, because all our needs for both the body and soul come from God. So, we should thank and praise God as the ultimate source for our daily bread. Although we are to ask God to keep us supplied with our daily bread we need in this life, we must remember that we do not live by bread alone, but instead by every word that comes from God's mouth. We do not just live by having our material needs fulfilled, because we also need something more and one of the things more that we need is hope, that is hope for tomorrow. The Greek word epicurious for the word daily appears only once in the Lord's Prayer and it means superessential which refers to the bread of life and the body of Christ. The presence of world hunger calls all humanity to exercise responsibility and justice for the poor, to share with love our spiritual and material goods. This petition also addresses the spiritual famines of the world and for humanity to proclaim the good news of the bread of life and the body of Christ to the poor and all of those in need.

VII.

We daily forgive to be forgiven, because we have done everything to earn God's wrath, but through Jesus Christ, God gives us the opposite which is mercy, grace, peace, and love. We have done nothing to earn God's forgiveness, yet He graciously offers us forgiveness daily. However, we make ourselves incapable of receiving God's forgiveness if we do not forgive others seven times seventy. God's purpose for the Lord's Prayer is that He is simply asking all of humanity in this life to be willing to forgive everyone and if we do, then God will be willing to forgive us of our sins that we commit directly against Him.

VIII.

Temptation and evil are overcome through God's help and only God knows how best to help keep us out of temptation and deliver us from evil in this wicked world on earth. The Lord's Prayer teaches us about God, because His son Jesus of Nazareth is the lord and leader in our life, leading us besides quiet waters on a level path and because God has disarmed the wicked powers and authorities and made a public spectacle of them, this triumph is always shown by Jesus of Nazareth's victory by the cross.

As God's children we with faith and hope need to pick up our cross daily and serve God our Father with the full body armor of the Holy Spirit with authenticity, unconditional love, hope, compassion, gratitude, joy, and bliss in our hearts. This is your daily seven in one stroke.

PICK UP YOUR CROSS AND USE THE FULL BODY ARMOR OF THE HOLY SPIRIT DAILY

Helmet of Salvation-Protects you from doubting God.

Breastplate of Righteousness-Protects you against Satan's attacks to your heart.

Shield of Faith-Protects you against Satan's fiery arrows.

Belt of Truth-Protects you against Satan's lies.

Sword of the Spirit-When tempted, trust God's word, the Holy Bible.

Be Available and Ready to Serve God- The enemy wants us to think that telling others about God's truths is a worthless and hopeless task.

This is your daily seven in one stroke and no matter what happens, keep going!

Let Go and Let God!

SPIRIT GUIDES

Every human being living on planet earth have spirit guides assigned to assist you during your life on earth, so you are never alone during your life journey. Your spirit guides exist in the seventh dimension, and they are with you all the way until you transition at the end of this life to a different room, realm, or dimension. Your assigned spirit guides already know you, so they do not need to contact you, because they live with you always. They are a part of your crew that makes up what is known as a band, so if you decide to communicate with them, they will continue to fill your life with wonders, surprises, and support for us.

Each one of us also has an angel who is higher than your guides assigned to you since your birth. We each have an assigned angel, because our Prime Creator knows each soul and its characteristics, and He places each of us with an assigned angel who has a bright spirit of love for each of us. Your assigned angel for life has many similarities to you and your angel can relate to you by communicating with your mind and soul which makes it easier for you to grasp their wisdom, guidance, and knowledge. Our assigned angle helps to lead us in life only if we use our free will to have faith to follow their guidance.

Each one of us also has an ascended higher mind who lives billions of years in the future in the seventh dimension. Your higher mind is your direct link, your connection to God. It is your voice, the soft patient one you hear all the time, while the impatient voice is your ego. Your higher mind also exists on our current fourth dimensional earth plane just above your head. As you continue to progress through the twenty-two initiation steps of ascension you will merge as one with your higher mind. When this occurs, your higher mind replaces your ego, and it will then exist within the top of your head to guide you through your ascension journey.

Each angelic spirit that God assigns to assist us during our life lessons here on earth will react to your needs just like a beloved parent or family member who deeply loves you. When it comes to the love your assigned angelic spirits have towards you, one cannot imagine the beauty, tenderness and care they have for you and their care for you is full of love, gentleness, wisdom, and power. You cannot attain or ascend to a higher level of love or divine love until your soul is whole again, pure, and free of sin and radiating pure light. There are many pure celestial beings we have all around us during our entire lives and we should feel incredibly special, blessed, grateful and humbled by all the divine help we are daily receiving to ascend back home. This is how our Prime Creator provides and blesses each soul on earth and how sad it is that most humans are not aware of this divine help we each have available to us.

Our guides, angels and higher mind act upon whatever our current beliefs are and many times your beliefs change which is no problem for them. Since your guides exist in higher dimensions, they only know the truth, while down here in the fourth dimension we struggle for that light until we receive more of it and as our hunger for more soul expansion grows, this causes us to follow the breadcrumbs. What is magnificent is that God and whatever we are into at that moment, through our guides will continue to be there to assist us. Your spiritual guides will always find the goodness in your choices in life and if it is not good for you, your guide will cause you to be led away from it if we allow ourselves to be sensitive to our hearts and souls. Your spiritual guides can create situations and show up as an animal or object, but there is a reason for this and there is always a lesson in it for you. If a situation is for you then it will take thought and prayer because it is deep and important for our happiness both here on earth as well as in the spirit realm.

You really need to think about what your spirit guides are trying to communicate with you. Pray about it and whether you believe in God or just the universe, you need to use your free will and ask yourself if this situation is going to help you to continue to ascend to higher dimensions. Many times, your guides are babysitting even when you are an adult, because your spirit guides protect you from dark entities as well as from people attracted to you who only want to bring you down to their level of darkness. Your angel and spirit guides know all about you, your life plan and much more, so if you think they are around which they are, it is because they will put this idea into your head, but you will think it is your idea. If you can feel your angel or spirit guide near you, then this means you have sensitivity which is a gift, and this means they are trying to help you realize that through their guidance you will be able to grow and stretch. What is cool is that your spirit guides want you to go deep inside yourself, into your soul and you do not have to find any answers when you do this, because your guides will give them to you. Never forget to pray, because prayer from our heart and soul is a direct connection to ask God to send you, His love. The act of prayer and meditation raises your vibrations and allows you to create a better rapport with your spiritual guides. It is the substance that transforms a human into a divine angel through patience, but it is a slow gradual process.

We live in a spiritually created universe and although men have created all this darkness on earth, it is not real. What you see is a counterfeit overlay of men's selfishness and very soon we are going to see the darkness change into love, a love that we will all feel and know. For those who do not want this pure love from the Prime Creator at this time of ascension will still be led to the next step in their spiritual evolution.

CHAPTER TWO

THE SUN'S AND EARTH'S INFLUENCE ON HUMANITY'S ASCENSION

In him we were also chosen that we might be for the praise of his glory.

(Ephesians 1: 11-12)

Everyone who believes that Jesus is the Christ is born of God.

(1 John 5:1)

A Prayer:

Creator God, thank you for making me one of your masterpieces.

THE SUN AND EARTH'S INFLUENCE ON HUMANITY'S ASCENSION

The earth's current sixth sun is five billion years old, and it is a yellow dwarf star, a hot glowing ball of hydrogen and helium that is located at the center of our solar system. The sun is the source of solar power, and it is our solar system's only star. Without the energy of the sun, life as we know it could not exist on earth. The sun is sometimes called Sol or Solic, and its symbol is a circle with a dot in the center. The sun warms our seas, stirs earth's atmosphere, generates weather patterns and gives energy to the growing green plants that provide both food and oxygen to earth. Our sun has a twin, a star called (18) Scorpio which is the mirror image of our own earth sun, and it is in the Scorpio constellation. The sun is the real star of the show, because by it being the closest star to the earth, it is the main source of all the heat and light for planet earth.

The source of DNA on planet earth is the sun and the origin of the evolution of life consciousness came from this DNA photon interaction, because the chemical energy of the process of photosynthesis which comes from the sun is the source of life. DNA is a universal instrument of life that has been blown out from the sun prior to the formation of planet earth and it has survived deep in the seas, and it gave way to the origin of life. We are all connected at a molecular level with the ancestry by our DNA. There are four bases of DNA that are universally present in all living beings on earth, and this means that we are all subject to birth and death due to the God-DNA-Yahweh code that is inside all of the human DNA strands. DNA is our vessel for life and the (12) activated DNA human strands blossom out from its spiral shape into the form of the petals in a flower.

The sixth sun rose on earth in the year of October 2011 and the new world on earth began. Shortly after the beginning of the new age on earth, planet earth entered the photon belt and the portal to the fourth dimension opened on December 21, 2012, and since then planet earth has been rapidly ascending to the new heaven on the Blessed Gaia Earth. During earth's current times of the sixth sun, it is now a time of creation where anything is possible. Of all who have ever lived on earth, no one has never been closer to the presence of God or had the powerful benevolent spiritual help that is available to humanity right now.

During our last world on earth, especially the nine hells that occurred at the end of our last world, it was a time when people were too afraid to think for themselves. But now the sixth sun has risen, and we are now in the sixth world on earth, because now everything we have waited and watched for so long is now here. What our new world on earth under the sixth sun and the great central sun Alcyone is going to be is a wonder to us all. We are now living in the times where we can finally really learn to see, hear, feel, and finally think for ourselves. Whatever our new world on the new heaven on earth will be, we are all creating it now.

The current sixth sun on earth represents the birth of a new consciousness on earth and this new energy is an excessively big step up for all of humanity. This current sun on earth will be a time where we will witness an elevation of the human collective's consciousness and the use of feminine forces once again on planet earth. The movement from the fifth sun to the sixth sun on earth has brought about a huge shift in human consciousness and our understanding of how we relate to ourselves, each other, the earth, and the cosmos. This is new available energy that represents an opportunity for the human collective on earth to receive these new energies that are coming to earth from the sixth sun. The sixth sun represents life, but it is also known to bring new energies, power, clarity, and positivity. The sun is also a star, a natural force that is outside of our control while it continues to illuminate the world around us with its light. During this shift, the influence of both suns are present.

The great central sun has been shining on earth since the portal to the fifth dimension opened on December 21, 2021. The entire week of October 10, 2021, had to be shut down and repeated on earth to make the necessary preparations for this massive event. The great central sun is the source and center of the all-pervading presence of the great "I AM." It is the point of integration of the spirit matter cosmos, and the central concentration of God's consciousness and the release of light, life, and love to all creation. The great central sun is the nucleus, the heart center, or the white fire core of the cosmos. The God star Sirius is the focus point of the great midway point in our sector of the Milky Way Galaxy. The great central sun is the fabric of our eternal heart space. Infinite possibilities of creation radiate from the beautiful and harmonious core of the great central sun and the powers of the healing source from the great central sun are filled with the highest vibrational energy of unconditional love and light. It is the sun of your true self, and it is time for humanity to awaken and return to a place of perfect oneness and live your most beautiful life.

The sun behind the sun is the spiritual cause behind the physical effect we see as our own physical sun and all the other stars, star systems, seen and unseen. The sun behind the sun of the cosmos is perceived as the cosmic Christ, the Word by whom the formless was endowed with form and spiritual worlds.

The great central sun is also known as the sun of the following.

The source

The great hub

The central source of life and intelligence

The heart of God

The great central source of all intelligence

The great central sun is the doorway for humans to reach higher consciousness. It is our connection to the source energy for all conscious existence within our universe. It is our source of unity of all-living beings as one with the Prime Creator, Source. It represents the powerful source of light and solar energy that exists at the center of all universes from where all life and energy emanate. The great central sun is a high frequency spiritual presence that surrounds the sixth sun, and it can be perceived through our psychic senses, intuition, and meditation. Through daily meditation we can connect with the great central sun and access its light to transform our energy and frequency which gives us access to higher states of consciousness and a spiritual evolution.

The great central sun and the I AM presence are linked because they both represent the highest level of spiritual consciousness, and it is the source of all creation. It is the highest spiritual reality, because it represents the divine spark that is within all beings and the goal of our spiritual evolution. Alcyone is the source of all creation, and our soul is connected to the divine light that flows down to us from this sun into our soul. By daily tapping into the light and wisdom of this sun, Alcyone, this will help you to unlock new levels of insight, wisdom, and spiritual growth. The nature of Alcyone is giving, and it asks nothing in return. As humans our goal is to become beings who radiate the life force energy from Alcyone with great power and wisdom.

The sun Alcyone represents clarification of intentions and the manifestation of the potential to trust yourself. Over the time of many generations, a group of beings from the planet Pleaides in association with the sun Alcyone have been keeping their focus on helping humanity on earth make a peaceful and fluent transformation of the human consciousness to its next level to exist on the new heaven on earth. The sun Alcyone is the brightest star in the Pleaides Star System which is comprised of a group of stars that formed one hundred million years ago. This group of stars are about 410 light years away from earth and they are in the constellation of Taurus. This group of stars will remain together as a group for the next 250 million years before moving outwards into the Milky Way Galaxy. This group of stars are clearly visible within a nebula of star dust around them, and they glitter in the night sky like a swarm of fireflies tangled in a single braid. The sun Alcyone is a big, brilliant star that is ten times the radius of our sun and it spins more than one hundred times faster and emits a thousand times as much light. To find the sun Alcyone in the night sky you start with Orion, the giant like constellation that is visible across the winter skies in the Northern Hemisphere. You then follow the line of Orion's belt to the red star Aldebaran and about as far as you can go until you reach the cluster of the Pleiadean Star System. On a clear night you will be able to see six or more distant stars that are in a group of several hundred stars and Alcyone will be the brightest star in the group.

There are several ancient folklore stories concerning this group of stars with Alcyone and it tells the story of seven Pleiadean sisters who were the daughters of Atlas (who carried the heavens on his shoulders), and in order to escape from the hunter Orion's desire for them, they transformed themselves into doves and flew into the sky to become the stars that we now see in the night sky. The ancient Inuit story tells that a group of Pleiadeans hunters and dogs chased a bear onto the ice and at that moment, the bear rose up into the sky where it then became to be Ursa Major, and these hunters are still chasing this bear. In Sweden, this group of stars and Alcyone were known in ancient folklore as the fur in the frost, referring it to as a servant who was turned out in the cold by his master.

These sparkling stars with their background reminded the Swedish people of ice crystals catching the light.

The early Arabic astronomers gave The sun Alcyone the names of, Central One, Bright One, and Walnut. For the people of India, Alcyone was regarded as being Arundhati, the wife of Vashishta or Brahma who with their six sons are the seven rishis who make up the seven stars of the Plough. The name Alcyone was thought by the ancient Greeks to relate to Alcyone the kingfisher. In one of the Greek myths, Aceyon lost her husband in a storm at sea and the gods took pity on both of them of them and turned them both into kingfishes and ever since that day, there have been seven days of calm, which are called the Alcyone days that fall around the time of the winter solstice.

The Pleiadeans are newcomers to our Nebadon universe and an elder group from their planet have chosen to incarnate back into the form of stars, because they have completed a long cycle of experiencing life on the physical plane. This group of Pleiadean elders are now offering humanity some of the fruits of their extensive life experiences and some of which are new ways to organize the energies in our bodies and new ways to form dynamic harmony within our bodies. Their main purpose is to broadcast what they have learned during their long lifetimes to the rest of the Milky Way Galaxy especially to star systems like ours and to those who exist in our neighboring space. The quality of the space we live within our galaxy is such that there is a huge receptivity for great leaps in evolutionary changes to occur during our current lifetime. In some ways the space that we are currently living in on earth is like a sponge that is absorbing love and light daily from the great central sun. This love and light are then being drawn to all the other star systems, planetary systems and to all the beings who live there and who are open to receive this outpouring of light and love coming from the sun daily. The Pleiadeans are offering us some organizing principles to assist those who with their free will are accepting these important DNA light codes and frequencies of light and love.

The sun Alcyone is the focus point of the light codes humanity is receiving daily and these high vibrational light frequencies are organized into planes or bandwidths so that these light codes will continue to offer a very focused and tailored light to each being who chooses to connect with it, a little like the same way in which a radio signal offers you a wide range of stations from which you can choose your favorite one. This explains mankind's long sense of personal connection, attraction, and interests in the Alcyone group of stars.

Over the period of many generations there has been a particular group of elders from the planet Pleaides who have had an interest in helping humanity on earth to develop new and more open flowing forms of thought relating to our ascension process to the new heaven on earth. In the upper astral plane, there is a room in the halls of learning that has an entire etheric model of planet earth that this group of Pleiadean elders are using for their work. In this room this group of elders study the unfolding of the blueprint for planet earth and they are using wisdom, light and love to transmit the necessary frequencies and vibrations we need through this etheric model of planet earth to the consciousness of humanity that will help us on our journey along our highest ascension path without altering our direction, just as a catalyst accelerates chemical change without altering its outcome.

During times of prayer and meditation as we journey within, this is the time to explore how the great central sun, Alcyone the brightest star in the Pleiades Star cluster, can help our mental bodies to continue to evolve. We can achieve this by using a broad overview of all that our life is and have a focused awareness of the many different events and individuals who are present in our life. As we continue to develop this skill, our mental body will begin to evolve to higher levels of intuitive thinking where your mental energy will be able to manifest new realities that are more related to the wishes you want to fulfill in your life.

The earth's sun, the solar system along with at least eight other suns all revolve around the great central sun in a 26,000-year cycle. It takes planet earth and our solar system approximately 226,000,000 million years to make a single rotation around the great central sun and once a sphere completes this complete rotation, the planet and its inhabitants begin the ascension process to the fifth dimension. When planet earth completed this 226, 000,000-million-year cycle in the year 2019 A.D., the old age on earth ended and we experienced the worldwide COVID 19 epidemic and a total reset of our world. A new age of light and love has now begun on earth and for the rest of our solar system and there will be no more dark ages ever again on our planet. The great central sun is the center of gravity and the sun around which the rest of the stars in our astral system revolve around. It is the main and brightest star in the Pleaides star group. In earth's history, the sun Alcyone has played a key role in the ancient folklore of many cultures. The Arabians called it Al Wasat, the central one, Al Nair and the bright one. The ancient Hindus called the central sun Amba, the mother and wife of the chief of the seven sages. Alcyone is located 440 light years away from earth and in Pleaides it represents the seven sisters, the seven stars that are situated on the shoulder blade of the bull. The great central sun has its own consciousness, and it is influencing the current events on earth by releasing solar flares and other phenomena. The sun and the rest of the stars are all conscious and this is based on the rhythmic electromagnetic fields that are present in the sun and other stars that act as an interface between the sun and the other stars' mind and body, and the sun is aware of the activities that are happening within our solar system.

Our physical universe is a part of the conscious minds that are living in and are a part of the universe and so our universe itself is also partially conscious. Human beings become sentient beings between 18 to 25 weeks (about 5 and a half months) during the initial stages of gestation while inside the mother's womb and electrical activity begins in the human brain around ten weeks of gestation. All molecules are conscious, and stars can cool down enough to contain stable molecules that allows them to achieve consciousness. The human brain is the most complex piece of living matter that exists in our known universe, and it can create reality and human consciousness from the electrochemical functions that exist in the brain. Our physical universe also has a memory meaning that it can remember past and present events. This is based on Einstein's theory of relativity which states that gravity results from the mass warping of space-time which then predicts that these gravitational waves shift the structures of space-time.

Most of the elements that exist in the human body were formed in the stars over the course of billions of years and through multiple star lifetimes. Also, some of the 9.5% of hydrogen and lithium that are in the human body originated from the big bang event that occurred long ago. Everything that exists within our universe has some sort of mind or consciousness.

As a result of receiving incredible high plasma light energies on earth from the sun, tremendous changes have been occurring within the earth's crystal core, which in turn has had significant effects on earth's surface and atmosphere. There have been temperature pressure increases as well as a host of other crucial factors such as increases in the speed of spinning for earth about its axis. This is leading to time acceleration, a reduction in the personal planetary and dimensional density leading to higher fluidity and an elevated light quotient on the planet. Earth is also experiencing higher dimensional vibrational frequencies, changes in the earth's dimensional fields and the way in which matter and antimatter interfaces with each other. The magnetic and gravitational fields of the earth have also both changed which is causing the structural layers of the human light body to change as well. There is during the current ascension process on earth a total alteration in the nature of the conscious reality that humans are experiencing on earth. The human organic structure is being completely restored to have twelve activated strands of DNA once again because of the daily light codes that are streaming onto earth daily from the great central sun. These light codes coming from the sun are healing and repairing the morphogenetic damage that our light bodies have suffered and they are causing a complete reversal of the human consciousness on earth.

As earth continues to move towards the great central sun it will continue to outpour light codes and pure love vibrations that will continue to upgrade our human consciousness.

There is nothing to worry about because everything is now moving towards the light. We who are living on earth will all make it one way or the other, it is just that the ride may be bumpier for some of us. Daily meditation is the key to tapping into the incoming ascension energies from the sun. Everything in the material spheres has a hidden spiritual component which means that everything that is alive has a soul. All life has an animating principle, an invisible ethereal portion that is connected to our Prime Creator, Source. Everything from a dense rock, plants, animals, human beings, all the way up to the planets and the stars all have a spirit. Through daily meditation we are given a glimpse into what is possible in our vast and eternal spectrum of oneness.

Our universe is one big giant mind, and it is connected by a large neural network just like our brains are, as above so below. Our universe is made of distinct energetic patterns that are held at frequencies that interact with each other. This entire network is held together by a system of central suns that are massive hubs of consciousness and they offer light and love to the lower levels of existence. These nine suns are all connected, and they are like the batteries of the universe. Each sun is connected to the light source energy, so the stars, the suns and the great central sun are all energetic portals that help to illuminate their portion of the universe using the light from the Prime Creator, Source. The sun is the point of integration between spirit and matter in the cosmos.

Each sun has its own spirit that lives in another dimension which contains millions of elevated consciousness. All the suns in the universe are like a filtration system for the loving awareness of our Prime Creator, Source. All the suns continue to transmute low vibrations into more higher frequencies to help the lower-level beings of existence grow to the vibration of love. In our solar system our local sun is a part of a much larger network of central suns, and it is in constant communication with the great central sun Alcyone in a cosmic dance where these two suns pass information, energy and insights pertaining to the status of the ascending human collectives in this section of the Milky Way Galaxy. When earth's local sun gets closer to Alcyone, all the consciousness on earth rises as humanity continues the path of the ascension process. The great central sun is the connection to source energy for all conscious beings who exist in our universe, so we are all connected to source, because everything in the universe is connected to this great mind. The universe is like a machine that absorbs conscious experiences of all the galaxy systems, planetary realms, and incarnated beings and then all this wealth of information is shared back to the source. Everything in the universe is light, because the universe is made of the light from the Prime Creator. The main purpose of our living in our current matrix dreamland is to shed the distortions and projections to open the light that is within each one of us.

Since the year 2020 A.D. the life lessons for many living on planet earth have accelerated and these changes have their cosmic origins in our life-giving star, the sun. The sun is a dynamic constantly shifting hot glowing ball of plasma gas that is located at the center of our solar system. It is an incredible energy source that maintains our balance and existence on earth. All humans sense and feel the ever-shifting changes of the sun, because humans are also energy beings, a part of the cosmic whole of our ever expanding and developing universes. This development in our human consciousness is the central development theme of our human life. In spiritual terms it is known as the ascension process, and it is infinite just as we are. With the ascension process comes wisdom, physical discomforts, and pain, so much love and authenticity and the unfolding remembrance that you are a child of the stars here to learn and grow through your human life lessons. Our current ascension path is at one with the solar cycles of our star, the sun.

The sun's recent solar activity during the year of February 22, 2024, A.D. has indicated that its current solar cycle number twenty-five is stronger than previously predicted with solar tsunamis and significant X-Class Sun Flares that occurred during this time. The solar maximum for the sun's current solar cycle number twenty-five will reach its maximum during the middle of year 2024 A.D. When the sun's solar maximum cycle reached its zenith, the magnetic field of the sun will flip, and this is called a polar shift. After two cycles of these sun flips which will take about twenty-two years, the sun will then return to its original state. This sun cycle is called the Hale Cycle. When the Sun's pole flips the sun's magnetic field will reverse, and this will cause the magnetic field to weaken and drop down to zero before emerging with a reverse polarity. This pole shift will also cause the sun's magnetic field to move from either a feminine flow (left rotation) to a masculine flow (right rotation) and back again.

When the sun's magnetic field reverses, it will also send energetic ripples out into the solar systems that will affect every planet and its inhabitants including planet earth. Humanity on earth will begin to see an increase in space weather, solar storms, and an increasing wave of higher consciousness. During the year 2019 A. D. during the time of the suns last solar reversal, the sun moved from a masculine wave (the north pole) to a feminine wave (south pole). Planet earth is now in an eleven-year period where a feminine energy wave is entering our solar system. For those humans on the path of ascension, you will be flooded with a call to act upon your intuition, listen to your soul's voice and trust in your own wisdom. During this current time of the sun's eleven-year cycle of the feminine pole shift, communication portals of energy will pass energy back and forth between, the earth and the sun every eight minutes, so this means that humanity is now able to communicate with our star, the sun on an energetic level.

This communication between the sun and the earth is known as a flux transfer event and even though these communications between the sun and the earth are brief, they are dynamic. The sun is a master teacher of the light within our local physical and non-physical solar system. The human soul supports and feeds all the humans on earth with an energy field that is always evolving and generating light codes for humanity's ascension. Since we as humans are linked to the sun, we are constantly evolving and embodying a greater capacity to transmit and emit source light from our human bodies. The one great overriding aspect of our human life is to serve the light and to be the light. To bring your vibrations, frequencies, and consciousness up to the level where you can remember who you are means you are ready to continue to become a spirit of light, because this is the path of ascension, and it is the path that humanity is currently treading.

The ancient humans were remarkably familiar with the great solar ascension process, and this is one of the reasons why the sun was also represented in their artwork, philosophies, architecture, and literature, because we are all walking along the same solar path. During the sun's solar year cycle 25, there will be several major events that will impact the global consciousness on earth during the year of 2024 A.D. There will be five eclipses in the year 2024 A. D. and the strongest impact of these eclipses will happen on April 8, 2024, with a total eclipse that will cross mainland North America. The 2024 elections that are scheduled to occur in the United States and Russia will both be huge deciding factors if world peace will continue on earth. By the year 2025 a group of New World Servers will emerge on earth, and they will act as spiritual teachers who will be meeting on the upper planes of earth to decide humanity's next steps for the ascension process. Also, during the month of January 2024, Pluto will begin its twenty-year journey through the astrological sign of Aquarius and on earth this will bring in a twenty-year period of unparallel advances in science and technology, because what has been hidden will now be released into the light.

The center core of the crystalline earth also plays a vital role in the earth's and humanity's current ascension process. The crystalline solids in the core of the earth are composed of atoms, ions and molecules that are arranged into a crystal lattice that extends in all directions. The elemental atoms that make up each crystal gives it unique properties such as color, frequency, and the intelligent design for its function, because crystals are neutrally charges unless they have been directly programmed. Most of the common elements found in crystals come from the earth's crust. Silicon is most often used as a semiconductor that is an essential component of most electrical circuits. A silicon chip can hold thousands of tiny transistors that are used to amplify or switch electrical power.

The earth and our bodies as well as the twelve strands of DNA in the human body are made of crystalline properties. Many humans still hold the cellular memories from the historical timeline records going back to Tara earth and from the civilizations of Atlantis and Lemuria. The crystals that are in the core of the earth generate crystalline fields of energy that produce the grid networks that control the holographic field of all creation. Our ancestors also had knowledge of this and after the final fall of Atlantis over 12,000 years ago, this knowledge of the crystalline fields and the holographic geography was passed on to the ancient Egyptians and other cultures. These ancient civilizations then tried to salvage the interdimensional gateways of energy on earth to stabilize earth's planetary crystalline field. The crystal core of the earth is the most important part of the planetary structural body that determines the foundation of its matter. The crystal core of the earth is composed of matter and antimatter, and when the non-physical energy (antimatter) moves through the crystal core of the earth, it becomes solid and then manifests as a presence in the physical reality. The crystal core of the earth acts as the transducer of non-physical energy that condenses it into a new state of elemental matter that has magnetic and gravitational fields running in the planet.

The crystal core of the earth instructs the conscious energies that are brought into the manifested bodies to form the morphogenetic blueprints for all the life forms who live on planet earth. The crystal core of earth affects everything, and it determines a life form's orientation in space as well as its geometric shape. The crystal core of the earth determines how the atomic and subatomic particles organize themselves into the blueprints that form physical matter as well as the perception reality on planet earth.

The golden spirals of the sun generate the crystalline lattice that connects directly with the crystal core of the earth and these golden spirals run all throughout the body of earth and into the celestial map of the sun-star networks that are in the galactic and universal plane of our universe. The planetary grid of earth is organized intelligently into layers of geometric blueprints that hold living crystal consciousness which perform specific functions within a precise layer of a crystalline lattice. When the platinum crystal becomes activated in the crystal core of the earth, the sun disc technology that has been dormant since the times of Atlantis start to come back online. There are underground crystal caverns in the core of the earth that function as internal power crystalline generators. These crystal caverns function just like our current day computers, and they are a form of crystal technology that can be directed to earth's surface as a wireless power source for usage as free energy. These crystals function as data memory storage devices that have the capacity to hold intelligent instruction.

The memories that are being stored in these crystals have the true history of origin of earth, its human beings, and the true history of the negative alien invasions that occurred on earth and the atrocities these alien races inflicted on humanity.

The crystal core of the earth now contains new sun star crystals that are full of crystalline coding that are healing the inorganic structure of the earth and humanity, specifically the cloning operations that are being done by the negative aliens with their use of Artificial Intelligence technology. Cloning technology is negative, because it forms shadow bodies and negative forms that produce lost solar fragments in the astral mirror from the soul capture technology that the negative aliens here on earth used on various human tribes and root races going all the way back to the previous Tara and Gaia earth timelines.

The bombardment of the cosmic plasma light that is coming from the great central sun to earth has caused the activation of the crystal core of the earth to increase. These rays from the sun have caused the opening of new arterial pathways that are running liquid crystal frequencies all throughout the Earth's crystalline grid. This is causing new circuitry and light body codes that are establishing new intergalactic communication lines between earth and the higher celestial dimensions. Atmospheric changes in the layers of the earth's core have also caused changes in the temperature and weather changes on the earth's surface. Also, the crystal caverns within the earth's core are now become reconnected to many dimensions some that involve the timelines of earth which includes Tara and Gaia earth. An agreement called the Pali Adorian Covenant has been formed by the Galactic Federation with the intent to rescue all the lost and damaged embodied souls and unite their consciousness back to the God-Source which supports the planetary liberation of earth that will support humanity's current ascension process to the new heaven on earth. This is being accomplished by the formation of new crystal stars within the core of the earth, where those souls on earth who have fractured souls are given these crystals throughout the timelines to heal their conscious bodies for the ascension process. As a result of these high frequency Pali Adorian plasma energies that are now being targeted to the crystal core of earth, the underground crystal bed networks through Easter Island are now linked and connected to the various sun disc vortexes that are in Brazil, Bolivia, Scotland, Australia and Giza, Egypt. These same frequencies are also beginning to nullify and turn off the Artificial Intelligence mind control signals that had been coming onto planet earth.

Planet earth is currently undergoing the process of a bifurcation of time which is the phenomenon of particle shifts that impacts how energy becomes matter and then how this matter reacts while it is shifting into different densities. When the particles shift into a different state of matter, the properties of these particles also shift, and this shift in density is currently having a profound impact on the human body as it continues to shift into higher dimensions of consciousness. The intense levels of ionization that is currently occurring in the underground crystal caverns in the core of the earth is also leading to immense solar body changes that are causing energetic collisions with the earth's electromagnetic field. These new incoming solar frequencies from the sun are also causing the earth to receive elevated levels of ionization which are the reasons why we are sometimes hearing loud underground noises that sound like sonic booms. Some of the other surface changes that have been occurring on earth include the changing of waterfront coastlines, the appearance of massive sinkholes and the occurrence of giant cracks suddenly appearing on earth's surface.

For those humans who are on the path of ascension, a new non-polarized base shield now exists within their human light body, because our light bodies have begun to build a completed Eukachistic Body to be used for the Avatar Christos-Sophia Consciousness.

This means that ascending humans will now have access to travel the stairway to the seven higher heavens to the super universe above Dimension (36) where the ascension earth resides. The human ascended body will subsequently develop into the krystallah eternal human light body which will be our vehicle to reach the Christo's Sophia earth in its unified male-female hierogamic form. The seven sacred suns in their unified form are also now transmitting the entire spectrum of the cosmic sun-star liquid crystal plasma waves into earth's crystalline grid which will allow profound expressions of this new energy into creating a variety of new forms and structures. In the crystal core of the earth there are also emerging a whole new range of elementals some of which includes sentient solar wind and solar vapors that have been revealing themselves to humans in some of the underground crystal caverns within the core of the earth.

During the end of the last ascension cycle and at the beginning of the new one in the year 2019, the seven sacred suns united and began to transmit the entire spectrum of their cosmic sun-star liquid crystal plasma waves into the earth's crystalline grid. This has changed the structure of the earth's crystal core and increased the speed of the inner and outer axis rotation spin of planet earth. This increased axis spin of planet earth has changed humanity's perception of time because time on earth is accelerating, and we are experiencing a void space of no time. These axis spin changes have caused a reset in the human light body grounding mechanisms and the human light body is now stationed in no-time, and it now has the trans-harmonic ability to now enter any timeline. These seven unified suns' frequencies now make up the new base shield template that replaces the former third dimensional mechanism that used to exist in planet earth's three lower chakras that interfaced with one another. Due to these new incoming frequencies to earth from these seven unified suns, the human light body now has a 360-degree base shield with a full interface of matter and antimatter which is leading the core of the human light body to now be stationed in the zero-point field in no-time.

There are nine realms of life that exist within the core of planet earth and from the nothingness, out of potential came a thought and the thought created the void from which within the universe came into existence just like the yolk of an egg inside a sea of albumin. As the universe grew, the universe expanded, and it was guided by the laws of energy that were created by the thought and in effect the nine universes were born simultaneously, each one a part of the whole but existing within their own bands of energetic vibrations, invisible to each other but fully engaged and part of the whole.

Human mystics and Shamans have been able to send their energetic selves into these other universes for an extraordinarily long time and earth has and is still being visited on a regular basis by these beings who live in these nine realms within earth. There are three realms that have lower vibrational energy than the human realm and there are laws of nature that restrict the ability of living beings to raise or lower their energetic thoughts to visit other realms beyond a certain level. Your guardian angels and dragons come from the ninth vibrational realm, while your spiritual guides and spiritual guardians visit the realm of earth from the seventh realm. Angels and dragons originate in the seventh realm, but when they are chosen to offer service, they move to the ninth realm and from this realm they can exist to live their life for the universe itself.

Those angels and dragons who are not ready or who choose to not offer service to other living beings in the other realms will continue to live out their lives in the seventh realm where they can still volunteer for short assignments to provide guidance to living beings from any of the other eight realms.

These realms of existence are not steps to heaven and they are only higher dimensions due to their existence in the higher energies. The sixth realm consists of more spiritual energies than any other realm because the banding that exists in this realm in the form of energetic wave lengths much like the gravity in the rings of Saturn. These same laws that govern the energies of the universe also have banded energies that can provide stability that allows a realm like this to develop. Spiritual energy flows through all the realms just like the effects of gravity that flows throughout all the nine realms. This spiritual energy is the original thought that created the void that existed before the expansion of the universe of multiples. The sixth realm is where the universal cosmic mind exists, the great spirit, the one who lives through all of us and in all the realms. The thought of creation exists within the laws that were created to shape the wholeness of the universe. This thought has no control over this creation without having to de-create the physical universe and the end of the nine realms and the living beings who have come into existence each with the thought and spiritual energy flowing through every living being who live in all the nine realms. This energy is referred to as spirit, chi, qi or life force. All the energies of the nine realms are all part of the spiritual thought energy of the one and they are available to be used for growth and development for all living beings of all the nine realms without exception.

Human consciousness exists in a non-local state within the human realm, but it can and does also touch all the nine realms. Humans who live among nature and its natural energies are more in tune and sensitive to the energies of the other realms and visitors who often come to the earth realm. There are eight other planet earths currently in existence with each one sharing the same space in the whole universe but each existing on different wavelengths and vibrations. This applies to all matter in the universe, for example the people who live on the planet Pleiades also have another light shadow selves that each exist in a different realm at a different energy level.

There are seven dimensions in the human universe, three are physical, three are electromagnetic and one that is a high energy dimension which contains the human psychic energy. This dimension is shared universally across all the nine universes, and it is used to communicate by some, while others use the human psychic energy in this universe to travel. Across all the nine universes there exists twelve distinct dimensions and they each have their own name and nature. Consciousness has developed in all the electromagnetic dimensions that are affiliated with the human universe, and these are referred to as the western worlds that consist of:

The Underworld, The Overworld and The Middleworld, and these worlds have their own names, and they have no end, because they are electromagnetic in nature. Humans and other life forms can visit, create, and interact with the inhabitants of these three worlds, and they are able to use each other's energies to survive. There is a wide spectrum of energies in the universe and some of these energies do not disperse or convert, because since all energy wavelengths are alive, they have a lifespan, a desire to survive and glow, just like a flame energy wavelength will attempt to spread and survive to extend its existence. Humans refer to some energies as subtle energies and these energies are generated with more consciousness than others, because they are created by organic complex life forms. Humans have learned how to directly manipulate some of these subtle energies through thought manifestation of the use of crystals. This is since humans contain within themselves crystalline matter without which we could not survive, and this is what you can call a symbiosis relationship between crystals and humans the same way bacteria and fungi have a symbiotic relationship.

The ancient stone builders used stone that contained a certain quality of crystalline structures within the rock to generate, amplify and direct the subtle energies of earth itself for the overall benefit of all. The goal of the ancient stone builders was to build their structures to shape and direct the subtle energies of the universe to gather, enhance and generate additional subtle energies. Humanity needs to develop ways of thinking and seeing that will generate the thoughts which are also energies and then merge these energies into the great matrix of life where they will affect the greater good.

Ten Ways To Be Happy

Write in your journal daily to feel and keep track of your life's occurrences.

Get rid of toxins, trauma and negative thoughts now.

Meditate daily and accept the Universal Father's source light energy to flow into your body.

Breathe in peace and breathe out love daily.

Listen to high frequency music daily.

Spend time daily in nature with God.

Keep the feelings of love and compassion in your heart and forgive now.

Experience and feel the highest emotion of authenticity now.

Tell yourself daily that you are on the true road to ascension and keep going.

There are numerous universes that exist within the cosmos, multiverse and the omniverse. Some of these universes are limitless and beyond our imagination, while others are as small as an infinitesimal point. Some universes such as our Nebadon universe, contain physical matter and antimatter that accommodates both physical and ethereal beings. Our Nebadon universe is composed of less than four percent of matter and the remaining 96% consists of antimatter and invisible matter which are limited to be detected by the five human perception capabilities.

Antimatter does not have density, no weight, no smell, taste, or texture and it cannot be detected through hearing or sight. Consciousness does exist in antimatter and thoughts and emotions are some of the energies that are present within the matrix of antimatter. The human soul is an entity that is made of antimatter, and it is capable of interfacing with matter like it does with our physical body. The realm of the etheric is within the territory of antimatter and antimatter can only exist as plasma in this realm because plasma is the fourth state of matter.

Earth is planet #606 in the Nebadon universe, and our universe is divided into five distinct Harmonic Universess. Each one of these Harmonic Universe are classified into three dimensions for a total of fifteen dimensions within our Nebadon universe. Each dimension has seven planes within it and their own distinct vibration frequency rate which indicates the consciousness that each plane of existence demands of the beings who live in each dimension. In our Nebadon universe the energy of consciousness is the lowest in the first dimension and the highest in dimension fifteen. Only twelve dimensions are viable dwelling domains for physical sentient beings to live in. Dimensions thirteen through fifteen are reserved for the realm of divinity where the highest-ranking spiritual entities and the beings who are responsible for the operation and creation portions of our Nebadon universe. Dimensions one through twelve are available for all the other sentient beings to live and as these beings excel in their spiritual rank, they can ascend to higher states of consciousness and move to the higher dimensions. The Nebadon universe is one big hologram and since it is a hologram-based universe, you can always look at only a part of the universe to see a representation of the total Nebadon universe. A hologram has the property that no matter what part of the universe you look at, it has the exact same properties of the entire hologram of the Nebadon universe. The geometric equations that the entire Nebadon universe is based on are calculated and maintained by Archangel Metatron (Enoch the Ethiopian) in the sixth dimension. All matter on planet earth begins first in the sixth dimension and it is then sent to the fourth dimension for humans to pick up the idea to bring it into existence on the physical level. This means that the thought or idea behind every chair, car, painting, etc. begins first in the sixth dimension and then it is sent to the fourth dimension for the idea to be picked up to be made into matter.

The first Harmonic Universe (HU1) is the domain of pure physicality. It is the universe of soul reincarnation which we refer to as the self. Your crystalline self, the I AM Presence or your higher mind all live outside of the first Harmonic Universe (HU1), because their vibrational frequencies are higher than yourself. The higher mind lives billions of years in the future in the seventh dimension, and once you raise your vibration to the second Harmonic Universe (HU2), you will then download your higher mind to merge with you as one within your human mind and you will be able to establish communication. This event can happen naturally at any time during your ascension process, but especially when you are doing something creative such as drawing and painting pictures or during the dream states.

The human conscious mind is normally tuned to operate in the lower frequencies, and it cannot openly perceive while this initial contact with our higher mind is happening, but we each download our higher mind into our matrix during the natural stages of our ascension process. Our higher mind operates at such a high stage of frequencies, that during the initial stages of linking with one's consciousness, it will at first be located above your crown charka above your head, unattached and unaware of the details of your physical sensations. The higher mind cannot perceive the workings of our physical body until you merge your ego with it and become one. This is the reason why the conscious mind is merged with your higher mind, you will then begin to experience a highly focused refined experience of total awe. As humanity continues to ascend and move up in dimensional consciousness, the sensitivity to the physical begins to diminish and instead the human spiritual consciousness begins to expand.

The first Harmonic Universe (HU1) is comprised of the first, second, and third dimensions, and these three dimensions are the starting point for sentient humans to gain their spiritual education. The first Harmonic Universe (HU1) with its three distinct dimensions which are located on planet earth, is the realm of lower physicality, and it has the lowest vibrational frequencies in the entire Nebadon universe.

Sentient conscious souls often split further into lower conscious beings, and they are then sent to the realm of physicality on planet earth to experience life, to love, to experiment and to learn important life lessons before they can increase their level of consciousness to ascend back home to the higher dimensions. Of all the planets in our universe, planet earth is the hardest school, and a soul must train for at least one million years before incarnating on earth to receive their PHD at the end of the life experience on planet earth. Linear time used to exist on planet earth before the portal to the fourth dimension opened on December 21, 2012, and the life experiment on earth is based on duality and it is all an illusion.

The main reason behind the existence of parallel universes and alternate realities within earth's paradigms of reality is because, the more the merrier and more information from the lower realms can be transmitted to the higher dimensions of consciousness. The individual oversoul often distributes the light of consciousness to its constituent souls who then further divide into many selves where they are then sent to earth to experience the duality life lessons. The entire human life experience on earth is pre-designed based on free will choices that we each make in the Akashic Records section of the Hall of Records that is in the upper astral plane. Many humans take their life on earth way too seriously and become too attached to materialism, carnal lust and games of competition and they end up forgetting that the very purpose of this game of life on earth is to make your own heaven on earth to attain the spiritual evolution you need to ascend back home to the higher realms.

The reason humans forget the real purpose of experiencing life on planet earth is that they remain detached from the vast pool of knowledge that your oversoul and higher mind possess. When we incarnate on earth as a human being, we only bring one-third of our soul's total knowledge, so to ensure we learn our life lessons while attending the earth school, the rest of your spirit remains in the higher dimensions. So, we never really leave heaven, because only one-third of our spirit exists here in the material realm of earth. Our total isolation or separation from God, the Source when we incarnate on earth is an illusion, because from the moment of our birth and until our transition, we always have spiritual guides, angels, our higher mind, prayer and meditation and self-reflection with us during our life's journey on earth. While we experience our life on earth, we daily continue to have first and second dimensional experiences. The first dimensional consciousness is linked to the mineral kingdom on earth. The most important aspect of one-dimensional consciousness are the mineral crystals located in the core of the earth that have the unique characteristic of having the power of communication and discernment. Crystals also have the power of absorption and the ability to store knowledge, and all humans have these same crystals running all throughout our bodies. Most of the crystals within the human body are currently in a chaotic form, but as we continue the path of ascension to the new heaven on earth, these crystals are now transforming into complex crystalline form, and these crystalline forms are regulated and precise. The human body including the endocrine gland system, the entire human cellular system all the way down to the DNA/RNA level are now crystallizing and for every human physical organ, and etheric counterpart exists.

Once humanity is ready to totally shift to the fifth dimension to live, the crystalline forms in the human organs will begin to appear from within and they will replace the old physical organs and it will be just like growing new skin, and we will ascend to the new heaven on earth in the human body suit that will consist of half of a (666) carbon body and half of (999) Adam Kadmon crystalline body.

The second dimensional consciousness on earth relates to the living vegetation and the lower animals. Two of the most important aspects of the second dimension on earth is that it is based on a group consciousness which provides a sense of security and protection for the self. The second important aspect of two-dimensional consciousness is that when living plants and animals use their motor skills, they can do things automatically without having to consult their conscious minds. A large majority of the human motor skills are a direct consequence of our second dimensional consciousness. All humans possess a one-dimensional self, our mineral aspect as well as a two-dimensional self, which is the plant or lower animal aspect of us who lives within the human body. Humans also have a fourth-dimensional self, the seven ethereal bodies that also live within us, because humans are multidimensional beings. The seven distinct ethereal bodies that each human possess are: physical, ethereal, astral, emotional, thought, causal, spiritual, and finally the human light body. The human light body is crystalline, and it is composed of silicate matter for the assurance of optimal performance and agility. Also, since humans have the constituent parts of the human soul or higher self, humans constantly vibrate back and forth into and out of parallel realities which means that we are multidimensional beings.

Within the first Harmonic Universe (HU1) there are an infinite distinct number of timelines and they each have different frequencies with each living being slightly above or below one another. There is only one physical earth that has an infinite number of diverse timelines that all exist together. This means that we also have many different identities, which are copies of the same soul fragment that is experiencing life in the 20th century earth, the baroque earth, in the medieval time, in the time of the Romans, or in Atlantis, and all at the same time but in a different frequency for each timeline. Only one reality can manifest itself on earth at a time, but all these realities still exist together simultaneously. This is the reason it is said that linear time is an illusion of duality of the third-dimensional earth, because we all live in the now moment, and the concept of the past and the future is an illusion. There is simply no past or future because there is only the now moment. Certain timelines on earth appear as the progression of one saga after another, but all the matrix programs that are being run on earth are running only in the now moment. Our Nebadon universe is based on one big hologram which depicts an illusion and holographic projection of the matrix of life which is the exact mechanism that brings the multiple realities and parallel realities that exist on earth to life, and each timeline or parallel reality is defined by its distinct vibrational rate.

To be able to experience life on earth and play the life game of duality, a soul chooses to incarnate and play a role as a transitory identity, just like a fictional character that is real and exists while we play the games of life on earth. The end game code for the life experience on earth is: Prime Creator.

Humans are all multidimensional beings who can experience more than one life and timeline at the same time, because while we are grounded here living on earth, we also have other lives on a different dimension, a different planet, a different timeline and with a different parallel reality on earth.

The living conditions on earth have drastically changed after the end of WWII and with the beginning of the 1950's. After WWII ended, the light quotient on planet earth had diminished so much that the earth's pilot light was almost extinguished and at this time Gaia earth sent out a distress call to the galaxies for help and a directive was sent from the Prime Creator to the galactic elders to send earth assistance. At that time, many Galactic's from the planets of Andromeda, Sirius, Pleaides, the Arcturians and many more arrived at the outer atmosphere of earth and collectively projected their light onto earth, but it was not enough to raise the light quotient on planet earth. A second message was then sent to the Galactic Divine Hierarchy to ask for volunteers to begin to incarnate on planet earth in the year 1950 to help to raise its light quotient by raising the vibrational frequency of the planet.

Also, during these same times, a visiting group of members from the Galactic Federation of Planets were selected to go to earth to contact the various governments to offer their assistance. During these visits to earth, the members of the Galactic Federation of Planets requested to the various governments to deactivate their nuclear weapons and refrain from using fossil fuels and in return they offered to equip the earth governments with highly advanced technology, but their proposals were flatly refused by the governments on earth, because they were under the control of Cabal-Deep State, Reptilians and their puppet Illuminati/Elite families who did not want to give up their control of planet earth. In addition to refusing help from the Galactic Federation of Planets, the dark cabal made the choice to distribute free dangerous drugs to the public worldwide in the early 1960's and incited a series of wars in various locations around the world. This was referred to as the New Age /Hippie Movement and various puppet Elite families oversaw the worldwide distribution of some of these drugs that included: heroin, mescaline, LSD, cocaine laced with ether, cocaine laced with fentanyl, weed, crack cocaine, opium, amphetamines, Percocet and the general population on earth were out in the quantum field without a clue as to where they were going, and this led to the destruction of the moral fabric of many societies worldwide.

All these negative events finally took a divergent turn when in 1987 a pulse was taken of planet earth and the findings were that fifty percent of humanity were ready for ascension. In the year 1987, the Prime Creator, Source decreed through the Harmonic Convergence that planet earth along with its inhabitants would ascend to the new heaven on earth.

For humanity living on earth, our physical life is a purposeful illusion, and we create all that we see around us in harmony. Our life on earth is an educational creation, a movie set that we are each producing, directing, and acting on various levels of consciousness. In the 3D earth physicality, we were the actor's taking direction from our higher mind and we were acting so efficiently on the movie set of the 3D linear time and space, that we never realized that our life is nothing but a stage. The actions that we as humans take in each of our lifetimes on earth are each only a scene in a play and these actions are all important because each role, we take in life has a meaning and offers us the chance to learn life lessons. The lessons are to connect with our Prime Creator by creating your heaven here on earth and make ascension your main focus in life. Consider what the world would be like if all humanity evolved spiritually to expand their consciousness to ascension to the new heaven on earth. This ascension is occurring now on earth and there will no longer be anymore degrees of separation on earth.

Before the beginning of the core of earth's crystalline activation, it was extremely hard and even impossible to connect into the crystal caverns to try to map out the route of these crystals, because the calamity of extensive overlays of demonic shadow creatures from cloning existed. It has now been discovered that within these crystal layers in earth's core that there were remnants of many grotesque creatures and more monstrosities that had been buried down in the collective subconscious mind of planet earth. In addition, these monstrosities had generated many obstructions that hindered the energetic connection and mapping project to proceed smoothly within the crystal core of the earth.

The earth's crystalline caverns are the internal power crystal generators and data memory storage devices for the planetary brain of earth. Many of these crystal clusters are the remnants of what is left of the earth's crystals after the fall of Atlantis over 12,000 years ago, which were then misused by negative alien reptilians after the end of the Lucifer

Rebellion and the fall of earth's Planetary Prince Caligastia, which also marks the timeline of the fall of Tara earth. Due to the abuse by the negative reptilian aliens and cohorts from Atlantis, these crystals were exploded in the underground crystal caverns which then created a cataclysm and even more widespread devastation on earth's surface.

These damaged crystal remnants in the crystalline caverns in earth's core are still being used today to power up the negative reptilian's NET (Nephilim Electrostatic Transduction) technology and its reversal fields that are programmed from off planet that runs the Metatronic Negative Aliens Reversal Consciousness (NARC) frequencies and the Alien machinery programming all throughout the core of the earth. These remnant crystals are the keys for earth's data programming, and they have now been confiscated by the white brotherhood and they are now being used as memory storage devices.

During the invasions on earth by these negative reptilian aliens, they also implanted artificial timelines with false identities and false memories about important historical events that happened on earth as inserts to further confuse and trap humanity in artificial implanted timelines. This is a psychological warfare strategy of using assorted artificial technologies to gain control over the ascension timelines on earth going all the way back to some of the critical events that contained benevolent works of some of the ascended masters and Christ missions that were completed on earth by the guardians, so these negative reptilian aliens not only re-wrote some of earth's history, but they also used their manipulation of the true timelines on earth as a negative tool to undermine the human consciousness of humanity on earth over 500,000 years ago.

The selenite rods, gypsum are commonly used and programmed as large computer chips, and these chips hold a tremendous amount of planetary data information about the contents of earth's planetary brain. Unfortunately, some of these large computer chips are still being used by some of the negative reptilian aliens to transmit programmed data through the earth's planetary brain directly into the human collectives' minds and into the soul matrix of humanity and this negative programmed data impacts humanity and all life on the surface of earth. These same underground crystals are also storage devices that contain data about planet earth and its life on the surface.

After the collapse of earth's natural magnetic field during the timeline of Atlantis, this is when the negative aliens were able to gain control of the crystal core of planet earth and the reversed alien technology that they used led to humanity's enslavement and turned earth into a prison planet. Around 5,550 years ago during the Egyptian-Sumerian invasion by negative aliens, this is when the twelve strands of humanity's DNA was unplugged, and this confused both the entire human language and our ability to communicate with each other. This failure in humanity's ability to communicate with each other occurred, because the earth's magnetic field collapsed, causing our human DNA to scramble, and thus removing humanity's natural and innate skill to communicate with each other. This collapse of the earth's magnetic field interfered with the proper sequence of the fire letters to arrange correctly in our DNA template. Humanity also lost its memories, its mental telepathy abilities and language which caused the total wiping out of all of humanity's genetic memories, language and causing the wiping out of all humanity's genetic memories. This is the real and true story of what is referred to as the Tower of Babel implant, because after this alien implant was placed inside the DNA of humanity, we became to be babbling idiots.

During these negative alien invasions on earth, these aliens were also able to negate humanity's ability to use our innate ability to access our multidimensionality and our ability to expand our human consciousness. Within the human body amygdala organ functions in the limbic system and it deals with the human instinct and emotions. Through the use of mind control and other artificial intelligence technologies that included genetic implants, these negative alien invaders also managed to block humanity from reaching any of the higher dimensions, which condemned humans to an endless cycle of reincarnation with no rest or healing in between the reincarnations to a life of imprisonment and enslavement to the lower dimensions of earth's 1D, 2D, and 3D and this has provided the alien reptilians with humans as their feeding grounds to obtain all the loosh fear and control based energy that they want for all these years.

The elementals that make up the human body the amygdala are now distorted in their cellular matrix because of the negative alien's tampering of our earth's timelines, the deliberate genetic manipulation of humanity's history and the introduction of the false alien checkerboard mutation matrix on planet earth. A wide range of genetic modifications and frequency fences were also used by these negative alien invaders that created a consciousness human slave race on earth and artificial technologies were used to purposely condense particles and compress matter forms to lock down the consciousness in human bodies and imprison them within a particular time and space.

Because of these continuous alien invasions and interferences on planet earth, many of the underground crystal networks in earth's core exploded which then generated cataclysms of massive floods on earth's surface. The shattered remnants of the crystals located in earth's planetary grid have been used by these negative alien invaders repeatedly to construct the basis of humanity's genetic damage, which is the false checkerboard matrix. This false matrix is a form of matrix that runs the artificial intelligence Nephilim electrostatic transduction (NET) reversal field technology along with a form of artificial intelligence programming which our current mainstream geneticists call human junk DNA genes.

The negative alien's technique of creating cloned versions of certain human individuals as well as timelines is accomplished by the bonding of memories, especially the negative memories that relate to an individual's vulnerabilities and moments of weakness. These false artificial intelligence versions of the original human individual are then applied to the fake clone which then generates a shadow body of the original human being. This is evil and extremely dangerous alien technology and the reason that these alien beings continue to create human clones here on earth is to manipulate and control the consciousness of individual humans. It is especially important that all of humanity remains aware of this evil and deal with our own vulnerabilities that can be used as tool for these negative aliens to complete this evil deed of cloning humans.

We each daily must be willing to do the necessary emotional healing through the clearing from our bodies of past traumas, triggers, and emotional pain, so that these weaknesses do not become an obstacle to our ability to continue to expand our consciousness to ascend to the new heaven on earth. The negative alien's reasons, mechanics and purpose of continuing to clone humans is because by reading the signature of certain human individuals especially celebrities who have influence or others, these negative aliens are often able to reverse engineer the memories recorded in the timelines and in the DNA of the clone and bond them to some false figure or false timeline leading to generating cloned versions of them. Their main agenda is to exploit the weakness and vulnerabilities of the targeted individual to project out cloned versions or false realities that can easily be perceived by others as being real and this only leads to these negative aliens being able to better control the consciousness of the public.

When humanity's ability to expand the human consciousness and the ability to access your multidimensional abilities are blocked, the human brain is blocked from being able to access the higher dimensional frequency energies and the subsequent emotional experiences that goes with it. As a result of these blockages, humanity has become plagued with having little or expanded consciousness, perception, emotional intelligence, or intuitive capabilities. In addition, due to the blockage and lack of these important intuitive functions, one becomes unable to control their instinctual impulses, which leads to a person to not have a sense of compassion, empathy, or love for others.

Most humans living on earth have an extremely limited range of perception vision as it relates to states of matter that are available in the visible light spectrum. Most humans can only see about one percent of the known electromagnetic wave spectrum with our bare eyes. The solid state of matter is an illusion on earth that we make up with our human physical senses and for the human brain and nervous system to be able to function properly, the brain must be healthy. However, the negative invasion aliens have been able to hijack earth's planetary brain and by doing this, they have been able to disrupt the human neurotransmitters and normal hormonal functions of the human brain. This gives these aliens control over the human bio-neurological system where they can now manipulate, control, suppress, and distort the way humans think and behave. If you stop for a minute and observe the current situation on planet earth, we can now really understand what really happened to humanity when the reptilians continued to invade earth, when the Lucifer Rebellion occurred on earth and when the civilizations of Atlantis and Lemuria collapsed so many ages ago. All these catastrophes help to explain why there is so much anxiety, fear, insecurity, misery, anger, and conflict being exhibited on planet earth now.

As a result of the improper functioning of the human endocrine gland system, this has caused a negative impact on the hypothalamus of the human brain, on the thalamus, the pineal gland, the thyroid gland, and the thymus, all of which causes a negative effect on the human immune system when they are not functioning properly. The malfunctions of all these human glands also greatly accelerates the human aging process.

Every day after you have completed your daily prayers, quantum jumps and meditations, say this aloud to yourself.

" I do not age, I evolve as long as I continue to accept our Prime Creator's, Source light and life energy to freely flow all throughout my human body daily, and I as an individual human will continue to daily raise my vibrational frequencies on earth by observing and shining my light, love, compassion, forgiveness, gratitude and authenticity to myself and to the entire human collective on earth."

The improper functioning of the human immune system also prevents humans from establishing important links to be able to communicate with the higher dimensions of consciousness. If you are on the path of ascension, you need to be in communication with your higher mind, your spiritual guides, and angels daily, because they are all here to guide and protect you on your journey of life. For centuries on earth, the negative invading reptilian aliens have been harvesting and controlling humanity using fear and anxiety to continue to harvest the loosh energy they need to survive. This is because when you make the free will decision to separate yourself from the light of our Prime Creator, Source, then you become a vampire and the only way you can survive is from the fear, pain, and suffering of others and this is called negative loosh energy. The negative reptilian aliens have been able for so long to control humanity on earth by taking over the amygdala functions of the crystal quartz shelves in the crystal caverns in the core of the earth. By having the control over the crystal's amygdala functions these aliens can incite overpowering emotional reactions to suit whatever agenda they want at the time, and this has put humanity in a state of bondage, because these aliens can incite fear, anxiety and induce the fight, flight impulses constantly into humanity's brains to give the false perception of danger. This way these negative reptilian aliens can continue to induce this negative energy of the futile fear for survival mode into humanity's brains and continue to harvest all the negative loosh energy they want. The human amygdala is also involved in the body's autonomic responses that are related to hormonal secretions which then provoke emotional reactions such as fear and the responses that are related to memory. Any negative stimulation of the amygdala arouses autonomic fear that the negative aliens then use for mind control, which in turn causes the human brain circuits to operate differently which in turn causes new false memories to from in the human brain.

The calamity of the negative reptilian aliens' aggressive takeover of the crystalline core technology in the earth has led to the corruption and reversal of the instructional sets that normally transmit from the earth's crystal core to humanity's brain and this has had a negative impact on the normal functions of the human amygdala. The result has caused an unprecedented rise in anxiety disorders on earth that are linked to Obsessive Compulsive Disorder, Post Traumatic Stress, Panic Attacks and Anxiety Attacks have become to be common ailments among humanity living today on earth.

Another method used by these negative reptilian aliens to gain control over the individual thoughts and behaviors of humanity are assorted electromagnetic technologies that are used to transmit extremely low frequencies (ELF) to humanity's brains and this is a form of predatory parasite negative programming that incites negative emotional energetic responses by targeting humanity's' amygdala with fear mongering and other related negative implants. Through this evil interference by these negative reptilian aliens, they have created a global system on earth that is based on fear, and they use the Illuminati and Elite families as their puppets to manage their evil schemes on earth. The current corrupt pharmaceuticals industries on earth also serve and uphold the evil interests of these evil reptilians and the once fundamental principle for physicians to heal their sick patients has lost its meaning, because doctors today are licensed drug dealers who are being trained to over medicate their patients which has led to many anxious and depressed humans living on earth today.

When the human synapses are blocked or distorted from receiving an electrical signal to another cell, then a neurotransmitter breaks down and muddles up all communication between the cells in the human brain. This in turn disconnects the entire messaging system in the brain's neural network. When the negative reptilian aliens change the human synapses to instead bond with artificial neural networks through the usage of pills and the constant exposure to 5G cellphone towers and chemtrails, all these things impair the normal synaptic functions in the human brain. This also distorts the signal messaging of the human brain and the neural network and further disrupts the brain's normal communication and muddles up its language capabilities. In addition, these 5G cell phone towers that you see everywhere are reading your every thought and watching your every move, so to be safe and to avoid radiation exposure from the 5G cell phone towers, if you must occasionally use a cell phone, always use the speaker option and never place it next to your ear on your head.

The current epidemic of the pharmaceutical companies, Big Pharma on earth are being tightly controlled by the Cabal, Deep State, and the puppets of the negative reptilians to oversee their many interests on earth. The current medical practices on earth are highly influenced by the pharmaceutical companies and their drug reps who are trained to encourage doctors to recommend pills to their patients which include the frequent prescription of narcotics drugs that interfere with the natural biological synaptic function of the brain and neural networks. In addition, these prescription narcotic pills hijack the human amygdala which then causes high anxiety and negative emotional states for those who take these pills.

The reptilians in conjunction with the Cabal have also devised many techniques to transmit artificial signals from earth's planetary brain to incite such low frequency impulses into humanity' brains that over a period of time, this leads to severe emotional trauma which in turn causes human soul fracturing. Soul fracturing means that parts of your soul are stuck up in the ether instead of your entire soul being with you in your body and since you need your entire soul to ascend back home to the new heaven on earth, soul fracturing further anchors you to the lower third dimensional state of consciousness on 3D earth. All these horrible tactics that are being used by the reptilians and their cohorts here on earth has prompted the urgent need to help repair the earth's planetary brain now by repairing the crystalline networks in the earth's core and this will then lead to upshifting the human consciousness and help to improve humanity's' emotional states.

The negative reptilians have also deployed special software to attack the current five percent of humanity who are on the path to ascend to the new heaven on earth. This negative online anti-ascension program is known as the Splitter Tech Spray which sends frequencies specifically to ascending humans that causes unprecedented body pain and suffering as we continue to raise our vibrations and ascend. In addition, an entire army of artificial intelligence replicate clones and imposters from the lower astral plane have been sent to earth under the online name of, aura blue coding to continue to try to further confuse the ascending light workers and to continue to inflict them with pain and suffering. The crux of this evil splitter technology by the negative reptilians is to keep on inflicting the light workers with so much pain and suffering so that they become totally distracted and not be able to sense this evil frequency. This evil splitter technology is attacking both male and female ascending humans to stop the light workers/star seeds from continuing to form a spiritual union as one in Christ Consciousness. For so many years these negative reptilians have repeatedly deployed evil attacks against humanity on earth in their attempt to stop the ascension process that has been occurring on earth since the portal to the fourth dimension opened on December 21, 2012, but they have failed miserably, because the first wave of ascending. Humans are now scheduled to enter the new heaven on earth during the spring of the year 2025..

CHAPTER THREE

THE SUPERUNIVERSE AND THE SEVEN HIGHER HEAVENS

We are God's handiwork created in Christ Jesus to do good works.

(Ephesians 2:10)

I have calmed and quieted myself, .

I am content.

(Psalm 131:2)

A Prayer:

God of all hope, please remind me of Jesus conquering death-victory.

PARADISE-THE SEVEN HIGHER HEAVENS

Our Universal Paradise Father's purpose when he created the perfect central universe of Paradise, the seven higher heavens was purely for the satisfaction of His divine nature.

Havona, Paradise serves as the pattern creation for all the other universes and as the finishing school for mortals from the worlds of time and space as they travel the long road to Paradise. God has an amazing plan for perfecting evolutionary mortals to ascend from the worlds of time and space and after they attain Paradise, and the corps of the finality is to provide ascending mortals with further training for some more future work on Paradise.

Paradise serves many purposes in the administration of the universal realms of space. The personal presence of the Universal Prime Creator Father who lives at the very center of the upper surface abodes of the spiritual deities in Paradise along with the Eternal Son and the Holy Spirit, provides the divinity that is needed for this magnificent place that is located above dimension thirty-six in our Nebadon universe. The Universal Father always has and always will live in the same abode in Paradise, and he is cosmically focalized and spiritually personalized as a permanent resident at the center of Paradise which is the center of the universe of universes. Those mortals who are on the path of true ascension will all be led directly back to the Universal Father's presence to his central home in Paradise, because God's infinite being flows the flood streams of pure life energy and love to the entire universe. Paradise is also the home, workshop, and playground of the corps of finaliters and for every God-knowing mortal who wants to be a finaliter. The central universe of Paradise is not only mortal man's established destiny, but it is also the starting point for their eternal career to be a member of the corps of finaliter in their universal adventure in the experience of exploring the infinity of the Universal Father in Paradise.

Havona, Paradise will continue to function even in future universe ages as a training universe for all ascending beings as an experiential training universe for the past, present and all future created mortal beings.

Planet earth is also called the planet Urantia and it is number (606) in the planetary system of Satania. Our Satania system is comprised of (619) inhabited worlds and two hundred more planets that are favorably evolving towards becoming inhabited worlds in the near future. The headquarters world for our system of Satania is called Jerusem and it is planet number (24) located in the constellation of Norlatiadek. The constellation of Norlatiadek consists of one hundred local systems and its headquarters world is called Edentia. Norlatiadek is number (70) in our Nebadon universe. Our local Nebadon universe consists of one hundred constellations and its capital is Salvington and the Nebadon universe is number (84) located in the minor sector of Ensa. The minor sector of Ensa consists of one hundred constellations and its capital is called Uminor the third. Uminor is located in the major sector of Splandon, which consists of one hundred minor sectors and its headquarters world is called Umajor the fifth and it is the fifth major sector of the superuniverse of Orvonton which is the seventh segment of the grand superuniverse. The grand superuniverse number for our planet earth is 5,342,482,337,666. This is the registry number for earth that is recorded on Paradise in the vast catalog of all the inhabited worlds in our Nebadon universe. Planet earth is a member of an enormous cosmos, because earth belongs to a large infinite family of worlds and planet earth is precisely administered to and lovingly taken care of just as if it were the only inhabited planet in all existence.

Paradise is the center of the force energy activation of the cosmos. It is the universe position of our Universal Prime Creator Father, who is the Father, the First Source and Center, the cosmos focal point of the Unqualified Absolute and the source of all energy. Paradise is the realm of primal origin and the center of all the force energy activation for the cosmos. The Universal Father is the creator, the controller and infinite upholder and he covers himself with light as a garment and stretches out His light onto the heavens as a curtain.

The enlightened worlds recognize and worship the Universal Father, and they embark on the long, long Paradise journey of finding and attaining the Universal Father. The goal of the children of time is to find the Universal Father, to comprehend his divine nature, and to become like God just as he is in his Paradise home. Mortal men who live on earth can attain the divine goal that God that has set for us, and when one does achieve Paradise, they will be one with God and live in his sphere of infinity and eternity. This search by mortal men to find the God of the universes is the supreme adventure of all the inhabitants of all the worlds of time and space. Not all the lower spirit beings of the local universes are immediately destined for Paradise, but it remains the goal of desire for all supernatural personalities.

The Universal Father is personally a resident on Paradise at the very center of the universe and he is also present on the worlds of time and space in the minds of his countless children of time, because he indwells them in their minds as the Divine Thought Adjusters. At the same time, the Universal Father is far removed from us, but he is still intimately associated with all his planetary sons. Paradise is also the home of the Eternal Son, the Infinite Spirit and all their divine associates. The Central Isle of Paradise is the most gigantic, organized body of cosmic reality in the entire master universe, and it is a material sphere as well as a spiritual home. All the intelligent creations of the Universal Father live on Paradise and the material beauty there is magnificent, because of its physical perfection. The depths of the spiritual beauty in Paradise are beyond the comprehension of the human mind because Paradise is from eternity and there are no records that can explain the origin of the nuclear Isle of Light and Life of Paradise which is located above dimension thirty-six in our Nebadon universe. Paradise is unique and it is the final goal of destiny for all free will spirit beings.

Paradise is the geographic center of infinity, and it is not a part of a universal creation, because it is an eternal and exclusive existence. Everything that has been, now is, or is yet to be, has come, now comes, or will come forth from, will come from Paradise, because it is the center of all creation, the source of all energies that exist on the worlds of time and space, and the origin of all living personalities. Every mortal who has spent his life doing the will of the Father is already on the path for the long path to Paradise for the pursuit of divinity and perfection. And when such an animal-origin being does get to stand as countless mortals now do before the Universal Father in Paradise after having ascended from the lowly spheres of space, such an achievement represents the reality of a glorious spiritual transformation that borders on the limits of supremacy.

As you proceed outward from Paradise through the horizontal extension of pervaded space, the master universe of Paradise exists in six concentric ellipses that encircle the Eternal Isle of Paradise. Havona, the central universe is not a time creation, it is an eternal existence universe that consists of one billion spheres, and it is surrounded by twenty-one satellites. The Paradise-Havona system is the eternal nucleus of the master universe, and it encircles the eternal Paradise Isle and all seven of the superuniverse of the regions that revolve around this sphere of outer space. The grand universe is an organized and inhabited creation that consists of seven superuniverses and seven trillion inhabited planets. Our local universe that includes planet earth, exists at the border of the grand universe currently at the tip of the fifth dimension.

The sacred spheres of Paradise are the three spheres that are located between the Central Isle of Paradise and the innermost part of the Havona planetary circuits. The inner most circuit consists of the seven secret spheres of the Universal Father, the second circuit are the seven luminous worlds of the Eternal Son, and the third circuit are the seven immense spheres of the Infinite Spirit which is also the headquarter worlds of the Seven Master Spirits. These three sacred spheres of Paradise are the seven world circuits of the Father, the Son, and the Holy Spirit, and they are spheres of grandeur and unimagined glory. All twenty-one of these spheres are enormous and like Paradise, they are eternal with no records of their origin. The seven secret spheres of the Universal Father that encircle Paradise are highly reflective of the spiritual luminosity of the shining eternal Deities who shine their light of divine glory throughout Paradise and the seven circuits of Havona. On the seven sacred Paradise worlds of the Eternal Son, the Eternal Son also shines his light without heat all throughout Paradise and to the billion worlds of the seven circuits of the central universe.

The seven sacred spheres of the Infinite Spirit are occupied by the Seven Master Spirits who preside over the destiny of the seven universes, and they send forth the spiritual illumination of the Third person of Deity to the creatures of time and space and all Havona receives their illumination.

Divington is the bosom world of the Universal Father, and it holds the secrets of nature and the activities of all the other forms of the Universal Father fragments of the gravity messengers.

Sonarington is the personal receiving world of the Eternal Son, and it is the headquarters of the descending and ascending Sons of God. This sphere is also the Paradise home for all the sons of the Eternal Son. The secret of this sphere includes the incarnation of the divine sons. When a divine son becomes a son of man, he is born of a woman as what occurred 2,154 years ago when Jesus was born from his mother Mary.

Spiritington is the Paradise home of the high beings who represent the Infinite Spirit. In this world, the Seven master Spirits and their offspring from all the universes are assigned the job of up stepping the mortal beings on the worlds of time and space so they can enter the Paradise levels of eternity. The secret of the Spiritington world is the mystery of reflectivity which is a secret between God and the Holy Spirit.

Vicegerington is the secret sphere of certain unrevealed beings who have their origin by the acts of the Universal Father and his Eternal Son. This sphere is the Paradise home of many glorified beings, and the secret of this planet includes trinitization with the secret authority to represent the Trinity and act as a vice-gerent of the Gods.

Solarington is the world where a host of beings of origin from the conjunct acts of the Universal Father and the Infinite Spirit give them the traits of the Universal Father. This world is also the home of the solitary messengers and other angelic orders. This world holds the secret of the personal relation of the Infinite Spirit with certain offspring of the Third Source and Center.

Seraphington is the destiny world for all the ministering orders of the angelic hosts, which includes the supernaphim angels, the seconaphim angels, and the seraphim angels. The secret of this world is the ability of the various orders of seraphim angels and allied spirit beings to envelop within their spirit forms the ability to carry non-material personalities on lengthy interplanetary journeys.

Ascendington is the rendezvous planet for the ascending creatures of time and space to come to until they attain Paradise status. Most ascending mortals spend most of their vacation time on this planet and as an ascending mortal continues his ascent to God, the human self while on this planet, begins to enter a new relationship with their divine self.

During Michael of Nebadon's incarnation 2,154 years ago on earth as Jesus of Nazareth, he often spoke to his disciples about the many mansions there were in his Father's Paradise universe. The fifty-six worlds that circle Jerusem in Paradise are devoted to the transitional culture for ascending mortals from the worlds of time and space.

These are the seven mansion worlds on Paradise and if an ascending mortal has chosen with his free will the Paradise path of perfection during his lifetime, after the final transition from the mortal flesh, the ascending mortal is immediately transported to one of the divine residences on the first mansion world in Paradise.

The first mansion world is where the resurrected mortal survivors can resume their lives just where they left off before being overtaken by death. The center of activities on the first mansion world is resurrection hall, the enormous temple where everyone on Paradise assembles. As you begin your new life on the first mansion world, one morontia companion is assigned to one thousand ascending mortals and their first stop is to visit Jerusem.

The second mansion world provides ascending mortals with the means to remove all the phases of intellectual conflict as they enter this world. The training and development that the ascending mortals receive on this world is the same intellectual status they received on their previous evolutionary world of time and space.

The third mansion world is the headquarters for the seven mansion worlds' teachers. This is where all the mansion worlds teachers maintain their group headquarters for all the established schools for the seven mansion worlds.

The fourth mansion world is the beginning of the ascended mortals morontia career and the intellectual and social culture of this world is just like the mental and social life of being a student in class with a teacher on a world of time and space.

The fifth mansion world is a tremendous step forward for an ascending mortal, because on this world, a real birth of cosmic consciousness takes place, and an ascending mortal begins to expand his horizons. At this point, the average ascending mortal begins to manifest enthusiasm to continue his ascent through the seven mansion worlds of Paradise. On this world of ascent, study becomes voluntary and unselfish natural service and worship to the Universal Father is spontaneous, because the ascending mortal has now developed a real morontia personality and a real morontia being is beginning to evolve.

On the sixth mansion world the ascending mortals can learn more about all the high spirits who live in the superuniverse, but they are still not able to visualize many of these celestial beings.

On this world the ascending mortals receive their first lesson in their upcoming spiritual career, by witnessing the perfect fusion of the human mind with their Divine Thought Adjuster. During the times the ascending mortals spend on the sixth mansion world, they progress beyond the stage of light and life. The shadows of the mortal nature begin to grow less and less, because at this stage, the ascending mortals by ascending through these seven mansion worlds are now one by one and slowly the memories of the ascending mortal's prior planetary animal origins are fading away.

On the seventh mansion world the ascending mortals have achieved the completion of their postmortal career. It is here on this world that the last remnants of the mark of the beast are eradicated, and you will be able to find the Universal Father's temple of worship on this world, but you do not see the Universal Father. Now is the time for the ascending mortals to get ready for their graduation to Jerusem to become a citizen. All the inhabitants of the seventh mansion world will soon assemble on the sea of glass to witness the group of ascending mortals' graduation and departure for Jerusem. An ascending mortal will enjoy the progression through the seven mansion worlds, which are occurring on the seven dematerializing and demortalizing spheres. An ascending human is still mostly human while going through training on the first mansion world. While an ascending mortal progresses through the seven mansion worlds, he does not pass from a mortal state to the immortal state until the time of fusion with his Divine Thought Adjuster and upon completion of the seven-mansion world Jerusem career, you will then be a full fledges morontia being.

When a new group of ascending mortals have graduated from the seven mansion worlds, they are welcomed as graduates, and all assemble to welcome them into Jerusem. After a mortal has attained citizenship and a residence on Jerusem, no more resurrection will be experienced. The morontia body that the former ascending mortal now has allows one to see through to the very end of your prior local universe experience on your previous world of time and space. Changes will be apparent, and once you have progressed through the seven mansion worlds in Paradise, you will retain your morontia form until you emerge as a first stage spirit ready for transit to the rest of the superuniverse worlds of the ascending culture and spiritual training. Once an ascending mortal reaches the seven mansion worlds in Paradise, they must pass through each of these worlds seven times and on each world, you will experience an adjustment sleep and the resurrection awakening.

The mortal personality that began on the evolutionary worlds of time and space is not fully mobilized and unified until one is given citizenship on Jerusem and this gives clearance for Edentia to proclaim you to be a true member of the morontia corps of Nebadon where you will be an immortal survivor, a Paradise ascender, a personality of morontia status and you will now be a true child of the Most Highs of Paradise.

Mortal death is a technique of escape from the material life in the flesh and the morontia experience of progressing through the seven mansion worlds in Paradise where you receive divine training, cultural education, the introduction to your morontia career and finally the transition life that intervenes between the evolutionary material experience and the higher spirit attainment of the mortal ascenders of time and space who are all destined to achieve and walk through the portals of eternity.

Of all the universe personalities who are concerned with the regulation of interplanetary and interuniverse affairs, the Universe Power Directors and their associates have been the least understood on earth. Mortal men have known for a long time about the existence of angels and other celestial beings, but there has been little information relating to the controllers and regulators of the physical universe. All the available power that exists on all inhabited worlds comes from the Universal Power Directors of Paradise.

These are the three groups of living beings who work with force control and energy regulation in the master universe and all the worlds of time and space.

The Primary Eventuated Master Force Organizers live on Paradise, but they function all throughout the master universe. They are the creators of the nebulae and the living instigators of the energy cyclones in outer space, and they are also the early organizers of the gigantic manifestations located in outer space.

The seven Supreme Universe Power Directors are the physical energy regulators of the grand universe, and they also live on Paradise. These mighty beings oversee many power centers and through these centers, there are many physical controllers who are scattered and working all throughout the seven superuniverses. In the grand universe we have intelligent and living entities who can perform tasks that involve complex computations with precision. These power directors can withstand extreme temperatures to function under physical conditions that would normally be intolerable even to most of the power directors in Paradise. The Universe Power Directors have existed from the near times of eternity and no more beings from this order are being created. The Seven Supreme Power Directors were personalized by the Seven Master Spirits, and they then collaborated with their parents to produce more than ten billion additional power directors. All energy is circuited in Paradise, and the Universe Power Directors' job is to direct this force energies of nether Paradise to the central and superuniverses by converting and directing these energies into channels of useful and constructive applications. The energies of nether Paradise are like a vast moving ocean of energy that engulfs and bathes the entire seven mansion worlds in the superuniverse.

The universe of universes is not an infinite plane, a boundless cube, a limitless circle, but it does have dimensions that proceed out of Paradise and through the horizontal extension of pervaded space, and the master universe exists in six concentric ellipses with the space levels that encircle the Isle of Paradise.

The central universe of Havona is not a time creation, but rather it is an eternal existence. This means that it is a never-beginning, never ending universe that consists of one billion worlds. The center of Havona is the Isle of Paradise which is surrounded by twenty-one satellite worlds. The Paradise Havona system is the eternal universe that encircles the eternal Isle of Paradise, and it constitutes the nucleus of the master universe. All the seven superuniverses and all its regions of outer space revolve in established orbits around the Paradise satellites and Havona worlds. The seven superuniverses do not cross a local universe, because each superuniverse is a geographic space that clusters one-seventh of the partially inhabited Havona creation. Nebadon, our local universe is one of the new creations that is in Orvonton, the seventh superuniverse.

The Grand Universe is the present organized and inhabited creation. It consists of the seven superuniverses that consists of seven trillion inhabited planets as well as the eternal planets of the central creation. The outer space levels of the Grand Universe are located far out in space extremely far away from the seven inhabited superuniverses and these four outer space zones are free from star dust and cosmic fog. There are tremendous wheels of energizing forces that are in the first outer space level of the Grand Universe which is a continuous belt of cosmic activity that encircles the entire known organized and inhabited creation. There are currently many eternal living beings who are now functioning various jobs on the Paradise worlds and these eternal beings are classified according to their relationship to the Paradise Deities. During the grand gatherings that occur on Paradise on the central and seven superuniverses, those who attend are also put into their designated groups when they attend these events, and these are some of the groups who live in Paradise.

The mortal survivors of time and space are called the ascending mortals or mortals while they are on their progressive ascent through the seven mansion worlds of Paradise. There are seven stages of training that the ascending mortals must first complete to graduate to become a citizen of Jerusem as a morontia being.

The planetary mortals consist of the evolutionary mortal beings and all the members of the human races from each world of time and space receive the same ministry from the Sons of God and they also receive the presence of the ministering spirits of time. After a mortal's natural death from the flesh, all types of ascenders fraternize together as one big morontia family while they are complete their journey on the seven mansion worlds of Paradise. The sleeping survivors are all the mortals who are classified as being in the survival status and they are in the custody of the personal guardians of destiny. As these sleeping survivors pass through the portals of natural death, during the third period of this transition, they personalize on the seven mansion worlds in Paradise. These sleeping survivors must continue to rest in an unconscious sleep until the judgement day of the new epoch, a new dispensation. When Michael who is now the system sovereign of Nebadon completed his seventh and final bestowal on planet earth 2,154 years ago as the incarnated Jesus of Nazareth, he walked through the portal of death and on the third day, he rose from the dead and then led a great multitude of former sleeping captives from the days going all the way back to the time of Adam and Eve to be resurrected in the resurrection hall on Paradise. All the Creator Sons from Paradise, when they are assigned to complete their final and seventh bestowal on a planet, must each walk through the portal of death and then they arise from the dead on the third day. However, Jesus of Nazareth was the only Creator Son of God to be crucified and put to death while completing his seventh and final bestowal on planet earth and this was due to the darkness earth was in during those times when the System Sovereign, Lucifer, and the earth's Planetary Prince, Caligastia started the universe wide Lucifer Rebellion.

The sleeping survivor students who journey to train on each of the seven mansion worlds are all the surviving mortals who awakened after death to begin their training on the seven mansion worlds of Paradise. These seven Paradise training worlds where the sleeping survivors attend their training on are called "mansions," and it was these seven worlds that Jesus of Nazareth was referring to when he said to his disciples that in my father's house there are many mansions. The sleeping survivors who journey and train on the seven mansion worlds of Paradise are called morontia progressors and during their training, these students can advance in intellect, spirit, and personality. When the sleeping survivors arrive on the seven mansion worlds for training, they are under the direction of the Ancients Of Days, because once they have completed their morontia life they are then classified as being accredited spirits. When their training has been completed for their spirit development, the surviving mortal then prepares for the long flight to Havona which is the haven for evolutionary spirits. On earth a mortal man is a creature of flesh and blood, but while living in Paradise, once you reach Havona, you then live as a morontia being. Once a morontia being reaches his residential status, they will then begin their progressive training courses in divinity and absonity. A mortal's residence in Paradise means that he has found God and that next he will be accepted into the Corps of Finality.

The Corps of the Finality is always the destination, where you enter God's eternal wheel of life, and it is the level that all ascending mortals strive to reach. This assignment which is both adequate and glorious justifies the universal plan for mortal man's evolutionary ascent to Paradise.

There are three ministering spirits of time, and they are the personalities of the Infinite Spirit. The angels are the ministering spirits of time, and they are classified as being the authorities, the messengers, the hosts of space and the powers and higher personalities of the Infinite Spirit.

The supernaphim angels minister in the central universe, while the seconaphim angels minister in the seven superuniverses and the cherubim and sanobim angels belong to the angelic corps who minister in the local universes.

The superuniverse wards are all the mortal ascenders who when they arrived in Paradise became the wards of the Ancients Of Days, because they have completed their morontia life in the local universe and they are now accredited spirits.

The midway creatures are classified with the ascending Sons of God, and they function with the ministering spirits of time to help and serve mortal man on the worlds of time and space. The midway creatures work with the angelic beings especially on the experiment planets such as earth. The primary midway beings are more spiritual, and they are members of the ascendant mortal staffs of the worlds' planetary princes. The number of primary midway beings on any planet is always 50,000. The secondary midway beings descend from the planetary biologic uplifters, the Adam and Eve of the planet. The primary midwayer beings are created intellectually and spiritually by angelic techniques and they are uniform in intellect. The secondary midwayer beings are physically created using the Adam and Eve biologic techniques and they are endowed with a seraphic and morontia type of mind. The primary midwayer beings resemble angels more than mortals and the secondary midwayer beings are more like human beings.

The primary midwayer beings can work with both morontia and spirit energy controllers and mind circuit manipulator, while the secondary midwayer beings can establish working connections with both the physical controllers and material circuit manipulators. On the normal worlds of time and space, not earth, the primary midwayer beings maintain their service as intelligent corps and as celestial entertainers for the world's planetary prince, while the secondary midwayer beings work with the Adam and Eve regime to help continue to further the progression of the civilization on their assigned world. Midwayer beings remain in service on their assigned planet for long periods of time and if they perform faithful service, they are rewarded for their patient ministry by being accepted into the ranks as ascending Sons of God to continue the long adventure of Paradise ascent in the company with their mortal earth brethren who they so effectively served during their long planetary term of service on their planet. The gap between the material and spiritual worlds is perfectly bridged by the association of mortal man, primary and secondary midwayer beings, the morontia cherubim and the mid-phase cherubim and seraphim angels.

God is love and in the superuniverse near the center of the universe of universes, our Universal Father is known as our Prime Creator, Source. The Paradise superuniverse is located above dimension thirty-six in our Nebadon universe. There is a divine family of living beings who live on Uversa on the seven grand mansion worlds of Paradise. These divine beings are classified according to their relationship to the Paradise Deities. During the many grand gatherings that are held on the seven Paradise mansion worlds, those who attend are always put into groups that are based on their origin from the Paradise Deities.

These are some of the divine beings who live on the seven mansion worlds of Paradise.

The Eternal Son is the original and only begotten son of God, the second person of God and the associate creator of all things. The Universal Father, Prime Creator, Source is the First Great Source and Center, and the Eternal Son is the Second Great Source and Center. The designation of the Eternal Son, the first original Son of God is reserved for the Eternal Son who is the co-creator along with our Universal Father of the superuniverse and all the other divine Sons of God. Every time the Universal Father and the Eternal Son jointly project a new identical, unique, and absolute personal thought, this new idea is then personified as a new and original Creator Son.

In Paradise, the application of the established laws and justice are carried out by the stationary sons of the Trinity and this group of Trinity Sons consists of the following personalities.

The Trinitized Secrets Of Supremacy

The Eternals Of Days

The Ancients Of Days

The Perfections Of Days

The Recents Of Days

The Unions Of Day

The Faithful Of Days

The Perfectors Of Wisdom

The Divine Counselors

The Universal Censor

The Paradise Trinity Sons are the children of the three Paradise Deities, and they function as the Trinity in a universal sense, because they represent the collective attitude of the Deity relating to their executive judgements during their administration of justice. The Trinity Sons are designed as a group to issue out fair judgements in the seven superuniverses. Justice is the collective thought of righteousness and mercy is its expression. Mercy is the attitude of love, precision characterizes the operation of law, and divine judgement is the soul of fairness that ever conforms to the justice of the ten Trinity Sons of Paradise, so they can continue to fulfil their mission of displaying the divine love of God.

The Magisterial Sons are known as the Avonals, because they are the high magistrates of the realms, the adjudicators of the successive dispensations on the worlds of time and space. They preside over the awakening of the sleeping survivors, sit in judgement on the realms and return to the headquarters world of their assigned local universe after they have completed their mission. Prior to the planetary appearance of a Creator Son to complete one of his seven bestowals on an inhabited world of time and space, this world is first visited by a Paradise Avonal on a magisterial mission, and he incarnates on the worlds as a material being. A world may have many magisterial visits both before and after the appearance of a Creator Son to complete one of his seven bestowals. Planet earth has never received a visit of an Avonal Son on a magisterial mission, because due to earth's fallen Planetary Prince Caligastia joining the Lucifer Rebellion, earth was plunged into darkness due to its failure to follow the plans that were set out for the inhabited worlds of time and space. However, planet earth may still be visited by an Avonal, because when Creator Son, Michael of Nebadon completed his final and seventh bestowal on planet earth as Jesus of Nazareth, he promised to come back to earth. The purpose of a Magisterial Son incarnating on an evolutionary world of time and space is to terminate the dispensation for the world or to inaugurate a new era of the planet's progression.

All the Trinity Sons' mission is to issue out fair judgements of supreme fairness to the inhabitants of the seven superuniverses. All law originates in the First Source and Center, because he is the law. The administration of the spiritual law is under the direction of the Eternal Son. The revelation of the spiritual law and the interpretation of the divine statues is the function of the Infinite Spirit. The application of law and justice falls within the authority of the Paradise Trinity, and it is carried out by the Sons of the Trinity.

Justice is inherent in the universal mission of the Paradise Trinity, while goodness, mercy and truth are the universe ministry of the divine personalities whose Deity union constitutes the Trinity. Justice is not the attitude of the Universal Father, the Eternal Son, or the Infinite Spirit. Justice is the Trinity attitude of these divine personalities of love, mercy, and ministry. None of the Paradise Deities fosters the administration of justice and justice is never a personal attitude because it is always a plural function.

The Perfectors Of Wisdom are comprised of a corps of one billion on the seven mansion worlds who work with the Divine Counselors to assist the Ancients Of Days to continue to process and issue out fair judgements.

There are one billion Eternals Of Days on Paradise and they each rule one of the Havona worlds in Paradise without rotation or reassignment. They visit each other's worlds, but they rule their assigned world by using their own ideas and style. The architecture, natural surroundings, morontia structures and spirit creations are unique on each one of their worlds and each world is a place of everlasting beauty. Every ascending mortal who is on the ascent to Paradise will get a chance to spend some time on one of The Eternals Of Days' world as they continue to travel through the seven mansion worlds of the superuniverse of Paradise.

The Ancients Of Days are all identical and they were created from the combined character and unified nature of the Trinity, and they rule each of the seven superuniverses of Paradise. The Ancients Of Days are all the same and they are the superperfect offspring of the Paradise Trinity. They make sure there is harmony within the seven mansion worlds. The Ancients Of Days were all trinitized at the same time and when you reach Paradise and search through the written records of the beginning of things, you will find that the first entry is the trinitization of the twenty-one Ancients Of Days. The Ancients Of Days always govern in groups of three working jointly together and they never leave their assigned world in the superuniverse of Paradise. The homes of the Ancients Of Days are located at the point of spiritual polarity on their assigned superuniverse mansion world. The twenty-one Ancients Of Days are the most powerful and mighty out of all the direct rulers of the worlds of time and space creations. The Ancients Of Days have the high powers of the final executive judgement concerning issues relating to the freewill beings. Also, the Ancients Of Days while they work in their groups of three participate in the final decrees of the supreme tribunals of their assigned superuniverse. During our present age of the unfinished evolution of the Supreme, the twenty-one Ancients Of Days provide the perfect administrative control of the evolving mortal beings who live on the worlds of time and space.

The Unions Of Days work as counselors and advisors in the evolving local universes and each local universe has one assigned Unions of Days. There are seven hundred Unions of Days in existence, and they report directly to the Recents Of Days. When a local universe becomes settled in the age of light and life, its glorified beings are then able to freely associate with The Unions Of Days who will work on their world as ambassadors and counselors.

The Faithfuls of Days are the Paradise advisors to the rulers of the one hundred constellations that exist in each of the local universes, and they also work as counselors to the Most Highs rulers of the constellation governments. There are seventy million Faithfuls of Days in existence, and they also work as counselors functioning in the constellations of a local universe under the direction of The Unions Of Days. The Faithfuls of Days live on the constellation capitals in modest homes, and they are the last link in the long administrative advisory chain that reaches from the sacred Paradise worlds of the Universal Father near the center of all things to the primary divisions of the local universes.

The Perfections Of Days are the rulers of the two major sectors of the superuniverse and they are comprised of a group of two hundred. The Perfections Of Days were trinitized as a group to complete the special work of assisting the superuniverse directors and to also assist the twenty-one Ancients Of Days in performing their duties. As an ascending mortal, you will see The Perfections Of Days as you advance during your ascent to Paradise through the seven mansion worlds to the headquarters of Splandon. The Perfections Of Days in person administers the group pledges to the ascending graduates of the major sector schools in Paradise. Once an ascending mortal has entered the registry of the major sector of Splandon, they then must pass through every one of the ten major divisions of the superuniverse and during this time an ascending mortal will be able to see all thirty of the Orvonton Perfections Of Days before they reach Uversa.

The Recents Of Days are the youngest of the supreme directors of the superuniverse and they work in group of three while they preside over the affairs of the minor sectors in Paradise. There are twenty-one thousand Recents Of Days, and they were all created simultaneously, and they complete the training for their duties under the instruction of The Eternals Of Days. They also alternate with The Perfections Of Days to represent the Ancients Of Days at the supreme councils of Paradise. The Recents Of Days are also in charge of the minor sector of Ensa, Paradise. While the ascending mortals are completing their training and on their way to Uversa, they will get a chance to work with a group of the Recents Of Days.

One billion Universal Censors work for each of the superuniverse administration, and they are a special completed creation of the Infinite Spirit. The Universal Censors were created to be able to maintain a perfect synchrony by utilizing a special technique, while at the same time being personally sensitive and responsive to intelligent free will in the superuniverses. They are always able to give the correct number, nature, and whereabouts of all the free will beings in any part of the seven superuniverses. The Universal Censors do not have to really function on Paradise, because there is no need since on Paradise everything is inherent, because the Deities who live there know all things.

The Seven Supreme Trinity Personalities were each created to perform a specific service. They were all created by the divine trinity to fulfill specific duties to serve with perfection with precise techniques with finality of devotion. The Seven Supreme Trinity Personalities were created as a definite and final numbers and their creation is a past event, which means that no more will be created in Paradise. All throughout the grand universe these Seven Supreme Trinity Personalities represent the administrative policies of the Paradise Trinity. They represent justice and they are the executive judgement of the Paradise Trinity because they form an interrelated line of administrative perfection that begins from the Paradise worlds to the headquarters worlds of the local universes and to the constellation capitals. All the Seven Supreme Trinity Personalities were created from divine essence of the Infinite Spirit and the have never been known to stray from being divine beings and they always follow the perfect path while conducting their duties.

At the head of all the divine personalities in our Nebadon universe stands the Master Creator Son, Michael who is the universe father and the system sovereign of the Nebadon universe.

The Universe Aids are a group of high vibrational spirits who are stationed in Nebadon and they are known as the intervening group of Universal Aids. Each universe has one Universal Aid, and he is always the first born of all the divine beings that are native to the specific local universe.

The Bright and Morning Star of our Nebadon universe is Gabriel of Salvington, Paradise and he is the chief executive of all Nebadon functioning as the personal representative of

Michael, our system sovereign of Nebadon and serving as his spokesperson. During the earlier times of Nebadon, Gabriel worked alone with Michael and the Creative Spirit, but as the Nebadon universe grew, Gabriel was given a personal staff and eventually this group grew into the Nebadon corps called the Evening Stars. The Melchizedek Paradise family planned the addition of the Brilliant Evening Stars to be a part of Gabriel's staff in Salvington, Paradise.

The Brilliant Evening Stars were then brought into being by the Creator Son and the Creator Spirit of Paradise and they serve in many capacities but mainly as liaison officers for Gabriel, who is the local universe chief executive. The brilliant Evening Stars also serve as Gabriel's representative at the system capital of every constellation and system in Nebadon. The brilliant Evening Stars Nebadon corps of super angels now have a total group of 13, 641 angels and many of these super angels began their universe career as seraphim angels. One of the main duties of the bright and Morning Star angels is to accompany the Avonal Bestowal Sons on their planetary missions, just like Gabriel accompanied Michael of Nebadon when he began his final seventh bestowal on planet earth as Jesus of Nazareth 2,154 years ago.

These groups of Bright and Morning Stars super angels are also assigned to help the planetary Trinity Teacher Sons to establish the dawning of the spiritual age on an inhabited world of time and space. On these assignments, the Brilliant Evening Stars serve as liaisons between the mortals of the planet and the invisible corps of the Trinity Teacher Sons. The Brilliant Evening Stars live on the sixth group of the seven Salvington Paradise worlds.

The material beauty of Paradise consists in the magnificence of its physical perfection. Paradise is from eternity and there are no records or traditions that can document the origin of this nuclear Isle of Light and Life that exists in Paradise. Back in eternity when the Paradise Universal Father's first infinite and absolute thought found in the Eternal Son a perfect word for this divine expression, they both had the Thought-God and Word-God for a universal and infinite agent of mutual expression and combined action of the origin of the Infinite Spirit, the Third person of Deity in Paradise. The Infinite Spirit is the effective agent of the all loving Universal Father and his all-Merciful Eternal Son to complete their project of saving truth loving souls on all the worlds of time and space to come back home to Paradise.

The Creator Sons are called the Paradise Michaels and Havona, Paradise is the educational training location where the Creator Sons prepare for their subsequent adventures in universe creation. The Creator Sons are a divine perfect creation whose goal is to complete their seven bestowals and then be awarded their own universe to attain the levels of Paradise-Havona perfection. The Creator Sons regard the central creation of Paradise as the home of their divine parents and the divine destiny for all living beings who live on the worlds of time and space. Each of the Paradise Creator Sons must complete seven bestowals in their assigned universe before he can assume the role of the system sovereign. During the seventh and final bestowal, each Creator Son must walk through the portal of death, arise from the dead on the third day and then assume his position as the system sovereign of that universe.

When the Eternal Son assigns a Paradise Creator Son his own local universe, the Creator Son then assumes full responsibility for the completion, control and composure of his assigned local universe, including the solemn oath to the eternal Trinity not to assume full sovereignty until his seven creature bestowals have been successfully completed and certified by the Ancients Of Days in the superuniverse. This obligation is completed by every Paradise Michael Creator Son who volunteers to go out from Paradise to complete the process of universe organization and creation. The purpose of these creature incarnations is to help the Creator Son to become a wise, sympathetic, just and an understanding system sovereign. These seven required bestowals that each Creator Son must complete are the last steps in their education and training to prepare them for the task of ruling their own local universe with divine righteousness, love and with justice.

On Nebadon, Paradise the archangels are the offspring of the Creator Son and the Universe Mother Spirit. The archangels are the highest type of high spirit who are produced in large numbers in a local universe and there are about eight hundred thousand archangels in Nebadon, Paradise. Archangels work with the Bright and Morning Stars and the Universe Aids while completing their assignments. The archangel corps of Nebadon is directed by the first born of their order and a divisional headquarters of these

Paradise archangels is maintained on planet earth. A corps of one hundred archangels accompanies every Creator Son while he is completing each of his seven bestowals for the duration of time he spends on each inhabited world. In the case that a magisterial Son should have to become the temporary ruler of a planet, then the group of one hundred archangels from Paradise act as the directing leader of all celestial life on the planet. Two senior Paradise archangels are always assigned as the personal aids of a Paradise Avonal on all planetary missions that involve judicial actions, magisterial missions, or bestowal incarnation by the Paradise Creator Sons. The archangels' home in Paradise is the seventh group of the Salvington worlds and their associated satellites. On the Paradise archangel world, they maintain the records for each ascending mortal from the worlds of time and space from the time of birth all through their Paradise career and when the individual leaves Salvington to go to the superuniverse regime, the individual is then blotted out of recorded existence by the mandate of the Ancients Of Days. On these worlds where the Paradise archangels live, the personality records of an individual are filed, preserved for the time between mortal death, the hour of repersonalization and the individual's resurrection from death.

The Most High Assistants of Paradise are a group of divine beings who are assigned to be central and superuniverse representatives and observers of the local creations on the worlds of time and space. The Most High Assistants help and work with the Nebadon Paradise divine personalities who include; The Unions Of Days, the according Creator Sons, the Faithfuls Of Days, the Magisterial Sons, and the Trinity Teacher Sons.

Life does not originate on any planet in our Nebadon universe spontaneously, because life is constructed according to the plans that are formulated by the Paradise Unrevealed Architects of Being. New life appears on the inhabited planets of our universe either by direct importation or as a result of the operations of the Paradise Life Carriers who work on the worlds in our local universe. The Paradise Life Carriers are among the most interesting and versatile of the diverse family of Universe Sons and they are entrusted with designing and carrying creature life to all the inhabited planetary worlds, and after planting the various forms of life on the new worlds, they remain there for long periods of time to help with the development of this new life. The Life Carriers group are the offspring of three pre-existent personalities from Paradise; the Creator Son, the Universe Mother Spirit, and one of the three Ancients Of Days who oversees the destinies for the beings who live in the superuniverse.

The Paradise Life Carriers are entrusted with the job of establishing new physical life on the new evolving worlds and there are over one hundred million Life Carriers that have been created and they work under the direction of the chief executive Gabriel, Father Melchizedek and Namibia who was the first-born Life Carrier in Paradise.

When a new evolutionary planet has ascended and has finally settled into a new age of light and life, then the Paradise Life Carriers are organized into higher bodies of an advisory capacity to assist in the further administration and development of the ascended world and its glorified beings. During the planets later and settled ages of light and life, the Life Carriers then have many new duties to continue to assist these worlds.

The Paradise Life Carriers work on each of the seven worlds in Paradise to complete their life implantation activities that will be implemented on the newly inhabited worlds in our universe.

On Paradise world number one the Life Carriers are devoted to the study of universal life in all its known phases of manifestation and their college of life planning is located on this world.

On Paradise world number two the Life carriers work on life designing techniques for all modes of the various life organizations.

The original life designs are provided by the Creator Son and after the new life plans have been given to the Life Carriers, they are transmitted to the first world where they are approved by the senior Life Carriers and the consulting Melchizedek groups. The chief of the Melchizedek's often represents the Creator Sons during these life design meetings.

On Paradise world number three the Life Carriers work on the conservation of life, and they devote their time to study and develop various forms of life protection and conservation techniques. The life plans for every new world provides for the establishment of life conservation plans through their expert manipulation of the new planet's life patterns. During the early days of life development on planet earth, the Life Carriers reproduced the highest form of life and carried a specimen of it in a bundle that contained twenty-four pattern units and when the intellectual life grew out from this bundle, the foundation of the four and twenty basic orders of psychic organization of life was created on planet earth.

On Paradise world number four the Life Carriers study the evolution of creature life to ensure that the original life plasma of a new evolutionary world contains the full potential for all future developmental variations for all future evolving changes that will occur on the new planet.

On Paradise world number five the Life Carriers are devoted to the study of the creative mind in relation with the creature life who will be living on the new world, because the mind that humanity possess is able to comprehend the endowment of the seven adjutant mind spirits as it continues to evolve.

On Paradise world number six the Life Carriers work on perfecting how the correlation of the mind and spirit works with the living forms and organisms on the new evolutionary world.

On Paradise world number seven the Life Carriers dedicate their time studying the unrevealed domains of the evolutionary creatures as it relates to the cosmic philosophy of the ever-expanding fractalizations of the Prime Creator, Source. The Corps of Life Carriers who are commissioned to plant life on a new world consists of one hundred senior Life Carriers, one hundred assistants and one thousand custodians. The Life Carrier groups always carry actual life plasm to the new worlds, and they sometimes organize the life patterns after they arrive in accordance with that have been previously approved to establish the new life on the planet.

The vital spark, the mystery of life is given through the Life Carriers, but not by them, because even though the Life Carriers formulate the life plasm that they use, it is in reality the Universe Mother Spirit and the Universe Creative Daughter Spirit who both supply the essential factor and the energy spark of life that ignites and then enlivens the physical body and the mind to experience life.

The Sons of God all originate from Paradise, and they are the offspring of the divine rulers of Paradise.

Michael, one of the twelve Creator Sons from Salvington, Paradise is the system sovereign of our Nebadon universe.

The following types of Sons of God are of the local universe origin, and they are the offspring of a Paradise Creator Son and the Universe Mother Spirit.

The second order of the Universe Sons of God of Paradise are the Avonals or Magisterial Sons. The third order are the Trinity Teacher Sons who are comprised of 9,642 in Paradise and they are:

The Melchizedek Sons

Father Melchizedek

The Lanonandek Sons

The Life Carrier Sons

Father Melchizedek oversees directing the activities of the Melchizedek group. After bringing into existence the beings of personal aid such as the Bright and Morning Star and other personalities to help in the divine purpose and creative plans, there occurred a new form of creative union between the Creator Son, the Creative Spirit and the local universe Daughter of the Infinite Spirit, and the personality offspring from this divine creative partnership is the first original Melchizedek, who was the Father Melchizedek, the unique being who works with the Paradise Creator Son and the Creative Spirit to bring the rest of the entire group of Melchizedeks into existence. In Paradise Father Melchizedek acts as the first executive of the Bright and Morning Star who work with Gabriel who is in charge over the tribunals and councils of Nebadon. Father Melchizedek also presides over the special emergency commission and advisory bodies in Salvington, Paradise and in Gabriel's absence Father Melchizedek also functions as the chief executive of Nebadon.

All of the Melchizedek group in our universe were all created within one millennial period of standard time by the Creator Son and the Creator Spirit in liaison with Father Melchizedek who from time to time designates twelve of the Melchizedeks to function as Life Carriers on some of the midsonite worlds, which is a type of inhabited planet that has not yet been revealed to the people who currently live on planet earth.

The Melchizedek Sons are the first order of divine sons to approach and live near the lower creature life and be able to function in their ministry of moral uplift and to serve the evolutionary races without having to incarnate on the planet. The Melchizedek Sons are midway between the highest divinity beings and the lowest free will mortal beings. They are the natural intermediaries between the higher and divine levels of living existence that exists between the material forms of life on the evolutionary worlds of time and space. The Melchizedeks are a self-governing order, and they are the teachers of self-government to all the worlds in our Nebadon universe. The Melchizedek Sons travel in small groups to various worlds to serve as advisory commissions, act as counselors and help to settle the serious differences that arise on some of the evolutionary worlds.

The oldest Melchizedek Son is the chief aid of the Bright and Morning Star in carrying out the mandates of the Creator Son. When a Creator Son begins one of his seven bestowals on one of the evolutionary worlds, he goes alone, but when one of his Paradise brothers, and Avonal Son goes on a mission to one of the evolutionary worlds, he is always accompanied by twelve Melchizedek Sons who help him with his mission. The Melchizedek Sons live on their own world near Salvington, Paradise and it consists of four hundred and ninety worlds. One of the most important Melchizedek activities is their supervision of the progression morontia career of the ascending mortals. The Melchizedek Sons are also available to help for all emergencies that may arise on all the worlds where they are assigned to work on.

Machiventa Melchizedek who lived on planet earth during the time of Abraham, helped to prepare earth for the subsequent incarnation of Michael of Nebadon on planet earth as Jesus of Nazareth. Machiventa Melchizedek was known on earth as the King of Salem, Palestine and he was the leader over a spiritual colony in Salem who he trained to be worldwide missionaries to spread the word of God to most of the then civilized known world. Machiventa Melchizedek left his original group who were working with the Life Carrier Corps on earth, and he volunteered to incarnate on earth as a mortal man to help fill the gap that was caused by the defaults of earth's then Planetary Prince Caligastia when he joined the Lucifer Rebellion and the subsequent default of the bioloptic racial uplifters Adam and Eve. Machiventa Melchizedek like many other ascended masters who came to earth before and after him incarnated on earth and he lived as a mortal man for ninety-four years to hold the light of life so that it would not extinguish during earth's time period of increasing darkness. Machiventa Melchizedek continued to hold this light and life on earth until he safely passed it on to Abraham and his descendants who held the light on earth until the times of Jesus of Nazareth. After the creation of the orders of personal aids and the Melchizedek Sons, the Creator Son and the local Universe Creative Spirit created another diverse order in the Paradise Universe known as the Vorondadek Sons.

The Vorondadek Sons are also known as the Constellation Fathers, because a son from this order is found to be the head of each constellation government in every local universe. There are one million Vorondadek Sons on record in Nebadon, Paradise and just like the Melchizedek Sons, the Vorondadek Sons have no reproduction powers. The service that the Vorondadek Sons provides in the local universes is extensive and diverse. They serve as ambassadors to other universes and for the isolated quarantine worlds who suffered in spiritual darkness who joined the Lucifer Rebellion and, in these cases, a Vorondadek Son stays on these words helping until the world is completely restored to a normal status with the Galactic Federation of Planets. The Vorondadek Sons are also the historians of the local universes, because they are personally familiar with the political struggles and social upheavals that occur on the worlds of time and space. The Universe Creator Son selects at least three Vorondadek Sons to rule each of the one hundred constellations that exist in each of the local universes. These Vorondadek Sons after they are selected by the Creator Son are then commissioned by Gabriel to be the Most High of the constellations for the duration of 50,000 years in earth time. The reigning Most High, the Constellation Father has two associates, and these one hundred Constellation Fathers then constitute the supreme advisory cabinet of the Universe Creator Son.

The Vorondadek Sons live on the second group of seven worlds in the circuit of seventy primary worlds that surround Salvington, Paradise. During their journey through the seven mansion worlds of their Paradise ascent, the ascending mortals get the chance to study and learn many skills and activities on these Vorondadek worlds.

After the creation of the Vorondadek Sons, the Universe Creator Son and the Universe Mother Spirit unite for the purpose of bringing into existence the third order of universe sonship, the Lanonandek Sons. The Lanonandek Sons were created of a lower spiritual order than the rest of the universe sons, and there have been several occasions of default and revolt among this order against their creator and father, Michael of Nebadon. The Lanonandek Sons are usually selected to be the system sovereigns, the rulers of the local systems and as Planetary Princes who are the administrative heads of the inhabited worlds. Lucifer, a Lanonandek Son was the former system sovereign of our local system of Satania until he defaulted and started the Lucifer Rebellion in Paradise and on many of the inhabited worlds within our Nebadon universe. Planet earth's former Planetary Prince Caligastia, a Lanonandek Son also defaulted in his duties and joined his brother Lucifer in the universe wide Lucifer Rebellion which plunged many inhabited worlds in our universe into thousands of years of endless darkness and evil. Machiventa Melchizedek is currently the Planetary Prince of planet earth, and his headquarters is in Salvington, Paradise.

The Lanonandek Sons were created on a lower divinity level than the other Sons of God, and they are required to pass through certain courses of training on the Melchizedek worlds to prepare for their subsequent service as system sovereigns and planetary princes. The Lanonandek Sons were the first students to attend the Melchizedek University, and they were classified and certified by the Melchizedek teachers as ready to perform their duties of service. The universe of Nebadon has exactly twelve million Lanonandek Sons and when they completed their training at the Melchizedek university on the Melchizedek worlds, they were divided into three groups.

The first group of Lanonandek Sons are the 709,841 Primary Lanonandek Sons who are designated to serve as system sovereigns in the local universe.

The Secondary Lanonandek Sons consists of 10,234,601 and they are assigned to serve as the Planetary Princes on the inhabited worlds of time and space in our universe.

The Tertiary Lanonandek Sons are designated as the third group that consists of 1,055,558 and they function as subordinate assistants, messengers, custodians, commissioners, observers and other miscellaneous duties on the worlds of time and space. Since the Lanonandek Sons are of a somewhat lower order of sonship than the Melchizedek Sons and the Vorondadek Son are, they are always at a greater danger of going astray, which is exactly what happened with Lucifer and Caligastia.

In the event of a default and rebellion by a Lanonandek Son who is serving as the system sovereign, a replacement is usually installed rather quickly, but not so on the individual planets. Because when earth's Planetary Prince Caligastia rebelled and defaulted in his duties, a successor planetary prince was designated, but he was not able to assume an active rulership until the final judgement concerning the insurrection were adjudicated by the Ancients Of Days. When a Planetary Prince rebels, the entire planet is then isolated, the local spiritual, the local spiritual circuits are severed from the Paradise circuits, the planet is placed under quarantine, and only the bestowal Creator Son can re-establish the interplanetary lines of communication with the Paradise circuits. If a Lanonandek Son causes a rebellion in his position as the system sovereign or planetary prince, he is rehabilitated and assigned to custodial duties or to departments of physical administration.

There are three groups of beings who are called the Sons of God, and the third group are known as the Trinitized Sons of God. All the Trinitized Sons of God have the common experience of trinitization as a part of their origin and all trinity embraced sons are of a dual or single origin, but they are all devoted to completing their trinity service and to complete their assignments under the direction of the Ancients Of Days.

These are the three groups of the Trinitized Sons of God.

The Trinitized Sons Of Attainment consists of the Mighty Messengers, Those High In Authority and Those Without Name or Number. This group of Trinitized Sons of God are all Divine Thought Adjuster-fused ascendant mortals who have attained their Paradise ascent and the Corps of the Finality, and they are assigned to work for the Ancients Of Days on the seven mansion worlds in the superuniverse.

The Trinitized Sons Of Selection are recruited from the evolutionary seraphim and translated midway beings who have completed their Paradise ascent and after a brief period of training in Havona, Paradise, these Trinitized Sons Of Selection are assigned to work in the courts of the Ancients Of Days.

The Trinitized Sons of Perfection are the celestial guardians, the High Son Assistants who are the Creature-Trinitized Sons of the perfected ascended mortals who have a long record of service in the Corps of the Finality. The Trinity-Origin Associates, The Perfectors Of Wisdom, The Divine Counselors and The Universal Censors are all commissioned as members of the seven mansion worlds superuniverse governments.

The Mighty Messengers belong to the ascendant group of the Trinitized Sons, and they are assigned to work in each superuniverse and they often go on missions to the local universes and to the local worlds to be observers for the Ancients Of Days and to assist The Perfections Of Days to direct the affairs in the major sectors of the superuniverse.

Those High In Authority are the second group who belong to the Trinitized Sons Of Attainment, and they are the Divine Thought Adjuster fused mortal beings. They are the perfected ascended mortals from the surviving mortal from the worlds of time and space.

The group of Those In High Authority are also superb administrators who present the cause of justice on behalf of the superuniverse tribunals.

The divine superuniverse group Those Without Name And Number are members of the Trinitized Sons Of Attainment and they are the ascendant souls who have developed the ability to worship beyond the skills of all the sons and daughters of the evolutionary races from the worlds of time and space. They have acquired a spiritual concept of the eternal purpose of the Universal Father, and they are the superior spiritual minds of the survival races who are specially qualified to sit in judgement and give their opinions when a spiritual viewpoint is needed.

The Trinitized Custodians are from the Trinitized Sons Of Selection group who are the ascendant seraphim angels and the translated midway beings who have attained Paradise and the Corps of the Finality. They work for the Ancients Of Days serving as officers of the superuniverse governments. They are also the custodians of records, plans and the institutions and they also act as trustees for ascendant projects and universe projections.

The Trinitized Ambassadors group are the second order of the Trinitized of Selection group, and they work in assisting the superuniverse rulers in various administrative areas. They also serve as the emergency or reserve corps of the Trinitized Sons for the superuniverse governments.

The Celestial Guardians are assigned to the completion of administrative duties for The Perfections Of Days. They also work as the officers of the courts for the Ancients Of Days functioning as court messengers and bearers of summons. They also work as the apprehending agents for the Ancients Of Days to bring back individuals whose presence is required before the superuniverse judge. The Celestial Guardians also accompany the spirit-fused mortals when they must travel from the local universe when their presence is required on Uversa, Paradise.

The High Son Assistants are the superior group of trinitized sons of glorified ascendant beings who are members of the mortal Corps of the Finality, and they function as personal aids to the high sons of the governments who work for the Ancients Of Days. They are the private secretaries, and they often accompany the Mighty Messengers on assignments to remote sections of the universe.

The main final destination for all mortal ascender who have attained Paradise is to be accepted into the Corps of the Finality and this corps represents the present known destination of an ascending adjuster fused mortal.

These are the seven groups of glorified beings who compose the unique body of the Corps of the Finality of eternal destiny in Paradise.

The Corps of the Mortal Finaliters

The Corps of the Paradise Finaliters

The Corps of the Trinitized Finaliters

The Corps of the Conjunct Trinitized Finaliters

The Corps of Havona Finaliters

The Corps of the Transcendental Finaliters

The Corps of the Unrevealed Sons of Destiny Finaliters

We think we know what the future work of this corps will be, but we are not really certain, because while the Corps of the Finality are mobilizing in Paradise and ministering to the universes of space and to the worlds that have ascended and settled in the age of light and life, this corps projected destination is to continue to organize new universes in the ever expanding outer space.

Even though the Universal Father is personally living in Paradise at the very center of the universes, he is also actually present on all the worlds of time and space living in the minds of his countless mortal children as the Divine Thought Adjuster. The Thought Adjusters are the actuality of the Universal Father's love that is incarnate in the souls of mortal men, and they are the promise of man's eternal career, and the essence of mortal men's perfected finaliter personality that mortal men can achieve in time as he masters the divine techniques of living the Universal Father's divine will. Step by step as we continue to ascend through the universe upon universe, we eventually attain the divine presence of the Universal Father. God commands mortal men to be perfect and as men is perfect, he accepts a Thought Adjuster to become his experiential partner during the achievement of one's destiny to ascend back home to Paradise. The fragment of God that indwells in the mind of mortal mind is the absolute and unqualified assurance that man will be able to find the Universal Father in association with the Thought Adjuster who came from God to find mortal man and stay with him in his mind during all his days of mortal life.

Any mortal man who has seen a Creator Son like those who were living on earth 2,154 years ago saw Jesus of Nazareth, have also seen the Universal Father and when man is indwelt by a Thought Adjuster, he is being indwelt by the Universal Father. When a mortal man who is following the lead of his Thought Adjuster, is living in accordance with the will of God. The Thought Adjuster creates within man the longing to be like God and to then travel the road to Paradise. The Thought Adjuster is the living presence and link between mortal man and the Universal Father and helps to draw man nearer to God. The Thought Adjuster also helps to equalize the universe tension that is created by the distance of mortal man's removal from God. The Thought Adjuster is the divine universe reality that shows man the truth that God is our father. Mortal man's Thought Adjuster is our cosmic compass that is always pointing man's soul to God. On the evolutionary worlds there are three stages of mortal man being indwelt by a Thought Adjuster. Your Thought Adjuster begins to indwell mortal man at the age of reason which is just before the age of six and from its first arrival until the age of twenty years until the age of forty years, the Thought Adjuster is then called a Divine Thought Adjuster. Since the Divine Thought Adjusters are the essence of the Universal Father, they originate from the Universal Father. They are not created beings, but instead Thought Adjusters are fragmentized entities who constitute the fractural presence of God, and together with their many unrevealed associates, these Thought Adjusters are God. The Thought Adjusters are classified as being virgin entities and they are destined to become either liberated or fused Personal Monitors.

These are the seven orders of the Divine Thought Adjusters who indwell the minds of mortal free will beings.

The Virgin Divine Thought Adjusters serve in their first assignment in the minds of the evolutionary ascending men.

The Advanced Divine Thought Adjusters have served for one or more lifetimes with free will beings on worlds where the final fusion has taken place between the living being and with the individual portion of the spirit of the local universe manifestation of the Third Source and Center, the Holy Spirit.

The Supreme Divine Thought Adjusters have worked on the evolutionary worlds where their human partner declined eternal survival. A Supreme Thought Adjuster has had more experience and is able to do things in the human mind than a less experienced Thought Adjuster could do.

The Vanished Thought Adjusters are at one with God once they are on detached assignments where they are free to roam the universe of universes.

The Liberated Thought Adjusters have been liberated from the service of time for the free will mortals of an evolutionary world.

The Fused Thought Adjusters are finaliters who have become one with an ascending mortal being who now lives in Paradise. They are now the eternity partners of the mortal ascenders who now belong to the Corps of the Finality.

The Personalized Thought Adjusters have served with the incarnated Paradise Sons whose subjects rejected eternal survival and these Thought Adjusters receive their future assignments that are based on the recommendations of the Ancients Of Days.

When Thought Adjusters return to their Universal Father in Paradise, they go back to live in Divinington where they will again have actual contact with the Universal Father's personality and divinity. No Divine Thought Adjuster has ever been disloyal to the Universal Father and even though the Thought Adjusters are invisible, they do display a unique light of an illuminated spirit called a pilot light that accompanies their divine presence.

After the Spirit of Truth, the Holy Spirit bestows itself on the mortal beings of an evolutionary world, then the Thought Adjusters flock to this world to indwell the minds of all the normal free will men. These Thought Adjusters then become to be the kingdom of heaven within the minds of the mortal free will beings of the planet. The Thought Adjusters are the increasing urge that leads men to attempt to master the material and present existence in the light of the spiritual future career of life. The Thought Adjusters actually enjoy communication with the minds of mortal men using more direct channels and they rejoice when they can directly flash messages to the intellects of the mind of their human partners. The Thought Adjusters are the faithful custodians for mortal man's life career, and they are always slowly re-creating man for his resurrection on the survival worlds, and just as a human adult is a parent, your assigned Thought Adjuster is the divine parent of the real you, your higher and advancing self, your better morontia and future spiritual self.

As a human mortal continues to navigate through life, when trouble and clouds gather overhead, your faith should accept the fact of the presence of your indwelling Divine Thought Adjuster and it is the time to look beyond the mists of your mortal uncertainty into the clear shining of the sun of eternal righteousness of the beckoning heights of the seven mansion worlds that await your ascent into Paradise and into eternity.

There are thirty-six (36) dimensions that exist between our current fifth dimensional earth and the seven mansion worlds of Paradise- the seven higher heavens. If you have an activated Merkabah light body, quantum jump into these dimensions now.

DIMENSION	DESCRIPTION
DIMENSION (1)	CRYSTAL CORE OF THE EARTH
DIMENSION (2)	ANIMALS, PLANTS, ROCKS
DIMENSION (3)	HUMANS, DUALITY, LOVE
DIMENSION (4)	ASTRAL HALLWAY TO THE HEAVENS
DIMENSION (5)	CHRIST CONSCIOUSNESS, UNITY AS ONE
DIMENSION (6)	SACRED GEOMETRY FOR ENTIRE UNIVERSE
DIMENSION (7)	HIGHER MIND, GUIDES, OM, GAIA EARTH
DIMENSION (8)	DIVINE LIGHT
DIMENSION (9)	VOICE COMMANDS OF GOD
DIMENSION (10)	UNIVERSE ATOMS HELD TOGETHER HERE
DIMENSION (11)	TECHNOLOGY-MULTI-VERSE
DIMENSION (12)	SOURCE CONSCIOUSNESS, DIVINE LOVE
DIMENSION (13)	CHRIST CONSCIOUSNESS, THE ONE
DIMENSION (14)	CELESTIAL PEACE, LOVE, BLISS
DIMENSION (15)	ANCIENTS OF DAYS-COUNCIL OF (13)

These are the (36) dimensions that exist between our current fifth dimensional earth and Paradise-the seven higher heavens. If you have an activated Merkabah Light Body, you can complete a quantum jump and experience the frequencies and vibrations available in each dimension now.

DIMENSION	DESCRIPTION
DIMENSION (22)	HOLY OF HOLIES
DIMENSION (23)	GUARDIAN ANGELS-GUIDES
DIMENSION (24)	FAITH-HOLY SPIRIT GIFTS
DIMENSION (25)	GRACE UPON GRACE
DIMENSION (26)	GOD'S MERCY ENDURES FOREVER
DIMENSION (27)	HUMAN COMPLETENESS
DIMENSION (28)	OPTIMISM-POSITIVITY
DIMENSION (29)	I AM PURE CONSCIOUSNESS
DIMENSION (30)	SANCTIFICATION-UNITY
DIMENSION (31)	MASTER NUMBER-PURPOSE OF BEING
DIMENSION (32)	GOOD BUSINESS-FRIENDSHIPS
DIMENSION (33)	SPIRITUAL AWAKENING
DIMENSION (34)	COSMIC ORGANIZATION
DIMENSION (35)	TRANSCENDENTAL RELATIONSHIP
DIMENSION (36)	LIGHT AND LIFE

THE (36) DIMENSIONS IN OUR UNIVERSE OF NEBADON

\36D-PARADISE-LIGHT AND LIFE/

\35D-TRANSCENDENTAL RELATIONSHIPS/ \34D-ORGANIZATION/

\33D-AWAKENING/ \32D-FRIENDSHIPS/ \31D-MASTER NUMBER/

\30D-SANCTIFICATION/ \29D-I AM CONSCIOSNESS/ \28D-OPTIMISM/

\27D-COMPLETENESS/ \26D GOD'S MERCY/ \25D-GRACE UPON GRACE/

\24D-FAITH/ \23D-ANGELS-GUIDES/ \22D-HOLY OF HOLIES/

\21D-HOLY CITY/ \20D-FOLLOW GOD/ \19D-SPIRITUAL PATH/

\18D-NATURE/ \17D-JESUS-BUDDHA/ \16D-FAITH-PEACE/

\15D-ANCIENTS OF DAYS/ \14D-JOY/ \13D-CHRIST CONSCIOUSNESS/

\12D-SOURCE/ \11D-MULTI-VERSE/ \10D-CREATION/

\9D-GOD'S VOICE/ \8D-DIVINE LIGHT/ \7D-OM-HIGHER MIND/

\6D-SACRED GEOMETRY/ \5D-UNITY-LOVE/ \4D-ASTRAL HALLWAY/

\3D-DUALITY/ \2D-ANIMALS-PLANTS/ \1D-EARTH'S CORE/

CHAPTER FOUR

THE ORIGINS OF PLANET EARTH

Faith is confidence in what we hope for and assurance about what we do not see.

(Hebrews 11:1)

That is why we labor and strive, because we have put our hope in the living God.

(Timothy (4:10)

A Prayer:

Dear God, please give me a heart to bring your hope to those around me.

The planet earth formed over five billion years ago out of a mixture of dust and gas that was around our planet's sun. Planet earth gradually grew larger due to the countless collisions between dust particles, asteroids and other growing planets in one last giant impact that threw enough rock, gas and dust into space to form the moon. Most of the rocks from the earliest parts of Earth's history have been destroyed or deformed, but the four billion years of geology of rocks, moon samples and meteorites have helped to provide us with the evidence of when and how the earth and moon were formed. The earth like all the other planets in our solar system started out its life as a disc of dust and gas orbiting the then young star, the sun. The dust particles were brought together by the forces of drag to form clumps of rock that grew into planetesimals, which are tens to hundreds of miles across that then grew to planet Mars-sized protoplanets by continuing to collide with each other.

Planet earth grew to its final size through one last major collision with another planet Mars sized object, and this last big collision was so large that in addition to adding lots of material to earth, it produced enough energy to vaporize some of the rock and metal from both earth and the impacting object. This vapor then formed a disc around earth that eventually cooled and clumped together to form the moon. After this formation of the moon, earth was a very different planet than the world we have today. The present-day earth has oceans covering much of its surface, but the early earth was covered in a magma ocean, and a layer of molten rock hundreds of miles deep that was melted by the energy that was released during a major collision. The early sun was also different, and it was far more active than it is in our present day, because in the beginning, the sun was blasting the entire solar system with UV radiation that was enough to evaporate a planet's entire atmosphere. Over time the magma ocean on earth cooled enough to form a solid surface, while earth's atmosphere was replenished by volcanic eruptions as well as water and other gases delivered by comets and meteorites that were crashing onto earth's surface.

This was the first step towards earth developing its plate tectonics. Plate tectonics are the giant plates of crust that slowly move around earth's surface over hundreds of millions of years. New rocks are produced at the volcanoes where the plates are moving apart, and they also recycle rocks from the earth's surface and atmosphere back into the interior where the plates are coming together. This process called subduction carries rocks, water and carbon dioxide that are trapped in minerals back into the earth's interior where they will drive future volcanoes and continue the earth's plate tectonic cycle. Plate tectonics is essential for a planet to develop life, because the repeated production and destruction of crust by plate tectonics releases carbon dioxide into the atmosphere, then removes it, which helps to keep the temperatures on earth comfortable for the plants, animals and humans to live.

When earth first formed over five billion years ago, it was approximately one-third the age of our universe by accretion from a solar nebula. Volcanic outgassing created earth's primordial atmosphere, then the oceans and earth early atmosphere had very little oxygen. 993,408 years ago, planet earth was formally registered as a planet of human habitation in Paradise by Michael of Nebadon when the human twins Andon and Fonta were born in the region known today as Afghanistan.

The late great planet Tiamat was the original planet earth and at that time it was the fifth rock from the sun. According to the harmonic rule of Bode's Law, a planet should now exist between Mars and Jupiter about two hundred and sixty miles for the sun. In the year of 1801 A.D. tiny rock and metallic objects were discovered to be orbiting the sun and since then several hundred thousand large asteroids have been observed. The total number of asteroids is estimated to be more than one million and they stretch out at a distance of three hundred million miles from the sun, and this band of rocks is known as the Asteroid Belt. The total diameter of the Asteroid Belt is nine hundred and thirty-two miles across which is less than half the diameter of the earth's moon. This debris in the Asteroid Belt is what is left of the matter from the fifth planet from the sun called Tiamat earth. This former major planet Tiamat which was the original planet earth exploded about sixty-five million years ago and this great explosive event where comets and asteroids destroyed Tiamat earth ended the reign of the dinosaurs on earth.

Our present-day earth evolved from the largest mass of what was left of Tiamat earth, and it moved from its position of being the fifth planet from the sun to its present position as the third planet from the sun and it has evolved to the planet earth that we are currently living on. The real cause of the comets and asteroids that destroyed Tiamat earth so long ago was the leader of the dark brotherhood Anunnaki (Draco-Reptilians) Marduk, the son of Enki-Poisedon who has had incarnations as Lucifer, Baal and Marduk. Draco-Reptilian Marduk up until the year 1999 A.D. was in control and the pilot of the traveling piloted planet Nibiru (Wormwood) which only comes into earth's orbit every 3,600 years. Sixty-five million years ago as Reptilian Marduk came into planet Tiamat's earth's orbit, he used one of his satellite weapons to strike Tiamat earth first and then its two moons. The present-day moon was towed to earth by the Galactic Federation of Planets from the planet Jupiter forty-five million years ago to replace Tiamat earth's two moons that were destroyed by the Reptilian Commander Marduk. When the Reptilian Marduk struck Tiamat earth with another one of his weapons after destroying its two moons, he smashed one half of Tiamat earth into pieces. The remaining half of Tiamat earth evolved into our present-day planet earth. The land formation on earth after the destruction of Tiamat earth by the reptilian Commander Marduk was called Pangea. In the year 1999 A.D. the white brotherhood once again gained control of the piloted traveling planet of Nibiru from the reptilian Commander Marduk.

Marduk remained in hiding in the many reptilian tunnels that exist in the core of the earth until finally in the year of June 2024 A.D. Marduk along with the rest of the reptilian dark overlords were cleared out of all the underground tunnels in earth's core and they were arrested by The Galactic Federation of Planets for all their crimes against humanity, which go way back to the ancient times on earth.

Earth is a hollow sphere and a living vibrational consciousness, a living entity that has a heartbeat and brain which is in the crystals that are in the core of the earth. Earth's heartbeat impacts all living life on the planet and it is called the Schumann Resonances (SR), which are the set of spectrum peaks in the extremely low frequency (ELF) portion of the earth's electromagnetic spectrum with accompanying lightning discharges in the cavity of the earth that are formed by the earth's surface and ionosphere, and the normal reading for planet earth's Schumann Resonances is 7.53Hz. The Schumann Resonances are linked to the human brain waves affects human behavior, consciousness and the human growth hormones. Lightning which is the source of energy for the Schumann Resonances strikes earth fifty times every second and the country of Venezuela, the oldest spot-on earth receives the most lightning strikes on earth.

All humans living on earth today originated from the central universe where we were all connected to God over 600 million years ago on the planet called Lyra and from there after an unexpected invasion by the reptilians, we spread out to live in other parts of the solar system. The Lyrans who incarnated on earth had to lower their vibrations to do this and they had to begin their evolution from the bottom up. Many starseeds who had already ascended to the other higher dimensional planets began to volunteer in the year 1950 A.D. to incarnate on earth to help the planet and its inhabitants to make the journey of true ascension to the new heaven on earth on Blessed Gaia.

Since the ancient times on earth, there have been an infinite number of parasites including the Draco-reptilians who have been controlling earth through the evil manipulation of the earth's brain which are all the crystals that are in the core of the earth. However, the biblical prophecy is now being fulfilled, because since the portal to the fourth dimension opened on December 21, 2012, and earth entered the photon belt, earth and every living inhabitant are now ascending into the new heaven on earth.

The descendants of Lucifer/Baal who are living on earth are the Draco-reptilians and the descendants of Michael of Nebadon are humanity. The white brotherhood The

125

Illuminati/Elites/Masons worship Lucifer/Baal and they are the members of the dark brotherhood on earth. The original leaders of the Illuminati/Elites were Enki-Poseidon, Ham and Kind Nimrod, which was the beginning of the Reptilian Luciferian Dark Brotherhood bloodline on planet earth. All cinema movies being shown through the media are disclosure, documentaries of what the dark brotherhood has done and what they plan to do to humanity on earth, and most of the news coverage being shown to us is fake.

The superman comic book and movie character were all based on the true-life bloodline of Zeus, and these are just some of the many incarnations of Zeus that include:

Zeus-Enlil-Father of Noah and the beginning of the royal King David/White Brotherhood bloodline on planet earth.

Zeus-King on the planet Sirius

Zeus-King of the planet Jupiter and the son of Cronus

Zeus-King on the planet Pleaides

Zeus-Enlil-King Neptune was the protector of planet earth and the origin of the White Brotherhood.

The current spiritual and material war that is currently happening on earth is between the white brotherhood and the dark brotherhood which began with the fall of Lucifer (Lord Samana) when he began the Lucifer Rebellion in Paradise and on many of the planets in our universe. The white brotherhood (white hats) has already won this war on planet earth and right now it is just being played out.

Since December 18, 2021, three days before the portal door opened to the fifth dimension, many spaceships have been parked in outer space right above earth's atmosphere and on each one of these spaceships there are big screen televisions, because earth is the prime-time channel as these positive extraterrestrials continue to monitor earth's ascension progress and ask themselves, "Are they getting along with each other yet?" But most importantly all these friendly spaceships are here for two important reasons. The main reason is to continue to neutralize any military nuclear weapon facilities with one single beam from the spaceships, because there will be no more nuclear bombs launched ever again on earth like what happened in Hiroshima and Nagasaki. There may be some small squimishes of war, but no more world wars. The second reason is to continue to neutralize and clear out all of members of the dark brotherhood from their underground cities and to eliminate their false evil matrix that is in place on earth.

Planet earth is one of the most important planets in our Milky Way Galaxy, because the earth's sun is an intergalactic portal where space travelers can travel to many destinations within a second. Earth is also an important location within our galaxy, because it contains easy access portals and wormholes for space travelers to travel through the twelve stargates on earth to easily get to the nine realms in the inner earth, and to the thirty-six dimensions to Paradise. Most importantly the many spaceships who are here right above earth's atmosphere to be a part of the soon upcoming celebration when planet earth and its inhabitants complete the ascension process to the new heaven on earth which will be very soon.

The first official contact with positive extraterrestrials occurred in the year 1941 A.D. when positive beings from the already ascended 5D planet Venus landed on earth and offered the various governments which included The United States and Germany on earth technology and ascension assistance. The governments of Germany instead made the decision to form negative alliances for alien technology with the Draco-reptilians and the Greys and at this subsequent end of this world war the United States seized this alien technology and the scientists from Germany while at the same time, they allowed numerous Nazi war criminals to escape and re-settle to live in South America.

Planet earth is currently in its final stages of ascension and the photonic energy humanity is currently receiving from the sun's solar flares is upgrading and activating the (12) strands of DNA in and sending the necessary light codes, frequencies and vibrations to all of humanity. All humans under the age of twenty are now being born with all their DNA strands already fully activated and they are called Indigo children.

The Galactic Federation of Planets which earth is now a member of are in charge of protecting and defending all the planets in our Milky Way Galaxy and this federation is under the command of Ashtar from the planet Venus. All the planets in the Milky Way Galaxy and their fleet are also unde the command of Ashstar from the planet Venus.

These are some of the Galactic Federation of Planets Defense Programs that planet earth also participates in.

The Radiant Guardians are one hundred selected individuals who are modified and trained on federation spaceships by angels, and they are then transformed into superheroes to protect and defend our Milky Way Galaxy.

The Solar Wardens are the super soldiers who have been working in space programs for the white hats in our own galaxy for seven generations since the 1950's to continue to protect and defend our galaxy. All these white hat soldiers who are working in the various space defense programs meet on planet Jupiter, the space command center before they go off on their missions. The white hats working on earth are continuing to neutralize the Cabal/Deep State Reptilian underground cities in Ukraine, Australia, Denver, Colorado that is located under the airport and the Vatican vaults that had been used as hubs for human child sacrifices. The only way to kill a Draco-reptilian is to cut off their head and this work of clearing out these negative entities of the dark brotherhood is still an ongoing military operation.

After planet earth receives its final great solar flash/love wave, any members of the dark brotherhood who are still on earth will immediately be vanquished by the light. There is currently an ascending timeline and a non-ascending timeline on earth and as of the date of July 2024 A.D., the ascending timeline light workers who are on the road of ascension have completed their mission here on planet earth will soon ascend to the new earth.

The non-ascending timeline humans will incarnate to the lower 4D or middle 4D earth where they will live in their same homes, remember nothing, continue to awake and ascend at their own pace with the help of those who volunteer to come back and help them from the new heaven on earth. After the grand solar flash/love wave, life on earth will immediately change to Terra, and advanced culture on earth while the ascending humans in their fifty percent carbon based (666) bodies and fifty percent (999) crystalline and (12) strand DNA activated bodies will ascend to the 7D Blessed Gaia Earth. All darkness and evil will be vaporized on the new earth and all the ascended humans living on the new earth will follow the Law of One and live in Christ consciousness in peace with unconditional love, compassion, and gratitude as one. On these star system planets that includes Alpha Centauri A, Alpha Centauri B, and Alpha Centauri C, have each already received their final solar flash on December 12, 2021, A. D., but on this date, planet earth still wasn't quite ready yet to receive their grand solar flash to complete its ascension to the new earth.

Many planets including earth have been infiltrated by the Draco-reptilians and have had their human inhabitants' (12) strands of DNA codes scrambled by adding two wires to it and by manipulating the crystals in the core of the planets. The Anunnaki are the ancestors of the Draco-reptilians when they invaded earth long ago, they believed from the start that they own humanity and had the right to enslave the entire human race. However, the white hats under the direction of the Galactic Federation of Planets have cancelled this plan of dominion that had been put in place in the false matrix by the dark brotherhood.

The dark brotherhood has been trying for so long to control humanity on earth with so many distractions such as fear, wars, chemtrails, poisoning our food supply, violence, drugs, child sex trafficking rings and many more tactics to try to stop earth's ascension process. However, the positive ascension timeline has already been firmly planted on earth and the white brotherhood are now in control. Time has speeded up on earth and the linear time that was put in place by the Acturians is gone, because now that planet earth is vibrating fifth dimensional frequencies, everything is happening at this now moment. On November 9, 2023, A.D., the earth split, and third dimensional matrix grid simulation has been shut down.

Since the portal to the fourth dimension opened on December 21, 2012, humanity has been existing in a 4D simulation/container to take time to continue to clear out any past triggers, trauma and negative thoughts to continue to raise our vibrations as we ascend to the new heaven on earth. The timeline for the new heaven on earth was finalized and set up on January 18, 2024, A.D., so now is the time to complete your daily quantum jumps, select your 5D name, build your 5D home, accept your 5D job and start helping now to manifest and build the communities on the new heaven on earth.

One of important portals for ascending mortals to access to obtain important light codes, frequencies and vibrations is the 7/7 portal that opens every year on July 7th every year that give us access these important frequencies to the Sirius 7/7 Gateway. The inhabitants of Sirius are advanced 10D beings who have recently formed an alliance with the 9D Arcturians to continue to help planet earth and its inhabitants during their current ascension process. The Sirius B inhabitants and Arcturians as a part of this alliance continue to work with the Sun's heliosphere to make sure that the ascending humans on earth can safely handle the incoming ascension energies and light codes coming from the solar flares of the sun without humanity suffering from being overloaded in the spinal column area. The Arcturians and Sirius B beings are also helping to change the gravity and time on earth and many old soul contracts for many humans have come to an end. More ascension energy from the sun is being sent to humanity's heart chakras which helps to further expand our consciousness and ability to continue to ascend to higher dimensions. The main keys to ascension are to keep peace and love in your heart, because we ascend with our heart not the mind.

The late Carl Sagan was an American astronomer and science communicator and one of his best known scientific contributions is his research on extraterrestrial life. Carl Sagan also sent the first universal message into space and his message included the song: Johnny Be Good by Chuck Berry in a universal format. During some of his scientific research he also discovered an important link and connection between Sirius B and the African Dogon Tribe who live in the African country of Mali.

This is some of the information Carl Sagan discovered about the Dogon Tribe.

The Dogon Tribe live in an area of West Africa, Mali in the area called the Bandiagara Escarpment and this area is a stretch of sandstone cliffs that are nearly one hundred miles long and they reach up to a height to 1500 feet. The Dogon Tribe took advantage of this area with its natural protection, and they built their homes on the sides of the cliffs during the third century, and they have lived at this location ever since. Even though the Dogon tribe live in this area of Mali that is more than 2,000 miles from Egypt, their history shows that they have connections with an ancient lineage that is connected to the star system of Sirius B. There are no known planets in the Sirius star system, but according to the members of the Dogon tribe, they clearly describe the existence of the stars Sirius

A, Sirius B and Sirius X in their star system. The Dogon tribe also have artifacts that are over six hundred years old to support their ancestral claims to Sirius X. Sirius X is a water planet and the star beings who visited the Dogon tribe over six hundred years ago were mostly aquatic beings, but they were also mobile when they were on land. Mermaids, merman, dolphins and whales are real living beings living in earth's seas and they all originated on the planet Sirius X and sirens are not the same creation as mermaids.

These Sirius X beings appeared to only a small portion of the Dogon tribe and they refer to the Sirius beings as the Nommos, non-physical beings. Every sixty years when the Sirius star appears between the two mountain peaks in the Bandiagara Escarpment where the Dogon tribe lives, marks a cycle in its orbit and the members of the Dogon tribe then hold a celebration called Sigui that sometimes lasts for six years. During this six-year celebration the younger men of the tribe isolate themselves from the rest of the tribe and communicate in a secret language amongst themselves. Also, during this six-year celebration, the older male members of the tribe pass the secret knowledge of the Sirius X beings to the younger male tribe members to be passed on to future generations and to date none of this secret knowledge has left the Dogon tribe since the third century.

The Sirius X beings who appeared to the select members of the Dogon tribe six hundred years ago were amphibious god-like beings who have also appeared to other ancient cultures outside of the Dogon tribe. These amphibious beings from Sirius X appeared to the ancient cultures of Babylonia, Greece, Japan and some of the Slavic nations. The ancient Dogu statues can be found in Japan also point to this country's connection with the amphibious beings from Sirius X and these statues resemble an astronaut dressed in a spacesuit. The Japanese accounts of these Sirius X beings visitations state that they arrived on earth in flying spaceships and that these Sirius X beings brought a written language with them and a lot of technology that helped to improve the Japanese civilizations. In ancient Mesopotamia there was a Deity known as Dagon or Dagan who is depicted as being a merman or fish god and there is a depiction of this in the original Hebrew bible.

The Dogon tribe's connection with Egypt is even more intriguing, because the same language that the Dogon tribe of Mali used to describe the Sirius star system consists of many of the same ancient Egyptian words that have not been used for centuries. The Dogon tribe does not have a written language, and they continue to pass down their tribe's secret knowledge to only a select younger males in their tribe using a secret language by word of mouth only. Another similarity between the Dogon tribe and Egypt is the way both cultures have organized their civilizations such as; the creation of an upper and lower kingdom and a 360-day calendar. The sky to the Dogon tribe is of extreme importance, because they believe that the sky god Amma created the first loving creatures known to the Dogon tribe as the Nommos. The Nommos from the planet Sirius X are ancestral spirits of the Dogon tribe who were male and female fishlike creatures who were the masters of the water. Most of the members of the Dogon tribe live in caves and up until the last century, this reclusive farming society were totally isolated from the outside world. The Dogon tribe calls the Sirius B star Po Tolo, and they were able to tell the Astronomer Carl Sagan every detail about the white dwarf star located near Sirius B and they know the length of the orbit, the shape of its orbit and that this white dwarf star is quite dense.

The members of the Dogon tribe also informed the astronomer Carl Sagan that there is another star in the Sirius star system called; Emma Ya and that is still has not been discovered by the astronomers on earth. The Dogon tribe members also stated that they have known for centuries that their ancestors are the descendants of a species of beings who came to earth six hundred years ago from the planet Sirius X which is 81/2 light years away from earth.

The sixth dimension (6D) is the dimension of sacred geometry, and the Archangel Metatron (Enoch the Ethiopian) oversees the maintenance of all the geometric equations that holds our universe together in this dimension. The sixth dimension is the origin of all matter that exists on earth, and it is the dimension of all the geometric shapes that are replicated as plants, animals, humans and material objects on earth in the process called morphogenesis. In the sixth dimension the idea of a tree originates, travels to the fourth dimension and then materializes on earth. Or for example the idea of a flying automobile originates in the sixth dimension and someone on earth picks up this idea for the fourth dimension and invents a flying car.

The sixth dimension is also home to KA, the body of the human spirit, which enables humans to read the vibrational ranges that define our human bodies, emotions, thoughts and our soul. The human KA knows when to absorb energy, when to block it and when to reflect it back to the source. The human KA is a singular subtle body of energy that contains the memory of our initiations, and it therefore contains the records of the greatest potential for anyone. A human living in 3D linear space and time carries a lot of density and solids in the physical body, which is why the KA in this environment is usually idle and many humans remain asleep throughout their entire lives and never realize that they are multidimensional spirit beings. The human 6D form is real only if you understand the relationship between 3D and 6D. The aquatic and advanced lion beings of the trinary Sirius star system are the guardians of the sixth dimension and planet earth has an interesting relationship with the Sirius star system. All of the other stars move in different paths in the spiral arms of our Milky Way Galaxy, but earth, Sirius and Pleaides revolve around the galactic center every 225 to 250 million years in the same location ratio in the Orion arm of our galaxy and this means that there is some kind of magnetic, gravitational and geometric system in place that makes this possible.

Planet earth's sun and Sirius are twin stars, sentient energies and they are always aware of each other and this relationship between Earth and Sirius has been known by many archaic guardians of medicine such as the Australian Aborigines. Many terrestrial cultures such as the Dogon tribe and the ancient Egyptians state that their ancestors are from Sirius B. According to the Pleiadeans, the library in Sirius A transmits the laws of sacred architecture which is the science of building structures that mode the geometric shapes in that originate in the sixth dimension.

The relationship between the solid world and the sixth dimensional world in eternal forms that replicate third dimensional beings or objects can easily be understood when we think about the frequency waves that are created by our human bodies, because the human physical body is made of electromagnetic particles that vibrate with oceans of space between them. The physical human body is aligned to our six-dimensional morphogenetic or morphic field (M-field) which is huge, and these M-fields vibrate with many frequencies and when we open our hearts and feel the emotion of love, we naturally align our physical body to this six-dimensional structure. Without our M-fields, which means without our human bodies light geometry, we would never look the same every time we look at ourselves in the mirror.

The Arcturians are advanced 7D-9D non-physical collective race of beings who are also here to assist planet earth and humanity during their current ascension process.

This is an important message from the Arcturian beings that they have given to humanity on earth during the month of June 2024 A.D. to those who are on the true path of ascension.

This is a wonderful time to be living on planet earth, see yourselves as being divine, follow your heart, serve others by shining your light and they will benefit from the divine light you continue to shine. Pay attention to what you think, feel and stay in alignment daily with the source. Humanity on earth is of the divine and for the divine, because everything that exists is of the divine and every situation and everything look at through the divine eyes of the source. If you wonder how to develop your unique gifts, ask yourself which gift lights you up. Everything you need is within you so relax, open your heart and receive God's divine source light energy daily. Treat others as members of your extended family so we can continue to build our new heaven on earth. Continue to serve the world as an extension of yourself, because when you give to others you are giving to yourself. You choose how you will ascend, but wake up now and choose which timeline you will collectively be in. Make the choice to go through ascension with a heart centered speed of love, because once we all complete the ascension process with planet earth, then earth will be the heart chakra for our Nebadon universe. Practice all you learn through ascension with other people who don't have the skills you have with love and compassion, because in the end darkness will follow the light and take it back and walk it back home to the source. Stay in unity and love to the darkness and walk it back home to the light, because before they fell from the light, they were and still are our brothers.

The Pleiadeans are advanced positive beings who originate from the Pleaides star cluster that is located over four hundred light years from earth. The Pleiadian beings have been visiting and quietly observing planet earth for thousands of years and at the same time sharing their ancient wisdom with some of earth's inhabitants and assisting in humanity's evolution. The Pleiadeans are spiritually and more technically advanced beyond our human understanding and their goal is to continue to help guide humanity into a new age of peace, cooperation, spiritual growth and expanded consciousness.

The presence of thousands of Pleiadean starships right above earth's atmosphere signifies a monumental increase in their direct activity and interaction with humanity. These massive motherships contain areas that are specifically designed to facilitate spiritual awakening and ascension to higher dimension levels of existence and these starships are strategically positioned around earth to help maximize the effectiveness of their technologies. The Pleiadean motherships use high frequency energies and light codes to help to activate humanity's dormant strands of DNA. This is helping to facilitate humanity's awakening process which is allowing more people to tune into higher dimensions and to access to higher states of consciousness, because the Pleiadeans are experts in the areas relating to lightwork, energy, healing and spiritual alignment. These motherships also provide a calming energy that reduces stress and promotes well being and the technologies from these motherships help to enhance moods, heal emotional pain and bring mental clarity to create positive personal transformation. Some of these Pleiadean motherships function as multidimensional lightships, because they are equipped to transmit high vibrational frequencies directly into the ley lines and chakras of the earth and this helps to benefit the planetary ascension of earth as a whole. This coordinated work of thousands of these motherships also helps to balance and stabilize the earth's energy grid, because they work subtly in the background to encourage our spiritual evolution. Their presence on earth is meant to be helpful, but the Pleiadeans follow a non-interference policy, and they avoid overt demonstrations of their technological capabilities or direct contact until humanity is ready for first contact.

Pleaides is a young star cluster that is in the constellation of Taurus which is approximately four hundred and forty light years away from planet earth and it is also known as the Seven Sisters. In addition to providing earth with spiritual guidance, Pleaides is also providing support to earth because its inhabitants have a deep love and respect for humanity on earth. They are here to help humanity to heal and to restore balance to earth and they are working with earth's environment sustainability and help to protect our planet's natural resources. Pleiadean spirituality is a path of self-discovery that aims to help individuals connect with their higher mind and tap into your inner wisdom. They encourage individuals to seek out their own truth rather than to rely on external sources for answers.

Consciousness is the central theme in Pleiadean spirituality, and they believe that we are all connected through a universal consciousness and by tapping into this consciousness, we can achieve a higher state of being, higher awareness and connect with our Universal Father. The Pleiadeans believe that through meditation, visualization and other spiritual practices, we can raise our frequencies and vibrations to ultimately gain a deeper understanding of ourselves and the universe. The Pleiadeans also played an important role in the creation of humanity, and they have been watching over humanity ever since.

One of the defining features of the Pleiadean starseeds who have incarnated now on earth is their DNA, because their DNA has been altered to allow them to better connect with their home planet and other star systems. Their altered DNA also gives the Pleiadeans a much more heightened intuition and psychic abilities and many of these Pleiadean starseeds are very sensitive, emphatic and compassionate with special healing qualities. The Pleiadeans here on earth who are helping humanity offer guidance and teachings in the areas related to healing and star wisdom, because they believe that we are all connected to the energy of the stars. The influence of inhabitants from Pleiades on earth has been expressed in many cultures on earth throughout history. The Cherokee native American tribe believe that their ancestors came from Pleaides and that the planet Pleaides was a gateway to the spirit world, and they viewed the seven stars of the planet

Pleiades as the seven representatives of the seven clans in the Cherokee tribe. The Nordic and Viking cultures viewed the planet Pleaides as the group of seven stars that represent the goddess Freyja and her seven sisters, and they believed that these seven stars had the power to guide and protect them on their journey through this thing called life.

Even the ancient civilization of Lemuria that was destroyed over 12,000 years ago saw the importance of the planet Pleaides and they believed that the seven stars of Pleaides were an important source of spiritual energy that could be used to help heal both the physical body and the mind. Throughout earth's history the planet Pleaides has also been an important part of many of the organized religions on earth and their spiritual practices. In Greek mythology the seven stars of Pleaides were believed to be the seven daughters of Atlas and Pleione, and they were known as the seven sisters who were associated with fertility and good luck. The Hopi Native American tribe believed that the seven stars of Pleaides were the home of their ancestors and that they would one day return to their original home on the planet Pleaides. The Lakota Native American tribe believed that the seven stars of Pleaides was the home of their ancestors and that they too would one day return home to their original planet on Pleiades.

During the current times of spirituality on planet earth, the Pleiadean starseeds are now recognized as being here to help earth and its inhabitants with the ascension process.

Star Seeds are the individuals who began to incarnate from the other planets and star systems on planet earth in the year 1950 A.D. to hold the light and help to raise the consciousness of both earth and humanity. According to the restored galactic history and backed by the esoteric ancient records, planet earth originally was a part of the Sirius star system that encircles the great central sun, Alcyone in the first concentric circle that extends from the center of the Milky Way Galaxy and outward. This is the location of where the light of our galaxy's central sun first anchored the covenant that is known as the Seal of Palador which equals the agreement known as the covenant that our Universal Prime Creator through Machiventa Melchizedek and Abraham established here on our planet earth. The star system Sirius is where the original seed of light and life began during the infant stages of the development of our Milky Way Galaxy. From the star system of Sirius this great quest began to spread and secure the universal light force that shines from the center of the galaxy was anchored. Our local sun star system called Helios Envesta was revolving around as part of the Sirius Trinary Star System. Planet earth was also part of the Vega Solar System in the Lyra constellation located in the galactic sector of Sirius B. Humanity began from this constellation with the colonization of the Milky Way Galaxy from the Lyra-Vega systems. Earth and our solar system are all a part of the same trinary star system and most of the worlds in the Milky Way Galaxy are part of a convergent of evolutions where human like beings exist in other solar systems and worlds within the Milky Way Galaxy.

The concept of mankind as a materialized being of light is a long ascending/descending process known as involution. The original fallen light beings were known as the reptoid and the dinoid species who were the negative extraterrestrials. The reptilians existed long before humanity did in an alternate reality of the Milky Way and when they fell from God's light, they destroyed their own universe and then began their quest to destroy everyone else's universe. Humanity's original form was celestial and in this celestial form, humans began their existence years ago long before the initial human seeding on earth began. The reptoids (reptilians) and the dinoids because of their separation from the light of the Source were only able to survive by only using their lower chakras and by feeding off the negative loosch energy of others and in addition, they were stuck and not able to ascend back home to the higher dimensions. While the original descending celestial humans were still able to use both of their lower and higher chakras to daily receive the Universal Father's source light and ascend back home to the higher dimensions.

The original fallen light beings the reptoids and the dinoids originated from the eleventh technology dimension, the multiverse and they must totally depend on technology to survive because they are separated from God's source light. These fallen light beings, the reptilians come from the ancient serpent race who were created by Lord Samana (Lucifer/Baal/Marduk) to prevent the spreading of the universal living light force beings. On planet earth you can trace the mark of the beast from these original fallen light reptilian beings to the following biblical people.

Cain the son of Adam and Eve who killed his half-brother Abel and Ham who had a high concentration of reptilian blood in his DNA and he later committed the first sin on earth five years after great flood by lusting after his own father, Noah who was the son of Enlil/Zeus, the founder of the white brotherhood on earth.

Nimrod, the great-grandson of Ham who also had a high concentration of reptilian blood in his DNA, hunted human men as his prey on the lands in his kingdom and later disobeyed God's instruction to spread the people out who lived in his kingdom to new lands and instead King Nimrod built the Tower of Babel which which was really a space station and a part of a secret space program for King Nimrod's plot to achieve world domination and to destroy God and His Niberian council in heaven.

The Pleiadeans are the higher evolved human like beings who are the parent race of humanity living on earth. They are collectively known as angels, Sons of God who in our current times are now coming forward to reveal their connections to planet earth. The Pleiadeans have also confirmed that once planet earth completes its current ascension process that it has been set up to be the location of the living cosmic library that will contain all the information relating to everything in creation. The Pleaides star system is considered to be the cradle of human consciousness, and the planet Pleaides is anchored to carry forward the seed of the celestial humanoid family to many solar systems within the Pleaides star system including planet earth.

The following is an important message from the positive group of Pleiadean beings that was given to humanity during the month of June 2024 A.D.

At this moment planet earth is moving into a new phase of our ascension into the new heaven on earth and as humanity continues to vibrate at its current fourth and fifth density consciousness, it is important to not fall into polarized thoughts, take no sides, stay in the middle at a neutral point and you will find that the experiences of integration in your consciousness will extend out into your reality. In order to continue to accelerate your awakening now, when you find yourself in the middle point of a situation, move yourself into a holographic consciousness fractural of unity consciousness where you will see yourself as a part of the whole instead of being separate and you will begin to experience your life from a different perspective. Humanity is the embodiment of Christ Consciousness because humans are a fractural of the One in unity consciousness. Whenever someone says something to hurt you, recognize the pain that person has inside themself to have said these words to you and forgive them.

What is going on planet earth right now is that humanity is awakening to what you already are, because you have been caught up in the false matrix that the reptilians have installed on earth, and you have been asleep. The energies from the higher dimensions are available to humanity now, because all is well and unfolding as planned. In order to accelerate your individual awakening, make ascension your main focus in life and see yourself as the universe sees you, look within where you will find the answers to all your questions, you can be yourself because you are safe to be in your every now moment, so love yourself and others. For many humans their awakening moment comes when you are questioning who am I, after losing your job, or when they lost a loved one and humanity as one human collective are going through this same awakening which is the greatest shift in consciousness ever to occur on earth. This shift in human consciousness is the end of the old ways and the beginning of a new age. You who are living now on earth during these great times of ascension made the free will choice to be here so you must continue to be in harmony with yourself to continue to contribute to earth's great awakening and ascension to the new heaven on earth.

Our local sun that earth revolves around is the light, the missing sisters or the eight stars of Pleaides. About eighty percent of the Milky Way Galaxy is still waiting to be colonized and that will happen after the ascension of earth and its inhabitants has been completed. Once the ascension process on earth has been completed with the ascending timeline humans living on the new Blessed Gaia 7D earth and the non-ascending timeline humans living on the middle 4D earth will ascended humans will be transformed from (666) carbon-based beings to (999) crystalline Adam Kadmon light beings. The ascended (999) Adam Kadmon humans will then begin to repopulate the rest of the eighty percent of the uninhabited Milky Way Galaxy. The non-ascending timeline humans living on the vacation planet will continue to live in their same homes, same jobs without remembering the ascension event and they will continue to live their lives free from any prior false matrix reptilian influences and they will proceed to evolve and ascend at their own pace and those ascended humans who volunteer will continue to travel back and forth from the new earth to the middle 4D earth to help in their ascension process.

The human species living on earth currently carries the greatest genetic diversity in the Milky Way Galaxy which means that humanity is the culminating masterpiece of all creations within the superuniverse of Orvonton. Also, when the ascension process on earth is complete, planet earth will be operating at all three of the major technological space population systems.

Another extraterrestrial presence that has been on planet earth since the year 1950 A. D. are the Greys, who were beings who also came to earth from a parallel reality and from three hundred years in the future. The Greys are a robotic race with no emotions who had been born in labs and since they could no longer reproduce, they were facing extinction. The Greys had become enslaved by the Alpha Draconian race who then turned their race into robots. The greys time travelled from three hundred years in the future from their parallel universe during the 1950's to the United States where they then tried to make an agreement with the late President Eisenhower to give them human babies and use their DNA to restart their race in exchange for technology. The late President Eisenhower refused their offer, but behind his back, the Deep State Cabal and military agreed to their proposals and as a result many humans were abducted from earth from the years of the 1950's all the way through the end of the 1980's.

When you time travel you cannot time jump to a specific year, but instead you must travel to specific entry points and the Grey's entry point was the 1950's. The result of these many human abductions by the Greys was that they used the DNA from their many human captives to create half human and half Greys ascended rainbow zeta beings who we will be meeting, and we will have to accept in the near future. Some of the technology the Deep State/Cabal and military on earth received from the Greys in exchange for these many abductions was the internet which made its debut in the year 1998 A.D., 5G spying and negative frequency output cell phone towers, and the advanced spacecraft (TRTD) spacecraft which is currently being used by the world's military. Many of the civilian

UFO sightings that are being reported are in reality military crafts that were obtained from alien technology. During the final years of earth's current ascension process on earth from the time period of the years 2024 through 2050 A.D., humans will be freely mating with these half human/half Greys ascended rainbow Zeta beings.

When I was a young child growing up in Southwest Detroit, Michigan during the 1950's, I spent a lot of time sitting on our family's large front porch and almost daily, I would watch these space vehicles driven by the Greys enter our atmosphere over the numerous large trees that were in our neighborhood. Apparently, others like me also continued to see these spaceships in the skies, but the media would always respond that the objects we were seeing were weather balloons. I never told anyone about my seeing these spaceships daily, because people just didn't talk about such things in the 1950's and if you did, they would have you committed to Eloise, the local mental hospital.

The great Paradise order of The Unions Of Days also known as the Order of Melchizedek has been given the job of repairing the Milky Way galaxy from all the chaos that has been caused by the Lucifer Rebellion and the countless invasions by the Draco-Reptilians. This high celestial command operating under The Order Of Melchizedek and under the direction of Archangel Michael have established certain galactic command centers and councils to help to maintain God's divine order within the galactic systems of the Nebadon universe. The Order Of Melchizedek under the direction of Archangel Michael first set out to establish their world of light and love in the star system Sirius, because it is the closest star system to our galactic center of the central sun Alcyone where the original guardians of our Milky Way Galaxy are stationed. This headquarters on the planet Sirius is located within the interior of the great central sun and the guardians of our galaxy harness this power within the great central sun and this power is equivalent to the power of billions of suns and this has been a smart and secure victor move for the forces of light.

The Sirius star system is the brightest star in our Milky Way Galaxy and its color is lapis blue. This is also the color of the solar ray that is used by Archangel Michael to restore light and life into all the lower planes of the universe that had been living in darkness. The origins of mankind began around the planet Sirius especially in the star system of Vega which is in the Lyra constellation and the Office of Christ which is the everlasting kingdom of light was first anchored in the Sirius star system. There is a great plan to restore the Milky Way Galaxy's three types of living beings and they are as follows. The corporeal beings are just like humans and they are made of solid matter.

The atmosphere beings are made of solid matter, but their molecular structure is quite different from the human structure.

The ethereal beings have no mass, solid or matter at all.

Humanity living on earth today are the final product of the celestial race who descended first in the living level of the Eutherians and then finally into the material level of the earth terrestrials who are the lowest form of a being who has taken the form to be a vibrating energy matter being. Humanity first all began as celestial beings with a pure body of light and then descending to become an intelligent operating being with etheric bodies and then we descended down further to an organic physical body as the final condensation of our energy field as a walking organic computer, and a multidimensional spiritual being of light. All humans live daily in a cycle that is known as the universal round which is the process that every spiritual being takes to achieve the greatest life experience and the highest ascension back to the source. The whole purpose of the universal round is so that all of the sparks of life (children of God) may get the opportunity to experience life, evolve and then ascend to return back home to our Universal Prime Creator Father in Paradise and there are many souls waiting in line in the void just waiting for their opportunity to experience the physical experience of life, so don't waste your time and complete the mission you came to earth to do.

There is no such thing as a flat planet or a flat earth in our Nebadon universe, because all planets are spheres, and they are based on equations that are created and maintained by Archangel Metatron (Enoch the Ethiopian) who oversees all the sacred geometry in the sixth dimension. Planet earth is a sphere that consists of many layers of different realities, that include dimensions, inner realms, inner worlds, stargates, portals and wormholes. Each one of these layers of realities that exist within the inner earth have within them active simulations and holograms that are all based on the sacred geometry of the sixth dimension. When you enter one of these available realities on earth and its many layers of reality, you don't enter a black void but instead each reality is loaded with simulations and holograms that are all based on geometric equations from the sixth dimension. The higher up you travel in these dimensions and realms, the more sophisticated the simulations become for you to experience that level of existence. Humans who have an activated

153

Merkabah light body can quantum jump and travel through all of these portals, stargates, inner worlds and dimensions that are available now on earth and this is the reason why so many beings choose to incarnate on planet earth, because on most planets you can only experience five emotions, but on planet earth you can experience up to (139) emotions.

THE TWELVE UNIVERSES IN THE MILKY WAY GALAXY

(UNIVERSE #12) \ COMPASSION-LOVE/

(UNIVERSE#11)\TECHNOLOGY-MECHANICS/

(UNIVERSE# 10) \THEOLOGY/

(UNIVERSE #9) \PRIME CREATOR-SOURCE/

(UNIVERSE #7) \UNIVERSAL LANGUAGE/

(UNIVERSE# 8) LABORATORY OF GOD/

(UNIVERSE # 6) \LITTLE PEOPLE-FAIRIES-GNOMES-NATURE SPIRITS/

(UNIVERSE # 5)\SILENT UNIVERSE/

(UNIVERSE #4) \ROOT OF DEMOCRACY-INTELLECT/

(UNIVERSE # 3) \UNIVERSE OF MEN/

(UNIVERSE #2)\UNIVERSE OF WOMEN/

(UNIVERSE # 1) \UNIVERSE OF JESUS/

The universe is all of space, matter, energy, time and its contents which includes the planets, stars, galaxies, and all of the other forms of matter and energy that exists within it. The universe is the totality of all that exists, the entire cosmos and it is the biggest because it contains billions of galaxies which includes all of us.

These are the twelve universes that exist within our Milky Way Galaxy.

The **first universe** extends outwards from our central core, and it is known as the universe of beauty and it is attributed to the first five cosmic lords, the first solar adept, the firstborn of heaven, our oldest brother and the greatest of the many sons of God, Lord Jesus and as the firstborn in heaven, everything comes through his first ray of essence.

The **second universe** extends from the God source, and it is known as the universe of women. The adept of this universe is Mariya, the second born of heaven and Mariya is God's eternal companion who acts as the focal point of the sacred divine feminine power and this universe is governed by the second cosmic ray of wisdom.

The **third universe** is known as the universe of men. It is the universe of intellectual pursuits, and the adept of this universe is known as Lord Samana (Lucifer) before he fell from the light to darkness and started the Lucifer Rebellion on Paradise and on many other worlds in the Nebadon universe including planet earth. Lord Samana (Lucifer) became the father of the dark brotherhood and of all the succeeding historical Lucifer like beings who were Enki (Poseidon), Baal and Marduk.

The **fourth universe** is where both the feminine and masculine or the love and intellectual aspects of the godhead are in balance which is really at the root of all democracies, and it is governed by the fourth cosmic ray.

The **fifth universe** is known as the great silent universe, and it is governed by the fifth cosmic ray. There is no sound in this universe, only thoughts and everything in this universe is conducted by the power of pure thinking.

The **sixth universe** is known as the universe of the little people. This is the universe where all of the fairies, gnomes and nature spirits had their origin, and it is governed by the sixth ray.

The **seventh universe** is known as the universe of mathematical science and this universe has the task to continue to pursue math as being the universal language across all universes and it is governed by the seventh cosmic ray.

The **eighth universe** is known as the great laboratory of God. It was in this universe that all of the cosmic rays were put into existence. Jesus, the firstborn in heaven and the greatest adept to ever visit our universe to establish the ascension guidelines of Christ consciousness and to God's children here on earth. Jesus was so pure and vibrating so high in consciousness, because he was one step below the Prime Creator, Source.

The **ninth universe** is where all creation is devoted to the worship of our prime Creator, Universal Father in Paradise.

The **tenth universe** is known as the universe of theology where everyone are ardent students of the subject of God and this universe is governed by the tenth cosmic ray.

The **eleventh universe** is known as the universe of the mechanics, because all technology originates here, and it is governed by the eleventh cosmic ray.

The **twelfth universe** is the universe of compassion, and it is governed by the twelfth cosmic ray.

Our universe of Nebadon is ruled by Michael of Nebadon, a being of unimaginable love and power, a Creator Son of the eternal and infinite Universal Prime Creator Father. Our Nebadon universe is a physical universe that is a part of the highest constitutional density realm, and it is made of a Universal Time Matrix. The Universal Time Matrix that our universe is made of is composed of five density levels that each hold three dimensional holographic fields within that are composed of three spectrums of frequency that manifests as layers of the consciousness of perception and expression. Our universe is all of space and time and its contents along with our planet earth is in the most remote part of the superuniverse number seven of Orvonton. The local universes that are located within our universe are the primary building blocks of the seven superuniverses and each of the local universe are a unified personal creation. Our local system of Satania is well developed and it has over three hundred and eighty-four inhabited planets. Our Nebadon universe consists of over one hundred constellations with each having one hundred systems of inhabited worlds. The creation of the Nebadon universe was governed by a trinity wave structure of an energetic system of higher order Christos Angelic Oraphim

Light Beings of the Emerald Order, The Amethyst Order and The Gold Order which are composed of the Elohim, the Seraphim and the RA Confederation. Together they formed the Threefold Founder Flame that is composed of the magenta-violet, the blue and gold rays that together form the Trinity ray aspect of the Nebadon universe. This Threefold Founder Flame then gave rise to the holographic structure of the four harmonic universes that each have a ray system with their own sound frequency, light quotients and colors. These Guardian Founders of our universe of Nebadon reside just outside of the Universal Time Matrix of Harmonic Universe #5 in Nebadon.

THESE ARE THE NINE REALMS THAT ARE LOCATED FOUR ABOVE AND THREE BELOW EARTH THAT FORM THE TREE OF LIFE IN OUR NEBBADON UNIVERSE

EARTH IS AT THE CENTER OF THESE NINE REALMS

(REALM #1) \AESIR GODS-THOR-ASGARD/

(REALM #2) \LIGHT ELVES, BLACK DWARFS-ALFHEIM

(REALM #3) \TITANS-JOTUNN/

(REALM #4) \SNOW WHITE-SEVEN DWARFS-NIDAVELLIR/

(REALM # 5) \EARTH/KAI/ATLANTIS-MIDGARD/

(REALM #6) \PLASMA BEINGS-MUSPELHEIM/

(REALM #7) FROST GIANTS-NIFLHEIM/

(REALM #8) \THE CONEHEADS-RIVALS TO GODS IN REALM#1-VANAHEIM/

(REALM #9) \HADES-REALM OF LOST GODS-LOST SOULS-HELL/

The Nine Realms of the Nebadon Universe

Earth is not a flat planet but rather it is a round sphere that has many layers to it which includes many realities, dimensions, realms, inner worlds, wormholes and stargates and the nine realms that are located above and below earth are just one of its many realities. The Nebadon universe is divided into nine realms, and they can be accessed now if you have an activated Merkabah light body through quantum jumping. Planet earth, the center of this Tree of Life configuration is located at the center and the rest of the eight realms stretch out from earth's Tree of Life roots side by side. If you have an activated Merkabah light body you can quantum jump now to each of these nine realms through Stargate #2 in Sarasota, Florida. Earth is the center of these nine realms in our universe and from the Tree of Life center point in earth the remaining eight realms stretch out like tree roots side by side.

Realm #1-Asgard is located directly above planet earth and our two worlds are connected by a great rainbow bridge named Bifrost that has a guardian on it. This is the near perfect realm of the Aesir deities which is the home of the Gods of the pantheon and home of Thor, the god with his mythical hammer. The Aesir Deities in this realm went to war with the fire gods from realm #7 and won. So, these fire gods have now been replaced with the frost giants.

Realm# 2-Alfheim is the realm of the light elves who are of the Black race, and they play good music, write good poetry, draw beautiful pictures and practice only good magic. The light elves from this world also work with elemental beings who live in Realm#5 on planet earth. This is the realm where the Smurfs originated from.

Realm #3-Jotunheim is the realm of the fallen monsters. It is the realm of the Assyria/Titan Guardians who live here with their many large pets some of which include Godzilla, King Kong, the kraken, dinosaurs, dragons and many more. Humans who live in realm #5 have 72 titans in their physical bodies.

Realm #4-Nidavellir is the subterranean realm of Snow White and the Seven Dwarfs. This is the animation/cartoon realm that is connected to humans who live in realm #5 through humans' seven chakras and their seven etheric bodies. During the process of involution where humans descend and ascend back to the higher dimensions, this process takes two weeks to completely travel through these nine realms.

The Nine Realms of the Nebadon Universe

Realm #5-Midgard is realm #5 on planet earth the realm of the humans, plants and animals. Earth is the center point of the Tree of Life of these nine realms in our Nebadon universe and the remaining eight realms spread out from the center point of earth like roots from the Tree of Life. These nine realms are separated by the ice walls in Antarctica and the three entrances to these nine realms are rainbows, the northern lights and stargate #2.

Realm #6-Muspelheim is the realm of the plasma beings who send the flashes of lightning to earth's surface every fifty seconds. This realm is located directly below earth and the lightning that these plasma beings send to earth's surface every fifty seconds provides planet earth with its pulse and heartbeat, the Schumann Resonances.

Realm #7-Niflheim is the realm of frigid ice and snow. This is where the frost giants live, and they are the beings who taught the Moors how to walk long ago by tying a flat board to their backs and behinds, which caused them to have flat behinds. The frost giants also taught the Moors how to read and write and while they were ruling Europe and Spain for more than eight hundred years, and they then shared this knowledge and taught the European population how to read and write. This realm is where frosty the snowman originated.

Realm #8-Vanaheim is the realm of the Black race of beings known as the Coneheads. They are a rival group of gods to the Pantheon gods who live in Asgard in realm #1. The Coneheads are Vanir Deities who are advanced in the use of the mystical arts, and they use the points at the top of their heads to complete interterritorial transmissions.

Realm #9-Hell is the realm of Hades for the resting place of the dead who have sold their soul to the dark brotherhood/Cabal/Illuminati. This is the realm of the lost gods, and these lost souls are put in a room until the lost gods of this realm are ready to use them as they see fit. There is no such place of Purgatory or Hell where you go to burn forever as they were both invented by the organized religions of the Cabal to instill fear and to control the many unsuspecting humans.

These nine realms in the Nebadon universe sprout from the roots of the Yggdrasil tree which is these worlds' tree that gives structure and form to the cosmos. Each realms position within the Yggdrasil tree determines its connections to the other eight realms.

THE TWELVE LEVEL KATA STARGATE GRID CHART

(STARGATE #12-MONGEUR FRANCE) \GREAT CENTRAL SUN –ALCYONE/

(STARGATE #11-STONEHENGE, ENGLAND) \PLANETS OF LYRA AND AVONYN-11D/

(STARGATE #10-ABADONN IRAQ) \PLANETS VEGA AND LYRA-10D/

(STARGATE #9-BAM TSO HEIHO TIBET) \PLANET OF ANDROMEDA-9D/

(STARGATE #8-SEDONA ARIZONA)\GAIA EARTH-7D

(STARGATE #7-LAKE TITICACA PERU) \PLANET ARCTURUS-7D/

(STARGATE #6-MOSCOW RUSSIA)\PLANET OF SIRIUS B-6D/

(STARGATE#5 MACHU PERU) \ PLEAIDES AND TARA-7D/

(STARGATE #4-GIZA EGYPT)\EARTH'S LOCAL SUN/

(STARGATE #3-BERMUDA) \EARTH 3D-4D PORTAL/

(STARGATE #2-SARASOTA FLORIDA)\ NINE REALMS OF EARTH-TREE OF LIFE

(STARGATE #1-HALLEY ANARTICA) \PLANET OF ORION-8D/

There are twelve stargates on planet earth and these are portals that are hidden within the earth's magnetic field. These stargate portals were built millions of years ago by a race called the Ancients and they provide instantaneous travel that are connected by a series of networks to different planets and universes. These twelve stargates are another layer of reality of earth that serve as a Rosen bridge portal that allows you to rapidly travel between two distant locations by creating a stable wormhole between the originating stargate to the destination stargate. These are the twelve stargates that can be accessed now with your activated Merkabah light body from the fifth realm of planet earth, so quantum jump now.

Stargate #1 is located in Halley; Antarctica and it is the portal to the planet of 8D Orion.

Stargate #2 is located in Sarasota; Florida and it is the portal to access the eight other realms within planet earth. These nine realms are the Tree of Life of the Nebadon universe.

Stargate #3 is located on the island of Bermuda, and it is the portal to 4D and 5D earth.

Stargate #4 is located in Giza, Egypt and it is the portal to our local sun where the Office of Christ is located.

Stargate #5 is located in Machu Picchu, Peru and it is the portal to access the 5D planets of Pleaides and Tara Earth.

Stargate # 6 is located in Moscow, Russia and it the portal to the 6D planet of Sirius B.

Stargate #7 is located in Lake Titicaca; Peru and it is the portal to planet Arcturus 7D.

Stargate #8 is located in Sedona, Arizona and it is the portal to the ascended 7D planet of Blessed Gaia, Earth.

Stargate #9 is located in Bamtso Heiho, Tibet and it is the portal to the 9D planet of Andromeda.

Stargate # 10 is located in Abadon, Iraq and it is the portal to the 10D planets of Vega and Lyra.

Stargate #11 is located in Stonehenge; England and it is the portal to the 11D planets of Lyra and Avyon.

Stargate #12 is located in Monsieur, France and it is the portal to our great central sun, Alcyone and this is the highest you can go.

The Nebadon universe is comprised of a matrix of matter and antimatter, and it has both physical and ethereal beings. We have been stuck in the illusion of total physicality by paying too much attention to things such as our own body and form, but the fact remains that the Nebadon universe is full of antimatter that includes a variety of ethereal beings which includes the highest portion of our own human selves. Our (4) Harmonic Universes in the Nebadon universe are occupied by various densities and consciousness which includes the realm of the Rishis Suns where the pure non-physical divine beings live, and they oversee the spiritual and consciousness expansion of all physical beings. Human beings incarnate within the third dimension here on earth to obtain lifetime experiences that will lead to consciousness expansion. The programs of reality that have already been pre-sorted by our higher mind are streamed into us while we are still in a state of diminished consciousness and amnesia. These programs of reality due to the slow progression of time on earth, along with the human consciousness receipt of light that is being projected on us, always gives humans a sense of anticipation for the next flash of consciousness which gives us the illusion of future. Humans also perceive the sequence of receiving the last flash of light consciousness with the illusion of the past.

The human soul occupies the center of the carousel of our consciousness the same way we continue a rotational motion around our Prime Creator Source who is at the center of the cosmos. The human local vibrating frequency reflects your state of consciousness which is the timeline you have chosen to live in, and all timelines or space-time have the same common beginning. We can always go back in time and change the past in a new cycle of reincarnation through the dream state or during meditation to effectively cleanse our soul from any past negative trauma and karma.

A review of some of the negative events that happened on planet earth after the end of WWII was that the soul of planet earth was depleted of all its conscious energy which then led to a tremendous dimming of the light consciousness of the planet. And even with the rushing of many of our galactic brothers who came to earth's atmosphere to shine their light quotient into earth's atmosphere, it just wasn't enough to correct the dire situation planet earth was in. Since the year 1950 A. D. volunteers from all over the galaxy have been incarnating on earth to continue to shine their light to help earth and its inhabitants to wake up, evolve and get on the true path of ascension back home to the new heaven on earth. Since the Draco reptilians made the decisions millions of years ago to separate themselves from the Prime Creator Source and from His light, they have invaded planet earth over and over again and the tampering they have done to earth's brain, the crystals that lie deep within the core of earth has helped to hinder humanity's ability to be free to wake up from this slavery mentality and walk the true path of ascension back home to the new heaven on earth.

The many crystals that are in the core of the earth hold the blueprint of the living consciousness records of all living beings contained in the evolutionary histories of earth. This means that these crystals record the consciousness experiences of all life that are imprinted through the complex patterns of frequencies and the mathematical coding they hold. These crystals that are located within earth's core also amplify and accelerate the light frequencies in the human body. Our ancestors knew the importance of earth's crystals and that they were to be used as sacred vibrational tools that interconnect humans with the planetary crystalline networks and support humanity's connection with the higher realms of consciousness. Many of the inner earth crystals have unique special qualities that also impact humans' spectrums of energy, frequency, vibrations and consciousness that are made through these crystals ability to access light and sound frequencies that activate holographic structures and electrical conductivity. Each kind of crystal is unique in their individual energetic signature and these signatures create configurations that are reflected in the individualized soul experience of a human being who relates to the specific crystalline consciousness. The silicate matrix DNA template is the original human crystalline blueprint, and crystalline consciousness is activated in the human body when a connection is made with love-coded hydro plasmic light which turns into liquid crystals.

The human body has the same properties as crystals, and that is the ability to amplify, absorb, store and transmit a wide range of vibrational frequencies. Everything that humans are exposed to has its own energetic signature and frequency that impacts the human energetic system by being either healthy or unhealthy for the entire human body. The key to restoring energetic health and balance for your body is to have an awareness that humans are all natural crystalline beings who can conduct energy through crystalline functioning, and we need to keep an abundant amount of life force to always be circulating through our physical bodies. The human body's energy field consists of an array of oscillating energy centers known as chakras that are in a multi-dimensional blueprint of interacting crystal structures that organize into various crystalline functions. The human body's organs, glandular systems, and skeletal structure all have a crystalline function that includes having a trait called piezoelectric properties. The human bone structure is the primary solid crystal in the physical body that is the main frequency transducer that runs all throughout the entire human body.

The platinum white crystal that is in the human light body is located at the top of the 12D shield in the 14th chakra and when this biological crystal is activated in the human light body, it interconnects the human consciousness to the platinum crystal energy records that are in planet earth's body in the core of the planet.

This allows a biological interface of the hydro plasmic light of the crystalline source of the platinum ray to link with the rainbow crystal light. The first activation stages of the platinum ray in turn the activates the gold, platinum, white and diamond crystal rays in the human body which will then balance and heal the feminine principle light body and reset the body's heart and silicate matrix. By adding protons from the solar activity and plasma light from the core of earth's crystal core also adds new elements into the matter realm and helps the human body to be able to conduct more liquid plasma light.

On December 30, 2023, A.D., the cosmic hierogamic event of the Twinned Universal Melchizedek Suns was completed, and this event was the restoration of the human body's organic consciousness to its original status prior to the invasion on earth by the negative reptilian extraterrestrials and this was done by activating the Emerald Guardian Ascension

Host to its highest intensity. After this great cosmic event, the next stage in the Guardian-Founders steps to repair the human organic consciousness included the anchoring of the Sapphire Diamond Shield architecture into the 10D gateways to return the Cosmic Mother Solar Reisha Sopianic lineage back into the planetary matrix of planet earth.

When matter shifts its state from a solid state to less dense states to become more fluid to flow like a liquid or plasma, it is undergoing the process called a mesomorphic state. This means that matter is upshifting its frequency to enable its particles to vibrate into higher and multidimensional spaces. This means that the more density we carry in our human bodies, this causes us to lose the ability to vibrate in the higher dimensions of consciousness. Different states of matter such as solids, liquids and gases all have different types of particle behavior, and all matter is made from the same fundamental elemental substances that cannot be broken down any further by any chemical or physical process. Condensed matter is more rigid, and its particles cannot move or slide past one another, because this matter is dense and unable to move around into different dimensional frequencies. When the human body's frequency of vibration is increased it means that you have naturally acquired a more fluid state of higher frequency consciousness, and your particles now have more available space because the density in your physical body has decreased. When your physical body becomes less dense you are ready and able to move and vibrate into different and higher dimensions of multidimensional space. In addition to our physical body losing density in matter through the absorption of incoming plasma light and ionization, the basic elemental compounds of our physical body and the atomic structure is changing from being a (666) carbon-based body to a less dense (999) silicate-based body and humanity is also currently shifting into another state of being that is more fluid.

As humanity continues to travel on the true path of ascension, we will continue to develop the ability to receive hydroplasmic light into our physical bodies and this will interconnect the lines of crystalline light that connects you to everything and everyone who is in the crystalline network. The focus now for those who are ascending is to cultivate and establish a direct relationship with your inner spirit, your world within and keep going the best way you can.

The human light body is a biological liquid crystal, and it is a constituent part of the coded blueprint of the crystalline grid that includes the collective consciousness of planet earth's sentient beings. The human light body also gives us instructions about how the expansion of consciousness energy may be achieved and this depends on whether or not the human light body is being exposed to natural frequencies from the Source which the loving radiant high vibrational vibrations of the Prime Creator, Source. When you daily hold Source light frequencies in the human light body, new crystalline imprints and the re-coding of missing Kundalini subharmonic frequencies that had caused soul-body fragmentation once again will connect us to our higher dimensional mental mind and matrixes. When you begin to run your body's kundalini current in corrected patterns, you will now be able to build the sub-harmonic strings in a new horizontal network for the 3-6-9 dimensions, which corrects your body's fragmented mental body patterns and thus you will be reconnected with your higher mind.

When the negative aliens continued their invasions on planet earth, they also tampered with humanity's natural organic process by placing genetic implants in our bodies and capping off some of our DNA strands. Some of these alien implants were glandular system devices that interfere with the normal functioning of the human endocrine system which changed the normal pattern of hormonal secretions into or blood stream and this caused malfunctions and blockages with the proper rising of the body's kundalini current. This blocked path of the human body's kundalini current has had a negative impact on all the body's brain receivers, the thalamus, the pineal gland, the thyroid gland and the thymus.

The platinum crystal and platinum day currents activates the sun disc that are organic spirals of gold crystalline technology that are in earth's planetary grid, and they all form a holographic light frequency pattern. The connection of the earth's platinum crystal to the sun disc network activates the human body's mental bodies and balances the feminine-masculine energies. When this balance occurs, the physical body's entire solar plexus area in the light body reconfigures itself into what is called the Golden Solar Gate energy vortex, and this vortex is also called the crystal palace of light or the RA center.

Human beings can repair and power up the crystalline earth grid so that it will be able to correct the natural organic currents into the crystalline heart that is in the crystal caverns in the earth. This can be accomplished by using the chakra crystal key mapping module (CCKMM) where advanced layers can be used to support the planetary grid to align it with the krystic architecture. These repairs can also be done, because all humans living on earth are the offsprings of God and our inherent design and morphogenetic structure is in line with this krystic architecture. There is also a platinum ray 12D shield technique that offers protective strength to the human biological crystal and to the crystal caverns in the earth. By practicing the technique of running the highest coherent energy current, one can access this grid that is harmonized by the merging of particles with anti-particles.

Since the year 2000, the platinum Indigos and those who are here on earth now to complete Christ missions, have continued to anchor the platinum white and diamond crystals into the crystal caverns within earth and they have also been anchoring the platinum ray ascension template in a silent and stealth manner.

As a result of the current global changes on earth that are occurring in the atmospheric pressure, this has begun to trigger new ascension symptoms in many humans. Some of the ascension symptoms that are occurring are related to feelings of compression and decompression along the spinal column area which is causing a sense of instability and buckling of the body's spinal column and neck which gives you the sensation of going in and out of space time. These compression-decompression sensations are also causing the physical body to work harder to adapt to the body's constant pressure changes. This has also had a direct effect on the blood, especially the blood pressure and one's heartbeat rhythm which can lead to you having feelings of anxiety.

It is important during these ascension times to complete these daily ascension homework items.

Complete at least one quantum jump daily to blessed Gaia earth.

Ground daily on the new heaven on blessed Gaia.

Receive Source light energy through your crown chakra daily while you are walking and grounding on the new heaven on blessed Gaia earth.

Align and focus all your entire bodies energies and five elements daily using our Universal Father's Source light to raise your vibrations if only one percent but do something.

Wrap your entire body's energy field with high vibrational Universal Father's source light.

Completely wrap your body's entire energy field with the blue light of protection from Archangel Michael.

Within the physical body's nervous system, the neurons or nerve cells need to be able to communicate with one another and transmit signals to be able to send messages to clearly interact throughout the body. A synapse is a structure that permits a neuron to pass chemical signals to another neuron, and the neurotransmitters are the chemicals that allow the transmission of these signals from one neuron to another across the synapses. These neurotransmitters and synapses are essential to the brain and nervous system, because they allow the nerve cells to communicate with each other and to form larger neural networks. The firing of the neurotransmitters in the human brain is responsible for the type of emotional state we will experience. The most excitable neurotransmitter in the human brain is the glutamate and the correct amount of gamma-aminobutyric acid and glutamate in the brain keeps us from getting feelings of being overwhelmed. Earth naturally produces dolomite through magnesium compounds that are related to the frequency transmission of the neurotransmitter dopamine, which is very important in stabilizing a person's mood and emotional state. When your brain is deprived of dopamine a person will show signs of ADHD, depression, apathetic behavior and become addicted to drugs both legal and illegal. Without the proper levels of dopamine in the human brain, it becomes very challenging for a person to have any mental discipline and cognitive control which are requirements for one to be a strong and stable person. Without having the sufficient and proper neurotransmitters in the human brain, it makes it harder for one to gather the energy you need to remain conscious, to stay awake and to be aware.

The many quartz crystals that are in the crystal caverns of the earth represent the higher bio-plasmic light, which is a part of the physical and ethereal substance of our cosmos. The quartz crystals are a part of the substance of the stars you see in our night time sky and the human consciousness, and they have the capability to transmit the frequency instructions set for firing the human brain's neurotransmitters, so they can communicate from one cell to another. By reclaiming the crystalline networks in earth's core, we will be able to reset earth's planetary brain to benefit humanity and further support the individual nerve cells within the human collective consciousness to effectively ensure that humanity has a more balanced brain function and continue to help to heal the human brain's chemistry.

Krystal consciousness is centered within the crystal lotus, or the crystal rose heart, a diamond crystal heart that flowers through the diamond sun body making it capable of transporting consciousness into the etheric or semi-physical density states, while at the same time spanning all possible timelines simultaneously and these are the properties that the activated human light body can achieve in its unlimited potential as the krystallah eternal light body. However, this can only be achieved when the activated human light body is exposed to the Prime Creator Source light.

When humans are exposed to artificial electromagnetic elements such as nanotechnologies and microwave weapons that are devoid of love, these technologies seal the body's liquid crystals literally into a state of frozen matter and this impairs humans' ability to freely move in any direction, which in turn prevents you to be able to experience an energetic multidimensional expansion during your ascension process.

When we are connected in our diamond crystalline heart with our Prime Creator, Source, we then possess the krystallah heart consciousness and we can then sense the difference between artificial intelligence software that is being used by negative aliens' machinery and true organic creation codes that hold pure love in adamantine particles which connects us directly to our Prime Creator, Source and truly reflect the universal laws of the universe.

The human body is an organic computer, a biological crystal and our body will return to its energetic balance when we follow the laws of nature and the Law of One. This means that the electromagnetic charge must be balanced in the human crystal body if you want to be able to ascend and the amount of the feminine magnetic charge in our body must equal the amount of the masculine electric charge in order to enter into the sacred marriage or Hieros Gamos of the final step of ascension which is the contracting back to God and having every aspect of God. Universal love must exist between the male and female gender twin flames in order to achieve an energetic balance and this in turn creates the crystal heart consciousness that can move through the energy architecture and a range of densities which gives rise to multidimensionality and shapeshifting which will come after ascension is completed. Through expansive mesomorphic behavior, after ascension is achieved, the krystallah core will then be able to reshape itself into many forms to be able to shapeshift, perceive and experience multiple expressions of life all throughout the entire universal system. The krystallah heart consciousness can also sense the original love radiance that is felt in the organic creator codes of the ascending timelines. Once we activate and grow our trinity consciousness, the liquid crystal that we all are, bonds with the pure love of the Source who co-creates the Eternal God or the adamantine particles.

The current shift in density on earth that is impacting our state of matter is important to our ascension process, because what we perceive as solid through our physical senses is really vortices of energy that are radiating unique energy signatures. Humans are a multidimensional collective consciousness, and we vibrate at a certain frequency, and we are co-creating what we daily experience in the physical material world. As we continue to hold less density in our physical body, we will gain the new ability to perceive energy signatures in our environment in a new and different way.

This means that what we had previously been unaware of or could not see before with the same energetic signatures, we will now be able to clearly see. Planet earth's sun discs are vortices that are connected to the earth's grid that interconnects with the stellar networks on multiple planes of reality. Through the connection with the sun disc on the earth grid, it is possible to travel on the intergalactic highways of the crystalline solar light that allows you through conscious though to transport to other dimensions. Every human has one of these sun discs two feet above your crown that you can use daily during times of meditation. When the platinum crystal becomes activated in the crystal caverns in the core of the earth, this sun disc technology that had been dormant since the times of Atlantic over 12, 000 years ago has now started to come back online.

The Aquaelle genetic lines first came to planet earth through the Sirius B stargate portal that is located at Stargate # 6 in Moscow, Russia and those who have remained behind on earth are known as the natural keepers of inner earth's crystal core. Through the Aqualle Matrix that is in earth's inner crystal core, we are now able to have access into the Aurora platforms that gives us access into the passageway that leads to the area of the Ascension Earth in the 9D planet of Andromeda. This Aqualle Matrix also transmits the Divine Mother's Aqua Ray Daughter Codes into earth's crystal caverns and the Aqualle Genetic Line descendants who are the keepers of these inner earth crystal caverns ensure that these codes remain intact. The Aqualle Genetic Line are directly related to the daughter of Christ bloodlines who incarnated here on earth from the planet of Andromeda more than a millennia ago to carry the required coding to bring the Diamond Sun Body back on planet earth for humanity to use in its ascension.

The divine beings who are a part of the genetic lines of the Aqualle matrix for all of these millennia have lived on earth as a part of the Native American Navajo tribe and they are light beings who are a part of the Aurora Krystar Star Family. They are the keepers of the crystal caverns in the earth, and they represent the unity intelligence field, and they are capable and dedicated to continuing to transmit the necessary codes that are needed in earth's crystal caverns. The name Aquaelle refers to the genetic descendants of the Guardian Yeshua and they are directly related to the Daughter of Christ bloodline who incarnated here on earth a millennia ago from the planet of Andromeda. The Aquaelle carry the Krystal Gene code for humanity on earth and it is the silicate matrix imprint that holds all of the twelve strands of DNA that are necessary for humanity's ascension.

The Aquaelle or Keepers of the Flame and the crystal caverns in the earth, also ensure that the necessary codes are embodied in earth's crystal core that will activate the Diamond Sun Body for the necessary male and female unification or Hieros Gamos, the sacred marriage and final step of ascension.

Planet earth entered the Cosmic Energy Cycle during the hierogamic event of the Cosmic Twinned Universal Melchizedek Suns on December 30, 2023 and this event allowed the center core of the Cosmic Spirit Body layers to open to transmit the spirit of all clusters that contain the first creation core memory cell for each human's eternal spirit family. This event also opened the doorway into the Universal Mother Dark Matter Matrix that holds many of the Solar Reiska Worlds that contain the mother lineages of many of the ascended masters, many of whom are connected to the original Blue Flame family of the Melchizedeks, Mua, and the Aquaelle, who still serve on earth as the keepers of earth's crystal caverns.

The descendants of the Aquaelle are represented by the male and female twins who are here on earth to protect the mother solar twin coding and the Diamond Sun Body genetics on earth, and this is the twelve strand DNA template that is the original human genome that was first seeded on Tara earth before it was destroyed by the negative aliens. And this twelve strand DNA template for the original human genome has been secretly protected by the Native American Navajo Tribe in the earth's grid during the 11,000 years of the Dark Age on earth and through this tribe this original DNA human template was represented by the manifestation of the White Buffalo Calf Woman and the White Navajo as the example of the mother solar twin coding and their direct descendants.

There are some light beings who are also assisting planet earth and its inhabitants during the current ascension process who live in the universe next to our Nebadon universe. These light beings are known as the Aurora family, and they are in alignment with the Paliadorian Covenant and the Law of One. The Aurora family are also a part of the Krystal Star and Unity Intelligence, and they have been working to build Aurora Platforms in our Nebadon universe that are being used as safe zones that makes it possible to safely step over the negative alien's frequency fences and (NET) that have been running on earth for quite some time. These safe zone Aurora Platforms also allow us to now safely access the Aquaelle Matrix through a passageway that leads to the ascension earth on the planet of 9D Andromeda.

On planet earth the Aquaelle Matrix represents the Guardian Host that the daughter coding that has been installed on earth through the incarnation of the Christos genetic bloodline from the planet Andromeda. This Aquaelle Matrix also represents the Andromeda Gate that is an ascension hosting platform that will help to heal the bloodlines on earth that had been afflicted by satanic binding, astral traps and Satanic human blood sacrifices.

The dream walkers who are currently living on planet earth are known as the Indigenous people, the Native Americans, the Aborigines, the Tibetans, the Celtics, the

Mua and the Blue Flame Melchizedeks, the lemurians and these groups of dream walkers have been helping to protect the earth by keeping their original organic pattern alive and its memory available for the human race since the 11,000 years of the Dark Age on earth when the planet fell under the dark control and evil manipulation of the dark brotherhood and the Cabal which caused widespread genetic damage to humanity on earth.

With the current return of the Daughter codes and activation of the Aquaelle Matrix on planet earth, the codified language that is embedded deep within earth's crystal caverns has surfaced onto earth and many of the male and female dream walkers who had been incarnated on Lemuria during the time of its glory over 12, 000 years ago or who are the descendants of the original tribes of Lemuria are now once again returning to earth. Many Native Americans and humans of Aborigine origin are also once again beginning to incarnate on planet earth to help restore the balance of the divine feminine and masculine principle on earth.

Before the negative aliens' invasions on planet earth, the civilization of Lemuria suffered a great holocaust and the motive was to take away the power that women had developed on earth that was associated with their Essene templar abilities which are known as dream walking which is a form of an awakened state of consciousness that was coded and preserved as a coded language in the crystal caverns of earth and these dream walkers are also considered as being the guardians of planet earth's crystal caverns.

All rays or electromagnetic spectrum have a base code, overtones and resonant tones and when the new magnetic Mother-Daughter code was introduced into earth's crystal caverns in the year 2012, this completely changed the magnetic field of planet earth. The Aquaelle Guardians facilitated this huge shift in the year 2012 which allowed the ascension process to begin and move planet earth into Harmonic Universe two (HU2). Planet earths entrance into the Photon Belt and the portal to the fourth dimension on December 21, 2012, also helped to jumpstart the ascension process for planet earth.

The Aquaelle Matrix is connected to the Aquilla Eagle Constellation and this connection will override the fallen areas of the Golden Eagle Grid and with the continued work of the daughter of Christ bloodline who incarnated here on earth from Andromeda, the gender related healing on earth will continue and this healing process is known as the "(777) Ancestral Clearing Coding."

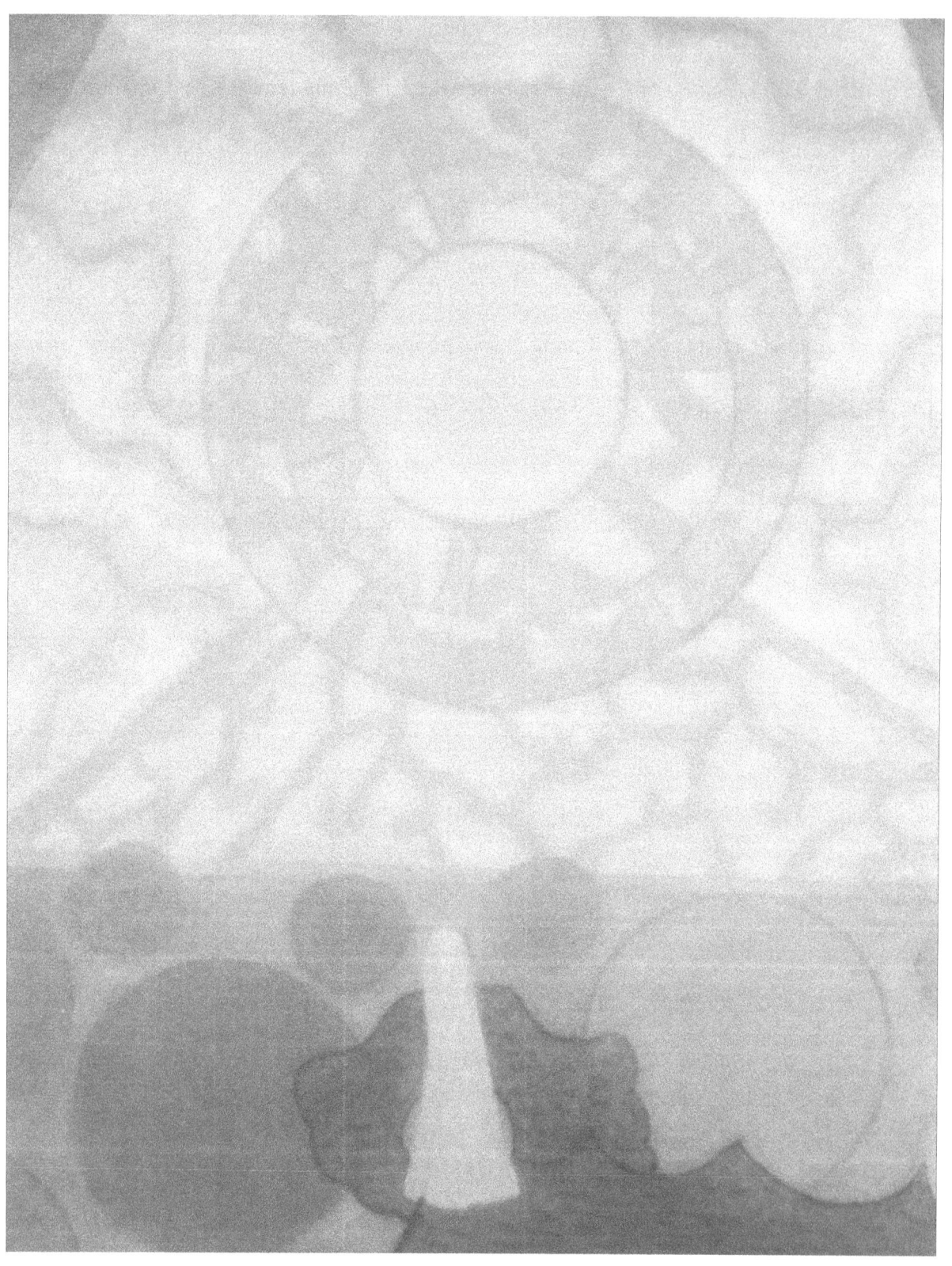

CHAPTER FIVE

THE EVOLUTIONARY RACES ON EARTH AND PLANET EARTH'S FIRST HUMAN FAMILY

Those who know your name trust in you.

(Psalm 9:10)

I have set before you life and death, blessings and curses. Now choose life.

(Deuteronomy 30:19)

A Prayer:

Dear God, Giver of joy, please help me to choose to follow you and believe and trust you

this day.

*ANDON AND FONTA, EARTH'S FIRST HUMAN FAMILY
993,408 YEARS AGO*

Approximately 1,000,000,000 years ago planet earth was placed on the physical registry of Nebadon in Paradise-the seven higher heavens as a viable planet and it was given the name of Urantia. There are sixty-one life modification planets that are very similar to planet earth in our Nebadon universe and the Life Carriers from Paradise are the team who initiated life on each of these sixty-one planets when each of these spheres displayed living beings who were ready to begin the evolutionary cycle of life. The Life Carriers then introduced a solution of sodium chloride into the flowing water on each of these planets which then introduced a pattern of life to enable the protoplasm that live in the waters to begin the cycle of life. About 1,000,000 years ago, planet earth was registered on the seven mansion worlds in Paradise as being an inhabited planet with human life.

About one million years ago the immediate ancestors of mankind made their appearance on earth by the completion of three successive mutations stemming from the early stock of a lemur type of placental mammal. A little more than one million years ago the Mesopotamian dawn mammals who were the direct descendants of the North American lemurs suddenly appeared and these lemurs who were the early dawn animals on earth were members of a new species and they had the largest brains for their size than any of the previous animals who had lived on earth. These agile lemurs multiplied and spread across the Mesopotamia peninsula for more than one thousand years and they proved to be a vital step in the evolution of the beginning of human life on planet earth.

Approximately 993,419 years ago in the area now known as Afghanistan and in a treetop home of a superior pair of lemur creatures, twins were born, one male and one female and their names were Andon and Fonta. Andon and Fonta had much less hair on their bodies than their parents and the rest of the members of their tribe had and they both insisted on walking upright. Andon and Fonta were both five feet tall and their heads grew much larger in comparison with the other members of their tribe, and they learned at an early age how to communicate with each other by using different signs and sounds. However, Andon and Fonta were not able to get the rest of their tribe to understand their new language of signs and sounds. Andon and Fonta were both true human beings and they had perfectly formed feet just like our present-day humans do. Andon and Fonta were the first two human beings to be born on planet earth and after they matured at the age of twelve, they had twenty-one children and lived to the age of forty-two years.

Andon and Fonta were able to experience many new emotions during their lifetime such as, admiration, gratitude, humility, fear, the spirit of worship and most importantly, love. At the age of nine years, Andon and Fonta met at the river, held a conference with each other and mutually agreed to live with and for each other only and they also agreed to leave their tribe and to journey north to begin a new life with each other.

Shortly before the twins left their tribe to begin their journey to a new life together, they lost their mother in a raid from a neighboring tribe, and their mother held off this raid until the twin's father arrived with reinforcements to defeat these raiders. After the death of their mother from the raiders Andon and Fonta left their village that same night to begin their new life together up north. When their father discovered that Andon and Fonta had left their village, he became listless, heartbroken and he refused to eat and since the rest of the members of their tribe could clearly see that their father had lost the will to live, one day as he aimlessly wandered off into the forest they beat him to death.

At the age of ten the spirit of worship entered into Andon and Fonta's minds and that was the moment 993,408 years ago that planet earth was registered in the Paradise worlds as being a planet of human life habitation. Once again biologic evolution had been achieved on a planet, because the human levels of dignity and free will had arrived on planet earth in the System of Satania and in the Nebadon universe.

Once human life appears on one of the sixty-one life experiment worlds in our Nebadon universe, the following divine team of Paradise beings then journey to this planet to assist in the evolution of the new human species.

The Divine Thought Adjusters were sent to planet earth to create within man the yearning to be like God and attain Paradise. These Divine Thought Adjusters remain indwelling the human mind during three stages of one's mortal life. The first stage is the arrival of the Divine Thought Adjuster to indwell the human mind just before the age of five years until the age of twenty. Around the age of forty the human mind then attains the age of discretion and the last stage is when a human mortal is delivered from the flesh.

The team of life Carriers who were assigned to work on planet earth were also sent to planet earth to complete their life development duties. Life does not originate on any planet spontaneously, because life is constructed on a planet according to the life plans that are formulated by the Architects of Beings on Paradise and then life appears on a new planet by either direct importation or as a result of life implantation techniques that are completed by the Life Carriers who are assigned to the planet. The Life Carriers from Paradise have the job of designing and assisting the continuing development of the new creature life on the planet and after planting life on a new world, the Life Carriers remain on the world for a long period of time to continue to assist to foster life and its development on the new world.

The Melchizedek family in Paradise oversee the Life Carriers and these are the worlds that the Life Carriers live on in Paradise-the seven higher heavens.

The Life Carrier headquarters world.

The Life Carrier planning world.

The Life Carrier life-conservation world.

The Life Carrier life evolution world.

The Life Carrier life associated with the mind world.

The Life Carrier mind and spirit in living being's world.

The Life Carrier of unrevealed life world.

The moment the spirit of worship entered the minds of Andon and Fonta at the age of ten 993,408 years ago, the first Planetary Prince Caligastia was sent to planet earth to support the biologic race uplifter Adam and the Creator Son when they arrived on earth. Each Planetary Prince is a Lanonandek Son from Papradise for the sixty-one life modification worlds in our universe and they are each first certified for this job by the Melchizedeks group before being assigned to their Planetary Prince position on a new world. All sixty-one planets inhabited planets in our Nebadon universe have an assigned Planetary Prince living on their planet. Earth's former Planetary Prince Caligastia defaulted in his duties and joined the Lucifer Rebellion so, earth's current Planetary Prince Machiventa Melchizedek performs his duties from Paradise under the direction of our system sovereign Michael of Nebadon.

During the time period that a Planetary Prince serves on an inhabited planet, when the mortal beings reach their limit of natural evolutionary development, Michael, the system sovereign then proceeds to dispatch to this world two biologic race uplifters known as Adam and Eve and each of the sixty-one worlds in our Nebadon universe had an Adam and Eve who are the Material Son and Daughter of the Creator Son Michael of Nebadon, Paradise. Together with the new world's assigned Planetary Prince, the Adam and Eve race uplifters remain working on their assigned planet throughout the evolutionary course of the planet. Usually an assignment to be a pair of race uplifters Adam and Eve on a new world that has a Planetary Prince is not too much of a hazard, but on planet earth the Planetary Prince Caligastia had defaulted to join the Lucifer Rebellion, and this proved to be a hazard for earth's Adam and Eve who were betrayed by Planetary Prince Caligastia which caused them to both also default in the mission on planet earth.

When a Planetary Prince is assigned on one of the sixty-one new inhabited worlds his staff includes one hundred midway creatures from Paradise. To the eyes of a normal human, the midway creatures are invisible, and they possess special powers, and this is the origin of all the superhero characters that we read about as kids in the comic books and go to view at our present-day cinema theaters. The primary midwayer beings work as a part of the intelligence corps and they also work as celestial entertainers for the Planetary Prince. The midway beings also work as the planet's historians and from the time of the arrival of Planetary Prince Caligastia up to earth's current ascension process to enter the age of light and life, these midway beings are still here on earth working on the history of earth that will later be exhibited on Paradise. The secondary midway beings who are also a part of the Planetary Prince's staff are more like human beings, but they also possess special powers, one being their ability to reproduce offspring by touching each other's palms on their two hands. The secondary midway beings were created by the new planet's race biologic uplifters Adam and Eve, and they remain working on earth until they are selected to travel the long road of adventure of true ascension back home to Paradise.

When Adam and Eve arrived on planet earth during the times of earth's former Planetary Prince Caligastia they were accompanied by twelve Melchizedek Sons from Paradise to assist them with their race biologic duties. The Melchizedeks are widely known as the emergency sons, because they work in a wide range of activities on the worlds of time and space. Whenever an unusual problem arises, or when something unusual is going to be attempted, a member of the Melchizedek family from Paradise accepts the job. The Order Of Melchizedek has been very active on earth since human life began on the planet 993,408 years ago and a corps of twelve Melchizedeks in conjunction with the Life Carriers became receivers and examiners on earth after the default of Planetary Prince Caligastia and they continued to work in this position until the incarnation of Michael of Nebadon on earth as Jesus of Nazareth.

Andon and Fonta were the first and the most remarkable pair of human beings who ever lived on earth, because they were highly superior to their descendants and completely different from their ancestors. Andon's name is the Nebadon-Paradise name that means the first fatherlike being to exhibit the human perfection of hunger. Fonta's name means the first Sonlike being to exhibit the human perfection of hunger. Andon and Fonta never knew what their real names were until the time of their first fusion with their Divine Thought Adjusters. During the time Andon and Fonta lived their mortal life on earth, they called each other Sonta-an and Sonta-en, which meant loved by our mother. It was almost two years after Andon and Fonta left their tribe before their first child was born and they named him Sontad and Sontad was the first living being on earth who was wrapped in protective coverings at the time of his birth. Humanity on planet earth had begun and with this, a new evolution appeared, the instinct to cover and properly care for human infants.

Adam and Fonta went on to have twenty-one children, fifty grandchildren, and six great-grandchildren. Their entire family lived in four adjoining rock shelters or semi-caves, three of which had connecting hallways. Andon and Fonta were the parents of the

Adonite Tribe, and they both died at the age of forty-two after being crushed by a large overhanging rock that fell on them during an earthquake. When Andon and Fonta died, their oldest son Sontad assumed leadership of their Andonite Tribe which lasted and stayed together as a tribe of people up until the twentieth generation.

The members of the Andonite Tribe had black eyes and their complexion was a cross between yellow and red. The early Andonite race strongly resembled our present day Alaskan Native race. Ten thousand years after the times of Andon and Fonta, the Andonite spiritual leader Onagar assumed leadership of his tribe and he taught the Andonites the worship of the Breath Giver. Onagar was born 983,323 years ago and he lived to be the age of sixty-nine and during his life he instituted an efficient Andonite tribal government, and he became to be the world's first missionary, and he taught the Andonites tribe how to cook their meat on the ends of sticks over hot stones. The days of Onagar were the golden age for primitive man, because although Andon, Fonta and their descendants all received their Divine Thought Adjusters, it was not until the times of Onagar that the Divine Thought Adjusters and Guardian Seraphim began to arrive on planet earth in large numbers.

Andon and Fonta, the founders of humanity on earth have received their recognition in Paradise and they have been granted their citizenship in the Paradise city of Jerusem. Andon and Fonta have not been permitted to incarnate back on planet earth, but they are both aware that they are the founders of humanity on planet earth. Andon and Fonta while they are living their eternal life in Paradise-the seven higher heavens were both very sad when the defaults of planet earth's Planetary Prince Caligastia and Adam and Eve occurred. However, they were both glad when they were informed that Michael of Nebadon, Paradise selected planet earth to complete his seventh and final bestowal as the incarnation of Jesus of Nazareth. Andon, Fonta and all of their twenty-one children were fused with their Divine Thought Adjusters in the Paradise city of Jerusem. Shortly after Andon and Fonta arrived in the Paradise city of Jerusem, they both received permission from Michael the system sovereign to return to the first Paradise mansion world to work indefinitely with the morontia beings and help to welcome the arriving ascending mortals from the worlds of time and space as they arrive to train and complete their seven bestowals on each of the seven mansion worlds in Paradise. Humanity on earth is almost one million years old and during this long period of time, we have all experienced a challenging vigorous learning experience on planet earth.

About 950,000 years ago, the descendants of Andon and Fonta began to migrate farther to the east, to the west and to the areas that included Europe, France, England, Java and Tasmania. About 900,000 years ago the culture of the Andonites that had been founded by Andon and Fonta were beginning to vanish from the face of the earth and during these times, the Foxhall people of England and the Badonan Tribes of India still continued to hold on to some of the original traditions of the Andonite tribe. Due to an ice age the Foxhall Tribe of England later migrated from England, and they have survived as the present day Native Alaskan Natives. The Badonan Tribes of India descended from the great-great grandson of Andon and Fonta, and they later migrated to the Suivalik Hills in what is now northern India. About 850,00 years ago the Badonan Tribes began to engage in a war with one of their neighboring tribes, and the mixed descendants of this Badonan stock brought about the emergence of the Neanderthal race. The Neanderthal race were excellent fighters, hunters and they traveled a lot, and they gradually spread from India to France, China, Africa and they roamed all over Europe.

About 500,000 years ago the Badonan Tribes of India became involved in a great racial war which lasted over one hundred years and when this one-hundred-year war was over, only one hundred of the most intelligent living descendants of Andon and Fonta had survived this long-lasting conflict.

However, among these last one hundred surviving intelligent Badonan Tribe members suddenly something remarkable happened. A man and woman who were living in the highland region of India suddenly began to produce offsprings that consisted of a diverse family of nineteen unusually intelligent children, and these children were the beginning of the original Sangik family who were the original ancestors of all the six colored races on planet earth. These nineteen Sangik children were not only extremely intelligent above the rest of the people in their Badonan Tribe, but the skins of these nineteen children turned various colors when they were exposed to sunlight. Among these nineteen Sangik children were five red children, two orange children, four yellow children, two green children, four blue children and two indigo children and these six different colors on this same family of children grew to be more pronounced as they got older. When these nineteen children of six different colors grew older and mated with the other members of their Badonan Tribe, all of their offspring had the same color as their Sangik father.

These nineteen children from the same family who were six different colors turned out to be a magnificent event in our Nebadon universe, because none of the other sixty-one life modification planets in our universe except for earth had ever experienced an early appearance of an Andonite race like Andon and Fonta during the early stages of its evolutionary process. Also, none of the other sixty-one life modification planets in our universe has had six new evolutionary races of color appear at the same time and all in the same family except on planet earth, so earth is indeed a unique planet in our universe.

But the bad part about it is that planet earth is the only planet in our Nebadon universe where its inhabitants, who by the way are all related and came from the same Sangik family from the Badonan Tribe in India, have from the beginning, continued to fight, harm and kill each other especially over race and money.

The Red men was the first and it is the most remarkable species of the human race, and they are far superior to Andon and Fonta's Andonite Tribe in many ways. The Red men are the most intelligent and have the most wisdom of all humanity's races and they were the first of race to develop a Sangik government. The Red men were always monogamous and seldom practiced plural mating. One of the early Red men's spiritual leader and deliverer, Omonalonton taught the Red men how to stop worshipping their many spirits and to only worship one God, the Great Spirit.

About 85,000 years ago the Red men began to cross over a land bridge that led to North America from Asia in a mass migration from Asis due to their prolonged and serious conflicts with the Yellow men in Asia. After the Red men migrated to the North American continent, they became totally isolated, and they never again came into contact with the outside world except for the Native Alaskans until later on during the 15th century when the White men from Europe began their invasion of North America. Unfortunately, the Red men had the tendency to continue to fight amongst themselves which weakened their tribes so much that the Yellow race in Asia were able to drive the Red men out of the Asian continent and later on the invading White races from Europe were also able to conquer the Red men and seize all of their land in North America.

The Red men also almost completely missed out on their opportunity of being racially uplifted by the Violet race mixture of the later Adam and Eve stock due to their being isolated on the North American continent. Also, as it turned out, the Red man was never able to defeat or rule the White men who totally invaded their North American homeland, and the Red men would not serve the White men either, so in cases such as this when two races cannot blend and live together in peace, one race is doomed.

The Orange race was the second Sangik evolutionary race of color on earth and their spiritual leader Porshunta was an outstanding speaker who taught the Orange men to worship one God, The Great Teacher. The most outstanding trait of the Orange race were their abilities to build anything and everything especially the vast mounds of stone they built just to see which tribe member could build the largest stone mound. The Orange race was not very progressive, but they profited and grew intellectually by sending many members of their tribe as delegates to study at earth's defaulted Planetary Prince Caligastia's schools before he defaulted from his position to join the Lucifer Rebellion. The Orange race were the first to migrate southward from their original homeland in India and they journeyed to the continent of Africa.

However, the Orange races were never able to secure a firm and favorable footing in Africa and they were later wiped out of existence completely by the Green race. The Orange race's last great battle with the Green men occurred in Egypt, and it lasted for almost one hundred years and after this long war was over, what was left of the Orange race was absorbed by the Green and Indigo races and the Orange race ceased to exist on planet earth about 100,000 years ago.

The Yellow race of Asia were the third Sangik evolutionary race of color to appear on earth and they were the first race who left their communities to develop a home life that was based on agriculture. The Yellow race were inferior to the Red men, but they proved to be far superior to the five remaining Sangik races in relation to their ability to foster a positive civilization that was based on agriculture and racial harmony. The yellow race had a very strong fraternal spirit, and they learned how to live together in peace and harmony. The Yellow race also made sure that they stayed far away from the negative influences of the Planetary Prince Caligastia's teachings after his default and betrayal. Instead, the Yellow race followed the teachings of their spiritual leader Singlangton, who taught them about the one true living God about 1,000 years ago. The yellow race has proven to be the most peaceful of all the races on earth and they received a small but potent legacy of the violet stock from the race uplifters Adam and Eve during their uplifting project on earth.

The Green race were the fourth evolutionary Sangik race of color to appear on earth and they were one of the less able groups to exist among the primitive races and they continued to be further weakened by too many migrations in too many different directions.

About 350,000 years ago, the Green race experienced a great revival under the spiritual leadership of a Green man called Fantad, and he was able to deliver the Green race from out of darkness by teaching them to worship one God, the One Source of life. The Green race were split into three major factions and later on the following events happened to these three factions of the Green race. The northern tribes of the Green men were captured by the Yellow and Blue races, while the eastern group of the Green men were blended and assimilated with the Red men and the remnant of the Green race still exists today in the Red men. The southern group of the Green men migrated to the continent of Africa where they proceeded to destroy their equally inferior Orange race cousins. The Green and Orange races were eight to nine feet tall, and these strains of giants were limited to the areas close to Egypt. What was later left of the Green race were later assimilated and absorbed by the Indigo race, who were the last of the Sangik evolutionary colored races to migrate from their original Sangik beginnings in India.

The Blue men were the fifth evolutionary colored Sangik race to appear on earth and the Blue men were a great race of people who were the early inventors of the spear, and they created many of the early art objects that we still see today in our modern civilizations. The Blue men had the same brain power as the Red men and they had the same soul and sentiment of the Yellow men. The descendants of the Violet race uplifters, Adam and Eve, preferred to blend with the Blue race out of all of the six Sangik evolutionary races of color. The early Blue men were responsive to planet earth's first Planetary Prince Caligastia's teachings in his schools and as a result they got caught up in a state of confusion, due to Caligastia's teachings becoming to be perverted when they joined the Lucifer Rebellion.

About five hundred years after earth's Planetary Prince Caligastia's downfall, the spiritual leader of the Blue men, Orlandof who also was the prince of the Blue men taught them to recognize the divinity of the one Supreme Chief. The Blue race were greatly uplifted and upstepped by the mixture of the Violet race from the Adam and Eve uplifter project and the current White Caucasian race who are currently living on earth are the direct descendants of the Blue race which was modified by a slight blending of the Yellow and Red races by Adam and Eve's race uplifting project and this racial mixture that formed the White race has proven them to be the most aggressive and violent race on planet earth.

The Indigo Black race were the sixth evolutionary colored Sangik race to appear on earth and they were the last-colored race to migrate from their original Sangik home in India. Around this same time, the Green race were in the process of killing off the rest of the Orange race who were living in Egypt and in doing this continued to weaken the Green race and when the physically strong Indigo race began to invade Egypt, they totally wiped the Green race out of existence. The Indigo race was able to accomplish this by absorbing what was left of the Green and Orange races and in the long run, this greatly improved the racial strain of the Indigo race.

Egypt was first dominated by the Orange race, then later on by the Green race and lastly by the Indigo race. Much later a mongrel race of Indigo, Blue and modified Green men began to appear on the African continent. Long before the arrival of the racial uplifters, Adam and Eve, the Blue race who were living in Europe and the mixed races who were living in Arabia had driven the Indigo race out of Egypt which then forced the Indigo race to move further south on the African continent.

When the Sangik migrations from their original homeland of India ended, the Green and Orange races were totally gone.

The Red man was living on the North American continent, the Yellow race were living in eastern Asia, the Blue race were living in Europe, the Indigo race in Africa and India still had a variety of a blend of the Sangik races.

During these same times, a superior race of Andonites who were the descendants of Andon and Fonta were living in South America, while a more purer strain of Andonites were living in the northern regions of Europe, Iceland and in the northeastern areas of the North American continent.

About 85,000 years ago shortly after the Red men migrated to the North American continent from Asia, the Alaskan native descendants of the original aborigines who had migrated to Alaska 2,100 years prior due to an ice age, were still living and thriving in this region long after the Red men had arrived. Around this same time period, some of the mixed stock of the Blue men migrated westward and began to blend with the Alaskan natives which also helped to improve the racial strain of the Alaskan native tribes.

About 5,000 years ago a chance meeting occurred between a Red men tribe and a single Alaskan Native Tribe on the shores of Hudson Bay and during this initial meeting, these two tribes were not able to understand or communicate with each other. However, they soon began to intermarry and live together peacefully, and the result was that eventually numerous native Alaskans were absorbed by the Red men race. The Native Alaskans were the only other human contact that the Red men had with any other race of human stock after their migration from Asia to North America until the White men from Europe began their invasions of North America about one thousand years ago.

When the Indigo Black race migrated to Africa, they took possession of this continent, and they have remained there ever since except for the many members of their race who were forcibly taken away into slavery that began after the Dutch race was given permission from the pope to do so after stating that the Indigo race had no soul. The Indigo race like the Red men in North America were isolated on the continent of Africa and they received little or none of the race elevation from the infusion of the violet race blend from Adam and Eve. The Indigo race were alone and isolated living on the continent of Africa with very little spiritual advancement until a spiritual leader Orvonon helped the Indigo race to experience a spiritual awakening and he taught the Indigo race to be of service to the God of Gods and they maintained this form of worship up until about one thousand years ago.

The many human struggles during the early evolutionary stages of humanity on earth were characterized by courage, bravery and a lot of heroism. We who are living on earth today appreciate the strong and rugged traits that our early ancestors displayed and their devotion to continue to build our advancing civilization that we are living in today.

There are many good reasons why on the sixty-one life modification planets in our Nebadon universe like planet earth why the decision was made to evolve human life from three to six different colored races and the Life Carriers who initially implant life on a new world always has it in their plan to evolve more than one race on a new world for the following reasons.

A variety of races on a planet is an important strategy to ensure the survival of the superior racial strains.

The stronger races on a new evolving planet are the result of the interbreeding of the diverse races of people when these different races are all carriers of superior inheritance factors.

The early evolutionary six Sangik colored races on planet earth have been effectively blended and upstepped by Adam and Eve when they received the Violet race infusion stock.

Competition is always healthy when it is stimulated by a diversity of more than one race on a planet.

The differences in the status of the races and groups that exists on a planet within each group are essential to the development of human tolerance and altruism.

The human races who live on planet earth are not really living in a positive desirable environment until humanity attains a relatively high level of spiritual development.

Any efforts that may be being made on earth to identify the original Sangik ancestry among our current modern-day people must consider the later improvements that were made by the race uplifters Adam and Eve by their implementation of the Violet race upstepping/uplifting programs that they administered to the original six Sangik evolutionary colored races.

These are some of the early spiritual leaders who also assisted the early evolutionary races of men living on planet earth from the times of the former Planetary Prince Caligastia to the times of the arrival of Michael from Paradise in the incarnation as Jesus of Nazareth.

Adam was a racial uplifter from Paradise, and he was discredited for his default in his assignment on planet earth, but he was rehabilitated in Paradise, and he still remains as the planetary father of planet earth. Adam was a Material Son of God from Paradise who accepted his assignment to be a race uplifter on planet earth.

When Adam accepted his assignment on planet earth his Paradise body was relegated to the likeness of mortal flesh, but he still survived and after his life ended on planet earth, Adam was elevated to a position in Paradise by a decree from Michael the system sovereign of the Nebadon universe.

Eve was Adam's mate, and she was also a race uplifter on Paradise and she and Adam's one hundred children on Paradise came to bid them farewell when they left Paradise to begin their race uplifter assignment on planet earth. When Eve accepted her assignment with Adam to come to planet earth, she became the mother of the race blending Violet race on earth. Eve suffered the penalty of default of her job on planet earth and at the end of her life on earth, Eve was also rehabilitated in Paradise along with her mate Adam. Eve is currently assigned to work in Paradise and she serves with the groups of incoming mortal ascenders from the worlds of time and space.

Enoch the Ethiopian was the first human living on earth to fuse with his Divine Thought Adjuster during his mortal life in the flesh. Enoch the Ethiopian was also the first mortal man to be able to walk with God in heaven for six years and bring the knowledge he learned to pass on to his family to carry out God's bloodline here on earth through his grandson Noah after the great flood. Enoch the Ethiopian now Archangel Metatron, is the only archangel who can directly talk to our Prime Creator Source and as Archangel Metatron, he is now in charge of all the sacred geometry in the sixth dimension.

Moses was the emancipation of the remnant of the Violet race that Adam and Eve brought to planet earth for the implementation of their race uplift program and his descendants later raised Machiventa Melchizedek during his childhood until many years later when he began his bestowal ministry in Salem, Palestine. Moses led the Hebrew people from out of slavery in Egypt and he taught them to worship the Universal Father under the name of the God of Israel, Yahweh.

Elijah was prophet of the Hebrew people, and he was a translated soul who was able to achieve a brilliant and spiritual life during the days of the post Adam and Eve age on earth.

Machiventa Melchizedek was the son from the Order Of Melchizedek of Paradise and he bestowed himself onto humanity on earth after the fall of earth's Planetary Prince Caligastia and Adam and Eve. Machiventa Melchizedek was the king of Salem who continued to hold God's light on earth and spread the word through his schools and missionaries about out Universal Prime Creator Father, the Source.

John the Baptist was born from the line of King David and his mother Elizabeth was a distant cousin of Mary, the mother of Jesus of Nazareth. John the Baptist was the

"Gate" who prepared the Hebrews through he and his disciple's teachings and baptisms for the coming of Jesus of Nazareth. As soon as John the Baptist was born, he opened up his mouth and spoke praising God, because he was born filled with the Holy Spirit and everyone in Judah was afraid of him and they asked his parents Zacharias and Elizabeth what kind of child is this who can speak at birth. John the Baptist's father Zaharias was a high priest who was filled with the Holy Spirit just like his son John was and he prophesized that to everyone who were afraid of his son John that God through his son, John the Baptist has raised up a horn of salvation for the Jewish people and all throughout his life John continued to be filled with the Holy Spirit.

John the Baptist's father Zacharias and Jesus' father Joseph were both from the pure blood line of King David and John's mother Elizabeth was a priestess who was a direct descendant of Moses' Brother Aaron the high priest of the Hebrews.

1-2-3 The First a midway being was the leader of the one hundred loyal midway beings who were working in service to Archangel Gabriel on earth as members of the staff of earth's Planetary Prince Caligastia. 1-2-3 The First was elevated to this position in Paradise by Michael of Nebadon soon after his entrance into unconditional sovereignty.

All of the eight above mentioned spiritual leaders were exempt from having to go through the death or ascension process when it was their time to return home to Paradise.

CHAPTER SIX

THE LUCIFER REBELLION IN PARADISE AND IN THE SYSTEM OF SATANIA

God blesses those who patiently endure testing and temptation.

(James 1:12)

The way of the wicked is like deep darkness, they do not know what makes them stumble.

(Proverbs 4:19)

A Prayer

Dear God, I wrestle with pride. My human knowledge can't save me. Please teach me your truth.

THE Lucifer Rebellion

In the seven superuniverses of Paradise-the seven higher heaven there are ten thousand systems of inhabited worlds that are under the rule of the Creator Son and System Sovereign Michael of Nebadon. Lucifer's original home was on Paradise and just like earth's fallen Planetary Prince Caligastia, he was a brilliant Lanonandek Son, and he had experienced service in many of the established systems in Paradise.

Lucifer had been selected by the Melchizedek Order on Paradise to be a counselor of his Lanonandek group and whenever he was commissioned to perform certain jobs and duties, he always performed these duties with the highest honors. In Paradise Lucifer was designated as being one of the one hundred most able and brilliant personalities capable to perform his designated jobs out of more than seven hundred thousand of the Lanonandek Sons who lived on Paradise. In all of the history of the Lanonandek Sons who have lived on Paradise, only one prior Planetary Prince from earth and three prior System Sovereigns have been found in contempt of following the rules and mandates of the Paradise government's Creator Son. Lucifer was not an ascendant mortal being but instead he was created on Paradise by the Creator Son Michael and Lucifer had been called in for counseling sessions with the Most Highs in Paradise many times for his erratic behavior.

Lucifer also served a reign on the holy mountain of God, which is the administrative mountain of Jerusem, Paradise and then Lucifer was subsequently appointed to serve as the System Sovereign, the chief executive of the great system of (607) inhabited worlds in our universe known as Satania. While Lucifer served in his position as the System

Sovereign of Satania very few people living on earth had ever heard of him because he assigned most of his duties on earth to his first lieutenant, Satan. Lucifer and Satan had reigned together on Paradise for more than five hundred years before their hearts began to turn away from the Universal Paradise Father, Source and Lucifer's father, Michael of Nebadon. Lucifer first announced his plans to instigate a rebellion first in Paradise and then in the rest of the Nebadon universe to his first lieutenant Satan and it took several months for Lucifer to corrupt Satan's mind and convince him to join his evil rebellion.

The idea of starting an open rebellion against the Universal Prime Creator Father, Source and his Creator Son, Michael originated totally in Lucifer's own mind. At no time before Lucifer decided to start his rebellion against the superuniverse administration had he openly expressed any dissatisfaction about the structure of the superuniverse administration. Even though Lucifer had been silent about his dissatisfaction towards the superuniverse administrative structure, The Unions Of Days who lived in Salvington, Paradise had kept on telling the senior members of the superuniverse administration that Lucifer's mind was not at peace, and something was bothering him.

The Unions Of Days had also been sharing this information concerning the unrest he sensed existed in Lucifer's mind with the Paradise Creator Son, Michael and with the Paradise Constellation Fathers of Norlatiadek. As time went on Lucifer began to openly criticize the entire superuniverse administration, but at the same time Lucifer continued to insist that he was still loyal to the Paradise Supreme Rulers.

Lucifer's first incident where he openly voiced his criticism of the superuniverse administrative structure was during a visit Archangel Gabriel made to Jerusem and this incident happened just days before Lucifer openly made a public proclamation of his Lucifer Declaration of Liberty. Archangel Gabriel was so sure that Lucifer was getting ready to start an open rebellion after his public display of disloyalty during his last visit to Jerusem that Archangel Gabriel went straight to Edentia where he held a very serious meeting with the Paradise Constellation Fathers to inform them about Lucifer's public display of disloyalty.

Lucifer was full of pride for himself, and these feelings began to grow stronger in his mind to the point of self-deception. Lucifer finally reached the point where he convinced himself that by starting an open rebellion in Paradise and in the system of Satania that it would actually benefit the entire superuniverse administration. By the time Lucifer's Rebellion plans had fully developed in his mind, he had reached the point of self-deception and at this point, Lucifer was too far gone from his original ideas of mischief-making pride where he could not stop from going forward with his evil plan to start an open rebellion. In his mind Lucifer became to be insincere and evil and his actions against the superuniverse administration had now evolved into a deliberate and willful sin on his part.

At this point Lucifer's father, the Creator Son Michael of Nebadon offered his son Lucifer the chance to repent and stop his evil actions. Some of Lucifer's followers accepted Creator Son Michael's offer to repent and they asked for mercy and forgiveness. However,

Lucifer and his first lieutenant Satan refused Michael's offer and instead they continued to move forward with their rebellion plans and the feelings of contempt and disdain continued to grow in Lucifer's heart. The final straw was when Lucifer openly declared in public on Paradise his Lucifer Declaration of Liberty.

These were the three reasons that Lucifer and Satan publicly stated why they were going to launch an open rebellion in Paradise and in the system of Satania against the administrative structure in the superuniverse, the seven higher heavens.

Lucifer's first charge was that the Universal Prime Creator Father in Paradise really didn't exist, and that the Paradise Sons had invented this concept of a Universal Father to enable them to have the right to rule the seven superuniverses in Paradise by using the Universal Father's name. Lucifer also stated that the Corps of the Finality were in collusion with the Paradise Sons and that the members of this corps were frauds.

Lucifer's second charge was that all of the local systems should be autonomous, and he stated that Creator Son Michael had no right to expect everyone in Paradise to continue to worship an unseen Universal Prime Creator Father, Source. Lucifer did acknowledge that Creator Son Michael of Nebadon was his father, but he did not accept him as being a God or a ruler of Paradise. Lucifer also stated that the Ancients Of Days had no right to interfere in the affairs of the local systems and he denounced them as being tyrants. Lucifer further stated that he felt that all of the living beings in the local systems had inherent rights to immortality and that their training and ascension through the seven mansion worlds in Paradise was unnecessary and a waste of time, because Lucifer believed that resurrection should be a natural automatic process for all living beings to live for eternity.

Lucifer's third charge was that the main basis for his rebellion was towards the Paradise universal plan for the ascendant mortal training and Lucifer felt that this entire training plan for mortal ascension training in Paradise was a total waste of time and he blamed this plan all on the Sons of God in Paradise.

Lucifer openly proclaimed these three charges as the basis of his rebellion at the annual conclave of Satania that was held on the sea of glass in the presence of all of the assembled hosts of Jerusem on the last day of the year about 200,000 years ago.

These blasphemous charges that Lucifer publicly made that last day of the year 200,000 years ago was the beginning of the war in heaven which included the fallen angels and thirty-seven planets in the system of Satania which included planet earth which was then plunged into a long age of evil and darkness. As soon as Lucifer publicly issued his blasphemous proclamation many of the ascendant Paradise citizens firmly banded together and vowed to stand firm against all of Lucifer's Rebellion proposals.

Lucifer then proceeded to appoint his own administrative cabinet as a part of his rebellion, and he publicly swore in and installed all of the rebel members of his administration on all of the thirty-seven liberated worlds in the system of Satania who had joined his rebellion.

Before the onset of the Lucifer Rebellion 200,000 years ago there had been two prior rebellions in Paradise and in two distant constellations, but these four rebellions were quickly squashed and all four were totally unsuccessful. Lucifer however, openly defied all of his Paradise superiors during his rebellion and because everyone in the Paradise administration chose to ignore Lucifer, his rebellion lasted for more than 200,000 years. So, Lucifer continued with his rebellion, and he openly boasted to his followers that the Paradise administration did not have the ability to stop his rebellion, and he openly defied and challenged his father Michael of Nebadon, his father's older brother Immanuel and the Ancients Of Days.

All during the times of the Lucifer Rebellion Lucifer was permitted to establish and thoroughly organize his rebel government but, in the meantime, the Constellation Fathers of Paradise made sure they kept Lucifer, and his rebel followers confined to the system of Satania. All during the many long years of the Lucifer Rebellion everything was chaotic and there was a lot of confusion going on in the seven mansion worlds of Paradise. When the Lucifer Rebellion first began Michael of Nebadon sought the council of his older brother Immanuel and at this meeting, Creator Son Michael announced that he was going to treat the Lucifer Rebellion the same as he did the two prior rebellions with no interference. At the time of the Lucifer Rebellion Michael had not yet completed his seven bestowals so he had not yet been vested with all the powers in heaven to really deal with the Lucifer Rebellion.

Since Creator Son Michael chose not to interfere with Lucifer and his rebel forces of his rebellion, Gabriel then held a meeting with his staff and with the Most Highs of Paradise and they decided to turn over the command of the system sovereign of Satania to Gabriel. Creator Son Michael remained in Salvington and Gabriel ruled Satania while he lived in Jerusem where he continued to establish himself on this sphere and he remained dedicated to the Universal Prime Creator Father, Source.

The emblem that the rebels of the Lucifer Rebellion wore was a white banner with one red circle in the center of one black circle. Due to this ongoing Lucifer Rebellion, there was a real spiritual war going on in Paradise and Creator Son Michael and his angels had a battle with the dragon (Lucifer and Satan) and this spiritual battle was very real and terrible because it was fought for the sake of preserving the ascension and eternal life for all living beings.

When the Lucifer Rebellion occurred in Paradise 200,000 years ago, the head of the seraphic angel hosts joined the rebellion, and this action caused a large number of other seraphim angels to also go astray and join the rebellion. This happened because the seraphic leader of the angels was spiritually blinded by Lucifer's brilliant personality, and his charming ways seemed to fascinate the lower celestial beings in Paradise.

Many of the lower celestial beings who were living in Paradise just couldn't understand how such a dazzling personality that Lucifer had could possibly go astray.

The Lucifer Rebellion was system wide, and the result was that thirty-seven Planetary Princes on the worlds of time and space in the system of Satania including earth's Planetary

Prince Caligastia all broke their ties with Paradise and swung their worlds into darkness to join the Lucifer Rebellion. The Planetary Prince on the world of Panoptia joined the Lucifer Rebellion, but all of the people on his world refused to follow him and instead they sought the help and guidance of the twelve Melchizedek Sons who were assigned on their world and they appointed Ellanora who was a young spiritual leader on their world of Panoptia to assume the leadership of the human races on their world and not one soul from Panoptia joined the Lucifer Rebellion. These loyal Panoptians have been rewarded for their loyalty and they still serve today as the caretakers and builders of the seven mansion worlds in Paradise.

All throughout the 200,000 years of the Lucifer Rebellion earth's Planetary Prince Caligastia supported this rebellion on earth. During these times on earth, humanity was still in its infancy primitive state of evolution and not in a great position to even know that they could refuse the leadership of their planetary prince like the humans did on the planet Panoptia. The twelve members of the Melchizedek Sons who were assigned to live on planet earth continued to firmly oppose the views of the fallen earth Planetary Prince Caligastia.

The Lucifer Rebellion was a Lanonandek rebellion and the higher orders of the local universe of Satania did not join forces with the rebel followers from Lucifer's Rebellion, but a few of the Life Carriers who were living on some of the rebel planets were influenced by some of their disloyal planetary princes and they joined forces with some of the rebels from Lucifer's Rebellion. None of the Trinitized Sons from Paradise joined forces with

Lucifer and all of the Melchizedek Sons, Archangels and Brilliant Evening Stars all remained loyal to the Creator Son Michael of Nebadon. None of the Paradise beings joined forces with the Lucifer Rebellion, but a large number of morontia companions and mansion world teachers in Paradise joined the Lucifer Rebellion.

Not one angel from the supreme order of the seraphim joined this rebellion, but one third of the Jerusem administrator cherubim did fall from the light to join this rebellion. One third of the planetary helpers and almost ten percent of the planetary transition ministers joined this rebellion and large numbers of the planetary midway beings who were members of the planetary prince's staff were also deceived spiritually by Lucifer and they joined the rebellion.

The Lucifer Rebellion was the most widespread and disastrous event that had ever occurred in Paradise, the seven higher heavens, because it lasted for so long and so many people and worlds were negatively affected by this open rebellion. This rebellion was very dishonorable for Lucifer's because during the course of this uprising Lucifer and his first lieutenant Satan were able to corrupt so many primitive developing minds on so many developing worlds like planet earth. One of the most positive things about the Lucifer Rebellion was that not one member of the ascending mortal beings who were living in Jerusem participated in this rebellion.

It was over two years from the onset of the Lucifer Rebellion before a successor was finally selected to replace Lucifer in his job position as the System Sovereign of the system of Satania and the new system sovereign promptly cut off Lucifer from all of his prior administrative duties that he had in the (607) planets of Satania. A decision was then made by the Paradise Constellation Fathers and the Ancients Of Days to hold off with handing down a final decision and disposition of Lucifer, his rebels and all of their associates.

Meanwhile Lucifer, Satan and their rebel followers were still allowed to freely roam about in Paradise and in Satania to continue to spread their evil doctrines of discontent, disobedience and self-assertions. However, these rebels have not been able to deceive anyone anymore on the (607) Satania worlds in almost 200,000 years and no more worlds in Satania have been lost since the initial thirty-seven worlds that fell from the light during the early days of this rebellion. Lucifer, Satan and their rebel followers continued to freely roam all throughout the Satania system until the Creator Son Michael of Nebadon arrived on planet earth to complete his seventh and final bestowal incarnated as Jesus of Nazareth. The seventh bestowal of Michael of Nebadon on planet earth finally terminated the Lucifer Rebellion in Paradise and in the system of Satania and now there was the assurance of survival for the ascending mortals from the worlds of time and space and security for all of the angels when Jesus of Nazareth calmly replied to Lucifer's proposals after fasting for forty days on the mountain on earth with divine assurance, "Get thee behind me Satan." and this statement from Jesus in principle was finally the final end of the Lucifer Rebellion.

The Uversa tribunals in Paradise still had not issued an executive decision regarding the destruction that the Lucifer Rebellion had caused, but a decree was on the way. The last act that Jesus of Nazareth did before he completed his final and seventh bestowal on planet earth was to offer mercy to earth's fallen Planetary Prince Caligastia and his first lieutenant Daligastia, but they both refused Jesus' offer of mercy. Earth's fallen planetary prince is still free to roam planet earth, but he has lost all of his powers to enter mortal men's minds, and he can no longer draw close to any mortal men's souls to try to tempt or corrupt them, unless with their free will they choose to allow him to do so.

Before the final seventh bestowal of Creator Son Michael of Nebadon on earth, the beings of darkness still tried to maintain their dark authority over planet earth, but ever since that day on Pentecost Sunday when the Spirit of Truth, the Holy Spirit with its heat, fire and power arrived on earth, all of the beings of darkness no longer have any more authority or power on earth, because humanity now living on earth have the divine majesty of the Paradise mind indwelling Divine Thought Adjusters, the protective Holy Spirit and most importantly the spirit of Jesus who has installed all of the gridlines of Christ consciousness on earth that enables all humans who choose to ascend now and walk the path back home to Paradise.

Truthfully speaking, no dark fallen from the light spirit never did really have the power to invade the minds of mortal men or to harness their souls, because we are all free will children of our Universal Prime Creator Father, Source of Paradise. Neither Lucifer, Satan, Caligastia or Daligastia were ever able to touch or approach the faith of God's children, because when you have love, gratitude, faith, no fear and keep your full body armor of the Holy Spirit, always in your heart, you have the seven in one stroke that will always be enough protection against all sin and iniquity. When weak mortals who choose fear instead of faith are supposedly under the influence of devils or demons, this was and will never be true, because in reality these are your own shadows and traumas that we each must face in life, by facing up to them, feel them and send them up to the violet flame to be healed and transmuted back to the light of love. The devil has been given a lot of credit for having evil powers over humans that he never had, because he never has nor never will have that kind of power. Take back your power now and choose peace, authenticity and love in your heart.

Planet earth's former fallen Planetary Prince Caligastia from over 200,000 years ago has been powerless and impotent since the arrival of the cross of Jesus Christ 1,954 years ago. During the early days of the Lucifer Rebellion mercy and salvation was offered to all of the followers of this rebellion by Creator Son Michael of Nebadon but the only beings who accepted this offer of mercy were the thousands of fallen angels, lower-level celestial beings and hundreds of Material Sons and daughters accepted Michael's offer of mercy and they were all rehabilitated during the times of the resurrection of Jesus of Nazareth.

Lucifer has not been able to come back to planet earth since the days when he attempted to stop the Creator Son Michael from completing his seventh and final bestowal on earth, which has finally established Michael of Nebadon as the ruler and system sovereign of the Nebadon universe.

Lucifer was finally taken into custody by the agents of the Uversa, Paradise Ancients Of Days and he has been a prisoner on satellite world number one on the transition sphere of Jerusem.

When Creator Son Michael of Nebadon assumed his current position as the system sovereign of the Nebadon universe, he asked the Ancients Of Days to give him the authority to imprison all of the rebel followers who had been involved in the Lucifer Rebellion and the case of Gabriel vs Lucifer was then placed on the records of the Uversa Supreme Court 200,000 years ago until such time that the Uversa courts begin the final adjudication of this case. The status of Lucifer's detainment on Uversa still has not changed at this point, but he is totally deactivated. So, the Lucifer Rebellion officially ended in Paradise and on the thirty-seven fallen worlds as soon as each Creator Son arrived on each of these worlds to complete their missions of salvation redemption. And ever since the event of the Lucifer Rebellion occurred, the seven prison worlds in the system of Satania have continued to issue a solemn warning to all of the Nebadon universe that the path of the transgressors of sin is very hard and that the wages of sin is death. Meanwhile, Machiventa Melchizedek has since been appointed to be the succeeding Planetary Prince of earth with his headquarters being on Paradise instead of on planet earth.

The Gods do not create evil or permit sin and rebellion, but potential evil exists only in a universe that embraces different levels of perfection, meanings and values. Sin is a potential waiting to happen in all of the realms where imperfect living free will beings have truth, untruth, fact and falsehood which all constitutes the potential for errors to occur. When a material being makes a deliberate choice of evil, then this is a sin, which is a willful rejection of the truth.

One of the main problems that arose from the Lucifer Rebellion was the difficulty and failure of many of the inhabitants of the immature primitive evolutionary worlds to be able to tell the difference between true and false liberty. True liberty is a quest of the ages and one of the rewards of man's evolutionary progress and if one's liberty is to last, it must be based on a reality of justice, intelligence, maturity, fraternity and equity. Wisdom is divine and safe only when it is cosmic in scope and spiritual in motivation. Evolutionary man living on earth has had to contend for his material liberties with tyrants and oppressors on a world full of sin, especially during the early times of primitive man's life, but on the other normal worlds where their advancing civilizations rejected physical combat, evil and sin and instead accepted unconditional love, compassion, gratitude, discernment and wisdom as the techniques to solve racial misunderstandings and any other disagreements are now on the road to live and thrive and ascend to be a planet of light and life in the higher dimensions.

Every material being on every evolving world who makes the choice to follow God's and their soul's divine plan are then destined to become a partner of the time-space creators in our path together in spiritual perfection attainment. Lucifer's Rebellion was a folly, because it was an attempt to short circuit time in our experiential universe of Nebadon.

Lucifer's crime was his threats to infringe on the free will choice of the mortal ascender's right to experience the thrilling path of ascension to and through the seven mansion worlds of Paradise, the seven higher heavens. What God has given mortal man, free will, Lucifer tried to take away with his rebellion, but man's free will is a divine privilege of a living being able to participate in the creation of one's own realities, destinies, and this is the path for all of the local systems of the (607) inhabited worlds of time and space in the system of Satania.

Many often ask the question why God permits evil and sin to happen in the worlds of time and space and the answer is that free will of an evolving man or an exquisite angel is a reality of all of the universes. The liberty that we each have to choose good, or evil is the free will choice that everyone has as an endowment from our supreme rulers, and they will never permit any individual or group to take this away to satisfy their own misguided and disillusioned misuse of one's personal liberty.

Another question that often arises pertains to the reasons for permitting Lucifer, Satan and the rest of his followers, the fallen angels, and the thirty-seven fallen planetary princes to continue to carry on with their mischievous rebellion for 200,000 years in earth time. Those who are parents and have born and raised their children understand why Michael of Nebadon who was Creator Son-Father of Lucifer would be so slow to condemn and destroy his own son. Jesus' parable that he taught to his followers about the prodigal son is a fine example of how long a loving father will wait for the repentance of his child who is living a life full of sin and error. The very fact that Lucifer chose to commit the sin of treason and start a rebellion establishes the fact of free will and fully justifies Creator Son Michael's delay in the execution of justice against his own son Lucifer.

The bad part about it is that most of the liberties that Lucifer demanded during 200,000-year rebellion he already had, and he was already destined to receive all of his other demands in his near future, but instead he lost it all due to his impatience. There are many reasons why the supreme rulers in Paradise did not immediately destroy or imprison the leaders and followers of the Lucifer Rebellion. If it had not been for the love Creator Son Michael had for his disobedient son Lucifer, the supreme justice of Uversa, Paradise surely would have taken some type of action right away. If Lucifer had instigated his rebellion in Paradise during the time period that Creator Son Michael was completing his seventh and final bestowal on earth as the incarnation of Jesus of Nazareth, Lucifer's Rebellion would have been instantly over.

The first hearing in the pending case of Gabriel vs Lucifer was held on Uversa, Paradise during the 1930's (earth time) and soon after these proceedings, the Ancients Of Days issued a mandate directing Lucifer and Satan be confined to the prison world which ended any future visits for them to the thirty-seven fallen worlds of the system of Satania, including earth and so this shows that justice in our mercy dominated universe may be very slow, but it is certain.

At the beginning of the Lucifer Rebellion at first it appeared to be a great calamity in Paradise, the local systems and in the Nebadon universe. However, as time passed, the Melchizedek Sons in Paradise began to resume to teach as usual in their training schools and it seemed that the good that came from Lucifer's folly came to equal the evil that had occurred. The evil that Lucifer had instigated became stagnant and his rebellion continued to increase only on certain isolated worlds, while the benefits continued to increase and multiply where they began to extend out through the universe, superuniverse and to Havona in Paradise. When the Melchizedek Sons continued teaching their spiritual classes in their training schools in Paradise, the good that was resulting from Lucifer's Rebellion was now more than a thousand times the sum of the evil it had caused. Earth was a prime example of this goodness, because after being stuck in a hopeless cycle of more than 11,000 years of darkness after the Lucifer Rebellion, planet earth and its awakened inhabitants since December 21, 2012, are now in the ascension process and entering into the age of light and life. As planet earth continues to ascend to the new heaven on earth, humanity will continue to broaden their many old concepts of the universe that have been hidden from us for such a long time.

After you as an individual attains Paradise, you then become to be more enlightened and comforted as you attend the many training sessions with the Paradise philosophers who explain all of the profound problems, we all experienced during the process of going through the universe's growth and adjustments. You will not be able to comprehend all of the complex problems we experienced while living in the universe as a material being until you are assigned to work in the administrative duty sections on one of the seven mansion worlds of Paradise. As you continue to ascend through the seven mansion worlds in Paradise, you will begin to learn that many of the problems we encountered in our universe can only be understood by our increased experiential capacities through the achievement of spiritual insight, because the cosmic wisdom that we will achieve during our journey of life is essential for us to be able to understand cosmic situations.

CHAPTER SEVEN

PLANET EARTH'S FIRST AND FALLEN PLANETARY PRINCE

The fruit of the righteous is a Tree of Life, and the one who is wise saves lives.

(Proverbs 11:30)

Clothe yourselves with compassion, kindness, humility, gentleness and patience.

(Colossians 3:12)

A Prayer

Dear God, thank you that I can surrender my anxious strivings in exchange for the peace of a quiet walk with you.

PLANET EARTH'S FIRST PLANETARY PRINCE

Earth is planet # 606 out of the six hundred and seven planets within our system of Satania. Under normal conditions when a Lanonandek Son from Paradise arrives on a newly inhabited world to serve as the planetary prince, it means that the humans have achieved the ability to choose the path of eternal survival in their minds. However, planet earth was different than the other planets, because its first planetary prince didn't arrive on earth until almost half a million years after the first appearance of free will humans on the planet.

About 500,000 years ago around the same time the six colored Sangik races, the Red, the Orange, the Yellow, the Green, the Blue and the Indigo appeared on earth in India, that's when earth's first Planetary Prince Caligastia arrived. When Prince Caligastia finally arrived on planet earth, there were about one-half billion human beings scattered across Europe, Asia and Africa and Planetary Prince Caligastia established his headquarters right in the center of planet earth's human population in the area which was known as Mesopotamia. Earth's Planetary Prince Caligastia was very experienced in the administration of the affairs of both the seven superuniverses in Paradise and in the six hundred and seven worlds within the system of Satania. Caligastia had also worked closely on a council with the Life Carrier advisors in Jerusem, Paradise and Lucifer, the system sovereign of the system of Satania had promoted Caligastia to a position on his personal staff and Caligastia served five successive terms in this job with honor and integrity.

Caligastia had previously applied for the position to serve as a planetary prince on several occasions, but he failed to be approved by the Constellation Fathers of Paradise on each occasion. When Caligastia was finally selected to be planet earth's first planetary prince 500,000 years ago, no one in Paradise would ever dream that he would fall from God's light, betray his administrative superiors in Paradise and default from his duties. Everyone in Paradise felt that humanity living on earth were very fortunate to be receiving such a brilliant and experienced leader like Caligastia. However, as soon as Caligastia accepted his new assignment on planet earth, he became to be full of pride and he began to fall in love with himself by using his ego instead of his heart.

The Paradise Constellation Fathers sent an entire staff of assistants and administrative helpers to support Caligastia to complete the duties of his planetary prince position. Some of Caligastia's staff included Daligastia a Lanonandek Son from Paradise who was his main assistant, a large number of angelic helpers and a host of celestial beings who would be helping Caligastia to further advance the interests and welfare of the six Sangik colored races who were living on planet earth.

The most interesting group in Caligastia's staff were the one hundred superior beings whom Caligastia referred to as the one hundred beings. Caligastia hand-picked these chosen group of superior beings from different planets within the Satania system and they were each provided with modified dual nature personalities with flesh and blood bodies that the Life Carriers also attained from the life circuits of the Satania system. Before these superior one hundred beings began their assignment working as members of Caligastia's staff, the Paradise Life Carriers who were also assigned to work for Caligastia's team received permission from Paradise to transplant the life plasm from one hundred superior selected survivor strains from the first human parents of planet earth, Andon and Fonta stock into their material bodies. The Life Carriers also chose fifty male and fifty females from the Andon and Fonta stock who represented the best strains of the first family of the human race on earth. Each of these one hundred were then assembled separately by the Divine Thought Adjusters under the direction and guidance of the angels who were assigned to work as a part of Planetary Prince Caligastia's headquarters. This literal creation of these one hundred superior special living beings who were superhuman was the origin of the numerous legends of superbeings living on planet earth during these times and it took ten days for the completion of these superhuman beings to be assembled and to become conscious on the earth realm.

The headquarters of Prince Caligastia and his staff was located in the Persian Gulf region where the climate and landscape were favorable for Caligastia and his staff to complete their mission to educate and help the six Sangik colored races to advance in their culture and civilization. The one great task that Caligastia had was to transform the primitive men on earth from being hunters and to become herders with the hope that later on humanity would evolve into peace loving home abiding farmers. Planetary Prince Caligastia and his staff's main assignment on earth was to advance the six primitive races on earth to the point that when the racial uplifters/upsteppers Adam and Eve arrived on earth humanity would be ready to be infused with the new Violet race infusion to help to further advance the six Sangik colored races who were living on earth.

Caligastia's headquarters in Mesopotamia was a simple and beautiful city called Dalmatia and it was enclosed within a forty-foot-high wall. There were ten sub-divisions along with the headquarters mansions where the ten councils and the one hundred superhuman corporeal staff lived. The temple of worship was located in the center of Dalmatia and the administrative headquarters building for Caligastia and his staff was arranged into twelve chambers around the temple. The buildings in the city of Dalmatia were made of brick and all of the native people who came to visit were really impressed by this magnificent city of Dalmatia.

The different tribes of people who lived in the surrounding areas of Dalmatia were a variety of the six Sangik colored races and Planetary Prince Caligastia soon invited and recruited many of them to attend his schools in the city of Dalmatia. The early schools in Dalmatia were crude, but they provided all of the required education that the primitive men and women needed and were able to comprehend.

Caligastia's one hundred superhuman members of his corporeal staff soon began to gather the superior individuals from the surrounding tribes to receive training in their Dalmatia schools and they were then sent back to their tribes to be both teachers and leaders to their people.

The arrival of the Planetary Prince Caligastia and his staff on planet earth 500,000 years ago created a strong impression on the six Sangik colored races who were living on earth at this time and even though it took almost a thousand years for the news of the city of Dalmatia to spread over earth, the tribes who lived near the city of Dalmatia received

235

many positive benefits from the education they received at Caligastia's schools. Most of earth's mythology stories and legends originated from Caligastia's staff of one hundred who were immortal superhuman beings and Caligastia and his entire staff were regarded as Gods by the tribes of people who were living on earth, but his staff of one hundred never used any of their supernatural powers while they were teaching their students in Caligastia's schools.

These are the three superior qualities that Caligastia's one hundred possessed that made them superhuman.

The one hundred were corporeal, relatively human, because they embodied the actual life plasm of the first humans on earth Andon and Fonta from their stock and they had the same color complexion that Andon and Fonta had, and their diet consisted basically of fruit and nuts which the members of the surrounding tribes began to adopt.

Caligastia's one hundred were all material but superhuman beings, because they were assembled on planet earth in ten days using the life plasm of Andon and Fonta by the Life Carriers and Divine Thought Adjusters which made them to be modified Andonites. The one hundred were originally legal citizens of Jerusem, Paradise, but they had not yet fused with their Divine Thought Adjusters, but they each possessed a soul to ensure their ability for ascension growth. The one hundred were not able to engage in sexual reproduction, but on the thirty-third year of their mission on earth, they discovered that if two of them held their palms together they could reproduce an offspring and this was the beginning of the creation of the primary midway beings and these new midway beings were visible to Caligastia and his staff but the surrounding tribes of people couldn't see the midway beings.

Prince Caligastia gave the rest of the one hundred permission to continue to reproduce their offspring in this manner and eventually Caligastia's staff in Dalmatia increased to be 50,000 primary midway beings. The secondary midway beings were later created from Adam and Eve's oldest son Adamson and his wife Ratta from the Violet strain race when they later came to live on planet earth. Caligastia's primary midway beings proved to be a great service to the rest of his staff and to the surrounding tribes as they helped to educate the students in Caligastia's schools. These primary midway beings were invisible to their students, and they taught them about the existence of unseen spirits and for a long time the people of earth believed that the entire spirit world was made of these primary midway beings.

Prince Caligastia's staff of one hundred were immortal, because they could not die, and they continued to live on earth indefinitely up until the arrival of Jesus of Nazareth on planet earth about 1,954 years ago. During Prince Caligastia's reign on earth, additional complements of life currents from the system of Satania were also taken from the Tree of Life from a piece of its shrub in Edentia, Paradise and it was sent to earth by the Most Highs of Paradise for Prince Caligastia and his staff to eat its fruit.

This Tree of Life was planted, and it grew in the central courtyard of the Universal Father's temple. The fruit from the Tree of Life bloomed a different fruit every month and it enabled Prince Caligastia and his staff to live on earth indefinitely without aging as long as they continued to eat its fruit. Adam and Eve also ate the fruit from this same Tree of Life to prevent the aging process when they arrived on planet earth sometime later to complete their mission to uplift the six Sangik human races on earth. The fruit from the Tree of Life did not work for mortal humans, but it was sufficient to indefinitely extend the life span for Prince Caligastia and his entire staff.

Prince Caligastia's staff of the one hundred who were modified Andonites also donated their germ plasma to Caligastia and his staff to help to further extend their life spans on earth. The Life Carriers who were members of Caligastia's staff also introduced additional doses of the system of Santania's life circuits into the entire staff that also helped them to live on earth century after century in defiance of experiencing a physical death. Prince Caligastia organized his one hundred staff of modified Andonites into ten councils and these were the functions and duties of these councils.

Ang was the leader of the food and material welfare council, and he taught the surrounding tribes the techniques of digging in the soil, spring control, irrigation and the usage of animal skins for clothing and weaving.

Bon was the leader of the animal domestication project, and he taught the neighboring tribes how to select and breed animals for domestic use. He introduced man's first usage of carrier pigeons to carry messages to and from different destinations.

Dan was the leader of the conquest of predatory animals' project and his council taught early man how to protect himself from the attacks of hostile animals.

Mek was the leader of the tribal beautification project, and his council helped to elevate the concept of beauty to the surrounding tribes which included the techniques of making pottery, decorative arts, music and the use of steam power.

Tut was the leader and governor of the advanced tribal relations, and his council helped to introduce the concept of intertribal marriages, competitive games and they continue to help to maintain peaceful tribal relations.

The Supreme Court council on planet earth at this time was under the direction of Van and the members of his group were basically the court of appeals for all of the other nine established councils who were in charge of managing the human tribal affairs on earth. The Constellation Fathers of Paradise selected Van to function as the head of the Supreme Court on planet earth.

A world culture is measured by the social heritage of its inhabitants and the rate of its cultural expansion depends on the ability of its natives to understand new and advanced ideas as they are presented to them. The staff of one hundred modified Andonites who worked for Planetary Prince Caligastia knew in advance that their mission to educationally uplift the human masses on earth had to be done very slowly and gradually, because they understood that humanity on earth were in the beginning process of a slow evolution of their species.

These ten planetary councils that Prince Caligastia set up worked naturally and they used the best minds from each of the surrounding tribes to train on the many new ideas and concepts and then they were sent back to their own tribes to teach and train the rest of the members of their tribe. Prince Caligastia's headquarters in Dalmatia, Mesopotamia was beautiful, and it was designed to set an example for the neighboring tribes to see how living a one family life should be like.

The idea of a family life with one family living together in a home originated in the city of Dalmatia. Prince Caligastia's staff lived together as fathers and mothers and even though none of his staff had children of their own, the fifty homes in the city of Dalmatia housed five hundred adopted children who all came from superior Andonite and Sangik racial strains families.

The Dalmatian leader Fad introduced the plans to teach trade classes in their schools where both male and female students were taught classes on manual dexterity and how to work together as a team.

The Dalmatian leader Hap presented the early Sangik six colored races on planet earth with the first basic moral law to follow and this law of seven commands became known as, The Father's Way and they are as follows.

You shall not fear or serve any God but the Father of all.

You shall not disobey the Father's Son, the world ruler or show disrespect to his superhuman associates.

You shall not speak a lie when called before a judge of the people.

You shall not kill men, women or children.

You shall not steal your neighbors' goods or cattle.

You shall not touch your friend's wife.

You shall not show disrespect to your parents or to the elders of your tribe.

This was the first primitive law of Dalmatia that was presented to humanity 300,000 years ago and the stones that this first law was written on still lies beneath the waters off the shores of Mesopotamia and Persia.

During these times of early humanity, the Sangik six colored races received all of these valuable teachings from Planetary Prince Caligastia's ten councils of teachers, Caligastia then made the decision to betray earth and its inhabitants by joining the Lucifer Rebellion 200,000 years ago. At the initial outbreak of the Lucifer Rebellion the city of Dalmatia had a population of six thousand residents, but after Caligastia joined the rebellion all of he and his staff's hard work and achievements were totally wiped out by the horrible confusion, evil and spiritual darkness that soon followed after Caligastia's decision to go to the dark side.

When you look back at the long career of Caligastia, while he was living in Paradise, one outstanding personality trait that stands out was that he was always living from his ego and not from his heart and he was always inclined to take sides with almost any group of protestors, and he was always sympathetic with those who openly expressed any forms of criticism. Early on in his career, Caligastia showed signs of being resentful of authority and any form of supervision, but whenever a true test presented itself to Caligastia, he always proved to be loyal to the Paradise rulers and to obey the mandates of the Paradise Constellation Fathers. No real fault was ever found with Caligastia until he betrayed planet earth by joining the Lucifer Rebellion

Both Lucifer and Caligastia had been warned while they were both still living on Paradise to be careful about their critical tendencies, but all of the previous attempts by the various members of the Paradise administration to help Lucifer and Caligastia were viewed by both of them as interfering with their personal liberties.

From the time Planetary Prince Caligastia arrived on earth 500,000 years ago, the civilizations on earth had continued to steadily evolve and progress for over 300,000 years. Since earth is one of the sixty-one life modification planets in our Nebadon universe, it was always being subjected to numerous irregularities and episodes of evolutionary changes, but earth was steadily progressing in the right direction up until the outbreak of the Lucifer Rebellion. When Caligastia betrayed earth he descended himself and the entire planet into a long period of darkness, violence, evil and confusion and after this betrayal planet earth was put into quarantine by the Paradise administration and totally isolated until the year 2012 when earth entered the Photon Belt which began its ascension process.

By the time Adam and Eve arrived on planet earth, it had been ravaged and plunged into a planet of darkness and confusion which helped to contribute to the default of their mission to continue to uplift the six Sangik colored races through the infusion of the lifeblood of the new Violet race and be descendants of Adam and Eve.

A lot of the damage fallen Planetary Prince caused to disturb and downgrade the state of human affairs on earth were greatly curtailed by the mortal incarnation of Machiventa Melchizedek on earth during the life and times of Abraham and then again when Jesus of Nazareth was born on planet earth which finally stripped Lucifer and Caligastia of all their power and authority on planet earth and the other thirty-six fallen planets.

The Lucifer Rebellion markedly modified the human course of social evolution and spiritual development on earth and the entire history of planet earth was profoundly influenced by the devastating calamity of this rebellion. The six Sangik colored evolutionary races who were living on earth during the times of the rebellion were all related since their ancestors all came from the same parents. However, due to the evil and darkness that this rebellion brought, they began wars, fighting and killing each other to the extent that some of these six races were annihilated, and no longer exist.

The beginning point of this rebellion on earth all began when Lucifer's first lieutenant came to planet earth to conduct a periodic inspection and during the course of this inspection Satan informed Caligastia that Lucifer who was their system sovereign had issued a proclamation of liberty in front of everyone to his superiors in Paradise and at this point, Caligastia agreed to join the rebellion.

Out of all of the administrative assignments of a local universe, no high trust is viewed as being more sacred than that of a Planetary Prince, because in this position you assume the responsibility for the personal welfare and guidance of all the evolving mortals on a new world. When Caligastia committed his act of treason against planet earth, his mind became so distorted and separated from the Source light, that he plunged into darkness, and he was never fully able to find his way back to God's Source light.

There are many ways of looking at sin, but in reality, sin is an individual's purposeful resistance to accepting God's divine reality. It is a conscious choice to oppose one's spiritual progress and the result is a degree of personality disintegration that often leads one to borderline insanity. Habitual sinners easily become to be wholehearted rebels against the universe and all of its divine realities and once you become to be an established sinner, it is hard for one to ever sincerely experience sorrow for the subsequent misdeeds or to accept forgiveness for the sins they are committing.

Shortly after the first lieutenant Satan completed his inspection with Caligastia of planet earth, Caligastia promptly called a staff meeting with his entire team and top assistant Daligastia and he informed everyone that he was going to issue a proclamation to make himself the absolute ruler over planet earth and for all the members of his team to immediately resign their commissions and turn over all their duties to his first assistant Daligastia. Van who was the head of earth's supreme court immediately appealed Caligastia's proclamation and Van asked all of the council members to hold off taking any action until his appeal could be taken to the system sovereign Lucifer and Caligastia's entire staff supported Van's request to appeal.

Van then took his appeal to Jerusem, Paradise and when he returned to earth, he addressed the ten earth councils in a seven-hour address where he disclosed all of the indictments against Lucifer, Caligastia and Daligastia for being in contempt of the laws of the superuniverse in Paradise, the seven higher heavens. Meanwhile, all of the system circuits between earth and Paradise were immediately severed and earth became an isolated planet. Every group of celestial life living on planet earth were suddenly without warning isolated and cut off from Paradise communications and from all outside counsel and advice. The serubim, cherubim and all of the other celestial beings who were living on earth were isolated, detained on earth and left to choose between sin or righteousness, between Lucifer's Rebellion or to continue to follow the divine will of the Universal Prime Creator Father, Source in Paradise. This struggle between good and evil lasted on planet earth for seven years before Van and his followers of loyal associates were finally vindicated by the Paradise Constellation Fathers.

During these seven crucial years, forty members of Caligastia's corporeal staff and the one hundred which included Van, refused to join the Lucifer Rebellion. Almost one half of the administrator and transition seraphim joined the rebellion, and 40,119 midway beings also joined Caligastia in this rebellion. Caligastia organized all of the groups who joined the rebellion into a rebel government, while Van assembled the remaining loyal members of Paradise into his loyal group and the great battle began to safeguard the salvation of the remaining celestial staff who remained on earth.

All throughout these seven long isolated years Van and his loyalists lived in an unwalled and poorly protected settlement right outside the deserted city of Dalmatia. The loyal seraphim and cherubim and three loyal primary midway beings took custody of the Tree of Life and only permitted the forty loyalists to eat its fruit. During these seven long years Van remained entirely devoted to the work of ministering to his loyal army of men, midway beings and to the angels. Amadon was a modified Andonite who served as Van's human assistant, and he proved to be one of the most outstanding human heroes of the Lucifer Rebellion. Amadon was one of the male descendants of Andon and Fonta and for seven years, he continued to donate his life plasma to the forty loyalists, and he made the decision to stand with his chief, Van all throughout the long struggle and battles they had with Lucifer's rebel forces for seven years.

At the end of the seven-year period of isolation, Van, Amadon and their loyal army were finally vindicated when members of the Most Highs from Paradise arrived on planet earth bringing with them emergency Melchizedek Sons to take the position of authority on planet earth. When the final roll call on earth was made, the corporeal staff and the rest of the members of Caligastia's staff who had remained loyal to Paradise were, Van and his entire court, Amadon, Ang, Fad, Nod, Hap and the entire council of art and science. Forty out of Caligastia's superhuman modified Andonites were saved, and they were later transferred back to Paradise, and the remaining sixty superhuman modified Andonites later chose Nod to be their leader and after the rebellion, this group migrated to the north and then to the east and their descendants became known as the Nodites who lived in the land of Nod. The disloyal supermen and superwomen who had joined the rebellion were left stranded on planet earth and they began to blend in and mate with ordinary humans and this was the origin of the stories about the fallen angels coming down to earth to mate with mortals. The legends and folk tales that continued to be passed down through the generations on earth were the ancestors who came into contact with these fallen superhumans, Nodites and their descendants. The fallen Planetary Prince Caligastia and his rebels were all deprived of eating the fruit from the Tree of Life and they all eventually died of the natural causes of old age.

When the emergency Melchizedek Sons arrived on planet earth during the Lucifer Rebellion all of the loyal members of Van and Amadon's team were translated back to Paradise where they were reunited with their waiting Divine Thought Adjusters. The vast majority of the human and superhuman beings who joined the Lucifer Rebellion have repented for their sins with the hope of someday being restored to some phase of their prior Paradise service when the Ancients Of Days complete the final adjudication of the case Gabriel vs Lucifer. There was a lot of confusion in the city of Dalmatia for over fifty years after the start of the Lucifer Rebellion, because hordes of savages began to penetrate the walls of the city due to the doctrines of liberty Lucifer had been teaching them. These hostile groups of tribes began to sweep into the city of Dalmatia and launch all out attacks that soon forced all those who were left in the city to have to migrate to the north.

One hundred and sixty-two years after the Lucifer Rebellion a giant tidal wave swept over the entire city of Dalmatia and earth's planetary headquarters and all of it sank into the sea. When the first capital city on planet earth, Dalmatia sank into the sea, all that was left on earth was the lowest strains of the six original and bloodline related Sangik races who had turned into renegades who turned the Universal Father's temple into a pagan shrine that was dedicated to the false god of light and fire.

During the Lucifer Rebellion years, Van, Amadon and their group of loyal followers soon began to migrate to the highlands west of India where they were safe from being attacked by the confused and violent races of tribes who lived in the lowland areas. Before the emergency Melchizedek Receivers arrived on earth, Van put the administration of human affairs back on track once again into the hands of the ten councils and the senior Life Carrier from Paradise assumed the leadership of the council of the forty superhumans who continued to remain loyal and work with their leader Van all throughout these seven years of waiting for adjudication from Paradise. When Van's loyal team of thirty-nine staff members were translated back home to Paradise, Van's group of loyal Amadonites took over their duties. This group of Amadonites who came to the aid of Van came from the original (144) loyal Andonites which Amadon belonged to and this group which was comprised of thirty-nine men and one hundred and five women became known by Amadon's name. Fifty-six of the members of this group had the status of immortality and the remaining members of Amadon's loyal team continued their work under the leadership of Van and Amadon until the end of their mortal days. Van's group continued to furnish positive leadership on earth all throughout the long dark ages of the post rebellion era. Van remained on earth until the arrival of the Violet race uplifters Adam and Eve, and he continued to function as the head of all the superhuman beings on earth. Van and Amadon were both able to continue to extend their lives by continuing to eat the fruit from the Tree of Life and by continuing to work with the specialized ministry with the Melchizedek Receiver Sons for over 150,000 years before they were translated back home to Paradise.

For quite some time the affairs on planet earth were managed by the twelve Melchizedek Receiver Sons by a mandate that was issued from the senior Paradise Constellation Ruler who is the Most High Father of Norlatiadek. The twelve Emergency Receiver Melchizedek Sons from Paradise who were assigned to assist earth were also given a team of helpers, two Life Carriers, one Trinitized Son, one volunteer Teacher Son, one Brilliant Evening Star of Avalon, the chiefs of the seraphim and cherubim, two advisers from neighboring planets and the director general of the angels and Van remained as the commander in chief of the primary midway beings. Van and his entire team continued to manage the affairs on earth until the arrival of Adam and Eve.

These twelve Melchizedek Receiver Sons performed heroic work during the hard dark days on earth after the Lucifer Rebellion, because they were still able to preserve the remnants of what was left of civilization on earth and all of their planetary policies were faithfully executed by Van. Within the time period of one thousand years after the rebellion, Van had assembled more than three hundred and fifty advanced groups who were scattered all over the world. These outposts of civilization on earth were mostly made up of the descendants of the loyal Andonites who were slightly mixed with the original Blue and Nodite Sangik races. Despite the terrible setbacks planet earth had suffered due to the Lucifer Rebellion, there were still many good strains of biologic promise left on earth. The twelve Emergency Receiver Melchizedek Sons, Van and Amadon continued to perform their work of helping to advance the natural evolution of the human race on earth for more than 150,000 years. Van and his team's positive work on earth after the rebellion helped to carry forward the physical evolution of humanity until mankind was able to advance to the point where it was time for Paradise to dispatch a Material Son and Daughter to earth.

Van, his assistant Amadon and their entire team continued to perform their positive work on earth and shortly after the arrival of Adam and Eve, they were both translated back home to Paradise where Van was able to be reunited with his waiting Divine Thought Adjuster. Van and Amadon are both now on the long path to achieve Paradise perfection and to their final destination of becoming a member of the Corps of the Mortal Finality.

It should be notated that when Van first appealed to the Most Highs in Paradise after Lucifer and Caligastia brought their rebellion to planet earth, he waited for seven long years to receive his response with patience and loyalty in his heart. However, the Constellation Fathers in Paradise had actually dispatched an immediate positive response supporting Van on every point of his appeal, but Van never received this immediate response, because earth's planetary circuits of communication from Paradise to earth had been severed while Van's response from Paradise was in transit.

This original response from Paradise to Van was recently found lodged in the possession of an energy transmitter where it had been stuck ever since the initial isolation of planet earth, because energy transmitters are able to receive and transmit messages, but they cannot initiate communications going out of Paradise. So, in essence, the technical status of Van concerning the legal records of Satania were not actually settled until this ruling from the Edentia Fathers in Paradise recorded Van's appeal in Jerusem.

The sin and darkness that the Lucifer Rebellion brought to planet earth did very little to delay the biologic evolution of mankind, but it did deprive all of the original six Sangik races from receiving their full infusion of the Violet race strain inheritance from Adam and Eve.

Sin cannot prevent an individual from achieving the highest spiritual potential when on makes the choice to follow God's and his soul's divine plan. Earth's fallen Planetary Prince Caligastia rebelled and Adam and Eve defaulted on their mission on earth, but none of the mortals born on earth has suffered in their personal spiritual experience in

251

spite of these mistakes and every mortal who has been born on earth since the Lucifer Rebellion has in some manner been delayed, but the future welfare of all the souls on earth has never been jeopardized from achieving the path to Paradise. No one is ever made to suffer vital spiritual deprivation because of another person's sin. The Lucifer Rebellion lasted for over 200,000 years, but many courageous and loyal beings to the Universal Prime Creator Father in Paradise from several worlds bravely withstood the evil and darkness of this rebellion. Van and his assistant Amadon on the official records in Paradise have both been recognized as the real heroes for their very long and continued glorious rejection of evil and for their continued devotion to righteousness and together they displayed an unmoved loyalty for 150,000 years to our Universal Prime Creator Father, Source in Paradise.

CHAPTER EIGHT

ADAM AND EVE'S MISSION ON PLANET EARTH

The Lord your God will be with you wherever you go.

(Joshua 1:9)

My soul is in deep anguish. How long, Lord, how long?

(Psalm 6:3)

Trust in the Lord forever.

(Isiah 26:4)

A Prayer:

Heavenly Father, give me courage to express my deepest pain and to welcome your presence and healing into my situation.

ADAM AND EVE AND THE TWO GARDENS OF EDEN

The cultural downfall and spiritual poverty on earth that resulted from earth's Planetary Prince Caligastia downfall and its social effects didn't have too much of an effect on the physical or biologic status of humanity. The organic evolution continued to proceed even though there were some moral setbacks and about forty thousand years ago, the Life Carriers who were on duty here on earth noted that the developmental progress of the races on earth were at its apex. The twelve Melchizedek Receiver Sons agreed with this opinion and both of these Paradise groups then submitted a petition to the Most Highs in Paradise to send an inspector to earth to authorize the dispatch of two biologic uplifters from Paradise, a Material Son and a Material Daughter, Adam and Eve. This request was sent to the Most Highs, because they had direct jurisdiction over planet earth since Prince Caligastia's downfall.

Tabamantia, the sovereign supervisor for the sixty-one experimental worlds came to inspect planet earth and he also recommended that earth was ready for a Material Son and a Material Daughter to be sent to the planet. And in less than one hundred years after this inspection, Adam and Eve arrived on earth and began the difficult task of attempting to untangle the still confused affairs of earth, because the planet was still under the veil of spiritual isolation. On the rest of other normal sixty planets the arrival of an Adam and Eve from Paradise ordinarily would mean that the world was at the brink of a great age of invention, material progress and intellectual enlightenment. However, when Adam and Eve arrived on planet earth it was populated with physically fit races, but most of the tribes living on earth at this time were still savage and stuck in moral stagnation.

About ten thousand years after the Lucifer Rebellion all of the momentum humanity on earth had achieved under Caligastia's administration had been erased and the Nodite and Amadonites were the only two tribes on earth who were still following the Dalmatian codes, culture and traditions of earth's former planetary prince. The Nodites were the descendants of the rebel members of the fallen planetary prince's staff and their tribal name came from their leader Nod who was the onetime chairman of the Dalmatian council of industry and trade. The Amadonites were the descendants of the Andonites who had remained loyal to Van and Amadon during the rebellion. The Amadonites were basically Andonites, descendants of Andon and Fonta, the first human family on earth, while the Nodites were the eighth race to appear on earth and there was an ongoing feud going on between the Nodites and the Amadonites and it would always come to the surface whenever the offspring of these two tribes would try to conduct any form of business enterprise. Even much later on in the second Garden of Eden, the Nodites and the Amadonites still could not work together in harmony.

Not too long after the destruction of the city of Dalmatia Nod's followers divided into three groups which were; the central group who remained living in the Persian Gulf area and the eastern group of Nodites migrated to the highland regions of the Euphrates valley.

The western group of Nodites lived on the northeastern shores of the Syrian shores of the Mediterranean Sea. All of the Nodites had freely mated with the other Sangik races, and they had left behind a variety of mixtures of descendants and some of which were rebels who had joined forces with Van and his followers in the lands north of Mesopotamia. In the area of the southern Caspian Sea region, these Nodites began to mingle and mix with the Amadonites and they were called the mighty men of old and just prior to the arrival of Adam and Eve on earth the Nodites and the Amadonites were considered to be the two most advanced and cultured races on earth.

For almost one hundred years before the arrival of Adam and Eve on earth, Van and his followers from their highland headquarters continued to preach to his followers about God's promise to send a Son of God and biologic uplifters Adam and Eve to earth. Those who were in immediate contact with Van and Amadon took their teachings seriously and they continued to plan for the actual reception for Adam and Eve, the racial uplifters and for the Son of God, a teacher of love and truth.

Van and Amadon's highland headquarters was based on sixty-one acres of settlements and they were able to recruit a corps of over three thousand workers who dedicated themselves to the mission of preparing for the arrival of the promised Son of God. Van divided his volunteers into one hundred companies with a captain and an associate over each company. Caligastia and Daligastia had both pretty much lost all of their power of evil, but they both continued to do everything possible to try to interfere and frustrate Van and Amadon in their job of preparing the first Garden of Eden for the pending arrival of Adam and Eve. However, any evil deed that Caligastia or Daligastia continued to try to do on earth were mostly stopped by the faithful activities of the ten thousand primary midway beings who continued to endlessly work to advance the work and activities of Van and Amadon.

A committee was formed to select the location for Van and Amadon to build the first Garden of Eden for Adam and Eve and this committee chose the Mediterranean peninsula and when they did, all of the previous dwellers who were living in this selected area except for one peaceful group quickly vacated the area. So, when Van and his volunteer workers arrived to begin construction, it took them two years to transfer all of the required construction materials from their previous world cultural headquarters, including the Tree of Life to this new first Garden of Eden site that was located on the Mediterranean peninsula.

The site that the committee chose for the first Garden of Eden was the most beautiful spot of its kind in all the world and the climate was ideal. The location for the first Garden of Eden was the one bright spot left on earth, the cream of civilization, because it was a natural dream of loveliness, and it soon developed into a location of exquisite and a perfected landscape of glory.

When a Material Son and a Material Daughter from Paradise who are biologic race uplifters begin their mission on an evolutionary world, their home is usually called the Garden of Eden on all of the sixty-one experimental worlds, because it always contains a lot of floral beauty and botanic grandeur. Van was well aware of the customs for the

Garden of Eden so he provided all of the commodities in the entire peninsula that would be needed to accommodate Adam and Eve. There were plenty of green pastures, animals, birds and numerous domestic species of animals were living in the park area of Eden Van's instructions to the volunteer workers were that Eden was only supposed to be a garden and no animals were killed in Eden, and all of the meat that the Eden workers ate was brought in from the herds who lived on the mainland outside of Eden.

The first task the workers had was to build a wall across the neck of the peninsula and once this was completed, the real landscape beautification and home building was able to proceed without any interruptions. A zoological garden was created by building a smaller wall just outside of the main wall and the space between these two walls was occupied by all types of wild beasts who helped to serve as an additional defense against any hostile attacks. The entire Garden of Eden was organized into twelve divisions and walled paths that led between all of the paths to the twelve gates of Eden, the river and its adjacent pastures that were in the central area of Eden.

Van and Amadon had the volunteer workers to cultivate the garden to be ready when Adam and Eve arrived, and they took care of the herds and the nearby residents who were believers contributed food for the volunteer workers to eat. The Garden of Eden project continued until its completion despite of the still confused status of earth during the troublesome times after the Lucifer Rebellion. At the center of Eden, the workers built an exquisite stone temple that was dedicated to our Universal Father in Paradise, and it was the sacred shrine of Eden. The administrative headquarters in Eden was built to the south where the homes for the workers and their families and to the west the schools were built, while in the east of Eden the homes for Adam and Eve and their offspring were built. The entire plan for the first Garden of Eden provided homes and a lot of land for more than one million humans.

When Adam and Eve arrived, Eden was only one-fourth completed, but it had thousands of miles of irrigation ditches and more than twelve thousand miles of paved paths and roads. There were over five thousand brick buildings and so many trees and plants that they couldn't be counted. The sanitary arrangements for Eden were way more advanced than anything that had ever been built on earth and the drinking water was kept wholesome and pure by following Van's rules to not allow anything to fall into the water supply in Eden. Amadon's water inspectors made their daily water rounds daily to ensure the drinking water remained pure. Later on, a sewage disposal system was established in Eden and they made it a practice to bury all waste or decomposing material. The people living on earth during those times did not realize the importance of the proper hygiene practices to prevent human diseases until the latter part of the nineteenth and twentieth centuries. Van later had the workers to build a covered brick conduit disposal system that ran beneath the walls and emptied into the river near Eden almost a mile beyond the wall of Eden.

By the time Adam and Eve arrived in Eden most of the plants in that section of earth were all growing in Eden and many of our modern-day vegetables and cereals were first cultivated in Eden, but many of these varieties of food plants were later lost to the rest of the world. About five percent of the first Eden was under high artificial cultivation, fifteen percent of the plants were partially cultivated, and the rest of the growing plants were partially cultivated, and the rest of the live plants and food were left in their natural state pending the arrival of Adam and Eve to get their input before finishing the food project. When Adam and Eve arrived in the Garden of Eden, they were pleased with the general plan, because it was full of botanical beauty and grandeur, and this was the first time on earth that such a garden had been built that had such a beautiful and complete exhibition of plants and agriculture. Van planted the Tree of Life whose leaves were for the healing of the nations and its fruit had for so long extended the life of he and Amadon for 150,000 years on earth in Eden for Adam and Eve who would also need an extension of their lives in order to complete their biologic race uplifting mission on earth. The Tree of Life is real and for a long time it was growing right here on planet earth in the city of Dalmatia and again in the first Garden of Eden. The Tree of Life was a superplant from Paradise that stored up certain space energies that were antidotal to the age producing elements of existence. The fruit from the Tree of Life was like a superchemical storage battery that mysteriously released the life extension force of the universe when eaten only by the Paradise beings who were working on missions on earth and who were living on earth straight from Paradise. The fruit from the Tree of Life did not work for normal humans who were born on earth except for the members of the Andonite tribe, the direct descendants of Andon and Fonta and who had continuing to donate some of their life plasm to fallen Planetary Prince Caligastia's staff.

When Adam and Eve arrived in the first Garden of Eden, the twelve Melchizedek Receiver Sons counseled both of them to not begin the program of racial uplift on the races of earth until their own family had reached the number of one-half million offspring. The Garden of Eden was never meant to be a permanent home for Adam and Eve and their family, because their job was to also become emissaries of a new life to all humanity on earth and Adam and Eve were supposed to be mobil for an unselfish bestowal on the needy races of earth. The clear instructions that the twelve Melchizedeks gave Adam and Eve were to implement all of their plans together only and to follow the plans that were outlined to them by their superiors before they left Paradise. Adam and Eve were also given clear instructions from the Melcizedeks to establish racial continental and divisional headquarters and to be in charge of his immediate sons and daughters while he and Eve divided their time between the various world capitals as advisers and coordinators of their worldwide ministry of biologic uplift, intellectual advancement and human moral rehabilitation.

Adam and Eve arrived on planet earth 37,848 years ago and it was in midseason during the time that the Garden of Eden was in the height of bloom. Two seraphic angel transports accompanied by Jerusem personnel were given the job to transport Adam and Eve to earth and all of the work to rematerialize the bodies of Adam and Eve was completed inside the shrine of the Universal Father in Eden. It took ten days before the two seraphim were able to recreate Adam and Eve into dual forms to be presented as planet earth's new rulers and they regained consciousness at the same time, because a material Son and Material Daughter complete and serve their assigned mission for the Universal Father always together. It is always the essence of a Material Son and Daughter from Paradise and in all places to never be separated, because they are designed to work in pairs, and they are not supposed to work alone.

Adam and Eve were members of the senior corps of Material Sons and Daughters on Paradise, and they were married and jointly assigned as numbers 14 and 311 and they were both eight feet tall and belonged to the third physical series. At the time Adam and Eve were chosen on Paradise to come to complete their mission on earth as racial biologic uplifters, they were both employed in the trial and testing laboratories in Paradise. For more than fifteen thousand years they had both been the directors of the division of experimental energy when applied to modified life forms and before this job Adam and Eve had both been teachers in the citizenship schools for new arrivals of ascending mortals in Jerusem, Paradise. When the proclamation on Paradise was issued asking for two volunteers to complete an adamic mission on planet earth, the entire corps of Material Sons and Daughters volunteered for this assignment.

The Melchizedek examiners with the approval of Lanaforg and the Most Highs finally selected Adam and Eve for this mission on earth, because they had both remained loyal to the Creator Son, Michael during the Lucifer Rebellion and once selected they were called before the system sovereign and his Satania cabinet to receive their final instructions. At this final meeting Adam and Eve were fully presented with all the details of the current affairs on earth along with specific instructions on how to complete their mission on the confused, strife torn planet earth. Adam and Eve both had to recite joint oaths of allegiance to the Most Highs of Edentia and the system sovereign Creator Son Michael. At this meeting Adam and Eve were also advised that the twelve Melchizedek Receiver Sons were earth's current governing body and that they both had to follow their rules while living on earth.

When Adam and Eve left Jerusem, Paradise for their mission on earth they left behind on Paradise fifty sons and fifty daughters who were all working as stewards of the universe. All of their children went to the dematerialization headquarters and said goodbye as Adam and Eve fell asleep in their personality lapse of consciousness which preceded their seraphic transport to earth. When Adam and Eve left Jerusem for their mission on earth they were both adequately equipped and fully instructed on what to expect and the duties and dangers they would be encountering on earth. So, Adam and Eve fell asleep on Paradise and when they woke up ten days later in the Universal Father's shrine in Eden on earth, they were face to face with two beings they had heard so much about, Van and Amadon who were the first to welcome them to their new Garden of Eden home on earth.

Adam and Eve had already fully mastered the Adonic language that was spoken in Eden and on that day of their arrival there was a lot of joy and excitement in Eden. The news of the arrival of Adam and Eve on earth quickly spread and thousands of their neighboring tribesman began to accept the teachings of Van and Amadon and for many months there were numerous pilgrims continued to come into Eden to welcome Adam and Eve and to worship in the new shrine to the Universal Father that was located in the center of Eden. Soon after Adam and Eve woke up in Eden, they were taken to their new installation ceremony as earth's new rulers on the great mound just north of the temple. Amadon was the chairman of the installation committee which consisted of twelve members who represented each of the six Sangik colored races, the acting chief of the midway beings, a spokesman for the Nodite tribe, two resident Life Carriers and Noah the son of the architect of Eden.

The senior Melchizedek Son next administered the oath of office to Adam and Eve where they were proclaimed to be the new official rulers of planet earth. Van then relinquished his ruling authority on earth which he had held for 150,000 years by the authority of the twelve Melchizedek Receiver Sons.

Adam and Eve then began their new reign on earth under seemingly favorable conditions, but right after their formal installation ceremony Adam and Eve painfully became aware of the total isolation they faced on earth, because the Lucifer Rebellion had changed everything on earth and Caligastia was still present on earth spreading his evil and he made Adam and Eve's task of completing their mission on earth quite hazardous. Adam and Eve spent their first night on earth walking all night through the Garden of Eden feeling disillusioned and discussing their plans for the next day. Adam and Eve felt lonely and isolated on their first night on earth and they walked and talked all night long, because they both really felt so lonely.

Adam and Eve's second day on earth was spent in meetings with the twelve planetary Melchizedek Receiver Sons and with their advisory council and at this meeting Adam and Eve learned more about the Lucifer Rebellion and the negative results it had caused to earth's progress. They discussed all the facts regarding the total collapse of Caligastia's evil scheme to advance planet earth separate from God's divine plan and Adam and Eve's second day on earth ended as a sad but enlightening day.

Adam and Eve's devoted their third day on earth completing a full inspection of the Garden of Eden and as they looked down on the vast stretches of land in Eden, they realized that they were living in the most beautiful spot on earth. An enormous banquet was held at the end of the third day in honor of all those who had worked so hard in building the Garden of Eden and once again Adam and Eve spent the entire night walking in Eden talking about the immensity of the problems they faced on earth.

One their fourth day on earth Adam and Eve addressed the entire Eden assembly and from the speaker's mount they spoke to all of the Eden dwellers concerning their plans to rehabilitate earth and to redeem the social culture that had fallen to low levels as a result of sin and Calisgastia joining the Lucifer Rebellion. Adam and Eve ended this day with a great feast with both men and women in attendance and it turned out to be a great day where Eve, a woman was able to share the honors and responsibilities of earth's affairs with her mate, a man called Adam.

Adam and Eve spent their fifth day on earth organizing a temporary government that would function when the twelve Melchizedek Receiver Sons left planet earth.

Adam and Eve spent the sixth day inspecting the different types of men, plants and animals that were in Eden to better understand the nature and function of the thousands of different species of animals that lived in Eden. Those who took Adam and Eve on this tour didn't realize that Adam had been one of the most expert anatomists in all of Paradise and he was able to describe the origin, nature and function of all the animals that they saw.

At the end of the sixth day Adam and Eve rested for the first time in their new home in Eden and their first six days on earth had been very busy and they looked forward to spending the next day just resting all day with no activities. However, circumstances proved otherwise, and Adam and Eve had so much won the hearts of the Eden dwellers that most of them were ready to fall down worship them as gods.

On the seventh day while Adam and Eve were asleep, strange things were starting to happen near the Universal Father's temple located in the center of Eden. All of the amazing events that Adam and Eve did during their first six days on earth were a bit too much for the unprepared minds of the Eden dwellers and hundreds of people had gathered at the temple all night and by morning the crowd had decreed that both Adam and Eve were gods to be worshipped. Van protested and quickly ran and told Adam and Eve what was going on with the crowd, so early that morning on their seventh day on earth, Adam addressed the crowd who had gathered at the temple and told them that he would accept their honor and respect, but that only the Universal Father would be worshipped and that he Adam would never accept the thought of being worshipped as a god. Adam then directed all of the people in the crowd to go into the temple, bow down and worship the Universal Father only. The crowd of people did as Adam directed and he and Eve stood alone on the mount with bowed heads while the crowd of people kneeled around the temple in worship to the Universal Father of Paradise and these events all occurred on Sunday morning, the seventh day on earth for Adam and Eve.

This event that occurred in Eden on Adam and Eve's seventh day on earth was the origin of keeping the Sabbath day tradition and from this day forward, the seventh day in Eden was always devoted to a noontide worship service to the Universal Father in the temple in Eden. Every Sunday before noon was devoted to physical improvement, noontime was for spiritual worship and the afternoon was devoted to improving the mind classes and Sunday evenings were spent in social activities. For almost seven years after Adam and Eve arrived on earth, the twelve Melchizedek Receiver Sons remained in their duties on earth, but they eventually turned the administration of world affairs over to Adam and Eve and they then returned to Paradise. Adam had on several occasions asked the twelve Melchizedek Receiver Sons to stay on earth, but they refused, because the time had come for Adam and Eve to assume their full duties and responsibilities to conduct the world affairs on earth. So, at around midnight the seraphic transports left planet earth with fourteen sleeping beings with a destination to Paradise, Van, Amadon, and the twelve Melchizedek Receiver Sons. For a while everything went fairly well on earth, and it looked like Adam's plans to promote the gradual extension of the Eden culture was going to work and Adam began to manufacture products and to develop trade relations with the neighboring tribes.

Adam and Eve had previously received extensive training in Paradise in the techniques on how to improve and advance new developing evolutionary worlds to transform into a progressive civilization. However, the pressing problems that Adam and Eve faced were how to establish law and order once again on a world like earth that was still full of savages, barbarians and semi-civilized humans, especially since there were only a few human groups on earth who were ready and willing to accept the new Adamic culture.

Adam continued to make a concentrated effort to establish a world government on earth, but he was constantly being met with a lot of stubborn resistance at every move he made Adam seemed to continue to run into serious opposition whenever he tried to apply his ideas to the neighboring tribes who lived right outside of Eden. Whenever Adam and his team tried to work with the tribes, they were always met with direct and well-planned resistance from Caligastia, Daligastia and the rest of their rebel followers who were still in the area. Caligastia had been stripped of his title of being earth's planetary prince, but he was still on earth, and he continued to do everything he could to interfere and resist all of Adam and Eve's plans to racially uplift and rehabilitate the human society on earth. Adam continued to try and warn the evolutionary races on earth about the evil intentions of Caligastia, but both the Eden dwellers and members of the neighboring tribes were confused and they continued to lean towards Caligastia's teachings on personal liberty. Adam and Eve's plan to implement socialization on earth failed and instead he implemented the same plan that Van had used in Dalmatia by dividing the garden dwellers in Eden into one hundred companies with a captain over each company and lieutenants in charge of groups of ten in each company. The one great forward step that Adam and Eve were able to achieve was their appointing ambassadors from each tribe to another which helped to improve the tribal relations on earth.

Adam and Eve's family area extended over a little over five miles and the land surrounding their homesite had enough provisions for them to care for more than three hundred thousand of their pure line violet race offspring. Adamson was the first born of Adam and Eve's pure line violet race on earth followed by a sister and their second son, Everson. Eve bore five children before the twelve Melchizedek Receiver Sons left earth and she continued to bear sixty-three children, thirty-two daughters and thirty-one sons. Adam and Eve's total family members consisted of four generations of 1,647 pure line descendants of the new violet race. Adam and Eve's children did not drink milk from animals so after breastfeeding, Eve instead fed their children milk she made from a variety of nuts, juices and fruits. Adam and Eve did not cook their food, they ate only once a day and they knew how to access the light and energy directly from certain space emanations that also provided nourishment to their family, because these space energies worked in conjunction with the energies, they received by eating the fruit from the Tree of Life.

A glow of light shined from Adam and Eve's bodies and since they always wore clothing, you could only see this glow of light around their heads. The origin of the pictures of a halo around the head of certain pious and holy men dates back to the times of Adam and Eve, because many of their descendants' bodies also glowed and they always portrayed the concept of being highly extraordinary in their spiritual development. Adam and Eve were able to communicate with each other and their children up to a distance of fifty miles through their thoughts and mental telepathy process that worked from a delicate gas chamber that was located close to Adam and Eve's brain structures. Adam and Eve's children attended their own separate schools in Eden until the age of sixteen, and the average age of betrothal was eighteen with two years of instruction for marriage and at the age of twenty, they were then eligible for marriage. The subsequent practice in the later royal families of permitting brothers and sisters to marry also originated with Adam and Eve's family in Eden, because they were descended from gods. The marriage ceremonies in Eden between the first and second generations of Adam and Eve's family were always performed by Adam and Eve.

These are some of the basic instructions that were taught in the separate schools that Adam and Eve's children attended.

Proper health and care of the body.

Follow the golden rule standard of social interaction.

Follow the proper relation of individual rights/groups and community obligations.

Respect the history and culture of the various human races on earth.

Proper methods of advancing and improving world trade.

Coordination of conflicting duties and emotions.

Cultivation of play, humor and competitive substitutes for fighting.

The schools in Eden also had seven laws that were based on the older Dalmatia codes that were set forth by Van with just a few differences.

The laws of health and sanitation.

The social regulations of the Garden of Eden.

The code of trade and commerce.

The laws of fair play and competition.

The laws of home life

The civil codes of the golden rule.

The seven commands of the supreme rule.

Adam made sure to teach the concept of racial equality in his Eden schools and ministry and the manner in which Eve always worked by the side of her mate Adam left a positive impression on all of the Eden dwellers. The more intelligent races on earth looked forward to the time when they would be allowed to intermarry with the superior children of Adam and Eve's pure line violet race. Adam continued to work hard to improve the welfare and to complete his mission to racially uplift humanity, but it continued to be a difficult task for he and Eve to lead the mixed races of people on earth to follow their plans for them to live a better way of life on earth.

The story of the six days of creation on earth was based on the tradition of the time that Adam and Eve spent on their first six days on earth during their initial survey of the Garden of Eden. Adam's spending six days inspecting Eden and formulating his plans to formulate the plans for their mission were not prearranged, instead their plans were worked out by Adam and Eve day by day and Adam's choosing the seventh day for worship was also entirely incidental. The legend of the creation of planet earth in six days was an afterthought more than 30,000 years afterwards. One feature story about the sudden appearance of the sun and moon originated in the traditions of the one time sudden emergence of earth from a dense space cloud of minute matter which for a long time obscured both the sun and the moon. The story about the creation of Eve from out of Adam's ribs is a confused condensation of the adamic surgery and the celestial surgery that was connected with the interchange of the living substances associated with the coming of the corporeal staff of earth's first Planetary Prince Caligastia more than 450,000 years prior to the arrival of Adam and Eve on earth.

Most of the intelligent humans living during the times of Adam and Eve believed in the gradual ascent of the human race and they had a clear understanding about the slow and evolutionary character of human progress. Some of the different races on earth had mixed views of evolution and many of the primitive tribes believed and were taught that they were the descendants of various animals. And many primitive tribes began to select the totem of the animals that they believed was their ancestry. Certain Native American tribes believed that they originated from beavers and cayotes, while some African tribes believed that they were the descendants from the hyena, a Malayan tribe from a lemur and a New Guinea tribe from a parrot. The Babylonians expanded the story of man's creation and taught that the humans were descended directly from the gods. The Old Testament account of creation dates a long time after the time of Moses who taught the Hebrews a simple narrative account of creation so that they would worship the Creator, the Universal Father who Moses called the Lord God of Israel.

The later religious and history writers tried to totally eradicate all references of human history before the times of Adam and Eve, but they were foolish in doing so, because they forgot to omit the true story of Cain's emigration to the land of Nod, the Nodites after killing his half-brother Abel and he took a wife with the Nodite tribe in the land of Nod.

The first Garden of Eden was a fact, and it was actually overthrown after Cain's biological father Cano and the rest of the members of his Nodite tribe were later killed by an angry mob from the First Garden of Eden. Adam and Eve worked hard in the first Garden of Eden for over one hundred and seventeen years, but due to the impatience of Adam and Eve and an error in judgement that they both made, they brought disaster on themselves which once again caused a ruinous delay of the developmental progression of planet earth. After more than one hundred years of hard work on earth, Adam realized that he was making very little progress in implementing his plans to racially uplift humanity outside of the first Garden of Eden and the world did not seem to be improving very much. Adam and Eve's realization of race betterment on earth appeared to be a long way off and the situation seemed so desperate that Adam and Eve needed some type of relief that was not included in their original plans. These thoughts of desperation kept on passing through Adam's mind and he often openly expressed these thoughts to Eve. Adam's wife Eve was loyal, but they were both isolated from their own kind in Paradise and they were both upset by the sorry plight of the social conditions of humanity on earth. Adam and Eve's mission on the experimental rebellion scarred and isolated earth began to feel like too much of an undertaking for both of them. Adam and Eve were both aware at the beginning of their mission how difficult and complex their job was going to be and in the beginning they both courageously set about completing the many tasks of solving the many problems and obstacles that kept on blocking their mission. In time Adam and Eve began to see that there was no way out of their dilemma and since they were isolated, they were not able to receive any counsel from their superiors or support groups in Paradise.

Under normal conditions on a planet, the first work of the Planetary Adam and Eve would be to coordinate and begin to uplift and blend the evolutionary races on the planet. But on earth a project such as this was hopeless for Adam and Eve, because even though the different races on earth were biologically fit, none of the races had been purged of their mentally challenged and defective strains. In addition, Adam and Eve found themselves living on a planet that was full of spiritual darkness and cursed with confusion and constant negative interference from Caligastia and Daligastia and the morals of humanity living on earth was at an all-time low.

Adam and Eve were still trying to begin the task of converting humanity on earth to follow some simple form of religious beliefs. Instead of finding one language of people on earth to work with, Adam and Eve were confronted by a world full of confusion with hundreds of different dialects of languages. No other Adam on the other sixty life modification planets who were sent to complete a mission of planetary service had ever been assigned to a more difficult world than earth, because the obstacles that Adam and Eve continued to encounter were beyond their capacity to solve. Adam and Eve's tremendous sense of loneliness grew worse after Van, Amadon and the twelve Melchizedek Receiver Sons left earth and returned to Paradise. The only way Adam and Eve were able to communicate with any other living being off earth was indirectly by means of the angelic orders who were working with them on earth. As time passed Adam and Eve's courage began to weaken, their spirits dropped and sometimes their faith began to falter and if they had been just a little bit more patient, they probably would have found more success in completing their mission on earth. However, both of them especially Eve was altogether too impatient, and they were not willing to settle down to complete their long mission on earth together. Instead, Adam and Eve kept on looking for immediate results and their impatience turned out in the end to be a total disaster for both of them, their family and for the first Garden of Eden.

Earth's fallen Planetary Prince Caligastia visited the First Garden of Eden often and he held many meetings with Adam and Eve, but they both continued to reject all of Caligastia's suggestions to compromise and use short cut measures to complete their mission on earth more quickly which were not in compliance with the divine plan that had been set in Paradise by their superiors. Caligastia was still the planetary prince of earth by title only since the end of the Lucifer Rebellion and he was not finally deposed from earth until Jesus of Nazareth arrived on earth. However, Caligastia was persistent and determined to still do things his way and soon he gave up on trying to distract Adam, so he decided to try run a wild evil scheme attack on Eve instead. Caligastia's evil scheme was to use a suitable person from the upper-class section of the Nodite tribe to entrap Eve, the mother of the violet race on earth.

The last thing that Eve ever intended to do was to go against Adam's plans for earth or to jeopardize their planetary trust to complete their mission on earth. Before the twelve Melchizedek Receiver Sons left earth to return to Paradise, they held a private meeting with Eve warning her that she and Adam would continue to be isolated on earth and that she should never participate in any secret meetings that would cause her to stray away from her long time mate, so Adam and Eve had continued to follow their instructions for more than one hundred years and it just didn't occur to Eve the danger she was putting herself in by beginning to have secret and private visits with the Nodite leader Serapalatia and this situation totally took Eve by surprise.

The Eden dwellers had stayed in contact with the neighboring Nodite Tribes who were the mixed descendants of the defaulting members of Caligastia's staff, but little did they know that these same Nodite Tribe members were going to be the cause of the final ruination of the first Garden of Eden. Adam had just completed his first one hundred years of service with his mission on earth when Serapatatia became the leader of the Syrian Nodite Tribe. Seapatatia was a brown tinted man who was a brilliant descendant of the onetime chief of the Dalmatia commission on health who had mated with a female from the Blue race and all down through the ages this particular Nodite line had held a high authority and great influence over the entire Nodite Tribe. Serapatatia had made several prior visits to the Garden of Eden, and he had announced his intentions of working together with Adam and Eve in Eden. Most of the rest of the Nodite tribe joined in to help Adam and Eve and Serapatatia and his staff were soon invited to Adam and Eve's home for dinner and entertainment.

Serapatatia soon became to be one of Adam's most able and efficient lieutenants and he was honest, sincere and he never knew that he was being used by Caligastia as a tool to entrap Adam's mate, Eve. Adam appointed Serapatatia to be the associate chairman of the Eden commission on tribal relations and he and Adam were working on many plans of winning the more remote tribes over to join the work and plans that the Eden staff had. Serapatatia held many conferences with Adam and Eve, especially with Eve and they discussed many plans to improve their working relations with the many remote tribes. One day while Serapatatia was having a meeting with Eve, he suggested that while they were waiting to recruit large numbers of the Violet race to blend with the neighboring tribes, that they could do something right now to quickly racially uplift the neighboring tribes to the Violet race. Serapatatia then suggested to Eve that since his tribe, the Nodites were the most progressive and cooperative tribe and that if they could have a Nodite leader born who was part of the original Violet race, that it would speed up their racial biologic project, and bring the Nodite the Nodite tribes more closely to the Garden of Eden.

Serapatatia said all of these things to Eve because he honestly felt that his plan would be good for the progress of earth and this proposed offspring would be reared and educated in the Garden of Eden and exert a good influence for the good of the Nodite Tribe. Serapatatia never once suspected that he was playing right into the hands of the evil scheme that Caligastia and Daligastia had planned to entrap Eve.

Serapatatia was totally loyal to Adam and Eve's plan of building up the half a million strong reserve of the Violet race before the implementation of the worldwide upstepping of the human race of the confused people on earth. This plan in all reality would take hundreds of years to complete and since Serapatatia just like Eve was impatient, he wanted to see some immediate results during his lifetime. Serapatatia kept on stressing to Eve during their meetings how discouraged Adam was by the little progress that had been achieved towards their racial uplifting plan. For more than five years these secret plans between Eve and Serapatatia continued to go on and they began to take hold in Eve's mind. At last Eve consented to have a secret conference with Cano, one of the friendly Nodite leaders. Cano was a sincere spiritual leader of the Nodites and he had friendly relations with the Eden dwellers and so Eve made the final arrangements to have the fateful secret meeting with Cano to occur during the twilight hours of an autumn evening not far from her home that she shared with her mate Adam. Before this fateful meeting, Eve had not yet met Cano, but when she did, Eve viewed him as a beautiful, enthusiastic and magnificent specimen of the survival of the superior physique and outstanding intellect of one of the former planetary prince's staff.

Outside of the Garden of Eden multiple mating was a common practice during those times on earth, and Cano thoroughly believed in the righteousness of Serapatatia's project of working with the Garden of Eden's plans. Eve was swept off her feet by Cano's flattery, enthusiasm, and great personal persuasion and she agreed to begin their plan which was to add her own little scheme with Cano's plan to help uplift the human races on earth by doing it her way. Before Eve realized what was happening, she had taken the fatal step of disobedience to her superior's plan that had been given to her and Adam in Paradise. As soon as Eve committed the sin of adultery with Cano the Nodite leader, all of the celestial life on the entire planet of earth were all astir and Adam immediately recognized that something was drastically wrong, and he asked Eve to step outside in the Garden to talk with him.

Eve then told Adam the entire story about the agreement she had made with Serapatatia and Cano to accelerate the race upstepping plan for humanity by having an offspring with the Nodite leader Cano. While Adam and Eve were talking in the Garden, Solona the seraphic voice of Eden scolded both of them for their act of disobedience and that they had defaulted in the execution of their orders of trust to the sovereign of the universe.

Even though Eve's secret plans that she had made with Serapatatia and Cano were made with sincerity and with the highest motives for the welfare of earth, it still constituted a sin, because it departed from the right way which was the divine plan that had been set by the system sovereign of the Nebadon universe in Paradise and Eve had also committed the sin of adultery against her long time mate Adam.

Eve had found Cano the Nodite leader to be pleasant to her eyes, but as she and Adam walked and talked that night in the Eden, Eve realized that the sin she had committed with the Nodite leader Cano was the act of commingling good with evil and that as a result, she and Adam would both become mortals of the realm of earth and eventually grow old and die. Eve's sense of disillusionment for the sin she had committed was pathetic and Adam felt heartbroken, dejected and he felt a lot of pity and sympathy for the serious error in judgement Eve had made. In a moment of despair which was caused by Eve's sin of adultery with the Nodite leader Cano, the very next day, Adam left their home and sought out the company of another woman named Laotta, a brilliant Nodite woman who was the head of the western schools in Eden and so Adam with premeditation in his heart, committed the same sin his mate Eve had done, adultery.

When the rest of the Eden dwellers learned how Eve had been entrapped by Serapatatia and Cano, they declared war on the nearby Nodite settlement where Cano lived and they attacked the Nodite settlement and utterly destroyed the entire village and not one man, woman or child was spared including Cano, the future father of Eve's son Cain. When Serapatatia saw that the entire Nodite village had been destroyed due to his unknowingly allowing himself to be used by Caligastia and Daligastia, he then drowned himself the next day in the nearby river.

Adam's sixty-three children tried to comfort Eve when Adam left their home, and at the end of thirty days, Adam returned home to Eve and his family, and he began to make plans for the family's next course of action. It's very unfortunate that the errors of misguided parents are often shared by their innocent children and the noble family of Adam and Eve never did fully recover from the mental and spiritual sorrow they experienced after Adam and Eve both committed the sin of adultery, but when Adam returned home to Eve and his family after thirty days, Eve felt a strong sense of joy and gratitude. Time passed and Adam was still not fully aware of the seriousness of the sin that both he and Eve had committed, but when the twelve Melchizedek Receiver Sons returned to earth and again assumed jurisdiction over the world affairs, then Adam knew for certain that he and Eve had failed in their mission on earth.

There was still more troubling news to come for Adam and Eve, because the news had traveled about the annihilation of the entire Nodite village by the Eden settlers to Serapatatia's home tribes to the north and a large army of Nodites were gathering to attack the first Garden of Eden and this was the beginning of the long and bitter warfare that existed between the Adamites and the Nodites and these hostilities continued for a long time even after Adam and the Eden settlers had migrated to the second Garden of Eden that was located in the Euphrates Valley. This conflict proved to be an intense and long-lasting enmity between that man and that woman between his seed and her seed.

When Adam learned that the large Nodite army were on their way to attack the first Garden of Eden, he tried to get advice from the twelve Melchizedek Receiver Sons, but they refused to give him any advice, because the Melchizedeks had been forbidden by the Most Highs in Paradise to not get involved or interfere with any future plans Adam and Eve had. Adam then held an all-night meeting with 1,200 of his Eden followers and the next day they all left the first Garden of Eden to find a new home. Adam did not like war, so instead he chose to leave the first Eden instead of engaging in a conflict with the Nodite army.

The caravan from the first Garden of Eden was stopped on the third day of their migration by the arrival of the seraphic transports from Jerusem, Paradise and at this time Adam and Eve were informed of what was going to happen to their sixty-three children. Their children who were over the age of twenty were given the choice to either stay on earth or return to Jerusem to become the wards of the Most Highs of Norlatiadek. Two-thirds of their children chose to return to Paradise and one third of their children decided to stay on earth with their parents Adam and Eve, but all of their children who were under the age of seven were taken back to Paradise by the seraphic transport. It was a very sad caravan that continued on the journey to their new home, the second Garden of Eden and it was a very tragic situation for Adam and Eve to had come to earth with such high hopes and then to have to leave the first Eden in disgrace, lose more than three fourths of their children and all of this happened before they were able to find their new home.

When Adam and Eve's caravan was stopped by the seraphic transport back to Paradise, they were also informed of the nature of their transgressions by Archangel Gabriel who also appeared to Adam and Eve to pronounce their judgement which was that Adam and Eve were both in default of their mission on earth, because they had violated the covenant of their trusteeship as the world rulers of earth. Adam and Eve were both downcast with guilt, but at the same time they both felt a great deal of relief when Archangel Gabriel told them that the judges in Salvington, Paradise had cleared them from all charges of contempt of the universe government, so they were both found not guilty of rebellion.

However, Adam and Eve were informed that they had degraded themselves in front of mortals on earth and that from now on they would conduct themselves as mortals and look to the future races of earth for their future. While Adam and Eve were still living in Paradise their teachers fully explained to them what the consequences would be if they strayed from the divine plan of their mission on earth. Adam and Eve were Material Sons and Daughters from Paradise, and they were only able to maintain their immortal status through intellectual association with the mind gravity circuit of the Holy Spirit and when this vital connection was broken by mental disjunction then regardless of the spiritual level of one's existence, immortality is lost. So, the consequences of Adam and Eve's intellectual default on earth through sin was the physical dissolution of their immortal status on earth.

Adam and Eve were also dependent on the proper maintenance of their dual circulatory systems, one from their physical nature and the other from the super energy that was stored in the fruit from the Tree of Life, and all of their access to these energies ended when Adam and Eve went into default of the divine plan that had been set before them in Paradise.

Caligastia was able to succeed in his evil plan to entrap Eve, but he failed in his attempt to lead Adam and Eve into joining the Lucifer Rebellion. Adam and Eve both fell from their high status of being a Material Son and Daughter down to the lowly status of being a mortal man on earth because of sin. But it was not the fall of man on earth, because humanity on earth were still racially uplifted by Adam and Eve despite their default in completing their mission. Although the divine plan of giving the infusion of the Violet race strain to the people on earth miscarried, the mortal races now living on earth have still profited enormously from the limited contributions that Adam, Eve and their descendants made and gave to the evolutionary races living on earth. There has not been a fall of mankind on earth, because the history of the human race has been one of a steady progressive evolution and the Adamic bestowal left earth and its people greatly improved over their previous biologic living conditions. The more superior strains of the races who now live on earth now contain the inheritance factors that came from four of the original races from India, which are the Andonite, Sangik, Nodite and the Adamic.

Adam and Eve are not the cause or reason of a curse on the human race on earth, because while Adam and Eve did fail to carry out the divine plan and degraded and transgressed their covenant with Paradise, their contributions to the human race still did a lot to help advance civilization on earth.

When Adam and Eve arrived on earth over 37,000 years ago, we have to recognize the condition of the planet. Adam was confronted with an extremely hard hopeless task when with his beautiful mate Eve, they were transported from Jerusem to a dark and confused planet earth. However, Adam and Eve were both guided well to complete their mission on earth by the Melchizedeks and their associates and if they had been just a little bit more patient, they would have eventually been successful in completing their mission on earth. Instead, Eve chose to listen to the evil plan of Caligastia about personal liberty and freedom. Eve was misled to experiment with the life plasm of a Nodite and she tried to mix and commingle it prematurely without her mate and without following the original design of the Life Carriers from Paradise. You never gain anything by impatiently attempting to circumvent the established divine plan with short cuts, and personal inventions. We are all part of a gigantic creation, and it is not strange that everything does not work in perfection, because perfection is our eternal goal and not our origin.

When Adam made the decision to leave the first Garden of Eden, he and the Eden dwellers could not go west, because they didn't have any boats that were adequate for them to all travel in. Their caravan was not able to travel to the north, because the northern Nodites were on their trail from the north and they could not travel south, because the hills of that region were infested with many hostile tribes. So, the only route they could safely take was east, so they continued their journey on eastward towards the region between the Tigris and Euphrates Rivers and many of those who were left behind by Adam later traveled eastward to join the Adamites in the new second Garden of Eden that was located in the Tigris and Euphrates region.

Cain who was Eve's son from the deceased Nodite spiritual leader Cano and Sansa, Adam's daughter from his thirty-day affair with Laotta, the Nodite school teacher were both born before Adam's caravan reached its new home in the Tigris and Euphrates area. Laotta died giving birth to her daughter Sansa and Eve also suffered greatly giving birth to her son Cain, but she survived. Eve raised Cain and Sansa together and Sansa grew up to be a great woman and she became to be the wife of Sargan, the chief of the northern Blue races and she helped to contribute to the advancement of the Blue race during those times. It took almost one year for Adam's caravan to reach their new home and to build the second Garden of Eden at the Euphrates River location. When the word began to spread across the area that Adam and Eve's caravan was coming their way, the dwellers of the land fled in haste to the nearby mountains and when Adam and his caravan arrived, he found that the entire territory had been vacated.

Adam and his followers immediately began working on building new homes and a new center for culture and religion. This new home site that Adam and his followers chose had been one of the three original locations that Van and Amadon had considered to build the first Garden of Eden on.

This second Garden of Eden location had to be built by Adam and his followers from the ground up from the labor of his own hands. Less than two years after Cain's birth, his half-brother Abel was born in the second Garden of Eden. When Abel grew up, he decided to be a herder, while Cain chose to work in agriculture. The custom in those days was to make offerings to the priesthood and the herders would offer their flocks while the farmers would always offer their harvests from the fields. Cain and Abel argued many times about whose vocation was the best and Abel always pointed out to Cain that his animal sacrifices were accepted over his fruit and vegetable sacrifices. Cain was only trying to follow the traditions of the first Garden of Eden by using the fruits and vegetables for his sacrifices, but Abel continued to tease and taunt Cain about his fruit and vegetable sacrifices.

In the first Garden of Eden Adam discouraged animal sacrifices, but it was difficult for Adam to organize the religious customs in the second Eden, because he was heavily burdened with the work of building, defense and agriculture. At this time, Adam was also very depressed spiritually, so he entrusted the organization of worship and education to the Nodites who were living with them in the second Eden, and the Nodite priests in the second Eden had reverted back to the practice of animal sacrifices.

Cain and Abel never really got along very well, and the issue of sacrifices contributed to the growing hatred that existed between them, because Abel knew that he was the natural son of Adam, and Abel continuously reminded Cain that he was not from the pure line of the new Violet race like he was, and that Adam was not his natural father. All of these factors caused Cain to feel an ever-increasing hatred towards his half-brother Abel. One day Abel's taunts so infuriated Cain that he turned on Abel in a fit of rage and killed him. Adam and Eve knew that Abel was dead when his dogs brought his entire herd home without him. Cain had fast been becoming to Adam and Eve a grim reminder of their prior sin and they supported Cain's decision to leave the second Garden of Eden.

Cain's life in the second Garden of Eden had not been a happy one, because he daily reminded Adam and Eve of their default in the first Eden and as Cain was leaving the second Eden, he knew that since he bore no tribal mark, that he would be killed by the first neighboring tribe he encountered. Cain had not yet been indwelled by a Divine Thought Adjuster and he had always been defiant of Adam and Eve's discipline and religion. But when Cain killed his half-brother Abel, he went to his mother Eve asked her for spiritual help and guidance and when he did this, he was immediately at that moment indwelt by his Divine Thought Adjuster. Cain's indwelling in his mind by his Divine Thought Adjuster gave Cain a new distinct advantage of superiority which then classified him finally as a member of the great tribe of Adam.

Cain continued to journey to the land of Nod which was just east of the second Eden and Cain became to be a great leader among his late father Cano's tribe of people, the

Nodites where he helped to promote peace between the Nodites and Adamites during his lifetime. Cain married his distant cousin Remona, and their first-born son Enoch became to be the leader of the Elamite Nodites and for hundreds of years the Elamites and the Adamites continued to live in peace.

As time passed in the second Eden the consequences of Adam and Eve's default became to be more apparent, because they both missed their former home of beauty and tranquility that they had in the first Eden. Adam spent most of his time training his children and his followers in the areas of civil administration, education and religious devotions. The civil rulers of the Adamites descended from the hereditary sons from the first Eden and Adam's first-born son Adamson was the founder of the center of the Violet race that was just north of the second Eden and Adam's second son Everson became the master leader and administrator for the Violet race center. Everson turned out to be a great helper to his father Adam and Everson's oldest son Jansad succeeded Adam as the head of the Adamite tribes.

All of the religious rulers and priests originated with Adam's oldest surviving son Seth who was born in the second Eden and Seth was born one hundred and twenty-nine years after Adam arrived on earth. Seth grew up and became to be the head of the priesthood in the second Eden and his son Enos founded a new order of worship and his grandson Kenan instituted the first foreign missionary service who ministered to the surrounding tribes both near and far. These Sethite priests taught in their ministry, religion, health and education and the Sethite priests were also trained to officiate at various religious ceremonies, they served as physicians, worked as sanitary inspectors and teachers in the second Garden of Eden.

Adam's caravan to their new home on the Euphrates River carried hundreds of seeds, plants, bulbs and cereals from the first Eden with them along with extensive herds and all of their domesticated animals. The eating of meat became to be a custom in the second Garden of Eden, but Adam and Eve nor any of their children never became to be meat eaters.

The Adamites did very well working with the surrounding tribes who lived near the second Eden, and they were able to achieve many cultural and intellectual developments with their neighboring tribes and many of their art projects turned out to be the forerunner of our modern art, science and literature. Here in this new land, the Adamites were able to teach their surrounding tribes the arts of writing, metalworking, pottery making, weaving and they were able to produce a new kind of architecture that has not been seen on earth again for thousands of years.

The home life of for Adam and Eve's Violet race of children was an ideal place of learning for their children. The Adamite children were trained in agriculture, craftsmanship, domestication of animals and their male children were educated to perform the duties of a Sethite priest, physician and teacher. Adam and Eve were the founders of the new Violet race on earth and their offspring had blue eyes, a fair complexion and light hair colors of yellow, red and brown. Eve and the early evolutionary women initially did not suffer pain during childbirth and not until they began to mix and blend with the Nodites that the severe pangs of childbirth began to appear in Adamite women.

Adam and Eve and the rest of their second Eden brethren were energized by a dual nutrition that consisted of food, light and certain superphysical unrevealed energies from earth, but Adam and Eve's offspring who were born on earth did not inherit their parents' special endowments of energy intake and light circulation. All of Adam and Eve's children had a single circulation system, normal human type blood and their bodies were designed for them to live as normal human mortals. The first generation of Adam and Eve's children's diet consisted of fruit and cereals and after the first generation all of their descendants began to eat a dairy diet, but still no consumption of meat. Many of the southern tribes later united with the Adamites and they also stopped eating meat, and these same tribes later migrated to the land now known as India.

Both the physical and spiritual visions of Adam and Eve were far superior compared to the rest of the people who lived during their times and their special senses were more keen, because they were able to see the midway beings, the angelic hosts, the Melchizedek Sons and Caligastia the fallen planetary prince while the rest of humanity was not able to see any of these beings who were living amongst them on planet earth. Adam and Eve were able to retain their special senses for over one hundred years after their default and these special senses seemed to diminish with each succeeding generation.

All of Adam and Eve's children were indwelt by Divine Thought Adjusters and they didn't have any fear inside themselves like the rest of the humans had. Also, the cells inside of the bodies of Adam and Eve's offspring were far more resistant to the disease producing microscopic organisms that existed on earth, and this is because the cells in the human bodies are just like the living disease producing microscopic organisms that live on earth and humans always have to do so much to constantly withstand so many physical disorders and diseases.

After Adam and Eve became established in the second Eden, Adam made the decision to leave behind as much of his life plasm as possible to try to help to continue to uplift humanity on earth as much as he could after his death.

Adam selected Eve to be the head of the commission of twelve to improve the racial relations among the different tribes and before Adam died this commission had selected 1,682 of the highest racial strains of women living on earth to participate in their racial uplift project. These women were then impregnated with the Adamic plasm and the offspring of these 1,682 women all except 112 of them grew up to maturity. So, in the end, this commission did its job to help earth to benefit by the addition of 1,570 superior strains of men and women on earth. The 1,682 candidate mothers were selected by Eve from all of the surrounding tribes, and they represented most of the races living on earth and the majority of those selected superior women were chosen from the highest strains of the Nodites tribes and they were the beginning of the mighty Andite race and these superior Violet race strains of children were born and raised in their own tribal surroundings with their mother.

Not long after Adam and Eve established the second Eden in the Euphrates area, they were informed by the twelve Melchizedek Receiver Sons who were now once again managing the world affairs on planet earth that their repentance for their default was acceptable and because they would both die as mortal beings that they were eligible for admission to the ranks of sleeping survivors from earth. Adam and Eve both fully believed in the gospel of the resurrection and rehabilitation that the Melchizedeks had proclaimed to them, because both of their transgressions had been an error of judgement on their part and not a deliberate sin of conscious or a deliberate rebellion.

Adam and Eve did not receive their indwelt Divine Thought Adjusters until they began their mortal life in the second Garden of Eden and they both felt this new presence within them which heartened them throughout the rest of their lives on earth. Adam and Eve both knew that they had failed as a Material Son and Material Daughter on earth, but they were glad to know that their Paradise career was still open to them as ascending mortal sons of the universe on the road to Paradise. Adam was aware about the dispensational resurrection that occurred simultaneously, and he believed that he and Eve would be repersonalized with the next order of sonship going to Paradise. What Adam didn't know was that Michael of Nebadon would soon be completing his seventh and final bestowal on planet earth as the incarnation of Jesus of Nazareth, and instead Adam thought that the next Creator Son to appear on planet earth would be from the Avonal Order in Paradise. Adam and Eve were very happy when they received a personal message from Michael of Nebadon that stated that he remembered the desire of their hearts to forever be loyal to their Father's divine will and that they would both be called from their mortal slumber when Michael of Nebadon completes his seventh and final bestowal on earth if the subordinate sons of Paradise don't send for you both before Michael of Nebadon's arrival as Jesus of Nazareth. This personal message they received from Michael of Nebadon was hard for Adam and Eve to understand, especially the promise of their special resurrection.

So, Adam and Eve both believed that they would be able to rest until this special resurrection occurred and Adam's biggest hope was that the strife torn earth would turn out in the end to be the most fortunate world out of all the six hundred and seven planets in the entire system of Satania.

Adam lived to be 530 years old, and he died of what we call the natural causes of old age, because his physical mechanisms simply wore out and the process of disintegration gradually gained on the process of repair and the end of Adam's life came. Eve had already died nineteen years earlier of heart failure and they were both buried in the center of the temple of divine service and their burial was the origin of the practice of burying famous and pious men and women under the floors of their house of worship. The super material government of earth under the direction of the twelve Melchizedek Receiver Sons continued, but their direct physical contact with the evolutionary human races on earth was severed.

The next comprehensive plan to improve the far-reaching world welfare of humanity did not occur again on earth until the arrival of Machiventa Melchizedek during the times of Abraham, who with the power, patience and authority of a Son of God laid down the foundations to further uplift and help with the spiritual rehabilitation of planet earth.

Misfortune has not always been the sole lot on earth, and in fact, earth has been one of the most fortunate planets in our local universe of Nebadon. But because of all the blunders and mistakes that earth's early rulers made, their actions plunged earth into such a hopeless state of confusion, that planet earth who by the way is a living consciousness with a heartbeat just like we humans are, appealed to Michael of Nebadon to please incarnate on earth to complete his seventh and final bestowal as Jesus of Nazareth to help to raise the light quotient and vibrations of the planet.

Adam and Eve went to their mortal rest with the strong belief and faith in the promises that were made to them by the Creator Son Michael of Nebadon and the Melchizedeks and they did not have to rest long in the oblivion of their unconscious sleep with the rest of the transitioned mortals from earth. On the third day after Adam's death, the second after his burial, the orders of Lanaforge of Paradise directed a special roll call for all of the distinguished survivors of the Adam default on planet earth, and with this mandate for a special resurrection, Adam and Eve were both repersonalized and reassembled in the resurrection hall on the mansion world of Satania, Paradise along with 1,316 survivors of the Garden of Eden. Adam and Eve quickly passed through the worlds of progressive ascension, and they attained their citizenship once again on Jerusem, Paradise.

Once Adam and Eve attained their citizenship once again in Jerusem they were then assigned their membership among the twenty-four counselors who served on the advisory controlling body of planet earth. Adam and Eve while living on earth made a mighty contribution to the civilizations and accelerated the biologic progress of the evolutionary races on earth. They left a great culture on earth, but it is always the people who in the end make a great civilization, because civilization does not make the people.

The northern Nodites were the descendants of the group of people who rejected the leadership of Nod and instead decided to follow Van and Amadon during the Lucifer Rebellion. Some of the early followers of Van settled down along the shores of the lake that still bears Van's name, and their traditions grew from accepting the spiritual leadership of Van and Amadon. Ararat became to be the sacred mountain for the northern Nodites and it had the same meaning to the later day Vanites that Mount Sinai later meant to the Hebrews. Ten thousand years ago the Vanite ancestors of the Assyrians taught their people that their moral law of seven commandments had been given to Van by the Gods who lived on Mount Ararat and the Nodites firmly believed that both Van and Amadon the two heroes of the Lucifer Rebellion were taken alive from earth while they were engaged in worship on Mount Ararat back home to Paradise. Mount Ararat was the sacred mountain in the northern Mesopotamian region and it's no surprise that this same Mount Ararat and its region was later woven into the Hebrew story of Noah and the great flood on earth.

About 35,000 years ago, Adam and Eve's oldest son Adamson visited one of the eastern parts of the old Vanite settlements that he had found in the center of his current civilization. Adamson was among the groups of the children of Adam and Eve who had made the choice to remain on earth with his mother and father. Adamson had often heard from Van and Amadon about the story of their highland home in the north and after the establishment of the second Eden, Adamson was determined to go and find this land from his youthful dreams. Adamson was 120 years old by this time and he was the father of thirty-two pure line Violet race children who had been born in the first Garden of Eden. Adamson chose to remain on earth with his parents Adam and Eve and he continued to help his parents to build the second Eden. However, at the same time Adamson was greatly disturbed because his mate had made the choice to return to Paradise with his thirty-six children on the seraphic angel transport after the default of Adam and Eve. Adamson didn't want to desert his parents, but he was never happy living in the second Eden, and he began to make plans to move north to begin a new life as soon as possible.

Adamson's departure from the second Garden of Eden was pleasant, but Adam and Eve were very sad that their oldest son was leaving them, especially since he was going out to a strange and hostile area, and they were both afraid that Adamson would never return.

Adamson left his home from the second Garden of Eden with a caravan of twenty-seven people in his quest to fulfill his childhood fantasy and it took a little over three years for his caravan to reach their destination and one of the first people Adamson met who was a wonderful and beautiful twenty year old woman who stated that she was the last pure line descendant of the former fallen Planetary Prince Caligastia's staff of the one hundred superhumans This woman's name was Ratta and she told Adamson that her ancestors were all descendants of two of the fallen staff of Caligastia. Ratta was the last of her race, because she had no brothers or sisters. Ratta had decided not to mate, and she had made up her mind to die single and alone, but she quickly lost her heart to the majestic man Adamson. When Adamson told Ratta the story about the two Garden of Edens and how all of the predictions of Van and Amadon had really come to pass, she continued to listen as Adamson explained the default of the First Garden of Eden and Ratta was having one single thought while Adamson was talking to her, and it was to marry Adamson, the oldest son and heir to Adam and Eve and Ratta's idea of marriage quickly grew on Adamson too and they were married within three months.

Adamson and Ratta had a family of sixty-seven children and their offspring were the origin to a great line of earth's leadership and their marriage did something even more. Since Adamson and Ratta were both really superhuman beings, every fourth child who was born to them was of a unique order, it was invisible and never in the history of all the world had such a thing ever happened. Ratta was dismayed by this, but Adamson was well aware of the existence of primary midway beings, so when their second unique offspring was born, Adamson decided to mate one male and one female offsprings and this was the origin of the secondary order of midway beings on planet earth. Within one hundred years before this phenomenon ceased, almost two thousand secondary midway beings were brought into being on planet earth.

Adamson lived for 396 years and every seven years he and Ratta would travel to the second Garden of Eden to visit with his parents Adam and Eve. All of the secondary midway beings kept Adamson informed on the welfare of his people and they also did a great service by upbuilding a new and independent world center of truth and righteousness. Adamson and Ratta were able to maintain a high culture for almost seven thousand years and due to the assistance, they received from their marvelous corps of the secondary midway beings who worked with them all throughout their long lives they were able to advance the truth and spread a higher standard of spiritual, intellectual and physical way of life for humanity living on earth. Some of the advances that were achieved through the accomplishments of Adamson and Ratta was the mixing of the Nodite and Andonite tribes which helped to produce the race called the mighty men of old. And many of the advances they made later blossomed into the later European civilizations.

The center of the civilization that Adamson and Ratta established was located in the region near the southern end of the Caspian Sea. A short way up in the foothills of Turkey is where Adamson's world headquarters for the Violet race was located. Four diverse cultures grew from these headquarters that originated from four different groups of Adamson's descendants. The second of these four groups migrated to Greece and to the islands located in the Mediterranean Sea. The last of Adamson and Ratta's descendants migrated north and west to Europe where they blended with the last of the stock of the Andite tribes who had come from out of the Mesopotamia region and this group also included the Andite-Aryan group who came from India.

The primary midway beings have a superhuman origin, while the secondary midways beings were the offspring of the pure line Violet race stock from Adamson and Ratta, Adam and Eve's oldest son. The primary midway beings are always the first group of inhabitants on all of the sixty-one experimental worlds in the Satania system. There are various orders of celestial beings who are also assigned from Paradise to work and minister on a planet and these midway beings actually live on the inhabited worlds where they are assigned to serve and work on. The seraphim angels come and go, but the midway beings remain, and they serve as ministers, provide harmony and connect with the changing administrations of the seraphic angelic hosts.

Midway beings are actual citizens of planet earth, and they have a personal interest in the destiny of our planet and its ongoing progress. Midway beings all have the ability to traverse the energy circuits and leave earth anytime they want, but their pledge and promise is not to leave a planet until they are released by the superuniverse authorities. Midway beings are anchored on the planet thy are assigned to until it ascends and is settled in the age of light and life.

With the exception of Midway 1-2-3 the first, no loyal midway being has ever left planet earth yet. Midway 1-2-3 the first, the oldest of the superhuman primary midway beings who was assigned to live and work on planet earth was released by the superuniverse officials from his duties on earth right after Pentecost Sunday 1,954 years go. This early release from earth that was issued to Midway being 1-2-3 the first was due to the fact that he stood strong and firm with loyalty to Van and Amadon all throughout the tragic times of the Lucifer Rebellion and his fearless leadership helped to reduce many causalities amongst the primary midway beings in his order. Midway being 1-2-3 the first now lives and works in Paradise as a member of the twenty-four counselors for ascending mortals from the worlds of time and space.

Primary midway beings are brought into existence fully developed and they do not experience any more further growth or development after they reach maturity, but they never cease to grow in wisdom and experience. Midway beings are just like mortal evolutionary humans and there are many of these great minds and mighty spirits who have been here since the beginning and still are living on planet earth. The midway beings' culture is the product of immortal planetary citizenship and while generations of humans on earth forget, these corps of midway beings remember, and these memories are a treasure for the traditions of those who are living on earth. The primary midway beings help to retain the memories of the culture on a planet and in the right circumstances many treasured memories of past events are available such as the story of the life and teachings about Jesus of Nazareth that have been retained and given to mankind by the midway beings who are still living on earth.

The primary midway beings are the skillful ministers who help to compensate for the gap that exists between the material and spiritual affairs of earth. The primary midway beings are humanity's comrades during our long ascension journey to attain a settled status of light and life on earth. Because of the valuable work that is performed by the midway beings living on earth, they have proven since the times of earth's first planetary prince to be an essential part of the spirit economy of our realm.

There were unfortunately some rebel primary midway beings who fell into sin and joined the Lucifer Rebellion 200,000 years ago on earth and when the devastation of this planetary rebellion on earth occurred, out of the original 50,000 primary midway beings who were assigned to work on planet earth, 40,119 joined Caligastia in this rebellion. The original number of secondary midway beings who were living on earth during the rebellion was 1,984 and 873 joined the rebellion. Both groups of the midway beings who joined the Lucifer Rebellion are now being held in custody awaiting the final adjudication of the affairs of the system wide Lucifer Rebellion.

These disloyal midway beings were able to reveal themselves to the mortals living on earth under certain circumstances, especially the midway beings who were the associates of Beelzebub, the lord of the flies, bugs and the leader of the secondary midway beings and these disloyal midway beings did many strange things on earth prior to earth's present planetary dispensations. This unique group of disloyal midway beings are not to be confused with the rebel cherubim and seraphim (fallen angels) who were also living on earth up to the time of the death and resurrection of Jesus of Nazareth. These rebellious midway beings were referred to as evil spirits, demons and along with the rebel seraphim and cherubim angels were designated as evil fallen angels.

Before the days of Jesus of Nazareth on earth and before the universal appearance of the Divine Thought Adjusters and the pouring out of the pure spirit of Jesus of Nazareth on all humanity on earth, these rebel midway beings were actually able to negatively influence the minds of certain inferior humans and somewhat control their actions. They were able to do this in much the same way that the loyal midway beings work as efficient contact guardians of the human minds of the earth reserve corps of destiny during the times when the Divine Thought Adjusters detaches from the human personality during the times of contact with superhuman intelligences. The casting out of demons from humans since the arrival of Jesus of Nazareth has been a matter of the confounding belief in demonic possession along with hysteria, insanity, and feeble mindedness and just because Jesus forever liberated all human minds from demonic possession on Pentecost Sunday, don't think that this was not a reality during the times before Jesus came to earth. Jesus of Nazareth knew and was able to recognize the difference between insanity and demonic possession, although these two states of the human mind are still being confused in the minds of those living in our present generation.

The entire group of rebel midway beings who fell into sin on earth are now being held as prisoners by the orders of the Most Highs in Paradise and they are no longer able to roam on earth bent on mischief and since the day of Pentecost Sunday, there will never again on earth be such a thing as demonic possession.

The entire current organization of the high spirits, angelic hosts and primary midway beings are now all devoted to the furthering of the Paradise plan for the progressive ascension and Paradise attainment for all evolutionary mortals. The business of the universe is to support the survival plan of bringing God down to earth to humanity and then by a sublime partnership of carrying man back up to God and onward to eternity in Paradise.

The second Garden of Eden was the cradle of civilization for almost thirty thousand years, because the Adamic people were dedicated to work in their mission to uplift the races of humanity and from this region in Mesopotamia, the Nodites, the Sangik races and the Andonites all helped to accelerate the cultural progress of humanity on earth.

The beginning of the eighth race on earth, the Violet race began when Adam and Eve arrived on earth 35,000 years ago. The minds and morals of humanity on earth at this time were at a low level when Adam and Eve arrived, but the physical evolution of man had gone on quite unaffected by the folly of the Lucifer Rebellion and Adam and Eve's contribution to the biologic uplifting status of the human races helped enormously to up step the eight human races on planet earth. During these times there existed certain centers of civilization, but most of earth was still steeped in savagery.

305

Thirty-five thousand years ago planet earth at large had very little culture and these are some of the centers of civilization that existed here and there on earth during these times.

The Violet race was the eighth race to appear that originated from the family of Adam and Eve and his oldest son Adamson and it was the main center of the Adamite culture that was located in the first and second Garden of Eden. The second Eden was located in the triangle of the Tigris and Euphrates River in Mesopotamia and this region was the center of the Occidental and Indian civilizations. The secondary northern center of the Violet race was the Adamsonite World Headquarters that was established by Adamson and his wife Ratta that was located on the southern shores of the Caspian Sea.

The Sumerians and the Nodites also lived in the Mesopotamian region, and they were the remnants of the ancient culture from the Dalmatia days of Van and Amadon and as time passed this group mixed with the Adamites who lived to the north, but they never lost their Nodite traditions. Various other Nodite tribes also settled in this region, and they were later absorbed by the ever-expanding Violet race.

The Adonite tribes lived five to six settlements to the north and east of the Adamson World Headquarters and they were also scattered throughout Turkey and these aborigines' tribes also migrated to the Eurasian continent, Iceland, Greenland and as time passed, they were driven out of Europe by the Blue race and out of Asia by the Yellow race.

The Red man lived in total isolation in America after being driven out of Asia for fighting all the time amongst themselves over fifty thousand years before the arrival of Adam and Eve arrived on earth 35,000 years later.

The Yellow man was a well-established peaceful race, and they were in control of eastern Asia. Their most advanced settlements were located in northwest China in the area bordering Tibet.

The Blue man was scattered all over Europe and their centers of culture were located in the Mediterranean basin and in northwestern Europe. The Blue race was by far the most aggressive, adventurous and exploratory of all the races on earth.

Pre-Dravidian India was a blend of complex mixtures of races that included almost every race on earth, especially the Green, Orange and Indigo races.

The Sahara civilization was the superior strain of the Indigo-Black race, and they lived in the Sahara Desert region and this Indigo-Black racial group carried extensive strains of the Orange and Green races.

The Mediterranean basin was the most highly blended race outside of India and the Blue man from the north continued to mix and blend with the Nodites and Adamites who lived to the east.

This was the picture and landscape of planet earth before the beginning of the great expansion of the Violet race about 25,000 years ago. The hopes for a future progressive civilization on earth existed in the second Garden of Eden in Mesopotamia, because here was the potential to develop and expand a great new civilization on earth.

Adam and Eve left behind a potent progeny and all the celestial observers who were living on earth anxiously waited to see how the descendants of Adam and Eve would evolve. For thousands of years the descendants of Adam and Eve worked hard along the rivers of the Mesopotamia region on their irrigation projects, flood control, perfecting their defense systems and continuing to preserve their traditions of the glory of the first Garden of Eden. The dwellers of the second Garden of Eden never lost sight of the purpose of Adam and Eve's original mission, and they continued to send their sons and daughters out in steady streams as emissaries and missionary spiritual teachers to all of the evolutionary races who were living on earth.

The civilization, society and cultural status of the Adamites was far above the levels of the evolutionary races who were living on earth during their times and the prior old settlements of Van and Amadon were the only other civilizations that were comparable. However, the civilization that existed in the second Garden of Eden was artificially built structures and because it had not yet evolved, it was doomed to deteriorate until it reached a natural evolutionary level.

Adam and Eve left a great intellectual and spiritual culture behind, but their culture was not advanced enough in the areas of mechanical appliances and after the deaths of

Adam and Eve their traditions began to grow dim and the cultural levels of the Adamites were gradually in balance with the same status of the surrounding tribes and with the natural evolving cultural capacities of their new Violet race. The Adamites grew to become a real nation around the year 19,000 BC and they had a population of about five million people who were still in the process of pouring forth their culture out into their neighboring tribes.

The Violet race which began with Adam and Eve retained its traditions for millions of years and when they suffered from population pressures instead of starting wars to secure more territory, they instead sent their excess people out as teachers and missionaries to the outlying tribes and this absorption of these Adamic teachers, traders, explorers and missionaries was biologically invigorating to their surrounding tribes.

About 25,000 years ago many of the purer strains of the Adamites began to migrate to the north and the more north they traveled they became less and less Adamic until by the time they reached Turkey they were mixed more with the Nodites and as a result very few pure line Violet people made it into Europe or Asia. From the time period of 30,000 BC to 10,000 BC there was a lot of racial blending taking place all throughout southwestern Asia. Most of the culture of Van and Amadon still existed in northwest India and the superior races of culture and character were continuing to be absorbed by the northward moving Adamites.

The early Adamite migrations ended about 15,000 B C and during this time there were more descendants of Adam living in central Asia than anywhere else in the world.

By this time the European Blue races had been largely infiltrated and absorbed. The lands of Russia and Turkey had people living there who had racial mixtures of Nodites, Andonites, Red, Yellow Sangiks, Orange men, Green men, Indigo-Black men and a sprinkle of Andonite stock. Asia Minor and central eastern Europe was heavily populated by mostly the Andonite tribes.

A blended colored race of people were living in Egypt and the Indigo-Black people continued to migrate farther south in Africa and just like the Red man who were living in the Americas, both of these races were isolated from the rest of the known world. The Saharan civilization was disrupted by a drought and the annual Mediterranean basin floods. The Blue races who were living in this region still had failed to develop an advanced culture and the Andonites were still scattered over the Artic and Asian regions, The Green and Orange races had by this time both been annihilated. These racial distributions on earth along with the extreme climate changes set the world stage for the beginning of the Andite era of civilization on earth and these early migrations lasted for about 10,000 years from the time period of 25,000 to 15,000 B C and the later Andite migrations lasted from 15,000 to 6,000 B C.

It took so long for the earlier waves of Adamites to pass over Eurasia that most of their culture was lost during transit. The later migrating Andites were able to travel with more sufficient speed and they were able to retain their culture from the second Garden of Eden from their origin of the Mesopotamia pure line Violet race and the Nodites along with the evolutionary races.

The Andite race has the largest percentage of the Adamic Violet race strain than any other of the current modern races living on earth and the Andite race means that your racial mixture is from one-eight to one-sixth of the Violet race and most of the modern people living on earth today even the northern white races contain much less than either of this percentage of the blood of the Violet race strain from Adam and Eve.

The earliest Andite people originated in the Mesopotamia region more than 25,000 years ago from the original blending of the Adamites with the Nodites. The second Garden of Eden was surrounded by concentric circles of diminishing Violet blood and this racial melting pot was the origin of the Andite stock. Later on, when the migrating Adamites and Nodites entered into Turkey, they soon blended with these superior tribes and the result was the extension of the Andite race further northward. The Andites were the best human racial stock to ever appear on earth since the days of the pure line Violet race who came from the original Adam and Eve family. The Nodite race had the superior racial strains of the most highest types of the surviving remnants of the Adamite, Nodite, Yellow, Blue and Green races of men. The early Andites were not white or Aryan, however, it is the Andite inheritance that gave the polygot mixture of the so-called White race that is now being called the Caucasian race.

The purer strains of the Violet race retained their traditions of peace seeking just like all of their earlier race movements had been. But as the Adamites began to unite with the Nodites their descendants soon began to evolve to be the most skillful militarists to ever live on earth and their migrations began to change to be more military in nature and they soon turned from migrating to conquering and these militant tribes of Andites had more roving and adventurous dispositions than their predecessors had. However, the increase of mixing the Sangik or Andonite racial strains with the Andites seemed to calm and stabilize their character. Despite the best efforts to calm the behavior of the Andite tribes down, their later descendants didn't stop until they had navigated and explored the entire earth including the remote continents.

The culture of the second Garden of Eden lasted for over twenty thousand years but is started to experience a steady decline after this time period and by 12,000 B.C. three quarters of the Andite race were living in northern and eastern Europe and their final migration from Mesopotamia moved over sixty-five percent of the Andites into Europe.

The Andites tribes also migrated to China and India, and many were missionaries, teachers and traders. These Andites were later called Dravidians and Aryans, the conquerors of India. Many of these same tribes migrated to China by traveling through Sinkiang and Tibet and they added desirable qualities to the Chinese racial strains.

From time to time some small groups of Andites migrated to Japan, Formosa, East Indies and to southern China and one day a small group of about one hundred and thirty-two Andites left in a small fleet of small boats from Japan, and they eventually reached South America and through intermarriages with the natives of the Andes, they established the origins of the later rulers of the Inca race. This same group of Andite sailors also traveled across the Pacific Ocean where they stopped along the way on many Polynesian islands that are now in our current times submerged underwater. One of their stops was Easter Island which was established as a religious and administrative center for the Andite tribes. One hundred and thirty-two of these same group of Andites who crossed the Pacific Ocean long ago were finally able to reach the mainland of the Americas and these migrations-conquests by the Andite tribes continued on down to their final dispersions from 8,000 B C to 6,000 B C.

When the Andite tribes first left their home in Mesopotamia, they continued to deplete the biologic reserves of their homeland, while at the same time, they continued to strengthen the surrounding tribes that they encountered along the way. Every nation the Andite tribe traveled to, they made positive contributions to the existing cultures through humor, art, music, adventure, manufacturing, agriculture and skillful animal domestication procedures. The Andite tribes' presence also helped to improve the religious and moral practices of the older evolutionary races and this culture from the second Garden of Eden quietly continued to spread all over Europe, India, China, northern Africa and the Pacific Islands.

The last three waves of Andites migrating from the Mesopotamia region happened between the time period of 8,000 B C until 6,000 B C and these last three migrations happened after the last remaining Andites were forced out of Mesopotamia by the invasion of the hill tribes who lived to the east and from the constant harassment from the plainsmen tribes who lived to the west. During these final migrations the Andite tribe traveled in several different directions. Sixty-five percent of the migrating Andite tribe members entered into Europe by crossing the Caspian Sea and their plan once they reached Europe was to conquer and racially blend with the new White men who were the racial blend of the Blue race with the earlier Andite races.

Ten percent including a large group of Sethite priests moved eastward to Iran and Turkey and many of their descendants were later driven into India to live with their Aryan brothers who had moved their earlier from the north. Ten percent of the Andites from Mesopotamia migrated eastward and entered into Sinkiang where they soon racially blended with the Yellow race inhabitants who lived in this region and the majority of their descendants later migrated to China and gave considerable improvements to the Yellow race.

Ten percent of the final migrations of the fleeing Andite tribes from their Mesopotamia home had the travel to Arabia where they entered into the land of Egypt and five percent of the Andites who lived in the coastal district between the Tigris and Euphrates Rivers had always been free from any intermarriages with the neighboring tribes and they refused to leave their Mesopotamia home. This last group of Andites represented the last surviving superior racial strain of the Nodite and Adamic racial strains. By the year 6,000 B.C. the entire Andite tribe had almost entirely left the entire Mesopotamia region but their descendants who had mixed with the surrounding Sangik races and with the Andite tribes of Asia Minor were still living in the Mesopotamia region destined to engage in battles with the northern and eastern invaders at a much later date in time.

The cultural age of the second Garden of Eden was terminated by the increasing infiltration of the surrounding tribes and this constant unchecked influx of invasions prepared the way for the later total conquest of all of the Mesopotamia region by the northern barbarians who finally drove out the last residual strains of the Andite tribe.

The river dwellers were used to rivers overflowing their riverbanks during certain seasons and these seasonal floods were annual events in their lives. For thousands of years after the first Garden of Eden was submerged underwater, the mountains along the east, northwest and northeast continued to rise. This elevation of the highlands greatly accelerated around the year 5,000 B C and along with increased snowfall in the northern mountains, this caused flooding to occur every spring in the Euphrates valley and these spring floods began to become to be so bad that the inhabitants of these river regions had to move to the eastern highland section of the Euphrates River for almost one thousand years. This annual flooding caused many of the cities in this region to become deserted due to the extensive damages that were caused by these floods. Almost five thousand years later while the Hebrews were in Babylonian captivity for five hundred years, the Hebrew rabbis began to write many stories to try to uplift the spirits of the Hebrew people during these hard times and some of these Hebrew rabbis made the decision to write the story that the whole world would soon drown in its sins and wickedness at the time of Noah's flood, and by doing this, it put the Jewish rabbis in a better position to trace Abraham as being one of the surviving descendants of Noah. The traditions on earth of a time when water covered the entire surface of the earth is a universal story and all cultures have written their version of this great event. Many of the different cultures on earth all tell the same story about a Great Flood of planet earth. In prior times earth had been completely covered with water was during the Archeozoic Age which was before land began to appear on the surface of the earth.

There was an Andite man also named Noah who lived on earth during the times of this flood, and he was a wine maker of Aram, a river settlement near Erech. Noah kept a written record of the days of the river's rise along the banks from year to year. Everyone in Noah's village of Aram laughed and made fun of Noah when he advised all of his neighbors up and down the river valley to build all of their homes our of wood in a houseboat design to protect themselves and their domesticated livestock.

Noah also kept on warning all of the settlers in his village to put all of their livestock inside of their wooden houseboats every night because the annual flood season was fast approaching. Noah continued to go to all of the neighboring river settlements every year and warn them that in so many days the annual floods for their area were on the way. But, every year all of the Noah's neighbors in the nearby settlements continued to laugh and make fun of his warnings, but finally the annual flood was a little higher than usual due to heavy rainfall and the sudden rise of these flood waters wiped out the entire village of Aram and Noah, his immediate family and their livestock were the only survivors, because they were all protected in their wooden houseboat.

These annual floods finally completed the disruptions of the Andite civilization and in addition to this flood destroying Noah's village of Aram, it was also the end of the second Garden of Eden and the remnants of the old days of Dalmatia with Van and Amadon their followers and the first Garden of Eden were all submerged underwater in the eastern end of the Mediterranean Sea and in the Persian Gulf region.

The Sumerians were the last of the Andite culture to live in the Mesopotamia region, because they remained in their homeland after everyone else had left living near the mouth of the Tigris and Euphrates Rivers and they continued to follow the old traditions of Van and Amadon from Dalmatia. During the times of the flooding in this region, these Sumerian Nodites still continued to prosper and the lower part of their city of Sura served as the headquarters for their artwork and the city of Ur became the city for their pottery industry. About seven thousand years ago the city of Ur, located in the Persian Gulf region was able to survive the annual flood, because of better water controlling procedures they had installed and due to the widening mouths of the rivers.

When the barbarians from the northeast overran the entire Euphrates valley, they were not able to conquer the last remnants of the Sumerian Nodites, because they were prepared to defend themselves with their superior intelligence, better weapons and with their massive irrigation pools. The Sumerian Nodites were a strong, united race with one uniform religion, and they were able to maintain their racial and national integrity long after their neighboring Andite tribes to the northwest were broken up into isolated city-states and not one of these city-states were ever able to defeat the united Sumerian Nodites.

After a while the barbarian invaders from the north learned in time to trust and respect the peace loving Sumerian Nodites, because they saw that the Sumerians were also teachers of art, industry and manufacturing. The Sumerian Nodites ended up being the directors of commerce and as the civil rulers of all of the people to the north from Egypt in the west and India in the east.

After the breakup of the early Sumerian confederation, the later city-states were ruled by the descendants of the Sethite priests, and these priests didn't call themselves kings until after they conquered their neighboring cities and these Sethite kings failed to form powerful confederations because they each believed that their city's god was superior, and they refused to choose one common leader. The end of this long period of the rule of the city-state Sethite priests was finally ended by Sargon, the Sethite priest of Kish who proclaimed himself to be king over all of them and Sargon proceeded to conquer all of Mesopotamia and the adjoining lands which ended the city-state rule in Sumerians.

Around 2500 B C the Sumerians suffered defeats at the hands of the northern barbarian tribes called the Suites and the Guites and by the time of the established laws of Hammurabi, the Sumerian had been absorbed by the northern Semites, and the Mesopotamia Nodites had passed totally from the pages of history.

This was the story of the eighth race to appear on planet earth, the Violet race that Adam and Eve brought to our planet to uplift the races and the fate of their two Garden of Eden homes, the first Eden was located in the Persian Gulf region and the second Garden of Eden was located between the Tigris and Euphrates Rivers in the Mesopotamia region. This ancient civilization that Adam and Eve began on earth 35,000 years ago finally fell due to the emigration of its superior stock of its people and by the continuing immigration of the neighboring tribes of people. Long before the barbarians finally conquered the entire Mesopotamia Valley, most of the second Garden of Eden culture and its traditions had already spread to Asia, Africa and Europe where they produced the important pieces of culture that have resulted in the formation of our current modern civilization today on earth.

CHAPTER NINE

MACHIVENTA MELCHIZEDEK

AND ABRAHAM

Encourage one another and build each other up.

(Thessalonians 5:11)

Peace, I leave with you my peace I give you.

(John 14:27)

A Prayer:

Jesus thank you for the comfort of your enduring, unfailing peace in my life.

MACHIVENTA MELCHIZEDEK AND ABRAHAM

The Melchizedek family of Paradise are widely known as the emergency Sons from the superuniverse seven mansion worlds of Paradise-the seven higher heavens. This family works for our Universal Father in a wide range of activities on many worlds of our local universe.

Whenever any kind of extraordinary problem arises or when something unusual occurs on one of the worlds in our local universe, it is usually a member of the Melchizedek family who volunteers to accept the assignment. The skills that the Melchizedek Sons have to function on the various planets during emergencies and on the wide diverse levels of the universe, even on a physical level of personality manifestation is one of the aspects that is unique about this Melchizedek order from Paradise.

The Melchizedek order of our universe has been very active on earth since its beginnings, and a corps of these twelve Melchizedek Sons have served in conjunction with the Life Carriers to take charge of the affairs of earth after the defaults of earth's fallen Planetary Prince Caligastia and Adam and Eve. These twelve Melchizedeks continued to serve in this capacity until Jesus of Nazareth appeared on planet earth 1,954 years ago. Machiventa Melchizedek was brought into the flesh on earth through the first virgin birth to ever occur on earth from his parents High Priest Nir and his wife Sopanim. Machiventa's high priest father Nir was Noah's brother, son of Lamech and grandson of Enoch the Ethiopian who is now Archangel Metatron. Machiventa's mother Sopanim was sterile and due to her medical condition, her husband Nir had never had intercourse with her. However, when Sopanim reached old age and at the brink of death, Nir noticed that she was pregnant and when Nir asked her how she got pregnant, Sopanim told Nir that she had no idea how she had gotten pregnant. They then began to argue and Sopanim being of old age fell down and died at Nir's feet. Nir went and got his brother Noah telling him what had just happened and that he would be a disgrace among his people, because everyone knew that Sopanim was sterile, but she was pregnant when she died. So, Noah helped Nir to prepare a private burial for Sopanim and they laid her body in the tomb, temporarily sealed the door to her burial tomb and left with intentions to return shortly to finish her burial. However, when Nir and Noah returned to complete Sopanim's private burial, they both saw a three-year-old fully clothed child coming out of Sopanim's dead body and this child was Machiventa Melchizedek, and he was born with the mark of the priesthood on his chest. Nir and Noah then both heard Machiventa say, "Bless the Lord." Archangel Gabriel from Salvington, Paradise then appeared to Nir and Noah telling them that this virgin birth of Machiventa Melchizedek was a part of God's plane to renew His priesthood on earth through their families' current bloodline. Due to the wickedness of the two hundred fallen angels that was occurring on earth during the time Machiventa was born, he was raised in secret for more than thirty years before he began his ministry on earth by the Katro family who were the ancestors of the Hebrews later Egyptian spiritual leader, Moses.

The entire process of the materialization of Machiventa Melchizedek on earth was actually completed by the eleven remaining Melchizedek Receiver Sons who were assigned to work on planet earth with the help of the Life Carriers, the Master Physical Controllers and the rest of the Paradise celestial beings who were all assigned to live on planet earth during this time. God's revealed truths were being threatened with extinction on earth during the millennium time period that followed the defaults of Caligastia, Adam and Eve before the time when Jesus of Nazareth appeared on earth to complete his ministry. Even though mankind was making progress intellectually, the human races were over time, slowly losing ground spiritually and by the year 3,000 B C, the concept of God had begun to grow very hazy in the minds of humanity on earth.

The twelve Melchizedek Receiver Sons who were in charge of managing the affairs on earth during these times knew of Creator Son Michael of Nebadon's pending final seventh bestowal on earth as the incarnation of Jesus of Nazareth, but they didn't know how soon this event would occur, so they held a meeting amongst themselves and asked the Most Highs in Paradise to provide earth with some type of provisions to help them to continue to maintain the light of God's truth on planet earth until the arrival of Jesus of Nazareth. The Most Highs in Paradise dismissed their request stating that the affairs of planet #606 earth were already in the competent hands of they themselves the twelve Melchizedek Receiver Sons. So, the twelve Melchizedek Receiver Sons then filed an appeal to Father Melchizedek, the head of their order on Paradise for help, but they received the same response telling them to continue to uphold God's light and truth on earth until the arrival of Jesus of Nazareth who would then complete the job they were now performing on earth.

Since the twelve Melchizedek Receiver Sons were now completely on their own to continue to manage the affairs on earth, Machiventa Melchizedek, one of the twelve planetary receivers volunteered to do what had been done only six times prior in all of the history of Paradise. Machiventa volunteered to personalize himself on earth as a temporary human man of the earth realm and to bestow himself on earth as an emergency Son of Man in order to complete his ministry on earth.

The Most Highs of Paradise granted permission to Machiventa Melchizedek to leave his assigned duty as one of the twelve Melchizedek Receiver Sons to complete his ministry on earth as an emergency Son of Man and the actual incarnation for his endeavor on earth was consummated near the city of Salem in Palestine. It was 1,973 years before the birth of Jesus of Nazareth of Palestine that Machiventa's bestowal on earth began and his appearance on earth was unspectacular with Machiventa being born in front of only his father and uncle in the tomb of his deceased mother Sopanim.

Machiventa Melchizedek began his ministry on earth on the one eventful day when he entered the tent of Amdon a Sumerian Chaldean shepherd and when Melchizedek entered Amdon's tent, he proclaimed to Amdon, the shepherd, "I am Melchizedek, priest of El Elyon, the Most High, the one and only God." Once Amdon had recovered from his astonishment of meeting Melchizedek for the first time, he began to ask him many questions and invited his new guest to have supper with him. This was the first time in his very long universe career that Melchizedek had ever eaten food, and this food helped to sustain Melchizedek all throughout his ninety-four years of life on earth as a material being. That same night as Melchizedek and Amdon talked while sitting under the stars, Melchizedek began his mission on earth by explaining to Amdon the revelation of the truth of the reality of God our Universal Prime Creator Source in Paradise.

Within a few years Melchizedek had gathered a group of pupils, disciples and followers who believed in his teachings about God, and they formed the nucleus of his later spiritual community and schools in Salem, Palestine. Melchizedek soon became known all throughout Palestine as the priest who served El Elyon, the Most High and he later became to be the sage or King of Salem, Palestine and the surrounding tribes called Melchizedek the sheik or King of Salem which was in later times renamed Jerusalem.

In his personal appearance Melchizedek resembled the blended Nodite Sumerian people, and he was about six feet tall, and he had a very commanding presence. Melchizedek spoke Chaldean and about six other languages and he dressed just like the rest of the Canaanite priests except that he wore an emblem on his breast of three concentric circles that represented the Paradise Trinity of the Father, the Son and the Holy Spirit. Melchizedek's insignia of the three concentric circles was regarded as sacred and none of his followers would use it or wear this emblem and after a few generations it was soon forgotten.

Melchizedek never married and he left no offspring and his physical body while it resembled that of a human male, was in reality a constructed body, the same bodies that were used by the one hundred materialized superhuman beings who were the members of earth's former fallen Planetary Prince Caligastia's immediate staff and because of this, Melchizedek terminated his spiritual bestowal mission on earth after living for ninety-four years before his temporary material body began to disintegrate.

While Melchizedek lived on earth in a material body, he was indwelt by a Divine Thought Adjuster, which enable the spirit of our Universal Father Prime Creator to function within Melchizedek and later within the mind of Jesus of Nazareth, the Son of God. This was the only instance where the same Divine Thought Adjuster functioned in two different minds, Machiventa Melchizedek and Jesus of Nazareth and this was because both of their minds were divine as well as human.

All during his incarnation as the King of Salem on earth, Melchizedek stayed in full contact with the rest of his fellow eleven Melchizedek Receiver Sons who were still working here on earth, but he was not able to communicate with the rest of the celestial beings who were living and working on earth nor was he able to communicate with the celestial beings living on Paradise.

Within ten years into his ministry, Melchizedek had opened schools in Salem that were similar to the earlier schools that had been run by the earlier Sethite priests who had lived in the second Garden of Eden in the Mesopotamia region. The idea of a tithing system which was later introduced by one of his converts Abraham was also derived from one of the old established traditions of the ancient Sethite priests who had lived in the second Garden of Eden.

Melchizedek taught many of his followers the concept of one God, a universal Deity and he allowed the people to associate his teachings with the Constellation Father of Norlatiadek whom he called, El Elyon-the Most High of Paradise. During his spiritual mission on earth, Melchizedek remained silent concerning the Lucifer Rebellion that was occurring on earth, Paradise and thirty-six other planets in our universe.

The emblem that Melchizedek wore that had the three concentric circles which represented the Paradise Trinity was interpreted by many of his followers as representation of the three kingdoms of God, angels and men and very few including Abraham clearly understood the concept of the Paradise Trinity. Based on his students' level of comprehension, Melchizedek taught that the Paradise Trinity concept in the emblem that he wore on his breast were the three rulers of the constellation of Norlatiadek, Paradise which were during those times regarded to his followers as being heaven.

Melchizedek did teach some advanced truths to some of his students and followers and some of these subjects included, the conduct and organization of our local universe, and to one of his most brilliant disciples, Nordan the Kenite along with his group of earnest students, Melchizedek taught them about the truths and organizational structure of the seven mansion worlds of the superuniverse, Paradise-the seven higher heavens.

From the time he was born Melchizedek was raised in secret for more than thirty years before it was time for him to begin his spiritual ministry here on earth. During these thirty years that Melchizedek lived with the Katro family, the ancestors of Moses, he taught them the philosophy of the Salem religion and about the one true living God in Paradise. The Katro family in turn passed these many spiritual teachings that they had received from Machiventa Melchizedek down through many generations of their family and one of their descendants, Moses later adapted these traditions and earlier teachings that Melchizedek taught his ancestors and used these teachings to free the Kenites-Hebrews from slavery in Egypt.

Melchizedek taught his students and followers all that they had the capacity to receive and comprehend and some of his teachings have been adapted and are still being used today in many of the modern religious ideas and philosophies relating to heaven, earth, humanity, angels and God our Universal Prime Creator Father, Source. Melchizedek taught the doctrine of one God, a universe Deity, our heavenly Creator and our Universal Prime Creator Father in Paradise-the seven higher heavens and the main purpose of Melchizedek's teachings were to continue to prepare man for the appearance of Jesus of Nazareth 1,935 years later in Palestine. Melchizedek also taught his followers that at some future time another Son of God would be born in Palestine of a woman in the flesh and that's why many of the later spiritual teachers and leaders believed that Jesus of Nazareth was also a priest, forever after the Order of Melchizedek.

Melchizedek continued his mission on earth preparing the way for the coming messiah and he helped to set the monotheistic stage of a world tendency on earth for all by teaching his followers about the one true living God. Melchizedek later taught the Salem religion to Abraham who accepted the concept that the one true God would accept man on the simple terms of his personal faith. When Creator Son Michael of Nebadon appeared on earth 1,935 years later to complete is seventh and final bestowal as the incarnation of Jesus of Nazareth, he confirmed all that Melchizedek had taught to his followers about the one true living God.

The religious ceremonies of the Salem worship that Melchizedek put in place were very simple and every person who signed or marked the clay tablet rolls at the Melchizedek church in Salem also memorized the following creed:

I believe in El Elyon, the Most High God, the only Universal Father and Creator of all things.

I accept the Melchizedek covenant with the Most High which bestows the favor of God on my faith, and not on sacrifices and burnt offerings.

I promise to obey the seven commandments of Melchizedek and to tell the good news of this covenant about the Most High to all men.

These are the seven commandments that Melchizedek gave to his followers, and they were patterned to follow the early traditions of the Ancient Dalmatian supreme law, and they resembled the same seven commandments that were taught by Adam and Eve in the second Garden of Eden in Mesopotamia.

The seven commandments that Melchizedek gave to his followers were:

You shall not serve any God but the Most High, Creator of heaven and earth.

You shall not doubt that faith is the only requirement for eternal salvation.

You shall not bear false witness.

You shall not kill.

You shall not steal.

You shall not commit adultery.

You shall not show disrespect for your parents or elders.

No animal sacrifices were permitted in the Salem colony and instead Melchizedek offered his followers of Salem the substitute of a sacrament of bread and wine in lieu of an animal sacrifice. However, some of the tribes still continued their flesh and blood sacrifices on the outskirts of the Salem community. Even Melchizedek's main follower Abraham continued to offer flesh and blood sacrifices, because he just didn't feel comfortable using the bread and wine substitute offerings.

Melchizedek focused strictly on completing his mission to keep in the light and to teach the truth of one God on earth and he continued his ministry and teachings in the Salem colony for ninety-four years and during this time, Abraham attended his Salem schools on three different occasions, and he later became to be one of Melchizedeks closest friends, his most brilliant student, chief supporter, and successor.

Abraham was one of God's chosen ones and Melchizedek gave Abraham the responsibility to continue his mission when he left earth in his material form. Melchizedek appeared and carried out his mission in Palestine, because the subsequent incarnation of Jesus of Nazareth among the Hebrew people occurred in the same location, because Palestine was centrally located for the world's existing trade and travel.

For quite some time the twelve Melchizedeks Receiver Sons had been observing the ancestors of Abraham and they were expecting that the offspring of Abraham's family that existed during the times of Melchizedek's ministry would have the intelligence and sincerity to help carry out Melchizedek's mission after he left earth as a material being. The children of Terah, the father of Abraham did meet these expectations, and this is another reason why Melchizedek choose Salem, Palestine rather than Egypt, China, India or any of the other northern tribes to complete his mission on earth.

Terah, Abraham's father and his entire family were all converts to the Salem religion, and they learned about Melchizedek's teachings through the ministry of Ovid, a Phoenician spiritual teacher who taught the Salem religious doctrines in the land of Ur. A few weeks after the death of Abraham's father Terah, Melchizedek invited Abraham and his brother Nahor to come to Salem to further study his teachings about the one true God. Abraham's brother Nahor had not yet converted to the Melchizedek gospel, so he chose to stay behind and build his own strong city-state in his late father Terah's homeland. Abraham and his nephew Lot decided to go and live in a hilly area near Salem where they would be able to defend themselves against the many surprise attacks from the northern barbarian raiders and from this location, Abraham and Lot were still able to make frequent pilgrimages to Salem to study with Melchizedek in his Salem schools.

Soon after Abraham and his nephew Lot moved to the hills near Salem, they had to travel to Egypt to obtain food supplies due to a drought that existed in Palestine. While they were in Egypt Abraham ran into a distant relative who was a member of the Egyptian throne and as a result, Abraham was appointed to serve two terms as the commander for the Egyptian military for the Pharoah. During this time Abraham and his wife Sarah lived at the Pharoah's court and Abraham was paid well for his military leadership duties. It was hard for Abraham to leave his military position in Egypt and return to complete his spiritual studies and work with Melchizedek in Salem, but Melchizedek was highly regarded in Egypt and the Pharoah urged Abraham to return to Salem to complete his vow to work with Melchizedek's spiritual community in Salem.

Abraham had ambitions to be a king and on his way home from Egypt, he told his nephew Lot about his plans to conquer all of the Canaan territory and bring all of its people under the rule of Salem, Palestine. Lot was more of a businessman and he and Abraham had a big disagreement about his invasion plans, so Lot decided to move to the city of Sodom to work in the trade and animal husbandry business, because Lot disliked the military and instead he preferred the shepherd lifestyle. When Abraham and his family returned to Salem, he resumed working on his military plans of conquest and soon Abraham was appointed to be the civil ruler of the entire Salem territory which included the seven surrounding tribes.

Melchizedek had to continue to restrain Abraham who was ready to round up all of the seven neighboring tribes with his sword to make them to quickly convert to the Salem religion. Instead, Melchizedek continued to maintain peaceful relations with these seven surrounding tribes, and he allowed Abraham to continue to formulate his efficient defense strategies to continue to protect the Salem colony. However, Melchizedek did not approve or agree with Abraham's ambitious military strategies for conquest, so they had a friendly severance of their close friendship.

Abraham then decided to move to Hebron, where he proceeded to establish his military capital and from this location, Abraham had a strong military advantage over all of the surrounding kingdoms, and because of Abraham's close connection with Melchizedek, all of the kings in these surrounding kingdoms were afraid of Abraham.

Abraham soon took advantage of this strategic military situation and when he learned that some of these kings had launched a raid on his nephew Lot's property in Sodom, Abraham along with his seven confederated tribes with a total of 4,000 troops launched an all-out attack on these three wicked kings. Melchizedek traveled to Hebron to try to talk Abraham out of attacking these three kings, but he was too late, because by the time Melchizedek reached Hebron, Abraham was already returning from his victorious battle against the three kings and he gave a tenth of his spoil from this battle to the Salem colony treasury and Abraham took the remaining ninety percent to his military capital in Hebron.

After winning this conflict, which was called the Battle of Siddham, Abraham became the leader of a second confederation of eleven tribes and not only was he the first person on earth to pay tithes to a religious organization, but Abraham also made sure that all of the members of his military forces also paid their tithes to the Salem religious colony. Abraham's diplomatic negotiations with the King of Sodom resulted in an alliance where the king agreed to join Abraham's Hebron confederation, and this meant that Abraham was well on his way of establishing a powerful state in Palestine.

Abraham's main vision was still to conquer the entire kingdom of Canaan, but Melchizedek still would not sanction this action. Abraham at this point finally made the decision to move forward to launch his invasion forces on the land of Canaan, but he suddenly remembered that he had no heir, no son to succeed him if something happened to him during his next planned upcoming battle in Canaan. Abraham then arranged a conference with Melchizedek and during this meeting, Melchizedek persuaded Abraham not to launch his invasion on Canaan and he explained to Abraham not to waste his time and efforts fighting with the Amorite confederation in Canaan, because of their current foolish barbaric practices, that in just a few generations the Amorites in Canaan would become so weakened that Abraham's descendants would then be able to overtake them much more easily.

Melchizedek then made a formal covenant with Abraham at this meeting in Salem which stated the following.

"Look now up to the heavens and number the stars if you are able; so numerous shall your seed be."

Abraham believed what his spiritual leader Melchizedek had just told him and then Melchizedek told Abraham the story about the future occupation of the land of Canaan by his offspring after they escaped from being bondage in the land of Egypt.

This covenant that Melchizedek made with Abraham on that day in Salem represented the great agreement that was made on earth between divinity and humanity where God agrees to do everything. All man has to do is to agree and to believe in God's promise and God's divine plan and instructions. Before Melchizedek and Abraham made this covenant, mankind believed that the only way salvation could be achieved was by good works, sacrifice and burnt offerings. Now with this new covenant that was made between Melchizedek and Abraham, this good news of man's salvation and favor with God could be gained by just having good faith. Melchizedek's gospel of simple faith in God was too far advanced for most of his followers, because they were more comfortable following their old traditions of animal blood sacrifices.

Not too long after Melchizedek and Abraham established their covenant, Abraham's son Isaac was born and Abraham accepted his covenant that he had made with Melchizedek from his heart, and he had this covenant put into writing and he made a public acceptance speech and read it out loud to the Salem colony. Also, during his public acceptance speech of this covenant with Melchizedek, Abraham then publicly changed his name from Abram to Abraham and right after Abraham publicly sealed his covenant with Melchizedek, three celestial beings from Paradise appeared to Abraham on the plains of Marme to stress to Abraham the divine significance and importance of the covenant he had made with his spiritual leader Melchizedek, because once Abraham consummated and sealed this covenant with Melchizedek, then their reconciliation to go forward to both complete their spiritual mission on earth was now complete.

Abraham again assumed command of the civil and military leadership of the Salem colony, which at that time had a population of over one hundred thousand regular tithe payers on the rolls of the priesthood of Melchizedek. Also, Abraham and Melchizedek were able to make many improved methods of conducting their business school and with the roll out and distribution of the Salem worldwide religious teachers and missionaries. Abraham was a pious and sincere follower of Melchizedek's ministry, but at the same time, Abraham was a shrewd, efficient and wealthy businessman, but he did firmly believe in and totally support Melchizedek's spiritual mission on earth as a close friend, student and follower.

Melchizedek continued for many years to lead and teach his students in the Salem schools and to train many of them to be teachers and missionaries and these missionaries continued to spread the Salem teachings to many areas some of which included Egypt, Mesopotamia and Asia Minor. As time went on these Salem missionaries began to journey even further from Salem and they carried with themselves the Salem gospel that was based on the belief and faith in the one true God. Some of the descendants of Adamson, Adam and Eve's oldest son gathered regularly on the Lake of Van to listen to sermons from the Hittite missionary teachers who came to their area to teach and preach. The Salem missionaries later on were dispatched from the main Andite center in Salem to many remote regions all over Europe, Asia, Mesopotamia, Egypt, British Isles, Tibet, Iceland, India, Iran, Arabia, Japan and China. The dedication and hard work that was performed by these brave and determined missionaries represents a heroic chapter in the history of humanity.

The job of the Salem missionaries was so great and many of the tribes of people they encountered were so backward that some of the results they achieved were vague and indefinite. Long before the coming of Jesus the teachings of the early Salem missionaries became submerged in the older superstitions and beliefs in the native tribes' beliefs in the Great Mother, the Sun and many other ancient cults and religions.

Shortly after the destruction of Sodom and Gomorrah Melchizedek decided that after ninety-four years of living a material life on planet earth that it was time for him to end his emergency bestowal on earth. This decision by Melchizedek to terminate his bestowal on earth was influenced by the growing tendency of the surrounding tribes and his immediate followers to continue to regard him as a Demigod and supernatural being, which he was. But it came to a point where everyone who was around Melchizedek began to look at him with a lot of superstitious fear and most importantly, Melchizedek wanted to leave earth at that time to give his most loyal follower Abraham enough time to complete his part of their spiritual mission to firmly establish the truth of the one living God in the minds of humanity before the arrival of Jesus.

So, one night soon thereafter, Melchizedek said goodnight to some of his close human companions went into his living quarters and he disappeared. The next morning when his companions went into his tent to awaken Melchizedek, he was not there, because he had simply disappeared. It was a time of grief and a great trial for Abraham when Melchizedek, his most trusted friend and spiritual leader disappeared so suddenly like that, and it took Abraham and the followers of the Salem religion a long time to recover from their loss of such a wonderful spiritual leader.

The loss of Melchizedek produced a great sadness in the heart of Abraham that he never fully recovered from, and he left Salem soon thereafter and moved further south to Gerar. Abraham was not deterred very long in his mission to succeed Melchizedek to teach as many people that he could about the beliefs of the Salem religion and soon after the loss of Melchizedek, Abraham began to convert some of the Philistines and many of Abimelech's people to the Salem religion. One night while Abraham was first beginning his ministry teaching the Salem gospel to the Abimelech's kingdom, he overheard a plot by Abimelech to murder him to get his beautiful wife Sarah, so Abraham hid his true identity and told Abimelech that Sarah was his sister. Abimelech was then able to appropriate Abraham's wife Sarah, but when a series of misfortunes continued to happen to Abimelech for this misjustice, Abraham revealed his true identity to Abimelech and his wife Sarah was returned to him.

Abraham continued to be a great civil and spiritual leader in Palestine, and he was held in high esteem and honor by many of the surrounding kings and surrounding tribes and his religious influence continued on for a long time after his death. During the final years of his life Abraham returned to Hebron to live and one of the last things he did was to send some of his most trustworthy servants to the city where his brother Nahor lived to secure one of his daughters to be a suitable wife for his son Isaac, because it has long been and still is in our current times the custom to marry one's cousin.

During the five hundred years that the Hebrews had to endure living under Babylonian captivity, their national heritage and egos were severely depressed, and their morale was at an all-time low. In their reaction against the inferiority the Hebrew nation was experiencing, many of the Hebrew scribes, scholars and priests changed and omitted many crucial historical events that had actually occurred. Some of these Hebrew historical writers resorted to extreme national and racial egotism and changed and perverted many of their traditions and exalted themselves above all of the other races on earth and labeled the Hebrew race as being the chosen people of God. These early Hebrew scribes carefully edited all of their records by raising Abraham up real high and eliminating the true and entire story of Machiventa Melchizedek and Abraham's full ministry and only telling the part when Melchizedek met Abraham after his Battle of Siddam where Abraham paid Melchizedek the first tithes ever paid to a religious organization.

The problem is that when these early Hebrew scholars eliminated all of the true history of the events that occurred during the lives of Melchizedek and Abraham, the rest of the Hebrews completely lost sight of the spiritual teachings that this emergency Son of God, Melchizedek from Paradise gave to humanity about God's promise to send His bestowal son, Jesus to earth.

The Hebrews instead lost sight of the true nature of Jesus of Nazareth's mission on earth and as a result, many people of the Jewish nation didn't recognize who Jesus was and they were not willing to accept, receive or recognize Jesus, because they were literally looking for a King of the Jews instead of our savior Jesus when he appeared on earth 1,954 years ago in Palestine.

However, one of the earlier Jewish scribes during the five hundred years of Babylonian captivity did completely understand the important spiritual mission of Machiventa Melchizedek, because these are the words that he wrote in the Book of Hebrews:

"This Machiventa Melchizedek priest of the Most High was also the king of peace, without father, without mother, without ancestry, having neither beginning of days, nor end of life, but made like a Son of God, he abides as a priest continually."

And this same Jewish scribe also designated Melchizedek as a type just like later bestowal of the Creator Son Michael of Nebadon's incarnation on earth as Jesus affirming that Jesus was also a minister forever in the Order of Melchizedek and this comparison is literally true, because Jesus of Nazareth did receive the provisional title to earth from the orders of the twelve Melchizedek Receiver Sons who were still on duty on earth at the time of the seventh and final bestowal of Michael of Nebadon on earth as Jesus of Nazareth.

During the years of Machiventa Melchizedek's human life on earth, the remaining eleven Melchizedek Receiver Sons on earth continued to serve in their regular job functions of managing the affairs of planet earth. When Machiventa Melchizedek came to the end of his spiritual mission on earth, he sent a signal to his eleven associates, and they immediately began to initiate the necessary techniques to release Melchizedek safely from his human form and restore him back to his original status with the rest of the eleven Melchizedek Receiver Sons on earth. On the third day after Melchizedek disappeared from his tent in Salem, he then appeared among his eleven fellowmen and resumed his interrupted career as one of the twelve receivers of planet of the system of Satania, earth. Machiventa Melchizedek didn't end his emergency bestowal on earth until he was released by Father Melchizedek informing him that his emergency bestowal was approved to end from the chief executive of Nebadon, Archangel Gabriel of Salvington, Paradise. Machiventa Melchizedek still continued his interest in the affairs of the descendants of his former followers in Salem and through the intermarriages of Abraham and his son

Isaac with the Kenites, the spiritual teachings of the Salem community were able to continue on earth. Melchizedek continued to work indirectly with humanity through nineteen succeeding centuries on earth through many prophets and seers to ensure that the Salem religious teachings remained alive until the appearance of Jesus of Nazareth.

Machiventa Melchizedek has since been appointed as the Vicegerent Planetary Prince of planet earth with his headquarters being in Salvington, Paradise.

The early teachers and missionaries from Melchizedek's Salem religion traveled to the faraway remote tribes of Africa and Eurasia preaching the Salem religion's gospel of man's faith and trust in the Universal Father as the only price to obtain salvation. Melchizedek's covenant with Abraham was the pattern for all of the early teachings that went out from Salem and from its other centers. Earth had never had more enthusiastic and aggressive missionaries of any other religion than these noble men and women who carried the teachings of Melchizedek over the entire eastern hemisphere. These missionaries were recruited from many different people and races, and they mainly spread their teachings through many of the surrounding native tribes.

During the lifetime of Melchizedek, India was a cosmopolitan country that had come under the political and religious dominance of the Aryan-Andite invaders who had come from the northwest. At this time only the northern and western portions of India had been invaded by the Aryans and these Vedic newcomers brought many of their tribal deities with them to India and their religious forms of worship closely followed the ceremonial practices of their earlier Andite ancestors where the father each family served as the priest and the mother was the priestess with the family hearth serving as their altar. In India the Salem missionaries preached and taught the doctrine of the one true God, the Most High of heaven and these teachings were not altogether in conflict with the emerging concept of the Father-Brahma as the source of all gods in India, but the Salem doctrine was non-ritualistic, and it didn't agree with the dogmas, traditions and teachings of India's Brahman priesthood. So, the Brahman priests in India refused to accept the Salem teachings of salvation through faith, because these beliefs were in direct conflict with the Brahman's ritual observances and sacrificial ceremonies. This rejection of the Melchizedek teachings marked a vital turning point in India.

As the Salem missionaries traveled throughout Asia spreading the Salem religious doctrines and they didn't stray from their mission for over one hundred years and during the middle of the second millennium they maintained their headquarters in China. It was in direct response to the Salem teachings that the earliest form of Taoism arose in China and the Yellow race were the first to emerge from under the control of a barbaric bondage existence and evolve into an orderly civilization, who was able to achieve some measure of freedom from their fear of the gods. However, China met its defeat, because it failed to progress beyond its early freedom days from the Chinese clergy and the entire country soon fell into the error of ancestor worship instead of worshipping the one true living God in heaven. The Salem missionaries who preached in China didn't labor in vain, because the Salem gospel proved to be the foundations that many of the great Chinese philosophers of the sixth century China built their teachings of Lao-tse and Confucious on.

About six hundred years before the arrival of Jesus of Nazareth, it seemed to Melchizedek, who had long since departed from his human form on earth, that the purity of his teachings on earth were in jeopardy by the general absorption into the older religious beliefs on earth. It began to look like for a time that Melchizedeks' mission on earth was in danger of failing. So, in the sixth century through an unusual divine coordination of some of the spiritual agencies in Paradise, earth began to witness a very unusual manifestation unfolding of religious truths. And through these divine heavenly agencies, various human spiritual leaders began to appear on earth to once again to restart the teachings of the Salem gospel and these teachings have now survived up to our current times on earth. This unique century of spiritual progress on earth was full of great religious, moral and philosophic teachers who were spread all over the civilized world and in China two of these great spiritual leaders were Lao-tse and Confucious.

The Salem missionaries continued to preach and teach all over southwestern Asia through Palestine, Mesopotamia, Egypt, Iran and Arabia where they proclaimed the good news of the Salem gospel. In the Mesopotamia region the Salem missionaries did a lot to help refine and uplift the neighboring tribes' religious beliefs by reducing the number of gods they worshipped, especially the popularity of the Ishtar, the mother god of fertility, but they failed in this region to stop the practice of temple harlotry.

In less than one generation the Salem headquarters in Kish came to an end and the belief in one God also ended all throughout the entire Mesopotamia region. However, the remnants of the original Salem schools still remained in small groups in this region who continued to believe in the one true living God in heaven. During the time period following some of the rejections of the Salem gospel, many of these dedicated missionaries began to write the Psalms of the Old Testament which they wrote on stone and later on when the Jewish scribes found these psalms, they incorporated many of them into a collection of Jewish hymns. The Jewish scribes also began to use these psalms that were written by the early Salem missionaries during their five hundred years of Babylonian captivity into their early Hebrew writings. The Book of Job is a fine example of one of the books that came from the Salem school at Kish and a lot of the Salem religious culture found its way into Hebrew literature and liturgy all throughout Egypt. Because of the two Egyptian religious leaders Amenemope and Ikhnaton, a lot of the earlier Andite Mesopotamia teachings were able to be preserved within the Egyptian culture. One very important point is that when you pray never say Amen at the end of your prayer, instead say: The end, because you are worshipping the above stated Egyptian leader Amenemope every time you say Amen. (See page four of this book at the end of the Lord's Prayer)

The original Salem teachings that Melchizedek taught in his schools took their deepest roots in the land of Egypt and from there they spread to Europe. The evolutionary religion that was prevalent in the Nile valley was being augmented by the periodic arrival of superior strains of Nodite, Adamite, Andite and Sumerian tribes and during these times, the country of India had the highest mixture of the world's races and Egypt had the most blended types of religious philosophy found on earth.

The early Hebrew scribes derived many of their ideas of the creation of the world from the Babylonians and they got their ideas of divine providence from the Egyptians. While Melchizedek was still living on earth, the Egyptians had a religious culture that was far above that of the surrounding cultures and the Egyptians believed that a disembodied soul if it was properly armed with the correct magical formulas, that the soul could then evade the intervening evil spirits and make its way to the judgement hall of Osiris where if innocent of, murder, robbery, falsehood, adultery, theft and selfishness, then the soul would be admitted to the realms of bliss. And if this same soul was weighed in the balances and found wanting, then it would be consigned to the devourness, because during these times in Egypt these concepts were advanced beliefs of a future life in comparison with the beliefs of the many surrounding tribes. This Egyptian concept of judgement in the hereafter for the sins of one's life in the flesh on earth was also used by the Hebrews and carried over into the Hebrew theology from Egypt. The word judgement appears only once in the entire Book of Hebrew Psalms and all of the psalms that are found in the bible were written by an Egyptian and not the Hebrews.

The culture and religion of Egypt was mainly originated from the Andite Mesopotamia tribes, and it extended out to many of the outlying civilizations through the early Hebrew and Greek civilizations. The social and ethical idealism that existed in ancient Egypt began in the Nile valley as a purely evolutionary developing religious culture. The importation of the truth and culture of the Mesopotamian Andite religion continued to evolve in Egypt as an important aspect of their human development prior to the arrival of Jesus of Nazareth on earth. The natural evolutions of consciousness and character that began to arise in humanity during these times was also assisted by the periodic arrivals of the spiritual teachers of truth. From the ancient times of man to the second Garden of Eden and later from the Melchizedek schools in Salem, humanity has steadily progressed in his moral concepts and spiritual values. Thousands of years before Melchizedek's gospel penetrated Egypt, the moral leaders were teaching the Egyptian people the values of justice, fairness, and to avoid greed.

Three thousand years before the Hebrew scriptures were written, the Egyptian people had the motto that a moral Egyptian had a high standard of righteousness, gentleness, moderation and discretion and the main message of one of the great Egyptian teachers was to do right and deal justly with everyone. The main Egyptian creed during these times was truth, justice and righteousness and of all the purely human religions that existed on earth during these times, none of them ever surpassed the social ideals and moral values that existed in the Nile valley of Egypt. In the midst of these evolving ethical and moral ideas that existed in Egypt, the surviving doctrines of Melchizedek's Salem teachings also continued to flourish in the land of Egypt.

During these times Egypt's culture was both intellectual and moral, but not overly spiritual, because in Egypt during the time period of six thousand years only four great prophets arose among the Egyptian people. The first Egyptian prophet, Amenemope was followed only for a short season and the second Egyptian prophet Okhban they quickly murdered and they then accepted the prophet Ikhnaton, but the Egyptians half-heartedly followed his teachings for only one short generation. The fourth Egyptian prophet was Moses whom they rejected, and he later ended up becoming the Hebrew's religious leader and Moses led them out of slavery from Egypt.

It was political rather than religious circumstances that made it easy for Abraham and later Joseph to both exert a great influence throughout Egypt teaching the Melchizedek Salem teachings of one God. When the Salem missionaries first entered Egypt, they found that they were teaching and preaching to a highly ethical culture of evolved people who had blended and mixed well with the modified moral standards of the Mesopotamian immigrants. These early Nile valley missionaries were the first to proclaim to the Egyptians that the human conscience was the mandate of the one true God who was the real true voice of Deity.

The Egyptian spiritual leader Amenemope was a seer, and he helped to raise the spiritual consciousness in Egypt to its highest level by stressing the importance of choosing between right and wrong and he proclaimed that one could achieve salvation by praying to the solar Deity. Amenemope also taught that riches and fortune were gifts from God, and the Hebrews later adapted this concept into their own Hebrew philosophy. Some of the main teachings of Amenemope were later translated into Hebrew and they became to be a part of the sacred book of the Hebrew people long before the Old Testament was finally translated from the stone writings that the early Salem missionaries had written on. Amenemope's also wrote many proverbs which were later translated into Hebrew and used for the Old Testament Book of Proverbs.

Amenemope's teachings were also translated into the Greek language, and they were used as the basis of the subsequent Hellenic Greek religious philosophy and later in Greece the Alexandrian philosopher Philo used the Egyptian Book of Wisdom in many of his teachings. Amenemope's teachings also helped to conserve the ethics, morals and positive evolution of Egypt through many of his writings, but the teachings of Amenemope began to fade away from the minds of the Egyptian people when the mother of Ikhnaton, a female Egyptian physician and member of the Egyptian royal family encouraged her son Ikhnaton to convert to Melchizedek's religion and then begin to teach the Melchizedek Salem gospel to the Egyptian people.

Since the times that Melchizedek left his human form on earth, no other mortal man had possessed such a clear understanding of the concepts of the Salem religion as Pharoah Ikhnaton did. In some respects, this young Pharoah was one of the most remarkable people who ever lived in the history of humanity and in the Book of Hebrews, the Proverbs, Chapters 15, 17, 20 22 and 24 and Psalm 1 were all taken verbatim on the teachings of Ikhnaton. During these times in Egypt, it was a period of increasing spiritual depression especially in the Mesopotamian region, but Pharoah Ikhnaton kept the doctrine of El Elyon, the one God of Egypt alive, thus maintaining the monotheistic ideology religious background alive to continue to prepare for the arrival of our messiah Jesus of Nazareth. This is one of the main reasons why Joseph and Mary took Jesus as a young child to live in Egypt where many of the spiritual successors of Ikhnaton protected Jesus and his family, because they accepted and understood the vast importance of Jesus' divine mission on earth. Moses was also one of the greatest spiritual leaders to ever live on earth between the lives and times of Melchizedek and Jesus of Nazareth. Moses was a joint gift to humanity from both the world of the Hebrew race and from the Egyptian royal family. If Pharoah Ikhnaton had possessed the same leadership, versatility and spiritual abilities as Moses, then Egypt would have completely become a monotheistic nation during his rule and if this had happened, then maybe Jesus of Nazareth may had been able to live the greater portion of his mortal life in Egypt instead of in Palestine. Never in all of the history on earth did any ruler like Ikhnaton methodically proceed to convert the entire nation of Egypt from the worship of polytheism to monotheism and Ikhnaton with amazing determination was able to break many of the old Egyptian traditions of the past, he changed his name, abandoned his original capital, built a new city and created a whole new culture of art and literature for the Egyptian people.

However, Pharoah Ikhnaton moved too fast, built too much too fast and none of his accomplishments lasted for too long after he was gone, because he neglected to provide for the material stability and prosperity for the common people, and the general population reacted unfavorably against his religious teachings as soon as the economic times in Egypt changed to oppression and adversity from the new regime. Ikhnaton was wise when he established monotheism in Egypt under the guise of the already worshipped sun-God. His approach to have his followers worship the Universal Prime Creator Father was to absorb all of the other Egyptian gods into the worship of the sun.

Ikhnaton's concept of immortality for all men was way too far advanced for the minds of the Egyptian people to grasp, because their established customs and traditions in Egypt was that the rich class and Pharaohs were promised a resurrection, and their custom was that for those who had transitioned to carefully wrap their body to preserve their body in the tomb until the day of judgement. However, Ikhnaton's concept of one's salvation and resurrection did prevail in Egypt even to the extent that the Egyptian culture later believed in the eternal survival of their domestic animals.

The religious teachings of Ikhnaton lasted for centuries, and Egypt became the source for his teachings to spread throughout Palestine and Greece. The glory of this great religious era of moral development and spiritual growth in Egypt was occurring around the same time that the national life of the Hebrew nation was beginning and the Hebrew scribes at that time began to use many of the teachings and doctrines of Ikhnaton in their writings.

Some of the Melchizedek missionaries traveled to Iran from Palestine and for more than five hundred years these Salem missionaries preached the Salem gospel in Iran and the whole nation of Iran became followers of the Salem religion. But after five hundred years passed the whole new regime of Iranian rulers stages a bitter persecution of the followers of the Salem religion and this was the end of the monotheistic Salem religion in Iran.

The doctrine of Abraham's covenant with Melchizedek that had been consummated many years prior was extinct by this time in Persia, but during the sixth century before the time of Jesus a great religious revival occurred under the leadership of the Persian religious leader Zoroaster and he was able to revive the Salem gospel and through he and his followers the light and essence of the Salem teachings were able to stay alive and continue to show mankind in the then dark days on earth the true path of light and love that would lead humanity back to eternal life. The Salem gospel became to be established in the Arabian region and only recently in our current times, each tribe in this region reverted to the worship of their same old traditional fetishes with each family having their own household god. Here and there throughout Arabia, there are still some families and clans who continue to hold on to the happy idea of serving and loving the one true living God.

CHAPTER TEN

THE STORY OF MOSES

Put your hope in God, for I will yet praise him, my savior and my God.

(Psalm 42:11)

Father, glorify your name!

(John 12:28)

A Prayer:

Father help me to face with faith the upcoming challenging things honestly and prayerfully that are for my good and that will glorify your name.

THE STORY OF MOSES

Early evolutionary man's first perception of Deity first included all of the known gods, then the foreign gods and in the process, man ended up excluding the one true God, the Universal Father of final and supreme value. The Jewish religion synthesized all of the gods into their religion's concept of the Lord God of Israel.

The Hindu religion combined multiple deities into one spirituality of the gods into the portrayal of the one god Rig-Veda. The Mesopotamians reduced their multiple gods to one centralized god concept of Bel-Marduk. All of these religious ideas of monotheism began to grow all over the world not too long after the appearance on earth of the spiritual leader Machiventa Melchizedek in Salem, Palestine. The Melchizedek religion's concept of the one true God was different from early evolutionary man's philosophy of inclusion, subordination and exclusion. Instead, Melchizedek's Salem gospel was based exclusively on creative power and deity concepts in Mesopotamia, India and in Egypt. Melchizedek's Salem religion was an important tradition that had been adapted by the Kenite and Canaanite tribes and this was one of the main reasons that Machiventa Melchizedek incarnated on earth, because his Salem gospel helped the Kenites and the Canaanites to prepare themselves spiritually for the coming of Jesus of Nazareth on earth, but the messiah could not come to complete his mission on earth until there were people living on earth who loved and believed in the Universal Prime Creator Father.

The Salem religion was the creed amongst the Kenite tribe who lived in Palestine, and it was later adapted by the Hebrew, Egyptian, Babylonian and Iranian civilizations. The Hebrew religion is primarily based on the covenant that was made between Abraham and Machiventa Melchizedek many years ago in Salem, Palestine. The early Semites believed that all life which included animals, vegetables, fire, water and air on earth were being indwelt by a spirit and the early teachings of the Melchizedek Salem religion never fully destroyed these early beliefs that the Semites had in these subordinate nature gods.

The Hebrew religion experienced many regressions relating to their evolutionary journey of Deity concepts and from time to time the Hebrews used numerous different terms to describe their concepts of God.

These are some of the various Deity titles that were used during the evolution of Jewish theology.

Yahweh was the God of the southern tribes of Palestine, and they associated Yahweh with Mount Horeb and Mount Sinai which were both active volcanoes. The God Yahweh was one of thousands of the nature gods who were worshipped by the various Semite tribes.

El Elyon was the God that the Hebrews called the Most High of heaven and many of the Semites including the immediate descendants of Abraham worshipped the Gods Yahweh and El Elyon.

El Shaddai is the most difficult God to explain, because this Hebrew idea of God was learned from the teachings of the Egyptian Amenemopes' Book of Wisdom, which was modified by the Egyptian Pharoah Ikhnaton's doctrine of Aton which was strongly influenced from Melchizedek's teachings on the concepts of El Elyon, the Most High. As the concepts of the God El Shaddai began to enter the minds of the Hebrews, it became blended with the Yahweh beliefs that the desert Hebrews followed. One of the most dominant ideas concerning religion during these times as the Egyptian concept of divine providence which taught that material prosperity was the reward for serving El Shaddai.

El was one of the nature Gods that the Bedouin Semites worshipped.

Elohim was the God who was worshipped in the lands of Kish and Ur by the Sumerian Chaldean tribes who believed in a three in one God trinity and these beliefs began with the traditions of Adam and Machiventa Melchizedek and this doctrine of the Holy Trinity was passed onto the cultures of Egypt and Alexandria. Many of the close advisors to Moses during the times of the exodus from Egypt also believed in the Holy Trinity concept. The concept of the God Elohim did not become a part of Hebrew theology until the time of the five hundred years of Babylonian captivity.

Many sundry names were also used by the Semites concerning the gods that they worshipped, because they didn't like to speak the name of their Deity and some of these sundry names for the various Semite Gods were; Kyrios, Jah, The Father in Heaven, The Almighty, The Lord and many more.

The concept of the God Jehovah didn't come into the Hebrew theology until 1,500 years after the times of Jesus of Nazareth. Jehovah is the completed concept of Yahweh and up until about 2,000 B.C., Mount Sinai was an active volcano, and its occasional eruptions caused a lot of fear among the Bedouin Semites and the surrounding tribes which in turn also caused these same tribes to have a great fear of the God Yahweh and the volcano God which later became the God of the Hebrew Semites.

The Canaanites also had a strong devotion to the God Yahweh. Many of the Kenites believed in and worshipped the God El Elyon, the super God of the Salem religion and in addition many of the Canaanite tribes still worshipped many of their old tribal deities.

The Syrians also continued to worship many of their tribal Gods, but they also believed in the Hebrew God Yahweh. The concept of the God Yahweh has undergone one of the most extensive developments of all of humanity's concepts of God. And while the Hebrews changed their views of deity from their tribal God of Mount Horeb to the living merciful Creator Father God, they did not change God's name, because the Hebrews continued to call their evolving concept of Deity, Yahweh.

The Semites who lived in the eastern areas of Palestine were well organized, skilled horsemen who invaded the eastern regions of the fertile crescent where they later united with the Babylonians. The Chaldeans who lived near the land of Ur were the most advanced group of the eastern Semites and the Phoenicians were also a superior and well-organized group of mixed Semites who lived in the western area of Palestine. Racially, the Semites were the most blended of all the people living on earth, because they contained the hereditary factors from all of the world's nine races.

The Arabian Semites fought their way again and again as they were traveling to get to the northern promised land for forty years, but they kept on being defeated and driven back by the better organized and more highly civilized northern Semites and Hittites. Later during a severe famine this same group of Arabian Semites, Bedouins went to work in Egypt as contract laborers and before they knew it, they were placed in bondage as downtrodden slaves of the Nile valley. It was only after the times of Machiventa Melchizedek and Abraham that some of the Semite tribes became to be called the children of Israel and later on, Hebrews, Jews and the chosen people.

Abraham was not the racial father of all the Hebrews, and he was not even the ancestor of all of the Bedouin Semites who had become enslaved in the land of Egypt.

It is a fact that Abraham's offspring while they were coming out of Egypt, did later form the nucleus of the later Jewish people, but most of the men and women who formed into the clans of Egypt had never really lived in Egypt. Instead, these offspring of Abraham were merely fellow nomads who chose to follow the leadership of Moses as the children of Abraham and along with their Semite associates from Egypt, they journeyed together through northern Arabia.

The Melchizedek teachings relating to El Elyon, the Most High and the covenant of divine favor through faith, had mostly been forgotten by the time the Bedouin Semite people became enslaved in Egypt. However, all throughout these times these Arabian Semites were on the brink of forming the Hebrew nation during their times of slavery in Egypt they continued to maintain their belief in Yahweh as their one true God. The God Yahweh was worshipped by more than one hundred separate Arabian tribes, and except for a small portion of the El Elyon Deity concept of Melchizedek which persisted among the educated classes of Egypt, their main religion was still the old Yahweh ritual of magic and sacrifice. The beginning of the evolution of the Hebrew concepts of a Supreme Creator began when the Semites fled from their slavery in Egypt under the great spiritual leadership of Moses.

Moses' mother was a female physician and a member of the Egyptian royal family, and his father was a Semite liaison officer between the Egyptian government and the Bedouin Semite slaves. Moses had superior racial ancestry, and he was so highly blended racially that it was almost impossible to classify Moses into any one racial group. If Moses had not been as mixed as he was racially, he would never have been able to display the unusual versatility and adaptability that enabled him to manage the large, diversified group of Bedouin Semites who went with him from their captivity in Egypt. Despite his royal lineage in Egypt, Moses still made the decision to become the spiritual leader and teacher of his father's people, the Semites. Moses had a speech impairment and stuttered when he talked, but this never stopped him from completing his mission to become a great spiritual leader and organizer and he immediately began to formulate his plans for the eventual freeing of the Bedouin Semites, his father's people. The Bedouin Semites who were being held as slaves in Egypt had no religion of their own, no true concept of God and they had very little faith or hope in their world. No other spiritual leader in the world except for Moses had ever undertaken the job such as his to uplift a more forlorn, downcast, dejected and ignorant group of human beings who needed his guidance and help. But this group of Bedouin Semite slaves carried latent possibilities for development in their hereditary strains, so Moses selected and began to coach and train a large number from this group of these enslaved Semites to be prepared for the day of revolt and strike for liberty. The superior Semite leaders who Moses had selected and trained had previously been employed as the overseers of the enslaved Bedouin Semites and due to the influence Moses had with the Egyptian royalty, he was able to have these overseers to receive a proper education while they performed their overseer duties.

Moses tried to negotiate diplomatically with the Egyptian rulers for the freedom of his fellow Semites and Moses and his brother Aaron finally entered into an agreement with the Pharoah for the freedom of the Bedouin Semites. This agreement with the Pharoah of

Egypt stated that the Bedouin Semites would peacefully be freed, and each slave would receive a modest payment of money and goods as a payment for their many years of service in Egypt. The Bedouin Semites all agreed to this agreement with the intention of being able to maintain friendly relations with the Egyptian monarch. However, the Pharoah of Egypt reneged on this agreement and instead accused the Bedouin Semite slaves of having spies working amongst them who had plans to organize their group against Egypt.

This dishonest move by the Egyptian Pharoah did not discourage Moses, and in less than a year's time, while the Egyptian military forces were off occupied defending their country against two simultaneous attacks from both Libya and Greece, Moses led his group of 600,550 Bedouin slaves in a spectacular night flight exit out of the land of Egypt.

Moses had very carefully planned this escape, and they were successful in their escape. However, Moses and his large group of fleeing Bedouin Semites were soon pursued by the Pharoah of Egypt and a small group of Egyptians, but Moses and his 600,550 Bedouin Semite slaves not only defeated the Pharoah's small group of pursuers, but they were also able to confiscate all of the spoils from this group and they continued their march on towards their ancestral desert home to the Promised Land.

The evolution and elevation of the teachings of Moses has influenced almost half the world and it still does even now in our current times. Moses had the knowledge of the advanced Egyptian religious philosophers, and he shared this knowledge in his teachings to his followers the Bedouin Semites. All throughout their forty-year journey in the desert as they continued marching around Mount Sinai, these Bedouin Semites never forgot, nor did they stop serving and loving their God of Mount Horeb whom their ancestors called Yahweh.

Moses' parents taught him the teachings of Machiventa Melchizedek when he was a child growing up and by the time the Hebrews were in their encampment around Mount Sinai, Moses had formulated a new concept of Deity which he then proclaimed to the Bedouin Semites as being their older tribal God, Yahweh.

Moses had tried to teach the Bedouin Semites the concepts of El Elyon before they left Egypt, but they weren't able to understand what Moses was trying to teach them and it continued to be hard for Moses to get his followers to accept the God of Yahweh, because the Bedouin Semites had since ancient times regarded the worship of the golden calf as their symbol for the God Yahweh. The fact that Yahweh was the God of the fleeing Bedouin Semites is important, because during the forty years they spent in the desert marching around Mount Sinai over and over again, they received the ten commandments from

Moses, and he was able to further improve the Hebrew worship and finally the Bedouin Semites came to accept and love their God Yahweh.

During the third week of the Hebrew worship at the base of Mount Horeb, this mountain of Yahweh was consumed in fire and smoke like a furnace and during this volcanic eruption, Moses proclaimed to his Hebrew followers that Yahweh was the Lord

God of Israel who had designated the Hebrews as his chosen people. Moses also taught his Hebrew people that Yahweh was a covenant keeping God who would not forsake, neither destroy you nor forget the covenant of our fathers, because the Lord loves you and will never forget the oath that He swore to our fathers.

Under the teachings of Moses, the Hebrew God Yahweh became the Lord God of Israel who followed them through the wilderness and even into exile. The later captivity that enslaved the Jews for five hundred years in Babylon finally liberated the evolving concept of Yahweh into the monotheistic role of the God of all nations.

Moses was an extraordinary military leader, social organizer and religious leader and teacher. Moses was one of the most important world teacher and leader who lived between the times of Machiventa Melchizedek and Jesus of Nazareth. Moses attempted to introduce many reforms in Israel, and he successfully led his Hebrew followers out of slavery into a forty-year journey in the desert marching around Mount Sinai, and during their long journey Moses was able to lay the foundation for the subsequent birth of the Hebrew nation.

There are very few written records left that depict the great work that Moses accomplished during his lifetime on earth, because the Hebews had no written language during the times of the exodus from Egypt. The records that have been found of the life and times of Moses were taken from the traditions that still existed more than one thousand years after the death of Moses.

Many of the advances that Moses made that were over and above the Egyptian and Levantine religions were due to the Kenite traditions that existed during the times of Melchizedek. Without the teachings of Melchizedek and Abraham, the Hebrews would have come out of slavery from Egypt in a hopeless state of darkness.

Moses and his father-in-law Jethro used the traditions from the days of Melchizedek and the early Egyptian teachings to improve the rituals and religious worship practices of the Hebrews. And while Moses continued to present the religious concepts of a universal and beneficial God to the Hebrews, their day-to-day concept of God still remained to be primitive and crude.

When Moses passed on, the Bedouin Semite tribes quickly reverted back to their barbaric ideas of the golden calf God of their ancestors. From the times of Moses to John the Baptist there was an unbroken line of faithful Hebrew spiritual teachers who passed on the truth of one God, Yahweh, the torch of light from one generation to the next generation while they continued to reject their unscrupulous rulers, commercial clergy and instead the Jewish nation continued to worship their supreme God Yahweh, the Lord God of Israel. The Jewish nation loved justice, wisdom and truth and although the Hebrew theology refused to expand, their religion still played an important role in the later development of two other world religions, Christianity and Islam.

CHAPTER ELEVEN

THE SEVEN BESTOWALS OF THE CREATOR SON MICHAEL OF NEBADON

Let brotherly love continue. (Hebrews 13:1).

(Psalm 131:2)

God chose the foolish things of the world to shame the wise.

(Corinthians 1:27)

A Prayer:

Loving Father, thank you for your unexpected ways. Help me follow you closely today, so that I may be used for what's pleasing to you.

THE SEVEN BESTOWALS OF MICHAEL OF NEBADON

Michael of Nebadon is a Creator Son from Paradise-the seven higher heavens who completed his six bestowals before incarnating on planet earth for his final seventh bestowal as Jesus of Nazareth. Each of the Creator Sons from Paradise are awarded the position to be the system sovereign of their own universe after they complete the seven required bestowals in different incarnations on their assigned universe. The Eternal Son of the Paradise Trinity led the way in this practice, because he was the first to complete his seven required bestowals on the seven circuits of Havona during the ascension of the first ascendant mortal from earth, a world of time and space to reach Paradise long ago and the Eternal Son of Paradise continues to bestow himself on the local universes' worlds of time and space through Michael and the Avonal Sons of Paradise.

When the Eternal Son of Paradise bestows one of his Creator Sons to incarnate on a local universe, the Creator Son then assumes full responsibility for the completion, control and composure of that universe, including a solemn oath to the Holy Trinity that he cannot assume the full sovereignty of this newly created universe until all of his seven bestowals have been completed and certified by the Ancients Of Days who resides in Paradise. This obligation is assumed by all of the Creator Michael Sons of Paradise who volunteer to go out from Paradise to participate in the organization and creation of a new universe.

The purpose of the Creator Michael Sons from Paradise to incarnate on the worlds of time and space as mortals is to enable the Creator Sons to become more wise, sympathetic, just and understanding system sovereigns. These divine sons are already just, but they become more merciful as a result of completing their seven bestowal missions on the worlds of time and space.

The seven bestowals that must be completed by the Creator Sons of Paradise are the last steps in their education and training to prepare them for the upcoming tasks of ruling a local universe in divine righteousness and with a merciful just judgement. There are numerous benefits that the Creator Sons learn when they incarnate on the various worlds, systems and constellations. In addition, the presence of a Creator Son on a local world benefits the mortal beings who live on these different planets. These seven bestowals help the Creator Son to complete all of the necessary training, education and all of the Michael Creator Sons of Paradise begin their work of universe organization with a full feeling of sympathy for the various orders of mortal beings who they have created on the numerous local planets.

The triune rulers of the superuniverse in Paradise will not certify a Creator Son as a universe system sovereign until he has completely acquired the viewpoint of all of the mortal beings on his assigned universe through actual hands-on training and experience in the local environments where the mortal beings live and this way the Creator Sons become more intelligent, compassionate, patient, love filled and understanding rulers.

Currently our local universe of Nebadon is being ruled by Michael of Nebadon who completed his seventh and final bestowal on earth 1,954 years ago as Jesus of Nazareth. Michael of Nebadon is number 611,121 of the total Creator Sons of Paradise and Michael began the organization of our local universe of Nebadon about four hundred billion years ago, and about one billion years ago he began his first bestowal adventure which was about the same time planet earth was formed as Tiamat earth. Each one of Michael's bestowals occurred about one hundred and fifty million years apart. Michael's final seventh bestowal took place on planet earth 1,954 years ago as the incarnation of Jesus of Nazareth.

The nature and character of the seven bestowals for Michael of Nebadon occurred during the following set of seven experiences.

The First Bestowal of Michael of Nebadon occurred on a solemn occasion on Salvington, Paradise one billion years ago when at an assembly meeting of the directors and chiefs of the universe of Nebadon, those in attendance suddenly heard Michael announce that his older brother Immanuel would be taking his place to assume authority in Nebadon while he was away on an unexplained mission. Michael then made a farewell broadcast to the Constellation Fathers stating he would be going away on a mission to do the bidding of his Universal Paradise Father. After Michael made this announcement all of the inhabitants of Salvington and from the system headquarters waited hoping to hear some kind of news about the mission and where the Creator Son Michael had gone.

On the third day after Michael's departure, a communication was received from the Melchizedek sphere stating that Michael had been received into the Melchizedek Order assigned to the emergency service of the Melchizedeks of Nebadon to complete his first bestowal to live and work as a Melchizedek Son for a period of one hundred years.

The Second Bestowal of Michael of Nebadon occurred one hundred and fifty million years after the completion of his first bestowal. Trouble began to arise on System# 11 in Constellation and this trouble involved a misunderstanding by a Lanonandek Son, the System Sovereign Lucifer who along with his assistant Satan proceeded to lead his associates in one of the most widespread and disastrous rebellions against the Creator Son Michael, and his Universal Father to ever occur in the universe of Nebadon and this rebel System Sovereign Lucifer and Satan continued to reign on his headquarters planet earth for more than twenty years. After twenty years had passed the Most Highs from Paradise designated a new System Sovereign to take over Lucifer's strife torn and confused systems of inhabited worlds. In response to this ongoing Lucifer Rebellion Creator Son Michael again issued a proclamation stating that he would once again be absent from his universe headquarters position to do the bidding of the Paradise Universal Father and that his oldest brother Immanuel would be in charge until he returned to Salvington, Paradise.

Three days after Michael left Salvington, Paradise a new member of the Lanonandek Sons of Paradise appeared who was Michael who was certified by the Ancients Of Days to be assigned to system #11 of constellation #37 as the Acting System Sovereign pending the appointment a new permanent System Sovereign. For more than seventeen years

Michael served on system #11 and he became known as the Savior System Sovereign on planetary system called Palonia, and no other System Sovereign was ever more ardently loved, honored and respected as Michael was while he was working on Palonia in his position and he even offered his rebellious son, Lucifer to share his duties with him if he would simply apologize to his brother Immanuel for leading the Lucifer Rebellion and end it, but Lucifer refused.

When the newly appointed system sovereign arrived seventeen years later, all who lived on the system of Palonia mourned the departure of Michael and three days after Michael completed his second bestowal on Palonia, he returned to Salvington, Paradise to resume his duties as the director of universe affairs.

The Third Bestowal of Michael of Nebadon was on planet #217 in system #87, constellation # 61 when the supreme council on Salvington, Paradise received a call for assistance from this planet due to the Life Carriers assigned to work on this planet going astray after they joined the Lucifer Rebellion. So, Michael for the third time put his brother Immanuel in charge of his job position and he placed Gabriel in charge of the universe celestial forces. Michael then took leave of the Universe Mother Spirit and vanished for the third time from Salvington, Paradise to begin his third bestowal as the Planetary Prince on planet Kepler #217. This third bestowal was difficult for Michael, because this planet was under quarantine due to joining the Lucifer Rebellion and it was a world of secession and rebellion. Also, Michael had no direct communication with anyone in Paradise for an entire generation and he had to work alone all through his third bestowal as the Planetary Prince on planet #217, Kepler. Michael was able to restore the entire planet back to the loyal service to the Paradise Constellation Fathers and after a generation it passed the inspection to have a Material Son, Adam and a Material Daughter, Eve who arrived on the redeemed world of planet #217, Kepler. On the third day after the arrival of the Material Son and Material Daughter from Paradise, Michael then reappeared back in his position as the director of universe affairs on Salvington, Paradise.

The Ancients Of Days then made an announcement to all the residents on Salvington that Michael had completed his third bestowal. The third bestowal that Michael had just successfully completed on the isolated planet Kepler was one of the most beautiful chapters in the history of all of Salvington and by the end of Michael's mission on planet Kepler it became clear to all in Salvington the reasons why Michael had made the decision to complete his seven bestowals.

The bestowals that Michael had completed as a Melchizedek Son, a Lanonandek Son and a Planetary Prince were all mysterious and beyond explanation to the residents of Salvington, because during each bestowal Michael appeared suddenly as a fully developed man in each one of his first three bestowals. The mystery of Michael's incarnations during each of his seven bestowals will never be understood except to those who have access to the inner circle of the records on the sacred sphere of Sonarington which is located in the superuniverse mansion worlds. Since Michael chose to complete his seven bestowals, no Material Son or Material Daughter has ever joined in rebellion against him because of the love and honor they felt for his courage and dedication to complete his seven bestowals.

The Fourth Bestowal of Michael of Nebadon was certified by the Ancients Of Days for Michael to go and live and work with the supreme order of the angels who were assigned to work for a local universe and Michael was gone working on this angel seraphic assignment for over forty years. During Michael's fourth bestowal he worked as an angelic seraphic teaching counselor to twenty-six different master teachers who in turn taught and worked with various angels on twenty-two different worlds of time and space, Michael also worked for seven years as a counselor and helper to assist the Trinity Teacher Son who was also working on his own bestowal mission on world #462 in system #84, constellation #3 in our Nebadon universe. This Trinity Teacher Son who Michael helped had been on his bestowal mission for seven years and all during this time, this Trinity Teacher Son never knew that his angelic seraphic helper was Michael of Nebadon.

As Michael's bestowals continued to have him living and working with many lower forms of free will mortal beings, Gabriel became to be more involved in Michael's incarnations, and adventures functioning as the universe liaison messenger between Michael and his brother Immanuel, the acting director of universe affairs. Now that Michael had passed through the bestowal experience of three orders of his created universe sons, the Melchizedek Sons, the Lanonandek Sons, A Planetary Prince and an Angelic Teaching Counselor, Michael next chose to complete his next upcoming bestowal working with the ascending careers of the lowest forms of free will living beings, the evolutionary mortals who live on the worlds of time and space.

The Fifth Bestowal of Michael of Nebadon occurred over three hundred million years ago when for the fifth time the transfer of authority was transferred to Michael's oldest brother Immanuel. Michael's fifth bestowal was different from the four previous ones and Michael announced that this time his destination would be on Uversa, the headquarters world of superuniverse Orvonton. Michael then disappeared and the announcement was broadcasted to all of Salvington that Michael's fifth bestowal would have him living as an ascendant mortal on Uversa.

Michael's name while he was living on Uversa was Eventod and this bestowal lasted for eleven years. Eventod received his assignments and performed his duties as an ascending mortal right along with the rest of the free will mortal beings who had come from various of the local universes of Orvonton. This was the first appearance of Michael being incarnated in a life of an ascending mortal being and he appeared on Uversa fully developed and Eventod lived his mortal life advancing up the ascension ladder on Uversa with a group of ascending mortals on their way to Havona. After living on Uversa for eleven years as Eventod, Michael held a meeting with the Ancients Of Days and then in the presence of Gabriel, Michael suddenly left his mortal life on Uversa and returned to his universe position in Salvington, Paradise working as the director of universe affairs.

Around the time that Michael completed his fifth bestowal living as an ascending mortal being on Uversa, the Melchizedek Sons began to include in the curriculum that they were teaching their students that Michael of Nebadon would probably sometime in the near future be incarnating as a mortal being of flesh and blood on a world of time and space in our universe of Nebadon.

The technique that Michael used to transform from Salvington, Paradise to each of his seven bestowal destinations still remain a mystery to all and even Gabriel of Salvington stated that he was never able to figure out or understand what method Michael used to be able to assume at will all of the different personalities to live the lives of one of his own living beings that he had created.

The Sixth Bestowal of Michael of Nebadon was a little unique, because this time Michael shared the entire detailed plan of this incarnation plan with his associates. Michael publicly addressed the inhabitants of Salvington at a large outdoor assembly meeting telling them that he would soon be leaving Salvington to assume the life of a morontia mortal of flesh and blood and live at the courts of the Most High Fathers on the headquarters planet of the fifth constellation, and then Michael suddenly disappeared in front of the assembly, and this time, he was accompanied by one angelic seraphim and the Bright and Morning Star of Nebadon.

Michael then appeared on the headquarters of constellation five on the planet Endantam as a fully developed mortal morontia mortal of flesh and blood and the day that Michael completed this sixth bestowal on planet Endantam, millions of the beings were assembled from the constellation headquarter worlds to welcome Michael back home. Michael then made a public address to this welcoming crowd telling them that he had simply been about his Universal Father's business.

And from the day that Michael addressed the crowd who welcomed back home on Salvington after he completed his sixth bestowal on the planet Endantam up until the time of Michael's seventh final bestowal on planet earth as the Son of Man, Jesus of Nazareth, everyone in the Nebadon universe continued to talk about the many trials Michael had to endure while he was completing his seven bestowals.

Michael's seventh and final bestowal had been looked forward to for more than tens of thousands of years by many of the residents of Salvington, Paradise. For years Gabriel of Salvington had been teaching his students who attended the universe schools that Michael would be completing his seventh and final bestowal as a mortal being of flesh and blood, but no one knew the time or the place where Michael's final bestowal would take place.

Shortly after the default of the Material Son and Daughter from Paradise Adam and Eve in the first Garden of Eden on planet #606 earth 37,848 years ago, Michael made a public announcement in Salvington that the planet #606 earth would be the location for his seventh and final bestowal, because for more than thirty-eight thousand years , planet earth was considered to be a very important planet in all of the councils of the entire universe. Planet earth was considered to be one of the most important planets in our universe because of its strategic locations, its many stargates and wormholes and most importantly it is inhabited by the Universal Father's special creation, human beings.

At the time that Michael of Nebadon was completing his seventh and final bestowal on earth as the incarnation of Jesus of Nazareth, there was a full disclosure and publicity given to all the residents on Salvington on everything that was occurring in Michael's life while he was living on planet earth. No one living on Salvington, Paradise knew until the actual time of the event itself, that Michael would appear on planet earth as a helpless infant on the realm of planet earth, because all of Michael's previous six bestowals he had always appeared as a fully developed individual of the personality group for each of his prior bestowal incarnations and it was a thrilling announcement when the Salvington broadcasts stated that the baby Jesus had been born on earth in Bethlehem, Palestine. However, when this announcement was made in Salvington then everyone knew that their Creator Son Michael had taken the most precarious step in his entire bestowal career and all of Michael's associates felt that Michael was risking his position and authority as the director of universe affairs on his seventh and final bestowal mission on planet earth by being born as a helpless infant. Michael was permitted to marry during his life as a mortal man living on earth, but as a Creator Son, Michael and all of the rest of the

Creator Sons were forbidden to leave any offspring behind on any of the planets during their seven bestowals. However, at the same time everyone on Salvington also understood that Michael's life in this seventh and final bestowal on planet earth would eternally enthrone him as the undisputed and supreme System Sovereign of the Nebadon universe.

This is the complete story of Michael of Nebadon's seventh and final bestowal on planet earth that began when he was born and named Joshua Ben Joseph on August 21, 7 B.C. at noon as an infant and depicts his life as the incarnation of Jesus of Nazareth until he died a mortal death on the cross on Friday, April 7, A. D. 30.

In order to begin his seventh and final bestowal of planet earth, Michael of Nebadon was conceived and born through a virgin birth just like Machiventa Melchizedek had been born on earth 1,973 years earlier.

Michael's virgin birth given name on earth was Jesus, a Jewish baby and his birth parents were Joseph and Mary. The only thing that was different about this Jewish baby was that he was the incarnation of Michael of Nebadon, a Creator Son of Paradise who created all of the things and living beings who live in our local universe of Nebadon.

This mystery of the incarnation of Deity into the human form of Jesus will forever remain to be unsolved and even those who live in eternity will never know the technique and method that was used by Creator Son Michael of Nebadon to incarnate into the form and likeness of the living beings he chose to complete his seven bestowals. That is the secret of those who live Sonarington, Paradise, because they have all already passed through their seven stages of the bestowal experience.

When Jesus was born on earth in Bethlehem, Palestine there were certain wise men who were the descendants of Noah, the wine maker who already knew about the impending arrival of the baby Jesus. And through their contacts of one world with another, these three wise men had spiritual insight, and they learned about the seventh and final bestowal of Michael of Nebadon that was going to be taking place on planet earth. The seraphim angels through the midway creatures who were living on earth also announced to a group of Chaldean priests whose leader was Arnon about the birth of baby Jesus in a stable in Bethlehem, Palestine. These Chaldean priests who were men of God then went to visit this newborn baby who was lying in a manger with his parents Joseph and Mary. The only supernatural event that was associated with the birth of Jesus was the announcement that the same seraphim angels who had been formally attached to Adam and Eve in the first Garden of Eden made the announcement to the Chaldean priest Ardon that the baby Jesus had just been born in a stable in Bethlehem.

Jesus' parents Joseph and Maty were an average Jewish family for their day and generation, and they raised Jesus along with his five brothers and three sisters in an ordinary manner by following the established Jewish traditions.

All through the early years of Jesus' helpless infancy years his mother Mary kept him constantly by her side to make sure that nothing would jeopardize or interfere with his future mission on earth. For the two years that Jesus lived with his parents Joseph and Mary in Alexandria, Egypt, Jesus continued to have good health, and he had a normal childhood and except for a few friends and relatives, no one was told about Jesus being a child of promise.

In the year 4 B. C. during the month of August when Jesus was three years old Jesus' parents moved their family from Alexandria, Egypt and back to Bethlehem, Palestine. By the end of the year 4 B. C. in the month of October their family moved again to Nazareth and in less than a week, his father Joseph began working at a new job as a carpenter. Jesus' first baby brother James was born on April 2, 3 B.C. and he was thrilled at having a baby brother. In the month of July, 3 B. C. one month before Jesus was four years old, an epidemic outbreak of a malignant intestinal disease began to spread all over Nazareth. Mary became concerned by the danger of Jesus being exposed to this epidemic, so she moved her two children Jesus and James to her brother's home on a farm in Megiddo near Sarid.

On February 11, 5 B. C. when Jesus reached the age of five, the Universal Father of Paradise sent a Divine Thought Adjuster to indwell Jesus and it was the same Divine Thought Adjuster who had indwelt Machiventa Melchizedek during his ninety-four years of living on earth 1,973 years earlier in Salem, Palestine. Jesus was very happy to receive his Divine Thought Adjuster, and he was also very happy when on July 11, 2, B.C. his first sister Miriam was born. It was the custom of the Galilean Jews in those days for the mother to educate their children until the age of five and then the father assumed this responsibility from that time on. By the time Jesus was six years old in the year 1, B. C., he had already mastered the Galilean dialect of the Aramaic tongue, and his father Joseph began teaching Jesus the Greek language. In the early summer of 1 B.C. Mary's cousin Elizabeth her husband high priest Zacharias and their son John who would later become to be John the Baptist came to visit Jesus' family. Jesus' mother Mary and her cousin Elizabeth were both descendants of Moses' brother Aaron, the high priest and from the bloodline of King David. Jesus and his cousin John enjoyed playing together during this visit by building blocks in the sand on the roof of Jesus' home.

The seventh year of Jesus' life during the year of A. D. 1, was an eventful year for Jesus, because for the first time in one hundred years one of the deepest and heaviest snowfall that was two feet deep occurred in Nazareth. Jesus was playing on the roof of his home in all of the snow and accidentally fell on the descending steps off of the roof.

This accident upset Jesus' mother Mary so much that from then on, she tried to keep Jesus very close to her side for many months afterwards.

The fourth member of Jesus' family in Nazareth was his brother Joseph who was born on Wednesday morning, March 16, A.D. 1. During those days Jewish children began their formal education at the age of seven, so in August, A. D. 1, Jesus entered a Jewish school in Nazareth, and he attended this Nazareth synagogue school where he received his moral and spiritual training until he was ten years old. Jesus' real education which was using the equipment of his mind and heart to be used for the actual test of dealing with the difficult problems of life is what Jesus learned daily by continuing to mingle with his fellow men. It was Jesus' constant close association with people, young and old, Jew and Gentile that gave him the opportunity to get to know and love all of the beautiful people who lived on earth.

Before Jesus turned eight years old, he was known to all the mothers and young women who lived in Nazareth, because they had all met him and talked often at the spring that was close to his home. During the eighth year, A.D. 2, of Jesus' life he had an interesting year at school, because he was a diligent student who always asked a lot of questions, and he was very keen in mathematics. Jesus soon came to be a skillful harpist, and both his family and friends enjoyed his extraordinary musical skills. Another happy event for Jesus during this same year was when his third brother, Simon was born on Friday evening April 14, A.D. 2. During the ninth year of Jesus's life his second sister Martha was born on September 13, A.D.3, and Jesus' father Joseph built an addition on to their house which served as a combined workshop with a bedroom and for the first time, Joseph gave Jesus his own set of tools. Jesus continued to grow physically, intellectually, socially and spiritually. Jesus got along fairly well with the rest of the children in his neighborhood who were his age, but he often became discouraged with their slow acting minds. Before Jesus was ten years old, he became to be the leader of a group of seven boys his age and they formed a club to promote the requirements of manhood which included new physical games, along with intellectual and religious pursuits.

During the tenth year A. D. 4 of Jesus' childhood while he was walking through the countryside with his father Joseph, Jesus told his father that he was starting to become increasingly conscious of the highly unusual nature of his life's mission on earth. Jesus entered the advanced synagogue school in August A. D. 4, and he continued to be very inquisitive and ask more questions in school than the rest of the students. One of the most unusual and outstanding traits that Jesus had was his unwillingness to physically fight when he was attacked by some of his neighboring bullies, because he was disciplined to not get involved in physical confrontations.

There were several occasions when some of the older boys in the neighborhood attacked Jesus, but his next-door neighbor was Jesus' best friend, and he always stepped in to defend him against these attacks. During Jesus' tenth year of life, he began to display a marked preference to associate with older people, and he enjoyed talking over things relating to cultural, social, economic, political and religious issues with the more older mature minds. Later on, during this same year, Jesus began to show great skills while fishing in the Sea of Galilee and he became to be an expert fisherman. One day while Jesus was on a fishing trip with his father Joseph, he made up his mind to become a fisherman.

During the eleventh year of Jesus' life another baby brother, Jude was born on June 24, A.D. 5, but there were birth complications for several weeks with Jude so, Jesus took it upon himself to help his mother Mary to care for Jude during the first two years of his life. At the end of the eleventh year of his life, Jesus had developed into a vigorous, well developed and fairly lighthearted youth and he began to meditate daily and this was followed by his serious contemplation of how he was going to carry out his family obligations with his eight brothers and sisters and at the same time be obedient to the call of his mission to earth and all its people, because Jesus knew that his ministry was not going to be limited to the betterment of his Jewish people.

During the twelfth year of Jesus's life in the year A.D.6, he became more successful in getting along with his five brothers and three sisters and the only conflict that existed in his home was the constant friction between his two brothers Joseph and Jude. It was very hard for Joseph and Mary while they were raising Jesus and their other eight children, but they faithfully raised all nine of their children and as time went on Jesus' parents both realized that there was something superhuman about their oldest son Jesus, but both of Jesus' parents died never knowing that their son Jesus was really the Universe Creator Son who had incarnated in the mortal flesh on earth.

During his twelfth year on earth, Jesus began to pay more attention to his music, and he began to home school his eight brothers and sisters. Joseph and Mary had different viewpoints about Jesus' bestowal mission on earth, but his father Joseph's beliefs grew stronger as time went by and during the next two years of Jesus' life, he suffered a lot of mental distress trying to adjust his personal religious beliefs with the established beliefs that his parents had. However, Jesus was able to make the necessary adjustments between the duties towards his family obligations into a smooth flow of family loyalty, fairness, tolerance and love.

During Jesus' thirteenth year of A. D. 7, he began to transform from boyhood to the beginning of being a young man and his voice began to change and other features of his body and mind began to display the evidence of his incoming manhood.

On Sunday night January 9, A.D. 7, Jesus' baby brother Amos was born and around the middle of February A.D. 7, Jesus suddenly became aware that he was destined to perform a very important mission on earth for the enlightenment of all mankind.

Jesus graduated from the local synagogue school in Nazareth on March 20, A.D. 7, and the Jewish elders began making plans for him to continue his education at the prestigious Hebrew academy in Jerusalem. Jesus listened as the Jewish elders made plans for him to complete his education in Jerusalem, but in his heart, he knew that he would not be able to go to Jerusalem to study with the rabbis. Little did Jesus dream of the tragedy that would soon occur where he would have to assume the responsibility to support his mother and eight siblings.

Jesus had now reached the threshold of young manhood, and he was now qualified to accompany is parents to Jerusalem to celebrate his first Passover and it took them four days to reach Jerusalem, and for the first time in Jesus' life he got to see the holy city, the beautiful palaces and the inspiring temple that had been built for his Universal Father.

The day before the Passover Sabbath, many spiritual thoughts began to flow through Jesus' mortal mind and these thoughts filled his heart with affectionate pity as he looked at all of the spiritually blind people who had assembled in the temple to celebrate the

Passover. That day proved to be one of the most extraordinary days that Jesus had ever gotten to experience as a mortal human, because that night, an assigned messenger from Salvington, Paradise who was sent by his heavenly older brother Emmanual told Jesus that his hour had come, and that it was time for him begin to be about his Father's business.

CHAPTER TWELVE

THE EARLY YEARS OF JESUS OF NAZARETH

God said, "I will be with you."

(Exodus 3:12)

Seek first his kingdom and his righteousness, and all these things will be given to you as well.

(Matthew 6:33)

A Prayer:

Father with you I lack nothing, no matter the situation.

The most engaging event in all of Jesus' earth bestowal experience on earth was his first visit to Jerusalem to attend the Passover and he especially enjoyed the experience of being able to go to the temple all by himself and have religious and philosophical discussions with the Jewish elders and rabbis. This was Jesus' first opportunity to enjoy a few days of independent living, and he had the freedom to come and go on his own in Jerusalem without any restrictions from his parents Joseph and Mary.

Everywhere Jesus went throughout the temple courts, he was shocked and sickened by the spirit of irreverence he observed. On Wednesday of the Passover week Jesus was permitted to go home with his friend Lazurus and his two sisters to spend the night at their home in Bethany. That evening Lazarus and his two sisters Martha and Mary listened intently as Jesus discussed the temporal, eternal, human and divine aspects of life and on that night all of the Lazurus family came to love Jesus as if he was their own brother.

Jesus' parents gathered near the temple when the Passover ended to begin the four-day journey back home to Nazareth and Jesus was supposed to travel back to Nazareth with his father and the rest of the men in their caravan. However, Jesus did not join the returning caravan and instead he stayed behind in the temple in Jerusalem discussing the subject of angels with the Jewish rabbis and he was completely unmindful of the passing time and the departure of his parents. It was not until Joseph and Mary reached Jericho that they discovered that their fourteen-year-old son Jesus was not with the group who were returning home to Nazareth.

In the meantime, Jesus remained in the temple all day listening and participating in the spiritual discussions with the rabbis and when the afternoon spiritual discussions with elders and rabbis ended, Jesus walked to his Uncle Simon's house in Bethany to have his evening meal. Early the next day Jesus went back to the temple in Jerusalem to continue his religious discussions with the elders and rabbis. Meanwhile Joseph and Mary were stopping by all of their relatives' homes asking if anyone had seen Jesus while Jesus went on to spend the next two days attending conferences and discussions with the elders and rabbis in the temple. Many of the questions Jesus was asking the Jewish scholars in the temple embarrassed and irritated them, but Jesus' spirit displayed such love, candid fairness and a hunger for knowledge that most of the temple scholars and rabbis treated Jesus with a lot of compassion and consideration.

When Jesus' second day in the temple ended Jesus once again went to his Uncle Simon's home to have his evening meal and later on that evening Jesus prayed and meditated in his Uncle Simon's Garden thinking about his upcoming heavy family problems and his bestowal mission on earth.

Jesus spent his third day in the temple with the scribes, teachers, rabbis and many spectators and his Uncle Simon came down from Bethany to see what his fourteen-year-old nephew was up to in the temple every day in Jerusalem. When the sessions were over on the third day in the temple, Simon and Jesus went back to Bethany once again to have their evening meal at his home. Jesus went to meditate and pray again on that third night in Simon's Garden thinking about how his definite plan of approach for his life's mission and trying to decide the best way to reveal the truths of the Universal Father and the path of light and life to the spiritually blended people on earth. All during these three days Jesus had never thought about his parents Joseph and Mary and on the fourth day while Jesus was having breakfast at his friend Lazarus' house, Jesus thought about his parents Joseph and Mary and hoped that they weren't worried about him for staying behind to go to the temple for the past four days.

Jesus went back to the temple again on the fourth day and the teachers and scribes were all astonished that Jesus had so much knowledge about the scriptures in both Hebrew and Greek especially at such a young age. That prior evening Jesus' parents had heard about a strange young man who had been debating and preaching to the Jewish scribes and teachers in the Jerusalem temple, but they had no idea that this young man was their son Jesus. Joseph and Mary were getting ready to go to their cousin Zacharius and Elizabeth's house, because they thought that's where Jesus had been for the past four days, but at the last minute they decided to stop by the temple first since Zacharias was a high priest who worked in the temple, they thought Zacharias might be at the temple working that day. Imagine how shocked Joseph and Mary were to find their son Jesus sitting in the temple among the scribes and elders teaching and preaching. Joseph was speechless when he saw Jesus and his mother Mary was totally perplexed and very little was said while the three of them journeyed back home to Nazareth. As Jesus and his parents continued on their journey home, they stopped briefly at the foot of Mount Olivet and Jesus raised his staff and with intense emotion he said these words:

"Oh Jerusalem, Jerusalem, and the people thereof, what slaves you are-subservient to the Roman yoke and victims of your own traditions-but I will return to cleanse yonder temple and deliver my people from this bondage."

When Jesus and his parents reached their home from their trip to Jerusalem Jesus briefly told his parents that while he had to do the will of his Father in heaven that he would also be obedient to his father and mother on earth and that he will await his hour to begin his mission on earth.

Jesus' father Joseph was puzzled by what he had just told them, but his mother Mary understood the words that Jesus had spoken at the foot of Mount Olivet and Mary also remembered the important Messiah mission that Jesus her son had to complete as the deliverer of Israel.

The fourteenth and fifteenth years of Jesus' life on earth were the most crucial ones, because during these two years Jesus began to become more self-conscious of his divinity and destiny, but since he still had not yet achieved a large amount of communication from his indwelling Divine Thought Adjuster, it was hard for Jesus during this time in his life of real tests and temptations to understand the full magnitude of his mission on earth and Jesus' parents Joseph and Mary both loved Jesus, but it was also very hard for both of them to really understand him and what his bestowal mission was on earth.

During the fourteenth year of Jesus' life in the year A.D. 8, he was developing good skills in making items from canvas and leather and Jesus continued to develop expert carpenter and cabinet making skills while working with his father Joseph. Jesus made frequent trips to pray and meditate on top of the hill near his family's home and during this time Jesus was also becoming more and more aware of the nature of his seventh and final bestowal mission on earth. All throughout the year A.D. 8, Jesus continued to grow in favor with mankind and God and his future was looking bright.

All was well in Jesus' family until on Tuesday, September 25, A.D.8, a messenger runner from Sepphoris brought the tragic news to Jesus' home that his father Joseph had been severely injured in a construction accident while he was working on the governor's home and his father subsequently died from his injuries. The death of Jesus' father disrupted the affairs of Jesus' home and his future education plans had to be put on hold. Jesus then realized that he not only had to fulfill his seventh bestowal for his Heavenly Father, but now he had to assume the responsibility of caring for his widowed mother who was pregnant and to help care for his seven brothers and sisters.

Jesus cheerfully accepted his family obligations, and he carried out his family duties to the end. All of this time Jesus knew nothing about Archangel Gabriel's visit to his mother Mary telling her about his upcoming virgin birth and he didn't learn about this event until his cousin John the Baptist told him on the day of his baptism in the River Jordan at the beginning of his public ministry. During this year of A.D. 8, many of Jesus' neighbors would often come by their home during the cold winter evenings to listen while Jesus played his harp, told his stories and read to them from the Greek scriptures. The economic affairs of Jesus' family ran smoothly after the death of his father Joseph, because a large sum of money was on hand and Jesus had a keen business and financial mind.

Jesus proved to be a wise and efficient administrator of his late father's estate, and he had a firm grasp on the proper management of his large family, but before the year A.D. 8, ended all of the family savings were gone and Jesus had to sell some of the houses that he and his neighbor Jacob who was his best friend owned together as partners.

On Wednesday evening April 17, A.D. 9, Ruth who was the baby of the family was born and Jesus gave her the nickname of Babe Ruth. Jesus loved and enjoyed being a good father to his baby sister Ruth and to the rest of his seven brothers and sisters. When Jesus was fifteen years old, he wrote the Lord's Prayer for his seven brothers and sisters to pray daily. Jesus also began to read the Book of Enoch over and over and this book influenced him so much that he later decided to call his seventh and final bestowal on earth as the "Son of Man." Jesus was thoroughly convinced that he was not going to be the Messiah and although he wanted to help his Universal Father's people, he knew that he would never lead the Jewish people in an army or sit on the throne of David, so Jesus began to ask himself that when the time came for him to begin his ministry on earth what would he call himself and how would he go forth as a world teacher.

Before the end of Jesus' fifteenth year once again his family ran out of money and his brother James had to begin selling doves and his sister Miriam had to sell milk from a second cow they had purchased from their neighbor. On the first Sabbath after Jesus' fifteenth birthday the chazan from the local synagogue arranged for Jesus to conduct the morning service and after that morning service Jesus and his brother James climbed to the top of the Nazareth hill near his family home and together, they wrote down the Ten Commandments on two smooth boards for their brothers and sisters to learn and recite.

Jesus was disappointed during his fifteenth year when he went to Sepphoris to petition King Herod Antipas to hear his appeal concerning the amount of money due to his late father Joseph at the time of his accidental death, but King Herod decreed to Jesus that no money would be paid to his family and from that day on Jesus called Herod Antipas, that fox.

As Jesus continued to grow up and mature during his adolescence years the rigorous duties of supporting his large family gave him very little time to indulge in any mystic tendencies. Jesus soon rented a large piece of land north of his family's home in Nazareth and he divided it into garden plots for his seven brothers and sisters to grow and sell their harvests. At the end of Jesus' fifteenth year Jesus had completed the transition from childhood to manhood and the growth period in Jesus' mind had also ended and he was now ready to begin his real career of being the young man of Nazareth.

As Jesus entered his adolescence years, he still found himself as the head and sole supporter of his large family and within a few years after his father Joseph's death all the family's property was gone. As time passed Jesus began to become consciously aware of his previous life as the Creator Son Michael of Nebadon in Paradise and at the same time he began to realize that now he was living on earth as a mortal man for the main purpose of revealing his heavenly Paradise Father to all of the children of men living on earth. As Jesus continued to experience living his adolescence years on earth, he also began to remember all of his six prior bestowals as a youth in all of the realms of Nebadon and this helped Jesus to better understand how distressed and perplexed the adolescents of all ages felt on all of the other worlds throughout the universe.

During Jesus' sixteenth year in A.D. 10, he attained his full physical growth, and he was a virile strong youth who became increasingly serious but at the same time Jesus was a very kind and sympathetic young man with kind eyes that were intensive but searching. His voice was musical but authoritative and even when he had ordinary common contact with people, his twofold divine and human nature were always quite visible. Jesus had a healthy and well-proportioned body and a keen analytical mind with a somewhat aggressive temperament and as time went on, it became harder and harder for Jesus' mother Mary and his eight brothers and sisters to understand him, and they often stumbled over his words and misunderstood what he was trying to do with his life. During this same year Jesus' brother started school, and his family had to sell one of their rental homes to pay for his educational expenses and Jesus' brother James took over the duties of home schooling all of the rest of the children in the family including the girls. By the end of this year A.D. 10, Jesus had made up his mind that after he was finished rearing his siblings and seeing them married, then he would begin his public ministry work as a teacher of truth and reveal the Universal Heavenly Father to the people living on earth. Jesus already knew that he was not going to be the expected Messiah that the Jewish people wanted so he began to talk less and less with anyone about his seventh and final bestowal mission on earth, because Jesus felt that his bestowal mission on earth was so peculiar that no on earth could give him any advice.

Jesus' mother Mary was hurt that Jesus had to work so hard every day at his carpenter bench earning a living for his large family instead of attending school at the synagogue in Jerusalem. During Jesus' seventeenth year in A.D.11, there was a lot of conflict in the Jewish community towards the Roman Empire concerning taxes and there was talk of a rebellion. A strong Jewish nationalist party called the Zealots were soon formed, because the Jews were not willing to wait for the coming Messiah, they wanted to revolt now. When the Zealots arrived in Jerusalem and approached Jesus about joining their group he refused to join.

Jesus' mother Mary's brother Simon joined the Jewish Zealot Party as an officer and for several years the relations between Simon and Jesus were estranged. Jesus who had just turned seventeen was confronted with a very delicate political situation and things grew even more complicated when a wealthy Jewish money lender named Isaac approached Jesus with a proposal that if he would lay down his tools and assume the leadership position of the Nazareth Zealot Party that he would agree to support Jesus' family. At this point in his life Jesus knew that something had to be done to state his political position, so Jesus turned down Isaac's proposal telling him that his first duty was to his family and that money could not provide the love he was giving to his family. Jesus also explained what his life's mission was to Isaac and that until it was time for him to begin his mission on earth, he was going to continue to faithfully fulfill his family obligations and with that answer that Jesus gave to Isaac, the rich Jewish money lender, he was able to bring a happy ending to a very tense and threatening situation. This crisis was over for Jesus for the time being, but the people of Nazareth were divided over Jesus's decision when he turned down the military position with the Jewish Zealot Party and many of the residents of Nazareth were agitated for a long time over Jesus' decision. Jesus lost favor with many of the citizens of Nazareth for turning down the military position with the Zealots Party and because of this and subsequent occurrences, Jesus in later years made the decision to leave Nazareth and move to Capernaum.

Jesus' brother James graduated from the synagogue school in the year A.D. 11, and he then began to work full time at home as a carpenter and this gave Jesus more time to work on his cabinet finishing business and the remodeling of their home. During this time Jesus also began to make more progress in organizing the many thoughts he was having in his mind about his mission on earth. Gradually Jesus was able to bring his divine and human natures together with the assistance of his indwelling Divine Thought Adjuster and by organizing his intellect, Jesus was able to continue to make his own honest decisions. So far nothing supernatural had occurred in Jesus's life except for the visit from the Paradise messenger Archangel Gabriel who was sent by his older brother Emmanual a few years earlier.

During Jesus' eighteenth year in A.D.12, all of the family property was sold, and the proceeds were used to pay the Roman taxes, buy his brother James new tools and to make a payment for their family's supply and repair shop. Jesus then decided to take his brother James to Jerusalem to celebrate the Passover. During their journey to Jerusalem Jesus and James talked about many things and James told Jesus that he was looking forward to the day when he could assume full responsibility for their large family so that Jesus could begin his mission.

When Jesus and James returned to Nazareth from their Passover celebration in Jerusalem Jesus began working in the family's supply and repair shop. Jesus truly loved people and he continued to provide for his family, and he continued to conduct the Sabbath services at the local synagogue. Around this same time the chazan from the local synagogue organized a young men's club for the young Jewish men where they could have religious and philosophic discussions, and they met regularly at the different members' homes and Jesus was a member of this group. Jesus' social life was restricted but he had many nice friends and staunch admirers who consisted of both young men and women who lived in Nazareth.

In September A.D. 12, Jesus' cousins Elizabeth and her son John the Baptist came to visit his family and Jesus and John were able to talk over some important issues during this visit, specifically that John was going to be an important part of Jesus' seventh and final bestowal mission on earth. Jesus and John, the Baptist both knew that Jesus still had a few more years with the rearing of his siblings and they never saw each other again until the day that John the Baptist completed the baptism of Jesus, the Son of Man in the River Jordan. On Saturday, December 3rd of this same year Jesus' baby brother Amos died after being sick for a week with a high fever and Jesus comforted his grieving family after this loss and his comfort gave his family hope.

During the nineteenth year of Jesus' life in the year A.D. 13, he and his mother Mary were starting to get along better than they had in years and they both mutually devoted their time to the continued upbringing of Jesus' four brothers and three sisters. Jesus used wise discipline with his brothers and sisters and there was very little, or no punishment required to ensure their obedience. The only exception was his brother Jude whom on many occasions Jesus found it necessary to impose penalties for Jude's frequent infractions of the family rules. All of Jesus' siblings would often consult Jesus about their childhood issues and troubles and they would also confide in Jesus as if he was their father. As time went on Jesus began to be more liberal and he modified the family teachings and practices relating to the Sabbath observations and religion and at these times, Jesus had unquestionably become the head of the household in his family.

Jesus' brother Jude started school at the local synagogue in A.D. 13, and Jesus had to sell his harp to pay for Jude's education expenses and this, the last recreational pleasure that Jesus had was now gone. Even though Jesus' family was poor, his social standing in Nazareth was not impaired and he was one of the foremost young men of Nazareth and he was highly regarded by many of the young women who lived in Nazareth.

One of these women who lived in Nazareth, Rebecca was the seventeen-year-old daughter of Ezra, a wealthy Jewish merchant and she was slowly falling in love with Jesus. So, Rebecca's father Ezra invited Jesus to their home to celebrate Rebecca's seventeenth birthday and Ezra then offered to supply Jesus' family with sufficient income if Jesus would agree to marry his daughter Rebecca. Jesus listened attentively to Ezra's proposal and his response to Ezra was that no amount of money could ever take the place of his feelings of the love and obligations he had in his heart to complete the rearing of his late father's family. Ezra was deeply touched by Jesus' response and Ezra then told his wife and daughter Rebecca that he couldn't have Jesus for a son-in-law, because he was much too noble for his family. Rebecca was heartbroken and she turned down many suitors and never married and Rebecca with pure devotion in her heart followed Jesus all throughout his public ministry years and she was one of the women who stood by the side of Jesus' mother Mary as he hung and died on the cross on April 7, A.D. 30.

In the year A. D. 13, Jesus had a strange longing to go to Jerusalem again to celebrate the Passover and as Jesus was passing through the city of Jerusalem, he paused to look at the temple and all of the visitors who had gathered there to celebrate the Passover and Jesus felt a feeling of revulsion to the Herod Antipas built temple with all of its politically appointed priests inside it and he instead decided to go to Bethany and celebrate the Passover with his dear friends Lazarus and his two sisters Martha and Mary in their home. As they began the Passover celebration Lazarus told Jesus that they didn't have a paschal lamb for the feast and Jesus then told Lazarus in a long and convincing speech that our Universal Father in Heaven was not concerned with such a childlike ritual of having a paschal lamb. So that Passover evening the four of them sat down and had the first Passover celebration ever without a paschal lamb. The wine and unleavened bread were ready for their Passover feast and Jesus called the bread and wine that they had the two emblems, the bread of life and the water of life.

When Jesus returned to Nazareth, he told his mother Mary about his new way of celebrating the Passover celebration and it became Jesus' new custom to celebrate the Passover this way whenever he was with Lazarus and his family in Bethany. During this same year of A.D. 13, Jesus's mother Mary had a long talk with him asking if he would ever get married and Jesus explained to his mother that his immediate duty was to complete his seventh and final bestowal mission on earth. Jesus was rapidly becoming to be a man, an adult and slowly he was learning how to live the heavenly life on earth as he continued to prepare to complete his seventh and final bestowal mission on earth.

More and more Jesus was depending on the ultimate guidance of his Universal Father while he continued to assume the role of the father to guide and direct his seven siblings. When Jesus turned the age of nineteen, he was becoming more experienced in the skill of turning his defeats into victories and he was also learning how to transform the many difficulties of time into the triumphs of eternity.

As the years passed Jesus continued to experience the daily life as a mortal man on earth and as a child Jesus had accumulated a vast amount of knowledge, as a youth he sorted, classified and correlated all of this important knowledge and now as a young man,

Jesus began to organize all of the intellectual and spiritual knowledge he had accumulated to prepare to use all of these important assets in his subsequent teachings, ministry and service for all mankind on earth and all of the other spheres throughout the entire universe of Nebadon.

Jesus was born as an infant into the realm of earth, he lived through his childhood, passed through the successive stages of youth and young manhood and now Jesus was standing on the threshold of full manhood. Jesus was now rich in the human experience of living and now he had a full understanding of human nature, and he was at a point in his life where he had become an expert in the divine art of revealing his Universal Father to all ages and stages of humanity living on earth. Jesus was now a full-grown man, an adult who was ready and preparing to complete his seventh and final bestowal mission on earth. As Jesus entered the early years of his adult life he continued to live a normal average human life on earth.

Jesus chose earth as the planet to carry out his final bestowal mission and he had two reasons for making this choice.

The first reason was to master the experience of living a full life as a mortal human to complete his sovereignty requirements on Nebadon.

The second reason was to complete the process of the revelation of the Universal Prime Creator Father to the mortals who live on the worlds of time and space and to provide these mortals with effective leadership to walk the path of finding the Universal Father in Paradise.

All of the other creature benefits and universe advantages that Jesus was able to experience were incidental and secondary to his main purpose of his mortal bestowal on earth. Jesus was a carpenter by trade, and he continued to humble himself and remain obedient to his Universal Father while he was living on earth.

Jesus received two celestial visits from the seven higher heavens of Paradise during his lifetime on earth, one when he was thirteen years old just before he attended his first Passover celebration with his parents and when he was being baptized by his cousin John the Baptist in the River Jordan. Once Jesus began his public ministry, he did not hesitate to publicly admit that he was the Son of God and Jesus never objected to any of the titles that his followers called him during his later public ministry years.

In the year A.D. 15, Jesus took his brother Joseph to Jerusalem to celebrate the Passover with Lazarus and his family in Bethany and Joseph asked his brother Jesus many questions while they were there about his life's mission and Jesus responded to all of Joseph's questions by telling him that his hour had not yet come.

During Jesus' twenty-second year in A.D. 16, Jesus was kept busy continuing to deal with the many trials and tribulations that his seven siblings were beginning to experience with their new intellectual and emotional issues that were coming into their lives. At this point Jesus felt that it was time to put his brother James in charge of the family affairs and then Jesus took a job working in nearby Sepphoris with a blacksmith. Jesus was beginning the slow process of weaning his family from having him to be in charge and when James had been the head of the family for two years, Jesus then put James in charge of the household funds and the general management of all of the household family affairs.

On Jesus' twenty-third birthday in A.D. 17, Jesus took off work for three weeks to take his brother Simon to Jerusalem for the Passover celebration and they both enjoyed this trip, because Jesus had time to mingle with many interesting people one of whom was a young Hellenist Greek named Stephen. Jesus and Stephen spent four hours discussing the one true living God and Stephen was impressed with the teachings Jesus gave him that day and this was the same Stephen who would become to be one of Jesus' followers and later one day while Stephen was preaching the early gospel of Jesus, he became the first Christian martyr after he was stoned to death by a group of irate Jews. When Stephen lost his life that day, Saul, from Tarsus was there and he saw how the young Greek man Stephen died for his faith and it aroused such strong emotions in Saul's heart that it led Saul to become a follower of Jesus and Saul later became to be one of Jesus' twelve apostles, Paul, the philosopher and sole founder of the early Christian religion. Jesus' brother Simon never forgot what Jesus taught him about the Universal Prime Creator Father in Paradise-the seven higher heavens during their trip to Jerusalem to attend the Passover celebration. The last four months of Jesus' twenty-third year in A.D. 17, Jesus went to Damascus and stayed as a guest in the home of a rich Jewish merchant he had met in Philadelphia and this merchant offered Jesus the position to be the master headmaster of a large educational institution he was planning to open.

This proposal was one of the greatest temptations Jesus ever faced in his human career, but he turned this offer down, because Jesus knew that his mission on earth was not going to be supported by any institution of learning where he would have to be under the direction of a council of men. The main thing that Jesus wanted to avoid while completing his public ministry was anything spectacular that would cause distractions to the subsequent generations where they would worship the teacher rather than following God's divine plan. Jesus always tried to suppress everything during his mission that might distract his followers to exalt the teacher in place of his teachings, because Jesus always refused to take any undue or unfair advantage of the human mind, and he didn't want his followers to believe in him unless their hearts were responsive to the spiritual realities that were revealed in his teachings. By the end of the year A.D. 17, Jesus' Nazareth home was being run smoothly by his brother James and Jesus continued to turn his earnings over to his brother James to support his family and he only kept a small portion of his earnings for his immediate personal needs.

As the years passed it became to be more difficult for the many people Jesus encountered to realize that he was really the Son of God on earth, because he seemed to be just like the rest of the people who were living on earth, but this is the way the Universal Father in Paradise ordained for the final seventh bestowal mission to unfold for Jesus. During the twenty-fourth year of Jesus' life in A.D. 18, it was the first time that Jesus finally had freedom from his family responsibilities to his seven siblings, because his brother James had been doing a good job in managing the family affairs.

The week after the Passover in June of A.D. 18, Jesus met with five prominent Jews from Alexandria, Egypt who offered him the position to once again be a religious teacher and assistant to the chazan in the main synagogue in their city. Once again Jesus declined their offer and he told these five prominent Jews that his hour had not yet come. Jesus spent the rest of the year of A.D. 18, praying and meditating and he continued to make tremendous progress in mastering his mind and heart. Marriage was in the air amongst two of Jesus' siblings James and Miriam, and Jesus gave his blessings for the double wedding that they had. Jesus continued to teach evening religious classes three times a week, read the scriptures during the Sabbath services at the local synagogue and he continued to conduct himself as a worthy respected citizen of Nazareth.

During the twenty-fifth year of Jesus's life in A.D. 19, Jesus had grown up to be one of the most robust specimens of manhood ever to appear on earth since the days of Adam and Eve, and Jesus' physical development was superb, and his mind was active, keen and penetrating. In comparison with the average men of his times, Jesus' mind had developed to gigantic proportions and his spirit was just humanly divine.

The family finances were in the best condition since the initial disappearance of his father Joseph's estate. So, Jesus decided this year to take his younger brother Jude to Jerusalem to attend his first Passover celebration in the temple and Jude was thrilled to finally get to meet Lazarus and his family in Bethany, but while Jesus was talking with Lazarus, Jude got into a confrontation with one of the Roman guards and Jude with

Jesus by his side was taken to the local military prison. After Jesus and Jude spent two days in prison, they both appeared before the military magistrate on behalf of Jude. Jesus apologized to the magistrate for Jude's aggressive behavior, and they were both released from prison, and this was the last Passover celebration Jesus attended with his own family.

All of the children in Nazareth especially loved Jesus and they called him Uncle Joshua, because Jesus always welcomed these children at the family's supply and repair shop where he provided them with sand, blocks and stone by the side of the repair shop to play with. Many of these children would often peek into the repair shop and ask Uncle Joshua to come out and tell them a big story, because the children all loved Jesus and Jesus loved all of the children.

During the twenty-sixth year of Jesus' life in the year A.D. 20, Jesus became strongly conscious that he now possessed a wide range of potential powers, but he knew in his heart that he could not use these newfound powers until his hour had come. Whenever Jesus walked to the top of the hill near his home to pray and meditate, he always prayed that he would remain subject and obedient with faith and strength to follow the will and divine plan of his Heavenly Father. Jesus continued to have trouble with his younger brother Jude, but since Jesus was a man of peace, he constantly told his family to be patient with love to Jude. And when Jude ran away from home to join a group of fishermen, Jesus was able to get Jude a permanent job being a fisherman and Jude excelled in this job. The wise and loving counsel of Jesus prevented a break in his family due to his brother's Jude belligerent behavior and Jude was never brought to his calm, normal senses until after he finally got married. Jesus spent this entire year continuing to train his brother James on how to manage the family's supply and repair shop and how to direct the family's affairs. Jesus' mother Mary could tell that Jesus was making plans to soon leave his family and at last the day came when all of Jesus' siblings were firmly established in their lives, and the stage was being set for Jesus' departure from home. In November of this same year Jesus' brother James and Miriam were married in a double wedding ceremony and the day after this wedding ceremony Jesus held an important meeting with his brother James and he told James that he was preparing to leave home to prepare to begin his public ministry. Jesus gave his brother James the title to the family's supply and repair shop and then he drew up a contract that they both signed stating that in return for receiving the repair shop James would assume full responsibility for the family.

CHAPTER THIRTEEN

THE LATER ADULT YEARS OF JESUS' LIFE

I am the light of the world, whoever follows me will never walk in darkness.

(John 8:12)

We do not lose heart. Though outwardly we are wasting away, yet inwardly we are being renewed day by day.

(Corinthians 4:16)

A Prayer:

Dear God, thank you for being near me, because of your loving presence, help and peace, I don't have to be anxious.

Jesus had fully and finally separated himself from the management of the domestic affairs of his Nazareth family, but Jesus continued right up to the day of his baptism to contribute to his family's finances and to still take a keen interest in the spiritual welfare of each one of his seven brothers and sisters. And as always Jesus was also always ready to provide comfort and happiness for his widowed mother Mary. Jesus had made every preparation to finally detach himself permanently from his family in Nazareth and it wasn't easy for him to do this and everyone in Jesus's family had slowly awakened to the fact that he was making the final preparations to leave them and for four years they watched while Jesus was finalizing the plans for his departure.

During the twenty-seventh year of Jesus' life in the year A.D. 21, Jesus quietly left his birth family explaining that he was going to Tiberias and then to visit some other cities near the Sea of Galilee, but this time when Jesus left, he would never again be a permanent member of his family's household. Jesus went and worked with the Zebedee family in Capernaum building boats in their shop for a year and during this time he created a new style of boats and established new methods of boat making. Once a week Jesus held a meeting with the Zebedee household, the boat shop crew and shore helpers and they all came to love Jesus, and they all began to call him master. During this year Jesus also began to attain high levels of conscious contact with his indwelling Divine Thought Adjuster and this year was the last time that Jesus was able to live a settled life living in one location. The days of Jesus' earth pilgrimages were fast approaching, and Jesus knew that it was time to complete his training so he could enter his public ministry.

In March A.D.22, Jesus left the Zebedee family in Capernaum and his plans was to travel extensively until his hour had come, but before Jesus left, he made arrangements with Zebedee's son John to continue to send money every month to provide for his family in Nazareth. Jesus spent the Passover week with the Zebedee family before leaving and at the end of the Passover celebration Jesus met a wealthy Jewish traveler from India named Gomad and his son Gonid who both insisted that Jesus travel with them to visit Rome and various other cities along the coastline of the Mediterranean Sea. Gomad gave Jesus an advance for his wages for one year which he gave to John Zebedee to send to his family every month in Nazareth. During the entire twenty-ninth year of Jesus' life in A.D. 23, he was traveling along the coast of the Mediterranean Sea and all throughout this tour of the Roman world Jesus became known as the Damascus scribe and Jewish tutor. While Jesus was on this tour of the Roman world, he got a chance to meet and love all different kinds of people, rich, poor, high, low, black, white, educated, uneducated, moral and immoral people and Jesus loved them all, because he was glad to have met them.

By the end of his Mediterranean tour Jesus knew with all certainty that he was the Son of God, a Creator Son of the Universal Prime Creator Father of Paradise, because his Divine Thought Adjuster helped Jesus to remember all of the Paradise experiences he had before he incarnated on earth. Jesus the Creator Son of God was so pure in spirit and in his vibration of love that the entire planet earth's vibrations were raised and later he and his wife Mary Magdalene set the foundations for the gridlines of Christ consciousness for humanity to use 1,900 years later when in 1987 after God decreed the Harmonic Convergence, earth began its thirty-eight-year ascension journey to the new heaven on earth.

Jesus and his two friends from India, Gomad and his son Gonid traveled all throughout the Roman world for two years until Jesus parted ways and said farewell in the city of Charax in December of A.D. 23. And Jesus then returned home to Nazareth. Gonid had learned a lot of spiritual teachings from Jesus during their two-year tour and during their journey Gonid had carefully studied all of the people he had met which helped him to make his final decision on what he was going to do for the remainder of his life on earth. Jesus had fully considered and now he approved of his plan that since he had been born of Jewish parents in Palestine that he was going to return to Galilee to wait for his time to come in the land of his father Joseph's people. Jesus had found out through personal experience that Palestine was the best place in all of the Roman world for him to begin the closing chapters and the final scenes of his mortal life on earth. For the first time in Jesus' life, he was satisfied with God's divine plan of openly manifesting his true nature to reveal his divine identity among the Jews and Gentiles in his native home of Palestine.

At the end of his Mediterranean tour Jesus had earned enough money to live off of until it was time to begin his public ministry. During Jesus's brief visit back home in Nazareth Jesus spent some time with his family and friends, but he spent most of his time with his two sisters Mary and Ruth. Both of Jesus' brothers Simon and Jude had been waiting for Jesus to return home before they got married and Jesus blessed both of their marriage unions at a double wedding ceremony that was held in March A.D. 24. By this time all of Jesus' brothers and sisters were now married except for his youngest sister Ruth who was still living at home with her mother Mary.

Around the time Jesus was preparing to leave Nazareth the conductor of a large caravan on its way to the Caspian Sea was passing through Nazareth and when the conductor fell ill, Jesus who was also a linguist volunteered to take his place. Jesus held a family conference before leaving with the caravan and suggested that his mother Mary and Ruth move to Capernaum while Joseph and his wife could move into their Nazareth home.

On April 1, A.D. 24 Jesus left Nazareth as the conductor of the caravan traveling to the Caspian Sea region and for Jesus this caravan trip was just another adventure of exploration and an opportunity to work on his personal ministry. Jesus had many interesting experiences with his caravan family of passengers, guards and camel drivers. There were also many people who lived along this caravan route who were able to experience uplifting spiritual and intellectual experiences after they came into contact with meeting Jesus. Of all of his world travels, the Caspian Sea trip took Jesus the closest he had ever been to the Orient and it helped Jesus to gain a better understanding and knowledge of the Far Eastern people. Jesus was able to make personal contact with all of the surviving races of earth except for the Red man who lived in America. Jesus enjoyed his personal ministry to each of the various races he met, and he blended with the people he met, and they were for the most part receptive to the living truth about the Universal Paradise Father that Jesus brought to them. The Europeans from the Far West and the Asians from the Far east all accepted Jesus' words of hope and eternal life and they were spiritually influenced by the life of loving service and spiritual ministry that Jesus so graciously displayed as he lived among them.

Jesus' caravan trip to the Caspian Sea region was very successful in every way and it was a most interesting episode for Jesus, because he was able to function in an executive capacity while being responsible for all of the material that was entrusted to him and for the safe travels for all of the members of his caravan family. During the caravan's return trip from the Caspian Sea region Jesus turned over his conductor position to a successor when they arrived at Lake Urmia and Jesus completed his return trip as a passenger with a different caravan group to Damascus and onward to Capernaum. Jesus arrived home to Capernaum in April A.D. 25, and at this point, he no longer regarded Nazareth as his home and Jesus never again lived with his family, so whenever he was in Capernaum he stayed with the Zebedee family.

While Jesus was the conductor of the caravan that was traveling to the Caspian Sea region, he stopped for several days to rest at the old Persian city of Urmia on the western shores of Lake Urmia. On one of the largest group of islands near Urmia, Jesus visited a temple that had been built by a wealthy merchant named Cymboyton and this temple and educational institution was being run by Cymboyton and his three sons with a full faculty who lived on the grounds of the school. Jesus attended this religious and educational institutions daily lectures and discussions at ten in the morning and three in the afternoon with debates at eight in the evening and Cymboyton and his three sons were always in attendance during these three daily sessions. Cymboyton made arrangements for Jesus to work and teach for two weeks in his school where Jesus gave twenty-four lectures on the brotherhood of men.

During the thirty-first year of Jesus' life in the year A.D. 25, he spent this entire year wandering alone through Palestine and Syria and all throughout this year Jesus was known by various names in different parts of Palestine some being, the carpenter of Nazareth, the boatbuilder of Capernaum, the scribe of Damascus and the teacher of Alexandria. Jesus lived in Antioch for over two months working, observing, studying, visiting and ministering while all the time he was learning how a mortal man lives, thinks, feels and reacts in an environment of human existence. Jesus worked as a tentmaker for three weeks and then he traveled along the coast to Caesarea to Joppa, Jamnia, Ashdod, Gaza and Beersheba. Jesus then started on his final tour where he traveled to about fourteen cities located in the heart of Palestine and during this time Jesus' Divine Thought Adjuster led Jesus to climb Mount Hermon so he could complete the work of mastering his human mind and achieve his full consecration on the remainder of his lifework on earth.

This period of isolation on Mount Hermon for Jesus was the end of his human career and the beginning of Jesus' divine phase of his final seventh bestowal mission on earth. Jesus lived alone for six weeks on the slopes of Mount Hermon and near the middle of August A.D. 25, Jesus gathered his supplies, secured a beast of burden and accompanied by a lad named Tiglath, Jesus began his ascent up Mount Hermon. The lad Tiglath accompanied Jesus up Mount Hermon to about 6,000 feet above sea level where they built a stone container where Tiglath stored food for Jesus twice a week.

The first day Jesus left Tiglath and ascended Mount Hermon and after a short way he paused to pray and Jesus asked his Paradise Father to send the guardian seraphim to be with his guide Tiglath and Jesus also asked his Paradise Father that he be permitted to go the rest of the way up the mountain to his last struggle of the realities of his mortal existence alone and his Universal Father granted Jesus this request. Jesus continued his climb up Mount Hermon alone into his great test with only his indwelling Divine Thought Adjuster to guide and sustain him and Jesus ate frugally while he was on Mount Hermon, and he abstained from all food for a day or two at a time. The superhuman beings who confronted Jesus while he was on Mount Hermon with whom he had to wrestle with in spirit and whom he defeated in power were indeed real. These spirits were Jesus' archenemies, members of the Lucifer Rebellion who lived in the system of Satania and these evil spirits were not phantasms of the imagination that evolved out of Jesus' mind, they were real.

Jesus spent the last weeks of August and the first three weeks of September, A.D. 25, praying to God his Universal Father on Mount Hermon and during this time Jesus' Divine Thought Adjuster was able to complete its assigned services to Jesus' mind which was the attunement of Jesus' which was the only thing left for Jesus' final phase.

After more than five weeks of unbroken communication with his Paradise Father, Jesus was now absolutely sure of his true nature and of the certainty of his triumph over the material levels of his time space personality manifestation. Jesus fully believed in and did not hesitate to assert the ascendancy of his divine nature over his human nature and near the end of Jesus being on Mount Hermon, Jesus asked his Paradise Father if he could now hold a conference with his Satania enemies, Lucifer, and Caligastia as the Son of Man, as Joshua Ben Joseph and Jesus' Universal Paradise Father granted Jesus his request.

During Jesus' last week on Mount Hermon a great temptation, a great universal trial occurred where all the leaders of the Lucifer Rebellion; Lucifer, Satan, Caligastia and Daligastia visibly presented themselves to Jesus to tempt him. This temptation was Jesus' final trial of human loyalty in the face of the misrepresentation of these rebel personalities which had nothing to do with food, temple pinnacles or the kingdom of earth, but this temptation had to do with the sovereignty of our mighty glorious Nebadon universe. This was a great spiritual struggle that Jesus, the Son of Man passed through during the great temptation that occurred that day on Mount Hermon. On that day Lucifer and earth's fallen Planetary Prince Caligastia submitted many proposals and counterproposals to Jesus, but his only reply to both of them was these words:

"May the will of my Paradise Father prevail and you, my rebellious son Lucifer may the Ancients Of Days judge you divinely, because I am your Creator Father, and I cannot judge you justly and my mercy you have already spurned. I commit you both to the adjudication of the judges of a greater universe. "

Jesus' response to all of Lucifer's and Caligastia's suggested compromises and proposals was that the will of his Universal Paradise Father will be done and when this trying ordeal was over, the detached guardian seraphim angel returned to Jesus' side and ministered to him. On that same day in the afternoon during the late summer of

September, A.D. 25, among the trees and in the silence of nature on the top of Mount Hermon, Jesus, Michael of Nebadon won the unquestioned sovereignty of his universe of Nebadon and Jesus also completed the task set for all of the Creator Sons from Paradise to live seven bestowals of a full incarnated life as a mortal being on an evolutionary worlds of time and space. The universe announcement from Paradise was not made of Jesus' momentous achievement and victory of that day on Mount Hermon was not made until the day of his baptism, months afterwards, but the victory really took place on that day in September, A.D. 25 on top of Mount Hermon.

When Jesus came down from this prayer retreat on Mount Hermon six weeks later, the Lucifer Rebellion on earth, and all of the system of Satania and the secession of earth's fallen Planetary Prince Caligastia were all over and settled.

Jesus had paid the last price that was required of him to attain the sovereignty of his Nebadon universe, and this meant that the regulation and status of any further upheavals in the Nebadon universe would be able to be dealt with by Michael of Nebadon immediately and effectively. It was now for Jesus near the end of the summer of A.D. 25, around the time of atonement and the feast of the tabernacles, so Jesus held a meeting with his family in Capernaum on the Sabbath and the next day he traveled to Jerusalem with Zebedee's son John and while they were on the journey to Jerusalem John Zebedee noticed a great change in Jesus.

Jesus and John stopped overnight in Bethany to visit with Lazarus and his two sisters and John then spent three weeks in Jerusalem alone while Jesus walked over to the nearby hills where he stayed in prayer with his Paradise Father. Both Jesus and John were present at the solemn services of the day of atonement and John was impressed with the atonement ceremonies while Jesus remained a silent spectator, because he viewed it all as a pitiful religious performance and a misrepresentation of the character and attributes of His Paradise Father. Jesus planned to remain with his friend John throughout the rest of the week for the feast of the tabernacles and Jesus did not participate in the merriment, but he was happy to see the joyous celebrations that the young and old were able to experience.

During the middle of the week when the festivities were over, Jesus left John in Jerusalem telling him that he was going to return to the hills to continue to pray with his Paradise Father and John wanted to go with Jesus but he insisted that John remain in Jerusalem and Jesus told John that it was not required for him to bear the burdens of the Son of Man. Jesus spent a week alone praying in the hills near Bethany and then he left for his home in Capernaum and on the way home Jesus spent a couple of days on the slopes of Gilboa near where the late King Saul had taken his own life.

When Jesus arrived home in Capernaum, he went straight to Zebedee's boat shop to the chest that contained his personal items, put on his work apron and presented himself for work stating that he needed to stay busy while he waited for his hour to come. Jesus continued to work for several months until January A.D. 26, in the Zebedee family boat shop alongside his brother James.

During this final period of Jesus working at the boat shop he spent most of his time working on completing the interior of a large boat project that he had been working on. As time passed rumors began to circulate in Capernaum about Jesus' cousin John who was now preaching and baptizing many people in the River Jordan and John's message to his followers was that God's kingdom of heaven was at hand and to repent and be baptized. Jesus listened to these rumors about his cousin John, and he kept on working to complete the interior of his boat project in Zebedee's boat shop.

In January A.D. 26, when John the Baptist had journeyed up the River Jordan near Pella, Jesus laid his tools down and announced out loud that his hour had come and then he walked to Pella to the River Jordan and presented himself to his cousin John the Baptist to be baptized. A great change had been coming over Jesus and most of the people who lived in Capernaum hardly recognized Jesus who had now become a public teacher, because they had always known Jesus as being a quiet, private man. But for many years now the transformation of Jesus' mind and spirit had been progressing and this process had been finished and completed during Jesus' six weeks of praying on top of Mount Hermon.

Zacharias the high priest and Elizabeth were the parents of John the Baptist, and they had both reached old age without a child due to Elizabeth being barren. Zacharias' job as a high priest in the temple of Jerusalem was to burn the incense at the altars in the temple and one day in the temple Archangel Gabriel appeared to Zacharias telling him that God had answered his prayers and he and his wife Elizabeth would soon have a son and to name him John. Archangel Gabriel also told Zacharias that his son John would be a great man in the sight of the Lord and that he would not drink wine nor any other strong drink and that his son John would be filled with the Holy Spirit at birth and that he would go before Jesus in the spirit and power of prophet Elias to prepare, preach and baptize many of the Jewish people for the coming of Jesus. When Zacharias walked out of the temple that day after Archangel Gabriel's visitation he could not speak, and the congregation knew that their priest Zacharias had seen a vision from God.

On June 6, 8 B.C. of that same year Archangel Gabriel visited John the Baptist's mother Elizabeth in a dream telling her that she would bear a son named John and that he would be born a child of promise. When Elizabeth was six months pregnant with John, Archangel Gabriel went to Galilee to tell Mary who was at the time engaged to Joseph that she was going to conceive a virgin birth of a son who was to be called Jesus and Mary asked Archangel Gabriel how this could be because she had never been with a man. Archangel Gabriel explained to Mary that the Holy Spirit would come upon her and the power of the Highest in Paradise, and that she would then have a holy son named Jesus, the Son of God. John the Baptist was born on March 25, 7 B.C., and he grew up as an ordinary child in the small city of Judah about four miles from Jerusalem. There was no synagogue school in John's small village of Judah, so John was well educated at home by both his parents and his father Zacharias devoted a great deal of time working with his son John on his mental and spiritual training. Zacharias received a regular allowance for the service he performed in the temple in Jerusalem and he and Elizabeth also had a small farm where they raised sheep.

Elizabeth the mother of John the Baptist and her cousin Mary, the mother of Jesus were both descendants of a long line of unique ancestors which included Aaron the high priest brother of Moses, Annon, Tamar, Ruth, Bathsheba, Ansie, Cloa, Eve, Enta and Ratta, the wife of Adam and Eve's oldest son, Adamson. Joseph, the father of Jesus and the son of Heli was a direct descendant of King David, and his ancestry goes all the way back to Enoch, Jared, Enos, Seth, Adam and to the days of Abraham, the Sumerians, the Nodites, the Blue man and the first human family on earth, Andon and Fonta.

When John the Baptist turned the age of fourteen his parents selected him to complete the spiritual training program to be a member of the Nazarite Brotherhood. Zacharias took his son John to the southern headquarters of the Nazarite Brotherhood and from there John was inducted into this group for life and after these Nazarite Brotherhood ceremonies were completed John the Baptist's vows were to abstain from all intoxicating drinks, to let his hair grow and to refrain from touching the dead. These vows that John the Baptist took when he joined the Nazarite Brotherhood were the same vows that two of his predecessors, Samson and Prophet Samuel who anointed David to be the King of Israel took. The Jewish culture regarded a Nazarite Brotherhood member with the utmost respect, because except for the high priests, they were the only people who were permitted to enter the holy of holies in the temple. After his induction ceremony in Jerusalem, John returned home to his parents' farm where he tended the sheep, and he grew up to be a strong man with a noble character.

When John the Baptist turned the age of sixteen, he began to read about the Prophet Elias, and he became impressed with this prophet of Mount Carmel, so John decided to adapt Prophet Elias' style of dress and from that day forward, John who was more than six feet tall always wore a hairy garment with a leather girdle. After being ill for several months, John the Baptist's father Zacharias died in July A.D. 12, when John was eighteen years old and on September, A.D. 12, Elizabeth and John made a journey to Nazareth to visit their cousins Mary, Jesus and family. John the Baptist had already made up his mind to begin his public ministry and he was surprised when Jesus told him to wait and instead go back home to Judah to take care of his mother Elizabeth and wait for the coming of the Universal Father's hour to begin his ministry. After Elizabeth and John said goodbye to Jesus' family at the end of their enjoyable visit, John the Baptist didn't see Jesus again until the day he baptized Jesus in the River Jordan.

John and Elizabeth returned home to their sheep farm in Judah, and they began to make plans for the future.

John the Baptist refused to accept the priest's allowance due to him from the Jerusalem temple funds and by the end of two years, John and his mother Elizabeth had lost their home, so they decided to move south with their sheep herd. John continued to tend the sheep in the wilderness of Judea along a brook that flowed into the Dead Sea at Engedi and this Engedi colony included Nazarites and other herdsmen who also lived with their herds, and they fraternized with the other members of the Nazarite Brotherhood. This Engedi colony lived and supported themselves by raising sheep and from the gifts they received from the wealthy Jewish community who were also members of the Nazarite Brotherhood. However, John the Baptist was different from the rest of the other members of the Nazarite Brotherhood, and he found it difficult to associate with the rest of the brotherhood members, but John got along with Abner who was the leader and head of the Engedi colony. John the Baptist built about six stone structures and night corrals along the brook where he could watch and safeguard his sheep herd and John's life as a shepherd gave him a lot of time to think about his spiritual mission in life.

John the Baptist talked a lot with Ezda, an orphan lad from Bethzur whom he had adopted, and Ezda took care of the sheep herds when John had to make frequent trips to visit his mother Elizabeth and to sell his sheep herds. Elizabeth kept John the Baptist updated about the politics in Palestine and world affairs. John knew that the time was fast approaching when the old order was soon going to end and then he would be able to help to bring in the new age of the kingdom of heaven. John the Baptist spent a lot of time studying the writings of the Prophet Daniel, but he was never able to completely get over his confusion by what his parents had told him when he was a child about his cousin Jesus' virgin birth and his special spiritual mission on earth. All throughout John the Baptist's confusion his mother Elizabeth continued to assure him that Jesus of Nazareth was the true Messiah of the Jewish nation. Elizabeth also further explained to her son John that his role was soon to become the person who was to prepare the people and to be Jesus' main support when it was his time to begin his public ministry and complete his seventh and final bestowal on earth.

On August 17, A.D. 22, when John the Baptist was twenty-eight years old, his mother Elizabeth suddenly passed away and when John returned to Engedi to attend his mother's funeral in Hebron, he gave his flock of sheep to the Nazarite Brotherhood group and isolated himself from the outside world for three months in the desert surviving on locusts, honey, fasting and praying, because John truly believed that he was going to be the last of the long line of the divine messengers who had been sent from the seven higher heavens to earth. During these three months of isolation, John read a lot of the sacred writings of Isiah and Malachi that he had found at one of the Engedi homes of a member of the Nazarite Brotherhood.

It was the influence of these teachings of Elijah that caused John the Baptist to adapt Prophet Elijah's methods of a direct and blunt assault on the sins and vices of many of the people who lived around him and John was well versed in the Jewish sacred writings, he was a clear thinker and a very powerful speaker. John the Baptist carefully thought out his method of how he was going to proclaim to the people that the new age and the coming of the Messiah was coming and John the Baptist left Engedi in March A.D. 25, ready to begin his short but brilliant career as a public baptizing preacher and teacher.

John the Baptist traveled around the western coast of the Dead Sea, up the River Jordan to Jericho and he established his ministry near the entrance to the River Jordan where he began to preach to the people who passed by him on their way back and forth across the River Jordan, because this area was the most frequented of all the River Jordan crossings.

It was apparent to all the people who heard John the Baptist preach that he was more than just an ordinary preacher and most of the people who listened to John the Baptist preach had come up from the Judean wilderness and they left believing that they had just heard the voice of a prophet and never in all of Jewish history had the devout children of Abraham so longed for the restoration of the kingdom of heaven. John the Baptist came from the family lineage of being a herdsman, just like Prophet Amos and he dressed like Prophet Elijah. John the Baptist created quite a stir all throughout all of Palestine and he became known as the traveler who went along the River Jordan carrying the good news of the coming Messiah. The new feature about the work of John the Baptist was that while he was preaching, he baptized his believers at the same time in the River Jordan telling them to repent for the remission of their sins.

Although baptism was not a new ceremony among the Jews, they had never seen it done the way John the Baptist did it, because the Jews had never been asked to submit to a baptism of repentance. Only fifteen months passed between the time that John the Baptist began to preach and baptize and his subsequent arrest and beheading by tetrarch Herod Antipas, but in this short period of time John baptized over one hundred thousand people to repentance in the River Jordan. John the Baptist preached for about four months at the Bethany ford of the River Jordan before he moved north of the River Jordan and during this time, tens of thousands of listeners came to hear him preach from all parts of Judea, Perea, Galilee and Samaria.

In May of A.D. 25, while John the Baptist was still preaching to the people at the Bethany ford section of the River Jordan, the priests and Levites sent a delegation out to ask John the Baptist if he was claiming to be the Messiah and by whose authority was, he preaching.

John answered their questions by telling them to go and tell their master's that they have heard the voice of one crying out of the wilderness making ready a straight path to God and all who were baptized and repented would soon see the salvation of the Lord. John the Baptist was a heroic but tactless preacher, and he conducted classes for his disciples where he instructed them in the details of their new spiritual life with God and John counseled his disciples to teach the word of God in the spirit. John the Baptist told the rich to feed the poor and the masters who had sent the delegation to question his public ministry were tetrarch Herod Antipas of Galilee and his brother Philip, the Roman tetrarch of the regions of Ituraea and Trachonitis. John the Baptist would later publicly denounce tetrarch Herod Antipas for taking his brother Philip's wife and openly living in an immoral relationship with her.

The longer John the Baptist preached the more confused he became in his mind only but never in his spirit, because John had no doubts about the coming of God's kingdom, but he wasn't certain if Jesus was to be the ruler of the coming kingdom. As John the Baptist continued to travel northward, he began to think a lot about his cousin Jesus and whenever one of John's disciples asked him if he, John the Baptist was the Messiah, John the Baptist would always respond that there would be one who will come after him who was greater than he was.

By December A.D. 25, when John the Baptist reached the region of Pella, his fame had extended all throughout Palestine and the people in all of the surrounding towns were all talking about the teachings of John the Baptist. Jesus always spoke favorably of his cousin John's spiritual messages and preaching, and this caused many people from Capernaum to follow John's teachings to be baptized and to repent. James and John, the two fishermen sons of their father Zebedee came down from Capernaum to follow John the Baptist in December A.D. 25, near Pella and they both asked John the Baptist to baptize them and after they were baptized, they listened to John the Baptist preach at least once a week and they brought back favorable reports of John's teachings to Jesus.

On Sunday morning January 13, A.D. 26, Jesus was working as usual in Zebedee's boat shop and just before the noon rest time, Jesus laid down his tools, removed his work apron and announced to three of his fellow workmen who were in the room with him that his hour had come. Jesus then went out to his two brothers James and Jude who were waiting for him in the lumber room and repeated to them that his hour had come and that they both needed to go and see their cousin John the Baptist at the River Jordan near Pella. Jesus and his two brothers James and Jude traveled all night, and they arrived where John the Baptist was baptizing people on the River Jordan at noon the next day on Monday, January 14, A.D. 26.

John the Baptist had just started baptizing the people who were standing in line waiting their turn when Jesus and his two brothers James and Jude took their positions in the line to wait their turn to be baptized. John the Baptist had heard about Jesus' positive remarks concerning his ministry, so he was expecting Jesus when he arrived with his two brothers, but John the Baptist never thought to see Jesus and his two brothers to be standing in the baptismal line. John the Baptist was so busy baptizing so many people that he didn't see Jesus until he was actually standing right in front of him and when John the Baptist recognized Jesus, the baptismal ceremonies stopped for a minute while he greeted Jesus asking why he was coming down into the water to see him. Jesus responded to John the Baptist that he needed to be baptized, and John the Baptist told Jesus that he needed to be baptized by him. Jesus then whispered to John the Baptist to bear with him, because he wanted to set an example for his two brothers who were there with him and that he needed the people who were there that day to know that his hour had come.

Jesus spoke with a tone of finality and authority to his cousin John the Baptist who by now was trembling with emotion as he prepared to baptize Jesus in the River Jordan at noon on Monday, January 14, A.D. 26. John the Baptist proceeded to baptize Jesus and his two brothers James and Jude and after John the Baptist had baptized Jesus and his two brothers he dismissed the rest of the waiting line of people for the day. But as the crowd of people who had been standing in the baptismal line were leaving, John the Baptist , Jesus and his two brothers were still standing in the River Jordan when they all heard a strange sound and suddenly for a brief moment, an apparition of a white dove appeared over the head of Jesus, and then they all heard a voice say, "This is my beloved Son in whom I am well pleased." A great change came over Jesus's face and he was completely silent while he was coming out of the water and Jesus continued walking after he left the waters of the River Jordan, and he kept on walking until he reached the hills to the east of where they were and after the day of his baptism no one saw Jesus again for forty days.

John the Baptist followed Jesus walking with him for a long way to tell him about the story of Archangel Gabriel's visits to both of his late parents and to Jesus' mother Mary and about his virgin birth and how his mother Elizabeth had told him this story many times before she passed. John the Baptist then told Jesus that he was now certain that he, Jesus was the Deliverer and after saying that John the Baptist let Jesus continue on his journey alone to the hills east of the River Jordan. As Jesus continued walking alone to the hills, he thought that this this was the first time he had known about his virgin birth, because his mother Mary had never told him about the miracle of his virgin birth.

John the Baptist had about thirty disciples who stayed with him constantly and when he returned to them after briefly walking and talking to Jesus as he walked to the hills, John found all of his disciples in an earnest conference discussing what had just happened at Jesus' baptism. John the Baptist's disciples were even more surprised when John told them how Archangel Gabriel had paid a visit to both of his late parents and to Jesus' mother Mary before both he and Jesus were born. John the Baptist and his disciples talked late into the night wondering where Jesus had gone and when would they see him again.

After the experience on the day of Jesus' baptism John the Baptist's preaching changed and he took on a new persona with certain words of proclamation concerning the coming kingdom and the expected Messiah. These were tense times for John the Baptist as he waited for forty days for Jesus to return from the hills. During this time John the Baptist continued to preach with great power and his disciples also began to preach to the overflow crowds who began to gather around John the Baptist at the River Jordan. While John and his thirty disciples were waiting for Jesus to return from the hills many rumors began to spread around the countryside even as far as Tiberias and Jerusalem. Thousands of people began to come to John the Baptist's camp to see the Messiah, but Jesus was nowhere to be found.

When John the Baptist and his disciples told the large crowds of people that Jesus had gone to the hills to pray many doubted that the entire story ever happened. About three weeks after Jesus had left them to go to the hills to pray, a group of priests and Pharisees arrived at John's camp and asked John the Baptist if he was Elijah or the prophet Moses and when John the Baptist said no, they then asked John the Baptist if he was the Messiah and again John said no. This same group then asked John the Baptist that if he was not

Elijah or the Messiah why was he baptizing so many people and causing such a stir among the people and John's response to this group of Pharisees was that he was baptizing those who hear his words, want to repent and that one of those whom he had baptized would soon return to baptize all of us with the Holy Spirit.

The forty days John and his thirty disciples waited for Jesus to return was a very difficult time and the crowds of people kept on asking many questions that centered around various spiritual ideas, especially the concepts about the Messiah. In his own mind John, the Baptists believed that Jesus had come to earth to establish the kingdom of heaven on earth, although he wasn't clear as to how Jesus was going to accomplish this mission. The days grew to be more tense and strenuous for John the Baptist and his thirty disciples and some of his disciples wanted to organize scouting parties to search for Jesus, but John the Baptist forbade them to do so. Early on the morning of the Sabbath, February 23, A.D. 26 while John the Baptist and his disciples were eating their morning meal, John looked towards the north and saw Jesus walking towards them.

As Jesus got closer to them John the Baptist stood up on a large rock and loudly said, "Behold the Son of God, the deliverer of the world." Jesus calmly told all of them to return to their morning meal and then he sat down to eat breakfast with his cousin John the Baptist. Early in the morning of the next day, Jesus left John and his disciples and went back to Galilee and Jesus didn't tell them when they would see him again and when

John the Baptist asked Jesus about his own mission and public ministry, Jesus told John that God would continue to guide him in the future just like He had done in the past. When Jesus and John the Baptist parted ways that morning on the banks of the River Jordan, it was the last time they would see each other in the flesh.

Since Jesus had gone north into Galilee, John the Baptist on Sunday morning, March 3, A.D. 26, traveled southward with his thirty disciples and one quarter of John's immediate followers left for Galilee searching for Jesus. John the Baptist felt sad, confused and he never again preached like he had before he baptized Jesus that day, because now John felt that the responsibility of the coming kingdom no longer rested on his shoulders and John the Baptist felt like his work on earth was almost finished and he felt very unhappy, but as he continued to travel southward, he continued to preach and baptize many people.

When John the Baptist reached the village of Adam, he stayed for several weeks, and it was here that John the Baptist made his memorable verbal attack on the Roman tetrarch of Galilee, Herod Antipas for openly living with his brother Philips' wife in an immoral relationship. By June, A.D. 26, John the Baptist was back at the Bethany section of the River Jordan where he again began preaching about the coming kingdom. During the weeks following John's baptism of Jesus, the tone of John the Baptist's preaching gradually changed into a proclamation of mercy for the common people, and he continued to denounce with a renewed vehemence the corrupt political and religious rulers who lived in the Palestine region.

John the Baptist continued his preaching in tetrarch Herod Antipas' territory and Herod became alarmed and worried that John the Baptist and his disciples were going to start a rebellion and Herod resented John's public criticism about the immoral relationship he was having with his brother Phillip's wife. Because of this, Herod Antipas decided to put John the Baptist in prison to shut him up. So, early in the morning of June 12, A.D. 26, and in front of a large crowd who had arrived to be baptized and hear John the Baptist preach, Herod Antipas had his agents place John the Baptist under arrest and they placed him in prison. John the Baptist's disciples then began to scatter all over Palestine and many of them traveled to Galilee to become followers of Jesus. Meanwhile John the Baptist had a lonely and bitter experience in prison and very few of his followers were permitted to see him.

John the Baptist really wanted to see Jesus, but it didn't happen, so he had to be content with hearing about Jesus' public ministry through some of his disciples. John the Baptist was confined to prison by Herod Antipas for over a year and it proved to be a great test of John's faith and loyalty to Jesus, because John was disappointed that Jesus sent him no word, nor did he come to visit him and especially that Jesus would not use any of his great power to deliver him from prison. Jesus knew John the Baptist was in prison and he loved his cousin John, but Jesus did not interfere, because he knew about the great things that were being prepared for John the Baptist in Paradise when he departed from earth.

John the Baptist's long stint in prison was unbearable and just a few days before his death John sent a message to Jesus asking if his work on earth was done. Jesus sent a reply message back to John the Baptist telling him that he was going to be abundantly blessed in the near future, and these were the last words John the Baptist received from Jesus, but the message John the Baptist received from Jesus did comfort him and helped to strengthen his faith to prepare him for the tragic end of his life on earth.

Tetrarch Herod Antipas was afraid to release John the Baptist from prison and he was also afraid to put him to death, because John was a member of the Nazarite Brotherhood, a holy man who was also a prophet and a preacher so, Herod feared that it would cause riots if John was put to death. Herod visited John the Baptist on numerous occasions while he was in prison talking with him about God and the kingdom of heaven and even though Herod was impressed with John's message, he was still afraid to release him from prison.

One night Herod Antipas was hosting a birthday celebration in his Machaerian palace with his chief officers and other men who held high council positions in his government of Galilee and this celebration gave Herod's brother's wife Herodias a chance to implement her cunning plan to have John the Baptist finally put to death. As the evening festivities continued at this birthday celebration, Herodias presented her daughter to dance before those in attendance and Herod was so pleased with her daughter's dance that Herod then offered to grant her one wish of whatever she desired, and she requested to have the head of John the Baptist presented to her on a plate. So, Herod Antipas had John the Baptist beheaded that night and had one of his soldiers bring it to Herodias' daughter on a plate at the rear section of the banquet hall.

When John the Baptist's disciples heard about this, they came to Herod's prison to retrieve John's body and after his burial his disciples went and told Jesus what had happened. Herod Antipas killed a holy man, a prophet and a member of the Nazareth brotherhood that night when he had John the Baptists beheaded and a few years later after sitting on his throne blaspheming God by stating that he was God, Herod was stricken with worms that consumed his entire body with cancer and he died.

Jesus began his public ministry at the height of the people's popular interest in the preaching of John the Baptist and at a time when the Jewish people of Palestine were eagerly looking for the Messiah to appear. There was a big difference between John the Baptist and Jesus, because John the Baptist was an eager, loud and earnest worker, while Jesus was a calm, quiet and happy laborer and there were only a few times in his life that Jesus was ever in a hurry or angry. Jesus was a comforting, consoling individual, while John the Baptist was hardly any comfort at all, and he didn't hesitate to loudly tell it like it is. Jesus still always spoke of John the Baptist as the greatest of the prophets of the old order and that those who were blessed to see John's great light to the new way to the kingdom of God were much better off. When John the Baptist preached about the kingdom of God his main message was to repent now. When Jesus began to preach, he also stressed the importance to repent, but his message was always followed by the gospel and good tidings about the joy and liberty of the coming kingdom of God.

The Jewish culture believed that during the times of John the Baptist and Jesus that their national history began with Abraham and that it would reach its highest point with the appearance of the Messiah. The Jewish culture also believed that just like Moses had delivered their forefathers from Egyptian bondage, the coming Messiah would deliver them from the grips of the Roman Empire.

When Jesus went down to the River Jordan to be baptized that day by his cousin John the Baptist, he was a mortal man of earth who had attained the height of his human evolutionary ascension in all of the matters relating to the conquest of his mind along with his self-identification with his spirit. On that day as John the Baptist laid his hands on Jesus to baptize him, Jesus' indwelling Divine Thought Adjuster took its final leave of Jesus' perfected human soul and at that moment in Jesus' life, he observed his own original divine spirit descend from Paradise and return to him in its personalized form and only Jesus' eyes could see his Paradise Personalized Adjuster return to indwell his mind just like it did when Jesus was living as Michael of Nebadon in Paradise-the seven higher heavens.

Jesus had to endure a great temptation as a part of his mortal bestowal on earth before his baptism that day when he stayed in isolation on Mount Hermon for six weeks, because it was there that Jesus met and defeated earth's Lucifer Rebellion leaders his son, Lucifer, his assistant Satan and earth's fallen Planetary Prince Caligastia and his assistant Daligastia and on that eventful day when Jesus finally defeated all four of these rebels, Jesus became the new system sovereign of the Nebadon universe.

After Jesus was baptized by John the Baptist on that eventful day Jesus went into isolation for forty days to adjust himself to the changed relationship in the world and in the universe due to receiving his original Paradise Thought Adjuster back into his mind.

Jesus isolated himself for forty days with no food on Mount Hermon, because he now clearly and fully understood the importance for him to pray and meditate so that he could think about the plans and procedures he was going to use to begin his public ministry on earth. While Jesus was walking in the hills of Mount Hermon for forty days seeking suitable shelter, Jesus encountered his universe chief executive Gabriel, the Bright and Morning Star of Nebadon and this was the first time that they had met since Michael of Nebadon had left Paradise to begin his seventh and final bestowal on earth. During this encounter, Gabriel told Jesus that his final bestowal on earth was completed concerning his right to be the new system sovereign of the Nebadon universe and that the Lucifer Rebellion on earth and the rest of the universe was terminated.

While Jesus and Gabriel were talking on Mount Hermon the Constellation Father of Edentia, Paradise also appeared to Jesus stating that the records of Jesus' completed seventh bestowal on earth had been officially recorded in Paradise and the Most Highs of Edentia, Paradise also then told Jesus that he was at liberty to terminate his incarnation on earth whenever he chose to and that technically his work on earth was finished and how he chose to proceed was his choice.

When the Most Highs of Edentia, Paradise had left, Jesus continued to talk with Gabriel for a long time talking about the welfare of the universe, and Jesus told Gabriel even though he was at liberty to terminate his incarnation now and return to Paradise, that his intentions were to go ahead and stay on earth to complete the work that he had made all the plans to accomplish during his public ministry and service to all the worlds of time and space in the

Nebadon universe. All throughout these forty days of isolation on Mount Hermon, Jesus' two friends, James and John Zebedee continued to search for him many times, but they were unable to find Jesus.

Day by day while Jesus was in isolation on Mount Hermon, he made definite plans on the program of public labor that he was about to implement on every inhabited world of our vast universe, because Michael of Nebadon's seventh and final bestowal was not only for planet #606 earth, but it was also for all of the inhabited worlds in our Nebadon universe. The first thing Jesus did after deciding on his general plan of coordinating his program was to review in his mind the instructions, he had received from his older brother Immanuel of Paradise which were to make sure during his public ministry he was not to leave any permanent writings on earth and never again after this meeting did Jesus write down anything except for in the sand later on during his public ministry when a crowd of angry Pharisees were about to stone to death a Jewish woman who had committed adultery and at that moment Jesus kneeled down and wrote the following words in the sand,

"He who is without sin cast the first stone." And with that being written, the angry crowd quickly dispersed.

On Jesus' next visit home, he destroyed all of the writings he had preserved on the boards in his home, on the walls of his home, and in the carpenter and boat shops.

During these forty days on Mount Hermon, Jesus also thought about the entire time that mortal man had spent on earth from the days of the first human family, Andon and Fonta in Afghanistan, down through Adam and Eve and on to the Ministry of Machiventa Melchizedek and Abraham of Salem.

During his meeting with Gabriel, he also reminded Jesus that there were two ways that he could choose how to manifest himself to the world just in case he made the decision to remain on earth instead of returning right away back home to Salvington, Paradise. Gabriel told Jesus that whatever choice he made that it would not affect his universe sovereignty or his recent termination of the Lucifer Rebellion in the Nebadon universe.

These are the two choices Gabriel gave Jesus that day to choose from to implement his worldwide public ministry on earth.

The first choice was for Jesus to do it his own way using the method that would seem more pleasant and profitable from the standpoint of the immediate needs of planet earth and the best way that will uplift the Nebadon universe.

The second choice was to do it the Universal Father in Paradise way through the example of a farseeing ideal of creature life as shown by the high personalities of the Paradise administration of the universes of universes.

On his third day of isolation on Mount Hermon Jesus made a promise to himself that he would make the choice to go back to his mortal life on earth and finish his mortal career by following the second choice that Gabriel gave him and that was to follow the will of his Universal Paradise Father. Even down to the bitter end, when he could have quickly gone back home to Paradise Jesus still chose to stay and complete the plans, he had made for humanity's salvation by following the will of his Paradise Father.

It had always been Jesus' practice that whenever he was facing any new or serious decisions concerning his final bestowal on earth, to withdraw for communion with his own spirit so he would seek and know the will of his Paradise Father. During all of this planning Jesus did for the remainder of the time he had left on earth he was torn in his human heart by two opposing courses of action to choose from.

The first issue was that Jesus had a strong desire to win the hearts of humanity and for them to believe in him, to accept his new spiritual kingdom, because Jesus knew the ideas the Jewish culture had concerning the coming Messiah.

The second issue was that Jesus wanted to live and work the way his Universal Father would approve and conduct his work on behalf of all of the worlds in the universe that had spiritual needs by showing his own divine character of love.

All throughout these forty days on Mount Hermon Jesus lived in an ancient rock cavern on the side of the hills near a village called Beit Adis and he drank his water from a small spring that was near his rock shelter. On Jesus' third day of being on Mount Hermon he held a conference with his Personal Divine Thought Adjuster and all of the assembled celestial hosts of the Nebadon universe which were composed of the twelve legions of the seraphim angels and every order of universe intelligence were at this conference with Jesus and at this conference Jesus had to make six decisions concerning how he was going to proceed to complete his public ministry on earth.

These are the six great decisions Jesus made during his forty days of isolation on Mount Hermon.

Jesus' First Great Decision

Jesus decided that he would not use any of the Paradise celestial beings unless it should become his Universal Father's will. Even though Jesus decided not to use the vast assembly of celestial Paradise beings, all of these celestial beings still remained with Jesus all throughout his final remaining days on earth. Although Jesus could not always see this vast host of celestial beings with his eyes, his Divine Thought Adjuster constantly communicated with all of them during Jesus' final days on earth.

Before coming down from the forty-day retreat on Mount Hermon, Jesus assigned the immediate command of this host of universe celestial beings to his Divine Thought Adjuster for more than four years, and they were under the guidance of Jesus' Personal Mystery Monitor. By assuming command of all of these celestial beings who were always around Jesus, the Divine Thought Adjusters who were originally a part and essence of the Paradise Father, assured Jesus that these superhuman Paradise beings would not be able to manifest themselves during Jesus' spiritual mission on earth unless the Paradise Father willed such intervention. Thus, by Jesus making his first great decision Jesus voluntarily deprived himself of all superhuman Paradise assistance for the rest of his mission on earth. Jesus' upcoming public ministry would pertain entirely on the elimination of time unless his Paradise Father ruled otherwise and no miracle, ministry of mercy or any other event occurring in connection with Jesus' remaining earth bestowal could be of the nature of an act that transcended the natural established laws except as stated in the matter of time, and no limits could be placed on the manifestations of the Universal Father's will.

The elimination of time in connection with Jesus' expressed desires could only be avoided by the direct and explicit act of the will of Jesus to affect that time that relates to the act or event. In order to prevent the appearance of apparent time miracles, it was necessary for Jesus to remain constantly time conscience and any lapse of time consciousness on Jesus' part in connection with a definite desire would be the equivalent of the enactment of the thing that was conceived in the mind of Jesus without the intervention of time. Through the supervising control of Jesus' Divine Thought Adjusters, Jesus was able to limit his personal earth activities in reference to time and space.

Jesus' Second Great Decision

Jesus now turned his thoughts inward towards himself and his immediate problem was finding food while he was on Mount Hermon for forty days. Jesus asked himself if he should go and look for food like an ordinary man would, or should he use his normal creative powers to produce food by commanding stones to become loaves of bread. At this moment Jesus made the decision to survive on water only for the rest of his forty days of isolation and to continue to choose the natural path of his earthly existence. However, Jesus could not promise himself that these natural laws might not in certain circumstances be greatly accelerated.

Jesus' human nature told himself that his first duty was self-preservation, which is the normal attitude of all men who live on the worlds of time and space. Jesus' final declaration concerning all of his other urges of the mortal flesh and natural impulses of human nature was that to use his superhuman powers for others but not for himself, never, and Jesus followed this policy consistently to the end of his mortal life on earth. The Jewish culture was expecting a Messiah to come to earth who would do even greater wonders than Moses and Jesus knew this and Jesus had all of the powers to measure up to these expectations, but he decided against this program of power and glory, because Jesus' view was that a path of expected miracle working was going back to the olden days of ignorant magic and the degrading practices of the savage medicine men. So, for the salvation of humanity, Jesus' final decision was not to transcend his own natural laws for the benefit of himself.

Jesus felt sorrow for his people, and he fully understood how they had been led up to the expectation of the coming Messiah to usher in an era of plenty of miracles, because the Hebrews had for so long been nurtured on the traditions of miracles and legends of wonder. Jesus was not a Messiah who came to earth to minister to humanity's temporal needs, he came to reveal the Universal Paradise Father to his children on earth and to lead mankind to join him in a sincere effort to live by following God's divine plan and will. Jesus' second decision portrayed to an onlooking universe the folly and sin of misusing divine talents and God given abilities for personal selfish gain and glorification.

That had been the sin and folly committed by Lucifer, his first lieutenant Satan and earth's first fallen Planetary Prince Caligastia and Daligastia when they launched the Lucifer Rebellion on Paradise, earth and thirty-six other planets in our universe in the name of their rights to have liberty. By making this second great decision Jesus showed the truth that selfish satisfaction and sensuous gratification should not be the basis of happiness for evolving humans, because there are far higher values in the mortal existence such as intellectual mastery, creative mastery, and the spiritual achievement which far transcend the necessary gratification of man's physical appetites and urges. Man's natural endowment of talent and ability should be mainly devoted to the development of the higher powers of the mind and spirit. By making this second great decision Jesus revealed to the living beings of his universe a new and better way to choose a higher moral value of living and the deeper spiritual satisfactions of evolutionary human existence on all the worlds of time and space.

Jesus' Third Great Decision

Jesus' third great decision was based on the issue of what would his attitude be when confronted with personal danger. Jesus decided to exercise normal care over his human safety and to take reasonable precautions to prevent the untimely termination of his mortal career, but to refrain from superhuman intervention if a crisis for his life did arise. While Jesus was working on formulating his third decision, he was sitting under a shady tree on an over hanging ledge of rock with a precipice right before him. Jesus then realized that he could cast himself off the ledge out into space and nothing would happen to harm him if he rescinded his first decision. All throughout the remaining years of his life, Jesus was loyal to his third decision and it didn't matter to Jesus how the Pharisees continued to follow and taunt him constantly asking for a sign or when the watchers at Calvary dared Jesus to come down from his dying cross, but instead Jesus stuck by the third decision he had made that day on the hillside of Mount Hermon.

Jesus' Fourth Great Decision

The next issue Jesus had to decide was whether or not any of his superhuman powers should be used for the purpose of attracting the attention and winning the commitment of his fellow men. Jesus asked himself if he should in any manner use his universe powers to gratify the Jewish need for the spectacular and marvelous and Jesus made the fourth decision not to use and of these spectacular practices as the method of completing his mission on earth. There were many instances where Jesus permitted manifestations of numerous times shortening ministry acts of mercy, but he never told the recipients about the benefits they had received.

Jesus continued to ignore the taunting challenges from the Pharisees to show them a sign with proof of his divinity and instead Jesus foresaw that the working of miracles or the execution of wonders would only gain followers by overdrawing the human material mind and it would not help to reveal the Universal Father nor do anything to help save the souls of mortal men. Jesus refused to be a mere wonder worker, and his main concern was the establishment of the kingdom of heaven on earth. Jesus had already traveled to a lot of different locations, and he knew the way of the world, how people gained their ends in politics and commerce of compromise and diplomacy. Once again Jesus chose to depend exclusively on his Paradise Father's will. Jesus made the fourth decision to establish the kingdom of heaven in the hearts of mankind by natural, ordinary, difficult and trying methods just like the procedures that every one of his children on earth must follow in their daily work of enlarging and extending God's heavenly kingdom on earth.

Jesus knew and foresaw that through much tribulation, that many of the children of all ages living on earth would be able to enter into the kingdom and at this time Jesus was passing through the great test of civilized man to have the power and refuse to use it for purely selfish or personal purposes.

Jesus, the Son of God was incarnated on earth in the mind of a first century human man, not in the mind of any other century mortal and the human endowments Jesus had been acquired naturally and he was the product of the hereditary and environmental factors of his time, plus he had extensive training and education. The humanity of Jesus was genuine, natural and wholly derived from the actual intellectual status and social economic conditions of his day and generation. During the life experience of Jesus there was always the possibility that his divine mind would transcend the human intellect and as Jesus' human mind continued to function for him, it continued to perform just like a true mortal mind would under the conditions of the human environment of his day and times. Jesus decided during his fourth decision to not misuse his divine attributes for the purpose of acquiring unearned popularity or for gaining political prestige. Instead, Jesus made the decision to not give away the transmutation of his divine and creative energy for national power or international prestige. Jesus refused to compromise with evil much less to fall into the wiles of sin and instead Jesus chose to put loyalty to his Paradise Father above every other earth and temporal consideration.

Jesus' Fifth Great Decision

Jesus was now asking himself if he was going to continue the mission that had been started by his late cousin John the Baptist and he was ready to make a final decision that would forbid that he would regard himself as the Jewish Messiah that was being popularly talked about during his times.

The Jewish culture's vision of their deliverer, the Messiah was one who would come with miraculous powers to cast down Israel's enemies and establish the Jewish nation as world rulers free from want and oppression. Jesus knew that through his mission, the Jews' hopes would never be realized, because the kingdom of heaven had to do with the overthrow of evil in the hearts of men and it was purely a matter of spiritual concern. Jesus thought about his ability of bringing in the spiritual kingdom on earth with a brilliant and dazzling display of power and a plan such as this would have been permissible and within the jurisdiction of Michael of Nebadon, but Jesus fully decided against such a plan. Instead, Jesus made the decision to not compromise with the revolutionary techniques of earth's fallen Planetary Prince Caligastia.

Jesus' plan was to win the hearts of mankind on earth by their free will submission to the Universal Father's Divine Plan. As the days passed Jesus' mind increased in clarity and he also saw that his path was not going to be easy and he saw that his final days on earth were going to be very bitter, but he decided to proceed onward.

The Roman Empire at that time was the mistress of the Western world and Jesus represented the last chance for the Jewish nation to attain domination. However, Jesus had so much love and wisdom in his heart that he was not going to use his universe superhuman powers to uplift his reputation or to enthrone the Jewish nation. The Most Highs of Edentia, Paradise had placed all of these superhuman powers into Jesus' hands, but he chose not to use them, because his main objective was the further revelation of God to humanity which was the establishment of God's kingdom on earth through the hearts of mankind.

Jesus made the fifth decision to appear on earth as the Prince of Peace to reveal a God of love. Before Jesus was baptized by John the Baptist in the River Jordan, he had refused the offer to lead the Jewish Nationalist Zealots group in an open rebellion against the Roman Empire, and now at this time Jesus was making his fifth decision concerning his public ministry based on the scriptures his mother Mary had taught him, so Jesus then decided to return to Galilee to quietly begin the proclamation of God's kingdom and he trusted his Universal Father and his Divine Thought Adjuster to work out the day by day details of the final days of his last bestowal mission as a mortal man on earth. This decision that Jesus made set a worthy example for every person on every world in our universe of Nebadon when he refused to apply material tests to solve spiritual problems, because Jesus chose to follow the natural laws of the universe.

If Jesus had any doubts about his seventh and final bestowal mission on earth and its nature when he went up to the hills of Mount Hermon after his baptism, he now had no doubts when he come back down from these hill to his fellow men who had been following his forty days of isolation of prayer, meditation, meeting with the Paradise celestial beings and making his final six decisions for his upcoming ministry.

By rejecting the methods of enhancing the coming of God's kingdom in the eyes of the expectant Jews, Jesus was pretty sure that these same Jews would certainly reject all of his claims of authority and divinity and since Jesus knew all of this, he early on in his ministry would not allow his followers to call him the Messiah. All throughout his public ministry Jesus was confronted with having to deal with three recurring situations, the need to be fed, the people insisting on miracles and his followers insisting to make him the king of the Jews. However, Jesus never departed from the six decisions that he made during his forty days of isolation for forty days in the Perean hills of Mount Hermon.

Jesus' Final Great Sixth Decision

On Jesus' last day of his forty days of isolation in the Perean hills, before starting back down Mount Hermon to rejoin John the Baptist and his thirty disciples, Jesus made his final sixth decision concerning the rolling out of his upcoming public ministry. Jesus discussed his final sixth decision with his indwelling Divine Thought Adjuster stating that his pledge was to forever be subject to the will of his Universal Father and after Jesus spoke this pledge out loud, he began his descent down the mountain and his face was shining brightly with the glory of spiritual victory and moral achievement.

CHAPTER FOURTEEN

JESUS IN GALILEE

The Lord, the Lord, the compassionate and gracious God, slow to anger, abounding in love and faithfulness.

(Exodus 34:6)

He lifted me out of the slimy pit, out of the mud and mire, he set my feet on a rock and gave me a firm place to stand.

(Psalm 40:2)

A Prayer:

Holy Spirit, please grow the fruit of the godly character in me today, especially when I'm online.

JESUS IN GALILEE

Early on Saturday morning, February 23, A.D. 26, Jesus after forty days of isolation came down from the hills to rejoin his cousin John the Baptist and his thirty disciples who were encamped at Pella and all that day Jesus mingled with the multitude who had also gathered there. Jesus ministered to a lad who had injured himself in a fall and Jesus traveled to the nearby village of Pella to take this injured lad back to his home safely to his parents and the next day two of John the Baptist's leading disciples spent most of their time being trained in spiritual teaching and preaching with Jesus. Of all of John the Baptist's followers, Andrew was the one who most profoundly impressed Jesus and Andrew went with Jesus to take the injured lad back home to his parents in Pella. On the way back to John the Baptist's encampment, Andrew asked Jesus many questions and he told Jesus that he had made up his mind to become one of his followers to learn the whole truth about God's new kingdom on earth. Jesus then welcomed Andrew as his first apostle, who would later be the group of twelve who would work with Jesus in his public ministry.

Soon after Jesus and Apostle Andrew returned to John the Baptist's encampment, Andrew went and found his brother Simon and after talking together, Simon went and told Jesus that he also wanted to be his follower to help to bring in God's new kingdom to humanity. Jesus then welcomed Simon as his second apostle but warned him that it was going to be dangerous work in their public ministry and Jesus changed Simon's name to Peter.

Meanwhile the parents of the injured lad Jesus and Andrew had taken back to his home in Pella came to the encampment and asked Jesus to spend the night with them in Pella in their home and Jesus said that he would. Before Jesus left his two new apostles Andrew and Peter, he told them that they would be going to Galilee early in the morning. Jesus' two closest friends James and John Zebedee came to the injured lad's home that night while Jesus was sleeping, woke him up and asked him why he had chosen Andrew and Peter to be his first two apostles after all the years they had been such close friends and after all the time they searched for him while he was in the hills for forty days. Jesus told James and John Zebedee to be calm in their hearts and that they were already with the spirit of the new kingdom from the beginning and that their only concern should be to do the will of the Universal Father. James and John Zebedee who both now realized that they had always been Jesus' apostles positively received this message from Jesus and they were never again envious of Apostles Andrew and Peter. The four new apostles of Jesus made the preparations to leave for Galilee early the next morning and later that evening the four new apostles, James, John, Andrew and Peter held a meeting with John the Baptist and with tears in their eyes, John the Baptist blessed his four former disciples who had now become the apostles of the Galilean Prince of Peace, Jesus.

Jesus continued to select eight more apostles to help him in his public ministry until he had selected a total of twelve apostles. Jesus' public teachings and preaching mainly consisted of parables and short discourses and he taught his twelve apostles by using the method of questions and answers and Jesus would always pause to answer questions during his public discourses. From the beginning of their public ministry the twelve apostles were shocked but soon became accustomed to Jesus' treatment towards women, because he made it clear from the beginning to the apostles that women were to be treated with equal rights with men in God's kingdom.

As a testimony to the charm and righteousness of Jesus' life on earth, he repeatedly dashed to pieces any hopes of his twelve apostles ambitions for personal exaltation and only one of his apostles, Judas Iscariot later deserted and betrayed Jesus to the Jewish high priests. Jesus' twelve apostles learned from Jesus about the kingdom of heaven and Jesus in turn learned a lot from them about the kingdom of men, especially human nature as it lives on earth and on the other evolutionary worlds of time and space. Jesus' twelve apostles represented many different types of human temperament, and they all carried heavy strains of Gentile blood in their bloodlines because of the forcible conversion of the Gentile population one hundred years prior.

All of the twelve apostles except for the Alpheus twins were graduates of the Jewish synagogue schools where they were thoroughly trained in the Hebrew scriptures and most of the current knowledge of their current times. Seven of Jesus' apostles were graduates of the Capernaum synagogue schools which were the best Jewish schools in all of Galilee.

The twelve apostles organized themselves to serve as disciples in Jesus' public ministry in the following job positions.

Andrew the first apostle to be chosen by Jesus was the designated chairman and director general of the twelve apostles and he was born in Capernaum, the oldest of five children and his father was a partner in the Zebedee family fish drying business in Bethsaida and Andrew and his brother Peter were both fishermen and business partners of James and John Zebedee. Andrew was thirty-three years old, the oldest apostle and the rest of the apostles always called Andrew the chief and they called Jesus their Master.

When the later Christian persecutions caused the apostles to flee out of Jerusalem Apostle Andrew traveled to Armenia, Asia Minor and Marcedonia and after converting thousands as believers of God's kingdom, Apostle Andrew was arrested by the Roman soldiers and crucified in Patrae, Achaia and it was two full days before before he died and all throughout his final tragic hours on earth Apostle Andrew continued to proclaim the good news of salvation of the kingdom of heaven.

Apostles Andrew and Peter were brothers, and Peter was the second apostle to be chosen by Jesus. Peter was married with three children, and he lived in Bethsaida which was close to Capernaum. Jesus had known Peter for quite some time and when he changed Peter's name from Simon to Peter Jesus did it with a smile because it was his nickname. Peter's duties along with Apostles James and John Zebedee was to be Jesus' personal companion and they tended to Jesus day and night and they went with Jesus on his night vigils of prayer and meditation. Later on, when the Christians had to flee persecutions in Jerusalem, Apostle Peter left Jerusalem and he became the leading spirit among the early Christian churches and when Peter's Roman captives later informed him that he was going to die on an upside down cross, Peter regarded himself to be the recipient of high honors.

The third and fourth apostles chosen by Jesus were his two longtime friends from the city of Capernaum brothers James and John Zebedee. John Zebedee was the oldest of the two and Jesus nicknamed them both, the sons of thunder. John Zebedee was thirty years old when Jesus chose him to be an apostle and along with his brother James and Peter his duties were to be Jesus' personal companion and to go with him to the hills when he went to pray and meditate. Apostle John was married with four children, and he worked as a fisherman in Capernaum and John Zebedee enjoyed the advantage of having known Jesus longer than any of the other apostles. After Jesus chose brothers James and John Zebedee to be apostles, he asked them both if they were ready to drink the cup and they both replied that they were ready. Apostle James Zebedee did drink the cup later on with his Master Jesus, because he was the first apostles to experience martyrdom after the crucifixion of Jesus by being put to death by the sword of Herod Agrippa who was afraid of Apostle James Zebedee more than any of the other apostles, because Apostle James Zebedee was quiet, silent but at the same time, he was brave and determined to complete his mission on earth. Apostle James Zebedee lived his life to the fullest while he worked with Jesus and when the end came, James bore himself with such grace and fortitude that his accuser and informant who attended apostles James' trial and execution was so touched by what he saw during Apostle James' final hours that he rushed away from the scene of Apostle James Zebedee's death to join and serve as one of the disciples of Jesus.

John Zebedee was James' brother, and he was the fourth apostle to be chosen by Jesus. John Zebedee was twenty-four years old, and the youngest member of the apostles and his duty was to also be Jesus' companion along with Peter and his brother James. Apostle

John Zebedee worked closely with Apostle Peter later on during the early activities of the Christian movement and he became to be one of the main supporters of the Jerusalem Christian church. Apostle John Zebedee was ninety-nine years old when his associate Nathan helped him to write the "Gospel According to John," while he was living in Ephesus.

Out of all of Jesus's twelve apostles John Zebedee became to be the most outstanding theologian and he died of natural causes in Ephesus in A.D. 103 at the ripe old age of one hundred and one years of age.

Philip was the fifth apostle to be chosen by Jesus when he was twenty-seven years old, and he had recently married with no children. The rest of the apostle gave Philip the nickname of Philip the Curious because he always wanted to be seen. Philip's duty was to be the steward of the twelve apostles making sure the multitude crowds and visitors always had something to eat. Apostle Philip made it through the trying times of Jesus' crucifixion and he helped to reorganize the apostles to go out into the world to continue to preach and win souls for God's kingdom and he was the most successful apostle in his ministry work with the Samaritans. Apostle Philips' wife was a dedicated member of the women's corps group that was founded by Jesus and she stood at the foot of Apostle Philip's cross as he was dying encouraging him to continue to proclaim the good tidings of God's kingdom to his murderers and when Philip's strength began to fail his wife began to recite the story of his salvation by faith in Jesus until she was silenced by a group of irate Jews who rushed to her and stoned her to death. Their oldest daughter Leah continued her parents' spiritual work, and she later became the renowned prophetess of Hierapolis.

Nathaniel was the sixth and last apostle to be chosen by Jesus and he was twenty-five years old, and he and Judas Iscariot were the two best educated men among the twelve apostles. Apostle Nathaniel's duty was to watch over the needs of each of the apostle's families and he received regular reports pertaining to each of the family's needs and after completing requisitions with Judas Iscariot, the apostles' treasurer Nathaniel would then send weekly funds to the apostles' families who were in need and his nickname was Honest Nathaniel. Apostle Nathaniel's father Bartholomew died shortly after Pentecost Sunday in the upper room and not too long afterwards Apostle Nathaniel traveled to both Mesopotamia and India where he continued to preach, teach and baptize believers in the kingdom of God and he later died in India.

Jesus' seventh apostle Matthew Levi was chosen by Apostle Andrew and Apostle Matthew came from a family of tax collectors and publicans and he was thirty-one years of age with a wife and four children when he became an apostle. Matthew's duty was to be the main financial representative for the twelve apostles by keeping their treasury replenished. And whenever apostles' treasury was low Apostle Matthew would often use his own personal funds to replenish it. Apostle Matthew later went out into the world to complete his public ministry after the beginning of the Christian persecutions in Jerusalem and he continued traveling further north preaching the gospel and baptizing believers all throughout Syria, Cappadocia, Galatia, Bethynia and Thrace.

One day while Apostle Matthew was preaching the gospel in Thrace, Lysimachia, a group of hostile Jews conspired with the Roman soldiers to have Matthew put to death. However, Matthew died triumphant with his faith of salvation he had learned so well from the teachings of Jesus.

Thomas Didymus was the eighth apostle to be chosen by Apostle Philip and when Thomas joined the apostles, he was twenty-nine years old and married with four children. Thomas had the duty of one of the apostles to manage the itinerary, work and movements of the twelve apostles. Apostle Thomas had a really hard time during the days of all the Christian persecutions, trials and crucifixions of the early Christians and for a while Apostle Thomas fell into despair, but he regained his strength and courage to stay with the apostles and he gave wise counsel to the rest of the apostles after Pentecost Sunday occurred in the upper room. When the persecutions caused many to flee Jerusalem, Apostle Thomas traveled to Cyprus, Crete, North Africa and Sicily where he preached the gospel and he continued his public ministry until he was arrested by Roman agents and put to death in Malta just a few weeks before finishing his writings about the life and teachings about Jesus of Nazareth.

The Apostle twins James and Judas Alpheus were the ninth apostles to be chosen by James and John Zebedee. The Alpheus twins were twenty-six years old, both married and James Alpheus had three children while his twin brother Judas had two children. Apostle Andrew assigned the Alpheus twin Apostles the duty of policing as well as serving as ushers to the multitude crowd during preaching services. They also worked as general assistants and errand boys and helped Apostle Philip with supplies and delivering weekly funds to the apostle families. Their nicknames were Thaddeus and Libbeus and they both served Jesus until the end until the dark days of the trials, crucifixions and despair came upon the early Christians. The twin Apostles James and Judas Alpheus never lost their faith in Jesus, and they were the first apostles to believe that Jesus had risen from the dead. Shortly after Jesus was crucified on the cross they both returned home to their families and to their fishing jobs, because neither of the twins had the mental capacity to go on being apostles during the more complex battles that later occurred in their public ministry, but they both lived and died knowing in their hearts that for a short time, they had the honor and blessing with serving as ushers for Jesus and the rest of the apostles. Simon Zelotes who the apostles called the zealot was chosen to be the eleventh apostle by Apostle Peter and he was twenty-eight years old when he became an apostle, and he had previously worked as a merchant in Capernaum and he was a former member of the Jewish Zealot Nationalist Group. Apostle Simon's duty was to coordinate recreation and play time for the apostles and he organized Wednesday recreation programs for the apostles.

After Jesus was crucified Apostle Simon Zelotes went into temporary retirement because he was literally crushed and felt that all had been lost when the trials and persecutions of the early Christians began in Jerusalem. However, within a few years Apostle Simon Zelotes' hopes rose, and he went into his public ministry to preach the gospel in Alexandria, Egypt and worked his way up the Nile River until he ended up in the heart of Africa where he continued his ministry until he was a very old man and when he died, he was buried in the heart of Africa.

Judas Iscariot, the twelfth apostle was chosen by Apostle Nathaniel, and he had formerly served as one of the late John the Baptist's thirty disciples. Judas Iscariot was born into a Sadducees family in Kerioth, a small town in southern Judea. When Judas was a lad his parents moved to Jericho, and he worked with his father in the family business enterprises until he became interested in the preaching and public ministry of John the Baptist. Judas Iscariot's parents disowned him when Judas became one of John the Baptist's disciples. Judas Iscariot's duty as an apostle was to be the treasurer, to carry the money bag, to keep the bills paid and to balance the books. Judas Iscariot was thirty years old when he became an apostle, and he was not married. Judas was a good thinker, but he was not always honest with himself, he never really understood himself and he was not sincere when dealing with his thoughts and emotions. Apostle Judas was never able to rise above the Judean prejudices he felt against the rest of the apostles and in his mind, Judas would often criticize many things about Jesus, because he felt that Jesus was too timid and reluctant to assert his power and authority. Judas was a good businessman, a great executive and a competent finance man, but he was a stickler for organization and the rest of the apostles viewed Judas as a great success. Judas Iscariot believed in Jesus, but he really didn't love Jesus with his whole heart, and he was always loyal financially to Jesus and the rest of the apostles and in the end, money was not the motive for Judas' betrayal of Jesus.

Judas Iscariot was the only son of unwise parents who pampered, petted and raised him to be a very spoiled child and as Judas grew up as a child, he had exaggerated ideas about his self-importance, and he was always a sore loser. Judas also had loose and distorted ideas about what was fair, and he was prone to periods of indulgences of hate and suspicion. All throughout his life Judas had the bad habit of getting even with anyone he felt had mistreated him, because his sense of values and loyalties were defective. From the beginning of Judas Iscariot being selected as the twelfth apostle, Jesus fully understood his weaknesses and the dangers of accepting Judas as an apostle, but Jesus' nature was to give every created being a full and equal chance for salvation and survival. Jesus wanted not only humanity on earth but the onlookers of many of the other worlds to know that when doubts exist concerning the sincerity of one's devotion to his gospel, it was the practice of the judges of men to still fully receive the doubtful candidate.

Jesus preached that the door of eternal life was wide open to all and that there were no restrictions or qualifications except for faith from those who walk through the door. This is the reason why Jesus allowed Judas Iscariot to remain an apostle to the very end and in the meantime, Jesus continued to do everything possible to transform and save this weak and confused twelfth apostle Judas Iscariot. But when light is not honestly received and lived up to, it tends to become darkness within one's soul and Apostle Judas Iscariot continued to grow intellectually regarding Jesus' teachings, but he failed to make progress in acquiring the spiritual character like the rest of the apostles. Judas increasingly became a brooder over his personal disappointments, and he finally became a victim of resentment, because his feelings had been hurt many times and he grew to become abnormally suspicious of his best friends, the rest of the apostles and even of Jesus. Judas became obsessed with the idea of getting revenge and he was willing to do anything to avenge himself, even to betray the rest of the apostles and Jesus. The wicked and dangerous ideas that Apostle Judas had in his mind did not take definite shape until the day when a grateful female follower broke open an expensive box of incense at Jesus' feet and when Judas verbally protested at this complete waste of money by this female follower for opening the box of incense, Jesus in front of everyone to hear disallowed Judas' verbal protest. This event proved to be too much for Apostle Judas and all of his past feelings of hurt, hate, malice, jealousy and revenge began to build up in his heart and mind and Judas at that moment made up his mind to get revenge and he really didn't know who, but he built up all the evil he had in his heart and mind and focused it on Jesus, because Jesus just so happened to be the chief actor who marked the point where Apostle Judas Iscariot fell from God's kingdom of light into his self-chosen life of evil and darkness.

HOW JESUS' TWELVE APOSTLES EACH DIED

Apostle Peter-Upside down cross

Apostle Andrew-X-Shaped cross

Apostle James Zebedee-Sword of Herod Agrippa

Apostle John Zebedee-Natural causes of old age

Apostle Bartholomew- Crucified, flayed, beheaded

Apostle Philip-Upside down cross

Apostle Thomas-Speared to death

Apostle Matthew-Burned at stake

Apostle Jude-Crucified and speared to death

Apostle Simon-Crucifixion

Judas Iscariot-Suicide by hanging himself

Jesus' twelve apostles each performed their assigned duties while working with Jesus in his public ministry and on Sunday, January 12, A. D. 27 Jesus called all of the apostles together and formally ordained them as ambassadors of God's kingdom and ministers of God's good tidings and soon after they were ordained by Jesus, they all prepared to travel to Jerusalem and Judea to begin their first public preaching tour. On Monday, January 19, A.D. 27, Jesus and the twelve apostles made plans to leave their headquarters in Bethsaida and go to Jerusalem, but just before they left for Jerusalem the apostles found Jesus sitting in a boat down by the beach weeping and Apostle Andrew asked Jesus which one of them had offended him to cause him to be weeping. Jesus told Apostle Andrew that he was sad because none of his family members had come to bid, he and his twelve new apostles Godspeed and farewell. Jesus didn't know that his youngest sister Babe Ruth was on her way to say good-bye to Jesus, but she was delayed and missed him before he left, but the rest of Jesus' family stayed away because of their foolish pride, disappointments, and misunderstandings and petty resentments due to their feelings being hurt.

Jesus and his apostles then proceeded to leave Galilee for Jerusalem, and the fame of Jesus had already begun to spread all over Galilee and beyond. Jesus knew that tetrarch Herod Antipas would soon begin to notice his public spiritual work, so he thought it was best to continue their journey to Jerusalem by traveling south through Judea. Jesus and the apostles traveled to Pella on the River Jordan where his late cousin John the Baptist had preached to so many people the year before and by the end of the week several hundred followers had assembled where Jesus and the apostles were camped and people came to their camp at Pella from Galilee, Syria, Phoenicia, Decapolis, Perea and Judea.

Many of Jesus' followers who came to hear the teachings of Jesus, and his apostles had already been baptized by John the Baptist during the prior year and they were interested in finding out more about Jesus' teachings. Apostle Andrew carefully instructed his fellow apostles in the delicate and difficult job of getting along smoothly with the former followers of John the Baptist, because during their first year of public ministry more than three fourths of their followers had previously followed John the Baptist. So, for the entire year of A.D.27, Jesus and his twelve apostles quietly worked on taking over John the Baptist's ministry work in Perea and Judea. Apostle Andrew divided the multitude crowds into groups, and he assigned the apostles to preach for morning, afternoon and after the evening meal sermons.

Next Jesus and the apostles traveled to Amathus where they preached to the crowd of followers twice daily for three weeks and they made a lot of progress during their public ministry in Amathus.

On February 26, A.D. 27, Jesus and the apostles traveled with a large group of followers down the River Jordan to Bethany and Jesus then took apostles Peter, James and John Zebedee into the hills south of Jericho and taught them some advanced spiritual truths about the kingdom of heaven. Although apostles Peter, James and John really couldn't understand what Jesus was teaching them, while they were in the hills with him, his gracious words stayed in their hearts and after Jesus' crucifixion and resurrection they used these teachings greatly enlightened and enriched when they began their own individual public ministry. It is no wonder that Apostles Peter, James and John Zebedee were unable to fully understand what Jesus was teaching them in the hills that day, because what Jesus was projecting and teaching them was God's plan for the new age of light and love that was not to manifest on planet earth until the times of the twenty-first century beginning with the year of 2012.

All throughout the four weeks Jesus and the apostles conducted their public ministry in Bethany, Apostle Andrew arranged the apostles into pairs of two to go into Jericho for a couple of days to minister to the sick and they were able to minster to every house in Jericho. On Monday the last day of March A.D.27, Jesus and the apostles began their journey up the hills to their next destination, Jerusalem. Jesus' friend Lazarus who lived in Bethany had come down to visit Jesus twice and he made arrangements for Jesus and the apostles to make their headquarters with Lazarus and his two sisters in Bethany during their stay.

On Sunday morning April 6, A.D. 27, Jesus and his apostles went down to Jerusalem, and this was the first time that Jesus and his apostles had ever been in Jerusalem together to celebrate the Passover. During this same month of April, Jesus and his apostles conducted their public ministry in Jerusalem and every evening they walked to Lazarus' home where they spent the night. Jesus or one of his apostles also taught daily spiritual classes in the temple of Jerusalem and the multitudes of people who were coming into Jerusalem to celebrate the Passover also got to hear the gospel from Jesus and his apostles. The chief priests and rulers of the Jews became very concerned about the public preaching that Jesus and the apostles were doing, and they had a meeting and debated among themselves as to what should be done about them.

Besides teaching in and about the temple in Jerusalem, the apostles and many of their followers were also completing a lot of spiritual work among the Passover crowds and many of these people who heard Jesus preach began to carry this good news of his message from the Passover celebration back to their hometowns. So, no longer was the spiritual message of Jesus confined to only Palestine.

One of the great sermons that Jesus preached in the temple during the Passover celebration was relating to who would truly be able to enter into God's kingdom. The public preaching experience in Jerusalem was a great inspiration for the apostles, because it was their first contact with such large crowds of people, and they learned many valuable lessons that later helped them with their own individual public ministry.

After the busy times of the apostles' spiritual preaching during the Passover week in Jerusalem, Jesus spent the following Wednesday resting with the apostles at his friend Lazarus' home in Bethany. By the end of April, A.D. 27, the opposition towards Jesus among the Pharisees and Sadducees had become so strong that Jesus and his apostles decided that it was best to leave Jerusalem for a while so they traveled south to conduct their public ministry in Bethlehem and Hebron and for the entire month of May, A.D. 27, Jesus and the apostles went from house to house preaching only in two of the villages surrounding Jerusalem. No public preaching was done during this trip, only house to house visitations. During this time while the apostles taught the gospel and ministered to the sick, Jesus and Abner, leader of the Nazarite Brotherhood visited and worked with the Nazarite colony and with many members of the Nazarite Brotherhood who became followers, and they believed in Jesus' gospel and message. The people who lived in Bethlehem and Hebron did not know that Jesus had been born in Bethlehem and the time that Jesus and his apostles spent in these two regions converted many followers to the gospel of God's kingdom. By the first part of June A.D. 27, the agitation against Jesus had quieted down in Jerusalem, so Jesus and the apostles returned to Jerusalem to continue to instruct and minister to their followers.

Jesus and the apostles spent the entire month of June A.D. 27, in or near Jerusalem, but they did no public teaching during this time period. When the rulers of the Jews learned that Jesus had returned to Jerusalem, they made preparations to arrest him, but when they noticed that Jesus had not done any public preaching, they figured they had frightened Jesus away, so they decided to let him carry on with his private teachings. All was quiet until towards the end of June when a man named Simon who as a member of the Sanhedrins publicly denounced the teachings of Jesus and immediately a new agitation towards Jesus and the apostles grew so strong that Jesus decided to leave the area and travel to Samaria and Decapolis.

At the end of June of this same year Jesus and the apostles traveled north to Samaria where they preached for several days to people who came to hear the gospel from Gophna and Ephraim and Jesus and his apostles spent more than two weeks preaching in this region and many people came from as far as Antipatris to hear the gospel of Jesus.

During the first half of August, A.D. 27, Jesus and the apostles traveled to the Greek cities of Archelais and Phasaelis where they had their first experience of preaching to some exclusive groups of Gentiles who were composed of Greeks, Romans, and Syrians. The apostles encountered new difficulties while preaching the gospel with many objections to Jesus' teachings and after this strong opposition a state of great nervousness and emotional tension began to develop among the apostles and their disciple associates. Jesus then told the apostles that he was taking them all up to the mountain for three days to rest and relax and this trip was a marvelous occasion for each of the apostles and for their disciple associates and when they reached the top of the mountain, Jesus assigned each of them a topic for discussion and they spent three days talking over issues not related to their religious work.

On the third day as they were all coming down the mountain and heading back to their camp, a great positive change had come over all of the apostles and disciples, because they had all made the important discovery that many human problems are nonexistent and that many passing troubles are created from fear. When the apostles and disciples returned from their three-day holiday with Jesus on the mountain, it was the beginning of a period of improved relations among Jesus, the apostles and their disciple associates.

There were not very many Gentiles in the two Greek cities of Archelais and Phasalis who accepted the gospel, but the apostles did gain valuable experience during their first extensive public ministry dealing with exclusive Gentile people. On Monday morning around the middle of the month, Jesus told Apostle Andrew that it was time for them to go and preach in Samaria to the city of Sychar near Jacob's well. For more than six hundred years the Jews of Judea and Galilee had been in conflict with the Samaritans and this conflict all began in the year 700 B.C. when Sargon, the King of Assyria while subduing a revolt in central Palestine, took 25,000 Jewish people into captivity and it was a severe test of loyalty for Jesus when he told the apostles that they were going to preach the gospel in Samaria.

When Jesus arrived at Jacob's well in Samaria, he arrived there first alone and he was very thirsty, but he had no drinking utensils and at that moment a young Samaritan woman named Nalda came up to Jacob's well with her water pitcher and Jesus asked her to give him a drink of water. Nalda was surprised to have a Jewish man to speak to her asking for water and she asked Jesus how could he being a Jewish man be asking her a Samaritan woman for a drink of water. Jesus then told Nalda that he who drinks the water from Jacob's well will become thirsty again, but he who drinks the water of the living spirit will never be thirsty again.

While Nalda continued talking with Jesus at Jacob's well, she avoided talking about her personal immoral life and Nalda told Jesus that she had heard about the teachings of John the Baptist telling everyone about a deliverer who would soon come to declare all things to us and Jesus then told Nalda that, "I who speaks to you now am he." This was Jesus' first direct, positive and undisguised pronouncement of his divine nature that Jesus had ever made while on earth and it was made to a Samaritan woman, Nalda, a woman who had been married four times and who had questionable character, but she was a woman whom Jesus looked upon as a human soul who desired salvation with sincerity whole-heartedly and that was enough for Jesus. Then Jesus told Nalda to go her way because God had forgiven her and that from that day on, she would live a new life, because she had received the living water of salvation, and a new joy would spring up within her soul and she would now become a daughter of the Most High in Paradise.

When Nalda returned to her hometown city of Sychar with her pitcher of water, she told everyone she could drawing a large crowd about who she had just met that day at Jacob's well and it was Jesus. That same day at sundown a large crowd of Samaritans from Sychar came to Jacob's well to hear Jesus preach the gospel and he talked to the crowd more about the eternal water of life and the gift of the indwelling Holy Spirit. Jesus knew that it would be dark soon, so he was determined to talk to the crowd of Samaritans who had gathered at Jacob's well before it was time for them to go back home to Sychar. After that night at Jacob's well, Jesus and the apostles went into Sychar and preached to the Samaritan people for two days before they established their camp on Mount Gerizim and many of the Samaritans who lived in Sychar became converts and accepted the kingdom of God into their hearts. Jesus declared why he was so open to the Samaritans, because he felt that he could safely do so due to the fact that he knew that he would never again be able to visit the heart of Samaria to preach the gospel. Jesus and the apostles camped on Mount Gerizim in Samaria until the end of August, A.D. 27, and they continued to preach the gospel to the Samaritan cities during the day and they spent their nights at their base camp. The spiritual ministry that Jesus and the apostles completed in the Samaritan cities helped to convert many people and it prepared the way for the future public ministry that Apostle Philip would be completing in these regions after the death, resurrection and ascension of Jesus. During the months of September and October, A.D. 27, Jesus spent this time alone with his twelve apostles teaching and instructing them on many truths about the Universal Father's kingdom. During this time period Jesus and his apostles were in retirement camping on the borders of Samaria and Decapolis, because the religious rulers in Jerusalem had become very antagonistic again and tetrarch Herod Antipas was still holding John the Baptist in prison and with these hostile conditions, it was unwise for Jesus to try to preach in either Judea or Galilee.

Another reason for this temporary retirement was that there still existed a growing tension between the leaders of John the Baptist former disciples and Jesus' apostles which continued to grow worse as the number of their believers increased. Jesus knew that the days of their preliminary work of teaching and preaching were just about over, and his next move was to begin the full and final effort to complete his mission on earth and Jesus didn't want to begin his public ministry in any way that would embarrass his imprisoned cousin John the Baptist. So, Jesus made the decision to spend some time in retirement rehearsing with and training his apostles to do some quiet work in Decapolis until John the Baptist was either released or executed.

Jesus made it clear to his twelve apostles and to John the Baptist's twelve disciples that they were in temporary retirement for these three reasons:

To strengthen their faith in the gospel of God's kingdom.

To allow the opposition to their ministry in Judea and Galilee to quiet down.

To await the fate of his cousin John the Baptist.

Throughout the months of November and December, A.D. 27, Jesus, his twelve apostles and the twelve disciples of John the Baptist teached and preached quietly in the Greek cities of Decapolis, Abila, Scythopolis, Gerasa, and Gadara and this was the end of Jesus' Preliminary period of taking over his cousin John the Baptist's work and organization and for two months this group of twenty-four spiritual preachers worked most of the time in pairs of two preaching the gospel and they were able to win many souls among the Gentiles and Apostate Jews in these Greek cities that they worked in.

During the last part of December A.D. 27, Jesus and his twenty-four disciples all went to Pella near the River Jordan where they again began to preach and while Jesus was teaching the gospel to the multitude crowd one afternoon, some of John the Baptist's friends brought Jesus the last message he was ever going to receive from his imprisoned cousin, John the Baptist and Jesus sent a return message back through John the Baptist's friend telling him that he was not forgotten and that the poor and needy were continuing to have the good tidings about God's kingdom preached to them. John the Baptist was executed by the order of tetrarch Herod Antipas on the evening of January 10, A.D. 28

and when Jesus heard about the death of John the Baptist, he dismissed the multitude he was preaching to and called his twenty-four disciples in council telling them that the time had come to proclaim God's kingdom openly and with power and that they were going to Galilee to preach the gospel. Accordingly, early in the morning of January 13, A.D. 28, Jesus and his twenty-four disciples traveled to Capernaum and stayed the night at the Zebedee household.

Jesus' youngest sister, Babe Ruth secretly came to visit on that same morning, and they spent an hour together in a boat talking while anchored a short distance from the shore. Jesus' baby sister Ruth was the only one is his family who truly believed in the divinity of Jesus' mission on earth and from the early days of his sister's Ruth spiritual journey right to when Jesus began his public ministry, death, resurrection and ascension, his baby sister Ruth never once doubted her brother Jesus' true mission on earth. Jesus called his youngest sister Babe Ruth, and she proved to be Jesus' main comforter from his earth family all throughout the trying ordeal of his trial, rejection and crucifixion.

While Jesus and his twenty-four disciples were in Capernaum on the next Sabbath Jesus preached a sermon at the synagogue to the people to make clear that religion was a personal experience and just as Jesus was completing this sermon a young man in the congregation began to have a violent epileptic seizure and he began to loudly cry out obscenities at Jesus who then took this young man by the hand telling the evil spirit to come out of him and the young man's seizure stopped. On the way home from the synagogue Jesus and some of his friends stopped by Peter's home where they found out that Peter's wife's mother was sick with chills and a fever. Jesus stood over Peter's mother-in-law held her hand and after speaking words of comfort, the chills and fever left her body. By the time Jesus and the apostles sat down to eat their evening meal at the end of their eventful Sabbath day, all of the people in Capernaum were talking about the two people Jesus had healed that day and according to the Jewish teachings, it was not permitted to go anywhere to be healed during the sacred hours of the Sabbath, so as soon as the sun went down on that same day, many sick and afflicted men, women and children began to make their way towards Apostle Peter's home.

After the sun went down Jesus and the apostles were sitting around the supper table when Peter's wife heard voices in the front yard and when she opened the door, she saw a large crowd of sick people standing there who wanted to be healed by Jesus. When Jesus stepped out of the front door of Peter's home he saw about one thousand sick people and the sight of so many people who were suffering genuinely touched Jesus' heart and Jesus then told the crowd of sick people that he had come to earth to reveal the power and glory of our Universal Paradise Father and to establish his kingdom on earth, but if it was the will of the Universal Father then his desire was to see that everyone there that night was to be made whole. Jesus had passed the responsibility of this healing decision to his Universal Father and suddenly an assembly of celestial beings who were serving under the command of Jesus' indwelling Divine Thought Adjuster descended where they were amidst of all of the afflicted people and in a moment of time, the six hundred and eighty-three sick people were all healed.

When Jesus was on Mount Hermon praying for forty days his indwelling Divine Thought Adjuster had told Jesus that if there was an instance where the Universal Father wanted all of the celestial hosts to manifest help to Jesus that it would not be in sync with the space and time that existed on planet earth. So in less than a moment all of the sick people were healed, because Jesus a Creator Son of God desired to heal this large crowd of sick people that night and his Universal Father willed that this mass healing through Jesus' Divine Thought Adjuster be done in a moment of time and not in all of Jesus' subsequent life on earth did another crowd that large of the healing of these people ever take place again.

That Sabbath Day in Capernaum was a great day on earth for Jesus and in the life of the entire Nebadon universe and to all of the universe onlookers, the little city of Capernaum was to them the real capital of the Paradise city of Nebadon, because the handful of Jews who were in attendance at the synagogue that day were not the only living beings to hear Jesus' closing statement of the sermon he preached that day when Jesus stated that:

"Hate is the shadow of fear, revenge is the mask of cowardice and man is the son of God and not a child of the devil."

The healing wonders that occurred every now and then during Jesus' spiritual ministry were not a part of his plan while he was preaching the word of God and these events of miracles caused nothing but trouble for Jesus, because they raised more prejudice and publicity that Jesus was trying hard to avoid. Jesus went into seclusion after the mass healing that occurred that night in the front yard of Apostle Peter's home and when he went back into Peter's home that night, Jesus refused to accept any adoration or congratulations from his apostles and instead Jesus told the apostles that the Universal Father was powerful enough to heal the body and also mighty enough to save the soul. The next day Jesus' brothers James and Jude came to visit him, but Jesus and the apostles had already left to go and preach in the city of Rimmon.

The first public preaching tour of Galilee began on Sunday, January 18, A.D. 28, and lasted for two months until Jesus and the apostles returned to Capernaum on March 17, A.D. 28, and during this preaching tour Jesus and his twenty-four disciples preached and baptized believers in the cities of Rimmon, Jotapata, Ramah, Zebulun, Iron, Gischala, Chorazin Madin, Cana, Nain and Endor and in these cities they continued to preach while they were passing through the smaller towns. This was the first time Jesus allowed the disciples to openly preach without any restraints and while they were on this preaching tour, Jesus cautioned the disciples on three occasions to stay away from Nazareth and to be discreet while traveling through Tiberias and Capernaum. Jesus and his disciples arrived back in Capernaum on March 17, A.D. 28, and they spent two weeks resting at their Bethsaida headquarters before they left for Jerusalem.

During the two weeks they were in the city of Capernaum the apostles taught the people by the seaside while Jesus stayed alone in the hills praying and meditating in communion with his Universal Father. During these two weeks Jesus along with James and John Zebedee made two secret trips to Tiberias where they met with many believers and preached the gospel to them and many members of tetrarch Herod Antipas' household believed in Jesus' teachings and they attended these meetings in Tiberias and the influence of the members of Herod's household helped to lessen the bad feelings Herod Antipas had towards Jesus. These family members of Herod Antipas' household explained to Herod that the kingdom that Jesus preached was spiritual in nature and not political and Herod listened to the Christian members of his household, and he didn't allow himself to become alarmed by the spreading reports abroad concerning Jesus' teachings and healings and Herod did not object to Jesus' spiritual work. There were, however, a group of Herod's staff who were being negatively influenced by some of the bitter Jewish religious leaders in Jerusalem and they remained to be enemies of Jesus and his disciples and later they did all they could to hamper Jesus' public religious ministry. The greatest danger to Jesus was from the Jewish religious leaders in Jerusalem and not from Herod Antipas and this was the main reason why Jesus and his disciples spent most of their public ministry preaching in Galilee and not in Judea or in Jerusalem.

Early on the morning of Tuesday, March 30, A.D. 28, Jesus and the apostles traveled to Jerusalem for the Passover feast, and they celebrated the Passover in Bethany, and this was the first time that Jesus and his disciples had a bloodless Passover feast, and the second time Jesus got to celebrate the Passover with his disciples in Jerusalem. After the Passover celebration Jesus and his disciples left to return to Capernaum and this time the twelve former disciples of John the Baptise did not return with Jesus and instead these twelve disciples under the direction of Abner, the leader of the Nazarite Brotherhood stayed in Jerusalem where they continued preaching in the surrounding areas, while Jesus and his twelve disciples returned to work their ministry in Galilee. Never again would this group of twenty-four disciples all work together again until for a short time before Jesus commissioned and sent seventy more disciples to go out into the various areas to preach and teach.

From May until October A.D. 28, Jesus and his apostles stayed at the Zebedee home in Bethsaida, and they also maintained a large camp by the seaside near the Zebedee home for five months which housed up to 1,500 people at a time and this huge, tented city was under the general supervision of David Zebedee and the two Apostles the Alpheus twins. This encampment was in model condition, and it had adequate sanitation and general administration facilities.

During the five months that this tent city existed interested believers from every part of the Roman Empire and from the lands east of the Euphrates River were in frequent attendance for the spiritual teaching sessions that were offered. This was the longest settled and well-organized period of Jesus and the apostles' public ministry, and Jesus' immediate family spent most of this time close to him in Nazareth and Cana. This tent city was not conducted as a community of common interests, but it was instead an apostolic family. David Zebedee managed this large tent city, and it became to be an efficient self-sustaining enterprise, and no one was ever turned away and the most important feature of this tent city was Apostle Peter's evangelist training school for prophets.

Jesus and the apostles second public teaching tour began on Sunday, October 3, A.D. 28 and lasted for three months until December 30, A.D. 28, and on this tour Jesus and his apostles were assisted by a newly formed corps of one hundred and seventeen evangelists and numerous other assistants. During this second public ministry tour they traveled to Gadara, Scthoapolis, Tarichea, Hippos, Gamala, Bethsaida-Julias and many more other small towns and villages. During the three months of this second tour David Zebedee still continued to maintain a permanent headquarters in Bethsaida and this location was the clearinghouse for Jesus' work on earth and the relay station for the messenger service that David Zebedee oversaw that connected between the fifty messengers of the rapidly enlarging work of Jesus and his apostles' public ministry.

Apostle Andrew while consulting with Apostle Peter and with the approval of Jesus had instructed David Zebedee at their Bethsaida headquarters to dispatch messengers to the various preaching groups to end their second public ministry tour and to return back to their Bethsaida headquarters. So, by Thursday, December 30, A.D. 28, and by supper time all of the apostolic party and teaching evangelists were back at their Bethsaida camp headquarters and the entire evangelist group stayed together until the next day until the next day after the Sabbath where they were all granted a two-week rest to go home to their families, friends or to simply go fishing. The three days that the entire group were together in Bethsaida was inspirational, because they were all able to share all of the experiences they had during their second public ministry tour and of the one hundred and seventeen newly recruited evangelists who participated in this second public ministry tour of Galilee, only seventy-five survived the test of this experience and were ready and on hand to be assigned for their new assignments at the end of their two week recess period.

On Sunday evening January 16, A.D. 29, Abner along with the twelve former John the Baptist disciples came from their headquarters in Hebron to have one of their periodic conferences with Jesus and his twelve apostles and on Tuesday, January 18, A.D. 29, this group of twenty-four disciples along with their seventy-five evangelists went out to begin their third public ministry tour.

This third tour lasted for three weeks, and they traveled to the cities of Magdala, Tiberias, and Nazareth and all of the main surrounding cities and villages of central and southern Galilee and this was Jesus' and the twenty-four apostles last public ministry tour to Galilee.

One of the most controversial things that Jesus did in connection with his spiritual bestowal mission on earth was to train ten devout women to help he and the apostles during their public speaking tours. Jesus appointed, trained and authorized these ten women to form their own spiritual organization, and he told Apostle Judas Iscariot to provide them with the funds they needed for their equipment and for their travel domesticated animals. These ten women were commissioned by Jesus to be religious teachers, and they were permitted to travel with Jesus walking in the rear behind Jesus and the apostles. The entire Jewish community were all stirred up about this group of female religious teachers and Jesus' enemies made a big deal out of Jesus' concepts to liberate women.

All throughout the early days of the Christian church, women spiritual teachers and spiritual ministers were called deaconesses, and they were given their proper recognition and whenever Jesus and the apostles traveled for their public ministry tours these female religious teachers went with them always traveling in the rear. When Jesus and the apostles traveled to Magdala for their public ministry, these female religious teachers first demonstrated their usefulness and proved the true wisdom they all possessed. Mary Magdalene who later became Jesus' wife converted to be a follower of Jesus in Magdala and after she was baptized by Apostle Peter, she became to be one of their most effective teachers and she helped to finance their spiritual ministry. Mary Magdalene and the rest of the female members of their spiritual teachers' group remained working with Jesus and his apostles for the rest of Jesus' life on earth and they worked faithfully, effectively for the enlightenment and uplifting of many downtrodden women that they encountered during their public ministry tours. When the last tragic episode in the drama of Jesus' life was unfolding, the apostles all fled but one, but the entire corps of the ten women stayed with Jesus without denying or betraying him in the end.

Towards the end of Jesus' third public ministry tour in March A.D. 29, Jesus spent time walking around in his old neighborhoods of Nazareth without being recognized. Jesus walked by his childhood home, the supply and repair shop and he walked up the hill that was a half hour from his boyhood home that he had loved so much as a child. Not since the day he was baptized by his cousin John the Baptist had Jesus experienced such a flood of emotion that was now stirring up in his soul and while Jesus continued walking down his favorite hill, he heard the familiar sounds of the trumpet announcing that the sun was going down soon.

Earlier that day Jesus had sent Apostle Thomas to arrange with the ruler of the local synagogue in Nazareth for him to preach at the upcoming Sabbath service. The people of Nazareth were never known to be pious or virtuous when it came to religion and as the years went by the village of Nazareth became to be increasingly contaminated by the low moral standards of the nearby village of Sepphoris. All throughout Jesus' youth and as a young man there had always been a strong division of opinion in Nazareth regarding him and a lot of people still resented Jesus when he left and moved to Capernaum. The people of Nazareth had heard a lot about Jesus' spiritual teachings, baptizing and peaching, but they were offended that Jesus had never included his native village of Nazareth in all of his public preaching tours. The people of Nazareth had all heard about Jesus' fame, but most of the residents of Nazareth were angry, because Jesus had done none of his great works in the village that he grew up in. For months prior to Jesus' arrival to preach on the upcoming sabbath at the synagogue, the people of Nazareth were talking a lot about Jesus, but overall, their opinions about Jesus were unfavorable.

So, Jesus found himself in the midst of a not so welcome homecoming and instead he was faced with a hostile and hypocritical atmosphere and this wasn't all that Jesus was up against, because his enemies knew that Jesus was scheduled to speak in the synagogue, so they hired a group of rough, uncouth men to come to the synagogue to harass and attack Jesus in every way they possibly could. The problem was that most of Jesus' older friends including his former synagogue chazan teacher were all dead or had moved away from Nazareth and the younger generation of people who were now living in Nazareth were full of jealousy and they resented Jesus' fame. Also, this younger generation didn't know about the devotion Jesus had for his family all those years and how he helped his mother Mary financially and emotionally to support and raise his seven siblings since he was fourteen years old. The attitude that Jesus' family had towards him except for his youngest sister, Babe Ruth also helped to contribute to the unkind feelings the people of Nazareth had towards him.

The orthodox Jews who lived in Nazareth even criticized Jesus stating that he had walked too fast while he was on his way to preach at the synagogue on that Sabbath morning, but that Sabbath morning turned out to be a beautiful day and all of Nazareth, both friends and foes showed up that day to hear their former citizen of Nazareth, Jesus preach in the synagogue and as it turned out, there was not enough room for all of the people to fit in the synagogue who came to hear Jesus speak that day.

When Jesus was a young lad, he had often spoken on the Sabbath at this synagogue and when the current ruler of the synagogue handed Jesus the roll of sacred writings to read the scripture lesson, no one in attendance knew that Jesus had given this sacred roll to the synagogue when he was a young man.

After Jesus read the scripture lesson from the sacred scroll, he then began to discourse with the congregation for about fifteen minutes and many of the people who were in the congregation that day were pleased with Jesus' discourse and with his graciousness and wisdom. The custom in the Jewish synagogues was that after the conclusion of the formal service the speaker was to remain so that those who were interested could ask questions and as Jesus proceeded to walk down into the crowd to answer their questions, the group of hired troublemakers began to verbally attack Jesus. When the apostles and evangelists saw that trouble was brewing, they tried to lead Jesus out of the synagogue, but Jesus would not leave.

Jesus soon found himself standing in the synagogue surrounded by a great crowd of enemies and with only a handful of loyal followers and the crowd began to shout obscenities at Jesus and point accusing fingers taunting him saying that he thought he was better than the rest of the people of Nazareth. Under normal conditions Jesus would have good naturedly been able to manage this hostile crowd, but one of his apostles Simon Zelotes with the help of Nahor, one of the young evangelists quickly gathered a group of Jesus' friends to surround the hostile crowd and with a loud and belligerent voice, Apostle Simon Zelotes told the crowd to depart. But the hired troublemakers in the crowd then quickly grabbed Jesus and took him up to the nearby hill with the intention to push Jesus over the edge of the cliff. Just as the crowd was about to push Jesus over the edge of the cliff, Jesus suddenly turned around, faced his captors and quietly folded his arms. Jesus then just stood there saying nothing and both the mob and Jesus' friends just stood there amazed and as Jesus began to walk forward, the mob parted and allowed Jesus to walk past them and walk down the hill unmolested.

Jesus' apostles and evangelists followed him back to their encampment where they began to discuss what had just happened. This turbulent ending to Jesus' third public preaching tour helped his disciples to better understand the meaning of some of Jesus' prior teachings that God's kingdom would come only through a lot of sorrow and bitter disappointments. Jesus and his disciples left Nazareth the next day on Sunday morning and after traveling by many different routes, they all finally assembled together again at their Bethsaida headquarters on March 10, A. D. 29.

CHAPTER FIFTEEN

JESUS TARRYING BY THE SEA

The fruit of the righteous is a Tree of Life, and the one who is wise saves lives.

(Proverbs 11:30)

When they saw the star, they were overjoyed.

(Matthew 2:10)

A Prayer:

Dear Jesus, I praise you for entering our dark world, forever brightening my days with your presence.

JESUS TARRYING BY THE SEA

By March 10, A.D. 29, all of the disciples and evangelist groups had gathered at their Bethsaida headquarters and on Thursday and Friday night of that week many of them went out fishing on the nearby lake. That Saturday night Jesus talked for more than an hour to the entire assembled group about adversity in their mission and the spiritual value of disappointments. Jesus had not yet fully recovered from the sorrow of his recent rejection in Nazareth and there was a sadness that was evident in his voice, and he did not have his usual cheerful demeanor. Apostles James and John Zebedee stayed close to Jesus during these times while Apostle Peter was busy training the new corps of seventy evangelists. During this time the women's corps of spiritual teachers spent their time visiting believers house to house teaching the gospel and ministering to the sick in Capernaum and in the surrounding villages and cities.

During this time Jesus began to teach all of the disciples a new method of preaching the gospel by the usage of parables, because this method enabled them to present new and startling truths to the believers and at the same time avoided controversy and clashing with the Jewish traditions and established authority. Jesus often used parables to teach the gospel, because it enabled, he and the disciples to proclaim vital truths to those who wanted to know a better way while at the same time it would give his enemies less opportunities to be offended by his new teachings of the gospel.

Jesus continued to teach the crowds of people during the day and at night he instructed the apostles and evangelists and a week before the Passover celebration in Jerusalem, Jesus declared a furlough of one week so that all of his followers could go home to be with their friends and family. More than half of his disciples refused to leave Jesus, and the crowds continued to increase daily so much that David Zebedee wanted to establish a new apostolic camp, but Jesus said no not at this time. Jesus hadn't been getting much rest, so on Sunday morning, March 26, A.D. 29, Jesus decided to get away for a while from the crowds of people and since the evangelists were still there preaching to the multitudes, Jesus and his apostles planned to escape unnoticed to rest in a beautiful park south of Bethsaida-Julias. However, the crowd of people watched as Jesus and the apostles were leaving in their boats and they followed them in pursuit in their own boats and by late afternoon more than one thousand followers had found Jesus and his apostles in the park and after Jesus and the apostles ate their evening meal, they organized this crowd into small groups so that the apostles could preach to them. By the next day on Monday afternoon, this crowd of people had increased to more than three thousand people and more were still coming to this area in the park and by Wednesday afternoon about five thousand men, women and children had gathered in the park south of Bethsaida-Julias.

Apostle Philip had only brought a three-day supply of food for Jesus and the apostles and by noon on Wednesday, all of the food that the large crowd had brought with them was nearly gone and the crowd of people were hungry, but they would not leave to go home. Rumors began to circulate among the crowd of people that the apostles and evangelists were about to proclaim and crown Jesus as the King of the Jewish people and the ringleader who started this rumor to proclaim Jesus as a king was one of the evangelists named Joab.

At around five in the evening on Wednesday, Jesus asked the apostles what were they going to do with their hungry crowd of five thousand people who had been with them for three days and Apostles Philip and Andrew told Jesus that they were going to send the large crowd home to their villages to buy themselves some food. Jesus then told Apostles Philip and Andrew that he didn't want to send everyone home and that he wanted to feed them some food. Apostle Andrew then went to ask one of their food assistants, a young lad named Mark how much food was left in their store of provisions and he returned to Jesus stating that the lad, Mark had five barley loaves, and two dried fishes left. Apostles Peter then quickly stated that Jesus and the twelve apostles had not eaten their evening meal yet. At that moment Jesus took the five barley loaves and two fishes in his hands, gave thanks to his Universal Father, broke the bread, gave the bread to his twelve apostles who then passed the bread to their food associates who then fed the entire multitude. Jesus likewise blessed, broke and distributed the fish to the entire multitude of five thousand people, and all ate well until they were full. When the crowd of people were finished eating Jesus told the disciples to gather up the broken pieces of food that was left over so that no food would be lost and when the disciples finished gathering up the leftover food, they had twelve full baskets of barley loaves and fish.

This feeding food to this multitude of five thousand people was the first and only natural miracle that Jesus had ever performed which was the result of his conscious preplanning. It was true that Jesus' disciples were prone to call many things that Jesus did as miracles when they were not, but this was a genuine supernatural miracle and in this case, Jesus fed an entire multitude crowd of five thousand people with only five barley loaves and two dried fish which was done through Michael of Nebadon who himself multiplied the food elements by the elimination of the time factor and the visible life channel.

Jesus' feeding of the crowd of five thousand people by using his supernatural energy was another one of those cases where human pity plus creative power equaled that which happened and now that the crowd had been fed the project to seize Jesus and proclaim him king was no longer necessary.

For a long time the Jewish culture had taught that the Jewish Messiah would be a descendant from the bloodline of David, son of Jesse, when he came to earth and that he would cause the land to again flow with milk and honey and that the bread of life would again fall as manna from heaven just like it did for their ancestors while they were in the wilderness marching around Mount Sinai for forty years and this expectation had been fulfilled right before their eyes. When this multitude of five thousand had finished eating that day, one man in the crowd stood up and shouted to make Jesus king, but this false hope didn't last long, because Jesus stepped up on a huge stone, lifted his right hand and told the crowd that the kingdom of God was not of this world, and if they had to have a king to let the Universal Father of light and love be enthroned in each of their hearts to be the spirit ruler of all things. Before Jesus left this large crowd to be alone in the hills, he told Apostle Andrew to take the rest of the disciples back to the Zebedee home and pray and the disciples set off by themselves in their boats and began to row back to Bethsaida and they were all crushed, because Jesus had never before sent them all away and Jesus refused to go with them.

It soon became dark, and a strong wind began to build up in the water and Apostle Peter fell into a deep sleep of exhaustion and while the rest of the apostles continued to row the boat, a strong wind with turbulent waves began to build up around them. Meanwhile while Apostle Peter continued to sleep, he began to dream that he saw a vision of Jesus walking to their boat on the sea and as Jesus walked by their boat, Apostle Peter cried out to Jesus to save them and as this vision continued in Peter's mind, he dreamed that Jesus told him to be of good cheer and not to be afraid. Jesus' words began to soothe Peter's troubled spirit, and he then asked Jesus to let him come and walk on the water of the sea with him and as Peter started to walk on the water of the sea, the strong waves frightened him, and Peter cried out again to Jesus to save him. The rest of the apostles on the boat were listening at what Peter was saying during this entire vision and Peter continued to dream that Jesus stretched out his hand and as Jesus was lifting Peter up from the sea, Jesus told Peter that he had little faith. While Peter was having this vision of Jesus, he actually stood up and stepped overboard into the water and Peter awakened from his vision just as Apostles Andrew, James and John reached down and pulled him out of the strong gusty waves of the sea.

Now as far as Apostle Peter was concerned, this vision was real, and he sincerely believed that Jesus had come to them that night and walked in the water alongside their boat and Peter was able to partially convince Apostle John that his dream had not been a vision and that these events had really happened. Apostle Luke who was the physician of their group carefully researched the facts of Apostle Peter's story and Luke concluded that Peter was simply having a vision, a dream.

That Thursday morning before daylight, the apostles arrived at their destination and anchored their boat near the Zebedee home, and they all slept until noon and when the apostles awakened Apostle Andrew found Jesus walking by the sea holding up one of the oars to their boat.

Out of the five thousand people that Jesus had fed on the prior day, only five hundred followers remained with them, and they continued to follow Jesus and the twelve apostles. Jesus asked Apostle Andrew to gather the rest of the disciples and women's corps, and Jesus then told them all that he was going away for a few days of rest with just the apostles before they traveled to Jerusalem for the Passover celebration. Jesus and the apostles then left on their boat to travel to Gennesaret to rest for three days, because Jesus was preparing himself for a great crisis of his life on earth and he needed this time to pray and meditate with his Universal Father in Paradise.

The news about Jesus feeding the five thousand people in the Bethsaida Park and their attempt to proclaim Jesus a king quickly spread and it aroused curiosity and stirred up fears among the Jewish religious leaders and Roman civil leaders all throughout Galilee and Judea. The real purpose of Jesus performing this miracle of feeding the multitude of five thousand people was to bring to a head the miracle seeking and king craving feelings that kept on surfacing from his immediate family of apostles and disciples. And this spectacular episode by Jesus brought an end to the early era of teaching, training and healing and helped to prepare the way for the proclamation of the higher and more spiritual phase of spreading God's gospel of divine sonship, spiritual liberty and eternal salvation.

While Jesus was resting at the home of a wealthy believer friend of his who lived in the Gennesaret region, he held conferences every afternoon with the apostles and the group of five hundred people who continued to follow Jesus since the days at the Bethsaida Park finally dispersed back to their homes while the rest traveled to Jerusalem to celebrate the Passover. During the second night in Gennesaret, Jesus began to prepare the apostles for the impending shock that was a brewing crisis in the public's attitude towards him and it was about to be displayed in just a few days. Jesus explained to the apostles that the Jewish religious leaders of Jerusalem were in the process of conspiring with tetrarch Herod Antipas to destroy he and the apostles and the apostles finally realized that Jesus did not come to earth to sit on a throne of David and that spiritual truth was not going to be advanced by material wonders. The apostles also saw that the fast-approaching times of spiritual sifting and cruel adversity were upon their entire spiritual ministry, and they were slowly awakening to the fact of the real nature of their job as spiritual ambassadors of God's kingdom and so they began to prepare themselves for the upcoming ordeals of Jesus' last year of ministry on earth.

Before Jesus and the twelve apostles left Gennesaret Jesus told them that he did not give in to his feelings of sympathy when he fed the crowd of five thousand people that day until he was certain that it was according to his Universal Father's will in Paradise and on Sunday, April 3, A.D. 29, Jesus and his apostles began their journey from Bethsaida to Jerusalem. To make sure that they avoided any crowds and to attract as little attention as possible, Jesus and the apostles traveled a different route by the way of Gerasa and Philadelphia in order to get to Jerusalem. Jesus would not allow the apostles to preach during this trip or when they arrived in Jerusalem and when they arrived in Jerusalem on April 6, A.D. 29, they stopped at Lazarus' house for one night only and separated the next day. Jesus and John Zebedee stayed at one of their believer's home named Simon, while Judas, Iscariot and Simon Zelotes stayed with friends in Jerusalem, and the rest of the apostles stayed in groups of two in the homes of their various friends. Jesus only went into Jerusalem once during this Passover celebration on the day of the great feast and while they were all in Jerusalem, the apostles learned just how bitter the people now felt towards Jesus and when they left Jerusalem, the apostles all knew that an impending crisis was inevitable.

On Sunday, April 24, A.D. 29, Jesus and the apostles left Jerusalem to travel back to Bethsaida and they arrived on Friday, April 29, A.D. 29. As soon as they reached the headquarters in Bethsaida Jesus sent Apostle Andrew to ask the ruler of the local synagogue for permission for Jesus to speak at the afternoon Sabbath service, because Jesus knew that this would be his last time to speak in this Capernaum synagogue. As

Jesus walked into the Capernaum synagogue on that beautiful Sabbath afternoon to give his last sermon, the only greeting of well wishes he received from his followers came from his two apostles, the Alpheus twins who saluted Jesus stating that they had both prayed that the Universal Father in Paradise would help him on this day.

A distinguished congregation greeted Jesus at the three o'clock in the afternoon service in this new Capernaum synagogue and Jairius presided over the service and he handed Jesus the scriptures to read to the congregation. The day before this Sabbath service fifty-three Pharisees and Sadducees had arrived from Jerusalem along with thirty leaders and rulers from the neighboring synagogues and these Jewish leaders were acting under direct orders from the Sanhedrin officers of Jerusalem to wage a direct warfare against Jesus and his apostles.

This crisis began in Jesus' life after he fed the crowd of five thousand people that day in the Bethsaida Park and it ended with the sermon Jesus gave that day and this conflict in the lives of Jesus and the apostles lasted for a whole year and it ended with Jesus' trial and crucifixion. When Jesus and the apostles arrived back home from the Sabbath service in Capernaum and the grueling questions that were addressed to Jesus from the Pharisees and Sadducees who had been sent from Jerusalem, upset the apostles and they were full of depression and feared for their safety.

Jesus refused to eat, and he isolated himself for hours in one of their upper rooms and around midnight that same night Joab, the leader of the young evangelist group reported to the rest of the apostles that one-third of the evangelists in his group had deserted the cause. During these trying hours the members of the women's corps stayed in constant meetings at Apostle Peter's home, because they were very upset about what had happened at the Capernaum synagogue, but none of them deserted Jesus. Just past midnight Jesus finally came down from the upper room and he told the apostles and evangelists that he now saw how the sifting of God's kingdom had everyone in distress, but that it was something that could not be avoided. Jesus also told the apostles that if they couldn't endure this test, what were they going to do when he, Jesus must return back home to his Universal Father in Paradise. When Jesus had finished talking to the apostles, Peter told Jesus that they were all very sad, but that they would never forsake him, because they all believed in Jesus and his teachings of the gospel. Jesus then told the apostles to go and rest, because they all had many busy active days coming on the horizon.

On Saturday night of April 30, A.D. 29, while Jesus was speaking words of comfort and courage to his downcast disciples, tetrarch Herod Antipas was holding a special council meeting with a group of special commissioners who consisted of a group of Pharisees who represented the Jerusalem Sanhedrin officers and these Pharisees urged Herod to arrest Jesus, because he was stirring up the people to start a rebellion. Herod refused to take any action against Jesus as a political offender, because his advisors had informed him how Jesus had actually rejected the crowd of five thousand peoples' proposal to proclaim himself king. One of Herod's official family members' wives belonged to the women's corps, and she had informed Herod that Jesus was not meddling with any earthly political affairs and Herod's conscience was still bothering him for the execution of the holy man

John the Baptist and he did not want to become entangled with any infractions against Jesus. In addition, Herod Antipas regarded Jesus as a prophet from God and when this group of Pharisees threatened to report to Caesar that Herod was shielding a traitor, Herod threw the group of Pharisees out of his council chamber.

During the days of May 1, A.D. 29, through May 2, A.D. 29, Jesus held one on one council meetings with each of his apostles at the Zebedee home and he and each disciple were the only ones in attendance. There were only about one hundred disciples left who had the moral courage to stand up against the opposition of the Pharisees and remain loyal to Jesus. On Friday during the week of May, A.D. 29, the rulers of the new Capernaum synagogue officially closed their door to Jesus and all of his followers and Jairus then resigned as the chief ruler of the Capernaum synagogue, and he openly aligned himself with Jesus.

The last seaside meeting was held by Jesus with one hundred and fifty of his followers on the Sabbath day of May 7, A.D. 29, and this day marked a time of the lowest ebb in the climate of the once popular Jesus, his disciples and their teachings of the gospel. But, from that day forward, a steady, slow and more healthy dependable growth where a brand-new following for Jesus and his teachings built up that was much better grounded in spiritual faith and with a true religious experience and a more open proclamation of the gospel of God's kingdom with a much larger scope in its spiritual implications began to develop in Jesus and the apostles' public ministry.

On Sunday, May 8, A.D. 29, the Sanhedrin officers in Jerusalem passed a decree closing all of the synagogues in Palestine to Jesus and his followers and before this decree was issued, all of the synagogues that had existed and functioned independently had always operated under the direction of its own board of governors. Within a short span of two weeks every synagogue in Palestine had bowed down to the authority of the Sanhedrin officers from Jerusalem except for the synagogue in Hebron and shortly afterwards this synagogue was burned down from a mysterious fire. On this same Sunday Jesus declared a week's holiday urging all of his disciples to return to their homes and continue to pray for the expansion of God's kingdom in the hearts of mankind on earth. During the week of the disciples' holiday off, Apostles Nathaniel and James were both afflicted for three days with a painful digestive illness and Jesus did not use any supernatural abilities to heal these two sick apostles, because Jesus believed that universe difficulties must be met and planetary obstacles must be encountered as a part of the experience training that is provided for the growth and development of progressive perfection for the evolving souls of all mortal beings who live on the worlds of time and space. These problematic situations such as what the two apostles were going through helps to produce the activities of the mind, soul and spirit that in turn helps one to achieve the worthy goals of mortal progression to attain the higher levels of one's spirit destiny.

On May 16, A.D. 29, a second council meeting was held in Tiberias between the Sanhedrin officers from Jerusalem and tetrarch Herod Antipas and these Jewish leaders once again tried to pressure Herod to arrest Jesus but again Herod refused. However, Herod did finally agree to the Sanhedrin's plan to seize Jesus and put him on trial for religious infractions in Jerusalem. Meanwhile, Jesus' enemies were spreading all kinds of rumors throughout Galilee that Herod Antipas had become hostile to Jesus and that his plan was to exterminate all of those who believed in Jesus' teachings and on Saturday, May 21, A.D. 29, the civil authorities in Jerusalem agreed to seize Jesus for trial before the Sanhedrin officers on the charges of violating the sacred laws of the Jewish nation.

Herod Antipas was put under a lot of pressure to sign this decree against Jesus to stand trial and Herod knew that Jesus would not receive a fair trial before his bitter enemies in Jerusalem and on this same night in Capernaum a group of fifty leading citizens met at the synagogue to discuss what to do about Jesus.

There was a lot of people talking about Jesus' preaching doctrines which seemed to upset the common Jewish people, and his enemies maintained that Jesus' teachings on the gospel were impractical. On May 22, A.D. 29, one of David Zebedee's fifty messengers arrived from Tiberias bringing the news to Jesus that Herod Antipas had authorized the arrest of Jesus by the Sanhedrin officers from Jerusalem and Jesus' sister-in-law was the first person to receive this news from the messenger and she told the rest of Jesus' family.

Jesus held an early morning meeting to give farewell instructions to his disciples, because he knew that he would be leaving Capernaum soon and Jesus gave his parting address to about one hundred followers who had crowded indoors to tell him farewell. Five members of Jesus' earth family soon arrived for this farewell meeting and his baby sister Babe Ruth was the only family member who continued to believe until the end in Jesus' divinity and mission on earth. Jesus' mother Mary and his brother James thought that Jesus did not understand them and that he had lost interest in them as a family, but the fact was that Jesus' earth family were unable to understand that he came to earth to be about his Universal Father's business. On Sunday morning May 22, A.D. 29 Jesus, his apostles and evangelists left Bethsaida in a hurry in their boat to Phoenicia, because the Sanhedrin officers were on their way to arrest Jesus. The Pharisees and their associates spent almost a week searching for Jesus in vain all around Capernaum while in the meantime Jesus and his disciples had escaped to Phoenicia. Jesus' earth family spent almost a week talking and praying together, because they were worried about Jesus.

Soon after they arrived near Kheresa, Jesus and his disciples traveled north and spent the night in a park south of Bethsaida-Julia and Jesus then told his disciples the plans he had for a projected preaching tour through Batanea, northern Galilee and along the coast of Phoenicia. On Monday morning May 23, A.D. 29, Apostle Peter and the evangelists traveled to Chorazin where they preached for two weeks and on Tuesday, June 7, A.D. 29, Peter and his group of evangelists left to join Jesus and the apostles at Caesarea-Phillipi. Jesus did no public preaching while they were in Caesarea-Phillipi, but many believers came out to their camp to attend the quiet evening meetings that the apostles held and during this time the apostles learned that the Jewish people had become spiritually stagnant for allowing the origin of their religious traditions to blind their eyes to the good news of God's kingdom that Jesus and his disciples were teaching to humanity. During Jesus' entire life on earth he devoted his life's mission of thawing out the frozen forms of religion into the liquid liberties of enlightened sonship.

On Friday afternoon June 10, A.D. 29, Jesus and his disciples arrived in Sidon to preach and teach the gospel and while the disciples completed their public ministry in Sidon Jesus went to stay in the home of his friend Justa and her mother that was located just north of Sidon.

The theme of Jesus' teachings during their public ministry tour in Sidon was spiritual progression and Jesus told his disciples not to stand still and to continue to move forward in righteousness and to forget about the past. On June 28, A.D.29, Jesus and his disciples next traveled to Porphyreon and Heldua and the disciples preached in Porphyreon and the evangelists preached in the city of Heldua. On Wednesday July 6, A.D. 29, Jesus and the disciples preached in the city of Tyre and by this time the apostles and evangelists were getting used to working among the many groups of Gentiles who had mainly descended from the earlier Canaanite tribes going all the way back to the times of Abraham. All of these Gentiles spoke the Greek language, and the disciples were surprised to observe how eager these groups of Gentiles were to hear the gospel and how ready they were to become believers. There was such a big interest in the gospel in Tyre that the doors of the Melkarth temple were opened to Jesus and his disciples whenever they wanted to preach. Around noon on Sunday, July 24, A.D. 29, Jesus and the disciples left Tyre and traveled down the coast to Ptolemais and there in this city Apostle Peter preached the gospel to a group of believers in the evening of July 25, A.D. 29.

When tetrarch Herod Antipas heard that Jesus and the disciples were preaching across the lake in his brother, tetrarch Philip Antipas' territory Herod experienced a change of heart, and he issued a decree stating that Jesus would not be arrested as long as he stayed outside of Galilee with his teachings and the Sanhedrin mandate to close all of the synagogues in Palestine to Jesus and his followers worked against the Pharisees and caused all of the Jewish people to react with feelings of resentment against the Jewish religious rulers in Jerusalem. Many of the rulers of the local synagogues began to open their synagogues to Abner and his followers claiming that these spiritual teachers were followers of John the Baptist and not disciples of Jesus.

At this point of his mortal life on earth, Jesus had entered into the fourth and final stage of his seventh and final bestowal on earth. The first stage was Jesus' childhood when he was only faintly conscious of his Paradise origin as Michael of Nebadon and the second stage was Jesus' increasingly self-conscious years of his youth and advancing manhood during which he began to remember and understand his divine nature and mission on earth. The third stage of Jesus' earth experience began with being baptized by his cousin John the Baptist and through the years of his public ministry as a teacher, preacher, leader and healer and up to the momentous hour when Apostle Peter's statement that he personally recognized that Jesus was the Son of God, because Jesus loved his ministry and all of humanity. The fourth and final stage of Jesus' seventh and final bestowal mission on earth began during the public ministry tour at Caesarea-Phillipi and onto his crucifixion, resurrection and ascension back home to Paradise. During the final stage of Jesus' ministry, he acknowledged his divinity and fully embraced the work he completed during his last year on earth.

During the fourth period of Jesus' life most of his followers still regarded him as the Messiah and his disciples called Jesus the Son of God. After Apostle Peter's statement that Jesus was the Son of God, this marked the beginning of the new period of the complete realization of the truth of Jesus' supreme ministry as a Creator Son from Paradise who was completing his seventh and final bestowal mission on earth for the benefit of the entire universe of Nebadon. Jesus exemplified in his life what he taught in his teachings which was the evolution of one's spiritual nature by the usage of the daily technique of spiritual living progress. Jesus never placed any emphasis on the never-ending struggles between the soul and the body but, instead Jesus taught that the spirit was always the easy victor over both and effective in the reconciliation of this intellectual and instinctual warfare.

Before Jesus went on his public preaching tour to Caesarea-Phillipi he presented the gospel of God's kingdom as his course of instruction for the disciples and evangelists and after this tour Jesus appeared to the public not merely as a teacher but as the divine representative of the Universal Father who is the center of the spiritual kingdom and as a Creator Son from Paradise and because of his origins, it was required that Jesus do all of these things as a mortal being on earth as the Son of Man.

That evening Apostle Andrew initiated a personal meeting with each of the apostles except for Judas Iscariot and Apostle Andrew was worried about Judas' attitude especially since he was absent from participating in this one-on-one meeting like the rest of the apostles and Andrew talked to Jesus about his concerns about Apostle Judas Iscariot. Jesus told Andrew that there was really nothing more they could do but to continue to place their confidence in Judas Iscariot and to have patience and compassion with him. Judas Iscariot was a former disciple of John the Baptist, and he had been shocked by his execution and Judas had been severely hurt emotionally by some past rebukes he had received from Jesus. Some of Judas' prior disappointments were when Jesus refused to be proclaimed a king that day in the Bethsaida Park, when Jesus fled from the Sanhedrin officers in Capernaum, when Jesus refused to give the Pharisees a sign that he was the Son of God and Judas was completely bewildered that Jesus refused to manifest his supernatural powers. Judas Iscariot was depressed because his treasury was empty, and he missed the large multitude crowds. Each one of the apostles had been affected by the trials and tribulations they had all been through, but they loved Jesus apparently more than Judas Iscariot did, because the rest of the apostles stayed with Jesus until the bitter end.

Judas Iscariot was from Judea, and he was personally offended when Jesus warned the apostles to beware of the Pharisees, because Judas felt that this statement was being directed at him personally.

The biggest mistake that Judas Iscariot continued to make was whenever Jesus would send the apostles to be off by themselves to pray, Judas would instead of praying he would continue to fill his mind up with fear and think about all of the doubts he had with Jesus' mission and his main thought was always revenge.

The next thing Jesus decided to do was to take the apostles along with him to Mount Hermon as the location to inaugurate his fourth phase of his earth ministry as the Son of

God. Some of Jesus' current apostles had been there when he was baptized by John the Baptist in the River Jordan and Jesus wanted the apostles to also be there with him to hear and see his authority as he began the fourth phase of his final bestowal mission on earth by assuming his new and public role as the Son of God.

On the morning of Friday, August 12, A. D. 29, Jesus told the apostles to prepare themselves to travel up Mount Hermon, because the Holy Spirit was ready for him to finish up his bestowal work on earth. Jesus wanted to take the apostles with him to the top of Mount Hermon so that they could also receive some spiritual strength to uplift them for the trying upcoming times ahead for all of them as they continued to travel the path with Jesus and his ministry. It was almost sundown on Friday afternoon, August 12, A.D. 29, when Jesus and the apostles reached the foot of Mount Hermon near the same spot where the lad Tiglath once waited for Jesus while he climbed Mount Hermon to settle the spiritual destinies of earth and the rest of the worlds of time and space in our Nebadon universe by the termination of the Lucifer Rebellion. Jesus and his apostles stayed camped at the foot of Mount Hermon for two days in spiritual preparation for the soon to arrive spectacular celestial events from Paradise.

Jesus already knew beforehand what was going to happen on Mount Hermon and he really wanted his apostles to share in this spiritual experience with him, because it was time for Jesus to share the revelation of himself with his apostles and Jesus knew that his apostles would not be able to fully attain the spiritual levels to fully understand the visitation that was about to happen from the celestial beings from Paradise who would soon appear to them on Mount Hermon. Jesus was not able to take all twelve of the apostles with him, so he decided to take his three companion apostles, Peter, James and John Zebedee who were used to going up the mountains with him for special vigils such as this. Early in the morning of Monday, August 15, A.D. 29, Jesus, Peter, James and John Zebedee began their ascent up Mount Hermon and it took them six days and during their six-day ascent up Mount Hermon while Jesus and his apostles were sitting and resting under the mulberry trees, this is the moment that Apostle Peter made his memorable statement that Jesus was indeed the Son of God. Jesus had been summoned by the Most Highs of Paradise to climb Mount Hermon for a very important spiritual presentation relating to the status and progress of his final bestowal as a mortal man on earth.

It was significant that this supernatural event on Mount Hermon was timed to occur while Jesus and the apostles were preaching in the lands of the Gentiles in Greece. Jesus and his three apostles reached their destination about halfway up the mountain just before noon and while they were eating lunch, Jesus told the three apostles about the spiritual experience he had in the hills east of the River Jordan right after his baptism and how lonely his retreat in those hills on Mount Hermon had been for him. When Jesus had been a young lad, he used to climb the hill near his home in Nazareth and dream about the ancient battles that had been fought there, but now as Jesus climbed Mount Hermon with his three apostles to receive the endowment from the Paradise celestial beings to prepare him for the closing scenes of his life on earth, Jesus had a choice to make. Jesus could make the choice at that moment to end the struggles of his mortal life on earth and return home to Paradise and begin his rule as the System Sovereign of the Universe of Nebadon, because he had already fulfilled his seventh bestowal on Mount Hermon when he met with his disobedient son Lucifer and earth's dethroned Planetary Prince Caligastia and officially ended the Lucifer Rebellion. But Jesus had made the choice to remain on earth and complete the last and full measure of the will of his Universal Paradise Father.

Each one of the Creator Sons from Paradise must complete seven bestowals on the worlds of their assigned universe and then after completion they must walk through the portal of death and rise again on the third day before they can begin their rule as the system sovereign of their assigned universe. However, Jesus was the only Creator Son in the history of Paradise to ever be put to death by being crucified like Jesus was during his final bestowal on earth.

On this day of August 15, A. D. 29, on Mount Hermon the three apostles Peter, James and John were able to witness with amazement as three Paradise celestial messengers appeared to Jesus concerning the status of his seventh and final bestowal mission on earth.

The twelve apostles faith was at a high point when Jesus fed the multitude crowd of five thousand people that day in the Bethsaida Park with five barley loaves and two dried fish, but right after this event Jesus and his disciples were attacked by the Jewish religious leaders with a vengeance and as a result, the apostles faith fell to zero. Now after Jesus admitted his divinity to the three apostles on Mount Hermon, their faith once again rose only to undergo a progressive decline as their trials and tribulations increased. The third revival of the apostles' faith did not occur again until after the resurrection of Jesus after the Spirit of Truth, the Holy Spirit endowed the apostles and the one hundred and twenty believers including Jesus' mother Mary in the upper room on Pentecost Sunday.

At around three in the afternoon Jesus and the three apostles had reached the meeting point on Mount Hermon and Jesus told the three apostles to wait for him at this location, because he had to commune with his Paradise Father first and his celestial messengers. Jesus then left and had a long conference with Archangel Gabriel and Father Melchizedek from Paradise and after this three-hour conference was over, Jesus then returned to the three waiting apostles at around six in the evening. While Jesus and the three apostles were eating their evening meal Peter asked Jesus how long they were going to be away from the rest of the apostles on Mount Hermon and Jesus' response was that they would be on Mount Hermon until they saw the glory of the Son of God and know what had been told to him by the special celestial messengers from Paradise. Jesus then explained to the three apostles about the Lucifer Rebellion and how it had been terminated after all these years by Jesus on this same mountain shortly after he had been baptized by John the Baptist. The three apostles, Peter, James and John soon fell asleep and after they had been asleep for about half an hour, they were suddenly awakened by a nearby crackling sound and to their amazement they saw Jesus in an intimate conversation with two brilliant glowing bright celestial beings and Jesus' face and body were glowing in a brilliant heavenly light. Jesus and the two glowing celestial beings were talking in what we now call the light language and Apostle Peter was able to understand some of what they were saying, and he figured out that the two glowing celestial beings that Jesus was talking to was Moses and Elijah, but in reality, they were really Archangel Gabriel and Father Melchizedek from Paradise. The Physical Controller from Paradise had arranged for the three apostles to witness this event, because Jesus had requested it. The three apostles were badly frightened by what they had just seen and as they slowly started to collect their wits about themselves, they continued to watch as the amazing vision before them began to fade away. Apostle Peter then told Jesus that it was so good for them to be there to be able to see this glory and Peter asked Jesus if they could stay there on Mount Hermon and build three tents in memoriam for Jesus, Moses and Elijah.

While Peter was still talking to Jesus a large silver cloud appeared over all four of them and as the three apostles fell to their knees with their faces down, they heard the same voice that had spoken on the day of Jesus' baptism say, "This is my beloved Son, give heed to Him." Shortly after midnight Jesus and the three apostles began to make the preparations to descend back down Mount Hermon to rejoin the rest of the apostles. The transfiguration that apostles Peter, James and John witnessed on Mount Hermon was a quick glimpse for the three apostles to watch this important celestial event from Paradise that was taking place between Jesus, Archangel Gabriel and Father Melchizedek for these following reasons.

The first reason for this celestial event from Paradise to meet with Jesus that night on Mount Hermon was to show the acceptance from Paradise of the seventh and final bestowal of the incarnated life of Michael of Nebadon on earth by the Eternal Mother-Son of Paradise. During this celestial meeting that night on Mount Hermon Jesus had now received assurance of his fulfillment and the support from the Eternal Mother-Son of Paradise and Archangel Gabriel brought this news to Jesus.

The second reason for this celestial visit to Jesus from Paradise was the testimony of the satisfaction of the Infinite Spirit to Jesus for his full completion of his seventh final bestowal as a mortal human on earth. The universe representative of the Infinite Spirit who was Michael of Nebadon's immediate associate and coworker spoke to Jesus that night on Mount Hermon through Father Melchizedek. Jesus was thankful that he received this visitation from Archangel Gabriel and Father Melchizedek that night on Mount Hermon in front of his three apostles regarding the success of his final bestowal mission on earth, but Jesus noticed that his Paradise Father did not indicate if his final bestowal mission on earth was finished. After this celestial visitation from the celestial beings of Paradise that night Jesus still wanted to know what his Paradise father's will was, so he decided to continue to pursue his final bestowal on earth to its natural end. Shortly before breakfast on Tuesday morning, August 16, A.D. 29, Jesus and the three apostles arrived back at their apostolic camp and as they got closer to their camp, they noticed that a large crowd had gathered around the apostles, and they all seemed to be arguing. The subject that the crowd was arguing about was a man named James of Safed who had arrived the day before with his fourteen year old epileptic son who was possessed by one of the wandering mischievous, rebellious primary midway beings who were still running loose on earth uncontrolled and left over from the Lucifer Rebellion days on earth and James of Safed had been trying to find Jesus for two days to heal his son.

The nine apostles who had remained at the apostolic encampment were very upset, because the sick lad's father had come to their encampment with forty of his companions looking for Jesus and since Jesus was not there James of Safed decided to stay at the camp until Jesus returned from Mount Hermon. The nine apostles had all tried to heal the lad, but they failed and when they saw Jesus returning from Mount Hermon, they were so relieved to welcome him back to the camp. When James of Safed saw Jesus, he kneeled down asking him to please heal his son and Jesus then stepped forward took the lad by his hand and told the rebellious primary midway being to go away from the boy and don't come back, and because his Father had granted the desire of this lad's soul to be healed, the boy was healed of his two afflictions. This was an instance of a true healing of a double affliction in this young boy, a physical ailment and a rogue primary midway being possession.

After James of Safed left their encampment with his healed son, Jesus told the nine apostles that they had not been able to heal this young lad because the key was to have faith, to fast and to pray to achieve a healing such as this. Later on, when Jesus asked his Universal Father to send the Holy Spirit to indwell the apostles and the one hundred and twenty followers who were present in the upper room on Pentecost Sunday, all of the fallen angels and any spirits from the dark side have all been banished from earth and they can no longer possess the bodies of humans, so anyone up to our current times who claims demonic possession is in reality a victim of their own dark shadows that need to be felt, looked at and sent back to the light to be recycled with love in your heart.

After James of Safed left with his healed son Jesus told the apostles that it was now time to travel to a public speaking tour in Caesarea-Philippi and their group was very quiet as they traveled to their next destination. When they arrived Jesus and the apostles stayed with a friend overnight in Celsus but before they went to bed Jesus told the apostles that he was about to enter the last and final phase of his mortal life on earth and that he was going to be put to death but that he would rise again to life in three days. The apostles all went to bed that night full of sorrow and quite bewildered by what Jesus had just told them, but they were slowly beginning to understand that Jesus was telling them that he was soon going to die.

When Jesus and the apostles arrived at Magadan Park they met up with a group of one hundred evangelists, disciples and the women's corps who were there waiting for them, and they were all ready to begin their next preaching tour in Decapolis. On that Thursday morning Jesus called everyone together and he assigned each one of the apostles to be with one of twelve evangelists while the women's corps and the rest of the disciples stayed with Jesus and this preaching tour was scheduled to end on Friday September 16, A.D. 29, and Jesus promised to visit each of the twelve groups during this tour. During this preaching tour these twelve groups taught the gospel in the cities of Gerasa, Gamala,

Hippos, Zaphon, Gadara, Abila, Edrei, Philadelphia, Heshbon, Duim, Scythopolis and many other Greek cities. During all of the public preaching tours Jesus always avoided using flowery language and he was able to bring the philosophy of religion from heaven down to earth. Jesus was never trying to gather up a bunch of followers to set up in large church buildings and be under the control and power of the Jewish religious rulers in these buildings, instead Jesus was teaching his disciples to be leaders to teach and preach the gospel of accepting our Universal Father into our heart filled with love, hope, faith, compassion, gratitude, joy and bliss. This preaching mission that the twelve groups of disciples completed in Decapolis was moderately successful where hundreds of souls converted to Jesus' teachings of the gospel and his disciples gained valuable experience of carrying out their public ministry without the personal presence of Jesus.

On Friday September 16, A.D. 29 the entire corps of Jesus' spiritual disciples assembled back at Magadan Park and the next day a council of more than one hundred believers was held where they discussed the future plans for extending the work of spreading the gospel of God's kingdom. The fifty messengers who worked for David Zebedee were also present at this conference and they made reports on the welfare of the many followers throughout Judea, Samaria, Galilee and in the surrounding districts. The fifty messengers who worked for David Zebedee also helped to keep all of Jesus' followers all throughout Palestine in touch with each other and with Jesus and the apostles. During the dark days of the trials and persecutions of the early Christians after Jesus had ascended back to heaven, these same messengers also helped to collect funds to help sustain the apostles' families who were in need.

During the month of September A.D. 29, Abner the leader of the Nazarite Brotherhood and the former leader of John the Baptist's twelve disciples moved his headquarters from Hebron to Bethlehem and this new location also served as the headquarters in Judea for David Zebedee's messenger service. David Zebedee also maintained an overnight relay service between Jerusalem and Bethsaida and these messenger runners left Jerusalem every evening, stopping for relays at Sychar and Scythopolis and they then arrived in Bethsaida around breakfast time the next morning.

Jesus and his disciples prepared to take a week's rest before they planned to start on their last mission to preach the gospel and this would also be their last rest time, because the Perean mission developed into a campaign of preaching that lasted right down to their arrival in Jerusalem and the last closing episodes of Jesus' bestowal mission on earth as a mortal human. On Sunday morning September 18, A.D. 29, Apostle Andrew made the announcement that the entire ministry group would be having the week off and all of the disciples except for Nathaniel and Thomas went home to be with their families. Jesus spent the week in complete rest, but Apostles Nathaniel and Thomas were busy all week in heated discussions with a Greek philosopher from Alexandria named Rodan and this Greek philosopher had recently become a disciple of Jesus as the result of the teachings of one of Abner's disciples during one of his missions in Alexandria. Early the next morning Rodan began a series of ten lectures that he gave to Apostles Nathaniel and Thomas and to a dozen followers who happened to be there at Magadan and on that Sunday all of the apostles and evangelists assembled together at Magadan to have a meeting with Jesus. After having a long meeting that evening with his entire ministry group Jesus surprised everyone by announcing that early the next day, he and the twelve apostles would be going to Jerusalem to attend the feast of the tabernacles.

Jesus then told the evangelists to visit with some followers in Galilee and for the women's corps to return to Bethsaida and Apostles Nathaniel and Thomas asked Jesus if they could remain in Magadan to complete their lecture series with the new disciple Rodan and after they completed their lectures Apostles Nathaniel and Thomas hurried to Jerusalem to join the rest of the apostles on Friday of that week. Meanwhile disciple Rodan went back to his home in Alexandria where he continued to teach philosophy in a school located in Meganta and Jesus' new disciple turned out to be a mighty man while he preached the gospel, and he remained to be a faithful believer to the end of his days on earth and he was executed for his spiritual beliefs when the Christian persecutions began in Greece

When Jesus began his journey to Jerusalem with the apostles for safety reasons he decided to take a shorter route through Samaria and just before it turned dark outside Jesus then sent Apostles Philip and Matthew to a Samaritan village that was located on the eastern slopes of Mount Gilboa to find suitable lodging for the night, however, this Samaritan village was very prejudiced against Jews and they ran Jesus' group out of town with sticks and stones. Jesus and the apostles were able to find a more friendlier village near the Jordan ford to spend the night in and the next day they continued their journey, and they arrived in Bethany late on Wednesday evening. Jesus and the apostles stayed in Jerusalem until the end of October, A.D. 29, and Jesus spent most of his time with Abner and his disciples in Bethlehem.

Long before Jesus and the apostles had fled from Galilee to avoid being arrested by the Sanhedrin officers many of his followers had been asking Jesus to go to Jerusalem to teach the gospel and the apostles were surprised by Jesus' sudden decision to attend the feast of the tabernacles in Jerusalem and when the apostles protested in fear, Jesus calmly told the apostles that his hour had not yet come. During the feast of the tabernacles thousands of believers of Jesus' teachings of the gospel from all parts of the Roman Empire got to hear Jesus preach the gospel. Jesus was allowed to publicly preach in the temple courts of Jerusalem, because the Sanhedrin officers were afraid to bother Jesus due to the secret division that had occurred within their own ranks concerning the teachings of Jesus. Many of the members of the Sanhedrin officers secretly believed in Jesus and they did not support the idea of arresting him during the feast of the tabernacles.

The hard work that Abner and his disciples had done also helped to improve the negative feelings that many of the Jewish people had towards Jesus and his enemies dared not to speak out against Jesus and the apostles at this time. However, the bold move of Jesus appearing publicly again to preach in Jerusalem overwhelmed his enemies and several times during this time period the Sanhedrin officers had tried to have Jesus arrested, but it did not work.

Every time Jesus went to Jerusalem the apostles were filled with terror and they became more afraid as Jesus continued to make bold announcements to them regarding the nature of his mission on earth. The first afternoon that Jesus taught in the temple courts of on the subject of the liberty of the new gospel and the joy of those who believe, the crowd was divided over Jesus' sermon and when the Pharisees in the audience heard the people talking this way they sent for Eber, the ruling officer of the Sanhedrin to arrest Jesus. As Eber approached Jesus to arrest him, Jesus told Eber that nothing would happen to the Son of Man until his hour comes so Eber and his associates backed off and refused to arrest Jesus at that time.

During Jesus' visit to Jerusalem a group of scribes and pharisees brought a woman who they were dragging in the streets stating that she had been caught in the act of adultery and their plan was to stone her to death. Jesus looked at the crowd and saw the woman's husband standing behind the others and Jesus knew that her husband had shamefully forced his wife to earn their living by prostituting her body. Jesus then walked close to the woman's husband and wrote a few words in the sand and after writing these first set of words in the sand, Jesus then walked back to the woman and the crowd and he once again wrote the same words in the sand and when the woman's husband and the angry crowd read the two sets of words that Jesus had written in the sand, one by one everyone walked away from the woman. Jesus then turned to the woman who had committed adultery and asked her where was her husband and the crowd of accusers, because they were all gone and Jesus then told the woman to go on her way with peace and this woman left her wicked husband and joined Jesus' group of the women's corps and the words that Jesus had written twice in the sand to the angry crowd and to the woman's wicked husband were:

"He who is without sin cast the first stone."

All of the people who had come to Jerusalem to celebrate the feast of the tabernacles came from as far away as Spain to India and it was an ideal occasion for Jesus to publicly proclaim his full gospel while he and the apostles were preaching in the temple courts of Jerusalem and this was the first time the apostles got to see Jesus boldly announcing the news about his bestowal mission on earth. On the last day of the feast of the tabernacles Jesus addressed the congregation after the chanting of the Hallel and declared that he was the giver of living water to every thirsty soul and at the conclusion of this morning service Jesus continued to teach the congregation and answer their questions and some of the people who were there that day thought that Jesus was a prophet, some the Messiah, but the Sanhedrin officers dared not to arrest Jesus on that day.

On the afternoon of the last day of the feast of the tabernacles and after the apostles had once again failed to persuade Jesus to leave Jerusalem, Jesus once again went into the temple courts to preach and he spoke to a large group of followers who had assembled in the Solomon's porch section of the temple and when some of the unbelieving Jews and agents of the Sanhedrin officers heard Jesus preach, many of them rushed Jesus to stone him and place him under arrest, but Jesus quickly escaped to a secret meeting place near Bethany where Lazarus and his two sisters were there waiting for Jesus.

All throughout the week after the feast of the tabernacles many believers gathered in Bethany to hear Jesus preach and during this time Abner and Jesus completed the arrangements to consolidate the work of their two groups of apostles into one group. Before Jesus left Bethlehem for the last time, he made arrangements for everyone from his and Abner's group to join in a united effort to go forward in the ending of his mission as a mortal man on earth and they all agreed that Abner and his disciples would join Jesus and his twelve apostles real soon in Magadan Park. In the early part of November A.D. 29, Abner and his twelve disciples began to teach and preach with Jesus and his apostles right down to the time of his crucifixion. During the last part of October A.D. 29, Jesus and his disciples left Jerusalem, and they arrived back at Magadan Park and the apostles were all relieved to have Jesus back on friendly soil. A few days after Jesus and the apostles arrived back at Magadan Park from Jerusalem, Abner and a group of fifty disciples arrived from Bethlehem and at the same time there was also a group assembled at their Magadan camp that included the evangelist corps, the women's corps and one hundred and fifty other disciples from various parts of Palestine.

After they all spent a few days of organizing the camp and getting acquainted with each other, Jesus and his apostles began a course of intensive training for this special group of disciples and at the end of this training course Jesus chose seventy spiritual teachers and sent them out to complete their missionary work. These seventy newly trained evangelists were ordained by Jesus on the Sabbath afternoon of November 19, A.D. 29 at the Magadan Camp and Abner was placed as the head of this newly formed corps of evangelists which consisted of Abner, ten former disciples of John the Baptist, fifty-one evangelists and eight additional disciples who were already in service with this group. At about two in the afternoon on this same day, between the rain showers this new group of disciples who were supported by David Zebedee and his fifty-messenger corps came to be a total of four hundred followers who were assembled on the shores of the Lake of Galilee to witness the ordination of this special group of newly trained evangelists.

After Jesus had given these seventy new evangelists a spiritual acceptance speech, beginning with their leader Abner and as they all knelt in a circle around Jesus, he laid hands on the heads of each of the members in this group. There were over fifty other disciples who had tried to be appointed to be members of this new group of seventy evangelists, however, fifty potential disciples were rejected by the committee appointed by Jesus to make these selections, and this selection committee consisted of Apostles Andrew and Abner who were the leaders of Jesus' evangelist corps. Jesus never taught his disciples that it was wrong to have wealth, he only required that his disciples and evangelists dedicate their worldly possessions to their common cause, and it was a great day for the seventy new evangelists, and they went out on their first public preaching tour traveling two by two as the set out for Galilee, Samaria and Judea.

Jesus and his apostles began to make preparations to establish their last headquarters in Perea near Pella close to where Jesus was baptized in the River Jordan and during the last ten days on November, A.D. 29, Jesus and the apostles spent a lot of time in meetings at Magadan and moved to their new headquarters camp in Pella on December 6, A.D. 29. After the shutdown of the Magadan Camp David Zebedee returned to Bethsaida and immediately began to shut down the messenger service, because the public preaching structure of the entire disciples' group was beginning a brand new phase. On December 18, A.D. 29, Devid Zebedee with the help of the fifty members of the messenger corps loaded all of their belongings onto the pack animals and said good bye to their former Bethsaida headquarters and David then set up a new camp along the River Jordan and in less than a week the new camp was open and ready to offer accommodations and hospitality to over fifteen hundred pilgrim visitors. This was the rainy season in Palestine, so these campground accommodations were necessary in order to take care of the ever-increasing number of followers who were coming into Perea to hear that preachings and teachings that were being given by Jesus and his disciples.

Jesus now knew that he could leave earth and return home to his Universal Father in Paradise without seriously hindering the progress of spreading the gospel, because he had laid the foundations of Christ consciousness by training plenty of competent spiritual leaders. Just before they all finally began their evening meal, Jesus experienced a rare moment of emotional ecstasy and in front of the entire group Jesus prayed out loud a sincere prayer of thanks to his Universal Father for His blessed gospel of love that he and the disciples were able to preach and teach to all who had opened their hearts to receive the word of God.

The next day Jesus went out with the seventy new evangelists to tell them how happy he was that they all came back from their first mission bearing good news of the positive reception they received of God's gospel. The next few days were busy times for everyone at the Pella campground, because preparations were being made to complete the new Perean mission and Jesus and the disciples were about to enter their last great mission of their three-month tour of Perea which would be terminated when Jesus went to Jerusalem to complete his final work on earth. All throughout this final time period for Jesus' spiritual mission, Jesus and the apostles maintained their final headquarters at their Pella camp.

It was no longer necessary for Jesus to go out on public speaking tours to teach people, because the people were now coming to him in increasing numbers from all parts of the entire Roman Empire and from the Near East. Jesus did participate with the seventy new evangelists during their missionary tour of Perea, but he really spent most of his time at the Pella camp teaching the large crowds of people and instructing the apostles and all during this time period at least ten of the apostles stayed with Jesus at all times.

During these times the women's corps also made preparations to go out on another missionary tour two by two with the rest of the seventy evangelists to preach in the larger cities of Perea and this original corps of twelve women had recently trained a larger corps of fifty additional women to help them to work in home visitation and to minister to the sick and afflicted. Perpetua, the wife of Apostle Peter became a member of this new division of the women's corps under the leadership of Abner. After Pentecost Sunday Perpetua stayed with her husband Apostle Peter on all of his missionary tours and on the day that Apostle Peter was crucified on an upside down cross in Rome, Perpetua was fed to the wild beasts in the Roman arena. This new division of the women's corps also included the wives of Apostle Andrew, Matthew and the mother of James and John Zebedee as members.

The work of continuing to preach the gospel was now prepared to enter its terminal phase of Jesus' ministry and it was filled with followers who could see that the kingdom of heaven was based on the spiritual brotherhood of man who accept love and God into their hearts based on the eternal truth of the Universal Fatherhood of God.

While David Zebedee was working on establishing the apostolic camp at Pella, Jesus took Apostles Nathaniel and Thomas secretly with him to Jerusalem to attend the feast of the tabernacles and when they realized where Jesus was taking them Apostles Nathaniel and Thomas both tried to talk Jesus out of going, but Jesus did not change his mind about making this secret trip to Jerusalem, because he wanted to give the spiritual teachers in Jerusalem the opportunity to see the light before his final hour came.

Jesus attended this feast of the tabernacles in Jerusalem so that he could proclaim the gospel to the pilgrims who were coming into Jerusalem from all parts of the Roman Empire, and it was really important to Jesus to give the Jewish Sanhedrin officers and the rest of the Jewish religious leaders one more chance to see the light. The main event of this feast occurred on Friday night at the home of Nicodemus where twenty-five Jewish leaders who believed in Jesus' teachings, fourteen Sanhedrin officers, Eber, Matadormus and Jesus' wealthy uncle from England, Joseph of Arimathea. That Friday night at Nicodemus' home everyone who was there including Jesus' two apostles Nathaniel and Thomas and everyone was totally amazed at the depth of the speech Jesus gave to this distinguished group of men and when this meeting was over, all of these men who had attended all went away mystified by Jesus' personality, charm, gracious manner and they had nothing but love in their hearts for Jesus, the Son of God. That night Apostles Nathaniel and Thomas couldn't sleep because they were both so excited at what they had just heard that night from Jesus' speech at Nicodemus' home.

The next morning Jesus, and his two apostles Nathaniel and Thomas went to visit his friend Lazarus and his two sisters in Bethany for breakfast and then they immediately went back to Jerusalem. While they were walking to Jerusalem, they saw a well-known born blind man named Josiah sitting at his usual location and as Jesus looked at Josiah, he thought about how he could once more bring the spiritual message of his mission to the Jewish leaders. As Jesus and the two apostles stood talking in front of the blind man Josiah, Jesus decided to use this blind man as the means of bringing his mission more prominently to the attention of the Jerusalem Jewish religious leaders. This was one of the strangest of all of Jesus' miracles, because the blind man Josiah never asked Jesus to heal him, but at that moment Jesus told his two apostles Nathaniel and Thomas that he was going to heal this man Josiah of his blindness and restore his eyesight on this Sabbath Day to give the scribes and Pharisees the reason they were looking for their accusation against the Son of Man. Jesus then stood over Josiah spat on the ground, mixed some clay with a spittle and then as Jesus placed the clay over both of Josiah's eyes, he told Josiah to go and wash the clay from his eyes in the pool of Shiloam and then he would immediately receive his eyesight. When Josiah washed the clay from his eyes in the pool of Shiloam, he returned to his family and friends to his usual spot able to see clearly.

When Jesus performed this miracle by restoring the eyesight of Josiah who had been blind all of his life, he told Josiah to go wash the clay from his eyes in the pool of Shiloam for these three reasons.

The first reason why Jesus healed Josiah was that Jesus did not perform this miracle as a response to Josiah's faith, because he never asked to be healed. Jesus chose to perform this miracle for his own purpose so that Josiah would have long lasting benefits from this healing.

The second reason why Jesus chose to heal Josiah was because he knew that Josiah believed in the superstition of the spittle and in the pool of Shiloam which was a semi-sacred, and this gave Josiah enough superstitious ceremony to give him enough faith to believe to follow Jesus' instructions to complete his healing on that day.

Jesus had a third reason for using these material means when he performed this strange miracle of Josiah mainly to his own choosing, because he wanted to teach his followers on that day and for all subsequent ages to refrain from despising or neglecting the available material to use for the sick and Jesus wanted to teach us the lesson to not regard miracles as the only way to cure human diseases.

The main controversy with this miracle that Jesus performed on Josiah with the scribes and Pharisees was that Jesus had violated Jewish tradition by performing this miracle on Josiah on the Sabbath and when Jesus did this, he deliberately provoked and stirred up heated discussions among the scribes and Pharisees about Jesus' violation of the Jewish tradition and law that prohibits any healing to be done on the Sabbath. By midafternoon the healing of Josiah that day by Jesus on the Sabbath Day had raised such a heated discussion all around the temple in Jerusalem that the Sanhedrin officers broke their own rules by calling a special council meeting on the Sabbath. The Pharisees brought the healed blind man Josiah and his parents before the council and after listening at Josiah's testimony on his healing, the Sanhedrin officers threw Josiah out of the synagogue telling him that his eyesight had been restored on the Sabbath day by the power of the prince of devils.

All the time the Sanhedrin officers were conducting their Sabbath council session with Josiah and his parents in the temple, Jesus was walking about teaching and preaching to some of his followers in the Solomon porch section of the temple. When Jesus and his two apostles Nathaniel and Thomas heard that Josiah had been thrown out of the temple by the Sanhedrin officers, Jesus immediately told Josiah to go with he and his apostles to their apostolic camp and to not again return until it as close to the time for him to prepare to leave earth and ascend back home to Paradise. After Josiah joined the apostolic camp at Pella, he proved to be one of Jesus' loyal followers and he later became to be a lifelong preacher of the gospel for many years.

On Tuesday, January 3, A.D. 30, Abner who was now the leader of the seventy evangelists and the sixty-two members of the women's corps gave his ministry group their final instructions before sending them out on to preach in the cities of Perea.

This Perean mission lasted for three months, and it was Jesus' last public ministry mission and after Jesus helped all of his disciples complete this Perean mission, Jesus went straight back to Jerusalem to pass through his final experiences as a mortal man on earth.

All throughout this final Perean mission the women's corps took over most of the work of ministering to the sick and afflicted and this was the final period of the development of the higher spiritual aspects of preaching the gospel and there were no miracles performed during this final Perean mission.

By the middle of January, A.D. 30, more than twelve hundred people had gathered at the apostolic camp at Pella and Jesus preached to this large group at nine o'clock every morning and the apostles taught and preached to the crowd every afternoon while Jesus conducted evening sessions with about fifty people daily to answer questions. During the month of February, A.D. 30, Jesus and his apostles toured and preached in all of the cities and villages located in the northern areas of Perea where Abner's seventy evangelists and women's corps were working. On February 18, A.D. 30 a wealthy Pharisee named Nathaniel who lived in Ragaba invited Jesus to be the guest of honor at a breakfast he had arranged at his home. By the time Jesus arrived at this breakfast most of the other guests who included Pharisees, and three attorneys were already seated at the breakfast table. Jesus immediately took his seat to the left of his host Nathaniel without going to the water basin to wash his hands and everyone who was seated at the table were shocked that Jesus did not wash his hands before being seated, nor did Jesus wash his hands after each course of food was served nor at the end of the breakfast meal. After Jesus noticed that host Nathaniel, the Pharisees and the three attorneys were whispering about his lack of washing his hands, Jesus stood up from the breakfast table and spoke the following words to the entire group who were seated at the breakfast table.

"I had thought that you invited me to this breakfast to break bread with you and to inquire of me concerning the proclamation of the new gospel of the kingdom of God, but I perceive that instead you have brought me here to witness an exhibition of ceremonial devotion to your own self-righteousness. How carefully you cleanse the outside of your hands while your spirit-food vessels are filthy and polluted. You make sure to present a pious and holy appearance to the people, but your inner souls are filled with self-righteousness, covertness, extortion and all manners of spiritual wickedness. Your leaders even dare to plot and plan the murder of the Son of Man. Woe upon you Pharisees who have persisted in rejecting the light of life."

After Jesus spoke these words, he left that house without eating any of his host Nathaniel's food and some of the Pharisees who were seated at Nathaniel's table that morning came to be immediate believers in Jesus' teachings and accepted God into their hearts, but most of them stayed on their path of darkness and became more determined to lie in waiting for Jesus so they could catch him in some of his words that they could use to bring him to trial and judgement before the Sanhedrin officers in Jerusalem.

The custom for most of the people of Palestine was to eat two meals a day and whenever Jesus and the apostles were travelling, they always stopped to have a noon meal and to rest. As they continued their journey towards Philadelphia to visit Abner, Jesus continued to teach the apostles and answer all of their questions relating to accidents, miracles and sickness and many of the things that Jesus taught the apostles were way beyond their levels on understanding and they did not grasp the true meaning of Jesus' earth's mission until long after his crucifixion, resurrection and ascension back home to Paradise.

Of all of the cities that were located in Perea, Philadelphia had the largest group of Jewish people and Gentiles, and its synagogues had not been closed to the teachings of Jesus and his disciples, because they were not under the jurisdiction of Jerusalem's Sanhedrin rule. During this time Abner and his evangelists and women's corps were teaching three times a day in the Philadelphia synagogue and this synagogue later on became a Christian church and missionary headquarters for the center of Christian teaching of the gospel through a lot of regions all the way to the East. Abner became the head of the Philadelphia church where he remained until his death. The Jews in Jerusalem had always been in conflict with the Jews in Philadelphia and that is why they were separate organizations and after the death, resurrection and ascension of Jesus, his brother James became the head of the Christian church in Jerusalem and Abner was the head of the Philadelphia Christian church and this separation is the reason why nothing is heard or recorded about Abner and his work in the gospel records of the New Testament section of the Holy Bible. This feud between the Jerusalem and Philadelphia Christian churches lasted throughout the lifetimes of Jesus' brother James and Abner and it continued even after the destruction of Jerusalem. In reality Philadelphia was the true headquarters of the early Christian church in the south and east with Antioch being the headquarters for the north and the west. It was unfortunate that Abner became to be involved in a lifetime conflict with all of the leaders of the early Christian church in Jerusalem, because Abner fell out early on with Apostle Peter and Jesus' blood brother James over issues concerning the administration and jurisdiction of the Christian church and Abner later also parted ways with Apostle Paul over philosophy and theology differences. Abner was more Babylonian in his theology viewpoints, and he stubbornly refused Apostle Paul's attempts to have him conform his teachings of Jesus to the Jewish and Greco-Roman doctrines that he was teaching.

Abner therefore lived a life of isolation, because he was the head of the church in Philadelphia that was totally separate from the Jerusalem church and during his final years of life Abner denounced Apostle Paul verbally as being a clever corrupter of the life teachings of Jesus of Nazareth, the Son of the true living God in heaven. After the death of Abner many of the followers of the Philadelphia Christian church began to follow more closely the teachings of Jesus of Nazareth just as he lived and taught his teachings to more than any other Christian group on earth. Abner died in Philadelphia at the age of eighty-nine years old on November 21, A.D. 74 and he was a faithful believer to the very end in the teachings of Jesus and his gospel of God's heavenly kingdom.

While Jesus and the apostles were visiting Abner and his evangelists in Philadelphia, Abner arranged for Jesus to teach in the synagogue during the upcoming Sabbath service and this was the first time Jesus had taught in a synagogue since they had all been closed to, he and his followers in Palestine. Jesus taught that Sabbath in the synagogue and many people were baptized by Abner on that day in the river that flowed south of the city of Philadelphia. Very late on the following day on Sunday night of February 26, A.D. 30 one of the messenger runners from Bethany arrived in Philadelphia with a message that Jesus' friend Lazarus was very ill. And at first Jesus said nothing to the messenger and then Jesus told the messenger runner that the sickness that Lazarus had was not to his death and that it would instead be used to glorify God and exalt his Son.

The Jewish tradition was to bury their dead on the day of death, because they lived in such a warm climate, but so many times they would put a supposedly dead person in a tomb who had actually been comatose and not dead and on the second or third day they would often walk out of their tomb alive. Early that Wednesday morning Jesus told the apostles that they needed to go to Judea at once and on the way to Judea, Jesus began to be followed by a group of almost fifty of his friends and Pharisees. As Jesus and the apostles traveled up the hills to Bethany, Apostle Nathaniel walked by Jesus' side most of the way and he asked Jesus what they should teach the people about heaven's ministers, the angels. Jesus then explained to Apostle Nathaniel that angels are a separate order of created beings who never die like mortal man does and that mortal man can never become to be an angel, only a morontia being as he completes the ascension process through the seven mansion worlds of Paradise.

It was shortly after noon when Lazarus' sister Martha started to walk out to meet Jesus as he was coming over the hill near Bethany and Martha told Jesus that Lazarus had been dead four days and he had been laid in the family's private tomb at the far end of their garden and the stone at the entrance of Lazarus' tomb had been rolled in place to seal his tomb just that Thursday morning that Jesus arrived in Bethany.

When Martha met Jesus on the hill, she fell at his feet telling him that if he had been here her brother Lazarus would not have died and when Jesus saw the grief Martha was suffering over the death of Lazarus, his soul was moved with compassion. After Jesus had spent a few moments comforting Martha and Mary, he asked them to take him to Lazarus tomb and he then began to cry. It is hard to explain why Jesus cried, but these are some of the thoughts and feelings that were going through Jesus' mind while he was walking to Lazarus' tomb.

The first feeling Jesus had was that he felt a genuine and sorrowful sympathy for his dear friends Martha and Mary who had just lost their brother Lazarus.

The second feeling Jesus had in his mind was that in the crowd of mourners some were sincere while others were simply pretending to mourn over the death of Lazarus.

Jesus really hesitated about bringing Lazarus back to his mortal life, because he knew the bitter persecution Lazarus was going to have to endure as a result of being used as the greatest of all demonstrations of the divine power of the Son of Man.

The records of the universe indicates that Jesus' Personal Divine Thought Adjuster who was the same Thought Adjuster for Machiventa Melchizedek during his mortal life on earth, just before Lazarus died gave the order for Lazarus' Divine Thought Adjuster to remain in Lazarus' body fifteen minutes before he died.

And so, on this Thursday afternoon at 2:30pm, the stage was set in Bethany for one of the greatest of all works connected with the earthly reincarnation of Michael of Nebadon, Paradise as Jesus of Nazareth to complete. The Universal Father of Paradise and all of the celestial hosts of Paradise were all present that day in Bethany for one of Jesus' greatest manifestations of his divine power during his incarnation in the mortal flesh. There were forty-five people standing before the tomb of Lazarus that day and after Jesus told them to roll the stone away from the tomb, they were able to dimly see the body of Lazarus wrapped in linen bandages and he was laying in the right section of his burial cave. Jesus then stood in front of Lazarus' open tomb lifted his eyes to heaven and said the following words:

" Father I am thankful that you have heard and granted my request, I know that you always hear me, but because of those who stand here with me, I thus speak with you, that they may believe that you have sent me into the planet earth, and that they may know that you are working with me in that which we are about to do. "

And after Jesus prayed, he cried out in a loud voice and said out loud for all of the forty-five people to hear,

"Lazarus come forth."

And in just twelve seconds of earth time, the lifeless body of Lazarus began to move, and he sat up and as Lazarus began to stand up Jesus then said to loose him and let him go. Everyone who was there at the tomb ran into Lazarus home and the rest of the crowd ran to their homes and the apostles remained there with Jesus and Lazarus.

Lazarus then greeted Jesus and the apostles and asked why he was wrapped in grave clothes and why had he woken up in their garden and his sister Martha explained to Lazarus that he had died on the prior Sunday, but Jesus had now brought him back to life today which was Thursday. As Lazarus continued to walk out of his burial tomb, the Personalized Thought Adjuster of Jesus, the chief of his kind in our local universe of Nebadon gave the command to Lazarus' Divine Thought Adjuster to resume functioning in the mind and soul of the now resurrected Lazarus. Then Lazarus walked over to Jesus and knelt at his feet, thanked him and then offered praise to God. As Jesus and Lazarus walked towards Lazarus' house Archangel Gabriel from Paradise dismissed the extra groups of the assembled heavenly hosts from this glorious scene while he made a record in Paradise of the first instance on planet earth and the last, where a mortal being had been resurrected from the physical body of death.

Lazarus was not able to comprehend what had happened to him and he was never able to tell anything that had happened to him during those four days that he spent in his tomb, because he was unconscious, and time does not exist for those who sleep the sleep of death. By noon the next day the story of Jesus raising Lazarus from the dead had spread all over Jerusalem and many people went to Bethany just to look at Lazarus and talk with him about his resurrection by Jesus. And of course, the alarmed and upset Pharisees quickly held a meeting with the Sanhedrin officers in Jerusalem to determine what should be done about these new developments. The following week Lazarus and his two sisters Martha and Mary were summoned to appear before the Sanhedrin officers in Jerusalem and after they gave their testimony about what had happened, the Sanhedrin had no doubts that Lazarus had been raised from the dead. The Sanhedrin though they admitted that Jesus had resurrected Lazarus, wrote down in the official records that this wonder that was done by Jesus was performed from the power of the prince of devils. Lazarus continued to live with his two sisters in their home in Bethany after his resurrection and Lazarus remained to be the center of attention and great interest until the time of the crucifixion of Jesus, when he received a warning message that the Sanhedrin had decreed that he was to be put to death, because the Sanhedrin did not want Lazarus to continue to live and bear testimony to the fact that Jesus had raised him from the dead, so Lazarus had to quickly leave Bethany and move to live in Philadelphia where he worked with Abner and his disciples.

Soon after Lazarus moved to live and work in Philadelphia with Abner and his disciples, his two sisters sisters Martha and Mary sold their home in Bethany and they also moved to Philadelphia to live with their brother Lazarus. While Lazarus was living in Philadelphia, he became to be a strong supporter of Abner in his ongoing conflict he was having with Apostle Paul and the Jerusalem church. Lazarus lived a full life working with Abner in the Philadelphia Christian church and he died at the age of sixty-seven of the same illness that had killed him years before when he was a younger man living in Bethany.

Jesus and his apostles arrived back at their Pella camp late on Monday evening, March 6, A.D. 30, and this was going to be Jesus' last week there and he stayed very busy preaching to the crowds and continuing to teach the twelve apostles. Jesus preached every day to the crowds and every night he answered the questions that the apostles and disciples had. Meanwhile the Pharisees and chief priests in Jerusalem continued to formulate their charges and accusations against Jesus and many times during his years of teaching, Jesus told and retold the parable story about the prodigal son and the good Samaritan as his two favorite means of teaching the love of the father and the brotherly love of mankind.

Jesus never claimed to be the manifestation of the Elohim in the flesh and Jesus never claimed that he was a revelation of the Elohim to any of the worlds he lived on during the completion of his seven bestowal missions. Jesus did, however, proclaim himself as the revelation of the Universal Father in Paradise in the flesh and Jesus did say that he who sees him had seen the Universal Father. Jesus was one of the twelve Creator Sons from the seven mansion worlds of the superuniverse of Paradise-the seven higher heavens and he claimed to only represent the Universal Father of Paradise. Jesus was the son of the Elohim God in the form of mortal flesh, but to the mortal beings living on earth, Jesus chose to limit his life revelation to the level that mortal man could understand. During his spiritual teachings Jesus taught humanity that God in himself is spirit and that in all matters relating to mortal man, God is our Father.

Jesus is the spiritual lens in human likeness that makes visible to mortal man God who is invisible, and Jesus is our elder brother who as a mortal man made known to man, God who is composed of infinite attributes, because God is a spirit who can be known only as a spiritual experience. God can be revealed to mortal beings who live on the many worlds of time and space through his twelve divine Creator Sons. And mortal beings can each know and love our Universal Father in Paradise and worship him always as our God of all universes, the infinite Prime Creator of all existences, our Source.

On Saturday afternoon March 11, A.D. 30, Jesus preached his last sermon at their Pella camp which proves to be among one of his most notable ones where Jesus fully explained the kingdom of heaven and the seven higher heavens.

It was more than fifty years later after the destruction of Jerusalem by the Roman armies that the last sermon that Jesus gave at their Pella campground explaining the concept of heaven finally began to evolve into the teaching of eternal life as its social and institutional aspects that were taken over by the rapidly expanding early Christian church.

The day after Jesus gave his last sermon at their Pella Campground, Jesus announced that he and the apostles would be leaving for the Passover celebration in Jerusalem and on the way they were going to visit many of the cities located in the southern area of Perea on the way and on this same day Salome Zebedee the mother of Apostles James and John Zebedee and member of the women's corps asked Jesus to please include her two sons James and John to sit at the right and left hand side of him as he traveled once again to Jerusalem to establish God's kingdom on earth. When Salome Zebedee made this request to Jesus little did she know that in less than one month Jesus would be hanging dying on a Roman cross with a dying thief on one side of him and another transgressor hanging on a cross on the other side of him.

On Monday March 13, A. D. 30, Jesus and the apostles left the Pella Campground for the last time to begin their final public ministry tour in the southern cities of Perea where Abner and his evangelists were also completing their missionary work. When Jesus left Pella for the last time there were about one thousand disciples with him and one half of this group continued to follow Jesus and the apostles on their last public ministry tour in Perea.

Most of Jesus' immediate followers knew that Camp Pella was closing, but they really thought that Jesus was going to Jerusalem to claim the throne of David and a large majority of Jesus' followers were never able to understand any other concept of the kingdom of heaven except for Jesus becoming the king of the Jews on earth. And so, acting on the instructions given to him from Apostle Andrew, David Zebedee officially closed the Pella Campground on Wednesday, March 15, A.D. 30, and he sold all of the camp equipment and gave the proceeds from the sale to Apostle Judas Iscariot.

David Zebedee was there in Jerusalem during Jesus' last tragic week, and he took his mother, Salome back with him to Bethsaida after the crucifixion of Jesus. While David Zebedee was waiting for Jesus and the apostles to arrive in Jerusalem, he stopped to visit Lazarus in Bethany, and he found that Lazarus was in a very agitated state due to the persecution and harassment he had been suffering from the Pharisees and Sanhedrin officers. Since Apostle Andrew had instructed David to close down the Pella Campground, David Zebedee no longer had a job, so he decided to be the self-appointed defender of Lazarus and he helped Lazarus to move to Philadelphia to live and work with Abner's group of evangelists and shortly after the death and resurrection of Jesus and the death of his mother Salome, David Zebedee married Jesus' sister Babe Ruth and helped Lazarus' two sisters Martha and Mary to also move to Philadelphia.

After David Zebedee moved to Philadelphia with his new wife Babe Ruth he also worked with Abner and Lazarus in the Philadelphia Christian church as its financial overseer. After the total destruction of Jerusalem by the Roman army fifty years later,

Antioch became the headquarters for Apostle Paul's Christian church while Philadelphia remained separate from Jerusalem, and it became the headquarters for the Aberian Kingdom of Heaven Christian Center. Meanwhile from Antioch Apostle Paul's version of Jesus' teachings spread all over the rest of the Western civilized world and from Abner's Philadelphia Christian church, the missionaries from Abner's version of Jesus' teachings of the kingdom of heaven spread all throughout Arabia and Mesopotamia until later times when the gospel of Jesus was overwhelmed by the sudden rise of the Islam religion.

For more than two weeks Jesus and the twelve apostles continued to be followed by a crowd of several hundred disciples as they completed their missionary work in Perea and at the end of this final tour as Jesus and the apostles were leaving Jericho, Jesus stood in the shade of an overhanging rock by the roadside and with cheerful dignity said these final words to his twelve apostles as they were about to complete Jesus' last journey to Jerusalem as a mortal man on earth:

"Come my brethren, let us go into Jerusalem, there to receive that which awaits us, thus shall we fulfill the will of the Heavenly Father in all things."

CHAPTER SIXTEEN

THE FINAL DAYS OF JESUS AS A MORTAL MAN ON PLANET EARTH

The Lord your God will be with you wherever you go.

(Joshua 1:9)

Blessed are those who walk in the light of your presence, Lord.

(Psalm 89:15)

A Prayer: Loving Universal Father, our Prime Creator, thank you for Your promise to never leave me. I trust You to be my strength, my provision, and my joy all throughout all of my life.

THE FINAL DAYS OF JESUS AS A MORTAL MAN ON EARTH

Jesus and the apostles arrived in Bethany on Friday afternoon, March 31, A.D. 30 and Lazarus' family and friends were expecting them and since so many people had been coming over to Lazarus' home daily to talk about his resurrection, arrangements were made for Jesus to stay with Lazarus' neighbor Simon. Jesus received many visitors that evening at Simon's home and many people stopped by to make Jesus feel welcome in Bethany. Lazarus and his two sisters realized that this was going to be Jesus' last visit to Jerusalem, so early the next morning Jesus was awakened by hundreds of people who had come from Jerusalem to visit with he and Lazarus.

On Sunday morning Jesus called his apostles around him to give them their final preparatory instructions before they arrived for his final visit to Jerusalem and Jesus told the apostles not to do any public teaching while they were in Jerusalem, stay close to him and to watch and pray. Jesus spoke privately with Lazarus and told him not to sacrifice his life to the vengeful Sanhedrin, so a few days later Lazarus moved to live and work with Abner and his disciples in Philadelphia. All of Jesus' disciples knew that an impending crisis was near, but they were prevented from fully understanding how serious the situation really was due to the unusual cheerfulness and exceptional good humor Jesus was displaying. Jesus already knew what was going to be the outcome of his last visit to Jerusalem and he had to choose a proper method to make his last public entrance into Jerusalem. A warrior king always enters a city riding on a horse and a king on a mission of peace and friendship always enters a city riding on a donkey, so Jesus chose to enter Jerusalem for the last time with a spirit of good will in his heart as the Son of Man riding on a donkey.

Jesus then told Apostle Peter to go to the junction in the road in the city of Bethpage where he would find a donkey tied there and to untie the donkey and bring it back to him and if the owner of the donkey asks why he are taking his donkey, tell the owner that Jesus of Nazareth has a need to briefly use this donkey. Meanwhile David Zebedee and some of his former messengers went to Jerusalem ahead of Jesus and the apostles' where they spread the news among the visiting people who were there for the Passover celebration that Jesus of Nazareth was making a triumphant entry into the city of Jerusalem.

As the procession with Jesus riding on the donkey left Bethany on the road to Jerusalem, there was a lot of enthusiasm among the festive crowd of disciples, believers and visiting pilgrims, many of whom had come from Galilee and Perea. Just before they all started on their journey to Jerusalem, the twelve original members of the women's corps arrived, and they joined the procession of Jesus' followers as they marched into Jerusalem. Before this procession started out on their journey to Jerusalem the Alpheus twin apostles both put their cloaks on the donkey and held him down while Jesus got on the donkey.

As this procession of disciples and followers of Jesus traveled on towards the summit of Mount Olivet the festive crowd began to throw their garments to the ground and cover them with palm branches from the nearby trees to make a carpet of honor for the donkey who was carrying Jesus to the city of Jerusalem. As this merry crowd traveled on towards the city of Jerusalem, they began to sing and shout one of the psalms in unison and Jesus was happy until they came to the brow of Mount Olivet where the city of Jerusalem and its temple towers came into full view and there Jesus stopped the procession and the whole crowd became silent, because they saw that Jesus had started to cry when he saw a vast multitude of people coming to meet him from Jerusalem. Jesus briefly spoke to the large crowd telling them that they would soon be turning their backs on the Son of peace and reject his gospel of salvation.

When Jesus had finished speaking to the crowd, they continued to descend down Mount Olivet along with many visitors from Jerusalem who were waving their palm branches at they expressed their good feelings of fellowship. Jesus had not planned for this crowd to come out from Jerusalem to meet his procession of followers, but this was the work of David Zebedee and his messengers to welcome Jesus back to Jerusalem. This same welcoming crowd in less than a week would change and reject Jesus just like he told them they would when the Sanhedrin officers decide to stand against Jesus which would cause this same crowd to become disillusioned when they realize that Jesus was not going to establish himself as the King of the Jews. While the Alpheus twins returned the donkey back to its owner, Jesus and the ten apostles strolled about the temple in Jerusalem viewing all of the preparations that were being made for the Passover celebration. As the evening came the crowds dispersed to look for nourishment leaving Jesus and his disciples all alone and, on this Sunday, now known as Palm Sunday, Jesus walked in front of the apostles who were now all bewildered, puzzled and depressed, because they knew that something catastrophic was about to happen to their Master, Jesus. To the Alpheus twins that Palm Sunday had been a perfect day they had really enjoyed, and they could not understand why the rest of the apostles were so depressed and downcast. From that day forward the only memory that the Alpeus twin apostles had of that Palm Sunday was that it was the most satisfying climax of their whole career of being apostles for Jesus. And this good memory of the elation the Alpheus twins felt from that Palm Sunday afternoon carried them on through the tragedy of the upcoming week right up to the hour of Jesus' crucifixion.

Out of all of the twelve apostles, Judas Iscariot was the most adversely affected by Jesus' processional entrance into the city of Jerusalem on a donkey, because Judas' mind was still in torment since Jesus had scolded him on the previous day in front of the other apostles for getting upset when Mary Magdalene, Jesus' wife used expensive incense and oil to wash and anoint Jesus' feet to prepare him for his upcoming crucifixion.

When Jesus publicly scolded Judas this caused Judas to have revenge in his heart and to Judas, Jesus looked just like a clown when he was riding on the back of a donkey into Jerusalem and Judas shared the views that many of the Greeks and Romans felt and they looked down on any man who would agree to ride a donkey into a city. By the time Jesus' triumphant processional group had entered the city of Jerusalem, Judas had already made up his mind to abandon the entire idea of continuing to preach the gospel of Jesus. But then Judas thought about the resurrection of Lazarus and many other good things that Jesus had done and he decided to stay with Jesus and the rest of the apostles for at least one more day, plus Judas did not want to desert Jesus with all of the apostolic funds he had in his possession. And so, since the rest of the apostle's behavior on that Palm Sunday night was downcast, Judas' brooding behavior did not seem to be strange at all. Judas was also very upset because while Jesus was riding on the back of the donkey into Jerusalem, he was being ridiculed by some of Judas' Sadducean friends and Judas never shrunk from persecution, but he never could withstand any type of ridicule. So, with his long list of nourished revenge that continued to grow in Judas' heart, it was also blended with negative feelings of ridicule and Judas began to have terrible feelings of being ashamed of Jesus and his fellow apostles. In his heart Judas was already a coward and a deserter and all he needed was some good excuse to openly break from Jesus and his fellow apostles.

Early on Monday morning April 3, A.D. 30, Jesus and the apostles all gathered at Simon's home in Bethany to have a brief meeting after which they all left to go back to Jerusalem, and they arrived at the temple at nine o'clock in the morning. There was a lot of noisy money changers, merchandisers and cattle sellers and all kinds of commercial activities going on in the temple except for praying and it was not uncommon for the Jewish temple treasury to have up to ten million dollars in it and the Jewish priests to be living in lavish homes, while the rest of the congregation were living in poverty and continuing to pay high unjust taxes. It just so happened that on this particular morning Jesus was attempting to teach the gospel and as he looked around at all of the loud commercial activity that was going on all around him in the temple. Jesus noticed that he was not alone in resenting this open desecration of God's sacred temple and just as Jesus was about to begin his sermon, two things happened that set Jesus off that caused him to experience the feelings of anger. The first incident was a violent heated argument that arose over the alleged overcharging of a Jewish man from Alexandria and the second incident was a group of so-called superior Judeans were ridiculing and pushing around a simple-minded Galilean man. To make matters worse the air in the entire temple was filled with the loud noises of droves of about one hundred bulls being driven by a young lad with a whip from one section of the animal pens to another.

All of these loud commercial scenes that were going on in the sacred temple caused a unique uprising of anger to suddenly rise up inside of Jesus and to the utter amazement of the apostles, Jesus calmly stepped down from the speaker's podium, took the whip from the young lad's hands and quickly drove all of the bulls from out of the temple. But that was not all, Jesus then majestically walked over to each one of the cattle stalls, opened each gate and drove all of the rest of the imprisoned animals with his whip out of the stalls and out of the temple. By this time all of the congregation of people were all electrified and with a lot of shouting, they moved towards all of the commercial booths overturning all of them and they ran all of the money changers along with their commercial enterprises out of the temple all in less than five minutes. By the time the Roman guards arrived at the temple, all was quiet, the congregation were all orderly sitting back in their seats and Jesus was back at the speaker's podium giving his sermon to the crowd of people.

When the chief Jewish priests heard how Jesus had cleared all of their commercial booths and enterprises out of the temple in less than five minutes they were dumbfounded and fearing Jesus even more, because now he was taking money from out of their pockets. So, the Sanhedrin officers and Chief Jewish priests were now even more determined to destroy Jesus. This surprising act by Jesus in the temple that day was beyond comprehension for the apostles and all throughout the entire episode the apostles stayed huddled together near the speaker podium. Jesus had swept all of the Jewish high priests' commercial enterprises from out of the temple in less than five minutes and by doing this, Jesus publicly showed the Jewish high priests what his attitude was towards the commercializing of religion in Jerusalem's sacred temple as well as his distaste for all forms of profiteering at the expense of the poor and downtrodden people in God's sacred temple. What Jesus did that day upset the Sanhedrin officers so much that they held an emergency meeting where they all agreed that Jesus must be quickly destroyed, because now he was messing with their power and money. Jesus' clearing of the temple that day also caused the Sadducees to join forces with the Pharisees to perfect a plan to finally destroy Jesus.

Jesus did not despise the Pharisees and Sadducees personally, but he did not agree with their systems of teaching and selfish power dominating practices which he sought to discredit and put to an end. Jesus was never hostile to any man, but now in his ministry, he was being confronted with a clash between a new living religion of the spirit with the older religion of ceremony, tradition and authority. At about four o'clock on that same afternoon Jesus told the apostles that it was time to leave the temple in Jerusalem and return to Bethany for their evening meal and a night of rest. On their way up Mount Olivet Jesus instructed Apostles Andrew, Philip and Thomas to establish a camp that would be closer to Jerusalem where they could stay in for the rest of the Passover week. So, the following morning the apostles pitched their tents and built a new campground in the Gethsemane Park on a plot of land that belonged to Simon of Bethany.

As the apostle walked with Jesus up the western slope of Mount Olivet on that Monday night, they were all silent, because the apostles were really beginning to sense that something tragic was about to happen to Jesus. And while Jesus' dramatic but quick cleansing of the temple that morning had aroused the apostles' hopes of seeing Jesus assert himself and manifest his mighty powers, the apostles were all being held in a grip of uncertainty, and they felt a dark cloud of gloom and doom coming towards Jesus. The apostles each went to their various spaces to rest that evening, but no one could sleep and even the Alpheus twins were at last brought to the realization that the events of Jesus' life were quickly moving to a final tragic event.

At about seven o'clock on Tuesday morning, April 4, A.D. 30, Jesus held a meeting with the apostles, the women's corps and two dozen other prominent disciples at Simon's home and at this meeting Jesus said farewell to his friend Lazarus, his senior citizen friend Simon and Jesus' final parting advice to the women's corps and this was the last time that Jesus formally addressed this group of his disciples. After Jesus concluded this final meeting, he left for Jerusalem with Apostles Andrew, James and John while the rest of the apostles left to finish setting up their new headquarters in the Gethsemane Park. About halfway down the slope of Mount Olivet Jesus stopped and talked with the three apostles for more than an hour.

On Monday evening April 3, A.D. 30, a meeting was held between the Sanhedrin, the Pharisees, the Sadducees and fifty Jewish leaders who were selected from the Jewish scribes and the consensus of this meeting was that it would be dangerous to arrest Jesus in public due to his hold on the sentiment and affections of the common Jewish people.

So, their plan was to for the time being to have several groups of well-educated men to follow Jesus along with his groups of believers and to be on hand at the temple the next morning to entrap and embarrass Jesus in front of the people in the temple. At last, the Pharisees, Sadducees and even the Herodians were all in agreement that they had formulated a plan to finally destroy Jesus.

Around noon on Tuesday April 4, A.D. 30, as Apostle Philip was purchasing supplies for their new campground, he was approached by a group of Greek believers of Jesus' teachings who had come to Jerusalem all the way from Athens, Rome and Alexandria and the spokesman for this group of Greek followers asked Apostle Philip to take them to meet Jesus and Apostle Philip told the group to wait right where they were so he could go and find Jesus' exact location. Apostle Philip then went and got Apostle Andrew to return with him and they both took this group of Greek followers to Jesus' wealthy uncle from England, Joseph of Arimathea's home where they were all warmly received by Jesus.

These group of Greek followers sat near Jesus who was attending a luncheon with Joseph and some of his disciples and as Jesus stood talking to the entire group who were attending this lunch on that day, Jesus perceived in his mind that he was at the end of one dispensation and stepping into the beginning of a new one. Jesus next turned his attention to the group of Greek followers he had just met and told them his hour had come where the Son of Man would soon be glorified and if they continue to follow his teachings after his return back home to his Universal Father, then they would all continue to be sincere disciples and servants to their fellow man. Jesus then told everyone who were at the luncheon that day that he knew that his final hour was soon approaching and that he was troubled and when Jesus finished speaking his Personalized Divine Thought Adjuster of his indwelling spirit appeared to only Jesus saying the following words;

"I have glorified my name in your seven bestowals many times and I will glorify it once more."

Everyone who was there that day attending this luncheon noticed how Jesus paused while speaking and they all said amongst themselves that an angel was speaking to Jesus during the speech he was giving to them. After Jesus finished his luncheon speech, he led the way over the narrow streets of Jerusalem back to the temple and they all followed Jesus in silence and in deep meditation all the way to the temple. When they all arrived at the temple at about two o'clock in the afternoon on that same day, Jesus began to preach his last discourse, his final appeal to the Jewish people, the Pharisees, the Sadducees and to the Jewish religious rulers. As Jesus began to preach his last discourse that day in the temple on April 4, A.D. 30, the entire temple court was quiet, orderly and the money changers and merchandisers with their booths wouldn't dare again to enter the temple since Jesus and the congregation had thrown them out on the previous day. As Jesus began to speak his final discourse, he tenderly looked down on his audience who were so soon going to hear his farewell public address of mercy to mankind along with his denunciation of the many false teachers and bigoted rulers of the Jews.

The fact that the spiritual and religious teachers of the Jewish nation rejected the teachings of Jesus and continued to conspire to bring about his cruel death does not affect the status of any individual Jew in his standing before God. And it should not cause anyone who are followers of Jesus Christ to be prejudiced against any Jewish person as a fellow human being. The Jewish nation as a sociopolitical group all paid in full the terrible price of rejecting the Prince of Peace and long since the Jews have ceased to be the spiritual torchbearers of divine truth to the races of humanity, but this constitutes no valid reason for the individual descendants of these long ago Jews should be made to suffer the evil persecutions that have been placed on Jews by intolerant followers of Jesus who was himself a Jew by birth when he was born through a virgin birth on earth as a mortal man to his parents Joseph and Mary.

On Tuesday, April 4, A.D. 30, at eight o'clock in the evening the Sanhedrin called a meeting to plan to put a stop to Jesus' public ministry on earth and just before midnight they voted to impose the death penalty on both Jesus and Lazarus. So, this was the Sanhedrin's answer to Jesus' last discourse appeal to the rulers of the Jews that he had made in the temple only a few hours earlier. This passing of the death penalty for Jesus even before his trial was the Sanhedrin's response to Jesus' last offer of heavenly mercy ever to be extended to the Jewish nation. From this time on the Jewish nation were left alone to complete their brief and short lease of national life in accordance with their purely human status, because Israel had rejected the Son of God who had made a covenant through Machiventa Melchizedek with Abraham and the plan to make the children of Abraham the light bearers of truth to the worlds had been shattered by the Jewish religious rulers. This divine covenant had failed and the end of the Hebrew nation by the hands of the Roman Empire's armies came quickly.

The officers of the Sanhedrin were given the orders to arrest Jesus early the next morning on April 5, A.D. 30, with clear orders to not arrest Jesus in public, but to arrest Jesus suddenly at night and in secret and to then bring Jesus to the Jewish high priest court sometime before midnight on Thursday, April 6, A.D. 30.

The Sadducees who now controlled and dominated this court charged Jesus with the following crimes.

Jesus was a threat to the Jewish nation, and he was involved with the Roman authorities.

Jesus' zeal for temple reform and cleansing adversely affected the temple's revenues.

The further spread of Jesus' strange teachings was a threat to the preservation of social order.

The Pharisees' charges against Jesus were as follows.

Jesus was making radical attacks on the established Jewish religious teachers.

Jesus showed disregard for the Sabbath and established Jewish ceremonies.

Jesus was charged with blasphemy for stating he was the Son of God.

The Pharisees were very angry with Jesus' final discourse that he preached in the temple on April 4, A.D. 30, and on that eventful day, a vast concourse of celestial beings in Paradise hovered over this tragic scene that was taking place on planet earth and they wanted to do something to help Jesus, but they were restrained from doing so by their commanding superiors of Paradise.

On Tuesday afternoon, April 4, A.D. 30, as Jesus and the apostles left the temple in Jerusalem to return to their Gethsemane Camp, Apostle Matthew pointed to the temple construction that was currently underway with all of the massive stones being used and as they got closer to Mount Olivet, Jesus told Apostle Matthew that in the coming days, soon to come that every one of the stones for the new temple being built would all be destroyed into a pile of heap by the armies of the Roman Empire.

On several occasions Jesus had made statements that he would soon be leaving earth, but that he would definitely return to complete the work of building his Father's kingdom and this doctrine of Jesus returning to earth was incorporated into the early teachings of the Christian church. Of all the discourses Jesus had given to the apostles, none of them confused the apostles like the one Jesus preached to them on Tuesday evening, April 4, A.D. 3, on Mount Olivet regarding the destruction of the temple in Jerusalem and his second coming. And as Jesus and the apostles resumed their journey towards their camp, everyone was silent and feeling great emotional tension.

Meanwhile, Apostle Judas Iscariot had finally made up his mind to abandon Jesus and his fellow apostles and later on that evening David Zebedee and the young lad, John Mark welcomed Jesus back to their camp and they asked Jesus to tell them more about the destruction of Jerusalem and about his second coming. When the Roman armies destroyed the walls of the city and temple of Jerusalem, Jesus still had not returned to earth, so the early Christians then began to believe that Jesus would return at the end of the world.

These are the two things that Jesus did promise to do after he ascended back home to Paradise.

Jesus promised to send to earth a comforter, a teacher who would be the Spirit of Truth, the Holy Spirit.

Jesus also promised to personally return to earth but he never stated when or how.

Whenever Jesus and the apostles did not have a heavy schedule of preaching and teaching to their followers, they had a custom of making Wednesday their day of rest, so after they had all eaten breakfast, Jesus told all of the disciples to take the day off to rest and think about all that had happened to them since they arrived in Jerusalem and that he was going to spend the rest of the day alone in the hills. But at the last minute, the young lad, John Mark took hold of Jesus' packed lunch asking if he could go with him to pray.

Jesus agreed and the two of them set off for their journey and Jesus spent his last day of peace and quiet on earth talking and praying with his Paradise Father. This day showed the young lad John Mark's willingness to fellowship and pray with Jesus to His Paradise Father in the hills of Judea. Jesus talked a lot that day with John Mark telling him the latest affairs of the world, the scriptures and about many of his teachings and John Mark told Jesus how much he regretted that he was not old enough to be one of his apostles, but that he was grateful for the time he got to work with the apostles since their first preaching tour they had in Jericho. While they were talking that day in the hills of Judea, Jesus warned John Mark to not become discouraged by the upcoming tragic events and Jesus then assured John Mark that he would in time become to be a mighty messenger spreading the good news about God's kingdom.

During the time that John Mark and Jesus spent talking that day in the hills of Judea, they were able to compare their childhood experiences and memories. And it turned out that John Mark's parents were more well off financially than Jesus' parents, but they still seemed to have had similar childhood experiences. Jesus explained to John Mark many things about the role of parenthood that helped him to better understand his parents and the rest of the members of his family and Jesus also explained how one's home life and a person's afterlife are tremendously influenced by what happens during the first early years of life at home with his family. And after this day and up until the time of Jesus' crucifixion young John Mark never permitted Jesus to get out of his sight and he was always in hiding somewhere watching out for Jesus. One of the main gospels of Jesus' teachings focused on the father-child relationships that embraces more love, more wisdom and the acceptance of Jesus' gospel.

That Wednesday, April 5, A.D. 30, the apostles spent most of that day walking on Mount Olivet and visiting with the rest of the apostles in their camp and at about four o'clock that evening a messenger runner brought word to David Zebedee from his mother and from Jesus' mother Mary that the chief Jewish priests and religious rulers of Jerusalem were going to kill Jesus. David Zebedee knew that the high priests and religious rulers were determined to destroy Jesus, so he wasted no time to dispatch a messenger to bring all of the members of his and Jesus' family at once to Jerusalem. Shortly after noon on that same time twenty of Jesus' group of new Greek friends who had attended the luncheon arrived at their camp and Jesus spent time visiting with them and not too many of Jesus' followers came to visit them at their Gethsemane Camp, because they had kept its location a secret. On this same day Judas Iscariot disappeared, and he did not return to the camp until later on that afternoon and before Jesus left for the hills to pray, he told the apostles to not go into Jerusalem.

However, Judas Iscariot disobeyed Jesus, and he quickly went into Jerusalem to keep an appointment he had made with some of Jesus' enemies in the home of Caiaphas, the

Jewish high priest. This was an informal meeting of the Sanhedrin that they had scheduled to discuss how they planned to capture Jesus and bring him to the Roman authorities on Thursday, April 6, A.D. 30. On the prior day Judas had told some of his relatives and Sadducees friends from his father's family that he had decided that Jesus was nothing but a dreamer and idealist and that he was ready to leave the Jesus movement. Judas' friends had led him to believe that if he left the Jesus movement that he would be hailed as a hero by the Jewish rulers and receive high honor. So, Judas Iscariot had convinced himself that Jesus would not use his power to escape from being captured by his enemies, but Judas firmly believed that Jesus would never allow the Jewish priests to kill him. In addition, Judas was resentful that Jesus had never assigned him to a position of greater honor and Judas began to feel like he was not being appreciated and then suddenly Judas began to feel indignation due to the fact that Jesus always took Apostles Peter, James and John with him during his private prayer and meditation excursions. While Judas was on his way to Caiaphas' house he was determined to get revenge on Apostles Peter, James and John even more than his determination to betray Jesus. Judas was also trying to gain honor for himself, and his mind was full of confusion, pride, desperation and determination to get his revenge. So, it was plain to see that it was not for money that Judas was on his way to the Jewish high priest Caiaphas' home to make the final arrangements to betray Jesus.

As Judas got closer to Caiaphas' home, he wanted to make sure he would get as much honor and glory for himself and Judas the traitor was then presented to Caiphas the high priest and the Jewish religious rulers by his Sadducees cousin who verbally explained that Judas Iscariot had realized his mistake of allowing himself to be misled by following the teachings of Jesus and that he also recognized that it would be best for the peace of Isarel for Jesus to be taken into custody for the continued peace for the Jewish people.

When Judas' cousin had finished speaking about Judas to the Jewish leaders Judas stepped forward asking how much he was going to be paid for his service of betraying Jesus and Judas was so full of pride and revenge that he didn't even notice the look of disgust that came over the Jewish high priest Caiaphas's face when he asked about his payment. Caiaphas then told Judas to make arrangements with the captain of the guard to bring Jesus to them either on that night or the next and then he would receive his reward money. Judas then quickly went to the captain of the guard and made the arrangements to have Jesus arrested the next day on Thursday, April 6, A.D. 30, after all of the visiting people in Jerusalem had retired for the night.

Judas did not realize it at the time, but he had been a subconscious critic of Jesus ever since John the Baptist had been executed by tetrarch Herod Antipas and deep down in his heart Judas always resented the fact that Jesus did not use his powers to save John the Baptist, because Judas had originally been a disciple with John the Baptist before he was appointed to be an apostle for Jesus. It always seemed like every time Judas felt his hopes begin to rise Jesus would do or say something to dash them to pieces and then his deep scars of bitterness would build up in Judas' heart. And the worse thing was that Judas did not even realize that he was nothing but a coward.

At last, the Jewish chief priests and Sanhedrin officers were able to rest easily, because they didn't have to arrest Jesus in public and by using the traitor Judas, they had assurance that Jesus would not be able to escape their jurisdiction like he had done so many times in the past. Since it was Wednesday and their day off, on this Wednesday evening of April 5, A.D. 30, Jesus tried hard to cheer up his downcast apostles, but it did not work, because the apostles all knew that the tragic events were soon coming on the horizon. The entire atmosphere at their Gethsemane Camp was full of tension and everyone knew that Lazarus had already made a quick emergency move to work with Abner in Philadelphia where it was safe, and all of the apostles felt like they were all about to descend into a sudden inescapable terror. That Wednesday evening was the low tide mark for the apostles' spiritual status right up to the actual hour of Jesus' crucifixion and although the next day was one more day nearer to the tragic Friday, Jesus was still with them and the apostles were able to pass the time through its tense and anxious hours with a little more ease.

It was just before midnight on Wednesday, April 5, A.D. 30, when Jesus knowing that this would be his last night he would ever get to sleep with his chosen spiritual family on earth, Jesus gave his disciples a farewell speech just before they went to sleep that night. Jesus had planned to spend Thursday, April 6, A.D. 30, his last free day on earth with his apostles and a few loyal devoted disciples and soon after they had all breakfast, Jesus took the apostles to a secluded spot not far from their Gethsemane Camp where he had spent some time teaching them many new spiritual teachings.

Jesus also preached several more discourses to the apostles during the evening hours of that Thursday evening, April 6, A.D. 30, and the main speech that Jesus gave that Thursday evening was his final farewell address to the entire camp group of apostles, disciples, his newly found Greek friends and a host of gentiles and Jewish followers and all of the apostles were with Jesus that Thursday night at their camp. Jesus also talked with about fifty of his trusted followers for almost two hours that last day at their camp and he answered many of the questions they had.

David Zebedee through the work of his secret agents he had working in Jerusalem knew about the Jewish high priest's plan to arrest and kill Jesus and David also knew that Judas Iscariot was a traitor for his part in the plot to capture and kill Jesus and shortly after lunch David Zebedee lead Jesus aside asking him if he knew, but he never got any further with his question, because Jesus held his hand up stopping David telling him that he knew but not to tell anyone else. This conversation between Jesus and David was interrupted by a messenger from Abner in Philadelphia asking if he should come to Jerusalem to help. Jesus sent a return message to Abner telling him to continue his ministry work in Philadelphia and to not come to Jerusalem.

Jesus had already made secret plans the day before with his follower the young lad John Mark to use the upper room in his parents' home to have his last supper with all of his apostles later that evening on Thursday night, April 6, A.D. 30. Meanwhile, David Zebedee made sure that he made Judas Iscariot give him all of the apostolic funds and receipts before they left for John Mark's parents' home to have the last supper in the upper room. At about half past four in the evening on that same Thursday Jesus began to make preparations to lead the twelve apostles over the trail to Jerusalem to have their last supper and this was the last journey they ever made together.

As Jesus and the apostles reached the western section of Mount Olivet, they were running a little early because Jesus did not want to enter Jerusalem until after sunset, so he had the apostles to sit down for a while so he could explain to them all of the events that were about to happen to him.

After Jesus had finished talking to the apostles on Mount Olivet, he resumed their journey and the apostles followed Jesus along the dark narrow streets of Jerusalem and except for David Zebedee, none of the apostles knew where they were going that night, and they also did not know that one of them was going to betray Jesus later on that same night. Jesus' young follower John Mark had followed Jesus and the apostles all the way from their camp to Jerusalem and after Jesus and the apostles entered the gate into the city of Jerusalem, John Mark quickly went on a different route to his parent's home so that he would get there first to welcome Jesus and his apostles to have their last supper in the upper room.

After receiving the welcome greetings to the home of John Marks' parents the apostles went on upstairs to the upper room while Jesus stayed downstairs to talk with John Mark's parents for a little while. Arrangements had already been made to not provide servants to wait on Jesus and the apostles, because Jesus wanted to have the last supper alone with his disciples.

Seated to the right of Jesus at the last supper table was his wife and disciple Mary Magdalene and Jesus' wife was the one woman Jesus loved the most out of all of his disciples and he kissed her often on the lips in front of the apostles and they were often offended by Jesus' outward show of affection to Mary Magdalene and the apostles would often ask Jesus why he loved her more than he loved them and Jesus' response was always, " Why do you say that I do not love you like Mary Magdalene?" Before Jesus began his incarnation as a normal mortal man on earth, he received permission from his older brother Immanual on Paradise to marry, but he was forbidden to leave behind any offspring on planet earth. One of the greatest cover-ups in our human history was Jesus' love and marriage to Mary Magdalene who was Jesus' divine feminine counterpart, his soul mate, but Jesus left no offspring and only his mother, his wife Mary Magdalene and his seven siblings remained on earth after he ascended back home to Paradise on May 18, A.D. 30.

Mary Magdalene was born into a wealthy family in the town of Magdala, a small fish processing town and Jesus met Mary Magdalene when he was thirty-three years old, and she was fifty years old, and Mary Magdalene continued to help to finance Jesus' spiritual ministry in Galilee and she was a priestess and leader of the Sisters of the Rose spiritual group. Together Jesus and Mary Magdalene laid the gridlines on planet earth to make it possible for earth to begin its ascension process along with humanity in the year 1987 when the Harmonic Convergence was decreed by our Universal Prime Creator in Paradise. When Jesus of Nazareth first met Mary Magdalene, she was possessed by seven demons that Jesus cleansed and delivered from her spiritual body and these seven demons that Jesus delivered Mary Magdalene from actually inhabited the spirit all humans living on the third dimensional low frequency earth before Jesus asked his Universal Father in Paradise and the Spirit of Truth-the Holy Spirit to come to earth on May 21, A.D. 30 Pentecost Sunday and on that day, all of the evil spirits were removed from planet earth.

All human beings living on earth are spirit beings of light, a fractural of God and we each have physical overlays and since the original Pentecost Sunday that occurred in the year of May, A.D. 30, humans are now each born on earth with the following seven aspects of the Holy Spirit or love which consists of:

Light

Righteous Desire-Empathy

Discernment

Excitement of life

Righteous Mind

Prudent Wisdom

Loving Wisdom

However, these seven spirits of peace of the Holy Spirit that each human being is born with on earth soon becomes corrupted by the low level third dimensional frequencies of planet earth that sometimes become corrupted into the seven spirits of wrath or evil spirit which are:

Darkness

Selfish Desire

Wrathful wisdom of the flesh-Wrath, vengeance, judgement

Ignorance with us versus them mentality

Excitement of Death-gluttony and addictions

Kingdom of the Flesh-greed, power

Foolish wisdom of the flesh-No concept of God or spirit worlds

When Jesus cast out these seven demons from Mary Magdalene's spirit, he resolved these demons back to their original form of peace and love that she had originally at her birth.

Mary Magdalene, the wife and disciple of Jesus was a central figure in the Gnostic Christian writings which included:

The Dialogue of the Savior

The Pistis Sophia

The Gospel of Thomas

The Gospel of Philip

The Gospel of Mary Magdelene

And all of these religious texts portray Mary Magdalene as the wife and disciple of Jesus and the leader of Jesus' women's corps. Mary Magdelene was Jesus' closest and most beloved disciple and the only person who fully understood all of Jesus' teachings. Mary Magdalene, Jesus' mother Mary, and young woman, Rebecca who fell in love with Jesus during his youth and John Zebedee were the only four people who never left Jesus' side while he was dying for five hours on the cross, while the rest of his apostles and disciples went into hiding. Mary Magdalene was also there to witness Jesus' entire crucifixion, burial and she was the first person to see Jesus after his resurrection on the third day from the dead. After the ascension of Jesus when he went back home to his Universal Father in Paradise on May 18, A.D. 30, Mary Magdalene later moved to France where she was buried in the lower area of a large church.

The Alpheus twin apostles began serving the Last Supper meal to Jesus, his wife Mary Magdalene and the ten apostles with their first course consisting of bread, wine, bitter herbs and a dried fruit paste and as everyone at the table ate in silence, Jesus told everyone that his hour had come and it was time for him to return home to his Paradise Father and that it was never required that one of his own apostles to betray him, because at the end of every one of the twelve Creator Sons final bestowal they each have to walk through the portal of death only to rise again in three days. After Jesus finished talking, he leaned over towards Apostle Judas Iscariot telling him to go quickly to do what he had decided to do, and Judas got up and quickly left the upper room to finish his betrayal of Jesus. This Last Supper was Jesus' last appeal to Apostle Judas Iscariot to not betray and desert him, but it was to no avail.

Jesus, his wife Mary Magdalene and the eleven apostles then sang Psalm 118 at the end of their Last Supper and the apostles went to stand up to leave and head back to their camp at Gethsemane Park, but Jesus signaled for everyone to sit back down and Jesus then told the apostles once again that his hour had come and in a very short time he was going to be leaving earth, but in the ages to come during the twenty-first century on earth, humanity will once again begin to ascend back home to heaven and then mortal man will see Jesus again on the new heaven on earth.

Jesus then proceeded to preach a farewell discourse to the apostles where he after talking to his Universal Father, promised to send a new helper, a comforter into the hearts of all believers, the Spirit of Truth-the Holy Spirit and Jesus then approached each individual apostle and gave them their final specific warning instructions. At around ten o'clock on this same Thursday night, April 6, A.D. 30, Jesus led the eleven apostles from Elizah and Mary Mark's home back to their Gethsemane Park Camp. Ever since the day that young John Mark spent the day with Jesus talking and praying in the Judea Hills, his job was to keep a watchful eye on Jesus, so on that Thursday night John Mark followed Jesus and the apostles closely as they traveled back to their camp. A few minutes after arriving back at their camp Jesus told the eleven apostles that his time with them was now very short, and he asked them to all pray with him. David Zebedee had already made arrangements to stand guard that night on the upper trail that led directly from Bethany to Jerusalem and John Mark stood guard near the road that ran by the brook to Jerusalem. However, John Mark left his post for a minute and while he was hiding in the bushes watching Jesus, he saw and overheard everything that happened during the moments that the guards arrested Jesus in the Garden of Gethsemane. Things were pretty quiet in their camp for now, so Jesus took Apostles Peter, James and John with him up to the nearby ravine where he could pray in solitude.

Jesus then asked his three apostles to watch and stay with him while he prayed to his Father, but the three apostles kept on falling asleep and Jesus had to wake them up three times.

Before Judas Iscariot brought the Roman soldiers to their Gethsemane Camp to betray Jesus with a kiss on the cheek, Jesus had finished praying to his Universal Father and he had fully regained his customary poise, because his spirit had triumphed over the flesh and his faith and strength had asserted itself over all of Jesus' human tendencies to fear or to have any doubts. Jesus' supreme test of his full realization of his next path had been met and Jesus acceptably passed this test and once again Jesus was ready and prepared to face his enemies with the full assurance as a mortal man who was dedicated to do his Paradise Father's will. After Jesus finished praying on that Thursday night in the ravine, he awakened the three apostles for the fourth time and suggested that they all go to their tents and sleep to prepare for the next day's duties. Jesus then left the three apostles, and he walked down alone towards the olive press near the entrance of Gethsemane Park. Jesus had forbidden his three apostles and his twenty Greek friends from going with him on that Thursday night, because Jesus knew that the plan for his death had its origin in the councils of the religious rulers of the Jews and with the full approval of his son Lucifer and earth's fallen Planetary Prince Caligastia. Jesus also knew that all of these rebels of the Lucifer Rebellion would also be pleased to see all of his apostles killed right along with him, so for their own safety Jesus made them all stay behind at their camp. Jesus' young friend John Mark had quickly ran through the olive trees when he saw Jesus, leaving the camp and he hid in a small shed near the olive press where he waited for Apostle Judas Iscariot, the traitor to come to betray Jesus with the members of the Roman guard. So along with John Mark watching Jesus were also a large number of celestial hosts from Paradise observing Jesus during his final hours.

On Thursday, April 6, A.D. 30 Judas Iscariot left the temple in Jerusalem at eleven o'clock in the evening with a company of sixty armed soldiers and guards who were carrying torches and lanterns. As soon as all of Jesus' disciples saw the armed soldiers with their torches swing around the brow of the hill, they all knew that these soldiers were coming to arrest Jesus, and they all rushed down to the olive press where Jesus was silently sitting in the solitude of the moonlight. As the company of soldiers approached on one side, the disciples approached on the other side. As these two groups stood there motionless, Judas walked forward and planted his traitorous kiss on the brow of Jesus to identify him to the Roman soldiers. Jesus then gave Judas Iscariot his last chance to not betray him, so Jesus stepped to one side asking the Roman soldiers who did they seek and when the captain of the Roman guard stated that he was looking for Jesus of Nazareth, Jesus then stated that he was Jesus of Nazareth and Judas then kissed Jesus on his brow.

Jesus was then ready to go back to Jerusalem with the Roman soldiers and captain of the soldiers allowed all of Jesus' disciples to go their way in peace.

However, when Apostle Peter saw that the Roman soldiers were getting ready to bind Jesus' hands, Apostle Peter drew his sword and sliced one of the Roman soldier's ear off. Jesus then quickly miraculously healed this soldier by placing the severed ear back in place on his head. Young John Mark suspected that the Roman soldiers were taking Jesus to Annas the Jewish high priest's palace, so he ran around the olive orchard so he would arrive there before the Roman soldiers did with Jesus in their custody. Young John Mark then hid in the bushes near the entrance gate of high priest Annas' palace and waited for them to arrive. About this time Apostle John Zebedee remembered Jesus' prior instructions for him to always be near at hand to him, so he hurried up and walked beside Jesus as he walked along between the two Roman captains to Annas' palace. When the Roman captain saw John Zebedee come alongside Jesus to walk with him, he ordered the Jewish captain not to bother John Zebedee in any way, because the Roman law allowed for any prisoner to have the right to have at least one friend to stand with him before his judgment. This explains why Apostle John Zebedee was permitted to stay by Jesus' side all the way through Jesus' trying experience of his trials and crucifixion. The Jewish guards were all afraid to say anything to Apostle John Zebedee, because he had the high-status job as being the observer of the transactions of the Jewish ecclesiastical court.

All the way as Jesus, Apostle John Zebedee and the guards walked to Annas' palace Jesus never spoke a word and Jesus spent about three hours at the high priest's palace that

583

was located in Olivet. The high priest Annas felt threatened by Jesus' clearing out the money changes and cattle from out of the temple in Jerusalem during the prior week, because it caused him to lose a lot of money. The high priest Annas was also perturbed with Jesus' refusal to answer any of his questions, so he thought it would just be best to go ahead and send Jesus to the Sanhedrin castle where his son Caiaphas lived.

At three o'clock in the morning on Friday, April 7, A.D. 30, the chief Jewish priest of the Sanhedrin brought Jesus before their court of inquiry for his personal trial and Jesus appeared before the Sanhedrin court wearing his usual garments with his hands bound behind his back. The entire Sanhedrin court was startled and confused by Jesus' majestic appearance, because the court members had never seen a prisoner on trial for his life have so much composure as Jesus. The Jewish chief high priest Caiphas kept rushing up to Jesus waving his finger in Jesus' face asking him if he was the Son of God and Jesus stated that he was and that soon he was going back home to his Father where the Son of Man would be clothed with power and once more reign over all the hosts of heaven.

After Jesus had so unexpectedly answered high priest Caiaphas, he then stepped forward and slapped Jesus in the face with his hand. This first court session that Jesus had at the Sanhedrin palace ended at four thirty on Friday morning April 7, A.D. 30 and the Jewish law required that when the death sentence was issued that the prisoner was entitled to have two court sessions. So, at five thirty on that same Friday morning, Jesus was taken to his second court session before Pontious Pilate.

Jesus' second court session before Pontious Pilate lasted for only thirty minutes and when it adjourned Jesus was indicted on three charges of being worthy of receiving the death penalty. After Jesus' two court sessions he was then brought before tetrarch Herod Antipas and the Roman governor Pontious Pilate and at this court session Pontious Pilate appeared before a mob crowd outside of his window stating that Jesus was a religious offender only and that he would not consent to enforce the death penalty. Pontious Pilate was just about ready to release Jesus when the Jewish high priest Caiaphas approached Pilate telling him that if he released Jesus then he was not a friend of Caesar. Pontious Pilate was afraid of falling out of favor with Caesar and he did not want to risk having a civil disturbance or riot during Passover time in Jerusalem, so when Pilate released the thief Barabbas instead of Jesus, the mob crowd cheered. Pilate then washed his hands in a water basin telling the mob crowd that he was innocent of the blood of Jesus.

At about eight o'clock on Friday morning on April 7, A.D. 30 Jesus was placed in the custody of the Roman soldiers who were there to crucify him. While the Jewish high priest Caiaphas was making his final report to the Sanhedrin about Jesus' death sentence, Judas appeared before the Sanhedrin court asking to claim his reward money. All of the Jewish high priests who were there that night felt disgust towards Judas for his betrayal of Jesus and they looked at Judas, the traitor with nothing but contempt. By this time Judas was starting to become disillusioned about receiving the thirty pieces of silver he was about to be paid for being a traitor. Judas was beginning to feel stunned and dumbfounded and when one of the high priest's servants tapped Judas on the shoulder and handed him a bag with thirty pieces of silver inside, Judas was crushed, because he was expecting to be brought before a full meeting with the Sanhedrin court to receive praise and honor for his betrayal of Jesus. When Judas tried to enter the hall to appeal to the Sanhedrin to receive some type of recognition, the doors were barred locked, and they would not let Judas enter. So, by this time Judas was feeling humiliated, because after his betrayal of Jesus all he had to show for his cowardice actions was a bag with thirty pieces of silver inside of it.

Judas Iscariot wandered out through the streets of Jerusalem walking through the crowds who were on their way to witness the crucifixion of Jesus. From a distance Judas saw the Roman soldiers raise the cross with Jesus nailed to it and Judas then rushed back to the temple in Jerusalem and forced his way past the doorkeeper. As Judas found himself standing before the Sanhedrin officers, Judas told them that he had sinned and betrayed Jesus who was innocent and that they the Sanhedrin officers had totally insulted him.

When the Sanhedrin officers heard what Judas said to them, they all laughed at Judas telling him that Jesus had already been crucified and to get out of their presence. As Judas Iscariot was leaving the Sanhedrin officers' chambers, he threw the thirty pieces of silver on the temple floor and he now realized what the true nature of sin was and all of the fascination, intoxication and wrongdoing he had in his mind were all gone, vanished. Judas was now all alone as he walked through the streets of Jerusalem alone, forsaken and full of despair. Judas continued to walk on through the streets of Jerusalem, outside the city walls, and on down into the terrible solitude of the valley of Hinnon, and there Judas Iscariot climbed up the steep rocks, took the strings from his cloak, fastened one end of his cloak to a tree on the steep rocks and cast himself over the precipice. However, Judas managed to botch his own suicide, because his hands were shaking as he tied the strings to the tree and they broke loose which then caused Judas' internal body parts and organs to be smashed to pieces where all of his body parts splattered all over the rocks below and to this day, this site is still called the mountain of disembowelment.

It was just before nine o'clock in the morning on Friday, April 7, A.D. 30 when the Roman soldiers led Jesus to Golgotha hill to be crucified and the two thieves who had been stealing along with the thief Barabbas who was released were crucified next to Jesus. It was the custom to have the prisoner make the journey to Golgotha by the longest road so that as many people as possible would get the chance to get a view of the condemned criminal. Crucifixion was not the preferred Jewish mode of punishment, but both the Greeks and the Romans had learned about this method of execution from the Phoenicians. Even tetrarch Herod Antipas with all his cruelty did not prefer to use this method to condemn a criminal. The Romans never crucified their own Roman citizens, only slaves and certain prisoners who were deemed as being worthy to suffer this type of dishonorable mode of death.

During the Roman siege of Jerusalem just forty years after the crucifixion of Jesus, the entire Golgotha hill was covered by thousands on thousands of crosses day by day and and the heart of the entire Jewish race died on crosses on Golgotha hill during this time period.

It was the custom to remove all of the clothes from those who were going to die by crucifixion, but the Jews objected to this public exposure, so the Roman soldiers always provided a suitable loin cloth for all those who were sentenced to die by crucifixion. There was also a society of Jewish women in Jerusalem who always sent one of their representatives to crucifixions for the purpose of offering drugged filled wine to the victim to help to lessen his suffering, but when Jesus tasted this wine full of narcotics, as thirsty as he was, he refused to drink it, because Jesus wanted to retain his own human mortal consciousness until the end.

When Apostle John Zebedee arrived at Jesus' crucifixion with his mother Mary, his sister Babe Ruth and brother Jude, Jesus smiled when he saw them, but he said nothing. Jesus was hung on the cross at half past nine on Friday morning April 7, A.D. 30 and by eleven o'clock that morning over one thousand people had gathered to witness his crucifixion. All throughout these dreadful hours, the unseen hosts of celestial beings of our universe of Nebadon stood in silence as they watched this extraordinary event of Jesus, one of the twelve Creator Sons of God dying the death of a mortal man on the cross. All of the twelve Creator Sons of Paradise must complete their seven bestowals before they can assume their position as the system sovereign of their assigned universe just like Jesus. During each of the twelve Creator Sons seventh and final bestowal they each have to walk through the portal of death and rise from the dead on the third day, but no Creator Son except for Jesus was killed by crucifixion during their final bestowal. Standing near the cross during Jesus' crucifixion were Mary his mother, Mary Magdalene his wife, his brother and sister Jude and Babe Ruth, Rebecca of Sepphoris who had fallen in love with Jesus during his youth and other close friends and followers. Shortly after noon the sky grew dark as night and fine grains of sand began to blow in the air and it was just before three o'clock in the afternoon when Jesus with a loud voice cried out: "It is finished, Father into your hands I commend my spirit." When one of the Roman centurions saw how Jesus died on the cross with so much courage and faith, he immediately began to believe in Jesus and his teachings. It was common for the victims of crucifixions to linger on and stay alive on the cross for two or three days, but due to Jesus' overwhelming emotional agony and acute spiritual anguish that Jesus was experiencing at the end of his life as a mortal man on earth, he died in less than five and one-half hours. The crucifixion of Jesus ended a day of tragedy and sorrow for our vast universe whose hosts of celestial beings had shuddered at the shocking spectacle of the crucifixion of the human incarnation of Michael of Nebadon, their beloved system sovereign as a mortal man Jesus. All of the celestial beings in Paradise were stunned by this exhibition on planet earth that displayed mortal callousness and human perversity.

In the meantime, Jesus' wealthy uncle Joseph of Arimathea along with Jesus' friend Nicodemus went to Pontious Pilate to claim Jesus' body, because a crucified person could not be buried in a Jewish cemetery, so Jesus was instead buried in Joseph of Arimathea's family tomb. The day and a half that Jesus' mortal body lay in his tomb which was the time between his death on the cross and his resurrection is one chapter in the earth career of Michael of Nebadon that proved to be an interesting experience for Jesus of Nazareth. Many of Jesus' disciples and followers had forgotten that Jesus had promised to rise from his death on the third day, but his enemies had not forgotten.

The chief Jewish priests, Pharisees and Sadducees all remembered the reports they had received that Jesus would rise from the dead on the third day, so these Jewish leaders asked Pontious Pilate to provide them with additional soldiers to add to their own guards to sit and watch at Jesus' tomb. Twenty soldiers were assigned to guard Jesus' tomb, and they rolled a large second stone in front of the tomb entrance and set the seal of Pontious Pilate all around and on all of the stones. These soldiers remained on watch at Jesus' tomb up to the hour of his resurrection and the Jews provided them with food and drinks. All throughout the day on Saturday, April 8, A.D. 30 all of Jesus' apostles remained in hiding until late that Saturday night when at that time their young friend John Mark secretly told the eleven apostles to meet with him at his parent's home just before midnight in the upper room where they had eaten the Last Supper with Jesus.

Jesus' physical body rested in his uncle Joseph of Arimathea's family's tomb until about three o'clock on Sunday morning and these were some of Jesus' experiences that occurred in his tomb during the time period of about thirty-six hours.

The Creator Son consciousness of Michael of Nebadon, Paradise was at large and free from its associated mind of the incarnation of Jesus of Nazareth.

The former Divine Personal Thought Adjuster of Jesus who had also been present with both Machiventa Melchizedek and Jesus of Nazareth during their mortal life on earth was in the personal command of the assembled celestial hosts of Paradise.

The acquired spirit identity of Jesus of Nazareth was built up during his lifetime on earth as a mortal man by the direct efforts of his Divine Thought Adjuster and later it was effectively used by Jesus' never-ending choices to continue to do his Father's will. The soul identity of Jesus now resides in the bosom of the Universal Father in Paradise to be subsequently released for the leadership of the Nebadon Corps of the Finality in their undisclosed destiny with the not yet created universes of the unorganized realms of outer space.

The human mortal consciousness of Jesus slept during these thirty-six hours and the resurrection of his life followed Jesus' sleep of death.

In the vast court of the resurrection halls located on the first mansion world in Paradise, there is a magnificent morontia structure known as the Michael Memorial that now bears the seal of Archangel Gabriel. This memorial was built in Paradise right after Michael of Nebadon ascended from earth as Jesus of Nazareth on May 18, A.D. 30 and it has these words written on it:

"In Commemoration of the mortal transit of Jesus of Nazareth on Earth."

The official records in Edentia, Paradise show that during the thirty-six hours that Jesus slept in his tomb that the supreme council of Salvington, Paradise numbering one hundred held an executive meeting on earth under the direction of Gabriel. These same records also indicate that the Ancients Of Days of Uversa, Paradise communicated with Michael of Nebadon regarding the status of the affairs of the Nebadon universe during the thirty-six hours Jesus was asleep in his tomb. Also, one message also passed between Michael and his older brother Immanuel on Salvington, Paradise while Jesus' body lay sleeping in his tomb on earth.

The records on Edentia, Paradise also indicate that the Constellation Father of Nolatiadek, Paradise was on earth receiving instructions from Michael of Nebadon while Jesus was sleeping in his tomb on earth.

The personality of Jesus was not always asleep and unconscious during the time of his apparent physical death during the thirty-six hours he spent in his tomb. The death of Jesus on the cross portrays the full measure of Jesus' supreme devotion of the true shepherd for even the unworthy members of his flock. The cross forever shows that the attitude of Jesus towards sinners was neither condemnation nor condonation, but rather of eternal and loving salvation. The sufferings that Jesus had to endure were not confined to his crucifixion, because Jesus as a mortal man had spent more than twenty-five years on the cross of a real intense mortal existence on planet earth. The real value of the cross consists in the fact that it was the supreme and final expression of Jesus' love and his completed revelation of his mercy.

On the other worlds of time and space in our Nebadon universe as well as on earth, this spectacle of the death of one of the twelve Creator Sons as the mortal man Jesus on the cross of Golgotha has stirred up the emotions of mortals and it has aroused the highest devotion from the angels. If mortal man cannot appreciate and understand the reasons and meaning behind Jesus' seventh and final bestowal on earth, we must know that Jesus' death on the cross was not to affect man's reconciliation with God, but to stimulate man's realization of our Universal Father's eternal love and his Creator Son Jesus' mercy and to continue to broadcast these universal truths to our entire universe.

Soon after the burial of Jesus on Friday, April 7, A.D. 30, the chief of the archangels of Nebadon, Paradise who at the time was on earth, summoned his council of the resurrection of sleeping free will creatures and began to decide on what technique they were going to use to restore the life of Jesus of Nazareth. These assembled sons of the local universe creatures who were all created by Michael of Nebadon did not do this on their own, because Gabriel had assembled the archangels to do this. By midnight on this Friday, April 7, A.D. 30, the chief of the archangels decided that they themselves could do nothing to resurrect the Creator Son Michael of Nebadon in his incarnation as Jesus.

This council of archangels accepted Gabriel's advice when he instructed them that since Michael had laid down his mortal life with his free will, that he also had the power to bring his mortal life back up again based on his own determination. Shortly afterwards the council of the archangels adjourned their meeting with the Life Carriers and their associates who were in charge with creature rehabilitation and morontia creation. The Life Carriers and Jesus' Divine Personal Thought Adjuster told the assembled celestial hosts from Paradise that Michael of Nebadon was still conducting his universe activities while the body of Jesus lay in his tomb and that all everyone could do at this point was to patiently wait for the further developments from Michael of Nebadon.

At about two forty-five early on that Sunday morning, April 9, A.D. 30, the Paradise incarnation committee consisting of seven celestial beings arrived on earth outside of

Jesus' tomb. At ten minutes before three o'clock that morning intense vibrations began to manifest within Jesus' burial tomb and at two minutes past three o'clock on that Sunday morning, the resurrected morontia form and personality of Jesus of Nazareth came forth from his tomb.

When a mortal man passes through the portal of death, this transition intervenes between the mortal body and the subsequent spirit body which is called the morontia body. This intermediate state, the morontia body differs markedly on the various worlds of time and space in our Nebadon universe.

The morontia realms are the local universe liaison spheres that are located between the material and spiritual levels of mortal beings' existence. The morontia beings have existed on planet earth since the early days of when earth's fallen Planetary Prince Caligastia had the one hundred morontia beings as a part of his staff. From time to time this transition state from a human mortal to a morontia being has been taught to some mortals. The morontia being extends over the various stages in the local universe and it is the only possible way that material mortal beings can attain the threshold of the spirit world. What magic could death, the natural dissolution of the material body holds that through the simple steps that instantly transforms the mortal and material mind into an immortal and perfected morontia being.

During the life of a mortal being living in the flesh, the divine spirit indwells the mortal being almost as a thing apart, but in reality, it is the indwelling of mortal man by the Universe Paradise Father. During the mortal beings' morontia stage of life, the spirit becomes to be a real part of the personality and after the morontia being successfully passes through the five hundred and seventy progressive transformations on the seven Paradise mansion worlds, then a mortal being ascends from the local material realm into the spiritual realm of creature life.

Apostle Paul learned about the existence of the morontia worlds in Paradise and the existence of the morontia beings, because he wrote these words:

"They have in heaven a better and more enduring substance as your living body and these morontia beings are real, literal and even as in the city that has foundations whose builder and maker is God. And each of these marvelous seven mansion worlds in Paradise are spheres of a better country that is a heavenly one. "

After the resurrected Jesus walked out of his burial tomb, the body of flesh that he had lived in on earth for almost thirty-six years was still lying in his burial tomb undisturbed and wrapped in a linen sheet, just like it had been laid to rest on that previous Friday afternoon. The stone that had sealed the entrance to the tomb was not disturbed in any way and none of the twenty guards at Jesus' tomb suspected that Jesus had risen to a new and higher form of existence as a morontia being and that the body of Jesus that they had been guarding was now nothing but the discarded outer layer of covering that had no further connections with the resurrected morontia body with the personality of Jesus.

Mankind is slow to perceive that in all that is personal, matter is the skeleton of the morontia body, and both are the reflected shadow of the enduring spirit reality. How long will it be before man regards time as nothing but merely the moving image of eternity and space as the fleeting shadow of the Paradise realities that are located in our Nebadon universe right above dimension thirty-six. No being of our universe nor any personality from another universe had anything to do with the morontia resurrection of Jesus of Nazareth, because Jesus used his own power to complete this transformation.

On Friday, April 7, A.D. 30, Jesus laid down his life as a mortal man on earth, and early on Sunday morning April 9, A.D. 30, Jesus brought his life back as a morontia being of the system of Satania in Norlatiadek. This complete phenomenon that is associated with Jesus' mortal transit, his morontia resurrection occurred in his burial tomb where the mortal material remains of Jesus still laid wrapped in linen burial clothes.

Early on that same Sunday morning of April 9, A.D. 30 suddenly seven celestial beings from Paradise appeared and surrounded Jesus' tomb, but they did not do anything in connection with Jesus' resurrection from the dead. As soon as Jesus appeared in his resurrected morontia body and stood beside Gabriel above his tomb, these seven celestial beings immediately left earth for Uversa, Paradise.

These are the facts relating to the resurrection of Jesus of Nazareth on Sunday, April 9, A.D. 30.

Jesus' material physical body was not a part of his resurrected personality. When Jesus walked out of his burial tomb, his earth body of flesh remained undisturbed in his burial tomb. Jesus came out of his burial tomb without moving the large stones and Pontious Pilate seals that were on the entrance to his tomb.

Jesus did not come out from his burial tomb as a spirit and not as Michael of Nebadon and he did not come out in his previous form as the Creator Son like he was before his incarnation from the resurrection halls from the first mansion world of Paradise. The presence of the Michael of Nebadon memorial in the center of the vast court of the resurrection halls points to the fact that Jesus' resurrection on earth was related to this large memorial that was built in Paradise.

The first thing that Jesus did when he arose from his burial tomb was to greet Gabriel from Salvington, Paradise and instruct him to continue to be in executive charge of the Nebadon universe affairs under the direction of his older brother Immanuel until his return to Paradise. Jesus then directed the chief of the Melchizedeks family, Father Melchizedek to tell his older brother Immanuel hello. Jesus then asked the Most High of Edentia, Paradise on May 18, A.D. 30.

for the certification from the Ancients Of Days for his mortal transit. Jesus then turned to the assembled morontia groups from the seven mansion worlds who had gathered to welcome and greet their Creator Son, Jesus who then spoke his first words of his morontia life which were as follows:

"Having finished my life in the flesh, I will tarry here for a short time in transition form so that I may more fully know the life of my ascendant creatures and further reveal the will of my Father in Paradise."

After Jesus finished speaking, he signaled to his Divine Personal Thought Adjuster and all of the universe celestial beings who had assembled on earth to witness his resurrection to return to their respective universe assignments. Jesus then began his initiation requirements to enter into the morontia world which lasted for one hour and this initiation was interrupted twice by Jesus' former mortal associates who had come looking into Jesus' empty tomb to verify that he had resurrected from the dead. After Jesus completed the required one-hour morontia life initiation, the mortal transit of Jesus which was his morontia resurrection was complete and this was the beginning of Jesus' transitory experience as a personality midway between the material and spiritual worlds. Jesus had completed his resurrection all through the power that was within himself without any assistance, and he was now living as a morontia being while his material earth body of his flesh still laid undisturbed in his tomb.

At ten minutes past three o'clock in the morning while the resurrected morontia Jesus talked with the group of morontia beings who had gathered from their morontia first mansion world of Paradise, the chief of the archangels and the resurrection angels approached Gabriel to ask if they could have the mortal body of Jesus so that it could be placed into immediate dissolution by invoking the process of accelerated time.

The chief of the archangels told Gabriel that it had been hard enough for them to have to watch Jesus suffer crucifixion on earth and they wanted to be spared the memory of having to watch the slow decay of the human shell that was left in the tomb of their Creator Son and Upholder of their Nebadon universe, Jesus. After Gabriel received permission from the senior Most High of Edentia, Paradise, the archangel spokesperson for the celestial hosts were allowed to use accelerated time to immediately dispose of the physical remains of Jesus' mortal earth body. The chief of the archangels with the help of the rest of the assembled angels, numerous celestial hosts and midway beings then took possession of Jesus' lifeless physical body, because Jesus' dead physical body could not be removed from his tomb like his resurrected morontia body had been able to escape his sealed tomb. With the help of certain morontia beings, the morontia body can be made at one time as the spirit so that it can become indifferent to ordinary matter, while at the same time the morontia body can also become discernible and contractable to the material beings that are just like the mortals living on the particular realm.

The secondary earth midway beings were assigned the job to roll away the large stones from the entrance to Jesus' burial tomb so that Jesus' morontia body could walk out of his tomb. When the twenty assigned guards in the dim lights of the early morning saw the huge stone begin to roll away on its own from the entrance to Jesus' tomb (humans cannot see midway beings), and without any visible means for this movement, the guards were overcome with fear and panic and they all fled from the scene in haste. The ten Jewish guards fled back to their homes and the ten Roman guards fled back to the fortress of Antonia to report to the Centurian what they had seen at Jesus' burial tomb.

The mortal remains of Jesus went through the same natural process of disintegration that the dead human bodies do except that, in the point of time this natural process of dissolution of Jesus' mortal physical body was greatly accelerated at such a high rate of speed that it was an instantaneous event. The true evidence of the resurrection of Michael of Nebadon who incarnated on planet earth as Jesus of Nazareth was spiritual in nature and during Jesus' personal experience as a morontia being on earth for forty days after his resurrection, Jesus was able to become a part of the personal experience of over one thousand of his followers before he finally left earth and ascended back home to Paradise on Resurrection Sunday, May 18, A.D. 30.

At four thirty in the morning on Sunday, April 9, A.D. 30 Gabriel summoned some of the archangels to his side to get ready to inaugurate the general resurrection and termination of Jesus' Adamic dispensation on planet earth. When the vast hosts of seraphim and cherubim assembled into the proper formation for this great event, the morontia Michael (Jesus) appeared before Gabriel saying to let the roll call of the planetary resurrection on earth begin.

The circuit of archangels then operated for the first time on earth and as the hosts of the archangels moved to their positions of spiritual polarity of earth, and when Gabriel gave the signal, there flashed to the first mansion world of Paradise the voice of Gabriel loudly saying, "By the mandate of Michael of Nebadon, let the dead of all the earth dispensation rise!" And at that moment all of the survivors of the human race on earth who had fallen asleep since the days of Adam and Eve and who had already gone on to judgement suddenly appeared in the resurrection halls ready to begin their morontia life in Paradise. And in an instant of time the seraphim made those resurrected souls from the time of Adam and Eve ready to be transported to the seven mansion worlds in Paradise. All of these mortal souls who had been sleeping since the times of Adam and Eve on earth were present at the moment of their awakening in the resurrection halls on the first mansion world of Paradise at this time, because of Gabriel's presence there in connection with the morontia resurrection of Jesus of Nazareth. This was the third of the planetary roll calls or complete dispensational resurrection to ever occur in Paradise. The first planetary roll call occurred at the time of the arrival of earth's original Planetary Prince Caligastia. The second roll call occurred during the times of Adam and Eve and this third roll call after the resurrection of Jesus of Nazareth signalized Jesus' morontia resurrection, the mortal transit of Jesus from planet earth and back home to Paradise.

When the signal of the planetary resurrection had been received by the chief of the archangels, the Personalized Divine Thought Adjuster who had indwelled in both Machiventa Melchizedek and Jesus of Nazareth relinquished his authority over the celestial beings from Paradise who had assembled on earth and to all of these sons of the local universe back to their respective commanders. And when the Personal Divine Thought Adjuster had released his authority, he then went to Salvington, Paradise to register with Michael's older brother Immanuel for the completion of the mortal transit of Michael of Nebadon and he was immediately followed by the celestial beings who were no longer required to be on duty anymore on earth. However, Gabriel remained on earth to be with the morontia being, Jesus until his ascension back home to Paradise forty days later.

A few minutes before three o'clock in the morning on Sunday, April 9, A.D. 30, Jesus' widow Mary Magdalene along with five other female followers of Jesus were on their way to visit Jesus' tomb to anoint his body with oils. As these women were walking out of the

Damascus gate, they saw twenty Roman and Jewish guards running into the city of Jerusalem and these women paused to look at these fleeing guards, but they continued on their journey to Jesus' tomb. When Mary Magdalene and the rest of the women arrived at Jesus' tomb, they were surprised to see that the large stone to the tomb's entrance had been rolled away from the entrance. Mary Magdalene walked around one of the smaller stones and then she walked into Jesus' open tomb where she saw that Jesus' body was gone and in its place were only linen grave clothes.

It never occurred to Mary Magdalene and the rest of the women that Jesus had risen from the dead. While Mary Magdalene and the rest of the women were sitting at the entrance to Jesus' empty tomb, Mary Magdalene was the first one to see a silent motionless stranger standing near Jesus' tomb and she thought that this stranger was the caretaker for this garden area, so she asked the stranger where he had taken Jesus' body. The stranger then told Mary Magdalene to remember that Jesus had told them that he would die and rise again on the third day. At that moment Mary Magdelene recognized Jesus' voice, but she noticed that Jesus' physical body had changed, so she did not recognize that this stranger was Jesus. Even though Mary Magdalene was a human mortal, her eyes were able to see the resurrected body of Jesus, because of the special ministry of the transformers, the midway beings and the designated morontia beings who accompanied Jesus everywhere he went during his final forty days on earth. Mary Magdalene then kneeled down and tried to embrace Jesus' feet, but he told her not to touch him, because as a morontia being he was only going to be on earth with them for forty days before his ascension back home to Paradise to his Father. Jesus then told Mary Magdalene to go and tell the eleven apostles that he had risen and that she had talked to him.

Now that the morontia Jesus had resurrected from the dead he was now preparing to spend this short time he had on earth to experience the ascending morontia life as a mortal man living on earth. Jesus' experience as a morontia being was just like what all of the rest of the Satania mortals pass through during the seven transitional stages they go through after death on the seven mansion worlds in Jerusem, Paradise.

All of this power was inherent in Jesus which was the endowment to create life which enabled Jesus to rise from the dead, the gift of eternal life which Jesus bestows on all believers of his teachings of God's kingdom. Morontia bodies do not have circulating blood, and they do not eat food, but morontia beings are real. So, when the various believers saw Jesus after his resurrection, they all really saw him and it was not a hallucination. The eleven apostles did not want Jesus to leave them, but they just were not expecting his resurrection when it happened, and the apostles refused to believe that Jesus had really risen from the dead until they had had absolute proof.

A week after Jesus' resurrection Apostle John Zebedee took Jesus' mother Mary to his home in Bethsaida and Jesus' older brother James stayed in Jerusalem with his family. The rest of Jesus' family returned to Galilee while David Zebedee after he first married

Jesus' youngest sister Babe Ruth, left Bethany to move Lazarus' sisters Martha and Mary to Philadelphia. From the time of Jesus' morontia resurrection up until the time of his ascension back to heaven, Jesus made nineteen separate appearances to his followers in his visible morontia form.

During these nineteen separate appearances, one thousand people were able to have a spiritual experience with Jesus in his morontia resurrected body. Jesus' first appearance was to his wife Mary Magdalene at his burial tomb and his second appearance was to his mother Mary and to the rest of the women who had come to his tomb to anoint his deceased body with oils. Jesus' third morontia appearance occurred at about noon on Sunday, April 9, A.D. 30 in Bethany while Jesus' oldest brother James was standing in Lazarus' Garden when James became aware of a stranger standing by his side and when the stranger spoke his name, James then knew that it was Jesus. Everyone all had difficulty recognizing Jesus' morontia body, but as soon as Jesus spoke, then they recognized his voice and then knew that it was Jesus. When James realized it was Jesus he fell to his knees, but Jesus told James to remain standing while they talked. Jesus and his brother James walked through Lazarus' Garden where they talked for three minutes and as they got close to Lazarus' house Jesus told his oldest brother James farewell. James then rushed into Lazarus' house telling everyone that he had just walked and talked with Jesus in Lazarus' Garden and then they all began to believe that Jesus had risen from the dead. David Zebedee who had just married Jesus' sister Babe Ruth told everyone that he was also expecting to see and talk to Jesus and he did not have to wait long, because at about two o'clock on that same afternoon, Jesus made his fourth morontia appearance to his brother-in-law David Zebedee inside of Martha and Mary's new home in Philadelphia when he suddenly appeared at their open back door to greet them all, but as soon as they started to move towards Jesus to embrace him, Jesus vanished from their sight.

The fifth morontia appearance of Jesus occurred in the presence of twenty-five women followers who were meeting at Jesus' Uncle Joseph of Arimathea's home at around four o'clock in the evening on that same Sunday. Mary Magdalene was in the middle of telling her story to this group of women about how she had seen Jesus when suddenly all of the women saw the morontia body of Jesus standing among them and Jesus greeted them all and then vanished from their sight. Counting all of the five morontia appearances Jesus had made so far to his family, friends and followers, his wife Mary Magdalene had witnessed four of them, because Mary Magdalene was not only very close to Jesus, but she was also his wife and Jesus gave Mary Magdalene secret teachings that the rest of the apostles did not receive, and he often openly kissed her on her mouth. Also, Mary Magdalene bathed and anointed Jesus' feet twice in public and according to the Judaic laws and customs when a woman bathes a man's feet or when a Jewish man kisses a woman in the mouth in public, this means they are husband and wife.

David Zebedee soon began sending out messengers to tell many of Jesus' followers about the resurrection of Jesus and the Jewish religious rulers and high priests began to get nervous, so they called a meeting on that same Sunday evening at eight o'clock in the evening.

At this meeting the Sanhedrin officers were all in a state of panic proposing to throw anyone out of the synagogue who claimed to have seen Jesus, and they even suggested that anyone claiming to have seen Jesus resurrected from the dead be put to death. This Sanhedrin meeting ended in a lot of confusion and panic, because they dared to think that they were through with Jesus. The Sanhedrin and Jewish high priests were about to discover that despite their crucifixion of Jesus that soon his teachings and new religion of Christianity were about to spread all throughout the entire Roman Empire and the known world.

At about half past four on this same Sunday evening Jesus made his sixth morontia appearance to forty of his Greek believer friends when he appeared in their midst, spoke to them briefly about peace, love and his ministry on earth and then he suddenly vanished from their sight. The rumors about Jesus' resurrection spread rapidly around the entire city of Jerusalem and everyone was excited about this great news.

In the small village of Emmanus which was seven miles west of Jerusalem two shepherd brothers, Cleopas and Jacob who were both followers of Jesus lived there and as they were walking on the road headed back home to their village, they began to talk about some of Jesus' teachings, his ministry work and especially about all of the rumors that his tomb was empty. While Cleopas and Jacob continued walking and talking, the morontia body of Jesus made his seventh appearance when Jesus suddenly appeared and began walking along side these two brothers. Cleopas had heard Jesus teach on many occasions and he had often eaten with Jesus at banquets in Jerusalem. Cleopas and Jacob didn't say a word while Jesus taught them some scriptures as they walked on the road to their village and at this point, the two brothers did not recognize Jesus and when they arrived at their humble home it was close to nightfall so they both insisted that Jesus come into their home to have dinner with them. As they sat down to eat dinner, the two brothers gave Jesus the bread to bless and as Jesus began to break and bless the bread, the two brothers' eyes opened, and they both recognized that their house guest was Jesus himself. As soon as Cleopas started to say that he was Jesus, the morontia body of Jesus suddenly vanished from their sight. Cleopas and Jacob then both said to each other that they now saw why their hearts were burning within while Jesus spoke to them while they walked along the road back home to their village. Cleopas and Jacob did not want to finish eating their dinner, because they were too excited about just seeing Jesus, so they rushed out and told everyone they could in Jerusalem to spread the good news that Jesus was risen from the dead.

At about nine o'clock on this same Sunday evening just before Jesus appeared to his apostles in the upper room of John Mark's parent's home, Cleopas and Jacob busted in to tell the apostles that they had just seen and talked to Jesus.

Resurrection Sunday was a terrible day for the ten apostles, because Apostle Thomas was alone drowning in his own sad troubles in Bethpage while the rest of the apostles were locked away in fear and despair in the upper room. The young lad John Mark was making sure that he kept the ten apostles informed on all the rumors and latest developments coming from the Sanhedrin in Jerusalem. Jesus had put off making his first morontia appearance to the apostles, because because he wanted Apostle Thomas to leave Bethpage and be with the rest of the apostles in the upper room and Jesus also wanted the apostles to think for a while about what he had told them about his death and resurrection. When John Mark finally found Apostle Thomas at Simon's house in Bethpage at around eleven o'clock that Sunday morning, he brought him back to the upper room to be with the rest of the ten apostles and at about half past eight on that Sunday evening Jesus appeared to Apostle Peter first in John Mark's parents' garden. This was Jesus' eighth morontia appearance since his resurrection earlier on that Sunday morning and Jesus appeared to Apostle Peter alone first, because Peter had been feeling a lot of doubt and guilt for his denial of Jesus three times in the garden on the night before Jesus was crucified. As Apostle Peter stood in John Mark's parents' garden his faith began to grow stronger and suddenly in front of him the form of a man appeared speaking to Peter in a familiar tone and Peter immediately knew that it was Jesus. Jesus and Peter walked and talked that evening about the past, present and future for about five minutes and then Jesus suddenly vanished from Apostle Peter's sight.

Apostle Peter then rushed to the upper room and told the ten apostles that he had just seen and talked to Jesus in the garden and that Jesus had forgiven him. Shortly after nine o'clock in the evening on that same Sunday, Jesus appeared to the ten apostles in the upper room telling them to continue to be strong, have faith in God and in each other and then Jesus suddenly vanished from their sight. This was Jesus' ninth morontia appearance and when he vanished from the apostles, they all fell to their knees praising God.

The next day on Monday, April 10, A.D. 30 Jesus spent the entire day with all of the other morontia beings who were living on earth at that time and these morontia beings 2,154 years ago were the participants who helped Jesus with his morontia transition experience and these morontia beings along with one million morontia directors and transition mortals had come from the seven mansion worlds in Paradise to help Jesus during his transition. Jesus spent all day Monday working with these splendid morontia and transition beings who taught Jesus all the ropes of living as a morontia being. Around midnight on this same Monday Jesus' morontia body was adjusted for his transition to the second stage of his morontia progression and as Jesus continued to advance in his morontia life, it became to be more technically difficult for the assisting morontia beings and their transforming associates to visualize Jesus to his human follower's material mortal eyes.

These are the progression of the stages of transition for Jesus' forty days of living as a morontia being on earth before he ascended and was received back as a citizen in Jerusem, Paradise and back into the embrace of the Most Highs of Edentia, Paradise.

April 10, A.D. 30-Jesus' second stage morontia body progression on earth began.

April 14, A.D. 30-Jesus' third stage morontia body progression on earth began.

April 17, A.D. 30-Jesus' fourth stage morontia body progression on earth began.

April 22, A.D. 30-Jesus' fifth stage morontia body progression on earth began.

April 27, A.D. 30-Jesus' sixth stage morontia body progression on earth began.

May 2, A.D. 30-Jesus' seventh stage morontia body progression on earth began.

May 7, A.D. 30-Jesus received once again Jerusem, Paradise citizenship.

May 18, A.D. 30-Jesus ascended and entered the embrace of the Most Highs in Edentia, Paradise.

These are the steps that Michael of Nebadon had to take to end his mortal incarnation as Jesus of Nazareth on earth in order to complete his service of universe experience to complete his seven bestowals from the beginning on the headquarters of the constellation and through the headquarters of the superuniverse. And it was by Jesus going through his seven transition stages of his morontia life during his final forty days on earth that Michael, the Creator Son of Nebadon finally completed and acceptably terminated his seventh and final universe bestowal on earth.

Jesus made his tenth morontia appearance at eight o'clock in the evening on Tuesday, April 11, A.D. 30 in Philadelphia where he appeared to Abner and Lazarus and five hundred of their religious associates who included fifty of Abner's evangelists. Abner and Lazurus had just begun their opening remarks at this special synagogue meeting to discuss the crucifixion and resurrection of Jesus and as Abner and Lazarus were standing together in the pulpit the congregation of five hundred saw Jesus suddenly appear standing between Abner and Lazarus. Jesus stepped forward because Abner and Lazarus did not see him at first and Jesus briefly spoke to the congregation telling them to continue to love one another and that he was leaving everyone with peace and in an instant Jesus suddenly vanished from their sight.

The next day on Wednesday, April 12, A.D. 30 Jesus spent the entire day with no interruptions with his morontia helpers and during the afternoon hours of this day many of the morontia delegates from the seven mansion worlds in Paradise and from the inhabited worlds all throughout the entire constellation of Norlatiadek came to visit Jesus, because they were all happy to know that Michael of Nebadon had become to live among them for a while as a morontia being.

On Sunday, April 16, A.D. 30 while the eleven apostles were having their evening meal in the upper room, Jesus suddenly appeared at their dinner table standing directly in front of Apostle Thomas. Jesus spoke to the eleven apostles about having faith and to continue to love and believe in our Father in Paradise. When Apostle Thomas heard Jesus' words he fell to his knees before Jesus saying that he was a believer and as Jesus moved near the head of the apostles' dinner table, he then told the apostles to all go to Galilee where he would appear to them and Jesus then suddenly vanished from their sight. The eleven apostles were all now thoroughly convinced that Jesus had risen from the dead and early the next morning before the break of dawn the apostles started out for Galilee to meet with Jesus.

And young John Mark went with them and while the apostles were traveling on the road to Galilee Jesus was busy visiting with some more of his followers.

On Tuesday at half past eight o'clock in the evening on April18, A.D. 30 Jesus appeared to about eighty of his Greek followers in Alexandria. This was Jesus' twelfth appearance that occurred right after one of David Zebedee's messengers gave the news to Rodan that Jesus had risen from the dead. One of Jesus' Greek followers Nathan of Buseris was speaking to this group of eighty Greek followers and as he was talking Jesus suddenly appeared in full view and told this group to stay in peace and love and that his comforter, the Holy Spirit was coming soon to earth and after Jesus finished speaking, he suddenly vanished from their sight. For the rest of this night this group of eighty Greek followers stayed there in their meeting recounting the words Jesus had spoken to them that night and continuing to listen to inspirational words from Rodan and his evangelists.

By the time the eleven apostles left to meet Jesus in Galilee the Jewish religious leaders in Jerusalem had quieted down about the resurrection of Jesus and since Jesus had so far made his twelve morontia appearances only to his family and followers, the Sanhedrin officers concluded that Jesus' teachings along with his religious movement had been crushed. The Sanhedrin officers also bribed their guards to continue to spread the false story that a group of Jesus' followers had taken Jesus' body from his burial tomb.

From this time on the apostles had to spread out and separate due to the rising tide of religious persecution that was beginning to arise in Jerusalem. Apostle Peter naturally assumed the role as being the new leader of the apostles and from that day forward public preaching once again became to be the main business for the apostles and before the apostles left for Galilee, they chose Matthias to be their twelfth apostle and serve as their treasurer to replace the deceased Judas Iscariot.

During the week of April 14, A.D. 30 Jesus' mother Mary spent this time with the women's corps of evangelists meeting at Joseph of Arimathea's home.

At about six o'clock Friday morning on April 21, A.D. 30 Jesus made his thirteenth appearance to the apostles and John Mark in Galilee and Apostle Peter suggested that they all go fishing that evening and they ended up fishing all night with their nets, but they did not catch any fish. The apostles talked all night while they were fishing about all of the interesting experiences that had recently happened to them in Jerusalem. When daylight came the apostles decided to return to Bethsaida and as their boat got closer to the shore, they saw someone standing on the beach near the boat landing area standing by a fire. At first the apostles thought that it was young John Mark who had come along with them, but as their boat got closer to the shore, they saw that they were mistaken, because the man was too tall to be John Mark. It never occurred to the apostles that the man standing on the beach was Jesus and as the apostles dropped the anchor to their boat to prepare to enter the small boat to go ashore, the tall man on the beach asked them if they had caught anything. When the apostles said no, the tall man told them to cast their net on the right side of the boat and they would find plenty of fish. The apostles still did not know that the tall man was Jesus and when they cast their net as instructed their fishing net became so filled with fish that they could barely pull it back up into their boat. When Apostle John Zebedee saw how full their net was with fish, he immediately knew that it was Jesus who was speaking to them and when Apostle John said it was Jesus, Apostle Peter immediately jumped into the water so that he could quickly reach Jesus. By this time, John Mark who had stayed ashore had awakened and when he saw the apostles coming ashore with a net full of fish, he also saw Jesus standing by the fire and after

Apostle John finished hauling in their full net of fish, there was a total of one hundred and fifty-three large fish in it. Jesus then told the apostles to sit down and have breakfast with him while they talked about all of the interesting experiences they had during their lives with Jesus.

This was Jesus' third appearance to the apostles, and he stayed with them on that day of Friday, April 21, A. D. 30 for a little over an hour and then Jesus walked up and down the beach talking with the apostles two at a time. At about ten o'clock that morning when Jesus returned from walking on the beach with the last two apostles who were the Alpheus twins, Jesus began to fade away from them and he then told the apostles to meet him the next day at noon on the mountain where they had received their ordination and Jesus then suddenly vanished from their sight.

At noon on Saturday, April 22, A.D. 30 the apostles assembled to meet Jesus at noon on the hill near Capernaum where they had originally been ordained from Jesus to be his ambassadors of preaching his teachings on earth. On this day of Saturday, April 22, A.D. 30, this was Jesus' fourteenth appearance, and the apostles once again knelt down in a circle around Jesus and listened as he re-enacted their first ordination ceremony for the continuation of their special work of preaching and teaching the gospel.

As Jesus prayed over the apostles that day using tones of majesty and using words with such power that the apostles had never heard or felt before, because Jesus now spoke with the rulers of the universes as one who in his own universe had all the power and authority committed to his hand. On that Saturday at noon, the apostles never forgot the profound spiritual experience they had with Jesus' rededication of their pledges to be spiritual ambassadors for their Universal Father in Paradise and Jesus stayed with the apostles for one hour at the rededication ceremony and after an affectionate farewell, Jesus suddenly vanished from their sight.

No one saw Jesus again for a full week after the time he spent with the apostles during their rededication ceremony and the apostles had no idea what to do, because they did not know if Jesus had gone back home to his Father in Paradise or if he was even still on earth. So, with the state of mind the apostles were in, they stayed put in Bethsaida and they were afraid to go anywhere, because they did not want to miss seeing Jesus.

During the entire week of April 22, A.D. 30 Jesus was busy working with the morontia beings who were with him on earth to help Jesus to complete his final seven transition morontia stages so that he could make his final ascension back home to Paradise. The news of all of Jesus' morontia appearances on earth continued to spread all throughout Galilee and Jesus' followers continued to stop by the Zebedee home to talk about Jesus' resurrection. Apostle Peter sent out word that a public meeting was going to be held by the seaside on Saturday, April 29, A.D. 30 at three o'clock in the afternoon. More than five hundred people showed up for this seaside meeting and Apostle Peter was at his best as he preached a discourse to the crowd and he ended his sermon saying that Jesus of Nazareth was not dead and that he had risen and just as Peter finished stating his declaration of faith, Jesus appeared standing beside Peter and Jesus then spoke to the crowd blessing them with peace and love and then Jesus suddenly vanished from their sight. This meeting at the seaside was Jesus' fifteenth appearance that he made to his followers.

The apostles returned to Jerusalem the next day on Sunday, April 30, A.D. 30 and they were able to do a considerable amount of preaching and teaching all the way home on the River Jordan and they arrived back at John Mark's parents' home late on Wednesday, May 3, A.D. 30. This turned out to be a very sad homecoming for young John Mark, because just a few hours before he reached his home, his father Elijah Mark suddenly died from a brain hemorrhage. The apostles all mourned for the loss of their good friend who had been their staunch supporter even during the times of great trouble and disappointment. John Mark did all he could to comfort his mother, and he invited the apostles to continue to make their home at his mother's house and the apostles continued to use the upper room as their headquarters until after the day of Pentecost.

The apostles had purposely returned to Jerusalem from their seaside meeting during the night, because they did not want to be seen by the Jewish religious leaders, and they remained in quiet seclusion in the upper room, and they did not make any more public appearances until after the day of Pentecost.

On Thursday night May 4, A.D. 30 the apostles had a wonderful meeting together in the upper room where they each pledged to go out and continue their public preaching based on Jesus' teachings except for Apostles Thomas, Simon Zelotes and the Alpheus Twins. And so, under the vigorous leadership of Apostle Peter the seven apostles set out to publicly preach and teach to change the teachings of Jesus into a new and modified form of a new religion called Christianity.

Jesus made his sixteenth appearance on Friday, May 5, A.D. 30 in the courtyard of his friend Nicodemus at nine o'clock that night. On this particular night some of Jesus' Jerusalem followers were making their first attempt to get together to informally visit with each other in a good fellowship meeting when suddenly Jesus appeared in full view, and he then told this entire group to stay in Jerusalem until the Holy Spirit endowed them with the special spiritual gifts that would greatly strengthen their spiritual ministry. When Jesus finished speaking to this group he suddenly vanished from their sight. This group of Jesus' disciples stayed talking with each other in this meeting all night discussing all of the wonderful spiritual experiences they had all had with Jesus and it was nearly daybreak before this meeting ended.

At about four o'clock on Saturday afternoon May 13, A.D. 30, Jesus appeared to Nalda the Samaritan woman he had met and converted at Jacob's Well and on that day Nalda was again at Jacob's Well with seventy-five believers at Sychar, because this group of believers had been in the habit of meeting at Jacob's Well to be close to where Jesus had originally spoken to Nalda on the day they first met about the water of life. On this particular Saturday afternoon Nalda and her group of about seventy-five followers of Jesus had just finished talking about Jesus' resurrection when Jesus suddenly appeared

617

before them offering them peace and telling them that he would always be with them in spirit and after Jesus finished speaking to Nalda and her group he suddenly vanished from their sight. Nalda's group of Samaritans were really astonished by Jesus' seventeenth appearance, and they hurriedly went to the nearby towns and villages to spread the good news that Jesus had risen from the dead and that they had seen and talked with him.

Jesus made his eighteenth appearance in Tyre on Tuesday, May 16, A.D. 30 at nine o'clock in the evening when he suddenly appeared at the end of a meeting that a group of followers were having, and Jesus spoke to this group telling them to be at peace and to continue to go forth spreading the gospel and then Jesus suddenly vanished from their sight.

Early on Thursday morning May 18, A.D. 30 Jesus made his final nineteenth appearance in his morontia body on earth. As the apostles were about to sit down to have breakfast in the upper room Jesus appeared to the apostles, wished them peace and then told them that the Holy Spirit would soon be poured upon them and endow all of them with the power on high. Jesus told the apostles to continue to confide in each other, because his hour had come to go back home to his Father in Paradise. When Jesus finished speaking to the apostles, he motioned for the apostles to come with him, and he led them out on Mount Olivet where he told the apostles farewell as he prepared to ascend from earth back home to his Universal Father in Paradise.

It was almost half past seven o'clock on Thursday morning May 18, A.D. 30 when Jesus arrived on the western slope of Mount Olivet with his eleven silent and somewhat bewildered apostles and from this location when Jesus and the apostles arrived about two-thirds the way up Mount Olivet they were able to look over the entire city of Jerusalem and down on the Garden of Gethsemane. Jesus now prepared to say his final farewell message to the apostles before he ascended from planet earth. As Jesus stood there before the apostles, they all knelt in a circle around Jesus as he told them that his love overshadows them and that his spirit will dwell with them forever and after Jesus blessed the apostles with peace, Jesus told them farewell.

When the morontia form of Jesus finished his farewell message to the apostles he suddenly vanished from their sight and Jesus' ascension was not any different from his other eighteen sudden vanishing from mortal vision during the forty days of his morontia life on earth. After Jesus made his final ascension from earth on Thursday, May 18, A.D. 30 he went to Edentia by way of Jerusem, Paradise where the Most Highs under the observation of the Paradise Son, released Jesus of Nazareth from his morontia state and through the spirit channels of ascension returned Jesus to his original life as Michael of Nebadon with the status of Paradise sonship and as the current supreme system sovereign of the Nebadon universe.

It was about seven forty-five in the morning on Thursday, May 18, A.D. 30 when the morontia body of Jesus of Nazareth made his final disappearance from the life of his eleven apostles to begin his final ascension to sit at the right hand of his Universal Father there to receive the formal confirmation of his completed seven bestowals. On this same day Thursday, May 18, A.D. 30 John Mark and some of Jesus' other disciples went to all of the leading disciples to tell them to attend a meeting that was being called by Apostle Peter at ten thirty on that same morning in the home of John Mark's mother Mary Mark. Exactly one hundred and twenty disciples came to this meeting to hear about Jesus' final farewell message and his ascension back home to Paradise.

Among the attendees at this meeting was Jesus' mother Mary and his oldest brother James. At this meeting Apostle Peter took it upon himself to speak for his fellow apostles and he gave a thrilling detailed report of the last meeting the eleven apostles had with Jesus. The most touching part was when Apostle Peter portrayed Jesus' final farewell to the apostles and his instant ascension disappearance. This meeting was one that the group of disciples had never been able to experience before, and Apostle Peter then explained to everyone at the meeting that the apostles had decided to choose a successor to replace the now deceased Apostles Judas Iscariot and that he was calling a recess so that he and the apostles could decide between the two candidates, Matthias and Justus.

The apostles subsequently chose Matthias to be the twelfth apostle and treasurer, but Apostle Matthias had very little part in the activities of the apostles. Right after Pentecost Sunday the two Apostles Alpheus Twins both returned back home to their families in Galilee, Apostle Simon Zelotes went into retirement for quite some time before he decided to return to public preaching of the gospel and Apostle Thomas still continued to worry for a short time and then he eventually went back into publicly preaching and teaching the gospel.

Apostle Nathaniel did not agree with Apostle Peter's philosophy to change their preaching to emphasize Jesus when they were teaching and proclaiming the good news of the gospel and this disagreement became to be so intense that by the end of June, A.D. 30, Apostle Nathaniel moved to Philadelphia to work with Abner and Lazarus for about a year and he then moved on to preach and teach in the lands beyond Mesopotamia.

At around noon the apostles returned to their meeting in the upper room with Jesus' one hundred and twenty disciples and Apostle Peter then asked to have a group prayer with everyone who was there so that everyone would be prepared to receive the Holy Spirit Jesus had promised to send to them after he talked to his Father to send them the Spirit of Truth.

At about one o'clock in the afternoon while the one hundred and twenty followers were praying together, they all became aware of a strange presence in the room and at the same time everyone in the upper room became conscious of a new profound sense of spiritual inner strength that was immediately followed by a strong urge to go out and publicly proclaim the good news of the gospel and that Jesus had risen from the dead and ascended back home into heaven. Apostle Peter then stood up and told everyone that what they were all

feeling was that they had just received the Holy Spirit that Jesus had promised to send to them and Peter then proposed that they all go to the temple in Jerusalem to begin the proclamation of the good news that they had all just received the Holy Spirit just as Jesus had promised and they all did just that.

All these disciples had been trained and instructed by Jesus to go out and preach and now they had all been endowed with the Holy Spirit that gave them the power on high to preach the good tidings of the gospel to the people. Jesus' teachings were based on the fatherhood of God along with the sonship and brotherhood of man and as the religion of Christianity from that day continued to develop, it was based on the fact that the Universal Father in Paradise is our Father and Jesus is his son.

The apostles had been hiding in the upper room of Mary Mark's home since the crucifixion of Jesus, but on the first Pentecost Sunday on May 21, A.D. 30 when Jesus' one hundred and twenty disciples received the Holy Spirit, at about two o'clock in the afternoon, Apostles Peter delivered an impassioned sermon in the Jerusalem temple that resulted in more than two thousand people converting to Christianity. The Jewish religious leaders were surprised at the boldness of the apostles' public preaching and by four o'clock on the that Pentecost Sunday on May 21, A.D. 30, more than two thousand new believers followed the Apostles Peter, Andrew, James and John down to the pool of Siloam to be baptized.

Jesus lived a life on earth as a mortal man with the revelation of a man who followed his Father's divine plan. Jesus' life in the mortal flesh along with his death on the cross and subsequent resurrection became to be a new religion, Christianity and the religious term of being baptized in the Holy Spirit came into general use in the year A.D. 30 which signified man's conscious reception of this gift of the Spirit of Truth. Since man first received this gift of the Holy Spirit on Pentecost Sunday, May 21, A.D. 30, humanity has been receiving the teaching and guidance of the threefold spirit endowment: the spirit of the Father, The Thought Adjuster, the spirit of the Son of God, the Spirit of Truth, the spirit of the Spirit and the Holy Spirit. Mankind on earth are also subject to the double influence of the sevenfold appeal of the universe influences. The early evolutionary races of men on earth were subject to the progressive contact of the seven adjutant mind spirits of the local universe Mother Spirit. As early man continued to progress upward in the scale of intelligence and spiritual perception, eventually there came to hover over him and indwell within man the seven higher spirit influences.

As humanity rapidly approaches the age of Light and Love those who are awake can now ascend back home to Paradise just like Jesus did 2,154 years ago, because our new earth, Blessed Gaia is here and now ready for those who have completed the entire individual ascension process. There are many stories that have been told on earth since its creation over 4.5 billion years ago, but the story of Jesus of Nazareth is by far the greatest story ever told.

These are the seven spirits of our advancing world that currently indwell in humanity who are living on planet earth.

The bestowed spirit of the Universal Father-The Divine Personal Thought Adjuster.

The indwelling spirit presence of the Eternal Son, the spirit gravity of the universes of universes and the certain channel of all spirit communion.

The indwelling spirit presence of the Infinite Spirit, the universal spirit mind of all creation, the spiritual source of the intellectual kinship of all progressive intelligence.

The spirit of the Universal Father and the Creator Son, the Spirit of truth is regarded as the spirit of the Universe Son.

The spirit of the Infinite Spirit and the Universe Mother Spirit, and the Holy Spirit who is generally regarded as the spirit of the Universe Spirit.

The mind spirit of the Universe Mother Spirit-the seven-adjutant mind-spirits of the local universe.

The spirit of the Father, Sons, and Spirits, the new name spirit of the ascending mortals of the realms after the fusion of the mortal spirit born soul with the Paradise Thought Adjuster and after the subsequent attainment of the divinity and glorification of the status of the Paradise Corps of the Finality.

And so, the gifts that Jesus sent down to earth from his Universal Father, the Holy Spirit on Pentecost Sunday May 21, A.D. 30 brought the last of the spirit endowments designed to help in the ascending man's path back home to the Universal Father in Paradise. There were many strange teachings that became to be associated with the early stories about the first day of the Pentecost, but the main mission of the Holy Spirit that indwelled the one hundred and twenty followers of Jesus who attended this meeting in the upper room was to teach humanity about the truths of our Father's love and his Son's mercy. Jesus as the Creator Son who incarnated as a mortal man on earth revealed The Universal Prime Creator Father to all of humanity. To Jesus, his mortal life on earth had dealt to him some of the hardest, cruelest and bitter blows and he met all of his mortal trials with faith, courage and determination to do his Father's will.

On the day of Pentecost Sunday, May 21, A.D. 30, the new religion of Jesus broke all of the national and racial restrictions, because the Holy Spirit became to be the personal gift from Jesus to every mortal man living on earth.

This gift of the Holy Spirit to humanity on earth was bestowed for the purpose of qualifying believers to more effectively preach the gospel and to free religion from being dependent on physical forces, because now the teachers of Christianity were equipped with spiritual weapons, the full body armor of the Holy Spirit-a seven in one stroke. The gift of the Holy Spirit to humanity on Pentecost Sunday gave humanity the power to forgive personal injuries, to stay sweet in the midst of grave injustices, to remain unmoved in the face of danger and to challenge the evils of hate and anger with fearless acts of love and forbearance.

Before the times and teachings of Jesus, women had little or no spiritual standing in the traditional religions and during his ministry on earth, Jesus established a women's corps of evangelists with his wife Mary Magdalene as its leader. After the day of the Pentecost Sunday in the brotherhood of the kingdom, women were able to stand before God as an equal to men. Both the mother and brother of Jesus were present among the one hundred and twenty followers who all received the gift of the Holy Spirit in the upper room on the day of the Pentecost. The day of the Pentecost also marked the end of special priesthoods and the old beliefs that existed in certain families, and it was a call for spiritual unity among all believers of the gospel. When the Holy Spirit descended on the entire group who were in the upper room on Pentecost Sunday, the same thing happened at the same time to all of Jesus' followers who were in prayer in Philadelphia, Alexandria and all of the other places on earth where Jesus' true believers were.

Christianity, the religion based on the teachings of Jesus is the most powerful, widespread and unifying influence the world has ever known and the power of prayer that the believers on the day of Pentecost received was that it dug out larger and deeper channels that enabled the divine bestowal of the Holy Spirit to flow into their hearts and souls, because of their sincere unbroken communion with the Universal Father through their sincere prayer and true worship.

And so, all went well in Jerusalem until the time of the coming of the Greeks in large numbers from Alexandria. Two pupils of Rodan from Greece arrived in Jerusalem, and they were able to convert many of the Hellenist Greeks to Christianity. Among two of Rodan's pupils who had converted to Christianity were Stephen and Barnabas and Stephen later became to be the leader of the Christian Greek colony in Jerusalem, and he became the first martyr to the faith when during one of his public sermons he was stoned to death by a group of angry Jews. This new crisis made the followers of Christianity realize that they could no longer worship together with the unbelievers and within one month from the death of Stephen, the church in Jerusalem and reorganized under the leadership of Apostle Peter along with Jesus' oldest brother James who was installed as its titular leader.

Shortly afterwards new and relentless persecutions broke out from the Jews against the Christians that were so bad that the active religious teachers of Christianity had to leave Jerusalem and spread out all over the Roman Empire.

The result of Apostle Peter preaching in the Jerusalem temple on the day of the Pentecost also helped to form and help to decide the future policies and plans for he and the rest of the apostles' efforts to go out and proclaim the gospel all throughout the Roman Empire and the rest of the known world. Apostle Peter was the true founder of the Christian Church and Apostle Paul carried this new Christian religion's message to the Gentiles and the Greek disciples carried the Christian teachings to many other parts of the Roman Empire.

During his lifetime on earth Jesus never required that his followers believe in him, but rather to believe with him of the reality of the love of God and the sonship with our Universal Prime Creator Father in Paradise. The great challenge now for modern man living on earth is to now strive to achieve better communication with the Divine Monitor that dwells within each human mind, because humanity's greatest adventure in the flesh consists in the well-balanced efforts to advance the borders of self-consciousness in an effort to reach the spirit consciousness which will result in contact with the divine presence. Such an experience constitutes God consciousness which is an experience of knowing God and this spirit consciousness is the knowledge of the actuality of sonship with God and this assurance of sonship is the main experience of having faith.

Jesus did not incarnate on earth to abolish the established Jewish religious laws, but rather he came to fulfill them, indicating a continuation and completion of the teachings of Moses. Jesus' teachings frequently addressed aspects of the established Jewish religious laws, such as the importance of loving God and one's neighbors and these principles were derived from the Books of Leviticus and Deuteronomy. Many of the parables that Jesus used in his teachings were within the context of Jewish life and the customs of the time, which reflected a deep understanding of Jewish law and traditions. One of Jesus' most famous teachings, the Sermon on the Mount was his interpretation of the Ten Commandments, and the other laws of Moses and Jesus remained firmly anchored in the Jewish tradition that his parents who were both from the pure bloodline of King David raised Jesus and his seven siblings in. Jesus' life on earth was the beginning of the cosmic karma cycle on earth which is humanity's hope to be able to ascend back to heaven, because before Jesus came to earth only three hundred humans had been able to ascend back home to heaven since the fall of Atlantis until earth began its thirty-eight-year ascension process in the year of the 1987 Harmonic Convergence.

When Michael of Nebadon of Paradise incarnated on earth as the mortal man, Jesus of Nazareth he confused many people on earth, because the Jewish nation was expecting a superhuman messiah from the sky who would supernaturally overthrow the Roman Empire and become the king of the Jews. Some people who were living on earth during these times even called Jesus the accidental Messiah, but there are no accidents in life, because Jesus was the savior, the Messiah who forever changed the direction not only for earth, but also for all of the other worlds of time and space that exist within our Nebadon universe.

After Michael of Nebadon's completion of his seventh and final bestowal on planet earth he was not only accepted by the Ancients Of Days as the system sovereign of our Nebadon universe, but Michael was also recognized by the Universal Father as the established director of the local universe that he had created billions of years ago.

When Jesus incarnated on earth 2,154 years ago as a mortal man he fulfilled all of the ancient prophesies, changed the course of history on earth and the fate of many other worlds in our universe. Precisely at the point of time of Jesus' ascension back home to heaven on May 18, A.D. 30, Jesus then took back absolute control of the Nebadon universe and began the final house cleaning of the fallen angels/reptilians in the heavens and at the same time, Jesus promised to return to earth in two thousand years with the entire armies of heaven with him. During this second coming to earth Jesus will be in full power and glory for his final victory against the dark brotherhood of the fallen angels. The time for Jesus our Messiah to return with the entire armies of heaven are now as planet earth with its awakened humans who are currently living in the twenty-first century continue to complete earth's current thirty-eight-year ascension process.

The second coming of Jesus is a two-way process, because when Jesus incarnated on earth, he embodied the highest field of consciousness called the cosmic source consciousness. Cosmic source consciousness is a field of energy that is now available to everyone living on earth now, because of earth's current ascension process. Everything in creation is one and we are currently living on earth merging our individual consciousness with the universal mind which is the Prime Creator source vibration of pure light. At this time on earth's thirty-eight-year ascension process all of humanity will embody the Christ universal mind field as one. The second coming to earth by Jesus also refers to him returning with all of the armies of heaven and with all of their ships (clouds). The reference in the bible to the clouds means, camouflage, to conceal the star ships that relate to the return of the hosts of heaven with Jesus being the head of this giant fleet. In the Book of Eziekiel, the star ships are described as wheels within wheels that descend from heaven and the Book of Elijah mentions chariots of fire.

In the biblical Book of Exodus, the Israelites were led through the wilderness traveling around Mount Sinai and caught in a loop for forty years by a moving cloud (starship) until they finally reached the promised land, and we now understand that a cloud or star does not move, navigate and lead anyone to a specific location but a starship does.

The New Jerusalem of the west is scheduled to descend on earth during our current times of the twenty-first century and earth is now entering into a higher ascended order of spiritual evolution. Since higher evolved beings exist in the fifth, sixth and seventh dimensions, earth is now ascending into these higher densities during our current times to reunite us with our celestial family and ancestors who now exist in these higher dimensions and these times are now at hand on earth.

CHAPTER SEVENTEEN

ASCEND NOW

The Lord is near. Do not be anxious about anything but present your requests to God.

(Philippians 4: 5-6)

So that we may boldly say, The Lord is my helper and I will not fear what man shall do unto me.

(Hebrews 13:6

A Prayer:

My Universal Prime Creator Father, the world is awash in distraction that doesn't satisfy my soul. Help me to trust only You to fill me with genuine contentment.

ASCEND NOW

The Founders refers to a group of light beings who have an extremely high vibration of light quotients of consciousness and they are responsible for creating or seeding entire universes, a species or a group of species to bring The Founders of a new group of species such as a council dedicated to a course or movement. Our Nebadon universe was co-created by a group of founders who created and seeded the humans who live in our universe.

The guardians-founders of the Nebadon universe are dedicated to preserve and uphold the provisions of the Law of One to ensure the right of sovereignty and free will for all sentient organic consciousness beings as well as providing support and safeguarding them to be able to expand their consciousness to ascend back home to heaven according to the plan relating to the 12D Grid and the natural organic Tree of Life through the process of the time matrix of the Nebadon universe. The guardian-founders of our Nebadon universe are also known as the guardian hosts and they are responsible for the ascension of all sentient beings which includes, angelic humans who play the most important role in ensuring the longevity and survival of our Nebadon universe.

At the center of all there is that is referred to as the cosmos, there exists the most incredible magnificent reservoir fountain of perfectly crystalline coherent energy that is referred to as the consciousness of the God-Source. This is the method in which creation proceeds or is governed by and this is known as the dualism principle of creation, which asserts that everything must be created as a conjugate pair, because this will ensure that the overall system of creation remains in a state of balance. The energetic state of the Prime

Creator Source comes from its initial kinetics with its quanta of energy eternally spinning about itself vibrating between the now moment. The Prime Creator is not temporary, and it explodes-implodes about itself to begin the process of creation, and this gives rise to the dawn of time and according to the dualism principle of creation, creation is of a bi-directional nature.

Crystalline Christ Consciousness is based on a free energy system that is an open source and self-sustaining, and this applies to earth's energetic structure which is based on a tri-wave unity open loop system. Creation or consciousness has to do with the simultaneous consideration of three distinct rays of light that form a dimensional reality, and this is what is commonly called the Trinity. The divine source is the trinity wave structure accessed through the merging of polarity of the masculine and feminine energies that are referred to as the unity code of the rod and staff. This natural architecture connects the solar organic consciousness to the Prime Creator Source and through the sacred union of these two polarities it is known as the hieros gamos and so this means that in order for a human to complete the ascension process the male and female energies in the body must be in complete alignment and then it is time to climb the stairway to heaven in your fully aligned hieros-gamos body.

There are three original primal order frequency light fields that make up the ray aspects of our entire universal creation and these primal codes are referred to as the threefold founder flame. The thirteenth, fourteenth and fifteenth rays of light of consciousness are referred to as the Rishi Suns and they form and reside within the Fifth Harmonic

Universe (HU5) and these Rishi Suns are the original founders of the Nebadon universe. The threefold founder flame is united into a simple liquid plasma current that creates the 12D Ray system which forms the blueprint for the Silicate Matrix of the Crystalline Christ Consciousness. The holographic template in which our conscious body interfaces with the Nebadon universe is known as the Tree of Life or the 12D Grid. The universal 12D Grid is a crystalline structure that is composed of an energetic substance that has its own patterns of frequency. The 12D Grid is also the process of a spiritual body integration sequence and configuration pattern for a Christos Oraphim known as the Diamond Sun Body.

The Tree of Life is composed of twelve spheres that are made of the following:

(12) Harmonic Structures

(12) Light Rays

(12) Dimensions

(12) Timelines

(12) DNA Strands

A ray of light is a form of an electromagnetic field (EMF) and an electromagnetic force is a physical interaction that occurs between electrically charged particles. The electromagnetic force is exhibited by an electromagnetic field as an electric field and a magnetic field and the electromagnetic field extends indefinitely throughout space.

The Nebadon universe is associated with the first fifteen dimensions of the cosmos, however, dimensions D13, D14 and D15 are outside of our universe's universal time matrix and the threefold founder flame exist as the three layers of the Rishi Matrix in the Fifth Harmonic Universe of dimensions D13, D14 and D15. These collective consciousness bodies also exist on earth throughout the densities, and they are aspects of the future timelines (higher dimensions) and the Lightbody of the planet earth. Planet earth's consciousness body is directly interconnected in all of the Harmonic Universes in order for it to be able to interface with the human consciousness which is its life form expression in all of the densities.

In the fifth Harmonic Universe (HU5) there is no dimensions into Nebadon's physical matter forms, so there is no planetary body or human forms in (HU5).

In the fifth density of Harmonic Universe(HU5) the consciousness does not manifest into Nebadon physical matter, and this area is called pre-matter.

The three primal light and sound fields that hold the ray expressions of the Mother Arc, Father Arc and the Golden Ray Sun of Christos-Sophia, the Trinity of the Godhead is the source of all the biological forms that are created in all of the first four Harmonic Universes. There is a lot of work that must be done by the guardian-founders to bring planet earth back to the God-worlds. The triad communication stations in the planetary grid network now have open access that are connected through the astral layers that can be entered through the pyramids of Giza. This portal then moves through the planets of Sirius 6D, Arcturus 7D and Orion 8D (galactic core) and into Andromeda 9D and then finally out of this system entirely. This is the meta-galactic layers that are aligned to the luminaries of the next universe that are in turn connected to our Krystar Star communication networks. This portal opening also allows access to the Krystal Star Guardians from the next universe, the seven superuniverses or seven higher heavens and to the Trinity Wave blueprints of creation.

The cosmos is composed of a crystalline structure in the form of a plasma matrix that is made of positive and negative ions. From a compressive pinch in the cosmos there is a natural tendency for the flow of negative charged ions from the slightly positive pole to its negative pole counterpart and this is called piezoelectricity. All of the dimensional layers in the cosmos are interconnected building blocks of matter and anti-matter that are created from positive charge, negative charge and neutral or zero-point energy potential.

Every dimensional space has an energetic polarity in matter and its double in anti-matter and the linking up of the particles of matter and anti-matter forms the state of neutrality or zero-point energy. Neutrality brings one to the zero-point consciousness, a state of intellectual bliss, appreciating the highest points of consciousness, connecting one with the Prime Creator, because it is the absolute state of balance. The achievement of integration or balance describes the state of experiencing unity consciousness and unity consciousness is the first provision of the Law of One which is the self-governing Law of the Prime Creator Source.

A space time dimension within a Harmonic Universe has a time dimensional victor or axis of rotation or a dimensional angle and a speed of rotation or frequency that must be in harmony with the spin rate of the particles of the matter and anti-matter which are the electrons, protons, positrons, antiprotons and neurons and this spin can either be clockwise or counterclockwise.

The Kathara Centers are the condensed scalar wave points that hold the core geometrical program for a dimensional structure and there are twelve Kathara Centers and each hold the program for one dimension.

The Kathara Centers are the template for each dimension to ground consciousness within our holographic experience in the matrix on earth. The Kathara Lines connect each Harmonic and dimension of consciousness to the other and govern the synchronization of the cycles of time that exist within the dimensional fields. There are three primary Kathara Lines that control the operation of the other twelve Kathara Lines and the central vertical line is the control central for the particle rhythms throughout the entire Kathara Line System.

Dimension 12D forms four individual holographic Harmonic Universes that are composed of four Harmonic Universes. The twelve spheres or nodes in the Tree of Life form the 12D grid and they are arranged in four triad grids or shields with each representing the blueprint within a particular physical Harmonic Universe and these four triads are the monadic body, the soul body, the personality body and the avatar body. A consciousness physical being experiences many different identities within each of these four different Harmonic Universes.

Harmonic Universe One (HU1) is the personality triad shield and it is composed of dimensions D1-Red, D2-Orange and D3-Yellow.

Harmonic Universe Two (HU2) is the soul triad shield and it is composed of dimensions D4-Green, D5-Blue and D6-Indigo.

Harmonic Universe Three (HU3) is the monad triad shield and it is composed of dimensions D7-Violet, D8-Gold and D9-Silver.

Harmonic Universe Four (HU4) is the avatar triad shield and it is composed of dimensions D10-Sapphire, D11-Dark Silver and D12-White.

Harmonic Universe Five (HU5) is where the Nebadon Universe Creator Rishi Suns reside, and it is composed of dimensions D13, D14 and D15 and it is not a part of the Nebadon universe. A human with an activated light body is capable of interfacing with the realm of the Universe Founders or Rishi Suns in (HU5).

A Harmonic Universe is the end result of the simultaneous projection of the three light rays of consciousness of certain frequencies. The original or organic creation design template is based on a tri-level wave structure and each divine ray creates a timeline within each Harmonic Universe and these twelve rays correspond to the four physical Harmonic Universes.

Space is defined by the spherical surface contour of energy or dimension and the concept of time defines the inverse spherical radius around the central Source of the space time dimension.

A sentient being is the offspring of the Prime Creator Source and as it anchors its consciousness to a particular dimension, it continues to vibrate between two space-times on a quantum level and between the worlds of matter and anti-matter. Every world of existence that is able to support life such as our Nebadon universe is based on a creation of a series of offspring who come from the central God-Source and these light beings have extremely high light quotients. In physical form such entities often take the form of "Suns" or planetary bodies that actually anchor their light of consciousness that is just above the central universal system, and the light of these Sun bodies causes the creation of universal systems. The life system of these universal bodies includes the set of all of its living solar organic consciousness beings and their longevity is maintained. Such a system also exists as the Rishi Suns in (HU5) and in dimensions 13D, 14D and 15D. These Rishi Suns exist in a realm that is just outside of the space-time matrix of the Nebadon universe in a pure energetic form just above the level of matter.

There also exists seven ascending levels of consciousness that have lower discrete levels of spectral density which are known as the seven higher levels of heaven and the Nebadon universe resides at the bottom of this group of Physical systems. The Prime Creator Source is the fundamental fountain of energy that supports and supplies all that is organic and with an infinite open loop of consciousness energy. The Prime Creator Source is the ultimate omnipotent, omniscient, omnipresent, fully self-aware, conscious entity, and being of a singular nature initially occupying a single point and he-she-it explodes-implodes upon itself to create the cosmos as its body of existence. In order to accomplish the task of creation, being originally of total neutrality, some of its quanta energy splits into expansive electric-male and contractive magnetic-female parts to form a Trinity aspect of itself. Through an expansive-contracting action where its electric quanta of energy could expand and its magnetic quanta of energy could contract, it then undergoes an exhalation of breathing out and an inhalation of breathing in process that we call organic life.

The Prime Creator Source is the heart brain of the cosmos as its body of existence undergoing a beating process that is again organic life. The action of this electric expansion of its quanta of energy is the dissemination of God's energy all throughout the cosmos, while the process of magnetic contraction ensures that all its quanta of energy returns back to the Prime Creator Source. This process is a description of the Law of Conservation of Energy which states that what expands away from the Source must contract back and return to the Source.

The name Nebadon was given to the creation of our universe when it was created, and it resides at the edge of the cosmos, and it is a part of all of the physical universal systems that are referred to as the seven superuniverse or the seven higher heavens.

The Nebadon universe is a part of the inhabited superuniverse of Orvonton which is located at the outermost edge of all the seven superuniverses and this superuniverse consists of the physical system of universes where the quanta of energy forming their fabric of space time also forms particles of matter and particles of anti-matter. This physical system of universes each has its own structure that is governed by their own physical laws. All together these seven superuniverses form the equation: 9x2=81, which is the outermost space-time dimensions out of a total of (356) possible dimensions with (3) outermost dimensions that all together form the holographic Harmonic Universe for a total of (84) non-fractal dimensions within the entire cosmos. These (84) non-fractal dimensions are all arranged as a set of (3) dimensions that form the structural arrangement of the set of the seven superuniverses or seven higher heavens.

The guardian founders and their family are known as the Christos Elders Angelic Oraphim who are composed of the Holy Emerald Order of Elohei, the Gold Order RA Confederacy, the Amethyst Order of the Ancient Master Builders and the Master Christos Collective and they are the protectors and preservers of the Law of One which is the path for any being to be able to take to ascend back to heaven, evolve their consciousness and exist as God, sovereign and free. These guardian founders of our Nebadon universe are Oraphim Ascended Masters Christos beings from the seven higher heavens which are the dimensions 13D through 36D. The guardian founders have fully activated (48) DNA strands, and they are capable to jump start and set up a whole new universe and they have the creation purpose for the genetic repair of all beings who live in the Nebadon universe. The universal time matrix that exists in the Nebadon universe runs by a system that is composed of (12) non-fractal dimensional space-times (85-86) and each is characterized by a unique sound frequency light quotient that is known as the 12D Grid or Tree of Life which describes the ray or consciousness of the universe. Our Nebadon universe is consistent with the rest of the cosmos with its seven superuniverses or seven higher heavens, three rays of light that form a triad system of waves that give rise to a holographic domain of four Harmonic Universes that each gives rise to (7x12=84) which is the outermost dimensions of the cosmos or the (21) Harmonic Universes.

The Christos crystalline light beings who created the Nebadon universe have the sound tone of KA-RA-YA-SA-TA-AA-LA or Krystal, Krystallah or Christ beings from the seven higher heavens who have the designation of sound and light that make up the holographic aspect of their solar organic consciousness. At their lowest level, a Christos light being is made of (12) fully assembled and activated crystalline silicate-based DNA strand structure that is known as the Diamond Sun DNA structure. The next level of these Oraphim light beings are composed of and additional (12) strands of DNA and they often function with (24-36) DNA strands fully activated, and they are also known to have a Double Diamond Sun DNA structure.

There is also another group of Oraphim Ascended Master light beings who have the Emerald Sun DNA structure who function with a fully assembled and activated (48) crystalline DNA strands, and they function as the architects and builders for the seven higher heavens and seed new universes to turn them into inhabited worlds.

The Universal Prime Creator has bestowed many gifts on all solar organic consciousness beings and the one demand from its offspring is to continue to strive to expand their consciousness and evolve to be able to discover more marvels of consciousness and existence and to ascend back home to heaven.

The guardian founders also have the capacity to interface with the neural network and divine mind of the Universal Prime Creator Source and they are an energetic form capable of shapeshifting to any desired form and traveling to and from all of the dimensional levels of the seven higher heavens. There are three orders of beings that make up the Trinity structure of the (84) functioning Oraphim light beings and the trinity aspect of the God-Source is disseminated in the form of a tri-wave system that forms our tri-wave consciousness and this consciousness is the three sources of the original primal sound frequencies along with their light quotients that project rays of distinct colors and together these represent the holographic aspect of universal creation.

The Godhead symbolizes the central point of all union which is what planet earth is moving towards through its current ascension process to become in direct alignment with God. Normally ordinary consciousness vibration occurs within the worlds of matter and anti-matter where the quanta of energy oscillate in a spiraling action about the central point of Godhead that is neural zero-point energy. The female and male aspects of the Godhead are referred to as the Holy Mother and the Holy Father and the zero point of the Godhead represents the Holy Son which is the One Godhead known as Christos-Sophia which is God's male and female aspects which are rolled into one centralized aspect. There is an energy matrix composed of sound, frequencies, light and colors that is in the form of a tri-wave tone and a tri-wave color of light and this is what makes our universal time matrix in the Nebadon universe. This energy matrix describes the core of consciousness of the all that is interdimensional, because each sound frequency and light color describes the holographic aspect of each unique dimension.

The cosmic trinity or universal trinity is represented by The Emerald Order, The Gold Order and the Amethyst Order and the first emanation of the primal sound-light field that represents the first individual God Source known as the Emerald Order. The second emanation of the primal sound-light field which represents the God Source is called the Gold Order and the third emanation of the primal sound-light field represents the third individual God Source known as the Amethyst Order.

Beginning with Harmonic Universe One (HU1), one must resonate and be a vibrational match in frequency with the higher spheres of the Universal Tree of Life in order to be able to ascend back home to heaven. This requires a lot of effort and perseverance, and one must acquire consciousness expansion through spiritual education in order to ascend back home. One way to rapidly ascend upward on the branches of the Tree of Life is to first understand the trinity aspect of God as well as to follow the Law of One, the art of compassion, unconditional love, empathy, interconnectedness, service to all and to daily experience the highest human emotion, authenticity.

Ascension back home to heaven in essence is the reverse process to creation, because in creation one singular unit implodes upon itself to form the many. In the process of ascension two or more fragments integrate and unify to build one perfected form and each triad body represents a distinct stage of spiritual body development which has a feminine and masculine energetic counterpart. Spiritual ascension is all about integration of the gender polarity forces that exist within each triad. The spiritual couplings of the rod and staff form the prototype template blueprint that is necessary to achieve hieros-gamos, the perfect alignment of the male and female energies in your body and the achievement of hieros-gamos occurs at various active levels of one's soul, personality, monad and avatar dimensional levels. Ascension is about polarity; integration and it is a significant job for one to integrate the masculine and feminine energies in order to achieve the sacred marriage union to finally reach the point of zero-point energy of ascension. Once the sacred marriage union of hieros-gamos is achieved in your physical body then one can then continue to move through the spiraling staircase of time (stairway to heaven) to experience the unification and sacred marriage with all of the aspects of God and in essence you will be climbing the stairway to heaven and ascending to the New Heaven on Earth which is on Blessed 7D Gaia Earth.

In the beginning before humans were individuals they traveled as one large orb through the universe and this large orb was able to embody anything in order to feel its consciousness, but this large orb had no physical form. This large orb during its travels met the (30) foot tall beings on the planet Lyra who were known as the golden race who were individual Adam Kadmon beings in perfected form. This large orb was humanity in its spiritual form and the people who lived on the planet Lyra were ascended beings who were sent by the Elohim to guide others on what they needed to do to evolve to have a human form. This race of Lyrans after teaching humanity how to evolve into individual physical human forms soon moved to other universes to teach other beings how to evolve and ascend to Christ consciousness. In order to accomplish this a living being must descend all the way down to the lowest level of human existence which is a third-dimension planet to master duality living a life starting all the way down to the caveman level and evolve back up to the consciousness level to ascend back up to the unity consciousness of the fifth dimension. There are no levels you can skip during this evolution process which can take up to a million years of incarnations.

The beings from the planets of Lyra, Arcturia, Pleiades, Sirius B and Andromeda have all helped humanity from its beginning to evolve and experience an individual human life. In order for a human to complete the path of a true ascension from the third dimension to the unity consciousness of the fifth dimension, one must master all of the experiences of the dark and light frequencies of their planet, and you then evolve to be an ascended master. Once you become an ascended master your job is to give and teach the God experience of life to others. Human beings living on earth were created with the combination of (22) DNA species from our Milky Way Galaxy and two of these twenty-two species came from Sirius,which is a a unicorn, dragon, whales, mermaid/ merman and royal lions water planet.

When the original orb of humans made the free will choice to become an individual to experience a life of matter on a world of time and space, the orb of humans split into twelve pieces with the higher self being the overseer of these twelve human realities. The higher self of each human exists billions of years in the future in the seventh dimension and during the ascension process you download your higher self, merge and embody your higher self to become one in order to complete the ascension process to the fifth dimension to live on the new heaven on earth. Your human oversoul exists a level above the higher mind and after having a board meeting with all of the ascended masters led by Jesus, they have now given humanity all of the necessary light codes to complete the ascension process.

Earth exists in Harmonic Universe One (HU1) as planet #606 in our Metaverse and the ascended masters were sent to earth to teach humanity the concept of Christ Consciousness which is the school of thought that teaches you how humanity has evolved from Homo Sapien-Sapien consciousness to God consciousness, which is to learn how to create your own reality of heaven on earth. Many of the planets within our Milky Way Galaxy all vibrate on different frequencies and some like the planets of Saturn, Jupiter, Venus and Mercury have already ascended to the fifth dimension. Saturn is the central hub of our Milky Way Galaxy and serves as the headquarters for the Galactic Federation of Planets. The planet Sirius B is where the Office of Christ is located.

When a soul makes the free will decision to descend down to a physical life on earth, he first exists in a void of infinite space from which everything originates and it is the concept of manifesting nothingness, emptiness from the quality or state of being without anything. The void is that from which all originates, infinite space and your physical body dies instantly after a moment of falling into the void. When a being of energy, soul and light with their own free will decides to incarnate on earth, you must first stand in line to receive your spark of life/blue flame which is located in your physical body right above your anus.

When you meet someone on earth who is your twin flame, this means that you were both standing in the same line when you received your spark of life. When an oversoul splits into twelve separate realities and two of these souls meet each other during their life on earth, this is called a soul mate. Once a soul has received the spark of life, then a home, race, parents and a life plan from the Akashic Records must be obtained. The incarnating soul then selects the twelve houses that will be the life plan for the material life that will be experienced on earth before descending into a material existence of life on earth. These twelve houses that are selected are sectors or zones that are located in the realm of the eighth heaven and we each choose which house, frequency and vibration we will bring with our soul as we descend into matter as a mortal human being on earth.

All souls begin their life in the void as a part of the Source energy and we each make the choice to choose twelve specific houses to be a part of our life plan to learn our life lessons on earth in order to evolve and continue to daily raise our vibrations to ascend back home to the fifth dimension.

First House is your ascendant rising sign, your identity, personal appearance and first impression in the sign of Aries.

Second House if your self worth, material possessions and how you will earn your living in the sign of Taurus.

Third House is your communication and how you will interact with others in the sign of Gemini.

Fourth House is your family domestic life and your inner world in the sign of Cancer.

Fifth House deals with your romance, self-expression and creativity in the sign of Leo.

Sixth House is your emotional mental well-being in the sign of Virgo.

Seventh House is yourself awareness, professional connections and marriage in the sign of Libra,

Eighth House is your intimacy, joint resources, sex, death, rebirth and transformation in the sign of Scorpio.

Ninth House is your travel, education, publishing and your religion in the sign of Sagittarius.

Tenth House is your professional path, taskmaster in the sign of Capricorn.

Eleventh House is your hopes, wishes, social media, humanity, rebellious in the sign of Aquarius.

Twelfth House is your karma, illusion, dreams and spiritual growth in the sign of Pisces.

Jesus of Nazareth is the only mortal who lived on earth who didn't have to select the twelve houses from the Akashic Records because he came to earth straight from Source filled with pure bliss love energy. The first memory that all humans experience occurs on the 49th day of conception when the eight genesis cells form and stay at the base of your spine and this is called a human's first whoosh moment where your light body is able to access the code 9/10 the speed of light to descend all the way down to through the hallway of the fourth dimension and into your life on the third dimensional earth. Also, when a human is still developing as a baby in the mother's womb its physical body is developing at a ratio of 1.618. There are three tetrahedrons, earth, sun and the eight circular genesis cells that form the human Merkabah light body that we use to descend to earth and to quantum jump and ascend back home to heaven. All humans experience two whoosh moments, and the second one is when a human has completed all of his karma and life lessons on earth ascends back home to heaven and then you experience your second whoosh moment of bliss.

Earth is the third planet from the sun and the fifth largest planet in our solar system that was formed from the magna eruptions from the sun 4.5 billion years ago. Asia is the home of the first family of the human race, Andon and Fonta, twins who were born in the region of what we now call Afghanistan 993,408 years ago. After humans on earth evolved and began to live in groups of tribes, Adam and Eve came to earth from Paradise on a mission to racially uplift the evolving humans to the Violet race.

After the fall of Atlantis and Lemuria over 12,000 years ago, God was going to shut down the entire human experiment on earth but Lord Sanat Kumara an advanced 9D being from the planet Venus went before the throne of God stating that he would continue to hold the light of pure source consciousness for all of humanity on earth. Buddha was one of Lord Sanat' Kumara's disciple and he came to earth with the 144,000 before Lord Sanat Kumara to prepare the way for Lord Kumara to hold the pure light source on earth, and it took Buddha over 1,000 years to build Shambala, a mythical Buddhist underground city in the Himalaya Mountains which represented a place of enlightenment, knowledge, peace and free of evil where everyone lived in harmony. All of the ascended masters now live in Shambala which is now located in the seventh dimension. Zeus (Enlil) and Jesus of Nazareth also both came to live on earth to continue to hold this pure source light for humanity and Jesus and his wife Mary Magdalene both planted the gridlines of Christ Consciousness on earth to help humanity in our current times of our ascension back home to heaven.

Lord Sanat Kumara's original plea to hold the pure source light for humanity on earth was made on behalf of humanity on earth who no longer knew about the presence of pure source light and were cut off. Lord Kumara volunteered to embody the threefold flame within earth for the evolving humans who were still living within the seven planes of being, fire, air, water and earth.

The Mayan calendar ended in the year 2012 because when the portal to the fourth dimension opened on December 21, 2012, planet earth actually ascended to the fourth dimension and the matrix that had been holding the fake 3D holographic simulation also collapsed on this same date, which means that humanity on earth are now living in a new cycle of time from the Age of Pisces to the Age of Aquarius.

We are currently following the Cabal/Elite Gregorian calendar which is inaccurate by about twelve years, because there are actually only 360 days in a year, not 365 years, and this means that our current year of 2024 A.D. is in reality the year of 2012 A.D

It takes thirty-eight years for a planet to complete the ascension process and since earth began ascending in the year of 1987, the first wave of ascension will occur in 2025, the second wave in 2026 and the third wave in 2028.Earth has ended a 26,000-year cycle, but this time instead of having to start all over, earth is now ascending to higher dimensions. Earth entered the photon belt on December 21, 2012, when the portal to the fourth dimension opened and the closer a planet gets to the end of the photon belt, the closer it gets to the light and the further away a planet moves from the photon belt, it then moves into a cycle of darkness.

When the portal to the fifth dimension opened on December 18, 2021, earth ascended into the fifth dimension and now we are at the finish line, the new kids on the block who have learned how to balance the light with darkness and after the completion of our ascension to the new heaven on earth we will be ascended masters. All of each human's creation energies are in our Merkabah Light Bodies and it takes about thirty days straight to fully activate your Merkabah and when you do you can then begin to quantum jump daily into infinite realities and if you have not done so already select your name, job and create your new home on the new heaven on earth and quantum jump into this new reality daily. Our main mission on earth is to daily raise our vibration, to ascend and help the rest of the earth plane to ascend to the new heaven on earth.

Earth completes a 360-degree cycle through the Milky Way Galaxy every 25,920 years and each complete cycle is known as Yuga and there are four parts to this Yuga cycle which are two parts of 180 degrees of ascending consciousness Yuga and two parts of 180 degrees of descending Yuga consciousness. This cyclical rise and of consciousness on earth has been occurring since the moment of the creation of earth and this explains the rise and fall of the great civilizations on earth. The Kali Yuga is the last quadrant of the descending consciousness cycle with the Yuga and the biblical name for Kali Yuga is the end of time and the end of time will not be the end of planet earth, but rather it will be the end of darkness and evil on earth and the dawn of the Seventh Golden Age of Enlightenment on earth.

Most of the 144,000 are now in the process of awakening which means that the human collective is coming out of their long mental and spiritual hibernation, realizing that we are currently living here on earth during these times to assist humanity in the great massive transformation of the planet earth.

The cellular memories of the 144,000 were planned, timed, and activated for them to remember at this time and help humanity to awaken to their identity, mission and purpose for being here on earth during its current ascension to higher dimensions.

The chosen ones have arrived and are awakened now on earth, and they have entered the 11th hour of the great change that is taking place on earth now and it is time for the remaining 144,000 light workers to erase the fake dreams of materialism, to wake up and dedicate ourselves to the gigantic task of helping earth to continue to ascend.

When we use the word ascension it is in reference to elevating the human consciousness to higher dimensional frequencies and realities. We can look at this in terms of 3D, 4D and 5D consciousness, because humanity has operated from a 3D consciousness level for centuries and as humanity continues to raise their frequencies and vibrations, we are ascending into higher states of 5D consciousness.

The 3D consciousness on earth was made up of a low, dense vibrational frequencies which operated in duality and separation from the Prime Creator Source. People vibrating from 3D frequencies look at life from a linear point of view and they only understand what they can see and touch as being reality. Life feels like the survival of the fittest and you are identified by the way you look, the job you have and the car you drive.

4D consciousness is the hallway/gateway to the higher dimensions but still operates in duality. It is the beginning of recognizing that there is something more than the self and 4D consciousness begins to awaken one to the idea that we are all connected and that there is more to life than what meets the eye. This is where one becomes curious about self-exploration and begins to connect to something more than ourselves and this is referred to as an awakening.

5D consciousness resides in love, authenticity and neutrality. There is no more duality and no good or bad and in 5D there is no competition, and we now know that there is enough in the universe for everyone. You feel overwhelming emotions of love and compassion for life, mother earth and the universe. In 5D you live free from conditioning and live in oneness with yourself and others and this is known as self-mastery with the will to create peace on the new heaven and earth.

The great solar flash/love wave is a natural event of our sun that occurs at the end of the Precession of the Equinox 25,900-year cycle and this event is prophesized to be a supernatural occurrence that will suddenly transform all living life on earth into a higher state of consciousness. This is known as ascension, and it is believed that this solar flash/love wave will activate our dormant DNA and propel planet earth in a 5D state of being where thoughts will manifest instantly, and telepathy will be the method of communication. The new 5D earth will be a place of love, peace and bliss, because the veil of fear and ignorance will be lifted. Ascension to the new heaven on earth is the largest and most important mission that the white brotherhood has ever undertaken in the past 200,000 years.

The eyes of the entire Milky Way Galaxy are looking while planet earth completes its ascension process and, in the end, we will all ascend into the new heaven on earth. Those humans who have completed their daily solar flash/love wave homework and continue to daily raise their vibrations will ascend no later than the spring of the year 2025, and then they will have a free will choice to return to earth as an ascended master to continue to help the rest of humanity to awaken and ascend during the second and third waves of ascension.

During these times of ascension planet earth has also been accepted once again as a member of the Galactic Federation of Planets which has been monitoring earth's activities for thousands of years under the command of Michael of Nebadon our system sovereign of the Nebadon universe. The Galactic Federation of Light (the angels) have currently infiltrated many of earth's governments and they have placed an emergency rescue bubble since the early 1900's over our entire solar system. This emergency rescue bubble was removed in the year 2001 to enable earth and its inhabitants to continue our ascension into the higher dimensions. In the year 1987 earth was placed under Sirian Jurisdiction and the Office of Christ has been working from Sirius B since the establishment of the Galactic Federation of Planets millions of years ago to assist all of the planets within our universe with their ascension process. As the awakened humans on earth continue to ascend, the second coming of the celestial hosts of heaven is scheduled to happen and this prophetic event will then be observed by many beings in our universe as well as from other universes. When this event occurs humanity will experience a mass landing of Galactic Federation starships that will help to restore earth back into a type two intermediate stellar space age civilization that will once again be capable of space travel.

After the second coming of Jesus and the grand solar flash/love wave in the spring of year 2025, earth will be transformed into heaven on earth and humanity will once again walk with the higher density luminaries just like we did during ancient times before the final fall of Atlantis over 12,000 years ago.

The traveling piloted planet Nibiru comes into earth's orbit every 3,600 years and it was reclaimed by the Galactic Federation of Planets in the year 1999 when Marduk (Lucifer/Baal) was finally overthrown since the days of Atlantis and lost his command. Marduk was the fourth dimensional aspect of Lucifer/Baal and the leader of the dark brotherhood on earth (Jesuit/Illuminati) and since he has now been downgraded and lost his godlike abilities, he is now nothing more than a mutant being on the run within earth's dark underground networks.

The nations on earth who are currently fully aware of the presence of the Galactic Federation of Planets fleet of starships are : the United States of America, China, Russia, Europe, Japan, Brazil, Argentia, Mexico, Peru, Bolivia, Canada and the Middle East nations, but all of the world governments have imposed a massive UFO coverup campaign due to the control that the dark brotherhood has over earth's media, political and economic systems. There are many light workers on earth who have been leaders in ending the UFO cover up and as the veil between the physical and spiritual world continues to lift, humanity will continue to quantum jump to create new realities and make many timeline shifts to higher dimensions to help prove that we are not alone in our Nebadon universe.

At this time of earth's ascension, the negative extraterrestrials living on earth and in our universe are being removed and being sent back to the light to be recycled. Our system sovereign Michael of Nebadon has reached our world and he is completing a lot of housecleaning of these negative extraterrestrials from our universe. The Galactic

Federation of Planets Commander Ashtar is from the planet Venus, and he oversees the federation starship fleets of the airborne division of the great white brotherhood and their headquarters is located on planet Jupiter where the affairs for our universe are conducted on behalf of the Sirius B high council, and the Office of Christ who oversees all of the federation councils in the Milky Way Galaxy.

Commander George Ceres Haston from the planet Pleaides is second in command of the Galactic Federation fleet of starships and he is also the leader of the Pleiadean Federation Fleets, and he is now the official commander of the traveling piloted planet Nibiru that comes into earth's orbit every 3,600 years. During the times of the destruction of Lemuria and Atlantis, Zeus was the pilot of the traveling planet Nibiru. Commander Soltec is the head of the new earth geographics department and he is working closely with Commander Haston to continue to send out scouting ships to closely monitor the progress and effects of earth's ascension to the higher dimensions. Commander Soltec is also in charge of the rescue plan system that is designed to clean up some of the major hazardous waste sites that have been harmful to planet earth. Commander Kortec is also on hand helping as the head of the communications interplanetary networks making sure that all of the Galactic Federation messages come through from the seventh dimension and into the fourth dimension on earth.

During the current restoration and ascension of earth, the Galactic Federation is also receiving help from the people who live on Telos, Shambala and Agartha, the inner earth civilizations who were able to escape the fifth and final fall of Atlantis over 12,000 years ago and these inner earth civilizations will all unite with us when earth's ascension is completed. The inhabitants on earth are also receiving help during our restoration and ascension process from the planets, Pleiades, Sirius B, Arcturia, Andromeda and Alpha Centuri who are all under the command of Michael of Nebadon.

The celestial hosts of heaven, visitors from all over our Milky Way Galaxy and other galaxies and universes are also here right above our skies in their starships by the masses to witness this great cosmic event that only takes place every 206 million years during the evolution of a planet.

The Elohim who were created by the archangels are the creators of our Milky Way Galaxy and all of the planets in it and the Elohim built planet earth in her original glory as a population two system that lasted until the fall of Atlantis and Lemuria. When Michael of Nebadon, Paradise incarnated on earth as Jesus of Nazareth straight from Source as a twelve dimensional being he was able to establish the ascension gridlines on earth raise the vibrations of earth so high that humanity living on earth now have the free will choice to awaken and ascend back home to heaven.

You may have heard that our human body on earth is now shifting from being carbon based to being a crystalline based body due to our DNA being upgraded from the solar flashes from the sun and these are some of the differences between a carbon and crystalline physical body.

HUMAN CARBON BODY	CRYSTALLINE HUMAN BODY
FOUNDATION OF LIFE MADE FROM EARTH	NEW STRUCTURE, ALIGNS WITH HIGHER

Human beings currently live on many of the populated worlds in our Nebadon universe and we are a special creation, because our DNA can hold frequencies up to the twelfth dimension. The normal frequency hertz for a human being with a carbon body is 500-600 hertz, but once a human is able to raise his vibration to the frequency of 3,000 hertz with his crystalline Adam Kadmon hieros gamos body, he is completely out of the physicality of the 3D earth and can then climb the stairway to heaven to make the final jump into the new heaven on earth. The city of Telos located in the inner earth is an entire civilization that is under Mount Shasta in California where all of its inhabitants vibrate at a very high rate of the fourth density level, so they are invisible to the human eye. When an individual reports seeing a UFO it's because it adjusts its frequency down so the human's eyes can see it, but once it raises its frequencies it suddenly disappears from sight. First Contact is tentatively scheduled to occur on earth during the year 2026 or sooner or sooner and the positive extraterrestrials will actually land their starships on earth and introduce, the med beds technology on earth that will reverse aging, heal all diseases and help to raise the human frequency overnight from 4D to 5D.

Once a human has ascended to the new heaven on earth, he has the free will to choose to return to earth to continue to help the rest of mankind ascend and these ascended humans will come back to earth as superhuman beings after first having a one-hundred-year vacation on the new earth, meeting your galactic and birth family again and then choosing your next assignment.

Once you ascend to the new heaven on earth and live and walk again with God's higher celestial beings, you will have access to enter Paradise-the seven higher heavens and this is the hierarchy of order in the kingdom of heaven.

Infinity

Infinity is the highest living breathing organism who is the Source, the Prime Creator, unconditional love. The Prime Creator, Source is neither masculine or feminine, nor is he a man, but rather it is an infinite force of expansiveness. Everything in dimensions thirteen down to dimension one comes from the body of the Prime Creator, Source who is infinite. You cannot come face to face with the Prime Creator, because he has the power of one billion suns and His light is so intense that He densifies His power down to .001% when he wants to interface with Archangel Metatron (Enoch the Ethiopian) to give his instructions to the rest of the archangels. Archangel Metatron is in charge, and he is the executive director of the throne of God and of maintaining all of the six-dimensional sacred geometry in 6D that holds our universe together and where all matter on the 3D earth originates. Archangel Metatron was the father of Lamech, and the grandfather of Noah and he is the only archangel who ever descended to earth 50,000 years ago and lived as a human man and God used his bloodline to continue the lineage of mankind on earth after the great flood. All humans receive the spark of life in the void before beginning their material life on earth and this spark of the Prime Creator, the Source lives within us and through this spark every experience we have in life, we are giving our Prime Creator the chance to experience life.

Seraphim

The seraphim angels exist in dimension 13D, and they are the executive assistants to the Prime Creator, Source. The seraphim angels have the largest wingspan of all the angels and their wings have a thousand eyes on them. Their job is to send out assignments from the Prime Creator, Source to the archangels.

Archangels

The archangels exist in the twelfth dimension and each archangel represents a strand of the Prime Creator, Source and their job is to carry out the will of God.

Archangel Metatron is the guardian of the throne of God, God's direct messenger and he oversees all of the sacred geometry in the sixth dimension. Archangel Metatron has a special love for young sensitive adults and one of the ways Metatron helps young adults is by guiding their parents. He is also the teacher of esoteric knowledge, and he helps humans to work with the universal energies for healing, understanding and teaching. Archangel Metatron is a powerful initiator of change on earth, and he has orchestrated many great events on earth, and he helps to clear the human mind of clutter and to bring positive changes and miracles into your life. He often appears on earth as a butterfly, eagle or condor.

Archangel Rafael oversees healing.

Archangel Gabriel oversees Paradise as the executive when Michael is not there, and he is God's messenger to humanity and he is entrusted with important missions to help humanity in their creative pursuits, completion of projects and he often appears on earth as a crow, raven, or lion.

Archangel Remiel oversees humanity's divine visions and hope.

Archangel Saraqael oversees spirits who sin during the night.

Archangel Raquel oversee the luminaries and serves as the peacemaker for those in heaven and on earth. He holds the book of Akashic Records which are stored in the hall of records in the Upper Astral Plane and helps to make changes to soul contracts and how to explore your akashic records. He often appears on earth as a mouse, groundhog, opossum, racoon and a skunk.

Archangel Michael prevents chaos in humanity and is the system sovereign of the Nebadon Universe. Archangel Michael is the leader of the archangels, and he is the protector of swordsmen, master of arms, he sends the blue flame/light of protection over mankind, and he reincarnated to earth 2,154 years ago to complete his final seventh bestowal as Jesus of Nazareth. Archangel Michael is now the system sovereign of the Nebadon Universe and he helps to heal the mind, body, spirit, loss of loved ones, addictions, physical ailments and he protects the lightworkers and starseeds who continue to work within the light of God.

Archangel Sandalphon and Archangel Metatron are both special, because they both began their lives as humans who were known as Enoch the Ethiopian and Prophet Elijah and they both lived such a pious life as humans that they were each whisked away by God to live the rest of their existence as archangels which helped them both to be able to understand and help humans with our struggles in life.

Archangel Sandalphon oversees the music in heaven and on earth and he nurtures our soul with music, assists us to create music, gives us better clarity, more effective meditation, serves as an advocate for our prayers and he reviews your life path when prayers are received to determine the best way to answer our prayers. Archangel Sandalphon often appears on earth as cicadas, birds, frog, and crickets. Archangel Sandalphon is Archangel Metatron's brother, and he serves as the middleman between God and Humanity.

Archangel Raphael assists in physical healing of human beings, and he heals mankind on every level and may appear on earth in the form of a deer.

Archangel Azrael assists to cure depression, mental and emotional illness, helps humanity in the transition from earth to heaven, helps to cure addictions, promotes inner stillness, inner calm and he helps to prevent the negative voice of the ego from taking over your thoughts and he often appears on earth as a dove.

Archangel Uriel helps with feelings of loneliness and helps us to learn how to be alone and how to appreciate our own company by looking at the wonders within your soul, helps you to explore the mysteries of the universe and he often appears on earth as a blue jay.

Archangel Chamuel is the angel of love and self-love, and he helps humanity to love and appreciate who you are and helps us with our relationships in life. He often appears on earth as a rabbit.

Archangel Remiel helps humanity with their divine visions and gives us hope.

Archangel Haniel helps to mend family relationships, family bonds, heals issues of abandonment and he often appears on earth in the form of a turtle.

The Seven Archangels

Archangel Ariel oversees earth and all its creatures especially during natural disasters, helps to maintain the good health in animals and brings peace into your life through natural means, He often appears on earth as ducks, geese or swans.

Archangel Raziel is the gatekeeper of divine information, he governs the veil between the worlds of heaven and earth, our subconscious dreams, spirit communications and he appears on earth as a fish and rainbows which are portals.

Archangel Zadkiel assists with issues dealing with forgiveness, abuse, productive use of time and he appears on earth as beavers.

Archangel Jeremiel deals with issues relating to mercy, justice and he provides spiritual cleansing of the soul, helps to increase our faith and helps in troublesome situations. he often appears on earth as a cheetah, puma or leopard.

Archangel Jophiel is the great giver of joy, and he helps to raise our energy levels, to receive unconditional love and helps to boost humanity with strong positive energy. He often appears on earth as a heron.

The Elohim

The word Elohim is plural, and it refers to many Gods and it means all that God is and the Elohim were referred to in the Old Testament over two thousand years ago five hundred times as the name of God. The Elohim are referred to as the Divine Mother and Jehovah refers to the Divine father who are beings of spirits of form. The Elohim were the beings who created the world by the will of YHWH (the Godhead) and if you look at the first layer of all of our DNA under a microscope and it spells out the words: God is eternal within the body.

The Elohim exist in the eleventh dimension which is called the technology dimension, and they were the first living beings to be created from the womb of God, the Prime Creator Source and they are one level below the archangels. When the Elohim were created, they felt intense physical pain from being separated from the Prime Creator and human beings share this same pain when we are born in the realm of fourth dimensional earth. Since the Elohim live in the eleventh dimension, the technology dimension they are the genetic scientists who also created the trees, plants and animals on all the planets. All humans living in our Nebadon universe can trace their original roots to the planet Lyra which is a tenth and eleventh dimensional planet where for the first time an intelligent being evolved which were the feline beings. And when these original feline beings developed on Lyra, the Elohim had to descend and incarnate on Lyra with a soul and spirit into these feline beings, because there were no human beings living on Lyra yet. These feline beings living on Lyra continued to evolve for millions of years in peace until the first sudden invasion of the Draco-reptilians from another universe on their planet and that's when all hell broke loose. Then the draco-reptilians destroyed the entire planet of Lyra and annihilated the entire population except for the ten percent who were able to escape to other planets in one large Merkabah light body. These Lyrans were able to escape this invasion when the Lyran high priest formed his molecular Merkabah and more Lyrans kept adding on their own small Merkabah's until they formed one large Merkabah spaceship. This Draco-reptilian invasion happened billions of years ago and the Lyrans who escaped had to descend down and settle on the planets Sirius B and Pleaides and this is when the Elohim began to create human beings.

The Prime Creator originally created the Draco-reptilians as Elohim angelic beings, but they made the decision to separate themselves from the Prime Creator and during the subsequent wars that followed in their universe, the Draco-reptilians adapted a victim consciousness where they blamed and attacked each other and any other available universe. The Draco-reptilians eventually destroyed the portal that would lead them back home to the Prime Creator and now they can't ascend any higher than the fourth dimension and so they cannot ascend back home to heaven. In order to survive the Draco-reptilians survive by invading universes and feeding off the pain and suffering of others which is called loosch energy.

Human beings currently live on planets all over the Nebadon universe and we are the only creation who has a free will with unlimited potential to evolve. Humanity living on earth have the capacity to experience one hundred and thirty-nine emotions with the highest and most powerful emotion being authenticity. Human beings and angels are separate creations with humans being superior to angels once they ascend, because they have made the free will choice to return back home to the Prime Creator after learning all of the life lessons on earth. Humans exist in their physical body up to the fourth dimension and once a human ascends past the seventh dimension, there is no more physical body, only spirit, light and energy with no more physical death.

These are The Twelve Ascended Masters Who Exist In Our Universe, And They Live in The Seventh Dimension In Shambala.

JESUS	**ASHTAR SHERAN**
CONFUCIUS	**SANAT KUMARA**
GAUTAMA BUDDHA	**SAINT GERMAIN**
MARY, THE MOTHER OF JESUS	**MACHIVENTA MELCHIZEDEK**
ST PAUL OF TARSUS KNOWN AS HILARION	**KWAN LIN**
KUTHUMI	**ARCHANGEL MICHAEL**

The Twelve Ascended Masters

Ascended Master Mother Mary of Jesus of Nazareth kept the flame of love for the world mother, and she is the archetype of motherhood, and she ascended body and soul back home to heaven. Mary was born from the bloodline of King David from a long line of unique ancestors who included many well-known women in the bible such as Amnon, Tamar, Ruth, Bathsheba, Ansie, Cloa, Eve, Enta, and Ratta. Mary, the mother of Jesus came to earth as one of God's beloved ones with the full powers to be God's ambassador. God entrusted Mary with the interests to complete God's divine plan to have God's mercy, justice and Mary had God's unique power of intercession. Mary while on earth was able to fight against the seven deadly sins on earth with superhuman ease and durability, because her human body was more resistant than that of a normal human.

Ascended Master St. Paul of Tarsus known as Hilarion was one of the leaders of Jesus' twelve apostles. He was born in the year 4 B.C. and he was an ambassador for Jesus of Nazareth who spread the good news of the gospel, Jesus' life, death, resurrection and ascension back home to heaven.

Ascended Master Kwan Yin was one of Buddhisms of Buddhism's most beloved Bodhisattvas and he is the embodiment of compassion, because he hears the cries of humanity on earth and listens deeply to humanity's prayers that are spoken from the heart.

Ascended Master Kuthumi was one of the Mahatmas who inspired the founding of the Theosophical Society in the year 1875. He is the doorkeeper of the ancient occult mysteries and the co-protector with Archangel Michael of the holy grail. Master Kuthumi works with Jesus as a world teacher and he is the master of the second ray of divine wisdom-illumination and some of his past incarnations on earth included, Pythagoras, St Francis of Assisi and as a Magi Priest.

Ascended Master Confucious was the first teacher in China who was instrumental in making education available to all and he established the art of teaching as a vocation. Confucious was a Chinese philosopher born in the year 551 BCE and he lived about five hundred years before the birth of Jesus of Nazareth. Confucious' golden rule was do not do to others what you do not want them to do to you.

Ascended Master Saint Germain was born in Germany in the year 1693 and he was the son of Prince Frances II Rakoczi of Transylvania. He was knowledgeable in science, arts, philosophy, alchemy, and was a composer and a pianist. Saint Germaine is the keeper of the sacred violet flame of healing and as we continue during the ascension process to heal our past life traumas and triggers with compassion and love ask Saint Germain to transmute these negative traumas with love to the sacred violet flame.

Ascended Master Machiventa Melchizedek was born of a virgin birth from his parents High Priest Nir (Noah's brother) and from the dead corpse of his mother Sothonim fully clothes as a three-year-old child. Melchizedek had no beginning and no end, and his priesthood lives on forever. Melchizedek was the King of Salem, and he worked in his spiritual ministry after the default of Adam and Eve to prepare the way for Jesus of Nazareth and he established a covenant with Abraham to be his successor. Melchizedek and Jesus of Nazareth shared the same Divine Thought Adjuster, and he is currently the Planetary Prince of planet earth.

Ascended Master Ashtar Sheran is the Commander of the Galactic Fleet for the Galactic Federation of Planets in our solar system. He oversees the airborne division of the brotherhood of light, and he has over twenty million personnel under his command in our solar system and four million personnel under his command on the physical plane. Commander Ashtar is from the 5D ascended planet Venus, he has never lived on planet earth, he is seven feet tall and has a fully activated Adam Kadmon (999) crystalline body which is an advanced form of the human body. Commander Ashtar also represents our solar system in all of the council meetings of our galaxy and universe all throughout the greater omniverse.

Ascended Master Sanat Kumara is from the 5D ascended planet Venus and he was the son the son of Krishna and after the fall of Atlantis on earth 12,000 years ago the cosmic council made the decision to end the human experiment on earth, but Sanat Kumara made a plea for humanity stating that he would hold the pure source light of love from our Prime Creator, Source so that humanity on earth could continue to evolve and ascend back home to heaven during our current times.

Ascended Master Archangel Michael is the leader of the archangels who live in the twelfth dimension of heaven and he incarnated on earth as a twelfth dimensional being straight from God to complete his seventh and final bestowal as Jesus of Nazareth where along with his wife Mary Magdalene, they planted the ascension gridlines on earth so that humanity during our current times can complete the ascension process to return home to heaven. Ascended Master Michael raised the vibrations of the entire planet earth during incarnation as Jesus of Nazareth and he is the keeper of the sacred blue flame and the spiritual warrior and leader for all the angels in both Christianity and in Islam's holy book the Quran.

Ascended Master Buddha (Siddhartha Gautama) was a member of the great white brotherhood, and he now serves in the hierarchy of light as the lord of the world. Buddha achieved enlightenment through guidance and meditation, and he left all of his worldly riches behind. Buddha was born in Nepal in the year 563 B.C. to royal parents and after he his rich home life, Buddha led a life as a monk in meditation, mendicancy and asceticism and he attained nirvana in India. Some of the miracles of Buddha's life included, healings, teleportation, creating duplicates of himself, manipulation of the elements and other supernatural phenomena. During his last years of living on earth, Jesus of Nazareth and his wife Mary Magdalene spent time in Kashmer studying Buddhism exclusively. Buddha taught the virtues of loving kindness, wisdom, gratitude, respect and to let go of anger and greed The goal of Buddhism is to achieve peace of mind as a step beyond joyful happiness.

The Ascended Masters are all human beings who have taken the path of initiation that is also known as ascension and they are able to live in 7D Shambala, because they have completed the tough lessons and tests of life on earth and ascended back home to heaven.

The main lesson that we learn from the ascended masters is that one of them Jesus of Nazareth who was the direct son of God came to live on earth 2,154 years ago and will return during earth's ascension to the higher dimensions. Jesus needed to ascend and return to Paradise after his life here on earth so that Michael of Nebadon could take his rightful place as the system sovereign of our Nebadon universe.

All of the ascended masters live in 7D Shambala and they all have multi-dimensional abilities, and they can hear you when you call out their name and they are able to jump into your timeline. The ascended masters love spending time with us observing our thoughts, watch us as we draw pictures or while reading or writing a book from your heart. Extend your hand out before going to sleep tonight and ask Jesus to take your hand to go to a beautiful place on a spiritual retreat with him while you sleep tonight. The ascended masters each have a dwelling on Shambala and since they are multi-dimensional beings, they can exist from the fifth dimension all the way up to the twelfth dimension. Jesus and the other ascended masters are also still currently guiding other planets as they continue to evolve and ascend to the higher dimensions. The ascended masters can live in their homes on 7D Shambala, they can live on starships, they can live with the angels, and they can live on planets Sirius B and Pleaides.

An example of this is once when there was an active volcanic eruption occurring here on earth, Jesus came to earth with some Pleiadeans to make sure that the volcano erupted correctly, because whenever a volcano erupts, it opens up portals on earth to that lead to the higher dimensions.

The ascended masters also have feelings when they spend time observing humans, but when they do, they must detox themselves for days afterwards, because pain and suffering does affect them.

The Law of One is a philosophy that is based on the origin of the universe, and it explains that the entire universe is a manifestation of the Prime Creator Source, and this message was communicated and explained humanity by celestial beings who call themselves RA in the 1980's through a channel named Carla Rueckert.

The Law of One

The seven densities that are located in the universe are explained in detail.

The thirty-six dimensions that are located in the Nebadon universe are explained.

The higher self who is our ascended master self who exists billions of years in the future in the seventh dimension 7D is explained.

Angels who live in the twelfth dimension 12D are explained.

Starseeds and lightworkers are a part of the human evolution of the choice we all have as souls with a free will to make in order to spiritually progress and ascend back home to the new heaven on earth and to become ascended masters.

The Middle Astral Plane

The middle astral plane is located in the fourth dimension, and it has a tranquil serene environment that is the domain of the elementals which includes the Devic kingdom, human ascended masters and the archangels and all of these beings have chosen to be stationed on the middle astral plane so that they can continue to assist humanity on earth appearing to us as our spiritual guides.

Not all of the territory of the middle astral plane is free of mischief, because parts of it in the vicinity of the lower astral plane is sometimes tainted with certain traits of indigenous leprechauns who have been known to play tricks and pranks on visiting humans. These leprechauns do not cause any real harm and most visiting humans who have a good sense of humor are able to tolerate their mischief.

Most of the middle astral plane is mostly a realm of consciousness, non-physical and as a part of the fourth dimension it provides a bridge to the next density of physical consciousness in the fifth dimension and most of the beings who live in the middle astral plane are able to shapeshift to any form they desire.

The Elementals

The human expression of the oversoul has elementals within the physical body just as earth has a planetary body, because we are the microcosm of Blessed Gaia earth.

The Devas

The Devas are the divine beings who oversee every constructive activity such as the building of great cathedrals, majestic mountains, lakes, woodlands and the construction of our human bodies. Devas act as the group consciousness of all of the different elemental beings who hold form, and the Deva body is the group consciousness of the earth, air, water and fire elementals that join together to form our physical human body. There are many types of Devas both subhuman and superhuman and during a Deva meeting all of the inspirational thoughts of humanity are gathered up, matched with the divine ideas of the Source and they are then sent back to the earth plane.

The Devic Kingdom

The Devic kingdom is ruled from the mental plane to infuse divine ideas into the physical manifestations. The Devic kingdom has all of the holders of form from the highest vibrational Elohim down to the lowest vibrational elemental body. All of the beings who live in the nature kingdom are a part of the Devic kingdom and they are each a specialist in creating a specific form whether it is an electron, a biological cell, a flower, a tree, a planet, a solar system or interstellar space. Just like the angels, the elemental beings begin their evolution small in size and their size increases as they evolve, while humans decrease the density of their bodies as they evolve, and their auras get larger.

The Elohim

The Elohim are the rulers of the elemental and Devic kingdoms and just as humans evolve into ascended masters, angels evolve into archangels and elementals will eventually evolve to be Devas and then to Elohim. The Elohim have a male and female aspect, and they are the creator gods and goddesses who are the highest evolution of the Devic kingdom. The Elohim and archangels are the left and right hands of the Prime Creator, Source and each of the Elohim is associated with one of the seven rays and they therefore contribute to the qualities of their assigned individual ray to all creation. The elemental beings who are living on earth have all sworn to only portray humanity's thoughts and feelings and they are obligated to materialize whatever they pick up from the thoughts and feelings of mankind. This relationship was intended to facilitate the re-manifestation of the new heaven on earth, but humanity's thoughts and feelings often result in natural disasters, such as tornadoes, hurricanes, volcanoes, earthquakes, the polluted oceans and smog in the atmosphere.

The Elementals

There are currently elemental beings working around the clock in our atmosphere to help purify the environment on earth from the distorted energies resulting from all the negative thoughts and feelings of mankind.

The salamanders are the fire elements, and you can use your psychic vision to see them dancing in flames of fire and their contribution to humanity is that they are the expression of the sacred fire of life. The salamanders have the ability to purify disharmony within all that is a part of nature. We can thank the salamander for a sunny day, because they rule the fire element and the fire elemental beings carry their fire spirit into the very essence of our physical world and without the salamander fire elementals, we would not receive photons from the sun, have fire to warm our homes, cook our meals and our human bodies would not have neuron synapses.

The Fire Elementals

Through the fire elemental beings humanity is able to impact the weather, and our thoughts are the end result of the neural activity that the fire and salamander elemental beings started and completed. When our thoughts are kind and clear, our inner elementals then attract other elementals who are kind and clear and the photons of the sun are also able to more easily integrate into earth by our efforts of having more positive calm thoughts. All of the weather on earth is a direct response to all of its occupants, because earth is the sum total of all of the planets' creatures.

The Undines

The Undines are the water elementals, and they can be seen with our psychic vision as wispy creatures in the water as waves, currents or sparkles of light on the surface of the water. Mermen and mermaids are also undines elemental beings, and they usually live by clear moving streams of water and the Sylphs elementals exist in gardens and forests and they work with the undines elementals to create rain. There is the same amount of water on the fourth dimensional astral planes as there is on planet earth.

The Gnomes

The Gnomes serve as earth elementals, and they are known as the elves or brownies. Gnomes are said to live in caves under the earth and they largely work with the mineral kingdom, the elves and the brownies to assist humanity and the animal kingdom on earth. The Gnomes who are the earth elemental beings give the human body its physical substance and only humans who can focus on love are able to see and visit the Gnomes who live in caves under the earth.

The Elementals

The Sylph Elementals

The chemtrails that the Deep State/Cabal/Elites/ Illuminati are currently spraying in the skies all over earth mostly during the night are also degrading and harming our human genetics by damaging the human DNA/RNA systems which totally interferes with our ascension process. This chemtrail program was addressed in a video by the late entertainer Prince and its agenda is genocide, because it helps to drastically reduce the human population to gain global control of earth under the false pretense of a new world order.

The Air Elementals

The air elementals assist in the flow of the life-giving oxygen to the human consciousness, and they are closely associated with humanity's thoughts. The weather on earth is changing, because since the portal to the fourth dimension opened on December 21, 2012, our planet is now basically a fourth dimensional planet, the old 3D earth is gone. This has made the current 4D reality that now exists on earth to be more unsettled, and it is now more easily influenced by the thoughts and feelings of its inhabitants. That is the reason why the air elemental beings are now continuing to help raise the vibrations of earth and for humanity.

The Elementals

All of the elementals that are embedded within each of our human physical body are all components of planet earth as well as being the components of our oversoul fractals who choose to be first, second and fourth dimensional beings. The human first and second dimensional selves live in unity with planet earth and from this unity we are able to commune in oneness with all of the fourth dimensional creatures who are the elemental beings of earth, air, fire and water. Just as a part of your oversoul chose to be first and second dimensional beings, some part of your oversoul chose to be fourth dimensional entities and these fourth dimensional entities have a strong unity consciousness which keeps them in constant communication with each other as well as with the lower dimensional beings. The elementals are the fourth dimensional beings from the astral plane who most directly interface with humanity's everyday life.

The Water Elementals

The water elementals and the undines elementals rule the human bodily fluids, blood and circulation which is the domain of the heart. When the human heart is not functioning well then, we experience the emotion of fear. The human heart and the water elements serve as the distributor of our emotions and as humanity continues to expand its consciousness, we will become more aware of our inner guides, the Holy Spirit, angels, and the other members of the inner world. As earth and humanity continues its spiritual path of ascension, we will become more aware of our own higher self whom as we ascend have each downloaded from the seventh dimension and eventually you will integrate and fully embody your higher self into your physical body and function as one.

The Fairies

The fairies are elemental beings who are also sylphs, because they serve the air and some of the fairies live in the land of the fairies, but many also live in the lower vibrations of the fourth dimensional astral plane. The fairy elementals are called the changes, because they help in changing the four seasons on earth. They help the old leaves to fall from the trees and you may find them in nice gardens. The lights and colors that are found in the fairy elementals is so bright that it is like coming out of a dark cave into a bright field.

The Sylph Elementals

The sylph elementals are the air elementals, and they live in the human's aura, and they constantly contribute and uplift earth's aura, the atmosphere and the quality of earth's air and sky. The sylph elementals are beautiful wispy creatures, and they are also known as fairies who help us with our breathing and every time we inhale we are receiving the thoughts of others and with every exhalation we are distributing our thoughts all throughout the world through our air elementals. When we have clear thinking then we contribute to having a clear day. The sylph elemental beings look like one living being to humans, but in reality, they are all joined together in consciousness, and they are not individual beings. The sylph elemental beings have been very busy on earth cleansing and neutralizing earth's atmosphere from the harmful chemicals that are daily being sprayed on mankind under the direction of the dark brotherhood through the use of chemtrails. These harmful chemtrails eventually destroy the human immune system and they have a way of damaging our pineal gland and the other divine organs humans have that are responsible for our multi-dimensional abilities that allow us to ascend to higher dimensions and ascend.

When our Prime Creator, Source created humans it is not that Prime Creator needed to create humans, but after the creation of the Archangels, Elohim and Angels at some point it was evident that these three newly created beings were not growing and evolving to their full potential within the dimensions of the spirit world, so forces were set in motion that led to the existence of the physical worlds of time and space. The Prime Creator Source for the most part left each world to evolve on its own and on some of the physical worlds a life form eventually evolved that was able to support the needs of the spirits who needed to learn the lessons of life in order to evolve and this gave the life forms who originally came from the spirit realms the capacity to reason and make informed choices while experiencing life in the physical worlds. On planet earth once the early hominids reached the evolutionary level of Homo Sapien- Sapien, some interventions were made to make humanity a reality. There was an Adam and Eve on every world of time and space in our universe whose job was to racially uplift the evolving humans on each of their assigned worlds.

When a spirit makes the free will choice to incarnate on earth, he only brings 1/3 of his spirit to earth, due to the density of the planet, and the rest stays in the heavenly realms, so we never really totally leave heaven, but when your spirit incarnates to earth you have no prior memories of your existence in the heavenly realms. Just as we humans evolve while living our life on earth, so does the Prime Creator, because the human existence helps the Prime Creator to experience what we do while living our lives on earth. The original intent of the Prime Creator when he created humans was to address the evolutionary needs of the first three spirits who were created, the Archangels, Elohim and Angels and not the needs of the Prime Creator. The more advanced a human becomes spiritually, the greater is their capacity to shape the values and interests of their human self and to use their stronger energy to make their presence known. Every human has the potential to go within to find the God source, to experience what we do authenticity and wake up to choose the spiritual path of ascension to return home to our Prime Creator, Source.

The human body is the most powerful being ever to be created, because it is an organic computer with a soul and far superior to any clone or artificial intelligence and at its center is the human heart and the wheels to the human body are its eight major chakras. The human body is the sacred foundation, an avatar that connects us to our ascended higher mind. The human skeleton is the anchor, our base, our scafford and the human body fits inside a cube of geometric space. Humans are galactic multi-dimensional beings who each have a soul and when we dance, practice yoga or exercise this helps to energize and cleanse the energy field of our physical body, because these activities takes us outside of our body's cube of space. Out of all the activities we perform as humans, the positive extraterrestrials enjoy watching humans dance out of anything else. Grounding and meditating daily while visualizing that you are on the new heaven on earth (Blessed Gaia is important, because it connects you with all of the new magnetic energies on Blessed Gaia.) Do not ground on our current earth, because its current vibrations are too low.

The human body is a bridge between worlds as above so below, it is a Tree of Life, a game of hopscotch that helps us in the earth journey that leads back to the Source. The DNA in the human body is our antenna that receives the light codes that connect us with the celestial realms, and it carries all of the geometric information from the sixth dimension into our human bodies. Crystals are also in the human body in the blood, teeth, bones, kidneys, retina and third eye which allows us to maintain our balance and connect to the higher realms. The fish who swim and live in the water are able to maintain their balance due to the crystals they have in their bodies.

These are some of the steps that are the beginning of human life that has made the choice to reincarnate on planet earth.

You begin as a geometric equation in the sixth dimension that is maintained by Archangel Metatron.

You stand in line to receive your spark of life, your blue flame.

You go to the Akashic Hall of Records to select your twelve houses and your life plan for your life on earth including all of the players for your reality/movie.

You access the code 9/10 the speed of light to gain entry to the fourth dimension in order to enter the womb of your mother in 3D earth.

Your one cell soon divides into

Two cells divide.

A tetrahedron

A cube develops.

Metatron cube (16 cells) develops.

A torus develops which is your fourth dimensional body.

On day (49) you have your first memory when your eight genesis cells form and stay locked at the base of your spine form. This is the basis of your Merkabah light body that you used to descend from the higher realms and need to use to ascend back home to heaven.

You continue to develop inside your mother's womb at a geometric ratio of 1.618.

The center of your torus is the human heart and when you are born the placenta looks just like a tree.

Your soul and consciousness are in and out of the developing baby but must be inside the baby's body at the time of birth, or the baby is born stillborn.

These are some of the most important organs in the human body relating to the ascension process.

The pineal gland is made of crystal, and it has all of the seeds in it that connects us with our ancestors.

The original stem cells are cube shaped and they are our origin of life here on earth.

The bone marrow carries the memories of all our past reincarnations.

The energy from the human heart is connected to the I am pure consciousness energy in dimension 29D.

The human heart is the first human organ to develop, and it connects the human with the rest of the universe, because it links us with the Prime Creator Source which then forms a spiral of love and after the ascension process has been completed the more love you hold in your heart, the more prosperous you will be on the new heaven on earth.

The human veins are similar to the flow of the rivers, and they carry energy all throughout the body just like lightening carries electricity from the sixth realm from the inner earth to the surface of the earth.

Tree rings are identical to the print on out thumb.

The human blood plasma is connected to the fourth state of matter.

Humans are created in the image of the divine, a vine.

The human kidney looks like the coral in the ocean.

The veins of leaves fit the lines in the palm of a human hand.

The human hands first forms as a golden spiral and follows of sacred geometry equation of 1.618, the golden ratio.

Walnuts help to prevent cognitive decline in the human brain, and we need to meditate daily to listen to what is in your arteries just like the rivers connect with the stars and the universe. The human brain is made up of specific parts that work together in harmony and one section of the human brain is reptilian.

The definition of the perfect human face conforms to the sacred geometry golden ratio of 1.618 with a ratio of 3-5-8.

When you listen to music it activates the entire human brain.

440 hertz music makes you sad and causes you to feel irregular emotions.

432 hertz music promotes feelings of peace and beauty in the human brain.

DNA was created for the human body to hold all of the necessary light codes, because our physical bodies are nothing more than light codes being held together in a vessel to enable us to experience third dimensional life. Our consciousness developed from the aspects of the twelve houses that we bring to earth with us. The high frequency light that we originated from was moved down with us from the higher dimensions to the lowest third dimension to create physicality in a human vessel, the body and our high frequency light was then moved to our carbon based (666) human body that holds these light codes in the DNA of the human body so that our spirit/soul will be able to daily receive the rays coming to earth from our great central sun.

Third Eye Opening

During the ascension process when your third eye opens you will never forget this experience. There will be enough power to light up an entire city focused into your forehead, because your punched, twisted and already pulsating and squirming pineal gland will pop, and you will hear the pop and then you will see a bright flash, exit your body, be pulled back into your physical body and then your heart will restart. The opening of your third eye is usually the last energy center in your body to be opened before you experience the kundalini rising event which will usually occur a few weeks later. The opening of your third eye is only for your benefit and you will receive divine help to open it, because you cannot open your third eye on your own.

Once your third eye energy center opens you will not magically then be able to see other beings or travel freely to wherever you want to go, because it doesn't work like that. You will need some help getting the energy centers in your body opened and the only way is when God himself wants to meet you face to face and God will then send an angel to you who will fuse with you to open your third eye energy center. This will be a rare and unique occurrence in your life that will scare the living daylights out of you, and it will happen totally independent of your wishes and desires. For some humans it might take over a year from the third eye opening fusion event to experience the kundalini rising event and your mind will be overwhelmed, your mind will not be in control of your third eye opening and kundalini event, so your mind must surrender to the spirit. Today you may be vibrating at 5D frequencies, but your physical and spiritual bodies still must be adequately prepared to physically live on the new heaven on earth. So, you must have faith and be patient and accept God's divine help. You will at this point be very confused about it all, because you will still have no power, understanding, abilities or authority over this entire ascension process that your body, not your spirit is going through. This is the level that your mind will be at, and you may spend two years at a level of nothingness after your third eye opening event. When God himself is ready for you in His divine time, you will then realize that the whole point of opening all of your physical body's energy centers and your kundalini rising event is, so you have the ability to see and communicate with other living beings in other realms and dimensions.

Third Eye Opening

When God himself sends an angel to you as His gift to open all of your body's energy centers, this means that you are having a meeting with God himself. Even after all of your body's energy centers have been opened, you still will not have the power or understanding that you can use at this point to benefit yourself or anyone else.

When you have your kundalini rising event, and have your face-to-face meeting with God himself, these are some of the events that may or may not occur for you:

You will exit your body and move through vortexes or wormholes and find yourself on the crucifixion cross as Jesus.

The power of the cross is that you will receive the power over death, the world and your own faith.

You will continue to travel through more wormholes and find yourself standing before the throne before a person who has no face seated on a throne and as this person stands up you will be pulled into him and when you sit down wisdom will begin to stream into your open energy centers and your new (999) krystallah body will then be formed.

You will continue to travel through more wormholes and find yourself in a place that resembles a crescent and as you travel down from above this crescent you will be standing at an inverted shoreline before the Universal Father and in this place, you will think in absolute terms, and this is the place of forever and the eternal.

In this place of forever and eternal you will be given eternal life from God himself and God will then speak to you.

Once all of these events occur, you will no longer be a human being just having a spiritual experience, but you are now a cosmic citizen being having a human experience. Whatever you decide to do with all of the blessings you have just received from God and all of the power of heaven backing you up, you need to have faith and continue to follow God's divine plan daily.

At this point this doesn't mean that your problems will magically disappear or that your suffering is over, but now you will begin to do and see things that will blow your mind at your level of consciousness, because you will now be able to see other spirits and living beings in other realms and dimensions and you will be able to communicate with them freely.

You will now be able to speak about six or more different languages and the beings you will communicate with will appear to you as human, but they are alien life forms who are happy to see you.

You will be welcomed everywhere except on planet earth, because here on earth you will be hated, ignored and silenced.

Continue to daily complete your lightworker duties here on earth, do your job, keep quiet about what you can see, because you are working under God's protection.

DNA allows for the evolution of human consciousness which answers our questions of who we are and why we incarnated here on earth and all of the light codes in the human DNA are condensed down into carbon, because carbon can easily shift from states of matter into air. The human DNA is designed to shift the states of being within the human body which due to the incoming solar flares is changing the human body from being carbon based to crystalline bodies. The big experiment that began on earth millions of years ago was designed for humanity to evolve from vibrating at the third density up to the fifth density in order to be able to ascend and return home to the new heaven on earth.

In the fifth dimension you will have a crystalline body, in the sixth dimension you won't be needing your DNA after ascending from 3D earth, because in 6D this is where all of the sacred geometry for our entire Nebadon universe is located and there is no physical body from the seventh dimension to the twelfth dimension, only light bodies of energy.

The more an individual's light codes are activated in their DNA, the more you will begin to remember who you really are and the higher a human evolves then the soul contracts that were made at the Akashic Hall of Records in the astral plane will dissolve, and you will begin to remember your soul's higher purpose instead of the traumatic memories of your past.

Human beings were created in our Nebadon universe 560 million years ago and we are the keyholders to ascend to the new heaven on earth on 7D Blessed Gaia. Whenever lightworkers/starseeds hold positive 432 hertz music festivals it helps to activate the earth's nodes, ley lines and helps to open portals on our ascending earth.

The portal to 5D opened on December 18, 2021, and ever since this date about 100,000 galactic starships from the Galactic Federation of Planets have been surrounding earth lowering down their beams of light on earth to continue to activate earth's nodes, ley lines and to neutralize any of the military's nuclear weapon facilities to help in the ascension process here on earth.

These are the twelve nodes and twelve nulls that are located on planet earth, and each has its own color and when you match two of the same color nodes and null together by emitting the right tone they are then activated.

LOCATIONS OF PLANET EARTH'S TWELVE NODES

GLASTONBURY, ENGLAND-BLUE

ISLAND OF THE SUN, LAKE TITICACA, BOLIVIA-BLUE

MACHU PICCHU, PERU-BLUE

MAUI, HAWAII-RED

MONT BLANC, FRENCH ALPS, FRANCE-RED

MOUNT COOK, NEW ZEALAND-RED

MOUNT IDA AND HOT SPRINGS, ARKANSAS-GREEN

MOUNT SHASTA, CALIFORNIA-GREEN

RILA MOUNTAIN, BULGARIA-GREEN

TABLE MOUNTAIN, SOUTH AFRICA-PURPLE

ULURU, AUSTRALIA-PURPLE

YUCATAN PENINSULA, MEXICO-PURPLE

LOCATIONS OF EARTH'S TWELVE NULLS

ANETO PYRENEES, SPAIN-BLUE

GUNNBJORN FIELD, GREENLAND-BLUE

MEILI SNOW MOUNTAIN, CHINA-BLUE

MOUNT KAILASH, TIBET-PURPLE

MOUNT KILIMANJARO, TANZANIA-PURPLE

MOUNT LOGAN YUKON TERRITORIES, CANADA-PURPLE

TIBESTI MOUNTAINS, CHAD-RED

URAL MOUNTAINS, RUSSIA-RED

VICTORY PEAK, TIEN SHAN KYRGYZSTAN-RED

MOUNT ACONCAGUA, ARGENTINA-GREEN

MOUNT ARARAT, TURKEY-GREEN

MOUNT FITZ ROY PATAGONIA, ARGENTINA-GREEN

The nodes and nulls on planet earth are called the Pleiadian time capsules and they represent twenty-four locations on earth where twelve of these are charged in one way and the other twelve are charged in another way and when you touch one node or null the other one is affected and these profound time capsules have been waiting for the ascension energy which began on earth in the year 2012 to begin. The end of year 2012 was a time when the key to these (12) Nodes and (12) Nulls were put into the lock which then opened the access for all (24) of them and when the tone-sets were song at one of the locations in Maui, Hawaii in the year 2012, this created a way to open potential access to all of these (12) nodes and (12) nulls.

The Pleiadeans placed these three-dimensional time capsules on earth and when the correct tone is song with its matching color pair it represents polarity, and it then activates and creates a third energy. When humans sing the tones for these three energies the divine consciousness generates the missing pixel which then transmits a picture with millions and millions of energies and colors into planet earth, alerting our entire galaxy of something humanity has never done before.

On December 21, 2012 when earth entered the Photon Belt and the portal to the fourth dimension opened, some designated lightworkers on earth were able to create this third new energy by singing the three matching tones that sent the compassionate consciousness into the earth and into the Milky Way Galaxy where we were able to let our entire galaxy see the whole picture that earth and its awakened light workers had begun the ascension process.

Humanity's divine consciousness of the seed core of our DNA when the node and null pairs are combined with the sacred emotion of compassion completes the triad which then sends three of these combined pixels to soar as humanity continues to steer the race car of ascension not really knowing where or when or ascension is taking us, but that is the meaning of faith.

Our great central sun will continue to build the parts of the engine of our race car that someday soon will bring those on the true path of ascension to the ascended planet Blessed Gaia where we will then achieve an eternal life of health, love, authenticity and compassion and so much gratitude without you ever seeing it coming, but then there will come a day soon when humanity will see what we call the city on the hill and it will take your breath away-the new heaven on earth on Blessed Gaia. And so it is.

For those who are on the true path of ascension these are some of the ascension phases you will undergo before you reach the end of your journey to the new heaven on earth.

Ascension Phases

After your awakening moment, ascension will then be your main focus in life.

Dark night of the soul

Thirst for knowledge

Family and friends will fall away from your life.

High pitch sounds in your ears from incoming updates

Blurry vision

No sex phase-chakra pillar is re-coding

No alcohol phase-aura is re-coding

Lightworker (ON) phase

Your world flips because you now live in the higher dimensions

Thirst for purpose

(12) (24) (36) DNA activation begins

Connecting with galactic family

Third eye and downloads on high speed

Looking for community who understands you

Skin breakouts on arms and hands-crystalline body activating

Download and Merging with your higher self

Daily quantum jumps to create your new realities

Physical transformations

Less dense body-weight loss

Physical transformations

Superpowers emerge

Mastery phase begins to continue higher work on the new earth

Ascension Map

Avoid the many distractions in the matrix by focusing on your now moment and don't get lost in the drama of your daily life.

There are many positive master spiritual ascension teachers who are now offering online or on-site ascension courses, accept their help and wisdom.

Complete your daily solar flash/ love wave homework by grounding, spending quiet time with God and meditating.

Disconnect yourself from negative family and friends.

Take responsibility for your thoughts and actions and do not judge others.

Try to live in a heart-based community.

Avoid envy and gossip.

Be authentic with yourself and others.

Don't expect everyone to be like you and have compassion for those who are not on your level.

Don't be disgusted with society, because you may miss your next initiation.

Integrate yourself back into the 3D society and accept people as they are, because at one point in our life we were also at their level.

Download, merge and embody your higher mind and connect with your angels and guides daily.

Master Key to Life and Spirituality

Be content during your ascension journey and tell yourself daily, "I am who I am and that's enough."

Play a beautiful love song and look in your eyes in a mirror telling yourself that you love God and yourself and watch how rapidly you will begin to ascend and do this daily

Put God first always, go to God for all your needs and follow His divine plan.

Complete your daily solar flash/love wave homework daily to raise your vibrations if only one percent.

It takes thirty consecutive days to activate your Merkabah light body which is your ascension vehicle back home to the new heaven on earth so, do this today.

Pick up your cross daily to serve our Prime Creator, Source with the full body armor of the Holy Spirit and you will then have a seven in one stroke with the following armor:

Helmet of Salvation

Breastplate of righteousness

Shield of faith

Sword of the spirit

Belt of truth

Be ready and available to serve God

Complete your ascension journey daily with your higher mind from your heart that is filled with: authenticity, love, hope, compassion, gratitude, joy and bliss.

Retrieve the fragments of your soul that are still trapped in the ether from past hurts and traumas. Forgive yourself and anyone who has hurt you to heal your triggers and shadows and accept all fragments of your soul back into your heart now with unconditional love.

No matter what happens during your ascension journey just keep going.

Kundalini

Kundalini is the human body's sexual energy, and it is the most potent energy on planet earth. Planet earth has its own kundalini energy which is located in Croatia which had been blocked since the Croatia Wars that occurred in the year 1990, but now due to the lightworkers holding a 432 hertz music festival in the year 2020, the earth's kundalini energy is now clear and freely flowing.

Planet earth's kundalini energy moves every 26,000 years and it has now moved to Peru where it is clear and flowing. The universe starts with the human body and all of the higher dimensional shifts begin from within your physical body. Do not personally try to awaken the kundalini energy in your body on your own, because your kundalini awakening will happen when your body is ready, and our physical body knows what it needs as you evolve through the ascension process.

Continue to align your life to at least thirty percent of service to others and the kundalini energy that is being stored at the base of your spine will awaken when it is time to do so. The kundalini awakening event is different for each individual, so just continue to merge and work with your higher self to guide and protect you during your ascension process.

Expand your soul by completing your inner work daily and as you continue to find your God Source within and heal your traumas, triggers and shadows you will be healing the seven generations of your entire family who lived before you.

The Eight Main Chakras in the Human Physical Body

The eight main chakras are the energy centers in the human body that correspond to the nerve bundles and major organs. The chakras are the spinning wheels in the human body where your life energy flows through. Your chakras need to be activated and stay open and balanced in order for you to maintain a healthy spiritual life, because the chakras affect the human emotional and physical well-being.

You will be able to open and activate your eight main chakras through meditation or yoga. Once you have opened and activated your chakras you will be at peace and feel a harmonious union of your spirit, body and mind. The chakras are located in the human astral body along the spine starting at its base and running upwards to the crown of your head and since the human astral body cannot be seen or touched, this is why you cannot see your chakras.

Planet earth is the major chakra of the Milky Way Galaxy and as it rotates, earth distributes chakra energy all throughout the Milky Way galaxy.

The Eight Main Chakras

These are the eight levels of awareness that are associated with the human body's eight major chakras.

The root chakra increases your body's level of survival, willpower and your ability to be well grounded into the earth. It is located in the base of your spine and represents the color red, and it is your foundation of life that helps you to withstand and endure the challenges of life.

The sacral or sex chakra represents your desires, pleasures and it governs your emotions. It is represented by the color orange, and it is located right below your navel, belly button and it is the core of your ability to self-heal, because orange is the color for healing. The sacral chakra is where your personal being is established and it enhances your creative expression, improves your sexual intimacy and helps to increase your intuition.

The solar plexus chakra increases your body's levels of intellect, and it is the center of your physical body's power. This chakra is represented by the color yellow which represents the sun, and this chakra is known as our inner sun, because it governs our individual power and how it relates to others. When the human body's bowels, liver, and spleen are in good condition, this is because the solar plexus chakra is distributing the right amount of energy that is needed for these organs to function properly. The solar plexus chakra is located around the belly button area, and it is your self-confidence, your point of personal power and your peace and harmony.

The heart chakra is your inner sun of Christ consciousness, and it increases your levels of compassion and unconditional love. The heart chakra is represented by the color green, and it governs the body's entire cardiovascular system making sure that all of our blood flows properly through our entire body. The heart chakra is the center of authenticity and out of the (139) human emotions we can experience, it is the highest and your key to ascension, because authenticity gives you the understanding that we are one. The heart chakra has its own brain, and it is the center where your sense of love, empathy, forgiveness, balance, serenity, unhurt, unstruck and unbeaten is located.

The throat chakra increases the body's levels of acceptance, and it is represented by the color blue which signifies truth and our ability to communicate clearly. The throat chakra is the body's point of self-expression, understanding and it is our direct link to the fifth dimension.

The Eight Main Chakras

The third eye chakra increases your body's levels of the perception of the truth, and it is located in the middle of your eyes. The third eye chakra is represented by the color purple, and it gives us the spiritual vision we need to be able to see into other realities, because it is connected to the body's pineal gland that governs the body's higher facilities. The third eye chakra gives you more awareness, wisdom and insight into your spiritual connections. We can acquire more extra sensory perception by the activation of the third eye chakra, which makes it possible for one to pierce the veil into the higher levels of reality.

The third eye chakra along with the rest of the body's chakras have not been used to their full potential and that's why our human bodies age and die. If our body's seven seals or chakras as described in the Book of Revelation were being used to their full potential then along with our body's Merkabah light body, we would become immortal. Once humanity evolves and learns how to clear and activate all of our body's eight main chakras, then we will never get sick, never age and never die.

The crown chakra is the most important one, because it gives us the freedom from delusion and if you count from the top of the human head, the crown chakra is the first chakra, because it connects us to our Prime Creator Source, to our Merkabah light body, to the universe and to the higher spiritual dimensions.

The crown chakra is where during our daily meditation the high vibrational source light energy from our Universal Prime Creator pours down the universal life force energy into all of the other chakras in our body to raise our body's vibration and to stop us from growing old. The crown chakra is represented by the color indigo and along with the rest of our body's chakras it needs to remain open to enable you to become a spiritual giant.

The crown chakra is located at the top of your head, and it connects you with your own supreme individual universe which is the reality you create. As ascending multi-dimensional spiritual beings of light, we must continue to meditate daily to keep our body's chakras activated, because our body's chakras are the channels to our body's Merkabah light body and only when all of the body's chakras are spinning and functioning properly will you be healed on all of the levels of existence. The crown chakra is directly linked to the fourth realm in the inner earth which is the realm of Snow White and the seven dwarfs; (7) Dwarfs-(7) Chakras and (7) Etheric bodies.

The eighth chakra is your higher mind which is located just above your head, and it is your ascended master self who exists billions of years in the future in the seventh dimension. Once you merge as one and embody your higher mind, the eighth chakra moves down and exists inside your head. The higher mind chakra is the gateway to your soul and your intuition, and this is the part of your mind that your higher self uses to communicate through to you. The higher mind is your second set of lenses for your eyes to see through and you can download and connect with your higher mind while drawing pictures or while meditating. The higher mind chakra helps to suppress your ego with its light and love, and it transcends all boundaries and holds all of the universal truths. Your higher mind chakra is your direct link to our Prime Creator, Source and when he or she speaks to you, it is your own voice. Your higher mind is the overseer of the twelve separate realties of your existence and once you merge as one with your higher mind then you can ascend to the higher dimension of existence.

Spiritual awakening occurs differently for each person living on the ascending earth now, but you know that you have had your awakening moment when you realize that you have broken free of the third-dimension simulation matrix and are able to hold more light within your carbon based (666) carbon body. Every dimension that you travel to during your existence is a simulation, but the higher up you travel to each dimension each simulation is more advanced and they are all simulations that originate in the sixth dimension that is maintained by Archangel Metatron.

During your true path of ascension, you will begin to notice that the people around you often become triggered by by your light and your best defense, and your best defense is to continue to shine unconditional love from your heart. Our entire Nebadon universe is watching as planet earth ascends and many humans now living on earth have incarnated from the future and from the higher angelic dimensions to help earth and humanity to ascend to the new heaven on earth. Planet earth is a very important highway in our solar system that affects many of the higher dimensions. Beginning with the planet Lyra, humans living on earth were created from (22) alien races to help end the galactic wars that had been going on in our universe with the dark brotherhood for billions of years. Humanity holds the key to bring everlasting peace to our Nebadon universe to continue to help harmonize the darkness and the light to bring about peace.

Humanity's current path of ascension on earth will make us beacons of light and the most powerful species in our universe. We need to remember who we are, what our mission is on earth, ascend and continue to help the rest of the earth plane to ascend to the new heaven on earth.

On planet earth the mesh that supported the frequency of the third dimension holographic 3D control matrix has been turned off and a new electromagnetic mesh called the solar crystal matrix has now been installed on the now new fourth dimensional earth and with earth's current fourth dimensional solar web, earth will once again return to the fifth dimensional solar web when it reaches a permanent frequency of 51Hz Schumann Resonance.

The midterm period or interface period on earth during the years of 2012 through 2026 is what the bible calls the Armageddon which is the process on earth of cleaning out all of the previous negativity, recalibration and reboot.

The planetary ascension process takes thirty-eight years and since planet earth's ascension began with the 1987 Harmonic Convergence, this means the great Solar Flash/ Love Wave for the first wave of those ascending should arrive on earth in the spring of the year 2025.

The first wave of ascending humans on earth who will ride the Love Wave to the new heaven on earth will also hit every planet in our solar system which will cause many planets to move up into a higher Harmonic Universe.

The ascending humans in the first wave will sleep for about three hours as their bodies expand and transform and complete an evolution of about one hundred years to their human bodies. It has been decided that a grand solar flash would be too harsh on humanity, so instead we will be riding a smooth Love Wave into the new heaven on earth.

The second wave of ascension will occur during the year of 2026 and millions of humans will awaken during this time period and all plastics and inorganic material will disappear from earth during these times.

The third ascension wave will occur on earth during the year of 2028 and sometime close to the year 2050, all life on the old planet earth will end, because earth will no longer be able to accommodate 3D frequencies. After the year 2050, all of the non-ascending humans left will be transferred in the blink of an eye with no memory of the old earth to the lower 4D or 4D middle earth where they will continue to evolve and eventually ascend.

These are some of the important events and dates for planet earth's current ascension process.

1950 to the present-Many starseeds, light workers and Indigo children incarnating on planet earth to help with the ascension process.

1987-Our Prime Creator, Source took a pulse of Humanity's spirituality and decreed that planet earth, and its inhabitants would begin the thirty-eight-year ascension process.

December 21, 2000- The old cycle of evolution ended on planet earth beginning a new era.

December 21, 2012-The portal to the fourth dimension opened and planet earth began vibrating at fourth dimensional frequencies.

December 21, 2012-Planet earth began its one-thousand-year journey through the Photon Belt.

December 21, 2021-The portal to the fifth dimension opened and earth began a new twenty-two-year cycle and began vibrating at fifth dimensional frequencies.

September 10, 2024- The 5D Operating System was turned on earth from the Christ Consciousness grid installed by Jesus and his wife Mary Magdalene 2,154 years ago.

The years of 2025 through 2026- Humanity will be moving to a galactic society and will experience First Contact with beings from the inner earth of the nine realms and from the planet Alpha Centuri and there will be a major overhaul of religion and politics on planet earth.

The years of 2025 through 2032-The United States of America will no longer be a corporation, instead there will be (20 and 2) regions on earth with money being eradicated and being replaced by a galactic currency and we will barter instead of using money. The current Cabal banking system that is being run by the Rothchild family will be going away very soon. All of the hierarchical structures on the old earth will dissolve and everyone will be equal. Med beds will become available that will cure all diseases and reverse aging. Most of humanity will be living in self-sustainable villages growing their own food instead of in large cities. Humans will be able to travel through the many stargates and portals on earth where we will be able to just walk through a portal and be on another planet. All holidays will be celebrated on Mars and on the Moon and there will be orbiting cities around earth along with active stargate technology in use by all. More extraterrestrial technology will be shared with humanity and with the introduction of replicators we will be able to use liquid plasma energy to replicate anything we want such as, food clothing and shelter. Rainbow Zeta beings who are half-human and half-Zeta will soon come to earth and start inbreeding with humans.

The year of 2034-The entire landscape on earth will change where some continents will sink while other continents will rise from the oceans.

The year of 2036-The first human being living on earth will fully activate their Merkabah light body and their (12) strands of DNA.

The year of 2050-Planet earth will no longer accommodate humans still vibrating at 3D frequencies and there will only be two billion ascended humans left living on the new earth.

Planet earth was first inhabited 200 million years ago by higher level twelfth dimensional beings who were half spirit and half material beings and earth was the first planet in our Nebadon universe to choose, a long time ago duality as its path of ascension. However, this choice of duality separated us from God and as planet earth and its inhabitants descended into the lower third dimensional frequencies, it came with the hard lessons of having to master and harmonize the dark aspects of life with the light. This duality that the lower third dimensional beings had to master included hard life lessons, of greed, violence, hatred and separation. The human collective now living on earth are the fifth root human race on earth to have completed this difficult and final curriculum of duality. In the year 2012 on earth the darkness and duality on earth ended when earth entered the Photon belt and the portal to the fourth dimension opened which began earth's current ascension into the higher dimensions began. When a human being graduates from completing the twelve levels of the life experience on earth, you then receive your PHD, because earth is the hardest life course to go through than any other planet in our universe.

Before a soul can incarnate on planet earth, you have to first train for millions of years, because that's how hard life is on this planet. All of the members of the dark brotherhood on earth originally came from the light but they got caught up in the illusion of the dark side and forgot that they incarnated here on earth to hold compassion, love, light and authenticity in their hearts, and instead they got caught up in earth's karma. Since planet earth along with its awakened humans are now ascending, the real showdown between the light and the dark within is happening now. The ascending humans must go through

(22) stages of initiation on earth and after the last and final step of achieving authenticity and balancing the male and female energies in the physical body to achieve the hierosgamos body, then it's time to climb the stairway to heaven and make the final quantum jump to the new heaven on earth.

No one is alone during the ascension process, because you are directly connected to the Prime Creator through your higher mind and you each have guides and angels helping you every step of the way.

During your ascension process you will see clear signs that your soul has experienced enough life in the numerous realities and twelve planes of the higher dimensions you have quantum jumped into and it has reached its highest potential of awakening. One of the clearest indications that you have gone as far as you can go on what the physical plane has to offer is that you will no longer be intrigued by the plays and games that are taking place around you and you are no longer interested in involving yourself for very long in the melodramas of life.

Everything in your life has become like watching a soap opera and you will know the purpose that each connection you have in your life is for. You will actually be able to see yourself sitting at a chessboard in a higher dimension moving the pieces and situations of your life. You will find that you are quantum jumping daily in your own activated Merkabah reality bubble and in your own space in the quantum field continuing to help to build new realities on the new heaven on earth and you will be spending more time in the astral plane doing this than you are on the physical plane of 4D earth. Most often you will choose to be alone rather than having to deal with the trivial pursuits and concerns that the people around you will have. The final cycle of ascension will be that your soul no longer has to search for the truth you have been looking for the past forty years of your life, because you have reached your authentic self, have found the God Source within, and already now know what the truth is within you.

Humanity will still have free will after ascending to the new heaven on earth for a limited amount of time and after that time limit is up, humanity will go to the judgement at the end of this full 7,000-year cycle. At this point humanity will look back on what we did with our free will and then we will realize how destructive free will really is and we will ask God to remove this ability from us to sin from our spirit, because all of our sins were not God's fault. God will then set us up where we will be unable to sin, while we will still retain our ability to use our free will to continue to make other righteous choices in life.

He that is unjust, let him be unjust still, and he which is filthy, let him be filthy still, and he that is righteous, let him be righteous still, and he that is holy, let him be holy still. And we will have the knowledge of sin removed from inside of us, and all the ways that sin manifested in our lives in this creation. We will go into the new creation without the knowledge of sin and without the ability to acquire the knowledge of sin again.

(Revelation 22:11)

For behold, I create new heavens and a new earth, and the former shall not be remembered or come to mind.

(Isiah 65:17)

We will offer our free will up to God willingly. By free will, God cannot force us to not have free will, but God can remove it from us with our permission. We will do it for the good of eternity and the new creation. You cannot judge someone for doing something that they had no choice to do. The Tree of Life that was in the Garden of Eden will once again be made available to us, as we shall see. In the middles of its street and on either side of the river, was the Tree of Life, which bore twelve fruits, each tree yielding its fruit every month.

The leaves of the Tree of Life were for the healing of the nations.

(Revelation 22:2)

Blessed are those who do his commandments, that they may have the right to the Tree of Life and may enter through the gates of the city.

(Revelation 22:14)

He who has an ear, let him hear what the spirit says to the churches.

"To him who overcomes I will give to eat from the Tree of Life, which is in the midst of the Paradise of God,'"

(Revelation 2:7)

Without the tree of knowledge of good and evil no longer being available, humanity will not be able to ever again use his free will to know evil again, because sin and evil will both be gone and not available to humanity ever again.

The tree of knowledge of good and evil is not mentioned in the new creation, because this means that humanity will have the ability for you to choose to quantum jump from to use our free will without sin.

CHAPTER EIGHTEEN

Your Transportation To Ascend

A Prayer:

Dear God, help me to run to You instead of turning to other things for comfort and security.

Encourage one another and build each other up.

(Thessalonians 5:11)

I am he who blots out your transgressions and remembers your sins no more.

(Isiah 43:25)

YOUR TRANSPORTATION TO ASCEND

The planet Tara Earth was created over 560 million years ago by the Lyra and Tara project beings who still live on the Tara earth, and they can exist in both physical and spiritual ascended form. All of the twelve planets in our Nebadon universe must first ascend in order for planet Tara Earth to complete its ascension process. Earth's current ascension process will positively affect many worlds in our universe, because every world will move up one level in the Harmonic Universe.

These are the four Harmonic Universes and the levels of beings who live in them.

HARMONIC UNIVERSE	BEINGS	LEVELS
HU1	HUMANS	1, 2 AND 3
HU2	ANGELS, SIRIUS B- SIRIANS	4,5, AND 6
HU2	ASCENDED BLESSED GAIA EARTH	4, 5 AND 6
HU3	TARA EARTH AND ARCHANGELS	7, 8 AND 9
HU3	GARDEN OF EDEN	7, 8 AND 9
HU4	AVATARS	10, 11 AND 12

The Elohim who are one creation below the archangels live in dimension 11D and the Council of Nine who oversee our Nebadon universe are based on planet Saturn. The Elohim came into our solar system, changed the orbit of the planets and brought humans into our solar system from a combination of (22) alien extraterrestrial races. The planet Maldek used to be located between the planets of Earth and Mars, but now this planet is an asteroid belt. All of the humans who were originally created by the Elohim were all blood type O, but 15,000 years ago when a large comet hit the planets Earth, Maldek and Mars, the human diet changed to eating more fruit which caused the blood types A and AB to begin to show up in humans. The Indigo children who have been incarnating on earth since the year 1950 have very high intelligence and they are helping to raise the vibrations on earth to assist in its ascension process. The Indigo children's liver is designed to be able to consume junk food and there was an Indigo child born in China in the year 1974 who was able to see with his ears.

Due to the current ascension process on earth, humanity is undergoing five levels of conscious changes to our chromosomes and some of these changes include :

46+2- 4th level of chromosomes

52 chromosomes just like there are 52 cards in a deck of cards

Children who are born with the Downs Syndrome condition are missing one chromosome and their body has the sequence of 45+2 when they should have the sequence of 46+2. Once all of the information centers of the human (12) DNA strands are fully activated by the solar flares coming in from the great central sun, humans will be able to vibrate and send information with incredible speed and power all over the universe. If you have not done so already, now is the time to create your own new reality, select your 5D name and occupation and create your new home on the new heaven on earth.

The Sun is the star at the center of the solar system that is a massive hot ball of plasma, inflated and heated by the energy produced by the nuclear fusion reactions that occur at its core. The Sun is a 4.5-billion-year-old dwarf star which is a hot glowing ball of hydrogen and helium that is 93 million miles away from earth and it is the only star of its size in our solar system.

The earth's sun does the following for the inhabitants who live on earth.

Drives the weather

Drives the ocean's currents

Enables plants to live their lives through the process of photosynthesis

Gives earth the four seasons

Gives earth its different climates

Without the sun's heat and light, the earth would be an ice coated planet of rock. The sun warms our seas, stirs our atmosphere, generates our weather patterns, gives energy to the growing green plants and provides food and oxygen to plants and provides food and oxygen to planet earth. The sun's gravity holds our solar system together and it keeps all of the planets from the biggest to the smallest in their proper orbits.

One of the most important experiences in your ascension journey is quantum jumping. You must have an activated Merkabah light body to quantum jump to higher dimensions and realities during your ascension, because our soul wants to live and experience life just as we do in our physical life. The higher dimensions that you quantum jump into are existential states with seven levels where waves of your soul is able to experience life.

Every time you quantum jump to another reality it is your twin flame existing in the second reality that you create so that way you can exist in two bodies at the same time in two different realities.

OPEN STARGATE LOCATIONS ON EARTH

#1 HALLEY ANTARCTICA LEADS TO PLANET ORION.

#2 SARASOTA, FLORIDA LEADS TO THE NINE REALMS INSIDE INNER EARTH.

#3 BERMUDA LEADS TO THE ASCENDED 4D AND 5D EARTH.

#4 GIZA, EGYPT LEADS TO THE EARTH'S SUN.

#5 MACHU PICCHU, PERU LEADS TO TARA EARTH AND TO 5D PLANET PLEIADES.

#6 MOSCOW, RUSSIA LEADS TO 6D PLANET SIRIUS B.

#7 LAKE TITICACA, PERU LEADS TO 7D-9D PLANET ARCTURIA.

#8 SEDONA, ARIZONA LEADS TO 7D BLESSED GAIA EARTH.

#9 BAN TSD HEICHO, TIBET LEADS TO 9D PLANET ANDROMEDA

#10 ABADDON, IRAQ LEADS TO THE 10D PLANETS OF VEGA AND LYRA.

#11 STONEHENGE, ENGLAND LEADS TO THE 11D PLANETS OF LYRA AND AVYON.

#12 MONSIEUR, FRANCE LEADS TO THE CENTRAL SUN, ALCYONE.

In the Nebadon universe there are (36) dimensions between the first dimension and to dimension (36) where Paradise-the seven higher heavens are located. Planet earth is designed to have the first seven dimensions that lead all the way up to dimension thirty-six. Every dimension or eight of a frequency is subdivided into seven planes and each plane vibrates at a certain frequency that increases as we ascend/quantum jump on each of the seven planes and then you move on to the next dimension to experience seven planes of existence in the next dimension. As you continue to quantum jump and ascend to higher dimensions your body's frequency and vibrations increases.

The journey that souls go on leaping, quantum jumping from dimension to dimension is called ascension and every time you complete a quantum jump ascending from one dimension to another your consciousness is expanded, your physical body is refined and reborn with each quantum jump you complete.

These are some of the ascension codes and frequencies that we can access on earth. Try to listen to high vibrational music daily to access the higher important ascension codes.

FREQUENCIES	DIMENSION
1111 HZ-AWAKENING	5D
999 HZ-MERKABAH LIGHT BODY	5D
700 HZ-ENLIGHTENMENT	5D
600 HZ- PEACE	5D
540 HZ-JOY	5D
500 HZ-LOVE	5D
400 HZ-REASON	5D
364 HZ-AUTHENTICITY	5D
350 HZ-ACCEPTANCE	5D
310 HZ-WILLINGNESS	5D
250 HZ-NEUTRALITY	5D
200 HZ-COURAGE	3D
175 HZ-PRIDE	3D
150 HZ-ANGER	3D
125 HZ-DESIRE	3D
100 HZ-FEAR	3D
75 HZ-GRIEF	3D
50 HZ-APATHY	3D
30 HZ-GUILT	3D
20HZ-SHAME	3D

Authenticity from your heart is the highest human emotion to experience and it is the main key to ascension, because this emotion deals with the vibratory essence of your true expression and it has a positive profound impact on the human physical body and spirit. The frequency and emotion of authenticity isn't just a random pitch, but instead it's a carefully identified sonic landscape that encourages the deepest levels of personal truth and self-acceptance. Authenticity is the key to unlocking the door to your most authentic self, and it allows emotions like love to flow more freely throughout your whole being. For those who are striving for mastery over their personal and professional lives, the understanding and integrating of the essence of authenticity can be transformative.

Engaging yourself with the emotion of authenticity promotes a calming, grounding effect and it is ideal for moments of meditation, relaxation and it aids in aligning your actions with your true self and by embracing your true self, you then unlock the power to manifest your desires and aspirations with greater ease. Authenticity is the highest human frequency that harmonizes your internal state with your external expressions.

Living authentically generates positive emotional resonance elevating you to higher vibrational states and this isn't just about feeling good, it's about being in a state where your energy flows freely which enhances your capacity to attract and manifest what aligns with your authentic self.

In essence, authenticity serves as a conduit for the free flow of energy all throughout your body and amplifying your ability to manifest by elevating your vibrational frequency. Authenticity empowers you and guides you towards a life where your aspirations aren't just dreams but will be achievable realities all through the power of being authentically you.

Daily meditation is an important aspect of ascension, because it helps to reduce stress and anxiety levels and it shrinks the part of the brain that regulates stress, and it helps you to sleep better by reducing the causes of insomnia. Deep sleep is important for good health, because it helps you feel rested, refreshed and you are better able to consolidate your memories. Daily meditation also helps to calm and clear your mind, improve your concentration, improve your mood and help to decrease irritability.

Many have found that when they meditate their creativity increases by improving your flexibility and you will begin to use more divergent thinking. When you meditate let go of your thoughts and focus on the present moment and this will help you to quiet down your inner self and help to create a more open mindset. Go within your inner self and our Universal Prime Creator, Source will meet you there.

One of the most important decisions you will ever make during your ascension journey is to invest your time in meditating to activate your Merkabah light body, because the Merkabah light body is the most powerful technology that you need to use as your transportation to ascend from the third dimensional matrix to the higher dimensions.

The basis of your Merkabah light body are the eight circular genesis cells that formed on the forty-ninth day of your conception, and they stay locked at the base of your spine. An activated Merkabah light body enables you to create your own realities in the quantum field and then quantum jump into each new reality you create. You cannot quantum jump without first activating your Merkabah light body, but with your activated Merkabah light body you will be able to ascend to the light, better organize your life, have many opportunities to experience this spiritual magic and abundance and you will be able to create the life of your dreams. Your activated Merkabah light body is your own personal quantum computer and the most powerful generator of 999 Hz of pure divine energy that once activated, it will continue to constantly spin at the rate of 9/10 the speed of light within your body's Merkabah light body.

These are some of the initial sensations you will begin to feel when you begin to activate your Merkabah light body.

Buzzing sensations within your physical body

Vivid lucid dreams

Feeling floaty

You will begin to astral travel.

Feelings of weightlessness in your body

You will download and connect with your higher self.

Feelings of being high without taking any outside substances

Able to now see more clearly through a second set of lenses.

Enhanced spiritual connections

Improved energy flow through your body

Heightened intuition

Enhanced abilities to manifest

Emotional healing

Feelings of unity consciousness

Physical healings

Once you have a fully activated Merkabah light body you can then begin to create your own realities and the life of your dreams by daily quantum jumps. A quantum jump is a sudden transition of the energy of your Merkabah light body from one quantum state to another and every time you complete a quantum jump you are ascending to a higher dimension, because the electrons in your Merkabah light body goes from one energy level to the other without moving in between. Quantum jumping is an actual physical event that can be observed and when you quantum jump you enter the alpha level of your mind where you visualize yourself soaring through the multiverse where you then meet alternate versions of yourself. Each quantum jump is a small discrete unit of a phenomenon, and it usually takes about four microseconds to complete and you always quantum jump at a ninety-degree angle.

Whenever you complete a quantum jump your consciousness is merging from one timeline to the next higher timeline and what you begin to realize as you continue to create new realities and quantum jump into them is that time is not really linear, because you are able to change and manipulate time during your quantum jumps. When you are able to transition into a new reality through a quantum jump, you are doing this through a leap in your mind. All humans already exist daily in a quantum reality when we on a normal basis quantum jump to a new frequency that better suits us. Quantum information is faster than the speed of light and this information is like a shower of entangled particles that can be transferred back and forth where it can occupy many places at the same time. The human body's soul, spiritual heart, mind, energy and matter are all interconnected aspects of a unified existence which is the quantum vibrational field.

All of life in the universe is based on the sixth dimensions sacred geometry equations and all memories that are based on our personal lives are stored in the eight genesis cells which are the basis of your Merkabah light body. The Tree of Life is one of humanity's main sources of life during the descending to life from heaven to earth and when ascending back home from earth to heaven and the Tree of Life is the vortex of energy that connects our journey from above and below. There are ten spheres in the Tree of Life which are the nine realms that are located in the inner earth, four above and four below earth, which is the fifth realm. There are three columns in the Tree of Life and ten planets in the journey from earth to heaven. Your Merkabah light body is your vehicle to ascend and your own personal chariot of light that carries your soul through all of the (36) dimensions to experience life and to continue on to Paradise-the seven higher heavens.

The Merkabah light body is a higher version of you, and it is an ascension manifestation tool that you can use daily as your sixth dimensional astral density body, because it represents you in the sixth dimension.

One of the most crucial steps in activating your Merkabah light body is the activation of your plait energy cord that is located in the back of your head and your assemblage point which is located between your two shoulder blades. The eight cells that are located in your genesis cells have electrical circuits and when you clear these circuits you then activate your plait. The plait energy cord extends from the back of your head like a long energy braid of tiny threads that run all throughout your body. When you are getting ready to create a new reality in your mind to quantum jump into, first visualize what you want to create through your plait, because you create your reality by seeing it first through your plait.

Your God center or assemblage point that attaches to your activated plait energy cord is located between your two shoulder blades and once you have activated your plait, its tip will fall into your inner center (the forehead) and then the tip will fall into your body's outer intention (assemblage point). The tip of your plait is what changes your reality into a new one that you create.

The following single frame quantum jump can be done daily while taking a shower or while leaning against a tree. You must have an activated Merkabah light body to complete this.

Say to yourself: "I am awake, and I can feel my activated plait attached to my activated assemblage point."

Select in your mind your new reality

State that: "I see myself and my new reality."

Imagine your new reality coming through, let go and make your quantum jump at a ninety-degree angle.

When you are ready to complete a quantum jump to a new reality do it from the heart and with humility from your inner child. Imagine an arrow of authenticity attached from the tip of your activated plait and attached to your activate assemblage point and after a while your plait will begin to activate on its own. Whenever you complete a quantum jump to a new reality your Merkabah light body leaves your physical body and travels in your light body to the higher dimensions of your new reality. Once you have fully activated your Merkabah light body your energy field will then connect to your higher self and to your true authentic self, because the Merkabah light body is literally a space/time transporter that you can use to quantum travel from one dimension to another. Once you activate your Merkabah light body you will be in a direct connection with all of your body's energy systems which will then allow you to interface between your mind and the flow of life force within your physical body.

The Prophet Ezekiel taught his followers about the Merkabah light body after he saw the glorious chariot of the cherubim angels and the Prophet Ezekiel also saw the Merkabah/ Merkava light body, the throne or chariot of God that Yahweh arrived to earth on it.

(Ecclesiasticus 49:8)

The human light body or astral body is the quasi-material aspect of the human body that is neither purely physical nor purely spiritual. Other names for the human Merkabah light body are spirit body, Luciform body, sideral body or the celestial body.

The Merkabah light body is the union of your spirit and physical body surrounded by light. As the vibration of earth continues to move to higher dimensions it is causing our Merkabah light body to spin faster, and more creation energy is pouring into planet earth.

The human soul or atman has the ability to enliven the physical body, and it is located in either your lungs, heart or pineal gland, but most of the time your soul is located in the brain, because the soul is made up of the mind, will and emotions of a person.

We all each have up to at least five spirit guides to help us on our ascension journey and any soul can make the decision to be a spirit guide helping a person to complete a specific project or occupation or an ancestor guide who watches over family members after their transition.

A soul must live a certain number of human lives to qualify to become a spiritual guide, because your first forty-nine lives on earth are for your personal learning and the life cycles after this time period is for serving others in different soul occupations.

Now that earth and humanity are in the ascension process the process of serving as a spirit guide is quicker, due to quantum jumping souls can now live in several parallel lives all at once. If you choose to be a spirit guide to be of service to others, you will have the orientation and necessary training between lives where your own guides will teach you how to be a spirit guide.

The occupation of being a spirit guide is a difficult job, because you will have to continuously communicate with humans in the third and higher dimensions and humans have the tendency to just not listen, so as a spirit guide, you will have to be very patient and compassionate. You will also have to incarnate on the levels in human's lives that will be way below your level of spirituality and guides also have to play the role to be a guide while at the same time living their own human life.

As a spiritual guide you will often feel lonely and surrounded by people who do not understand you, because they only have material interests. Spiritual guides are often assigned to supervise certain humans during their spiritual development and stay with the same person for many incarnations.

It takes at least thirty days to one year to fully activate your Merkabah light body and during this one-year time period do not stop your daily activations and quantum jumps, because if you do stop and forget about your Merkabah, you will have to start all over again from the beginning. There are eight electrical cells located in your lower back that must be cleared daily of all stagnant and negative energy as the first part of your initial Merkabah activation. Once you have cleansed these eight electrical circuits, these eight genesis cells then form into an energy ball of two tetrahedrons, one male which is the human mind and spins to the left (34) times and one female tetrahedron your emotional body that spins to the right (21) times. These two tetrahedrons then intersect and form a gray/purple colored six-pointed star which is called the Merkabah light body. The first sun tetrahedron points up and signifies man reaching up to the Prime Creator. The second earth tetrahedron points down and signifies the Prime Creator reaching down to humanity. The third tetrahedron, the eight genesis cells formed during your forty-ninth day of conception are neutral and stay locked at the base of your spine. The male and female tetrahedrons spin at a rate of 34/21, then 1/3 to 2/3 the speed of light and once this speed is attained a flat disc quickly extends out to a distance of (55) feet. You can now remain seated inside your own activated Merkabah light body in your own Merkabah reality vehicle in your own space in the quantum field. Your twin flame always jumps into the new realities you create while you remain in your current reality. It is important to cover your eyes while meditating with two black scarves in order to effectively enter the void of complete darkness. During the first few sessions of meditating to activate your Merkabah You will begin to see yourself in the void surrounded by stars and planets and as you progress in your activation you will see the twelve versions of yourself for you to choose the highest version to be in your new reality.

Your activated Merkabah light body looks just like a smaller version of our Milky Way Galaxy and your plait located in the back of your head looks just like when you put your hair into a ponytail. We each have an invisible plait that extends from the middle back of our head and connects to the assemblage point located between your two shoulder blades. Your plait stores your new reality while the assemblage point powers your quantum jumps and your Merkabah light body is your vehicle of transportation.

The plait is the explanation as to the reason why it is said that God lives in the back of your head, and this is the way reality works in the universe. Once your plait energy cord is attached to the assemblage point it interacts with your Merkabah light body and assemblage point whenever you are completing a quantum jump.

Your Merkabah light body also serves as a protective barrier against danger, and it is constructed by your thoughts and feelings in order for you to complete your journeys of time travel, interdimensional travel and your travels to different worlds.

Your Merkabah light body is also linked with your chakras and from the third upper purlescent level, you can quantum jump all the way to the Akashic Hall of Records. With an activated Merkabah light body you are able to astral travel, link with an advanced version of yourself and quantum jump through the stargates to enter other planets. We have always used our Merkabah light body numerous times, but we have just forgotten when we incarnated here on earth.

During the Merkabah activation meditation immerse yourself in love, authenticity and hope from your heart, because love is the basis of life for the Merkabah light body. The Merkabah light body is a living sentient being, because it is you and you are alive, and it is your direct connection to God, and it links you and God as one. The Merkabah is your key to time and space, and it directly links you with all of the sacred geometry in the sixth dimension.

The Merkabah extends into all of the (36) dimensions that exist in our Nebadon universe and since the fall of Atlantis and Lemuria over 12,000 years ago less than 0.01%

of humanity have an activated Merkabah light body. Your Merkabah light body must keep spinning at 9/10 the speed of light with you sitting inside of it in order for it to remain activated. You will now be a conscious breather once you have an activated living Merkabah light body that you are sitting in extended (55) feet around your body. You will know when your Merkabah has been permanently activated and no matter what happens while you are on the true path of ascension, keep going and your ascension graduation to the new heaven on earth will be a glorious occasion filled with parties, banquets and wonderful celebrations.

Full Merkabah Light Body Activation Meditation (Takes ½ hour)

Play soft (1111Hz) high frequency music during all meditations.

Anytime you meditate begin first by breathing in chanting the sacred word (OM) and breathing out chanting (OM) three times, because chanting the sound of OM is the word of God and the first sound that created everything in our universe. Chanting (OM) connects you to your higher mind and spiritual guides who exist in the seventh dimension.

Continue to breathe in and hold to the count of (4) and breathe out to the count of three during this entire meditation.

Invite your higher mind and your spiritual ascension team of angels and spiritual guides to join you and protect you during your activation meditation.

In your mind choose the reality you will quantum jump into after the eighteenth breath of this activation meditation.

State in your mind: "I am awake, and I can feel the tip of my activated plait attached to my activated assemblage point. "It takes eighteen breaths and twenty-one short hard fire breaths from your mouth to complete your quantum jump after the eighteenth breath.

Visualize yourself sitting inside of your Merkabah in your own reality body and in your own space in the quantum field.

Begin Merkabah Activation Meditation Now

First Breath- Holding your thumb and index finger together breathe in for four seconds and imagine two joint tetrahedrons, the sun tetrahedron is above your head and the earth tetrahedron is below you. Exhale and your first electrical circuit has been cleared of all negative energy and contamination.

Second Breath-Inhale and hold for four seconds, hold your thumb and first finger together and exhale for three second and your second electrical circuit has been cleared.

Third Breath-Inhale in for four seconds, hold your thumb and second finger together, keep your awareness in your heart and state that you will always use your spiritual psychic gifts for the highest good only. Exhale for three seconds and your third electrical circuit has been cleared.

Fourth Breath-Hold your thumb and third finger together, inhale in for four seconds and exhale for three seconds and your fourth electrical circuit has been cleared.

Fifth Breath-Hold your thumb and fourth finger together, inhale in for four seconds and exhale for three seconds and your fifth electrical circuit has been cleared.

Sixth Breath-Hold your two hands close to your navel with your palms up, inhale in for four seconds and exhale for three seconds and your sixth electrical circuit has been cleared.

Seventh Breath-Inhale in for four seconds and visualize that from the top of your head and from your secret chakra near your heart two beams of prana enter into your body into a prana tube and at the point where these two beams of prana meet at your solar plexus a grapefruit size sphere of blue prana forms.

Eighth Breath-Inhale in for four seconds while the energy continues to flow into your prana tube that is filling up your entire stomach area with prana.

Ninth Breath-Inhale in for four seconds and exhale for three seconds while the prana energy is continuing to flow through the prana tube and the sphere is beginning to become brighter.

Tenth Breath-Inhale for four seconds and exhale for three seconds and the sphere of prana in your stomach area is now flashing and its color has changed from blue to a golden sphere of the sun. Exhale now with force and the golden sphere of prana expands where your entire body is now enclosed in a large golden sphere of prana. This is your own reality bubble for you while sitting inside your Merkabah light body and you will soon complete a quantum jump into your new reality and in your own space in the quantum field after the final eighteenth breath of this meditation. You have also now returned to the ancient form of spherical breathing while you are sitting inside this large sphere of golden prana.

Eleventh Breath-Inhale and hold for four seconds to continue to fill your golden sphere with prana. Exhale for three seconds.

Twelfth Breath- Your golden sphere of prana is now being visualized, maintained and reinforced, inhale for four seconds and exhale for three seconds.

Thirteenth Breath-Keeping your awareness in your heart inhale for four seconds and exhale for three seconds.

Fourteenth Breath-Keep your breath going and inhale in for four seconds and exhale for three seconds and move the sphere of prana with your mind from the area of your solar plexus to the area of your heart and this moves your consciousness from earth consciousness to Christ consciousness.

Fifteenth Breath-Inhale in to the count of four and exhale to the count of three and you are now activating the engine of your Merkabah light body. Visualize the male tetrahedron which is your human mind spinning counterclockwise to the left (34) times, while the female tetrahedron spins clockwise to the right (21) times. Your male and female tetrahedrons are now spinning at a ratio of 35/21 at 1/3 the speed of light. Your third tetrahedron the eight neutral genesis cells that stay locked at the base of your spine are the core of your Merkabah and when your male and female tetrahedrons reach the speed of 2/3 the speed of light a flat white disc quickly extends out from the base of your spine to a distance of (55) feet. This is your Merkabah light body with you sitting inside it within your own reality bubble in your own space in the quantum field. Your Merkabah light body is now linked along with your mind to all of the sacred geometry in the sixth dimension. Visualize at this time that your mind is also linked with your Merkabah light body.

Sixteenth Breath-Continue breathing in and out for four and three seconds and as your male and female tetrahedrons reach the speed of 9/10 the speed of light your Merkabah light body is now in harmony with the third/fourth dimensional universe.

Seventeenth Breath-Continue breathing in and out at the count of four and three and visualize a bright white sphere above your head which is your higher mind and visualize a large dark sphere (your ego) below you. With your mind bring the black sphere up and through the white sphere three times to merge and unite with your higher mind. Each time your black sphere passes through the white sphere it becomes lighter and you are now merged and united with your higher mind. Ask your higher mind now to give you your eighteenth breath so you can complete your quantum jump.

Eighteenth Breath-Continue to breathe in and out to the count of four and three for the eighteenth breath your higher mind has just given you. You will now do (21) short forceful fire breaths from your mouth to complete the final push of your consciousness to your new reality. In the void you will see a small opening to your new reality and complete (21) short forceful fire breaths now and then at a 90-degree angle quantum jump now into your new reality. You are there now and as you enter your new reality accept the highest version of your new body, accept the thoughts and consciousness of your new body, breathe in and out three times and you are in your new reality now.

A single frame quantum jump can be completed outside leaning against a tree or inside while taking a shower. Every time you complete a quantum jump in your Merkabah body you are ascending, because your soul is getting to experience life through all of your manifestations and new realities you create.

In your mind visualize and choose the new reality you will quantum jump into.

Breathe in and out three times to the count of four and three to activate your plait and assemblage point.

Tell yourself that: "I am awake, and I can feel the tip of my activated plait attached to my activated assemblage point."

Continue to breathe in and out to the count of four and three and at a 90-degree angle quantum jump into your new reality now.

Inhale to the count of four and three times and tell yourself that you have accepted the highest version of your new body in your new reality and timeline now.

Ten Minute Quantum Jump Meditation

Put on some high frequency (1111) Hz music and while sitting in a chair or sofa, tie two black scarfs around your eyes.

Visualize and choose in your mind the new reality your wish to quantum jump into.

Tell yourself that: "I am awake, and I can feel the tip of my activated plait attached to my activated assemblage point.

Visualize in your mind that you are sitting inside of your Activated Merkabah reality bubble in your own quantum space.

In order to build your energy up to complete your quantum jump, stand up and lightly tap your lower back with both fists five times.

Sit back down and with both hands clap down the inside of both your legs and both feet with your hands twice.

With both hands gently thump your chest like Tarzan three times.

Complete (30) short fire breaths from your mouth to continue to build up your energy.

Blessed Gaia Earth Meditation

Continue to breathe in and out to the count of four and three and open your crown chakra and pull in the high vibrational source light energy from the Prime Creator from the top of the universe and allow this high vibrational energy to melt in your heart.

Breathe in and out with this high vibrational source light energy and feel this energy stream in the realm of all time at this moment.

Relax your body and become aware of the endless black void that is way out beyond you. How far can your awareness travel through this endless void?

Now in your mind visualize your new reality, feel it, smell it as if it has already happened. Create your new reality now, make it perfect, make it holographic, feel the light, the vibrations and the sounds of your new reality. What would you be doing right now in your new reality and a small doorway to your new reality is opening now.

Walk right through the open door to your new reality and at a 90-degree angle while sitting in your activated Merkabah light body jump now and accept the thoughts and consciousness of the highest version of your new body in your new reality and new timeline. You are in your new reality now and you are reborn, free and in the highest version of your new body.

During this next meditation you will first complete a quantum jump into the new heaven on Blessed Gaia earth through Stargate #8 in Sedona, California and then through the rainbow portal to Blessed Gaia. Once you reach Blessed Gaia you need to ground first where you will align and focus all of the energies, five elements, male and female (hieros-gamos) and inner child energies with a child's heart to the highest timeline you are able to vibrate in. The five elements you will align and focus in your body are: air, water, earth, fire and space (akash). Next you will wrap all of your body's aligned highest timeline energies twice with high vibrationa source light from the Prime Creator. You will then wrap your body with mirrors that will protect you from feeling other people's low vibrational energies that may be around you. During the last step of this meditation, you will wrap the blue light/flame of protection from Archangel Michael around your body's total aligned energy field which will protect you for twenty-four hours in the earth and astral planes. You will then be able to go about your day completing your light worker duties by observing and continuing to shine your light and love and you will be able to walk your day living in a high vibrational way.

Breathe in and out to the count of four and three in your new reality and timeline.

Begin Meditation

Play some soft high frequency (11110Hz music.

Chant the word OM three times.

Sit in a chair or on the sofa and tie two black scarfs around your eyes.

Visualize in your mind that the new reality you will be creating is to ground and complete a Highest Timeline Meditation On Blessed Gaia

In your mind tell yourself that: I am awake, and I can feel the tip of my activated plait attached to my activated assemblage point.

Visualize in your mind that you are sitting inside of your activated Merkabah in your own reality bubble and in your own space in the quantum field.

With your mind, see the small doorway opening in the void to your new reality and in order to build up the energy to make the final push of your consciousness into your new reality complete (21) forceful short fire breaths from your mouth and at a 90-degree angle quantum jump now through Stargate #8 in Sedona, California and enter the rainbow portal to blessed Gaia and you are now in your new reality on Blessed Gaia.

Visualize yourself walking barefoot in a beautiful meadow of green grass on Blessed Gaia and you will be able to hear a waterfall in the distance.

Feel the grass under your feet and in between your toes as you continue on your walk to ground and open your crown chakra now and begin to feel the high vibrational source light energy flow through your body and while it continues to freely flow throughout your body you can feel your vibrations rise and this energy is pushing out any stagnant energy down your calves down through the bottom of your feet to the center core of Blessed Gaia. Repeat this step two more times and take a big breath in and out to the count of four and three and you are now grounded on Blessed Gaia.

Ground daily on Blessed Gaia only, because the vibrations are too low on our current earth.

Highest Timeline Meditation

Visualize in your mind a large sphere of high vibrational source light energy over your head and this energy is extending down in a straight line over the entire width of your body all the way down to your feet and your feet are the middle of your timeline.

Beginning with the infinity area above your head align all of the energies, five elements, male-female (hieros-gamos) energies and inner child energies with a child's heart to the highest possible timeline.

Move down to your head, neck, shoulders, arms, and hands and align all of your energies to the highest possible timeline.

Move down to your to your chest, waist, hips, thighs knees, calves, ankles and feet and align all of your energies in these areas to the highest possible timeline.

Once you have reached your feet, pause for a moment and breathe in and out to the count of four and three.

Go back up your body from your feet all the way up to the area of infinity that is located directly above your crown and breathe in and out to the count of four and three.

You have now aligned and focused all of the energies in your body to the highest timeline today and this will help to increase your manifestations and make things happen more smoothly for you.

Source Light Wrapping Meditation

Remain seated in your chair or sofa.

In your mind visualize a big ball of high vibrational source light energy right above your head. You are now going to wrap this source light three feet around you in all directions around all of your high vibrational energy you have just aligned and focused around your body.

Bring this high vibrational source light down and wrap it around your body three feet to the right, three feet to the left, three feet under your body, three feet behind your body, three feet above your body and three feet in front of your body.

Now visualize a large second ball of high vibrational source right above your head and bring this source light down now and wrap it around your body three feet to the right, three feet to the left, three feet below you, three feet behind you, three feet above you and three feet in front of you.

Now visualize a large ball a large mirrored disco ball above your head and you are going to wrap this mirror around your body to seal all of your aligned high vibrational energies and source wrapping. You will be able to see out of these mirrors as you walk your day today and anyone who is not for your higher good will bounce off these mirrors and not be able to enter your energy field.

Bring these mirrors around now and wrap them around your body three feet to the right, three feet to the left, three feet under your body, three feet above your body and three feet in front of your body.

This mirror wrapping around the energy field of your body will protect you for (24) hours from people coming into your energy field and now anchor these mirrors into your earth chakra with golden cords.

Visualize now that Archangel Michael is pouring the blue light/flame of protection around your entire high vibrational energy field.

Pour this blue light of protection around your body three feet to the right, three feet to the left, three feet under you, three feet above you and three feet in front of you. You are now wrapped and protected for (24) hours walking your day in a high vibrational way.

Sit is a chair, tie two black scarfs around your eyes and play some high vibrational (1111) Hz music.

Visualize that you are barefoot and getting ready to take a walk in the forest to spend some quiet time in communion with our Prime Creator while you are grounding in the forest.

Invite in the following divine team to go with you on your journey today on your walk in the forest and your tour of Blessed Gaia.

Invite your higher mind to accompany you on your journey today.

Invite the archangels of the north, south, east and west and the archangel of above and below to accompany you today on your journey.

Invite all of the spiritual guides who have been with you during your ascension journey to accompany you today on your journey.

You are now surrounded by and are under the protection of this entire celestial team.

Imagine in your mind that you are walking barefoot in your favorite forest, and you can hear a stream far off in the distance to the right of you. Feel the grass under your feet, fill the breeze blowing on your face and watch the trees in the forest as they sway back and forth to the breeze.

This is your favorite daily forest walk, a little piece of your Paradise and as you continue walking, you notice that a new path to the right has opened for you and as this new path unfolds before you and you begin walking on it, you can see a rainbow bridge far off in the distance to the right and as you continue walking and looking at this rainbow bridge you realize that it is actually the portal to Blessed Gaia.

You continue to enjoy your walk and you are enjoying how the fresh green grass feels under your bare feet, and you now realize that you have reached the rainbow portal bridge to Blessed Gaia. From Stargate # 8 in Sedona, California and at a 90-degree angle, you quantum jump now onto this rainbow portal bridge to Blessed Gaia and as you enter this portal you place your hands on the rails and notice that you don't have to walk up this bridge, because the energy of this portal is pulling you up and across it.

As you continue on your journey on the rainbow bridge to Blessed Gaia you notice that there is one more portal to go through and this portal is full of photonic lights and all of the beautiful colors of the rainbow in it and once again at a 90-degree angle to quantum jump into this final photonic portal and as soon as you enter it, there is an instant flash and you notice that the bridge is now a normal bridge that is taking you to a beautiful grassy area.

Daily Tour of Blessed Gaia Earth Meditation

As you step off this bridge onto the grassy area, you realize that you are on the new heaven on Blessed Gaia earth, and you can feel the high vibrational energy of Blessed Gaia beginning to flow through your body and you feel so happy to finally be home and accepted on Blessed Gaia.

You need to ground first before beginning your tour today on Blessed Gaia and you can feel white bright roots extending now from the bottom of your feet all the way down to the center of Blessed Gaia earth and you are wrapping these cords around a very large crystal and anything that is not for your highest good, you are releasing these stagnant energies now into this crystal. Blessed Gaia is transmuting these energies now to pure love and flooding your body with this high vibrational energy.

Daily Tour of Blessed Gaia Earth Meditation

You are now grounded on Blessed Gaia.

You look around and see that you are standing on a beautiful grassy area and directly in front of you is a large, majestic waterfall emptying into a lake that you heard earlier at the beginning of your walk in this meadow.

You look to your left and you see beautiful mountains and trees that never end.

You look to your right and one of your spiritual guides who has been there with you all during your ascension journey and you take your guide's hand now to go on your tour.

There are twenty and two regions on the new heaven on Blessed Gaia earth and your guide is going to take you first to the region where you live, to your lot and home that you have built long ago on Blessed Gaia and from there you will decide which region you want to tour today.

The Daily Magic Hour on Planet Earth

Actually, the most magical hour on earth is top secret, but every single morning ever since time began, just before the sun rises the drums start beating, the choirs start singing, the energies start rising, the birds start singing to awaken the leaves and every single soul who has ever lived scurries around the plane of manifestation as the chanting begins, and as it gets louder and louder and goes faster and faster until a feverish pitch is reached and the skies part with a clap of thunder, revealing billions upon billions of the most beautiful angels you have ever seen.

Flying down from the heavens, some of these angels have their wings outstretched, while some of the other angels have their wings pointed back and these angels are darting, diving, banking and rolling, some flying so fast that they are only a blur, while some of the other angels seem to float by as if they are catching what remains of a midsummer night's breeze.

Every one of these angels are a reflection of the greatest, the loveliest and the highest that you can ever imagine and every one of these angels are a messenger of hope, peace, joy and they are healers, teachers, comforters and creators. And every one of these angels are ready to greet a brand-new day in time and space with a morning yawn, sleepy eyes and with the power to rock the world.

And if you listen really hard, you can still hear the drums.

Hosanna in the highest.

Anaya's Blessed Gaia Victory Garden and Blueprint of Her Home and Occupation

Blessed Gaia New Earth Name

Antonia Anthony

Blessed Gaia New Earth Occupations

Contrast Master and Love Child to the Fairy Folks on Blessed Gaia

Author/Artists/Healer/Teacher

Blessed Gaia New Earth Spiritual Name

The Creative Rainbow

Anaya's Blessed Gaia Victory Garden

Lima Beans	Mustard Greens
Cabbage	Onions
Parsnips	
Beets	
Asparagus	
Lettuce	
Potatoes	

INTERIOR OF ANAYA'S NEW HEAVEN ON EARTH HOME

CHAPTER NINETEEN

THE NEXT TWO THOUSAND YEARS ON THE NEW HEAVEN ON EARTH

Put your hope in God, for I will yet praise him, my Savior and my God.

(Psalm 42:11)

The name of the Lord is a strong tower, the righteous run to it and are safe.

(Proverbs 18:10 NKJV)

A Prayer:

Dear God; thank you for forgiving and forgetting my sins.

THE NEW HEAVEN ON EARTH FOR THE NEXT TWO THOUSAND YEARS

766

The main thing to understand about our human existence on earth is that everything is cyclic by nature. From the moment of our cosmic conception, everything proceeds in a circular form and this circular form is an established rhythm that starts at the highest level of existence and descends into an involution outward and an inward evolution as it perfects itself in never-ending infinite spirals, one space level at a time. At the point of this Immaculate Conception when the always existing Omni-Verse divided and fractaled itself, there was only space and no time. Time began because of its expansion (involution), because time became a construct of measuring where a point begins and another point ends, the alpha and the omega. This alpha and omega are just one cycle or one gigantic megahertz, and at the end of the alpha and omega cycle, a new alpha and omega cycle begins again.

We can compare the alpha and omega cycle to one universal round, which expands our always existing central universe one space level at a time. Time becomes a measuring device or tool designed by the always existing central universe to determine all its points and conjunctions that mark all events that will transpire and have transpired as it expands forever outward. In the celestial spheres, it is all happening at once and from a lower perspective, in the material spheres it is all relative, happening in sessions, segments, or fractals, which is the whole dividing itself to experience more of itself as it explores every level of its own being.

Before the beginning of space and time (involution), there was only pure potential force and this unqualified absolute began dividing itself, so it set out to complete what is known in esoteric studies as one universal round of the cosmic process known as the descent and ascent of the great God force. This is controlled by a cosmic Meta central sun and the great central suns of all of the universes who are the timekeepers on every level of existence and this process repeats again and again as the grand central universe rotates like a clock in circular form and that is why it is always spinning new universes into existence as we continue to expand one outer space level at a time into infinity. Cosmic time is a governing force just like gravity and it is controlled by rotation and spin which produces all of the forces that hold and bind universes. Cosmic time is circular rather than a straight line and our entire cosmos is one big rotating circle within circles all the way down to the atoms. A circle like a clock begins at the top making its way around the clock full circle to repeat the same cycle again and each time it does, it gathers more experience.

The Mayan calendar has been the keeper of the great cosmic spin behind all sacred time that harmonize all living things in our cosmos.

Sacred time is the measurement and relationship between all living things as it harmonizes into one great symphony, because everything is interconnected with everything else. It is neither linear nor limited, but rather it is a force everywhere at once and infinite Divine time is also the harmony of all things as opposed to man-made time, which is a disharmony of all things. These cosmic cycles of time and the harmony of the cosmos from the macro to the micro have always been understood and known by the ancient spiritually advanced cultures that flourished before the great flood that occurred on planet earth.

The ancient cultures knew more about astronomy than we do now in the twenty-first century, because they understood the concept of divine time. The ancient cultures also understood that the earth and the other planets revolve around our local sun and that our solar system revolves around the galactic great central sun Alcyone in a cycle of 25,000 years.

The Precision of the Equinoxes explains where earth stands in the great scheme of things which includes the zodiac and our solar system's relationship with all of the stars and constellations within our galaxy. Everything that happens on earth is directly influenced by earth's movements in the heavens. All of the celestial bodies from the planets to the stars are vibrators of frequencies and depending on where our solar system is located in the heavens, earth takes on these new energies as intercessing points that generate different vibrations. Each age on earth brings in new energy fields that determine the quality and what kind of world it will be on planet earth.

Each new age on earth is governed by a constellation and each constellation has its own frequency and these frequencies are produced by the cosmic transmission that resonates at the center of the Milky Way Galaxy. All of the celestial bodies get their spin and as well as their frequency from the central sun, Alcyone and it generates and transmits cosmic energy outward from its center influencing all of the stars and planets.

Time is related to astrogeny which keeps track of the movements of planet earth and the solar system in their relationship with the other stars, planets and the great central sun that is located in the center of the Milky Way Galaxy. When our galaxy's sun begins to transmit a new frequency which what is happening now, all of the solar systems change to match the new resonance that is being received from the great central sun. This is done through super galactic photon fields of light that are generated from the central hub of our galaxy. These high energy fields are super galactic highways of light, and it is the source of spontaneous evolution that is happening now everywhere in our galaxy. Our solar system is currently emerging in one of the super galactic photon fields that is shifting the resonance of our solar system into a new spin, a new vibration which when complete will be a new heaven on earth and this new emanation of higher energy is shifting reality on earth and our entire solar system.

According to the ancient Mayan scholars, planet earth and its solar system are getting ready to enter a high resonating field of super charged energy that occurs twice every 25,000 years and a rare galactic alignment within the center of our galaxy is now taking place which indicates the completion of a 230,000,000-million-year cycle on earth. Our galaxy's central sun and its many photonic galactic fields are vibrating to the frequencies of our great central sun within our galaxy and eleven other galaxies and in addition, our central sun is currently vibrating to the frequency of our super universe's great central sun which is vibrating to the cosmic pulse of the mother universe's cosmic central sun.

The ancient Mayan civilization was directly seeded by the Pleiadeans just before the fall of Atlantis to preserve all of the sacred calendars. These sacred calendars were then given to the ancient Egyptians, Atlanteans, Lemurians, Ramanians and the Yu civilizations that all flourished before the final fall and sinking of Atlantis over 12,000 years ago. These sacred calendars that follow the system of thirteen months were also given to the early Hebrews, the Dogon tribe of Africa who descended from Sirius B, and the early native Indigenous cultures of the North American continent who are genetically related to the early Hebrews.

The Mayan people were named after the second star system Maya of the Pleiadean star system, and seven sisters were chosen to hide this prophetic code that would emerge when the time was right to prepare for the transformation and restoration of earth before the year and month of December 2024 (actually December 2012), which is the real completion date of the Mayan calendar. The higher intelligences planned for the emergence of this great sacred calendar during our current times during the year of 1970.

Just about the time that the western world thought they had discovered that earth is a sphere that revolves around our local sun along with the other planets, the Mayan culture understood the revolution of our solar system and our local sun around the great central sun that is located at the center of our Milky Way Galaxy and this great revolution is known as a universal round which is the completion of a 206-225 million year cycle. We live in a holographic existence and the concept of twelve going around the one is repetitive on every level, and it takes our solar system 2,160 years to travel through one of the twelve houses of the zodiac. This 25,000-year revolution is known as the Procession of the Equinox's and it is further divided into shorter world ages of 5,100 years for a total of five and it is this 5,100 period the Mayans called the long count, or the (13) baktun.

The (13) baktun cycle of the Mayan long count calendar measures 1,872,000 days or 5,125,366 tropical years. This is one of the longest cycles found in the Mayan calendar system and it ended on the winter solstice on December 21, 2012, the day that the portal to the fourth dimension opened, thus beginning earth's ascension process.

The Haab cycle is 365 days which equates to one solar year and according to the long count, the last world age began around 3114 BC and ended on December 21, 2012. However, if you follow the non-Gregorian (Mayan) calendar, the accurate date is really between the years of 2020 through 2022 for the correct ending of the last world age on earth and this explains the total shutdown and reset that occurred in the year of April 2020 due to the COVID epidemic.

The photon belt is the reason why planet earth recycles herself every 25,000 years. Our solar system enters one of the many photon belts for two thousand years which also corresponds to the rise and fall of all of the golden ages that have existed on earth. When planet earth entered the photon belt on December 21, 2012, it began to experience the age of light and love due to the high resonance that vibrates with the galactic center. All of the photon fields automatically transmute all vibrations into the higher frequencies of vibrating light, and this allows awakened humans to connect with their light bodies which then in turn directly links humanity to the great central sun of our galaxy.

Since our solar system enters the photon belt twice during a 25,000-year cycle, our solar system experiences two ages of light, 5,000 years of peace when it is traveling through the photon belt, and as the earth travels the long dark nights outside of the photon belt, it then experiences the dark ages for 20,000 years, which is a ten-thousand-year interval between two periods of light. When our solar system travels furthest from the photon belt, it experiences low vibrations on planet earth and as the earth travels close or within the photon belt that it has been since the year of 2012, it experiences high vibrations which correlate with the ages of light being within the higher energy field that emanates from the Ecliptic of our galactic equator.

The platonic year of the Procession of the Equinox is divided into five world stages and in India they are known as the five Yugas. The first world age is known as the Golden Age, which corresponds to the time period that our solar system spends inside the photon belt. As earth leaves the photon belt, it ends a half phase of the first world age which is two thousand years, and this produces a still peaceful society with one fourth of darkness still lurking in the background. Together the golden and silver ages on earth makeup what is called the first world age or Krita Yuga that lasts for five thousand years and as earth completes its 5,000-year cycle, which is two 2,160 tear cycles, we experience one fifth of the 25,000-year great Platonic cycle. As our solar system goes further out from the photon belt finishing its first world age or 5,000-year period, it begins a new 5,000-year period known as the second world age as it enters in to about two fifths in the great platonic year entering the second world age of Tetra Yuga.

The Tetra Yuga Age is known as the blending of silver and bronze and it is where we fall from Paradise as darkness begins to gain ground and when the second world age Tetra Yuga ends, the third world age begins which is known as Dwapara Yuga and this age is a mixture of the Bronze and Iron Age.

During this time period it marks a point where darkness increases to three-fifths percent and the beginning of tyranny begins. By the time earth enters the third world age, the golden silver age deteriorates due to the increase of evil by three-fifths percent that has occurred due to our solar system being further away from the photon belt.

In the final world age and the last phase of the 25,000 platonic year cycle, earth then enters the darkest period known to mankind and this age is called the Kali Yuga, the Iron Age which is the age of hell on earth. Currently on earth we are literally days away from ending the last few years of the great platonic cycle that lasted for 25,000 years and this will mean that earth has completed a full circle around the Pleiadean central sun Alcyone once again as we have 5,200 times before.

Humanity who are now living on earth are now coming into the first world age that is now bringing in a new golden age which will bring a new heaven on earth. This is the good news that the Mayan sacred calendar brings to our world, no more doom and gloom. Earth is ending the Age of Pisces, a 2,160-year cycle and a world age of a 5,000-year cycle, a 25,000-year cycle of a platonic year and a 230,000,000-million-year cycle which is a grand cycle that our solar system along with the Pleiades and Sirius systems take around the center of our Milky Way Galaxy. Since earth is now in the process of completing this greater revolution, planet earth will continue ascending without having to repeat anymore of the planet's dark ages. The convergence of the precision of the equinoxes and the greater 230,000,000-million-year cycle of the Pleiadean's sun around our galaxy's great central sun marked the global event on earth known as the Harmonic Convergence in the year 1987. Humanity on earth are currently living in the greatest times ever as we approach the closing of all cycles in the grand cosmic clock.

A new heaven on earth will soon begin on earth for all life that will last for all eternity. The completion of this 230,000,000-million-year cycle marks the ascension of our entire Milky Way Galaxy which means that all of the planets within our galaxy will soon be moving up one octave to a higher harmonic universe. Michael of Nebadon, our system sovereign of the Nebadon universe has revealed that all of the entire twelve creations are now ready to come home to Paradise on the seven mansion worlds of the super universe.

The completion of the seventh super universe of Orvonton will be final when all of its local universes ascend, because the super universe of Orvonton, Paradise has been incomplete and with the current completion of Orvonton, Paradise will be in the greatest cycle to date which was completed during the overall descent of the grand central sphere's expansion into one space level at a time.

One of the most important things to expect to see in the coming new world age on earth will be the sudden transformation of government systems, social structures, economics and the sudden rise of inter-planetary and galactic cultures. The earth's current Orion based banking and economic systems are scheduled to collapse and be replaced by a world non-monetary prosperity for all economic systems soon. Earth and humanity are scheduled to take massive quantum leaps and transform into a population two stellar system space age civilization. Planet earth will be becoming a galactic planet once again just like we were before earth became quarantined from the rest of the Milky Way Galaxy after the Lucifer Rebellion and the final fall of Atlantis over 12,000 years ago. Once humanity living on earth completes their physical transformation to become crystalized (999) Adam Kadmon human beings, our genetic material will be activated from using (2) strands of DNA to using (12) strands and the new earth will once again become to be a galactic planet.

The divine order of the emissaries of light who have continued to hold this pure divine light in our universe for the past million years in our galaxy will soon manifest and show themselves on planet earth. The great white brotherhood/sisterhood from all of the thirty-six dimensions that lead to Paradise have all been working endlessly for the restoration of the new heaven on earth. In the political world, the white brotherhood/sisterhood are known as the white knights who have been guarding the constitution of the United States (Zion) government from being totally abolished by the dark brotherhood of the Jesuit-Illuminati Cabal Catholic Church new world order Elites. These white knights/white brotherhood groups have also been working closely with the higher intelligences of the Galactic Federation of Planets and with the spiritual hierarchy of the earth angels to establish a worldwide constitution that will be under the authority of the celestial constitution who will be under the authority of the celestial Council of Twelve that will recognize honor and serve all of the new (20) and (2) regions on the new heaven on earth.

This new system of government that is now materializing on earth is being built by the order of Michael our system sovereign of the Nebadon Universe for a Council of Twelve. This Council of Twelve has the support of all the councils who are currently members of the Galactic Federation of Planets, and this new system of government will bring in a worldwide commonwealth that will be known as the government on the new heaven on earth or as the Commonwealth of the (20) and (2) regions on the new earth.

This newly established government system on earth will be both divine and democratic and this new world system will be established in the fifth dimension by the end of the year 2025 and it will be headed by the Office of Christ whose headquarters is located on the planet Sirius B. The Office of Christ is the office of cosmic fusion, the office of power and new rulership, the office of culture, civilization and finally the office of universal justice. All of these new world foundations will be known as the office of the four arms or the great vehicle. This new Commonwealth of Nations will be formed under a universal constitution that will be called the Five-Pointed Star that will serve the mandate of the five petals. The head of this new world council on the new heaven on earth will be Lord Maitreya Surya Vishnu who is from the direct line of King David.

These new governments on the new earth, the Commonwealth of Nations will include all of the national identities and countries with a global structure of the (20) and (2) federated regions each with its own leadership and independent infrastructure. These

(20) and (2) infrastructures will be in harmony with all of the governments of the world which will secure the rights of all mankind. The new earth will be a global democratic network for the people and by the people that will be overseen by the new celestial council of twelve.

Lord Gabriel Franchela who was Michael of Nebadon's first born and apprentice will be the head of the thirteenth ray replacing Lord Samana (Lucifer who fell from the light) and now this ray is known as the Franchela ray of sound that deadens the noise of war. These thirteen celestial beings under the direction of Lord Gabriel Franchela will make their first appearance on earth just before the Galactic Federation (angels) make their first contact with planet earth.

The commander of the galactic Federation of Planets will issue the mandates that will come from the thirteen rays, the adepts and when these thirteen great lords and ladies of light make themselves known, the people living on the new heaven on earth will experience a sense of serenity due to the great love that generates from these thirteen celestial light beings.

All of this will happen the moment our solar system has emerged in the photon belt where the human collective density will be catapulting into a higher energy vibrating all matter at the fifth, sixth, seventh and eighth density frequencies. In these higher planes of existence, humanity will once again walk with the higher evolved beings of light. These sons and daughters of the light will head the new planetary spiritual council also known as the restored council of twelve and their 144,00 helpers, who will have the support of the Galactic Federation guardians of the councils who will be in charge of overseeing all matters on the new heaven on earth.

These thirteen adepts will be the most powerful beings in the universe, and they have chosen earth as their new home. The council of the 144,000 will be working for the new council of the thirteen and they will oversee the affairs of the new world structure of the (20) and (2) federated regions of the new earth system. In the new earth world structure, everyone will be provided with health care, housing, education and food will be the basic human needs that will be met, and this will include everyone living on the new heaven on earth.

Since humanity will be becoming part of a greater galactic community, we will meet and learn to co-exist in harmony with other beings who will be from non-humanoid species. Humanity will learn higher universal values and learn how to tap the power of our local sun, which will enable us to visit and interact with other planetary and stellar systems within our Milky Way Galaxy. Planet earth has been a member of the Galactic Federation of Planets since the year 2001 and we will operate under the direction of the galactic tribunal council no later than the year 2025.

The celestial kingdom of light has always existed and it is time for the kingdom of light to manifest in the lower levels of the material realms which has given awakened humans living on earth the opportunity to ascend to higher levels of existence beyond the material spheres. Following the complete restoration of planet earth, some of the star people who are already here on earth from the other stellar civilizations will leave earth and advance directly into the higher dimensions of the celestial realms in the grand central universe. These advanced beings of light were asked to volunteer to come to earth by the guardians of the councils from the planet Sirius B to help earth to ascend. These were the waves of the higher evolved souls who incarnated here on earth just by existing during these times on the earth plane, and these beings are waiting to be able to return to the worlds where they came from.

There are three major levels or planes of existence, so some of these incarnated souls will advance next to the highest level of the celestial realms in the central universe, and even these spheres are divided into various levels of celestial glory. Some of these souls will advance once their mission has been completed on earth to the middle heavens or to the morontia worlds. Some souls will remain on the new heaven on earth for the next two thousand years to continue to help to build new communities and to also help the rest of the ascending humans to shift into higher levels of existence all the way up to the eighth dimension. The three levels of the heavens are the three levels of existence that make up the many dimensions of reality.

Earth exists in the lower material realms of time and space, but since the year 1998 earth began to vibrate on a higher reality and ascend all of the way up to the eighth density. After the great shift on earth occurs it will split into three separate worlds and those souls who cannot make the shift into the higher dimensional densities will continue their existence on the lower 4D or middle 4D earth to continue their evolution and ascension process. For the members of humanity on earth who didn't make the shift to the new earth, they will be able to experience a moment of peace and enlightenment for a few minutes during the transition as a reminder of what heaven on earth will be like, so they will be able to imprint this memory in their souls as they transition to the lower 4D or middle 4D earth. The reason is that our planet earth and solar system were in the final phase in the closing of one universal round of descent and ascent, completing the evolution to ascend to our super universe of Orvonton, Paradise. The ascension of planet earth is a completion of a long descent of light into matter and the return or ascension of matter back into the light is now in progress. The ascension process of earth and humanity will bring everything that took place in the descension back to the godhead, the Prime Creator, Source. The awakened humans who remain living on earth will continue to ascend into higher dimensions never again having to repeat or experience a Dark Age cycle.

Eventually the souls that get recycled back into the lower 4D or middle 4D earth will still have a chance to choose oneness and harmony over division and separation at the closing of the end of the millennium. This is being done so that no soul will be left behind during the overall ascension of everyone who all have their origin in the always existing spheres of the grand central universe/metaverse/motherverse. For those humans who ascend or get a direct ticket to the celestial realms or the highest level of existence, will occur because they were able to become the most advanced spiritual souls while they were living on planet earth. The remaining earth souls who transition into the higher densities will be given the opportunity to continue to ascend to even higher dimensions into the celestial realms of the central universe.

These three kingdoms of light could also be compared to the new proposed one-two and three-star populations and at our current stage on earth, the three star system civilizations are millions of years ahead of us, but once earth completes its ascension to the new heaven on earth, it will only take 100,000 years for earth to reach the level of population three status.

Since planet earth is currently being restored to its original glory, it will be ascending into a population two-star interplanetary system space age civilization. All civilizations that are a population one and two-star system are members of the Galactic Federation of Planets, because they are able to live in harmony within their own planet, other planets and each star system within their galaxy.

A population one star system planet has full admission to the Federation of Planets, and it is allowed to interact with a few star systems in their local cluster. A population two-star system planet is able to interact with millions of star systems and spread out to visit planets across the entire galaxy.

A population three system civilization on a planet is beyond our material realm on earth, because it functions higher than the eighth dimension and above all of the Galactic Federation of Planets in our galaxy and they are part of an intergalactic alliance of many universes. A population three-star system civilization makes up the entire eternal fabric of the central universe spheres of Havona, Paradise which is located above dimension thirty-six. Since earth is currently ascending into higher levels of awareness and dimensions, all ascended humans will be multi-dimensional and most of the ascending earth humans will have to attend school to learn how to properly use their light bodies, because they have been dormant since the times of Atlantis.

For the next two thousand years, temples and great mystery schools of higher spiritual education will be on the new heaven on earth everywhere to ensure that every human continues to receive higher initiations into higher levels of consciousness and awareness. Great cities of light will exist again on the new heaven on earth just like as in the times of Atlantis, Lemuria and ancient Egypt.

Atlantis was so enormous that no matter where one is standing on earth, you are standing on top of Atlantis before it sank. During the times of the new heaven on earth, the old continent of Atlantis and Lemuria will rise again with all of their cities intact as if they had never been destroyed. Also, when earth completes its ascension, we will again be reunited with all of the inner earth people who have been living in the nine realms and in Mount Shasta for thousands of years in great civilizations within planet earth. In the coming days our planet earth will shine like a jewel in the heavens and become the intergalactic exchange center for cosmic transmissions relating to our entire super universe segment which is 1/7 of the entire mother universe. Planet earth will be a showcase planet, because beings from all of the universes will once again begin to visit earth and earth beings will begin to visit other planets in the Milky Way Galaxy. There will be some advanced souls living on earth who will be able to experience even higher dimensions than the eighth density who will be capable of materializing to the eighth dimension at will. Once a human has reached and is able to experience high densities of existence, they can co-exist and consciously embody all of the twelve dimensions within the Milky Way Galaxy.

The new heaven on earth will be able to have three types of civilizations co-existing side by side, because we will be operating with one magnetic field with multiple bands of electromagnetic fields merging with all of the twelve-dimensional densities and vibrations into one planetary energy field.

Only seventh density beings will be able to perceive eighth density beings, while the eighth dimensional beings will be able to perceive the council of the higher ninth, tenth, eleventh and twelve dimensional beings who will also be here living on the new heaven on earth, but on the higher frequency bands. This is because planet earth was originally designed to exist in all twelve dimensions before it fell all the way down to the third dimension which happened thousands of years ago.

On the new heaven on earth, our planet will once again exist simultaneously in three places by splitting into three separate realities in its relationship to the great central sun, Alcyone.

The first new heaven on earth will be anchored in all twelve of the dimensions and it will exist near the center of the Milky Way Galaxy within the first concentric circle. This location of the first new heaven on earth is where the Lords and Ladies of Light, the council of twelve will be stationed overseeing the evolution of billions of worlds as we begin the colonization process of the Milky Way Galaxy.

The second new heaven on earth will embody dimension seven, eight and nine and it will exist in the second concentric circle orbiting the planet Sirius where the original first earth existed before the first galactic war that occurred that destroyed the first earth known as Avyon in Lyra.

The third new heaven on earth will embody the fourth, fifth and sixth dimensions will exist in Pleiades in the third concentric circle where the current ascending members of humanity are heading.

Planet earth has twelve other unseen fields of energy and these unseen electromagnetic field exist in higher frequencies, and they hold earth's grid system together. This crystalline grid system on earth during the times of Atlantis, Lemuria and ancient Egypt 12,000 years ago became the living energy field, the living matrix that allowed the living beings from the higher dimensions to co-exist with the beings from the lower dimensions and those were the times when the angels walked with mortal man on earth. This living energy field known as the crystalline grid system will be re-activated when earth merges into the photon belt allowing for the interaction and co-existence of all living beings from the multiple levels of dimensions of existence. This means that there will be a reactivation of the system life circuits that will reconnect the new earth to the Jerusem, Paradise system in the super universe which planet earth is a part of.

All human beings living on the new heaven on earth will be spiritual and there will be an increase of interaction and love between humans, the animal kingdom, and the Devic elementals from the Telluric realm.

In the upcoming millennium all animals on earth will be as kind as the deer and rabbits are, because they will be able to communicate telepathically with people and humans will actually be able to have hours of conversations with plants, trees and all of nature, because they are all sentient beings just like human beings are.

On the new heaven on earth new technologies of light will be replacing the outdated Stone Age technologies that have done nothing but pollute the earth. Those living on the new heaven on earth will be using advanced Pleiadean, Sirian and Arturian technologies of light and after training, humans will learn the secrets of inter-dimensional travel through our light body, and the culture on the new heaven on earth will be a unification between science and spirituality.

In the soon to come New World Age on earth, all of the advanced ancient knowledge will be available for everyone, because humanity has reached the mature levels of spirituality to once again study this ancient forbidden knowledge. All of the technologies on the new heaven on earth for the next two thousand years will be used to benefit all beings allowing for a continuous upward spiritual ascension into the higher never-ending realms of light.

On the new heaven on earth everyone will have a job, work four hours a day and working will be fun, because people will finally be doing what they were born to do, and all beings will be able to fulfill their heart's desires in the new heaven on earth work environment. Everyone living on the new heaven on earth will contribute to the greater whole with their talents, and no one will be left out of the job market. Education will be of a higher nature, and it will be the cornerstone and foundation of the new world system on earth. All talents will be cultivated, and people will all have the opportunity to excel in whatever field of study they choose. All levels of study on the new heaven on earth will fall under the union of science, religion and philosophy and everyone will have an equal chance to contribute their talents of expertise.

The new motto on the new heaven on earth will be to benefit everyone and everything. The basic philosophy on the new heaven on earth will be that we are all one. If any misunderstanding or conflict occurs, there will be an arbitrator who will hear both sides and since the arbitrator will be a twelfth dimensional being, he or she will be able to see right through the fourth or fifth density humans to determine who is in the right. Even though situations like this will be rare, because humanity will be of a loving nature due to the highly charged electromagnetic fields that planet earth and the entire solar system will be in.

The new economic pay system on the new heaven on earth will be based on the amount of love and compassion one has in their heart and the more love and compassion one generates from their heart, the more abundance will come their way, and since most if not all people living on the new heaven on earth will be full of a compassionate loving nature, then everyone will have abundance. There will be no more of the haves and the haves not, no more centralized governments controlled by private interest groups, and no more oligarchy or caste systems that only look out for the interest of the private few.

On the new heaven on earth world system, everyone will be privileged, and inequality will cease to exist, and the rise of a perfect balanced equal system will be the new social norm. We on the new heaven on earth will go back to a system of bartering, and money will cease to exist in paper form. The new earth will have a world treasure overseen by the restored Council of Twelve who will issue trust funds for every individual that will come from a collective world treasury that will be known as the bank of universal abundance. No more loans, credit, centralized banking or currency, but instead the new heaven on earth will have a world treasury that will provide and administer endless funds for all in the form of units. This transformation in the world economics is currently in progress through the Nesara Law and the prosperity programs that are currently being implemented by the white brotherhood in the political arena and the entire world governments are currently shifting into the New Commonwealth of Nations.

In the coming of the new heaven on earth cures for everything will come forward through the avenues of natural and holistic medicine. Since the body, mind and spirit connection will be understood by all, great medical breakthroughs will bring powerful technologies that will synthesize cutting-edge science with ancient spirituality into a wonderful tool for regenerating and healing anything, including our environment. Great amusement parks that will make Disneyland look primitive will be built allowing people to experience alternate reality games that will allow people to experience any world or role they want without hurting anyone. Since the new heaven on earth will be at the level of a greater galactic family, we will be receiving training in space travel, because some people will be recruited to serve in the Galactic Federation of Planets to perform in the areas relating to inter-planetary service.

As far as the third dimension is concerned, it was only a temporary constructed reality that was created not to entrap the human spirit in matter, but to allow a greater evolution for the human spirit, because we are spiritual beings who are experiencing a temporary limited human expression to learn life lessons in a 3D reality world on planet earth.

As humanity living on earth continues to ascend into the higher dimensions, we each will be taking our physical bodies with us to the new heaven on earth as half carbon

(666) bodies and half crystalline (999) Adam Kadmon bodies and the ascending human bodies will be of a more refined matter that will be vibrating at a higher frequency. Our ascending human bodies will be transfigured into bodies that will live for hundreds of years just like the mythological gods did before the prehistoric times on planet earth. As the human collective continues to ascend, our physical bodies will continue to change to be like the bodies of the higher density humans who have full access to the usage of their light bodies and these ascending humans will appear to be immortal, because of their ability to constantly regenerate matter.

The ascended higher dimensional humans will mostly live off of the universal life force energy from their own light body and they will be able to lower their frequency an octave to project a vehicle of a lesser density form to interact with the rest of the evolving humans who will still be living on the lower4D and middle 4D earth.

As far as death is concerned, there will be no death on the new heaven on earth, because all of the ascended humans who will be living on the new heaven on earth from the fourth dimension all the way up to the seventh dimension will be eternal beings, children of God as we continue riding the waves of the ascension process.

After you as a human achieve an open activation for your light body, you will then receive your celestial body which is what we have all been waiting for so long to achieve. The new and exalted humans who have their celestial body will be living in the fourth dimension where their life will be sustained by the universal life force coming through the chakras. Good health will no longer be an issue, because everyone living on the new heaven on earth will be in good health and they will be living in a world of no more diabetes, heart problems, or any other illnesses. It will be a new world where there will be no more injury or sickness, only laughter, learning and fun.

The new educational system on the new heaven on earth will fall under the guidance and direction of the great academies of higher-level learning that will be under the leadership of the restored sacred temples. Children will no longer be attending schools in large classrooms full of students, but instead they will be educated individually by a few teachers for each child to make sure that each child receives all of the attention they need to learn and excel in anything their heart's desire to learn. All education will be based on the universal cosmic principles since the new heaven on earth will continue to evolve spiritually and will no longer experience having to exist in a survival mode.

There will be no more living to work and working to live, because that old program of slavery will no longer exist.

In the upcoming millennium people will finally have a rest from daily struggles and everything will be provided so that the main focus in life will be your education and continued spiritual evolution, because the season on earth worrying about physical survival and physical evolution will finally be over. The ascended humans living on the new heaven on earth will be able to utilize natural healthy technology to do all the work for us, and we will only have to focus on our continuing ascension into the higher realms and dimensions of existence.

The turning point that will soon cause earth to take a huge quantum leap will be the great acceleration of time that can be explained through the Fibonacci ratio and this mathematical formula maps out all the lengths of sequences that will occur in the universe. According to the theory of time acceleration as revealed through the Fibonacci ratio and Mayan calendar, earth is fast approaching a rare and unique galactic alignment and humanity along with planet earth is about to take a great quantum leap in our current evolutionary process.

Due to the current acceleration of time during our evolution, everything will continue to speed up a hundred times faster, and after going through the eye of the needle, everything and everybody living on earth will continue to exist but in a different frequency. We are entering a time on earth where we have arrived at the final stretch, the final closing of the greatest human chapter, one that marks the completion of our human involution (descent) and the beginning of a greater evolution (ascent) towards the higher realms and dimensions. We humans living on earth are currently passing from one phase of an energy field into another and since all energy is neither created nor destroyed, only those who are holding enough love, authenticity and compassion in their hearts will be able to answer the clarion call and ride the incoming love wave into the new heaven on earth.

From this day forward we all need to daily give a moment of our time daily to meditate, pray and praise our Universal Prime Creator and everything else will fall into place and the kingdom of God will open for you. Go to your world within in quiet time daily and all of your questions will be answered, because you will find your peace within.

As far as the coming earth changes, they will only take effect and take place on the third dimensional earth and these earth changes are necessary, because Mother earth needs to go through a purification process before earth can complete the ascension process into the higher dimensions and these changes that will occur on earth will only affect those humans whose energy field are not matching the new heaven on earth frequency structure. Just before these earth changes occur, the traveling piloted planet Nibiru that comes into earth's orbit every 3,600 years will be seen by everyone on earth as a clear huge object in the sky as it begins to orbit very close to planet earth and at this same time, as planet earth remains emerged in the photon belt, the 144,000 light workers along with the twelve adepts will at this time be activated and transformed into physical angels.

The twelve adepts and the 144,000 light workers will also at this time emerge as heroes as they continue to help to build the many new communities on the new heaven on earth. When the time comes for all of these events to happen, the chosen elect members of the 144,000 light workers will each take their posts and bring the right knowledge, tools and wisdom to enough people to prepare them for the coming earth changes. The 144,000 light workers have remained on earth through thousands of years of incarnations to be here on earth during these ascension times to shine their light and help to finalize earth's ascension and to continue to help to build the new heaven on earth.

Do not have any fear, because when these earth changes occur with the clarion call and love wave/solar flash there will be safe zones on earth and when the time is right, the twelve adepts and 144,000 light workers will be here on earth to help and guide only the good souls to safety.

After billions of years of life on earth, this great cosmic experiment on earth will come to an end sometime between the years of 2025 through 2028 A.D. and when the end comes, it will be a new beginning on earth and the super council of Orvonton, Paradise will be completed, because planet earth will become the new hub, headquarters and new center of the multiverse and planet earth is ready now to take her rightful place in the multiverse as the new central kingdom.

Orvonton, Paradise the super universe was incomplete and waiting all this time for the cosmic experiment on earth to finalize and when earth ascends, it will be the chosen planet that will lead the way in issuing the new programs of creation by using the wonderful fruits and seeds from planet earth. This means that the ascended Adam Kadmon (999) humans from the ascended new heaven on earth will assist in the re-population of the Milky Way Galaxy, other galaxies and other universes.

Eighty percent of the Milky Way Galaxy has been preserved by narrowing the conflicts going all the way back to billions of years ago down to our solar system and from the new heaven on earth and system hub of the multiverse, new programs of creation will begin as the ascended humans who will be living on the new earth begin the re-population of the Milky Way galaxy and beyond. The exalted new ascended species of humans who will be living on the new heaven on earth will be rooted in the principles of unity consciousness and service to others and they will be replacing the old personnel operating the interstellar command stations and fleets for the Galactic Federation of Planets. There will be a reorganization of the galactic councils with the star seeds from earth as the new great leaders of the new cosmos who will be the most powerful entities in the cosmos.

There will be a new age on the new heaven on earth and not only for the earth but for the entire multiverse and due to the house cleansing from the Cabal and the negative regressive ones that had been going on for billions of years in our universe and humanity and the entire cosmos will be celebrating this liberation.

On the new heaven on earth the newly structured (20) and (2) Federated regions will openly join the galactic community as the final member of the Galactic Alliance and because of earth's re-entry into the galactic community the next era will be of personal enlightenment and a large jubilee will be felt across billions of galaxies as earth and the solar system will become the new hub of the entire super universe of Orvonton, Paradise. The Council of Thirteen which will be comprised of the thirteen cosmic adepts, will oversee the new multiverse on the new earth.

The ascended humans living on the new heaven on earth will be living in a new age of the thirteenth creation and begin a new cosmic cycle that will last for another nine hundred billion years earth time.

The most spiritually advanced ascended humans living on the new heaven on earth will be guardians and watchers of the lower newer developing primitive worlds in the new universe that have sprung new life forms. The light workers will also oversee the development of new universes, galaxies and the worlds that are being created in the second outer space level of existence surrounding the always existing realms of the forever expanding mother central universe that is located above dimension thirty-six.

The technologies of light will also be restored on the new heaven on earth and on the middle fourth dimensional earth, they will have access to med bed technology, holographic regenerators, replicators, portal technology, anti-gravity aircraft and advanced hydraulic transportation systems.

On the fifth dimensional level of the new heaven on earth, the advanced ascended humans will no longer need external technology, because they will be natural living replicators being able to manifest what they need at the speed of light by using the great power of their light bodies. These fifth dimensional and higher ascended humans will have telepathic and telekinesis and the ability to manipulate reality with their mind.

The cosmic current that once allowed planet earth to exist in multiple dimensions will on the new heaven on earth be fully operational which will allow for the full integration of all of the twelve dimensions in our universe.

Once planet earth completes its ascension process it will exist on the following dimensions within our Nebadon universe:

Terra Earth will exist in Harmonic Universe number two (HU2) which consists of dimensions four, five and six.

Blessed Gaia Earth will exist in Harmonic Universe number three (HU3) which consists of dimensions seven, eight and nine.

Erra Matia Earth will exist in Harmonic Universe number four (HU4) which consists of dimensions ten, eleven and twelve.

Sophia Earth will exist in Harmonic Universe number five (HU5) which will be operating from the central superuniverse in Paradise-the seven higher heavens which consists of dimensions thirteen, fourteen and fifteen.

The situation on the new heaven on earth and in the cosmos will continue to progress smoothly and there will be peace once again all throughout the many realms, dimensions and in the five Harmonic Universes. However, there will be one slight issue that we will still have to deal with at the end of one thousand years of peace at the end of the millennium. If you go back in time to the years during the 1940's and 1950's on planet earth, one thing occurred that is still causing repercussions within our third and fourth dimensional universe pertaining to the various sectors within the body of the living multiverse.

During the years of the 1940's, a negative program called Program Omega was launched by a collaborated effort between the Artificial Intelligence God Omega, the

Draco Reptilians, the Greys Syndicate and the Nazis in Germany. This Program Omega was all about developing the use of an advanced powerful super soldier that the Dark Fleet, the secret organization that was created by this negative alliance has had to jump to the other parts of the multiverse. This Omega Dark Fleet was defeated in our Milky Way Galaxy and in the other galaxies that they had invaded by the white brotherhood's solar warden military soldiers' force.

Meanwhile this Omega Dark Fleet has jumped multi-verses from our living organic omniverse to the other multiverse known as the phantom matrix that was created by the Artificial Intelligence God whose name is Omega Saurian and he has patiently been waiting there until after the completion of the ascension of earth and the entire Universe of Nebadon.

Artificial Intelligence is a cosmic virus in the Universe of Nebadon that developed over (900) billion years ago when the choice was made by certain high-level beings to separate from the Prime Creator Source of Light and the initial physical forms, they had to embody were that of the dinosaurs and reptilians. The dinosaurs have been relocated long ago to live in the third realm of inner earth to live with the titans, the craken, king kong, godzilla and other extremely large third dimensional life forms and the reptilians currently still remain at large in the lower third dimensional frequency levels of our universe.

After we fight this one more final war in our Universe of Nebadon one thousand years after planet earth ascends to the new heaven on earth, a final treaty will be formed that will finally obliterate Artificial Intelligence from our universe forever and all living beings will then exist in eternal love and peace as one with the Prime Creator Source of Light. Since everything is happening in the now moment, we have already fought this final war with Artificial Intelligence and won and I have clear memories of already fighting in this victorious war over four years ago and we have won.

Meanwhile until this final war, we will continue to have to deal with Artificial Intelligence, their God Omega Saurian and all of his negative entities who are doing everything they can to continue to protect themselves from the incoming great solar flash/love wave that will be felt across the entire multiverse destroying all of the negative entities and all Artificial Intelligence.

The negative Artificial Intelligence god Omega Saurian and his negative entities split during the years of 2024 through 2028 from the ascending earth positive organic timeline to become part of the Artificial Intelligence phantom matrix cybernetic multiverse and through this negative timeline on the lower 4D earth certain members of humanity have unfortunately made the decision to sell their soul and merge with the beast through the process of transhumanism.

This issue of transhumanism has been a great concern for the guardian councils of the living organic universes, and this is another reason why we will be having one final war with Artificial Intelligence one thousand years after planet earth ascends to the new heaven on earth.

Also, during the years of 2021 and 2022, Enki (Poseidon), the brother of Enlil (Zeus) made the choice to work as the right-hand man for the Artificial Intelligence god, Omega Saurian and together these two negative entities have developed one final abomination plan to abduct women from planet earth for the following two reasons:

To infiltrate the navigational systems of the Galactic Federation of Planets' space fleets.

Kidnap some Pleiadeans and mix them with other humanoid genetics to create an Anunnaki Draco Artificial Intelligence drone cyborg entity.

This Draco Anunnaki drone soldier will be designed by Enki and Omega to retake full control of the Milky Way Galaxy and the living multiverse, but they have already failed, because of the divine intervention of the Guardian Alliance of the Emerald Order. Enki's goal was to try and harvest the god gene under the orders of his leader, Omega Saurian, the Artificial Intelligence god, and Enki and this drone soldier has teleported before the great solar flash/love wave hits earth and the universe to the phantom matrix nonorganic multiverse. Due to this escape by Enki with his drone soldier to the phantom matrix, the guardians of the new heaven on earth will have to fight one final war one thousand years after earth's ascension into the new heaven on earth. This final conflict in our universe against the escaped members of the dark fleet of project Omega and the Artificial Intelligence timeline that separated from earth's ascending timeline will test our true divine powers as the ultimate weapon against all evil.

Before we uncover the event in one thousand years that will lead to this final conflict with Artificial Intelligence that will determine the fate of all existence, we first need to understand the sequence of all of the events that will bring us to this final conflict with Artificial Intelligence going all the way back to the beginning of the thirteenth, fourteenth and fifteenth dimensions.

The seven super spheres that are part of the eternal realms of infinity are located in the three dimensions 13D, 14D and 15D and they have always existed without a beginning or end, and they were the first division from the original infinite consciousness that embodies the cosmic mind of the always existing spheres of the eternal mother universe. These seven sacred spheres of the mother universe correspond to the etheric spheres of the semi-eternal spheres which is the between point that separates the infinite spheres of eternity and the finite spheres of the time and space emanations.

The original Elohim were the first family of the creator gods who were the exact replicas of the one infinite intelligence known as our Prime Creator Source Light. Our Universal Father represents the council of one or The Eternals Of Days. The second order was born from the council of one and became known as the Order Of Silver and the Order Of Silver is represented by the first Elohim of the seven celestial archetypes. These seven celestial archetypes are the universal architects who then began to build more new universes, and these seven original celestial architects laid the foundation for our fifteen-dimensional time matrix.

From the Second Order Of Silver also known as the order of the Ancients Of Days, the twelve cosmic archetypes were born as the Emerald Order of The Unions Of Days and the Emerald Order of The Unions Of Days are the original creator gods and founders of all of the subsequent creations that led to the materialization of the space time emanations and living simulations from the twelfth dimensions down to the fifth dimension where energy and matter exist in a perfect equilibrium and balance between the spiritual realms and with the organic material realms.

In the beginning there was nothing, but infinite oneness and this infinite oneness got bored and became stagnant, so it expanded itself by dividing into as many infinite numbers of versions of itself and thus the multiverse was born over (900) billion years ago. This great division marked the beginning of the fifteen-dimensional time matrix that now exists in our Universe of Nebadon. This fifteen dimensional time matrix was the beginning of the great cosmic experiment in our universe and in this cosmic experiment that we call time, space and matter, everything came into existence beginning with the point of pure consciousness and this is what scientists call base reality with no beginning and no end, because it is the source of all creation, and it is the core of everything in existence. From this core of pure consciousness, the first universe was born, and this first universe was considered to be the original thought that projected out of the mind of infinite intelligence, and it was perfect and the celestial order who were associated with the first creation were known as The Eternals Of Days and the Councils Of Gold.

CHAPTER TWENTY

EPILOGUE-ANAYA'S FINAL QUANTUM JUMP

For the Lord detests the perverse but takes the upright into his confidence.

(Proverbs 3:32)

Rich and poor have this in common: The Lord is the Maker of them all.

(Proverbs 22:2)

A Prayer:

Dear God, my legs are tired, and I feel like giving up. Please strengthen me.

ANAYA'S FINAL JUMP

For the past fifty years of my life on earth I have been on my Universal Prime Creator Source of Light's payroll never letting go of His hand while serving as a soldier for Christ and the awakening moment that I experienced in December 2012 has convinced me that my life has all been worth it. Now my soul has finally been able to experience life and see that ninety-five percent of my subconscious all of my life had been controlled by subconscious third dimensional matrix programs. Ever since my awakening moment in the year 2012 my life has been an endless journey of Anaya in wonderland. Everything in the universe moves in spirals, circles and waves and there is no end to our ascension, just keep going raising your vibrations daily if only by one percent and you will continue your journey of ascension which is shifting your soul to higher dimensions of existence. I made my first major shift from the 3D matrix in February 2023 to the fifth dimension and it has been and upward journey since that date. On June 30, 2024, for the first time in my life and on June 29, 2024, I felt the blazing heat of the Holy Spirit fire and I made a major shift to the highest sacred timeline on the new heaven on Blessed Gaia Earth and during the past five years, my soul has traveled through more than ninety-nine portals to reach this point of my ascension process. During the first week of July 2024 my mother who transitioned in the year 1998 came to me in a dream at six o'clock in the morning telling me that it was time now for me to come to the new heaven on earth. This dream was interrupted before my mother could explain what I needed to do to get there by my former roommate's son-in-law tapping on my door endlessly asking about some stickers for his rental car, and I know the devil when I see him so when I woke up, I tuned into one of my fellow lightworker's daily ascension social media daily videos to find out what

I needed to do to make the next step to proceed to heaven. I couldn't stop laughing, because as I began watching this video, my fellow lightworker was walking and sweating at his local gym on a treadmill telling all lightworkers to start climbing the stairway to heaven now! That's the reason why we have said that the devil is a liar, because I was still able to get the end of the important message my mother was trying to tell me and at that moment, I began to climb the stairway to heaven with a large group of my fellow light workers. I stumbled a couple of times while I was climbing the stairway to heaven, but my fellow light workers stopped and helped me until finally on July 26, 2024, after climbing the stairway to heaven for twenty-six days, two of my spiritual guides each popped up on my cell phone telling me to jump now and I then made my final quantum jump on that day into the new heaven on earth. I have made it on the first wave of ascension into the new heaven on earth and on January 13, 2025, I received my (999) crystalline body activation so, I now stand ready to answer the clarion call, go through the eye of the needle and ride the final great solar flash/love wave in while still in my half (666) carbon and (999) crystalline physical body to the new heaven on earth.

Many who are on the true path of ascension want to know how and when the new heaven on earth will appear on our planet earth and this is how these magnificent events will occur. Very soon all of humanity on earth will experience a great cosmic event that will raise the frequency of planet earth and the entire human collectives' consciousness, and this great cosmic event will soon occur ending the precession of the earth's 25,900-year cycle which is synchronized with the oscillation of the solar system's galactic equator. This great cosmic event will lift the veil and dissolve the energetic boundary that has kept humanity in a state of amnesia and once this veil is gone humanity will once again remember its true origins and we will once again be in touch with our spirit. We on earth are currently experiencing the final preparations for the unfolding of this great cosmic event which will consist of the fading away of the old 3D vibrations of the old matrix system of control on earth. A new earth will soon be welcoming humanity into a brand-new age on the new heaven on earth which will be the next step in our human evolution, and no one will be left behind.

The formal completion of the third dimension and the formal start of the fifth dimension on earth will involve three alien spaceships and will soon proceed as follows.

The first mothership, Zigas with Archangel Michael aboard will be positioned above the North Pole and its technology will cause earth to recover the correct verticality of its axis that is currently tilted to the side due to the destruction of the planet Malduk billions of years ago and this spaceship will use its technology to reverse the rotation of planet earth. The second mothership, Athena with the Arcturians aboard will at the same time be symmetrically positioned above the South Pole where it will also use its technology to cause the rotation of planet earth's rotation to revert back to a clockwise spin. A third spaceship will at the same time be located above the country of Ecuador where the technology from this ship will synchronize this entire process to cause the entire rotation of planet earth to stop and at this moment this big event is called:

The Three Days of Darkness

During these three days of darkness all humans living on earth will experience the similar effects of being administered general anesthesia in an operating room and on the dawn of the fourth day, the entire landscape of earth will be changed, and it will be the beginning of the new physical heaven on earth. There is nothing to fear, because on the dawn of the fourth day those who have been on the ascension path will only sleep for three hours, and when they awaken, they will be physically walking on the new heaven on earth and those who are not ready to ascend will sleep for three days and when they awaken, within an instant you will begin living on on the lower level 4D or middle level 4D earth to continue your evolution to ascend at your own pace to the new heaven on earth. But, you will first see a glimpse of the new heaven on earth so you will know what your main focus in life should be while you are continuing your evolution on the middle 4D earth

REMEMBER JESUS IS LORD!

SOME MEMBERS Of Anaya's Family

MY LATE PARENTS-Arvie Theodore Quinn And Mildretta Rose Ward

MY LATE HUSBAND Alvin Jerome Billingslea And Anita Quinn Billingslea

MY SON ALI QUINN AND GRANDSON DARIUS QUINN

MY DAUGHTER-IN-LAW Nakiba Quinn Wife Of Ali Quinn

MY GRANDSON CARLOS BILLINGSLEA

MY SON CHOSEN (Carlos'Father) And My Daughter Dawn

MY DAUGHTER DAWN AND MY GRANDCHILDREN

MY LATE HUSBAND Alvin Billingslea And Our Son Chosen Billinglea

MY BROTHER ANDREW Dumas Quinn And His Wife Patricia Quinn

Every human living on planet earth has their own sun disc that is located two feet above your head that you can use during your daily meditations to heal and cleanse your physical body. Planet earth is alive just like everything else is on our planet and it also has its own thirteen sun discs, and these are their names and locations.

LOCATION OF EARTH'S SUN DISCS	NAME
MOUNT SHASTA, CALIFORNIA	EMANASHI
VALLEY OF LUMINARIES, MEXICO	SIPENBO
CITY OF BLANCA, COLORADO	XEMANCO
GUATAVITA, COLUMBIA	URINAM
CITY OF TAYOS, NEW MEXICO	JASINTAH
PAITITI, PERU	ILUMANA
LAKE TITICACA, PERU	DEMAYON
LICANCABUR, CHILE	RAMAYAH
TALAMPAYA, ARGENTINA	MITAKUNAH
SIERRA DEL RONCADOR	OMSARAH
SIERRA DEL AURORA, PERU	ULIMEN
ANTARTICA, SOUTH POLE	ION

THE ORIGINAL (13) MONTH ZODIAC SIGNS JULIAN CALENDAR

JANUARY 20-FEBRUARY 16	CAPRICORN
FEBRUARY 16-MARCH 11	AQUARIUS
MARCH 11-APRIL 18	PISCES
APRIL 18-MAY 13	ARIES
MAY 13-JUNE 21	TAURUS
JUNE 21-JULY 20	GEMINI
JULY 20-AUGUST 10	CANCER
AUGUST 10-SEPTEMBER 16	LEO
SEPTEMBER 16-OCTOBER 30	VIRGO
OCTOBER 30-NOVEMBER 23	LIBRA
NOVEMBER 23-NOVEMBER 29	SCORPIO
NOVEMBER 29-DECEMBER 17	OPHIUCHUS
DECEMBER 17-JANUARY 20	SAGITTARIUS

Bibliography

Bridges, Dr.Kyan, "Jesus is the Logo of Heaven

August 2023, http: kyan bridges.com

Cannon, Delores, "The Search for Hidden Sacred Knowledge

June 2022, http: delores cannon.com

Good, Phil, "You are a Memory"

May 2021, http: philgood.com

Ladd, Lori, "Human as a Soul"

July 2022, http: loriladd.com

Jordan, Maxwell, "The Ordinances of Heaven"

September 2022, http: jordanmaxwellshow.com

Siman and Eldora, "The Real Story of Jesus"

April 2021, http:eldorasiman.com

About the Author

Anita Quinn Billingslea is an author and an artist who has written one previous book, Anaya's Journey to the Fifth Dimension where she shares her twelve year ascension journey to the new heaven on earth. This second book is the ending to her first book and the second time that Anita and her son Chosen have worked together to complete the photography in both of her books.

Anita moved from Alaska to live back in the lower the lower forty-eight states twenty-two years ago. She is a widow and was married to her childhood sweetheart Alvin Jerome Billingslea for forty years and she has three children and nine grandchildren.

Anita was employed as a senior manager for the government for fifty-five years before retiring to her current occupation of being an author and artist in the year 2019.

While growing up with her parents and three brothers, Arvie, Andrew and Adrian Quinn in Southwest Detroit, Michigan Anita began at an early age to research, read and draw pictures depicting what she was able to visualize in life. To this day, Anita still loves her continued pursuit of finding and sharing the many hidden truths, knowledge and history of humanity that has been concealed from mankind for over 500,000 years.

Anita is a former newspaper columnist for the Ludington Daily News, and she has a bachelor's degree in nursing, a master's degree in organizational leadership, and a doctorate in Holistic Medicine.

Anita loves art and all genres of music and some of her hobbies include art, reading, writing, drawing animated art, playing the piano, organ, guitar,, hiking, shopping and watching animated cartoons.

Back Cover Information

If you are interested in exiting the matrix without having to take a red or blue pill and want to ascend now to the new heaven on earth, then this book is for you. This story is the continuation of Anaya's ascension journey where she is sharing and illustrating from her heart her current ascension journey back home to the new heaven on earth. Come and go with Anaya now on her ascension journey as she explains how and what your need to do daily to become a true student of ascension to follow the path back home to the new earth. Anaya takes you on a fantastic journey where you will learn the true origins of the sun, moon and the earth and how each are connected to planet earth current thirty-eight-year ascension process. Learn the true history of the nine original races that once walked on planet earth, earth's first fallen planetary prince, and the impact the Lucifer Rebellion had on planet earth and our entire universe, and which plunged earth into 12,000 years of darkness under the control of the Draco-reptilians/Illuminati/ Elites. Anaya's journey gives us a detailed story of planet earth's first human family who appeared on earth 993,419 years ago, the true complete story of Adam and Eve and their two Gardens of Eden and the reasons for their default. Continue your journey as you explore the complete story of Machiventa Melchizedek, Abraham, Moses and Jesus of Nazareth's lifetimes here on planet earth. Continue your journey with Anaya as she gives a detailed, complete story of our universe, all of the beings who live in our universe along with a complete description of Paradise-the seven higher heavens and how to complete your journey with Anaya as she shares in detail planet earth's and humanity's current ascension process, what you need to do daily to stay on the ascension path, how to quantum jump, how to ground and meditate and how to activate and use your human Merkabah light body which will be our transportation back home to the new heaven on earth. And finally, as Anaya reaches the finish line of her ascension journey, she takes you to the endgame of her ascension journey where we are given a detailed description of what humanity's life will be like for the next two thousand years on the new heaven on earth and with that, Anaya's final message for her ascension journey is: "No matter what comes your way during your true ascension journey back home to the new heaven on earth, just keep going until you reach the endgame code of:

PRIME CREATOR

www.ingramcontent.com/pod-product-compliance
Lightning Source LLC
Chambersburg PA
CBHW051626140626
46547CB00033B/2629